THE
INSIDERS' GUIDE®
TO
Santa Fe

THE
INSIDERS'®
GUIDE
TO
Santa Fe

by
Anne Hillerman
and
Tamar Stieber

Insiders' Publishing Inc.

Published by:
Insiders' Publishing Inc.
105 Budleigh St.
P.O. Box 2057
Manteo, NC 27954
(919) 473-6100
www.insiders.com

Sales and Marketing:
Falcon Distribution Services
P.O. Box 1718
Helena, MT 59624
(800) 582-2665
www.falconguide.com

•

FIRST EDITION
1st printing

•

Copyright ©1998
by Insiders' Publishing Inc.

•

Printed in the United States
of America

•

Publications from The Insiders' Guide®
series are available at special discounts
for bulk purchases for sales promotions,
premiums or fundraisings. Special
editions, including personalized covers,
can be created in large quantities for
special needs. For more information,
please write to Insiders' Publishing Inc.,
P.O. Box 2057, Manteo, NC 27954, or
call (919) 473-6100 Ext. 241.

ISBN 1-57380-052-X

Insiders' Publishing Inc.

Publisher/Editor-in-Chief
Beth P. Storie

President/General Manager
Michael McOwen

Creative Services Director
Giles MacMillan

Art Director
David Haynes

Managing Editor
Dave McCarter

Regional Advertising Sales
Greg Swanson

Local Advertising Sales
Bruce Adams
Nadine Buscher

Project Editor
Molly Harrison

Project Artist
Jason Cope

Preface

Santa Fe is a jewel of a city. And like a jewel, either in the rough or finely cut, it has many facets, not all of which present themselves at first glance — or even after 30 years, the combined length of time the authors of *The Insiders' Guide®* to Santa Fe have lived in this beautiful and complex town. As journalists, we've probed the city from the outside in. As residents, we've explored it from the inside out. We come to this project with different experiences and differing perspectives but with a shared affection and abiding respect for the city we call home. We've tried to impart our knowledge and enjoyment of Santa Fe in an illustrative, entertaining and thoroughly candid fashion.

This guide is not meant to be an exhaustive account of what Santa Fe has to offer, however. That's why we have telephone books. The purpose of *The Insiders' Guide®* to Santa Fe is to give you a taste of this extraordinary city, including its natural and cultural history, its physical and spiritual beauty and, of course, suggestions about where to eat and sleep and what to see and do while you're here. Whether you're staying a couple of days, a couple of weeks or the rest of your life, we're confident you'll find information in these pages you won't see in other travel guides. Even locals, who will probably look upon this book as more of a curiosity than a guide, may learn a thing or two, just as we did in the course of our research.

As you can see from the size of this book, Santa Fe has an enormous variety of attractions — its natural beauty and clean, crisp mountain air being high on the list — and dis-tractions, ranging from the down-home to the urbane. For many visitors to the capital of New Mexico, a "backwater" state that some Americans don't even realize is one of our 50, this is a surprising revelation. But keep in mind that despite its sophisticated trappings, Santa Fe is really just a small town in size and at heart. With some exceptions, you're not going to find the same level of service and efficiency here that you would in, say, San Francisco or Miami. What you will find is a beautiful little city with friendly people and a fascinating history that predates Plymouth Rock. You'll also find a city and county deeply in touch with their cultural roots, perhaps more so than most places in the United States. And you'll find ageless mystery here — a magic that has drawn humankind to this very spot for literally thousands of years.

Please keep in mind as you read *The Insiders' Guide®* to Santa Fe that people and places change, especially in an area undergoing as much metamorphosis as Santa Fe has in recent years and probably will continue doing right into the new millennium. We can't guarantee that the quality — or even the places — we discovered during our visits will be the same during yours. Please let us know if you've had either a bad experience or a good one. We care. We update the guide every year, so if you have comments, suggestions or recommendations, visit our website at www.insiders.com and send them to us from there. Or write to us in care of:

Insiders' Publishing Inc.
P.O. Box 2057
Manteo, North Carolina 27954

About the Authors

Anne Hillerman arrived in Santa Fe (from her birth state of Oklahoma) as a frisky three-year-old and has lived there most of her life. As a girl, she attended Loretto Academy and rode her bike through the open fields from her home in Casa Alegre to the swimming pool at Perez Park.

The oldest of author Tony Hillerman's six children, Anne began writing as a teenager and became a journalist despite good advice to get into a profession where she could make money. After attending the University of Massachusetts and graduating from the University of New Mexico, she got a job as a reporter covering the state legislature in Santa Fe. She met her husband through her next job, education and arts reporter for *The (Santa Fe) New Mexican*. Anne is now editorial page editor for the *Albuquerque Journal North*, the edition of the statewide newspaper that serves Santa Fe.

Anne is the author of three books for children and a nonfiction adventure, *Ride the Wind USA to Africa*. Her writing has appeared in *New Mexico Magazine*, *Santa Fe Woman*, *New Mexico Almanac*, *Spirit* (Southwest Airlines) and other airline magazines, *The Los Angeles Times* and the *Peak Ski Guide*. Among her memorable projects are creating an interactive video to teach managers to improve their communications skills, developing a morning television newscast, writing travel articles on Alaska's Glacier Bay and, of course, working on *The Insiders' Guide to Santa Fe*. She recently finished her newest book, a collection of stories that feature children from different cultures as heroes.

Anne has won awards for her articles from the National Federation of Press Women, New Mexico Press Association, New Mexico Associated Press Managing Editors and New Mexico Press Women. In addition to honoring as a writer, New Mexico Press Women also named her "Woman of Achievement."

When she's not working, Anne likes to ski, read, do volunteer projects with children and travel. She, her photographer husband and their 13-year-old son live in the Santa Fe foothills where they enjoy the sunsets and not having a lawn to mow.

For **Tamar Stieber** Santa Fe was merely a stopover on the way to Texas rather than a final destination point. It was the spring of 1988, and she was driving from her home in Berkeley, California, to visit a sister in Austin. With a few weeks to burn, she had mapped out a long, scenic route that would take her through Nevada, Utah, Colorado and New Mexico before winding up in Texas. Santa Fe was her next to last port of call.

In took less than two days for the high desert city to seduce her. Like countless others who have passed beneath the shadows of the Sangre de Cristo Mountains, she was astounded by the region's natural beauty and intrigued by its unique blend of Indian, Hispanic and "Anglo" cultures.

Despite her abiding love for northern California, where she had lived for nine years, Tamar was unable to shake her attraction for New Mexico. In 1989, she left her job at the *Vallejo Times Herald*, where she had arrived only six months earlier after a year and a half at the *Sonoma Index-Tribune*. She got a job covering northern New Mexico for the *Albuquerque Journal*. A year later, she won a Pulitzer Prize for a series of stories connecting an over-the-counter food supplement with a disabling blood disorder she uncovered first in New Mexico.

Now freelancing, she has written for such publications as *The Nation*, *Glamour* and *New Mexico Magazine* and is a regular contributor to *The Denver Post*. Her stories have also appeared in the *San Francisco Examiner* and the *Sacramento Bee*. She has won writing awards from the Associated Press Managing Editors,

the New Mexico Press Association and the Albuquerque Press Club. She was also a finalist in 1990 for the prestigious Livingston Award.

Originally from New York — she was born in Brooklyn, raised in the 'burbs and lived in Manhattan for five years — she spent three years in London in the early 1970s, using that city as a base from which to travel throughout Europe.

In 1980, she moved to San Francisco, where she got her start in journalism a year later as a secretary for the Associated Press. She quit in 1983 to go back to school, graduating in 1985 from the University of California, Berkeley with a degree in film, high honors and a Phi Beta Kappa key. She also graduated with high honors in 1988 from the Police Reserve Academy at Napa Valley College in California's wine country.

An avid movie fan, she still gets a thrill when the lights go down in a darkened movie theater and the screen comes alive with images. She is a voracious reader and a tireless, if not particularly gifted, athlete.

About the Photos . . .

Don Strel of Southwest Assignments Ltd. gathered the photographs for *The Insiders' Guide®to Santa Fe*, and many of the images used are his own. Strel has been photographing Santa Fe and the Southwest for the last 30 years. His work has been featured in national and international magazines and newspapers including *Ski*, *Skiing*, *Los Angeles Times*, *Detroit Free Press*, *Atlanta Journal Constitution* and the *Albuquerque Journal*. His photographs were also included in two recent books — *Ride the Wind, USA to Africa* and *Christmas Celebration, Santa Fe Traditions, Foods and Crafts*. If you would like to contact Strel regarding his work, write to him at Southwest Assignments, 304 Calle Oso, Santa Fe, NM 87501, or call (505) 983-5615.

Acknowledgments

Introducing your beloved home town to strangers, even interested strangers, is a tremendous responsibility. I find Santa Fe endearing, and I hope the city will shine brightly in your eyes too.

I was honored when publisher Beth Storie chose me as one of the writers on this Insiders' Guide® and humbled by the responsibility too. Despite having been a Santa Fe resident for more than 20 years, I quickly realized I had a lot to learn. Luckily, Santa Fe is filled with eager teachers. I spent a fast six months visiting museums and galleries I hadn't yet seen, eating in restaurants I'd always meant to get to and reading what other writers had to say about Santa Fe.

Santa Fe is a beautiful town filled with interesting, original people. It's a place justly proud of its history and its multicultural richness, which are reflected in the arts, architecture, the names of the streets and on the faces of the people you'll meet here.

I'd like to thank all the people who helped me with this project, beginning with my husband, Don Strel, who was always available to brainstorm ideas, to read rough drafts and to offer encouragement and constructive criticism. I appreciate all the words of support from my parents and my siblings. I'm grateful to my friend, writer Sharon Lloyd Spence, for her loan of Santa Fe materials and for her willingness to listen to me complain when the job seemed overwhelming.

I owe historian Stanley Hordes more than just thanks for the time, effort and energy he spent reviewing the History chapter and trying to steer me on the right path.

Without the hands-on research help of Cindy Bellinger and the advice of Peggy van Hulsteyn and Kathleen Donlan, Insiders' readers would know less about shopping in Santa Fe. DeeDee Clendenning spent many hours on the phone helping me make sure that phone numbers and addresses were accurate. Chris Zappe helped with this fact checking too.

Thanks to the many cheerful and gracious public relations staff members, secretaries and other people who answered questions and provided information for me to work with.

Special recognition goes to Janet Wise at the College of Santa Fe; Nancy File with the Santa Fe Community College Early Childhood Program; Nancy Bennett at Santa Fe Community College; and to Beverly Friedman of the Santa Fe Public Schools. The Education and Child Care chapter benefitted from the insights of Barbara Bellomy Hagood and Brenda Bentley. Brother Richard Kovatch helped me learn more about the contribution of the Christian Brothers to Santa Fe. Ken Mock explained the intracacies of putting on the Santa Fe Airshow.

Jose Villegas at the New Mexico State Archives helped me find what I needed. I appreciate the time Merrily Pierson, Susan Varela, Patty Ashton and Anna Marie Baca spent educating me about Santa Fe real estate and neighborhood designations. Thanks, too, to all the real estate office managers who took time to complete our questionnaire and to the staff at the Santa Fe City planning department for keeping informative publications on hand.

Lucy Bourke of the Santa Fe Opera, Joyce Spray of the Museum of New Mexico, Joyce Bond of the Wheelwright Museum, Lou Ann Jordan at El Rancho de las Golondrinas, Penny Landry at the Santa Fe Children's Museum and Sarah Laughlin of the Portal Program were generous with their time in support of the book. Thanks, too, to the many Santa Fe gallery owners who answered my requests for information.

I appreciation the help of Gilbert Martinez and the staff of the Santa Fe Convention and Visitors Bureau and the cooperation of the Santa Fe Chamber of Commerce. Thanks to Ed Berry for putting up with many questions about the Taste of Santa Fe, and Rosanne Gain and Rodeo de Santa Fe for their help with Western Days Events. Mike Pitel with the state tourism department gave me good advice.

Alexis Sabin shared her insights into quality activities for children in Santa Fe. Al Lucero helped me understand the scope and prestige of Santa Fe's restaurant business. I appreciated the information obtained from Steve Lewis and Ski New Mexico and the help I received from Maureen O'Dowd of the Santa Fe Ski Area, J.P. Rael at Taos Ski Valley, Wally Dobbs from Red River, Greg Morton from Angel Fire and Sara Kauppila of the Parajito Ski Area.

Finally, thanks to my co-author, Tamar Stieber, and to our editor, Molly Harrison, for their help. It was a pleasure to work with such professionals.

— Anne

With gratitude to those who were constant in helping this project flow: writer and film historian Joseph Dispenza for his friendship and encouragement; former state historian Stan Hordes for his enthusiasm, historical acumen and cultural sensitivity; Santa Fe public librarian Judy Klinger for her selfless, detailed research at the drop of a hat; Carl Miller, Sandra Thomas and the rest of the gang at Carl and Sandra's for keeping me healthy and in good humor even after far too many all-nighters; Ben Neary for the inside scoop on hunting and fishing, repeatedly coming through in a pinch and his unwavering moral support; Orlando Romero, director of the Fray Angélico Chávez History Library, for his interest, his keen local perspective and for sharing some of the myths behind the stories and vice versa; Florence and Fred Stieber for more than they'll ever know; Jerry West for his eagerness to share information, for entrusting me with much-loved books from his personal library and for his utter understanding of deadlines; Mildred West for her indomitable spirit and sense of humor that 96 years hasn't eroded; and, of course, to my co-author, Anne Hillerman, her support and a neverending supply of clippings, books and suggestions, and to our editor, Molly Harrison, for her unshakable calm, patience, encouragement and empathy, even under the most trying of circumstances.

Thanks go, too, to the many others who went the extra mile to provide vital information, share a personal perspective or, in some cases, offer a shoulder: Kim Alderwick, the Rev. Talitha Arnold of United Church of Santa Fe; Richard Atkinson, manager of the Public Lands Information Center; Loranne Burkey of Open Hands; Mike Chapman and Tony Farrar of New Mexico Bike-N-Sport; Baptist Church historian Betty Danielson; Camille Flores; Don Jones; Steve Jackson; the Rev. Webster Kitchell of the Unitarian Church of Santa Fe; Lydia M. Loice of the Santa Fe Police Department; Anthony Martinez of the Santa Fe Chamber of Commerce; Shane Miller; Terry Nefos, director of Santa Fe Transit Services and Aviation; state tourism spokesman Mike Pitel; Ed Powers of Hastings Books, Music and Video; Sebastian Puente; Chrissy Salazar of Presbyterian Medical Services, Albuquerque International Sunport spokeswoman Maggie Santiago; Jean Schaumberg of Railyard Books; Ron Shirley, the City of Santa Fe's Parks Division director; Sharon Stieber; Marcos Tapia of the First Judicial District Attorney's Office; Lauren Tiano of Tom Tiano's Sports Center; State Historian Robert Torrez; Stephanie Trane; Peggy van Hulsteyn; Ingrid Vollnhofer and Norma McCallan from the State Library's Southwest Room; Pueblo historian Dave Warren; Santa Fe Economic Development Planner Steve Whitman; Arbitron's Dave Willinski; and Danielle and Lee Wilson.

And a very special note of appreciation to the late Fray Angélico Chávez, whose books on northern New Mexico — in particular, *My Penitente Land* — proved invaluable in helping to unravel some of the misconceptions about my chosen home without diminishing one iota from its myriad and wonderful mysteries.

— Tamar

The Museum of Fine Arts houses one of the finest collections of
New Mexican and Southwestern art in the country.

Table of Contents

Directory of Maps

Santa Fe and Surrounding Area

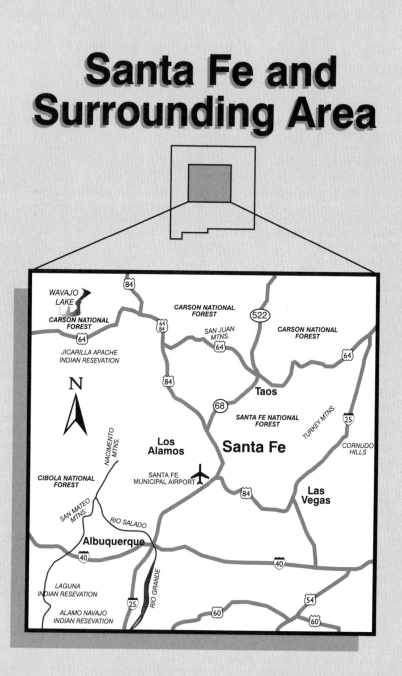

Santa Fe

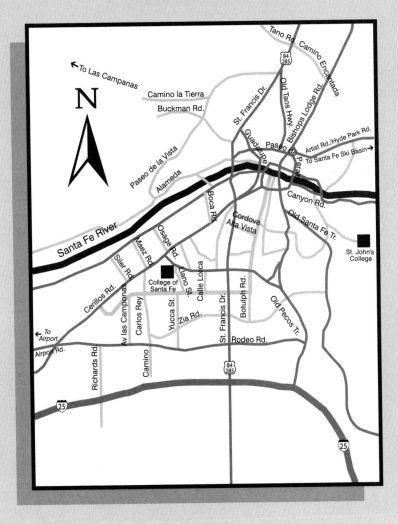

Downtown Santa Fe

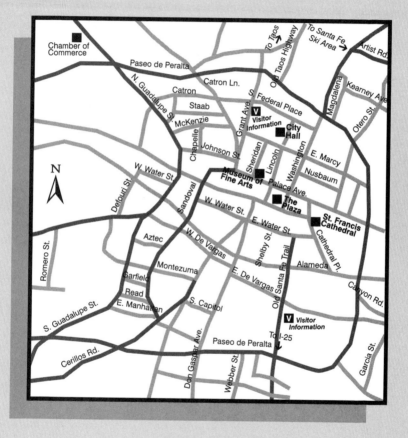

How to Use This Book

Where you start reading The Insiders' Guide® depends on your needs. One of the things we've liked about writing this book, and one of the things we hope you'll appreciate as you read it, is that each chapter is packed with useful information designed to be accessible and, we hope, entertaining.

If you're on the plane heading for New Mexico, you'll probably want to look at the Getting Around chapter to help you figure out the best way to get from the Albuquerque airport to Santa Fe. If you're using the book to plan a vacation, take a good look at our extensive accommodations chapters for help in finding a motel, bed and breakfast, deluxe resort or vacation rental. Use the Annual Events chapter to find out if something special is going on when you plan to be in town. The maps will help orientate you to Santa Fe's sights and attractions.

We've got it covered in terms of what to do and where to go when you get here too. The Attractions chapter gives you a comprehensive overview of Santa Fe's historic buildings, museums and other places of interest. Kidstuff offers an overview of what to do to keep the little ones happy. Add the Parks and Recreation, Nightlife and Arts chapters, and you have a cornucopia of ideas, from good art to golf, from mountain biking to Mozart, from pottery classes to poetry readings.

To help visitors gain a greater appreciation for our town, the book includes a readable thumbnail history of the city from its pre-history days as an Indian hunting camp to the present, post-atomic age. You'll find a layman's explanation of the American Indian and Hispanic cultures as reflected in the city's contemporary life and some suggestions on shopping for their handmade arts and crafts. Our book includes a close look at the diversity of religions and spiritual practices available here, and information on education, mainstream and alternative health services and child care. If you're considering a move to Santa Fe, be sure to look at our Neighborhoods and Real Estate chapter for a comprehensive overview. The index can help you track references. Throughout the text you'll find tips that provide an Insider's look into our beautiful city. The close-ups offer additional insight into various aspects of Santa Fe living.

We've attempted, above all else, to give you information you can use to enrich your visit here. If you've used other books in the Insiders' Guide® series (and if you haven't, we hope you will), you'll find this book similar in terms of content and design.

The area code throughout New Mexico is 505. A call from Santa Fe to most other communities — Albuquerque, Pecos, Las Vegas or Espanola is long distance. (A call to Los Alamos is not.) We did our best to double check addresses and phone numbers — but the currents of change run strongly here. We've done our best to include the high spots, to get the facts right and to help you make your way around Santa Fe.

Santa Fe is the oldest capital city in the United States, predating the establishment of New England's more famous Plymouth colony by 10 years.

History

Early Indian Days

It's difficult to re-create the history of Santa Fe's earliest residents because they left no written records save their carved petroglyphs. From archaeological evidence, though, we know that Indians camped in the Santa Fe area on hunting trips for bison and other animals as long ago as 10,000 B.C. You could consider them the area's first visitors.

By about 5,500 B.C. the hunters had established permanent annual camps in the area. Recent work on a new highway northwest of Santa Fe uncovered some of the old camping sites to which Indian bands returned year after year. From the few clues that remain about these early residents, we know they hunted deer and antelope with obsidian points on primitive spears or atatls and ate piñon nuts and seeds as part of their diet.

As the seasons rolled on, the Santa Fe area attracted permanent residents. Archaeologists have found pit houses, cave-like homes built partly underground, along the Santa Fe River and its tributaries. For about eight centuries, Indians lived in what is now known as Santa Fe, first in pit houses and later in organized pueblos, some with hundreds of rooms and community plazas. A suspected 13th-century eastward migration of the ancestors of today's Pueblo people, also known as Anasazi, from such places as Mesa Verde on the Colorado plateau temporarily swelled the area's population. The presence of water was the single-most compelling factor for settlement in what's now known as the Santa Fe area and elsewhere throughout the arid Southwest.

Exact figures are unavailable, but the combined population of the pueblos near the current site of Santa Fe may have been several thousand. At least seven major pueblos existed within a 20-minute drive of where the Plaza now stands. Archaeologists gave the pottery made by these communities its own distinctive names, among them Santa Fe Black on White, Agua Fría Glaze on Red and Cienegilla Polychrome.

The Tano Indians occupied a number of large villages south of Santa Fe for centuries. Archaeologists have discovered evidence of pueblo communities beneath Agua Fría Village on the west side of Santa Fe, in Arroyo Hondo and Galisteo to the south, Cerrillos to the southwest and near the current Fort Marcy park, a few blocks from the Plaza. Another pueblo may have occupied the very site on which the Plaza now stands. Archaeologists speculate that sometime after A.D. 900 Indians built the Pueblo of Ogapoge, as it is called by tradition, on or near the site of Santa Fe's Plaza and spreading south. By the time the first Spanish arrived in the 16th century, however, Ogapoge had been abandoned for more than a century.

The Arroyo Hondo Pueblo had 1,000 rooms built around 10 plazas by 1330. The pueblo's population fluctuated, and at one point the Indians moved out, probably because of lack of rainfall, but later reoccupied it. Then the rain stopped again, and the population began to decline. Archaeological evidence shows that in 1410 a fire destroyed the pueblo, and the Indians left Arroyo Hondo for the last time. After many generations of life in and near the present site of Santa Fe, the Pueblo Indians moved away between the years of 1400 and 1425, possibly settling at the villages of Tesuque, Pecos and Cienegilla, in the Galisteo Basin and along the Rio Grande. The clues these people left behind point to drought as the prime motivator for the move. Skeletons of children and young adults buried in the ruins at Arroyo Hondo Pueblo, for example, exhibit evidence of extreme malnutrition. Tree-ring data indicate that this period saw the worst drought in 1,000 years. Nearby settlements of

Tesuque, Nambé and San Juan remained and continue to be occupied to this day.

The Spanish Arrive

Historians tracing the story of the early Spanish presence in Santa Fe face a major challenge. An Indian revolt — the only successful native uprising against European settlement in the United States — destroyed the city's official records dating from the early Spanish explorations until 1680. Nonetheless, using copies of some of the documents that survived in the Vatican, in Mexico City and in Spain, along with archaeological evidence and the journals and letters of explorers who came later, we have a fairly good idea of what life was like here in the 17th century.

When wealthy and well-placed Juan de Oñate became the first person to receive permission to establish a colony in New Spain — at his own expense — he was one of many who believed he would also enjoy some of the riches of the region. For years, rumors of cities of gold had spawned Spanish exploration. Wealth, however, only provided part of the motivation. The Spanish explorers and colonists were also interested in land of their own, in converting more souls to Catholicism and in providing an area of defense against the other Europeans who had settled in the new world. Oñate, accompanied by 129 soldiers and their families and a small group of friars, settled near San Juan Pueblo in 1598, approximately 25 miles north of the ruins of Ogapoge. They called their encampment San Juan de los Caballeros. The colonists found life difficult here, and Gov. Oñate spent most of his time exploring. By 1600, the Spaniards had moved their capital across the Rio Grande to a new location, which they called San Gabriel, at the confluence of the Rio Chama and the Rio Grande. The fledgling colony struggled to survive and sent no riches back to Spain. Ever optimistic, Oñate and his men explored much of the rest of New Mexico seeking gold, submission of the Indians to the Spanish crown and their conversion to the Christian God.

At Acoma Pueblo, Indians attacked and killed 13 Spanish who visited the pueblo requesting provisions. One of those killed was Oñate's nephew. The colony declared a "holy war" on the pueblo based on the assumption that there could be no peace in New Mexico until the Indians were either subdued or destroyed. At the governor's command (and with the approval of the friars), 70 Spanish soldiers went for revenge on the Acoma. Another Oñate nephew, the brother of the killed leader, took Spanish troops to the pueblo. They demanded the surrender of the Indians responsible for the deaths and the Acomas' acquiescence to the king. The Indians fought, but the Spanish, who were better armed, defeated them after three days of battle and hundreds of deaths. The Spanish destroyed the pueblo and brought those whom they believed were responsible for the earlier Spanish deaths to Santo Domingo Pueblo for trial. Oñate meet the party there and dealt with the Acoma prisons.

The Acoma, and people from other pueblos who may have watched the trial, probably didn't comprehend the formality of Spanish law, but they understood the results. The governor sentenced some 20 Acoma males age 25 and older to have one foot hacked off. They, along with the captured Acoma women and young boys, had to serve 20 years as slaves to the Spanish. Two Hopi Indians caught at Acoma had their right hands cut off and were set free, "in order that they may convey the news of this punishment," Oñate commanded.

Life in the colony resumed, with Oñate continuing his search for the riches that would repay his personal investment and bring honor to Spain. The governor headed west to the Colorado River and then south to the Gulf of California, taking possession of more new land

---

INSIDERS' TIP

The pen used by President William Howard Taft to sign the document authorizing New Mexico's statehood is on display at the Palace of the Governors, 107 W. Palace Avenue. New Mexico became the 47th state in 1912.

The accomplishments of Don Diego de Vargas are commemorated at the Santa Fe Fiesta.

for his king. His efforts left him exhausted and used up his family fortune. Meanwhile, rather than living the easy life as they'd envisioned, the colonists had to work hard to survive in this demanding land. They resented the chronic lack of food and the failure to find gold. The poverty and desolation, the suffering of the women and children, the bugs in summer, cold of the winter and the sullen looks of the Indians who disliked the Spanish intrusion disheartened the settlers.

Historian John Kessell in his book, *Kiva Cross and Crown*, reported that the colonists had a saying about New Mexico: "*Ocho meses de invierno y cuatro de infierno!*" which translates as "Eight months of winter and four months of hell!"

When the governor, half of the colony's armed men and a couple of friars left once again to search for wealth, most of the colonists and all but one of the friars deserted, heading back to Mexico. Only two dozen settlers and one Franciscan remained. When Oñate and his men returned, the governor ordered the fleeing colonists pursued, but they had too much of a lead to be captured. When the defectors reached Mexico, they reported the expedition's lack of success in converting the Indians or finding gold. The viceroy of Mexico, with the concurrence of the king of Spain, decided that the colony should be abandoned.

And it would have been, except for a plea for fairness toward the Christianized Indians. (While estimates of the number of converts differed considerably, all agreed that some Indians had become Christians.) Rather than abandon these new converts or force them to leave New Mexico, secular and religious authorities decided to keep the new areas as mission territory. The viceroy named a new governor, Pedro de Peralta, but ordered Oñate to remain until Peralta arrived. Embarrassed and disgraced, Oñate resigned in 1607.

When Peralta arrived, Oñate and his son, Cristóbal, left for Mexico City, but on the journey Cristóbal died. Oñate was charged with failure to obey royal decrees, lack of respect for the friars and mistreatment of the Indians, especially of the Acomas. He was fined, banned perpetually from New Mexico and returned to Spain.

Conventional history places the establishment of Santa Fe, where Peralta moved the capital, at 1608, though some historians say Oñate or his son founded Santa Fe as early as 1605. But even the 1608 date makes Santa Fe the oldest capital city in the United States, predating the establishment of New England's more famous Plymouth colony by more than

10 years. Gov. Peralta and several settlers from San Gabriel selected a site on the southern end of the Sangre de Cristo Mountains, a place with a higher elevation, which meant cooler summers, and a location better situated for defense against the attacks of the Apache, Navajo and Comanche tribes. The new location also relieved the pressure on the San Juan Pueblo. The Spanish laid out the town, which they called Santa Fe (meaning "Holy Faith") according to instructions from Spain.

The city grew from the mud with small, one-story adobe buildings situated around a rectangular plaza. Most historians believe the original Plaza was at least an additional block larger than its current size. Land that could be cultivated lay beyond this town square, and the city spread along the Santa Fe River — a decision the settlers came to regret. The most important building was the *Casas Reales*, as the Palace of the Governors was then called. The governors and their families lived there, with adjoining rooms for municipal offices, meetings of the town council, storage and a jail. Many settlers moved from San Gabriel to the new city, attracted by the promise of land and water rights if they stayed for 10 years. Other newcomers trickled in over *El Camino Real*, the road leading into the territory from Mexico. All roads in the province — and there weren't many — led to Santa Fe.

In the early 1600s, the population of Santa Fe was approximately 1,000, including Mexican Indians who came to Santa Fe as servants of the Spanish and who lived separately in Barrio Analco across the Santa Fe River. Santa Fe's other early settlers included some of pure Spanish blood, many *mestizos*, or people of mixed race, and others from France and Portugal. Some were black, and at least one came from Flanders. Santa Fe and New Mexico grew slowly as more colonists arrived and babies were born. The statue of *La Conquistadora*, which was to become Santa Fe's most revered religious object, arrived in 1625. Santa Fe's Spanish settlers were uniformly Catholic, including some of Judaic heritage whose ancestors had been baptized rather than face deportation or death from the Inquisition. The economy ran largely on the barter system. While in some ways life was hard on the frontier, in other ways the settlers were freer than they may have been in Spain or Mexico. Gambling flourished in the new settlement as it did in most frontier towns.

The arrival of the supply caravan from Mexico City over *El Camino Real* every three years was cause for village-wide celebration. Although the central purpose of the caravans was to bring supplies for the missions and official correspondence, they also delivered a few precious luxury items such as silver, silk, lace, tobacco, saddles, writing desks and chocolate.

By 1680, three generations of Santa Fe residents had been born, some of whom had Indian mothers. Ninety percent of the city's population was native to the province. The village had two major areas of conflict. Continuous friction between the church and state over who should have the final voice in ruling the Indians and the colony sometimes reached such a degree that colonists had to choose to follow either civil or religious authority. And the Pueblo Indians grew increasingly unhappy at their economic exploitation and the periodic attempts to undermine their spiritual, political and social traditions. The colony established the *encomienda* system, which granted certain settlers the right to collect tributes from Indians who lived on designed parcels of land.

As historian Kessell explains it, the *encomienda* system was born of the 1573 colonization laws, which stated that Indians should be persuaded to pay moderate amounts of tribute in local products. "In no legal sense did a grant of Indians in *encomienda* ("in trust") imply that the recipient had use of native land or labor, but rather only the collection of tribute — usually maize and *mantas* (woven ma-

INSIDERS' TIP

New Mexico Gov. Manuel Armijo rented rooms in the Palace of the Governors to travelers who arrived in Santa Fe along the Santa Fe Trail.

terial) and animal skins — in kind as personal income." In exchange, the Spanish *encomiendero*, or the man who received the tribute, was supposed to protect the colony by answering the governor's call to arms whenever the need arose. And the Indians, whether they liked it or not, received the benefit of Christianity and of becoming subjects of the king of Spain.

Spanish law made it clear that Indians had to be paid at least minimum wage if they worked for the colonists. But New Mexico was a long way from Spain, and Pueblo Indians were often forced to labor against their will by the *encomienderos*. Adding to the uproar, raiding Comanche and other non-farming Indians frequently stole the crops and livestock of both the Pueblo Indians and the Spanish settlers.

But the Indian-Spanish relationships weren't exclusively antagonistic. In the worldview of the Franciscans, Indians were souls worthy of God's salvation. In the years since Oñate's arrival, many Pueblo Indians and Spanish had married. They had served as godparents for each other's children and had established friendships based on mutual respect and the need to cooperate. This wasn't enough, however, to stay the building forces of revolution.

In 1675, the Spanish flogged a large group of Pueblo religious leaders, including Popé from San Juan Pueblo, for practicing witchcraft. The event, which followed an earlier incident in which 1,600 ceremonial masks, prayer sticks and fetishes had been burned, had ramifications for New Mexico for many years to come.

The Pueblo Revolt

After his flogging, Popé fled to Taos where he began to work with other Pueblo Indian leaders and in the Hopi country to organize a sophisticated rebellion. The cautious conspiracy went on for five years, hampered by the fact that the Indians did not share a common language. The Indians agreed to join forces to drive the Spanish invaders out. They timed the rebellion to fall in the year before the supply train arrived so the settlers would be low on food and ammunition. On August 9, 1680, runners with knotted ropes signifying the exact day of the revolt went from pueblo to pueblo, telling the people that the time had come.

Popé originally planned the uprising to coincide with the Feast of San Lorenzo but moved it up when he realized that the Spanish were on to the plan. In fact, Santa Fe's Governor Antonio de Otermín discovered the plot two days before the date of the rebellion but was unable to marshal any organized defense.

Photo: Don Strel/Southwest Assignments

Besides its Indian and Spanish influences Santa Fe also reflects the charm of the Old West.

The Indians' plan split the Spanish settlements in New Mexico into two groups, one in Santa Fe and one in Isleta, succeeded. They tried to convince each group of settlers that the other had been killed and that their situation was hopeless. The Pueblo warriors burned and sacked missions, killed priests, attacked settlers and stole or stampeded livestock.

When word of the uprising arrived in Santa Fe, Governor Otermín sent messengers to warn all settlers in the outlying districts to defend themselves. Those who lived between Taos and Cochití Pueblo literally ran for their lives to the walled city of Santa Fe. Settlers between Cochití and Socorro sought safety at Isleta Pueblo, which remained friendly to the Spanish. Settlers living on the western side of the province, from Ziá and Jémez Pueblos across to Zuni and Oraibi, had to fend for themselves. Most were killed.

At the Palace of the Governors, Otermín distributed weapons to the male colonists, and they prepared for a siege. Each new group of refugees brought grim reports of how the murder and rebellion had spread. Otermín sent soldiers to assist settlers who had held out in Los Cerrillos and La Cañada, helping them reach Santa Fe. The Spanish made sure that *La Conquistadora*, the 3-foot image of the Virgin, was safe inside the thick adobe walls.

By August 13 the Indians arrived in Santa Fe, and a nine-day siege began. Some 1,000 men, women and children, along with a few of their animals, waited inside the Palace. The Indians cut off the *acequia* that supplied water to the Palace. To preserve precious food and water, the colonists let their animals die. The Indians burned Santa Fe, and the besieged band watched the glow of flames from their homes and crops in the evening sky. The Pueblo leader sent a delegate to the settlers with a red flag and a white flag. The Spanish could pick the white flag, surrender and leave. If they picked red and chose to fight, they should prepare to die. Otermín scolded the emissary and instructed him to tell the Indians that they should abandon the revolt and ask God to forgive them. The Indians scoffed at the message.

Finally, Otermín had to make a decision. Rather than perish of thirst and starvation, the Spanish decided to attempt to fight their way out of the Palace at dawn. Otermín advanced with a small force of handpicked soldiers and caught the Indians by surprise. Although the rebels numbered about 1,500 warriors, the Spanish claimed to have slain 300, captured 47 and temporarily driven away the rest.

When the Spanish left their fortification for water, they saw the extent of the devastation the Indians had wrought. They led the weakened livestock out to the ruined fields to scrounge for food. With their possessions destroyed, homes burned and crops ravaged, they knew they could not stay in Santa Fe. On August 21, 1680, Otermín signed an affidavit that he and the surviving Santa Fe settlers would abandon the villa. The party divided all clothing, food and livestock among the surviving families and, in military formation, marched southward down *El Camino Real*, the route their optimistic ancestors had taken into New Mexico 82 years earlier.

The Spanish had lost 21 clergymen and between 380 and 400 settlers — a devastating blow to the new colony. At least 20 more were missing, either left behind as captives or in hiding from the Indians. Many, including Otermín himself, were wounded. The disheartened band headed downriver toward El Paso, joined on the way by other terrified settlers and Indians who had befriended the Spanish

---

INSIDERS' TIP

Agua Fria Village, a historic area that has been encompassed by the city's growth, was built on the site of Pindi Pueblo. Indians occupied the pueblo's several hundred rooms between 1250 and 1350. The Laboratory of Anthropology organized its excavation in 1932 and 1933. The ruins of another major pueblo, Arroyo Hondo, lie 8 miles south of Santa Fe and were the focus of extensive archaeological and ecological research by the School of American Research between 1970 and 1974.

and feared for their lives. Otermín, stunned by the defeat, planned to reconquer the territory and led two unsuccessful expeditions. In 1683, his term as governor ended.

After Otermin, other Spanish *conquistadores* attempted to reclaim New Mexico, but all were rebuffed. Spain viewed the loss of the territory as an embarrassment. The Indians ruled New Mexico for 12 years, during which time they attempted, with wide success, to obliterate all traces of the European settlers and their religion. They destroyed most of the Spanish buildings and replaced them with cornfields, saving only the *Casas Reales*. (The walls and foundation of San Miguel Mission — New Mexico's oldest church — also remained.) Indians burned the Spanish records, crosses and other traces of the foreigners. Some moved into the *Casas Reales*, modifying it to suit their needs. Some historians believe that they also built a pueblo on the Plaza.

When things settled down, many of the Indians left Santa Fe and returned to their home pueblos. The Indian coalition dissolved, despite the efforts of some leaders to keep it together. In 1690, the king of Spain appointed Diego de Vargas to be New Spain's new governor, and Vargas agreed to reclaim the territory for Spain at his own expense. Vargas traced his family back to a famous senator of imperial Rome and felt he had the necessary military and organizational skills, along with the requisite courage, to face the Indians and succeed. He planned a two-stage reconquest; first a military presence and then the return of the settlers.

The Spanish Return

On September 13, 1692, at 4 AM, Vargas and a band of 40 Spanish soldiers and 50 Indian allies arrived at the pueblo that had once been Santa Fe. Vargas had given the order: No one was to fire a shot unless and until Vargas so signalled. The Spanish approached the Palace in the early morning darkness, crying in unison, "Glory to the Blessed Sacrament of the Altar!" With the help of Spanish soldiers who spoke the pueblo language, Vargas told the Indians that he had come in peace to pardon them and accept their obedience to God and the king of Spain. The Indi-

ans initially refused to acquiesce. Vargas instructed his men to encircle the stronghold, positioning himself in front of the main gate. Taking his cue from Otermín's experience, he ordered his men to shut off the *acequia* that allowed water to flow into the fortification. The Spanish brought forward a cannon they'd hauled all the way from El Paso. The Indians began to surrender.

As the native leaders appeared, Vargas climbed down from his horse to embrace them. They invited Vargas and his men inside the Palace. The Franciscans celebrated mass, absolved the Indians of their sins and baptized the children born since 1680. This is the peaceful reconquest that the Santa Fe Fiesta celebrates, a credit to Vargas' faith in God and in himself. However, the story was far from over.

Vargas and his men returned to Mexico and came back with 70 families of settlers, about 800 people. They left El Paso in mid-October of 1693 and got to Santa Fe on December 16 after camping in snow and bitter cold for two weeks. With them, they brought the statue of the Virgin, *La Conquistadora*, home to Santa Fe to stay. This time the Indians declined to abandon their home and its food supplies, and a fierce battle ensued. Vargas and his men succeeded in seizing the *Casas Reales*. Vargas ordered the execution of 70 of the Indian defenders he had captured. Some 400 others became slaves to the Spanish for 10 years. It took the Spanish years of battle to subdue the rest of New Mexico, but by 1696 all the pueblos had been reconquered. The longest and most successful uprising of Native Americans against colonists was over, and Spanish rule was reestablished. Twenty-six Spanish governors followed Vargas. Some represented Spain with honor, wisdom and integrity, and others were ignorant and corrupt. All faced hardships in ruling a poor isolated colony besieged by raids from Apache, Navajo and other Indians and requiring almost constant support from the mother country.

18th-Century Santa Fe

Although New Mexico's reinstated Spanish government and settlers faced many of the same problems as before, the *encomienda* system never functioned again. The Spanish

Photo: Don Strel/Southwest Assignments

Early travelers to Santa Fe traveled along *El Camino Real*,
now partly preserved at El Rancho de Golondrinas.

abandoned attempts to integrate the Pueblo Indians into Spanish society, probably with relief on both sides. The Indians and the friars made peace; as long as the Indians officially professed to be Christians, the friars generally ignored their ceremonial dances and other non-Christian rituals.

In 1712 the residents of Santa Fe established a fiesta to celebrate Vargas' initial entry into the city. Santa Fe's defensive walls came down, and some settlers moved to homes along the Santa Fe River to protect their fields from animals and marauding neighbors. Like most villages in New Spain, Santa Fe struggled to survive during the 18th century, with the settlers fighting poverty, disease and the whims of the weather. But life wasn't all hard work, even on the frontier. People loved the *fandan-*

gos, or social dances. Utilitarian folk arts of many kinds flourished in part because of the colony's isolation from manufactured products. Spain discouraged foreign trade, and as a result, many New Mexicans learned crafts such as folk painting, weaving and wood carving, which they refined over generations.

Santa Fe remained Spain's capital in the northern provinces for the next 125 years. Visitors from Spain and Mexico often noted their impressions of Santa Fe in their journals. Fray Francisco Atanasio Domínguez, who came in 1776, described the town as "a rough stone set in fine metal" — a reference to the city's lovely environment — and noted, "it lacks in everything."

The first known map of Santa Fe, drawn by army officer Joseph de Urrútia in 1768, includes "Camino de Galisteo" and "Camino de Pecos," which seem to be near the routes of present Galisteo Street and Old Pecos Trail. The Santa Fe depicted by Urrútia was made totally of adobe with a garrison of soldiers to protect it.

Almost continuous raids by the Comanches, Apaches, Navajos and Utes against both the Pueblos Indians and the Spanish settlements marked life in 18th-century Santa Fe. The Spanish launched frequent campaigns of reprisal and retaliation; their attacks in turn prompted the Indians to seek revenge, and the cycle continued. Frontiersman Juan Bautista de Anza, Governor of New Mexico from 1778 to 1787, made peace with the Comanches, a happy condition that continued through 1794.

Santa Fe, along with Taos, Pecos and Abiquiú, hosted annual trade fairs between Spaniards and the nomadic Indians. By the end of the century money had begun to circulate in New Mexico, and Santa Fe, as the capital, led the trend.

Santa Fe's population grew slowly. The 1790 census shows farming as the main occupation of the 2,542 residents. The survey also found adobe makers, carpenters, blacksmiths, barrelmakers, muleskinners, shoemakers, weavers and tailors. Only one teacher is identified in the old document; nonetheless, many historians have been impressed with the high quality of the written records that remain..

Some historians believe the Louisiana Purchase in 1803 signaled the end of Spanish control over New Mexico. The purchase inspired U.S. residents to move westward. Although American trappers had trespassed in the territory for decades, in 1805 Zebulon Pike led a group of explorers westward into new Spain under orders from Thomas Jefferson. The Spanish arrested Pike and jailed him in Santa Fe. The governor treated Pike to dinner, outfitted him in new clothes and sent him down to Durango, Mexico, where he was further questioned and released. He later wrote about his adventures, fueling curiosity about New Mexico and Santa Fe.

For almost 300 years, *El Camino Real* was the major thoroughfare for missionaries, colonists, soldiers and commercial caravans into New Mexico. The longest of America's trails, it ran 1,200 miles from Santa Fe to Mexico City. Until the opening of the Santa Fe Trail, it was virtually Santa Fe's only link to the outside world. The passage from Mexico to Santa Fe took months and put the travelers in danger; in addition to severe natural forces, the fear of attack by Indians was ever-present.

Once they arrived in Santa Fe, the Mexican caravans would pause several weeks or months, buying local products with which to return south. Beginning about 1709, the caravans became annual events from Chihuahua, and the northern part of *El Camino Real* became known as the *Camino de Chihuahua*. When the initial profitablity of trading in Santa Fe began to wane for merchants who took the Santa Fe Trail from Independence, Missouri, some U.S. wagons used the Chihuahua trail to continue into Mexico.

The Mexican Period

In the late 18th century, Spain, preoccupied with the Napoleonic War, began to lose its grip on its New World colonies. Mexico gained its independence from Spain, and New Mexico, then part of Mexico, came along with it. Although Mexican independence had little initial effect, the winds of change again swept over Santa Fe with hurricane force.

Santa Fe remained the provincial capital during Mexican rule, as it had during centuries of Spanish authority. With a population of almost 5,100 at the turn of the century, Santa Fe was the official seat of government for a territory that stretched to Arizona and included parts of Colorado and Utah. Conflict with Indians and lack of adequate finances continued, and the understaffed and underfunded Mexican government provided even less to New Mexico than Spain had. Albuquerque-born Manuel Armijo, whom some historians regard as a cowardly scoundrel and others believe was a pragmatic leader and successful administrator, was New Mexico's governor during most of the Mexican period. Armijo acted notoriously independent of the Mexican government, often refusing to enforce Mexican laws he considered inappropriate for the colony. Armijo declined to collect taxes, saying that service in the militia was enough of a burden for New Mexico's poor residents.

In 1835 the Mexican government replaced Armijo with Albino Pérez, a Mexican nobleman with a taste for luxury. In 1837, the residents of New Mexico rebelled against the Mexican rules and Pérez, who, unfortunately, personified their resentment. A mob savagely murdered him and 16 other civil servants and elected José Gonzales, a Taos Indian, to rule them. Gonzales appointed Armijo as part of a delegation to go to Mexico and reassure the Mexican officials that all was under control. But, sensing an opportunity, Armijo instead marched to Santa Fe with a small army and officially "reclaimed" the city for Mexico. Gonzales resigned. In 1838 the Mexican government confirmed Armijo as governor once again. In 1844 Armijo resigned and was replaced with a governor from Mexico who reinstigated war with the Utes and was removed from office in 1845, replaced again by Manuel Armijo.

Unlike the Spanish governors who preceded him, Armijo welcomed Anglo American traders, seeing tremendous economic advantage to Santa Fe — and himself — from the caravans. He also realized the United States could pose a threat to Mexican rule and repeatedly pleaded with Mexico for more trained soldiers, weapons and supplies. Mexico, overwhelmed with its own problems, ignored his requests.

The same year Mexico won its independence, William Becknell, the man who became known as "The Father of the Old Santa Fe Trail," arrived in Santa Fe on an exploratory mission with pack mules loaded with items for trade. The Mexican governor, Facundo Melgares, encouraged Becknell to return and to tell other Anglo Americans that Santa Fe would welcome them. By 1822, caravans were on the move down the Santa Fe Trail. (Although Becknell gets the credit for "founding"

the trail, the route was originally blazed by Spanish explorer Pedro Vial in 1792.)

For decades, the arrival of the caravans brought buyers, sellers, animals and goods of all sorts to the territory. The wagons made a 900-mile trip from central Missouri on the edge of the American frontier to Santa Fe's Plaza. The trail entered and left the Plaza at its southeast corner, near the present intersection of San Francisco and Shelby streets. The traders and their merchandise came down what's now Shelby Street with a jog east at the present Water Street, then followed the modern Santa Fe street named Old Santa Fe Trail south to near the intersection of Old Pecos Trail. Even today, homeowners who live slightly out of town along the Old Santa Fe Trail can see ruts in their yards made by the heavy wagons.

By 1866 — just as the transcontinental railroad reached Kansas — the trail had seen 5,000 wagons. In keeping with the Spanish custom of hospitality, boisterous parties welcomed the caravans, especially the early ones. For Santa Fe residents, the trail meant a less-expensive supply of manufactured goods and a link to the outside world. Previously, the residents acquired anything they needed that they couldn't make themselves from Chihuahua on *El Camino Real* or at the Indian trade fairs. The goods from Mexico were less diverse and more expensive than the assortment of things now available from the Santa Fe Trail.

In the early years of the Santa Fe Trail, the travelers did not pass a single permanent settlement between the western boundaries of Missouri and San Miguel del Vado, about 50 miles east of Santa Fe. The trip put them to the test as they faced water and food shortages, Indian attacks, disease, freezing storms, floods and starvation. The wagons seldom covered more than 15 miles a day. Santa Fe looked good to these weary travelers, but they were quick to note how different the city was from the places they knew. For most, Santa

INSIDERS' TIP

Pedro Hidalgo is New Mexico's Paul Revere. After nearly being killed by Indians at Tesuque Pueblo in the Pueblo Revolt of 1680, he made his way back to Santa Fe despite his wounds. He informed the governor that the Indian uprising had begun.

Fe was the first foreign city they'd ever visited. The locals dressed differently, ate different food and spoke different languages.

Most of those who arrived in Santa Fe had never encountered Spanish culture but had heard the "Black Legend." A common Anglo-American misperception maintained that the Spanish conquerors and settlers were unusually cruel to the Indians. The image was frequently reinforced in England and the Protestant countries of Europe with publications that illustrated Spanish mistreatment of natives with scenes of torture, maimings and hangings. Since much of Europe was at war with Spain, this material could be considered anti-Spanish propaganda. While some individual Spanish were cruel and tyrannical, on the whole there is no evidence to demonstrate the Spanish treated the Indians any more or less cruelly than did other arriving conquerors.

The city's adobe look was strange to the newcomers; many didn't even recognize the small brown boxlike buildings as houses at first. Some travelers compared Santa Fe to a prairie dog town, perhaps not realizing that the mud bricks were ideal material for keeping out the day's heat and, once warmed by the fires from wood stoves in the winter, they retained heat far better than a log home. Inside, the homes lacked the furnishings common to the United States. Instead of formal beds, for instance, Santa Fe's practical residents folded their sleeping mattresses to double as couches during the day.

But the differences were more than just superficial. Unlike blacks and Indians in the United States, those living in New Mexico and other Mexican territories had full rights of citizenship as provided by the Mexican Constitution, a document which also gave all residents free speech. The Mexicans abolished the old Spanish caste system, rigid social rankings based on a person's degree of Spanish blood. At the Governor's Ball in 1839, for example, an American visitor noted that the poor and rich alike attended and even danced together.

Another strong difference was the status of women. Santa Fe women enjoyed much more freedom than women in America and were not considered their husbands' property. They retained their maiden names after marriage. They smoked, danced and enjoyed gambling as much as the men. The women dressed less formally and in styles considerably less confining than those worn by women in the early 19th-century United States. Women in Santa Fe had property rights and legal rights denied their U.S. counterparts. They worked for wages in jobs such as bakers, weavers, card dealers and, of course, prostitutes. Women could own rental property and flocks and were not legally required to share their money with their husbands. Both wives and husbands could take spouses to court for legal redress of their grievances.

The U.S. travelers also entered a territory that was largely on its own in terms of religion. The Mexican government had offered no financial support to the Catholic Church — the only religion in the territory other than that of the American Indians — and priests were included in orders for all Spanish-born citizens to leave the country. Historians report that only five to eight priests remained to minister to the far-flung population. As a result of the lack of clergy, lay Catholic orders developed in rural communities to keep the faith alive. These brotherhoods became known as the *Penitentes* for their severe penance during Holy Week. As another result of the scarcity of priests — and the high fee on marriage — more than half of the couples in Santa Fe lived together without the church's blessing.

Commerce and information flowed both ways along the Santa Fe Trail. In addition to selling the American products they brought by the wagonload, the caravans returned to the United States with hides, pelts and Indian weavings from New Mexico. Some Santa Fe merchants journeyed to the United States themselves to make purchases and return with goods that could be sold at a substantial profit. One of Santa Fe's best-known merchants was Gertrudes Barcelo, or "La Tules." La Tules made her money gambling and invested it in American goods, which she had shipped to Santa Fe to sell at a profit. Another trader who profited from the wagons was Gov. Manuel Armijo himself. In addition to the benefit of their trade goods, the U.S. merchants paid customs duties on their cargoes, money which supported New Mexico's government and paid the Santa Fe soldiers' salaries. Some travelers from the United States became citizens and lifelong residents of Santa Fe, holding office and helping the territory in many ways, including fighting Indian raiders as members of the citizen militia. Others were arrogant and lawless, trapping animals illegally, cheating their customers, demeaning the territory's Spanish-speaking people and their culture and selling guns to hostile Indians.

Besides bringing merchandise, the trail brought massive cultural change. In June 1846, New Mexico's governor received word that the United States had declared war on Mexico. The war put Armijo in a terrible position. His duty as governor would be to fight the Americans in what was sure to be a doomed effort. After assembling several thousand disheveled troops for battle in Apache Canyon outside of Santa Fe, Armijo decided not fight and fled to Mexico. He was tried and acquitted of treason in Mexico City and returned to New Mexico, where he died under U.S. rule. Questions remain about Armijo's motivation: Was he bribed to leave or did he decide that avoiding bloodshed was in the best interests of New Mexico?

U.S. Gen. Stephen Watts Kearny and his staff rode into Santa Fe unobstructed to meet with New Mexico's acting governor, who greeted them politely and served them dinner complete with wine imported from El Paso over *El Camino Real*. The next day, Kearny made a speech to Santa Fe residents, attempting to alleviate their fears. He promised that their religion and language would be protected, that all provisions needed by the U.S. soldiers would be purchased, not stolen. He assured Santa Fe residents that they would have a voice in new government and a role in the area's future. In 1850, New Mexico became a U.S. territory and remained as such for more than 60 years.

Santa Fe, U.S.A.

Kearny and his forces had taken Santa Fe without firing a shot, and the Stars and Stripes now flew over the Plaza. Five days after his arrival, the general instructed the soldiers with him to begin building the garrison of Fort Marcy on a hill overlooking the city. The next 10 years, until New Mexico became involved in the Civil War, were largely spent fighting off Apache and other Indian raids and protecting new immigrants along the Santa Fe Trail.

In 1847, not long after the U.S. captured New Mexico, the state's first territorial governor, Charles Bent, was assassinated in Taos. The conspirators planned to attack and kill all Anglo Americans in northern New Mexico as well as all New Mexico natives who had accepted positions in the new government. On the night of January 18, conspirators killed Bent and five others and paraded Bent's scalp through the town. The rebels attacked and killed seven others a few miles north of Taos; more were shot in Mora. The U.S. forces responded with troops from Santa Fe and Albuquerque. After a battle at Embudo, they continued on to Taos, to discover that the rebels had fortified themselves in the church at Taos Pueblo. U.S. artillery broke down the church walls, and after 150 New Mexicans were killed, the rebels fled or surrendered. U.S courts tried the prisoners and hanged six of the leaders for their role in the bloody attempt at revolution.

The Taos rebellion was the last organized revolt against American authority in New Mexico, but raids and uprisings continued through 1847. One of the most visible signs of the American occupation was the presence of English-speaking soldiers who protected the Santa Fe settlers from Indians. Another was the new State Capitol, intended to replace the Spanish *Casas Reales*. Construction began in 1850, but the money ran out before the work was done. Of more immediate value was the establishment of regular twice-a-month mail service beginning in 1857. Stage coaches added Santa Fe to their line, and the city enjoyed a temporary economic boom in the 1850s, a period described by historian Marc Simmons as the heyday of the Santa Fe Trail.

Among the travelers the trail brought was

INSIDERS' TIP

Santa Fe's first general city plan was developed in 1912 and called for the preservation of the city's narrow, winding streets.

A Santa Fe Timeline

1150-1400 — Pueblo Indian villages thrive along the Santa Fe River.

Early 15th century — Indians abandon the villages closest to Santa Fe such as Pindi, Ogapoge and Arroyo Hondo pueblos.

1598 — Juan de Oñate claims New Mexico for the Spanish and establishes the first Spanish settlement in New Spain near San Juan Pueblo northwest of Santa Fe.

1608-10 — Pedro de Peralta establishes the city of Santa Fe as New Mexico's capital. The Palace of the Governors is built. *El Camino Real* runs from Mexico City to Santa Fe as a supply route for the Spanish missions and colony.

1680 — The Pueblo Indians drive the Spanish out of Santa Fe and New Mexico. The Indians burn Spanish records and remodel the Palace of the Governors to serve their needs.

1692 — Diego de Vargas brings a Spanish military expedition back to Santa Fe and reclaims Santa Fe for the King of Spain.

1693-1696 — Vargas returns to Santa Fe with a band of settlers. After a fierce battle, the Indians give up the Palace of the Governors. Vargas spends the next few years reconquering the outlying pueblos.

1712 — Santa Fe celebrates its first official Fiesta in thanksgiving for the reconquest.

1777 — The first known map of Santa Fe is drawn.

1778 — Juan Bautista de Anza arrives in Santa Fe as governor and begins making peace with the Comanches.

1792 — Pedro Vial blazes a trail from Santa Fe to St. Louis and returns the following year, making the first complete journey over what was to be known as the Santa Fe Trail.

1807 — American explorer Zebulon Pike and his party are arrested as intruders in

Photo: Don Strel/Southwest Assignments

Spanish New Mexico. The Spanish government institutes protective trade measures to restrict American influence in New Spain, including Santa Fe.

1821 — Mexico wins independence from Spain. Trader William Becknell arrives in Santa Fe to do business.

1822 — The first wagons roll into the Santa Fe Plaza over the Santa Fe Trail, leading the way for millions of dollars of trade goods and new ideas and cultural influences in Santa Fe.

1833 — The first gold mines west of the Mississippi open in the Ortiz Mountains between Santa Fe and Albuquerque.

1834 — New Mexico's first newspaper, *El Crepúsculo de la Libertad* — the Dawn of Liberty — is published in Santa Fe.

1837 — A group of northern New Mexican farmers and Indians band together to

Pedro de Peralta, who replaced Don Juan de Oñate as New Mexico's Spanish governor, is depicted in a statue on Grant Avenue.

— continued on next page

protest new taxes imposed by the Mexican government. Gov. Albino Pérez is killed. Manuel Armijo resumes his post as governor.

1846 — The United States declares war on Mexico. U.S. General Stephen W. Kearny occupies Santa Fe without firing a shot after Mexican governor Armijo flees.

1847 — Territorial Gov. Charles Bent is assassinated in Taos. U.S. forces quell the rebellion in an attack that seriously damages the mission church at Taos Pueblo.

1848 — The Treaty of Guadalupe Hidalgo is signed. Mexico cedes New Mexico to the United States.

1850 — New Mexico becomes a U.S. territory.

1851 — The first English language school is founded in Santa Fe by Bishop Jean Lamy.

1861-62 — Confederate soldiers from Texas invade Santa Fe and occupy the Palace of the Governors. The Battle of Glorieta, near Santa Fe, ends Confederate control in New Mexico and squelches their plan to capture the West.

1869 — Construction of St. Francis Cathedral begins.

1870 — The territorial governor disposes of many of the official records of New Mexico. Only about one-fourth are recovered.

1874 — Workers lay the foundations for Loretto Chapel.

1879 — Governor Lew Wallace writes a portion of *Ben Hur* in the Palace of the Governors.

1880 — The Atchison, Topeka & Santa Fe Railroad arrives in Santa Fe over a spur line from the main station in Lamy. Travel along the Santa Fe Trail dies away.

1881 — Santa Fe installs its first water and telegraph systems.

1891 — The City of Santa Fe is officially incorporated.

1892 — New Mexico's new territorial capitol building burns in Santa Fe. Arson by Albuquerque boosters who want the seat of government moved south is suspected but never proven.

1907 — The Palace of the Governors, saved from demolition, becomes a museum.

1912 — New Mexico becomes the 47th state.

1913 — The Palace of the Governors is remodeled with a Pueblo-Revival-style portal. Soon many other buildings receive similar treatment, and new architecture also adopts this look.

1917 — The Museum of Fine Arts, another example of Santa Fe style, is dedicated.

1922 — The Southwestern Association on Indian Affairs establishes the annual Indian market, a show and sale that remains part of modern Santa Fe's cultural life.

1926 — The Old Santa Fe Association is formed to help preserve city landmarks.

1942 — The federal government selects Los Alamos Boys School site for a secret project to develop an atomic bomb. Scientists and their families begin coming to Santa Fe on their way to the research site.

1945 — Scientists working in Los Alamos produce the world's first atomic bomb.

1948 — Indians receive the right to vote.

1957 — Santa Fe adopts its Historic District Ordinance to help protect landmark buildings.

1957 — John Crosby founds the Santa Fe Opera.

1964 — St. John's College of Annapolis establishes a second campus in Santa Fe.

1966 — New Mexico's present state capitol building, the Roundhouse, is dedicated in Santa Fe.

1975 — Extensive archaeological work begins at the Palace of the Governors.

1975 — Democrat Jerry Apodaca becomes New Mexico's first Hispanic governor since 1918.

— continued on next page

1975 — The Santa Fe Chamber Music Festival is established.

1980s — Celebrities "discover" Santa Fe. The city begins to become trendy; real estate prices start to climb. New Age seekers begin to come to Santa Fe as a spiritual center.

1983 — Santa Fe Community College is created.

1987 — The Santa Fe City Council adopts an archaeological review ordinance protecting artifacts older than 75 years.

1989 — Santa Fe Children's Museum is founded.

1994 — Debbie Jaramillo becomes Santa Fe's first woman mayor.

Santa Fe's first bishop, Frenchman Jean Baptiste Lamy. Lamy recruited adventurous priests, nuns and brothers from Europe to help establish schools, hospitals and orphanages in New Mexico and to care for the territory's sprawling population of Catholics. Lamy began construction of St. Francis Cathedral and Loretto Chapel. He introduced reform into New Mexico's long-neglected Catholic Church but declined to show what many residents believed was sufficient respect for New Mexico's indigenous religious traditions.

Lamy's imposition of northern European cultural values on New Mexico's Catholics, who had been largely independent of church authority for many decades, led to resentment. His clashes with native clergy and what many considered his disrespect for northern New Mexico's indigenous arts and culture — much of which had been created for the glory of God and the saints — brought conflict that continued throughout his long tenure as bishop and archbishop.

Other settlers of the 19th century came to Santa Fe as traders who wished to establish businesses or as sheep raisers, ranchers and homesteaders looking for a fresh start. The people of Santa Fe called them "Anglo" — a word used to mean people who were not Spanish or American Indian. Many Spanish women married Anglos, but whether they did or not, women lost many of the freedoms they'd enjoyed prior to U.S. occupation.

As a concession to the ethnic realities of the area, territorial government was conducted in both English and Spanish, and the legislature itself was primarily Hispanic until 1886. Hispanics outnumbered non-Hispanics by about 50 to 1. The influx of Anglo settlers was prompted by cheap land and the rumor that the New Mexico climate was good for one's health. Health seekers and artists, who also appreciated Santa Fe's brilliantly clear air and high-country climate, continued to visit and move to Santa Fe off and on throughout the city's history.

Reflective of the changes that overtook the territory, Santa Fe received its first Protestant church — the first in New Mexico — built by the Baptists at the corner of Grant and Griffin streets in 1854. The Presbyterians acquired the property in 1857 and remodeled it several times, ending with the Pueblo-Revival style building that exists today.

Despite the area's geographic isolation, the Civil War found New Mexico. In February 1862, a Confederate general leading troops from Texas invaded, won several crucial battles and took control of Santa Fe. But Confederate rule didn't last long. On March 26, Union and Confederate forces met about 15 miles from Santa Fe. The Union troops destroyed Confederate supplies in the Battle of Glorieta, and the Texans went south, abandoning their dreams of capturing the West.

The end of the Civil War didn't bring peace. Conflicts with the Plains Indians increased during U.S. rule partly because the American government failed to protect Indian lands, as the Mexicans and Spanish had done. Reflecting the cultural values of the day, the U.S. government openly suppressed Indian rights and worked to destroy Native American culture by forcing children to go to boarding schools where they could not speak their native languages, practice their traditional religion or stay in close touch with their families. As more settlers moved in, the problems worsened.

Conflict between the territorial government and the citizenry continued. One governor, William Pile, angered Santa Fe residents when he ordered workers to dispose of all historic documents in a room at the Palace of the Governors, as the *Casas Reales* was now called. Outraged Hispanic and Anglo residents attempted to recover the priceless papers. Some were found as waste paper or meat wrappers; many were lost forever.

Once the Anglos gained political power in Santa Fe, an ugly anti-Hispanic prejudice took its toll on the area. The treaty of Guadalupe Hidalgo specified that Spanish and Mexican land grants in the territories acquired by the United States after the Mexican War would be respected. But the differences in the systems of law made it difficult for many land-grant owners to substantiate their land titles. Although some of Santa Fe's prominent longtime families managed to keep their land and their power, most fared badly. Not speaking English or understanding the American legal system, they were easy prey for unscrupulous lawyers and politicians. The Spanish and Mexican judicial system required only that *alcaldes*, or judges, know how to read and write; the U.S. system called for trained lawyers. Anglo lawyers soon concentrated in Santa Fe, and many grew rich.

One of Santa Fe's most powerful men during this period was Thomas Catron. Catron moved to Santa Fe from Missouri, learned to speak and write Spanish and amassed more than a million and a half acres of land-grant property. Catron, a lawyer, involved himself in local politics and ruled the powerful Republican party, then worked as an advocate for statehood and became one of New Mexico's first two senators. During his day and afterward, many accused him of unethical practices, but his defenders say he accumulated his fortune and power legally and died bankrupt.

Accusations of fraud, political corruption and malfeasance flowed freely in territorial New Mexico. Finally, the U.S. Secretary of the Interior suspended New Mexico's Gov. Samuel Axtell and named Lew Wallace in his place. Wallace is the best known of the state's territorial rulers, not so much for his politics, but because he worked on his famous novel, *Ben Hur*, while living at the Palace of the Governors. In addition to the problems of Spanish families, who felt they were being unjustly deprived of their land, Wallace had to deal with Indian uprisings, raids by Billy the Kid in southeastern New Mexico and growing conflict between cattle and sheep ranchers. He coined the often-repeated expression: "Every calculation based on experience elsewhere fails in New Mexico." During Wallace's administration the first successful effort was made to preserve and catalog the existing priceless documents from Santa Fe's Mexican and Spanish periods.

In 1880 the railroad made its presence felt. Even though it was named Atchison Topeka & Santa Fe, the company planned to bypass Santa Fe because of engineering problems. A group of city boosters prevailed on the railroad to run an 18-mile spur to serve Santa Fe. Without rail service, they feared that Santa Fe would lose its prominence to rail towns such as Las Vegas and Albuquerque. Rail service quickly brought the end to the Santa Fe Trail and delivered curious tourists to the city's doorstep. The spur line cut through the western part of the city, and railyards and depots were built using bricks brought by the trains.

The look of Santa Fe began to change. The railroad delivered quantities of new building materials, among them wood and glass. Santa Fe residents enjoyed new options; some wished to duplicate the homes they'd known in the East or Midwest. Preservationists and the city promoters worried that the town would shortly sacrifice its distinctiveness and that the popularity of the new materials would mean the end of adobe. They feared that the unique character of Santa Fe would erode. If Santa Fe lost its charm, they believed, it would also lose the tourist dollars that had begun to flow.

These city boosters, among them artists, archaeologists, civic leaders and merchants, began to develop a plan for Santa Fe's future that included a unique architectural vision. The Pueblo-Revival style, also known as Spanish Pueblo style, combined modern convenience with the city's traditional look and came to be known as "Santa Fe Style." In the 1880s, a new State Capitol building and a governor's mansion were constructed on vacant land south of the Santa Fe River, shifting these functions away from the Palace of the Governors and the Plaza. The new capitol burned under mysterious circumstances in 1885 — some said the cause was arson by Albuquerque partisans who wanted their town to become the state capital. Another new capitol, complete with pillars and a dome rather than Santa Fe-style *vigas* and a *portal*, was built in 1900.

But Santa Fe won a larger battle. The city persuaded the Territorial Legislature to renovate the Palace of the Governors and transform it into a museum instead of demolishing the old building. Later a Fine Arts Museum was constructed in the new style, a modification of traditional pueblo construction. La Fonda Hotel, the School of American Research and the old Post Office building across from the Cathedral Place all testify to the early popularity of this look, which has become an enduring trademark of modern Santa Fe.

Lew Wallace wrote enthusiastically about his new home and was one of many 19th-century writers and artists who spread the news of Santa Fe's attraction. Although the territory had its problems, its romanticization began. The railroad made it easier to come West, and visitors did.

With wonderful foresight, the territory established the Bureau of Immigration, a precursor to the modern department of economic development, in Santa Fe in 1880. The department offered information to outsiders who hoped to make money here, but also received inquiries from artists, writers and anthropologists drawn by Santa Fe's physical beauty and Hispanic and Indian cultures. Santa Fe's business community came together in 1882 as the Santa Fe Board of Trade, spearheading the movement that led to the incorporation of the city in 1891. By the end of the 19th century, many community leaders recognized that Santa Fe's economic future hinged on two factors: tourism and government employment.

Statehood and Beyond

When Gen. Kearny first brought U.S. rule to Santa Fe, the city's population was estimated at between 2,000 and 4,000. By 1910, that figure was 5,600, with an additional 9,200 people living outside the city proper. Santa Fe marked the early years of the 20th century with an ongoing cry for the rights of statehood. Three attempts at admission to the Union had failed, at least partly because of continuing anti-Catholic, anti-Spanish sentiment in Congress. New Mexico suggested joint statehood with Arizona in 1906, but Arizona rejected the idea. Finally, on January 6, 1912, President William Howard Taft signed the bill making New Mexico the 47th state.

Although it has been amended several times, the state constitution has never been rewritten — but the idea arises frequently. Generally a conservative document, the constitution specified that Spanish was equal to English in both public education and legal discourse and included a bill of rights that again stressed that the rights provided in the Treaty of Guadalupe Hidalgo must be upheld. William C. MacDonald was New Mexico's first U.S. governor, living and working from Santa Fe, which continued to be the state capital.

In 1916, the old Fort Marcy headquarters were demolished to make way for the construction of the new Fine Arts Museum. A few years later, a group of artists and newcomers resurrected the Santa Fe Fiesta, including secular events and more parties to give the festival additional appeal. The custom of honoring *La Conquistadora* had survived, but when Santa Fe became a Mexican city the community began to celebrate Mexican independence rather than the exploits of Vargas — who became known in Santa Fe as "DeVargas."

In the 1920s, Santa Fe's art colony thrived, and visitors returned to the city seeking to become permanent residents. Painters captured the city's beauty on canvas and spread the word with their work. Before World War I, Sheldon Parsons, Victor Higgins, Gerald Cassidy, William Penhallow Henderson, B.J.O Nordfeldt and many more artists enriched the city in many ways. Will Shuster — now best known for creating Zozobra — and four other Santa Fe painters became known as *Los Cinco Pintores* and spread the glory of Santa Fe's scenery and people with their art. John Sloan, George Bellows and Leon Kroll — important names in 20th-century American art — had spent some time visiting and painting in Santa Fe. Edward Hopper and Marsden Hartley lived here in the 1920s and '30s, as did Robert Herni and Andrew Dausburg. In 1925 author Mary Austin and group of artists and collectors founded the Spanish Colonial Arts Society to encourage Hispanic artists to continue working in the traditions of the 18th century and to sell and promote their work. The 1920s also saw Santa Fe's first Indian Market, which became a long-standing community event. Leading Southwestern anthropologist Clyde Kluckhohn arrived in Santa Fe in 1925. In addition to "real" art, Santa Fe of this era also was filled with curio shops for tourists, including travelers who came on the Indian Detours circuit, a popular Southwestern touring business based in Santa Fe.

In the 1930s Santa Fe architect John Gaw Meem accelerated the trend to re-create Santa Fe's traditional look. The National Park Service Headquarters, built during the New Deal era, is a beautiful example of Pueblo-Revival style. In the 1930s, due partly to the pressure applied to the federal government by some of the city's well-placed Anglo residents and changing cultural views, the repression of Indian culture eased. The U.S. Indian School, a boarding school that brought Indian students to Santa Fe, was allowed to open an art department. The result renewed interest in Indian art among both American Indians themselves and in the broader culture.

Toward the Millennium

In the 1940s New Mexico assumed growing national importance due to its role in the development of the atomic bomb. The U.S. government took over Los Alamos Ranch School in 1943 as a secret center for nuclear research, and the project brought a steady stream of scientists and their families through Santa Fe for the clandestine work. By 1945 more than 3,000 civilian and military personnel were living there. Atomic bombs built in Los Alamos were dropped in Nagasaki and Hiroshima. Los Alamos National Laboratory (LANL), operated by the United States Department of Energy through a contract with the University of California, continues as a major contributor to Santa Fe and northern New Mexico's economy. The lab conducts a variety of scientific and technological research including work on nuclear weapons. With approximately 7,000 on staff and millions of dollars worth of contracts with northern New Mexico businesses, LANL's presence is seen by some as a blessing. Others believe that weapons research should have no place in the modern world, much less in northern New Mexico.

Through the 1950s, Santa Fe continued to grow, spreading southwest. However, during the 1960s and '70s urban renewal, highway construction, State Capitol expansion projects and the construction of large office buildings for state workers changed the city's urban pattern. The project caused realignment of roads and division of neighborhoods. Shopping centers, which offered lower rents and convenient parking, drew local customers away from downtown; Plaza businesses began to cater more to tourists and art buyers.

The construction of the Santa Fe Opera and its subsequent rise to national prominence helped keep Santa Fe's arts community in the spotlight. Established in 1957, the Opera successfully involved Santa Fe and New Mexico residents and businesses in its fund-raising. The Opera also attracted major corporate and out-of-state donors and now draws an international audience. The establishment of the Santa Fe Chamber Music Festival in 1975 added to Santa Fe's stature as an arts center. (See our Arts chapter.)

In 1957, the city created a historic district encompassing the Plaza and the eastern part of town. After the construction of two large buildings downtown in the 1970s and '80s, the city again tightened its protection for historic properties. Since then the designations have been expanded, and the rules and regulations for protecting historic properties in other neighborhoods clarified. Excavation at the Palace of the Governors in 1975 uncovered evidence from all periods of the history of the building. Visitors to the Palace today can see storage bins from 1693 in a glass-covered pit beneath the floor boards.

Santa Fe's status as an educational center was enhanced by the establishment of St. John's College in 1964. The creation of Santa Fe Community College in 1983 made it possible for the first time for Santa Fe students to continue their learning at a public college without leaving home. (See our Education chapter.) Beginning in the early 1980s, Hollywood and music celebrities "discovered" Santa Fe, many buying homes in the area and others vacationing here regularly. Their presence, and Santa Fe's growing attraction as a place for millionaires to build second homes, led to more gourmet restaurants, first-rate art galleries and luxury shops. It also lead to accelerating rents and real estate prices, higher property taxes and the dislocation of some longtime residents. Santa Fe also attracted many "New Agers" and has became a center for the study and practice of alternative medicine. By the late 1990s, the city's population reflected the influx of non-Hispanic residents; Hispanics became a minority here for the first time in the city's history.

Modern Santa Fe contends with issues that face many cities in the United States: traffic, the need for affordable housing, problems with the public school system, crime and growing demand for city services. In 1994, Santa Fe elected its first woman mayor, former city councilor Debbie Jaramillo. Jaramillo's anti-tourism comments and the hiring of her brother and brother-in-law in major city jobs led to considerable controversy and brought negative national attention to Santa Fe. But the Jaramillo administration also inaugurated a successful affordable-housing program, purchased the railyard property and initiated new services for children and teenagers.

The city's reputation as an intellectual center was boosted with the opening of the Santa Fe Institute, a high-tech think tank which draws scientists, computer experts, writers and intellectuals from around the world. In the '90s Santa Fe was also home to more than 50 publishing companies. As the city looks toward the millennium, Santa Fe's economic base remains tourism and government, with a recent influx of small entrepreneurial companies including spin-offs of technology developed by Los Alamos National Laboratory.

The city's population combines American Indians with the ancestors of the founding Spanish families, great grandchildren of merchants who arrived over the Santa Fe Trail and new immigrants from California, Texas and elsewhere who find the city's culture, history and natural environment irresistible. Readers of the upscale *Condé Nast* travel publications consistently rank Santa Fe among their top-10 national and international destinations. The city's visitors bureau estimates that 3 million tourists spend time here over the course of a year.

If you want to learn more about Santa Fe's rich and long history, wonderful books await you. Check the shop at the Palace of the Governors or any of the city's bookstores. Now that you know a little about the forces that shaped modern Santa Fe, please use this guide to get the most out of your visit.

Undoubtedly, the most striking thing about Santa Fe is the loveliness and grandeur of the landscape and its brilliant azure skies.

Area Overview

It was a scorching day in New Mexico's capital city, and the heat spell, going on nearly a month, was starting to take its toll on the high-desert community unaccustomed to prolonged temperatures in the 90s. Located in the north-central mountains of the state — just 60 miles north of Albuquerque but a full 2,000 feet higher — Santa Fe's 7,000-foot elevation normally precludes more than a handful of such blistering hot days each summer. Still, except for the soaring mercury, it felt like just another weekday in the bustling, quaintly beautiful downtown, as locals and tourists alike lounged in the Plaza, seeking shelter from the unforgiving sun under trees or with the cool comfort of an ice cream cone from one of the busiest Häagen Dazs stores in the country.

But July 17, 1997, was no ordinary day, not even for a town where the peculiar and the remarkable are often perceived as banal, hence Santa Fe's moniker, "The City Different." On Johnson Street, just a few blocks northwest of the Plaza, some 5,000 people were lining up in a queue that overflowed into neighboring Grant, Griffin and McKenzie streets. Many would wait up to an hour and a half to be among the first to cross the threshold of the sparkling 13,000-square-foot Georgia O'Keeffe Museum on opening day.

As Oscar-winning actor Gene Hackman — one of Santa Fe's many celebrated residents and a board member of the new museum — gave the keynote speech, the staff at nearby Woolworth's was reeling from a different sort of news. In just a few months, the five-and-dime would close its doors forever, never to sell another handkerchief, hair net or one of its famous original Frito pies. For more than 60 years, Woolworth's was a stalwart Plaza landmark, one of the last vestiges of old Santa Fe in a downtown overflowing with upscale galleries, restaurants and trinket shops.

It was a striking juxtaposition of events and completely serendipitous. Woolworth's corporate offices in New York surely had no idea that their announcement to close every Woolworth's in the nation would coincide with the grand opening of a Santa Fe museum dedicated to O'Keeffe — an East Coast emigree whose red hills, bleached bones and cerulean skies would, for millions around the world, become synonymous with New Mexico and the American Southwest.

Here was a perfect metaphor for what Santa Fe had become, perhaps what it has always been — a confluence of contradictions where the old and the new, the practical and the luxurious, the working stiffs and the well-to-do live side-by-side in a constant state of often creative, occasionally troublesome, tension known as "tricultural harmony."

History

For those of you who still believe the Pilgrims were the first Europeans to settle in what would become the United States of America, throw away your old Anglo-centric text books and ideas and take note: Santa Fe was founded around 1608. That's 12 years before the Pilgrims landed on Plymouth Rock, making Santa Fe the oldest capital in the United States and the country's second-oldest city. Only St. Augustine, Florida, founded in 1563, is older.

You can almost feel the history buzz be-

INSIDERS' TIP

The average weekly wage in Santa Fe in 1996 was about $450. A one-bedroom apartment rented for an average of about $520; two-bedroom places went for about $650.

neath your feet as you walk the narrow, winding streets of downtown Santa Fe to the Plaza — the social, commercial and historical heart of the city. The Plaza is the site of the original settlement of Santa Fe. It's also where the Santa Fe Trail — the 19th-century trade route that originated in Independence, Missouri — ended and *El Camino Real*, the 16th-century "Royal Road" or "King's Highway" from Mexico City, began.

A few structures, such as the Palace of the Governors on the Plaza's north side, actually date back to the 17th century. But most downtown buildings have been renovated or newly built with facades of adobe-colored stucco to blend in with the early 20th century Spanish-Pueblo Revival architecture whose reddish-brown earth tones, flat roofs, small, deeply set windows, and protruding *vigas* (log beams) and *canales* (rectangular overhead drainage pipes) imitate construction methods used for centuries by the Pueblo Indians. You'll also see examples of the Territorial style, a relative of Greek Revival architecture that first came to Santa Fe in 1846 with the U.S. occupation. These buildings, both old and new, are characterized by red-brick facades, slender exterior columns, detailed cornices and larger windows and doors than in classical Spanish-Pueblo Revival buildings like the Museum of Fine Arts and La Fonda Hotel near the Plaza. Whatever and wherever the architecture, you're likely to find a pendulous red chile *ristra* hanging welcomingly from a *viga* or *portal* (porch). Despite its face-lift and proliferation of tourist-oriented businesses, the Plaza remains the soul of Santa Fe — a meeting place for old timers and newcomers, for lunch breaks and lovers' trysts, for political rallies and historical festivals, or just to put your feet up and sleep.

Tricultural Harmony

Though many ethnic groups coexist in Santa Fe, the three that dominate are Hispanics, Native Americans and "Anglos," a category that refers to anyone who's not Hispanic or Native American, including such distinctly non-Anglo ethnicities as Italians, Jews and Poles and sometimes even Asians and African-Americans. Together they create a fascinating mosaic of cultures and values that overlap and occasionally conflict. Voices are sometimes raised, as are fists — the latter only figuratively as a rule. Much of the reason lies with ethnic and economic reapportionment.

Only 30 years ago, Santa Fe was a relatively poor, primarily Hispanic town where Anglos comprised a mere 35 percent of the population. Today, Hispanics are in the minority for the first time in recent history — 48 percent to Anglos' 49 percent. Though the margin is tiny, it is hugely symbolic of a growing sense among Hispanics that wealthy Anglos have invaded what was once a tranquil little town and, however unwittingly, overshadowed their traditional culture. To a lesser, or at least less vocal, extent, Santa Fe's Native American community shares some of these sentiments. Though only 2.1 percent of the city's population, Indians exert a far greater influence in the city and county than their numbers imply.

The result is an occasional outbreak of resentment directed not only at "newcomers" — a euphemism for even longtime Anglo residents — but also toward Santa Fe's bread and butter: tourists. Certainly there's nothing new about tourist towns biting the hands that feed them. But in Santa Fe, tourism has supplanted even government as the state capital's chief employer, bringing with it massive waves of change and a city unsure how to deal with it. Because tourists come with cash — lots of it in many cases — they unintentionally highlight the growing gap between Santa Fe's haves and have-nots. Sadly, this disparity tends to break down along ethnic lines, creating what the city has termed an "Us versus Them" society.

INSIDERS' TIP

Voted by readers of the *Santa Fe Reporter* as the best place to take visitors, walk dogs, watch people, spot celebrities and hang out, the Santa Fe Plaza may not literally be in the geographical heart of the city, but it's certainly in the heart of city residents.

Consequently, visitors sometimes encounter, in a city renowned for its friendliness, a reluctant welcome from overzealous Santa Feans who want to avoid the "Californication" of their home town, as a bumper sticker popular several years ago proclaimed. Locals are understandably worried that their beautiful little city will turn into a mini-Los Angeles or Phoenix, the prototypes of unbounded growth and insidious urban sprawl. And without official intervention, it surely would.

But the city and county are striving to safeguard the region's special blend of traditions, cultures and natural beauty — assets that paradoxically draw more newcomers — while at the same time developing economies and housing that will meet the needs of present and future residents.

Growing Pains

Like an adolescent whose psyche can't keep up with its physical development, Santa Fe is facing an identity crisis. It's asking itself what it wants to be when it grows up. And growth is definitely a burning issue — perhaps the greatest single issue the city and county face. *Condé Nast* rated Santa Fe the top tourist destination in the world in 1992 and the third-most popular spot in the nation last year. Santa Fe's beauty, reputation for tolerance of all lifestyles and, in recent years, trendiness have attracted so many new residents to Santa Fe County that its population has tripled over the past 50 years to about 120,000 residents. Of those, 65,000 live within the city limits. That's up nearly a third from the 49,299 who called Santa Fe home in 1980.

Unfortunately, income, housing and even water haven't kept up with the influx of new bodies. In other words, welcome to Santa Fe, but don't count on a job that will leave much spending money after you've paid your rent or your mortgage.

Although the average weekly wage in 1996 for Santa Feans — $420.52 — was comparable to the national average of $410.72, housing costs on average were 25 percent higher than the rest of the country. For example, one-bedroom apartments rented for an average of $522.16 per month. A two-bedroom apartment cost another $131.85. Meanwhile, the median

cost of a house that same year ranged from $139,500 in the cheapest area (the southwest quadrant) to $378,500 in the chi-chi northeast corner of the city.

The question is not only *how* people manage, but also *why*? In a phrase: quality of life.

Quality of Life

Whatever their differences, Santa Feans agree on at least one thing — they live in a very special place that ranks high on the quality-of-life scale. It's why people come here; it's why they stay.

Quality of life means different things to different people. In Santa Fe, it almost universally refers to the unique combination of small-town atmosphere in a centrally located, urban setting with access to a wide variety of cultural activities that range from the urbane to the rustic — all this against a backdrop of extraordinary natural beauty and a healthy climate with crisp, clean mountain air.

Undoubtedly, the most striking thing about Santa Fe is the loveliness and grandeur of the landscape and its brilliant skies (see our Natural Environment chapter for details). Artists, particularly painters, have been attracted to northern New Mexico since time immemorial, lured by natural light that is like no other in the world. It's both dazzling and subtle and eternally difficult to capture on canvas. Many have tried, few have succeeded. Even those who have managed to lasso some of the luminescence of a New Mexico sky will tell you their work doesn't touch the real thing.

Of course, this is all part of the mythology of Santa Fe and the West. And it's why artists like Georgia O'Keeffe, a relatively late arrival, migrated en masse to Santa Fe, Taos and elsewhere in northern New Mexico beginning in the late 19th century. They found themselves enthralled not only by the colorful combination of cultures, but also by the austere beauty of the physical surroundings. For many of them it was the most exotic place they'd ever seen. They attracted more intellectuals who attracted still more intellectuals and, voilá, Santa Fe and its northern neighbor, Taos, turned into artists' colonies.

An hour's drive in any direction will quickly tell you why. The vistas are as fascinating as

The Plaza is the heart of Santa Fe.

they are beautiful, changing from minute to minute and mile to mile. A bend or two in the road can take you from gently rolling hills pocked with piñon, juniper and scrub brush to flat-topped mesas standing dark and aloof against streaky, iridescent blue skies. Another few miles and you're in the forest among white-barked aspen, ponderosa pine and — depending on the season — snow.

Snow? Seasons? In the desert? Indeed, many visitors come to Santa Fe with the mistaken notion that because it's desert, it's always hot. Wrong! This is *high* desert; mountain country. That means four distinct seasons, including winters that get an average of 30 to 34 inches of snow each year and attract in the neighborhood of 250,000 skiers from around the world.

Santa Fe sits in the foothills of the Sangre de Cristo mountain range at an elevation of 7,000 feet. While the nearby mountains are rugged — Santa Fe Baldy reaches higher than 12,600 feet, and Wheeler Peak in Taos measures 13,161 feet — they also protect the region below from the elements, affording Santa Fe relatively mild weather conditions.

Still, Mother Nature likes to flex her muscles every once in a while with dry, scorching hot spells or brutally cold winters, so be prepared for all possibilities. Generally, however, the seasons are fairly predictable, each arriving with its distinct brand of beauty — perhaps none more vibrantly than fall.

In autumn, the hillsides explode with reds and orange, pinks and purple and the shimmering gold of aspen groves that streak through the mountains. The colors force even the most jaded locals to stare in awe at nature's artistry. Many join tourists at the Santa Fe Ski Area to take a lift up the mountain and get a birds-eye view of the leaves (see our Annual Events chapter).

Springtime in Santa Fe County is also a sight to behold. The high desert virtually comes alive with wildflowers, the winter-barren earth bursting forth in colorful blooms and — hay fever sufferers beware — pollen. Bring plenty of extra-strength Allerest but, whatever you do, don't hide indoors.

Things To Do

If you insist on staying indoors, you can choose from a host of activities: world-class museums for art, history and native culture; historic buildings and churches; and more than 250 art galleries in a city reputed to be the third-largest art market in the country. Classical music lovers can enjoy the Santa Fe Chamber Music Festival and Santa Fe Desert Chorale in summer, Santa Fe Pro Musica from September to May and the Santa Fe Symphony Orchestra and Chorus year round.

Santa Fe also offers a nightly assortment of live music and dancing from piano bars and cabaret to salsa, jazz, blues, rock and much, much more. Flamenco fans can look forward to summer when the dazzling María Benítez Teatro Flamenco returns. It's also the season when St. John College hosts the annual Shakespeare in Santa Fe, an outdoor festival where even those who couldn't possibly sit through another performance of *The Tempest* or *The Merchant of Venice* can find something to enjoy. When all else fails, there's shopping. Whether you're in the market for jewelry, ceramic pots, clothing or a chile *ristra*, you'll be overwhelmed by the number and variety of places to explore.

If you're willing to venture outdoors, a whole other world awaits you including the internationally acclaimed, summer-only Santa Fe Opera, where world-renowned performers play to an open-sided amphitheater with a stunning view of the Jémez Mountains. July and August bring Spanish and Indian markets which, combined, attract up to 150,000 visitors each year. September means the annual Fiesta de Santa Fe, commemorating Don Diego de Vargas' reconquest of New Mexico 12 years after the 1680 Pueblo Rebellion. Several days of pageantry and parades culminate in the burning of "Zozobra" — a 40-foot-plus effigy of "Old Man Gloom." (See our Arts and Annual Events chapters for more about these events.)

Then, of course, there's the real outdoors — camping, hiking, bicycling, swimming, tennis, golf, rock-climbing and horseback riding all within a few miles of town. Hunting, fishing, rafting and hot-air ballooning will require a bit of travel. But few will complain about the scenery along the way. Winter sports include downhill skiing, snowboarding and even inner-tubing down the slopes of the Santa Fe National Forest. Cross-country skiers and snowshoers can blaze their own trails through the Santa Fe National Forest. (See our Parks and Recreation and Winter Sports chapters.)

Local Color

Santa Fe Style

Santa Fe has a unique style that's instantaneously recognizable in many places around the world. Whether it's art or architecture, food or clothing, home decor or entertainment, it's always colorful, casual and downright earthy. Architecturally, for example, it doesn't get much earthier than adobe, which after all is mud brick. Even faux adobe buildings are earth-colored and, like the real thing, often trimmed with turquoise window sills and doorways; dark brown, rough-hewn *vigas* (log ceiling beams); and bright red chile *ristras*. Inside you're likely to find terra-cotta *saltillo* tile on the floor; hand-painted ceramic tile in the kitchen or bathroom; colorful, geometric-designed Navajo rugs on the walls or floors; perhaps a wooden *santo* (religious sculpture) or an Indian pot in a small *nicho* (niche) built into the wall; maybe even a *banco* (earthen bench) on either side of a corner *kiva* fireplace. Some homes feature handcrafted Santa Fe style furniture, which is rustic and expensive. The price reflects the intricate, hand-carved details whose irregularities and imperfections lend it a rough beauty. Staining or etching in turquoise or other colors can add another few dollar signs to the cost.

Santa Fe also has a distinctive clothing style, conspicuous not only for its color and flair but also for its casualness. You'll rarely see anyone wearing a business suit here — except lawyers, and then only when they're in court, or state legislators (many of whom are lawyers), and then only when they're in session. Santa Fe men would rather wear Dockers or denims and bolo ties than business suits and silk ties, while women seem to be more comfortable in prairie skirts and boots than dresses and heels (though there's certainly plenty of that too). Even in Santa Fe's most expensive restaurants diners are as likely to be dressed in jeans or broomstick skirts and fancy cowboy boots as Armanis and Donna Karans. And day or night, it's a sure bet you'll see lots of jewelry and accessories — silver bracelets, watchbands and rings trimmed with turquoise, onyx and other stones; *concha* or silver-buckled belts; bolo ties; squash blossom necklaces; big, dangly earrings with crystals and gems on women; and small studs or hoops on men, even at City Hall. You'll see lots of cowboy hats, too, but probably not as many as you expected.

Of course, Santa Fe style is easy to overdo, and you'll see examples in real life and in parody. In your travels around the Plaza, be sure to look for a now-famous cartoon poster entitled "Another Victim of Santa Fe Style." It shows a woman dressed head-to-toe in haute Santa Fe fashion — cowboy boots, broomstick skirt, concho belt, squash blossom necklace, big earrings, etc. — lying lifelessly on her flawlessly tiled, Navajo-rug-covered floor as one of the brightly colored wooden snakes that previously lived on her wall slithers across the floor toward an open door.

Politics

Stop a half-dozen Santa Feans on the street and ask what the favorite local pastime is, and they may hesitate for a millisecond before answering, "Politics." While this may be less than shocking in a state capital — especially one in which nearly every third worker has a government job — the tremendous interest residents take in local issues is still striking. One need only glance at the op-ed pages of *The Santa Fe New Mexican,* the *Journal North,* or the weekly *Santa Fe Reporter* to see the astounding number of letters to the editor that debate regional politics. But it doesn't stop there. Santa Feans debate regional politics over breakfast, lunch and dinner, at work, at play, on street corners, in the malls, at the library and via e-mail. Local government garners so much interest that Channel 6, the cable public access station, televises meetings for those who can't attend in person.

Some people show up or tune in just to watch Mayor Debbie Jaramillo, notorious for her off-the-cuff, often intemperate comments. She was up for re-election in March 1998. Among the many controversies surrounding the

INSIDERS' TIP

Don't assume that because you're out of the big city, you're out of the woods when it comes to crime. Santa Fe has a high rate of thefts, especially from automobile break-ins, which accounted for nearly 40 percent of all property crimes in 1996. Lock your car at all times and avoid leaving tempting items in plain view. Try to park in well-trafficked areas or at least well-lighted ones.

Tall aspens put on a colorful show in fall.

mayor was appointing her brother to be city manager. The city council fired him after he named the mayor's brother-in-law as the new police chief when their hand-chosen chief — the first African American to head the city's police department — resigned after an 18-month reign fraught with dissension and accusations of racism.

Among the most contentious items of recent times — one that split the Democratic Party in an area where Democrats have traditionally outnumbered Republicans by more than two to one — was 1997's special congressional election. The dark-horse Republican — a little-known conservative Anglo minister from affluent Los Alamos — defeated a career Democrat Hispanic to replace Democrat Rep. Bill Richardson, also Hispanic and an unbeatable incumbent who held on to his northern New Mexico seat for eight terms before becoming U.S. ambassador to the United Nations. Democrats accused the Green Party of splitting the vote. The Green Party accused the Democrats of nominating without voter approval a party cog with a checkered political past. Northern New Mexicans are still arguing the issue

Also stirring up Santa Feans is the prospect of having truckloads of nuclear waste pass through their fair city en route to the Waste Isolation Pilot Plant (WIPP) — an underground nuclear dump near Carlsbad, New Mexico, where mixed radioactive materials are to be buried 2,150 feet below the ground in 225-million-year-old rock salt deposits.

One of 1997's great debates was the county's decision to allow the Santa Fe Ski Area to raze 9 acres of national forest to build a parking lot. The county approved the plan only after a commissioner who had gone on record opposing it ducked out of the meeting moments before the crucial vote. The city sued both the county and the ski company to halt construction but withdrew the lawsuit, calling it an expensive exercise in futility. Meanwhile, some citizens chained themselves to trees to prevent loggers from cutting them down.

Food

Eating is another favorite pastime in Santa Fe, especially when it comes to local cuisine. While the ingredients might be the same ones used in other cultures — Mexican, Tex-Mex, Spanish, etc. — the food here is a culinary blending of American Indian and Mexican influences that is as distinct as the dialect. That's largely due to the ubiquitous chile pepper. Whether you like it hot or mild, whether you prefer green or red or even "Christmas" (some of each), you're going to encounter New Mexican chile in many different forms, usually in traditional native foods such as enchiladas, tamales, carne adovada (marinated and baked pork) or posole (stewed hominy), but also in hamburgers, on pizza, even in apple pie. Don't be shy about using a sopaipilla — a hollow, deep-fried yeast bread eaten with honey — to wipe up that last drop of chile from your plate.

Many of Santa Fe's more than 200 restaurants, regardless of nationality, will use locally grown chile in at least one of their dishes, whether it's a five-star restaurant — and Santa Fe boasts many — or McDonald's. Celebrated for its fine New Mexican fare, Santa Fe is also deservedly famous for the variety and quality of its many restaurants, from nouvelle cuisine with a Southwestern twist to Chinese, French, Greek, Indian (from India), fine Italian, Japanese, Middle Eastern, Native American, Thai, Tibetan, vegetarian . . . the list goes on.

INSIDERS' TIP

New Mexico's official state symbol is the Zia, an ancient sun sign taken from a design seen on a late-19th-century water jar from Zia Pueblo. The New Mexico flag — designed in 1923 by Reba Mera and officially recognized two years later — features a Zia symbol in red on a field of bright gold. Those were the colors of Queen Isabel of Castilla, which the Spanish *conquistadores* brought with them to the New World.

Language

Spanish is the second official language of Santa Fe — the first language for an estimated 10,000 residents. Locals pepper their conversations with colorful Spanish words and phrases that have no adequate translation in English. Even newspapers and magazines have liberal sprinklings of Spanish throughout, with tildes (~) and accent marks appearing as a matter of course. Some have all-Spanish language sections.

But don't come to Santa Fe planning to speak Spanish with the natives. While a huge portion of the population speaks Spanish at home — around 35,000 according to the last census — English tends to be the language of choice here. Remember, New Mexico is one of the 50 United States — the 47th, to be precise. Apparently some Americans are unaware of that fact — enough to warrant an anecdotal column in *New Mexico Magazine* called "One of Our Fifty is Missing."

Among the most infamous anecdotes — one that appeared in *Time* magazine and other national publications as well as on television and radio — recounts how a Santa Fe man called Atlanta to order volleyball tickets for the 1996 Olympics. When he gave the agent his New Mexico address, she told him she could only sell tickets in the United States; he'd have to call his country's national committee for tickets. He tried to explain, first to the agent and then to her supervisor, that New Mexico joined the Union in 1912 and is as American as Georgia peaches, but to no avail. He finally had to give an address in Phoenix to get his tickets.

Tolerance

By the late 19th century, Santa Fe had already earned a reputation for tolerance, primarily because of the artists who "discovered" it and lived quietly among the natives. The area was still enough off the beaten path to attract some of society's outcasts and eccentrics — artists, healers, spiritualists or simply individualists. Today, however, the beaten path leads directly to Santa Fe's door, where everyone is welcome provided they "don't move the furniture," as Mayor Debbie Jaramillo put it.

She was referring to what a North Carolina acquaintance of ours calls RAREs — Recent Arrivals Rearranging Everything. These are the people who move to Santa Fe for its unique beauty and relaxed, small-town charm, then immediately want to change things once they get here. It understandably causes resentment.

RAREs are a relatively recent phenomenon — and a rather conventional one at that. As a beacon for alternative lifestyles and ideologies, Santa Fe has also attracted more than its share of Aquarian Age adherents. It began in the 1960s with the hippie movement which found, if not open arms, at least passive ones in northern New Mexico. Today, Santa Fe is filled with old and young flower children as well as aura readers, channelers, Iron Johns, non-native shamans, white Rastafarians and women who run with wolves. Once merely the state capital of New Mexico, Santa Fe is now the New Age capital of the United States.

Santa Fe's more traditional spiritual community offers options as diverse as they are plentiful from Assembly of God to Zen Buddhism as well as Baha'ism, Hinduism, Islam, Mormonism, Sikhism, Sufism and Unitarian Universalism, to name just a few. There's never a moment's doubt, however, as to which religion dominates. One need only look up at the mountain range that reigns regally and protectively over the region — the Sangre de Cristo ("Blood of Christ") Mountains — to be reminded that Catholicism runs deeply in the veins and the hearts of northern New Mexicans.

Running just as deeply in northern New Mexicans is an abiding respect for traditional herbal medicine administered either by Hispanic healers called *curanderas* or Indian medicine men. Perhaps for that reason, Santa Fe has long been a mecca for alternative healthcare. Even a brief glance in the Yellow Pages offers a mind-boggling array of "modalities," including acupuncture, chiropractors, hypnotism, massage therapy, homeopathy, energy healing, biofeedback, herbs and spiritual healing.

Bienvenidos

New Agers, old-timers and trust funders;

Our magnificent scenery will overwhelm you.

Hispanics, Native Americans and Anglos — they're all part of the fabric of Santa Fe, a cloth tightly woven from a variety of belief systems, traditions and lifestyles. The only way to know it is to experience it — and even then it could take a lifetime.

So ¡Bienvenidos a Santa Fe! And remember, don't move the furniture.

New Mexico's pueblos hold numerous feasts, dances and other celebrations throughout the year that are open to non-Indians.

Local Cultures

Northern New Mexico is a land of conquest and reconquest, sometimes accomplished by forceful means, other times without a drop of blood spilled. The region has changed hands and complexions many times, starting with the Pueblo Indians, whose agrarian cliff-dwelling forebears settled the region as far back as the 1st century B.C.

Pueblo culture as we know it today took root at the beginning of the 14th century and flourished for 300 years — until its first encounter in 1540 with Europeans, who brought guns as well as a new world of diseases against which the natives had no natural defenses. Through force in some cases and friendly but firm persuasion in others, Spanish *conquistadores*, priests and settlers claimed the region in the name of the motherland and the Catholic Church, only to lose it in 1680 during the Pueblo Revolt (see our History chapter). Spain reconquered the territory in 1692 and held onto it for more than a century. In 1821, Mexico claimed the New Mexico area by default when it won independence from Spain. Twenty-seven years later, after losing a two-year war to its northern neighbor, young Mexico ceded the territory to an even younger United States under the terms of the 1848 Treaty of Guadalupe Hidalgo.

Hispanic Culture

The result of this checkered history is a checkerboard of cultures, with Anglo Americans among the last to arrive. "Anglo" culture is a category that today in New Mexico encompasses everything from white bread Americans to African Americans, Arabs, Asians, East Indians, Tibetans, Irish, Italians, Jews, Poles, Russians and anyone else not of Hispanic or Native American origin.

Despite the subtle and not-so-subtle encroachment of Anglo culture over the past 150 years, the dominant flavor of northern New Mexico is without a doubt Hispanic. What that means, however, has been an ongoing — and often heated — debate in which many *Hispanos* have shunned their Mexican roots in favor of their Spanish heritage, while a few have taken the opposite stance. Today, however, the consensus seems to be that local Hispanic culture has its roots in Spain *and* Mexico as well as in Native America.

Whatever the precise definition, it's a combination unique to New Mexico — one you'll see, hear and feel the moment you emerge from the airplane into the Albuquerque International Sunport or step out of your car at any Allsup's gas station/convenience store in Santa Fe or points north. It's all around you — in the art and the architecture, the music and the clothing, the food and the language . . . especially the language.

Here we live in flat-roofed *adobe* homes on *caminos* and *calles*. Outside, our *portales* (porches) are decorated with bright red chile *ristras*. Inside, our *casas* have corner *kiva* fireplaces and log *vigas* that hold up *latilla* ceilings. Our walls are decorated with built-in *nichos* displaying handcrafted *santos* — religious images carved by *santeros* — that glorify *Díos*. We wear *bolo* ties and *concho* belts. We dance to *ranchero* music, *mariachi* or *salsa*, which is also something we eat with tortilla chips and guacamole before digging into plates filled with enchiladas or burritos with red or green chile and perhaps a side of posole or chicos. Chicos are also children, whom parents affectionately call mi hijo or mi hijita — elided to m'ijo or m'ijita — sending them off to school where they recite the Pledge of Allegiance first in English, then, in some cases, in Spanish.

That's a far cry from the time between the 19th century and the mid-20th century, when New Mexican children were punished for speaking español in school. Today, students learn early on that the Spanish arrived in New Mexico years before the real Anglos — the English Puritans — landed at Plymouth Rock. They're fully aware that Santa Fe is the oldest state capital and the second-oldest city in the nation.

In schools and elsewhere throughout New Mexico, there's a pride in Hispanic heritage that has produced local artists and artisans whose work is recognized nationally and internationally. Traditional or folk artists utilize native materials — wood, tin, silver, straw, etc. — and techniques that in many cases their families have been using for generations. While the Spanish and Mexican influences are apparent in their work, the styles are uniquely New Mexican — and often unique to a particular family. Contemporary hispano artists, like their brethren around the world, work in every imaginable medium. Sculpture, painting, photography, jewelry and, yes, those elegant, traffic-stopping labors of love called low riders (see our tip in this chapter) all play an integral role in the northern New Mexico art scene. So do Hispanic literature, film, theater, dance, music and lore.

Of course, Hispanics — who represent nearly half the population of Santa Fe — play major roles in all walks of life, not just the arts. They're accomplished doctors, dentists, lawyers, teachers, priests and politicians, to name just a few professions. In fact, the two most powerful men in the state legislature are Hispanic and have each been in their respective positions — speaker of the House of Representatives and Senate president pro tem — for more than a decade. In Santa Fe, the majority of city coun-

FYI

Unless otherwise noted, the area code for all phone numbers listed in this guide is 505.

cilors and county commissioners are Hispanic.

But la cultura hispana is far more than what people do for a living, the clothes they wear, the food they eat or even the language they speak — though the latter is closer to the crux of the matter. Here in northern New Mexico, Hispanic culture is la gente (the people). La familia (family) comes first, followed by la comunidad (community). Sometimes they're one and the same.

Embedded in the culture is a deep-rooted sense of hidalguismo — an aristocratic lineage that hearkens back to the founding of Santa Fe in 1608 by the nobility (los hidalgos) in concert with the Catholic Church. While el hidalguismo and the entitlement that came with it is today merely a vestige, the Catholic Church has survived intact. Indeed, el catolicismo touches all aspects of la vida in northern New Mexico, regardless of one's faith. From the Sangre de Cristo (Blood of Christ) Mountains that loom over the northern Rio Grande Valley to the myriad churches, missions and moradas (see the close-up on Penitentes in our Worship chapter) dotting the landscape; from invocations at government functions and school sporting events to Las Fiestas de Santa Fe which, despite its secular trappings, is Catholic at its core; from the festive farolitos that light rooftops and driveways throughout the Christmas season to the annual Easter pilgrimage to the Santuario de Chimayó — there's no question that northern New Mexico, and particularly La Villa Real de Santa Fe (Royal City of the Holy Faith), was founded as a far reaching bastion of the Spanish Catholic Church. It remains tied to those roots at its deepest levels.

Spain's influence in New Mexico goes beyond religion and art. Spanish colonizers who survived the perilous six-month trek along El Camino Real — the 2,000-mile "Royal Road" or "King's Highway" from Mexico City to Santa Fe — brought with them mining and forging equipment and techniques. They showed the Indians how to use metals for weapons, tools and art. They brought the wheel, introduced horses to the continent and taught the Pueblo

Visitors to Santa Fe will feel the impact of pueblo culture.

people how to raise cattle and sheep. They engineered the efficient and aesthetic *acequia* irrigation system still used throughout New Mexico today.

Despite armed conflicts between the two cultures, the settlers in time found they had more in common with their immediate neighbors than they did with distant Spain, if only because they shared an enemy in the hostile Plains Indians. Years of commingling among the Spanish, Mexicans and Indians eventually gave rise in New Mexico to a unique *mestizo* culture of its own — one rich with tradition, much of it oral. *La curandera* heals with unwritten methods passed down to her, and which she will pass on to the next generation; *el mayordomo* consults no manual to direct the annual cleaning of the *acequias* (irrigation ditches); *la cuentista* (storyteller) needs no script to relate *cuentos* (tales) and *leyendas* (legends) that have been refined and embellished over hundreds of years.

What we've described thus far is a colorful portrait of Hispanic life in northern New Mexico. But this multifaceted culture that has flourished here since the 16th century has of late been confronted with a dark side. In Santa Fe, where

until recently *Hispanos* were in the majority, the unemployment and poverty rates among Hispanics are disproportionately high. As a result, so is the dropout rate, homicide rate and domestic violence. The powers that be attribute this largely to a movement away from what was once primarily a land-based culture to a free-market, wage-dependent economy where traditional skills such as farming and ranching are no longer marketable. Add to this volatility an invasion of visitors and new, moneyed residents, and perhaps you can understand why many in the Hispanic community feel disenfranchised. They sense they're losing their land, their voice and ultimately their culture to the highest bidder.

For the survival of their rich heritage and a legacy to pass on to future generations, it's vital that Santa Fe cling to its roots. The answer lies not in isolationism, but rather in preserving the cultural vitality of the region without exploiting it.

Pueblo Culture

Centuries before Europeans reached the Americas, New Mexico was home to a thriving native population called the Anasazi — "the ancient ones," according to the most familiar translation from the Navajo, though the term literally means "the enemy of my ancestors." At the height of its civilization (approximately A.D. 900 to 1350), the Anasazi lived in a territory that stretched from central Utah and southern Colorado south to Mexico and from western Arizona into the Texas Panhandle. Their abandoned cities of cliff dwellings, pit houses, underground ceremonial *kivas* and petroglyphs etched in rocks are silent testament to the richness and resourcefulness of their culture. Many of New Mexico's 19 existing Indian pueblos — nine of them within 65 miles of Santa Fe — trace their origins directly to the Anasazi. The Navajo and Jicarilla Apache tribes, located in or near the remote Four Corners region in northeastern New Mexico, and the Mescalero Apaches in south-central New Mexico descended from the nomadic Athapascan tribe that arrived later. With some notable exceptions — among them the 1680 Pueblo Revolt, the raids of Spanish, Anglo and Pueblo Indian villages by Apache, Navajo and Plains peoples (see our History chapter), and more recently the fight to build and operate tribal casinos — Native Americans in the Southwest have kept a low profile, both politically and socially. Yet their artistic, architectural and culinary influence on the region is unmistakable. Native culture permeates all aspects of life here to some degree.

It was the Pueblo Indians whom Spanish explorers first encountered when they arrived in New Mexico in the late 1500s. They found a flourishing, agrarian and relatively peaceful population living in compact, apartment-like dwellings made of stone or adobe. The explorers christened them "pueblo" Indians from the Spanish word for village — a term that refers to the entire culture rather than a specific tribe. Spanish settlers adopted the native architecture and adapted the Indians' sophisticated underground irrigation system to their own *acequia* system. At the time of the first encounter, some historians estimate that close to 50,000 Indians lived on more than 100 pueblos. By 1857, they numbered only 7,000. Their civilization had been decimated by disease, starvation and execution, and their culture was threatened by assimilation — both forced and voluntary — and intermarriage. Still, the tribes managed to preserve many traditions by externally adopting the ways of the various paternalistic governments that occupied their native lands while secretly continuing to practice their own pantheistic religions and customs. Many of the new ways stuck, most notably Catholicism, which is widely practiced on the pueblos, though it has been adapted to native practices. This is particularly evident on feast days, which combine elements of the native religion with commemoration of Catholic saints.

www.insiders.com

See this and many other **Insiders' Guide®** destinations online — in their entirety.

Visit us today!

Modern Pueblo Life

Today, the 19 New Mexico pueblos count an estimated 30,000 members, including many who live away from their tribal lands. The pueblos share many characteristics, including similar customs and native languages — Tewa, Tiwa, Towa and Keresan. (Zuni Indians speak Zunian, which is unrelated to the other four languages.) But each pueblo is a unique, sovereign entity with individual governmental, religious and social structure. Every tribe also has a distinctive style in jewelry, weaving, basketry, carving and especially pottery, which is considered among the finest of all North American tribes. The black-on-black pottery made famous by María Martínez, for example, is recognized internationally as being from San Ildefonso Pueblo, while geometric black and white pots are clearly from Ácoma Pueblo, "The City in the Sky" west of Albuquerque.

INSIDERS' TIP

In case you missed our reminder elsewhere in this chapter, don't forget to read our close-up on pueblo etiquette before you visit. It will save you from embarrassing yourself or offending others.

Underlying the art and the very culture of the Pueblo Indians is a deeply personal and religious connection to the earth. Sometimes this is literal, as in the earth-toned, close-to-the-ground, mud and clay pueblo architecture that inspired the Spanish Colonial construction and today is known informally as "Santa Fe style." Other times it's reflected in dances or other religious ceremonies. One doesn't own the land, one belongs to it. As such, land is not a resource to be exploited but rather one to be respected. The land defines your origins as it defines your destiny. It provides shelter and food. It's the source of native art.

Until recently, land was the basis of the pueblos' economies — through agriculture, livestock and the sale of pottery, jewelry, baskets and other crafts. Today, however, a land-based economy is rapidly being supplanted by casinos as the main source of income for many pueblos. This has stirred a tremendous debate both within and outside the Indian community. Casinos have brought jobs and dollars to communities where unemployment has been as high as 45 percent and where staggering poverty and its associated ills — malnutrition, alcoholism, poor education, domestic violence and an alarming increase in violent crimes — have over the years become the norm.

With revenue from casinos, many tribes for the first time can afford to build sorely needed infrastructure and social programs. Fewer young men and women are leaving the pueblos, while many who took off for urban centers are returning home. As a result, tribes are gaining the human and material resources necessary to compete with their non-Indian neighbors on a more level playing field. And, indeed, they're taking a more active role in local, state and federal policy-making. But many say it's a Faustian bargain that comes with its own set of problems, among them gambling addictions, increased drug abuse, the potential for corruption and especially a clash of values. The latter is unique to the pueblos, which are trying to balance culture and tradition with political and economic pragmatism in what may well be a "New Federalism" of state, federal and tribal governments. Yet New Mexico remains divided about legalized gambling on lands that are supposed to be sovereign nations. Seeing the writing on the wall, many tribes are taking steps to diversify their economies. But the genie is out of the bottle, leaving behind a colossal political, cultural, social and economic hot potato with still unimagined implications.

Dances and Feast Days

There's no doubt that the pueblos are undergoing dramatic change. Through it all, they continue to practice their old and largely secret ways. These include ceremonial dances, which link the pueblo people to their physical and spiritual ancestors and to nature. Although some dances are open to the public, they are not entertainment. Dances are religious ceremonies, most of which are tied to seasonal or life-cycle events such as hunting, sowing, harvesting, initiations, rites of passage, etc. The pueblos perform dances to sanctify an event, to give thanks or to influence nature — for bountiful crops, for example, or a successful hunt. Non-Indians are privileged to watch selected dances on the pueblos at various times during the year, typically on Christmas Eve, Christmas Day, New Year's Day, Easter and on selected days throughout the summer. The rest are closed to outsiders — a result, in part, of centuries of persecution by

Photo: Don Strel/Southwest Assignments

Mariachi music adds to the Santa Fe Fiesta.

non-Indians who have misunderstood and misinterpreted native rituals. The tribes believe that secrecy has helped their religion survive. For that reason, you're likely to be met with a stony silence if you ask questions about dances or volunteer comments on their symbolic or spiritual meaning. Please refer to this chapter's closeup on pueblo etiquette.

Feast days, on the other hand, are a vestige of the pueblos' encounters with Europeans. Yet they're a uniquely Indian event. When the Spanish arrived in New Mexico in the late 16th century, missionaries assigned a patron saint to each pueblo in an effort to convert the Indians to Catholicism. In time, the saints' days became aligned with the pueblos' native religion because they coincided with tribal rituals. Today, feast days are a time when friends and family gather to eat together and participate in native ceremonies. They're also a time when tribal members invite complete strangers into their homes for a meal of green or red chile, posole (stewed hominy), fry bread, cookies or any of a number of other dishes. Forget the diet when you visit a pueblo on a feast day. It's considered impolite to refuse an invitation to eat. By doing so, you will have spurned your host's hospitality and generosity. At the risk of repeating ourselves, be sure to read the close-up in this chapter on etiquette.

Feast days are held around the same date every year. Dances take place at various times and may be scheduled a year or just a few days ahead of time. We suggest you call the pueblo before visiting to confirm any dates listed here or elsewhere, even in pueblo literature. Schedule changes are common. The pueblo can also provide you with information about taking photographs or making recordings or drawings, any or all of which may be prohibited or for which there may be a charge.

Following are individual descriptions of what are called the Eight Northern Pueblos, all within a two-hour drive north of Santa Fe. Each entry includes a brief history as well as the date of the pueblo's annual feast day. We have included a complete, tentative schedule of dances and other events at the end of this chapter. Most begin mid-morning and last until shortly after dusk. Again, please be sure to call the pueblo before attending an event to make sure the date and times haven't changed.

Eight Northern Indian Pueblos Council

San Juan Pueblo, S.R. 74 • 852-4265, (800) 793-4955

The Eight Northern Indian Pueblos Council is a cooperative group that works to promote joint projects and improve the economy, education and ceremonial efforts of the eight pueblos due north of Santa Fe. The council, a consortium of the pueblo governors, sponsors the Eight Northern Indian Arts and Crafts Show, which takes place in July at one of the northern pueblos. The show features Native American arts and crafts, dancing and traditional food. Unlike Indian Market (see our Annual Events chapter), the Eight Northern Indian Arts and Crafts Show is an Indian-run enterprise.

Nambé Pueblo

Rt. 1, Box 117BB, Nambé • 455-2036

Patron saint is San Francisco de Asís (St. Francis). Feast day is October 4 with pre-feast celebrations and dances on October 3.

Pronounced Nahm-BEH, the name of this pueblo is Tewa for "Mound of Earth in the Corner" — a poetic and apt description for the 19,076 acres that are home to an estimated 600 tribal members. It is one of the smaller of the northern pueblos. Occupied since 1300, Nambé was a religious and cultural center for Pueblo Indians throughout the region long before the Spanish arrived. As such, it became a target for *conquistadores* and priests whose mission included converting the natives to Catholicism. The tribe took an active role in the Pueblo Revolt of 1680, in which their priest was killed and their church destroyed.

Today, the tribe is highly assimilated to the surrounding community, which is primarily Hispanic. Over the past decade, however, members have taken an active interest in reviving traditional arts and crafts, which are a mainstay of the tribe's economy. You'll find many residents selling pottery, jewelry and other crafts out of their homes. The pueblo also houses a sculpture gallery and studio displaying both traditional and contemporary art. Nambé Pueblo also offers recreational opportunities galore, including camping, fishing and boating at Nambé Falls Recreation Area. As the name implies, the recreation area affords a close look at three natural waterfalls as well as a lake and stunning views of the Sangre de Cristo Mountains. You might also catch a glimpse of the tribe's buffalo herd, which at last count had 21 animals. The pueblo holds its annual Nambé Falls Celebration on July 4th with a variety of traditional dances, food vendors and arts and crafts.

Directions from Santa Fe: Take U.S. Highway 84/285 N. 16 miles to the junction with N.M. Highway 503 north of Pojoaque; then head east 2 miles on N.M. 503.

Picurís Pueblo

Off N.M. Hwy. 75, 13 miles east of Dixon • 587-2519

Patron saint is San Lorenzo (St. Lawrence). Feast day is August 10 with pre-feast celebrations and dances on August 9.

Once one of the largest of the northern pueblos, today Picurís [pick-kuh-REES] — or *We-lai*, which means "Those Who Paint" in Tiwa — is among the smallest with fewer than 350 members living in a secluded valley of the Sangre de Cristo Mountains about an hour north of Santa Fe. The Picurís ancestors arrived in the region around A.D. 750, settling first in a larger pueblo called Pot Creek before moving in or around the year 1250 to its current location, about 20 miles south of Taos. The Picurís were historically more aggressive than other pueblos, perhaps because of greater contact with the aggressive Plains Indians. Picurís Indians were deeply involved in the 1680 Pueblo Revolt, killing their priest and all the Spanish in the area. They paid a heavy price for it when the Spanish returned in 1692 and literally taxed them into starvation.

Picurís was 3,000 members strong when the Spanish arrived. By the end of the 17th century, only 500 were left, and they abandoned their pueblo. But they reclaimed their ancestral land in 1706 — 14,947 acres that today boast a number of excavated ruins and an above-ground ceremonial *kiva* that's at least 700 years old.

The pueblo's centerpiece remains the San Lorenzo de Picurís mission, an old adobe church that took 12 years to restore by hand. The tribe operates an on-site museum, gift shop and restaurant and is the majority owner of the Hotel Santa Fe in the capital city. The pueblo has a small buffalo herd and two trout-fishing lakes. Tours are available for Anasazi, pueblo and church ruins. In addition to the Feast of San Lorenzo in August, the pueblo hosts a feast day for St. Paul (San Pablo) on January 25 and another for St. Anthony (San Antonio) in June. The Weekend High Country Arts and Crafts Festival, usually the first weekend in July, is another major event on the pueblo.

Directions from Santa Fe: Take U.S. 84/285 N. 24.3 miles to the junction with N.M. 68 in Española. Go 20 miles north on N.M. 68 to the junction with N.M. 75 in the vicinity of Dixon, and go 13 miles east on N.M. 75.

Pojoaque Pueblo
Rt. 11, Box 21GS, Pojoaque • 455-2278 (governor's office), 455-3334 (Poeh Cultural Center)

Patron is Our Lady of Guadalupe. Feast day is on December 12.

With an estimated 280 members, Pojoaque (po-WAH-keh) is the smallest of all the northern pueblos. Its name is a Spanish derivative of *P'o-Suwae-Geh*, which is Tewa for "Water Drinking Place." Because of its abundance of water, Pojoaque was a major gathering place for Pueblo Indians of the Rio Grande prior to the Pueblo Revolt of 1680. The 11,063-acre pueblo sits between Nambé and Tesuque (Teh-SOO-keh) pueblos along U.S. 84/285, the northbound highway out of Santa Fe. Pojoaque is the site of the first Spanish mission in New Mexico, San Francisco de Pojoaque, founded in the early 1600s. The pueblo is notable for twice rising from near extinction. The first occurrence was in 1706 when five families resettled on tribal lands, which had been ravaged during and after the Pueblo Revolt of 1680 and were completely deserted by the time of the Spanish returned in 1692. They rose again in 1934 when 14 individuals returned from nearby pueblos and states to which the Pojoaque tribe had scattered after a turn-of-the-century smallpox epidemic nearly wiped out all its members. A drought and encroachment by non-Indians added to the pueblo's demise. But like the Phoenix, the pueblo quite literally rose from its ashes, with survivors rebuilding it physically and culturally.

Its church, built in 1706, is still used today. Among the pueblo's newer buildings is its handsome adobe Poeh Cultural Center and Museum. In addition to showcasing arts and crafts of Tewa-speaking people, the cultural center also offers classes in pottery, sculpture, textiles and art business management to tribal members and other Indians. The tribe manages a shopping center and a tourist information office that sells artwork from a variety of Tewa-speaking pueblos. But the pueblo's pride and joy without a doubt is its Cities of Gold Casino, a 40,000-square-foot gambling hall that employs 550 people.

Directions from Santa Fe: Take U.S. 84/285 north 15 miles.

San Ildefonso Pueblo
Rt. 5, Box 315A • 455-3549 (tourism office), 455-2273 (governor's office)

Patron saint is San Ildefonso (St. Ildefonse). Feast day is January 23. Pre-feast ceremonies are held on January 22.

Named for a 7th-century archbishop from Toledo, Spain, San Ildefonso's Tewa name is *Po-Woh-Ge-Oweenge*, or "Where the Water Cuts Down Through." A small pueblo, San Ildefonso is also one of the most beautiful.

Located 22 miles northwest of Santa Fe, the 26,198 acres of tribal land run from the Rio Grande to the upper elevations of the Jémez Mountains near Los Alamos. Cottonwood (*alamo*) trees line the riverbanks, deer and elk roam the land, and from all directions you can see Black Mesa — a dark, lonely hill sacred to the pueblo because it's the site where San Ildefonso and other pueblos valiantly but unsuccessfully defended their lands against the Spanish in 1694.

The San Ildefonso Indians are believed to have migrated from the Mesa Verde Anasazi colony in southwestern Colorado, whose ancient cliff dwellings, which date back to the 1st century, are now a national park. They settled first in Bandelier near Los Alamos, which today has been set aside as a national monument. A drought sent them to lower ground at the end of the 13th century, when they settled in their current location.

San Ildefonso is perhaps best known for its striking black-on-black pottery, especially that of the late María Martínez, whose pots today fetch high prices. Martínez and her husband, Julian, were largely responsible for the resurgence in the 1920s of traditional arts and crafts on San Ildefonso and other pueblos.

Tewa is the indigenous language for most of the tribe's 298 members. The pueblo hosts a feast day in June for San Antonio (St. Anthony).

Directions from Santa Fe: Take U.S. 84/285 15 miles to the junction with N.M. 502 in Pojoaque; go 6 miles west on N.M. 502.

San Juan Pueblo
S.R. 74 • 852-4400

Patron saint is San Juan (St. John the Baptist). Feast day is June 24.

Located some 25 miles north of Santa Fe along the Rio Grande, San Juan is the largest of all the northern pueblos with 2,500 to 3,000 members and a total population of about 5,500 people. Tribe members share complex and closely guarded social and belief systems based on their traditional clan system.

The tribe's 12,238-acre pueblo sits across the Rio Grande from the original San Juan Pueblo, the site of the first Spanish settlement in New Mexico in 1598 and the first capital of the territory. San Juan was also the birthplace of Popé, the man credited with organizing the Pueblo Revolt of 1680, which succeeded in banishing the Spanish from the region for 12 years. San Juan has retained a reputation for leadership among Tewa-speaking people, hence its name, *Oke Owingeh*, "Place of the Strong People." The pueblo is home to the offices of the Eight Northern Indian Pueblos

Hornos, beehive-shaped outdoor ovens, are common at New Mexican pueblos.

Photo: Chris Corrie

Council (see earlier entry) and the Bureau of Indian Affairs Northern Pueblos Agency.

San Juan has two central plazas with two rectangular *kivas*, the 19th-century, red brick St. John the Baptist Catholic Church and an even older chapel built from volcanic rock across the street. Tourists may visit the tribal lakes and a recreation area and view buffalo, the latter by reservation only. The pueblo operates several attractions, including the Tewa Indian Restaurant; the Oke Oweenge Crafts Cooperative, which displays and sells the pueblo's distinctive red pottery along with wood and stone carvings, weavings, paintings and jewelry; the Ohkay T'owa Gardens Cooperative, which grows and processes traditional native food products; the Ohkay Casino; and the top-rated Ohkay RV Park.

Directions from Santa Fe: Take U.S. 84/285 north 24.3 miles to the junction with N.M. 68 in Española; head 4 miles north on N.M. 68 to the junction with N.M. 74. Go 1 mile west on N.M. 74.

Santa Clara Pueblo
1 Kee St., Española • 753-7326

Patron saint is Santa Clara (St. Claire). Feast day is August 12.

With an estimated 2,400 tribal members and 45,965 acres, Santa Clara is the second-largest in population and physical size of the Eight Northern Pueblos. Located west of the Rio Grande and adjacent to San Ildefonso Pueblo, Santa Clara Pueblo offers majestic landscapes and stunning views. The people of Santa Clara trace their ancestors to ancient Pueblo Indians who occupied the Puyé Cliff Dwellings beneath and along the mesa tops above the pueblo. They're believed to have arrived in the 12th century, when they carved cavelike "apartments" into the soft volcanic rock along the Pajarito (pa-ha-REE-to, Spanish for "little bird") Plateau leading into the Jémez Mountains. They later moved to the top of the mesa, where they built adobe structures whose remains extend more than a mile along the plateau. A drought forced these ancestral Pueblo Indians to abandon Puyé about 600 years ago. They settled in the what is now the Santa Clara Pueblo, or *Kha p'o*, which is Tewa for "Valley of the Wild Roses." The Puyé ruins are accessible year round on foot or by driving to the top of the mesa. The pueblo also offers guided tours by reservation only.

Another huge attraction at the pueblo is Santa Clara Canyon, a beautiful recreation area that offers trout fishing in several well-stocked lakes, 86 campsites with tables, lean-tos and RV parking, and picnicking. The canyon is open to visitors from April through October. The pueblo is famous for its lustrous black and red pottery made from clay molded from individual coils and refined by hand, then decorated with carved or painted designs, hand-polished with a smooth stone and finally finished on an open wood fire. The pots, along with other arts and crafts, are for sale in a number of shops on the pueblo. In addition to its patron saint, Santa Clara commemorates St. Anthony with a feast day on June 13.

Directions from Santa Fe: Take U.S. 84/285 N. 24 miles to the junction with with N.M.

INSIDERS' TIP

Low-riders are sleek, customized cars that sit low to the ground — in some cases low enough to be grounded by a speed bump. Many are fitted with hydraulics that raise and lower the vehicle at the flick of a switch. Chrome is often a prominent feature on low-riders, as are eye-catching, incredibly intricate paint jobs. Some are literally works of art, including one from New Mexico that's in the Smithsonian Institution in Washington. To catch a glimpse of low-riders in Santa Fe, head on over to Alameda Street on a Saturday night. If you're driving, don't plan to be anywhere in a hurry because the low-riders are cruisin'. Española, just a half-hour north of Santa Fe, is the "Low Rider Capital of the World," according to MTV.

Pueblo Etiquette

Remember that old adage, "When in Rome, do as the Romans do?" It applies doubly when visiting Indian reservations. Please don't be lulled into a sense of complacency because people on the reservation speak English. The pueblos are sovereign lands with their own

culture and a different code of etiquette than the one with which you're most likely familiar. The language may be the same, but it's a completely different culture. Please take to heart the following suggestions for courteous behavior so as not to offend your hosts or make future guests unwelcome. Please take special note of the rules at the end of this section for taking photographs.

General Etiquette:

• Every pueblo has its own government and its own set of rules for visitors. Please learn the rules and regulations of each pueblo before entering and obey them during your visit.

• While the pueblos are open to the public during the day, private homes are not. Do not enter anyone's house without permission.

• If you are invited into someone's house on a feast day, don't linger at the table after you've finished eating. Your host will want to serve many guests throughout the day.

• By all means thank your host, but it's inappropriate to offer any payment or tip.

• Pueblo dances are religious ceremonies not staged performances. Observe them with the respect and quiet attention you would maintain in a house of worship. Please don't talk or wave or otherwise disturb nondancers. It's considered impolite to ask questions about dances or make comments about their meaning. Applause is inappropriate.

• Refrain from talking to dancers and don't approach them as they are entering, leaving or resting near the *kiva*.

• *Kivas* and graveyards are sacred places and not to be entered by any non-pueblo person.

• Don't wander beyond areas open to tourists.

• Don't climb walls or other structures. Some are hundreds of years old and fragile.

• Do not take or even pick up artifacts such as broken pottery or other objects.

• Obey all parking and traffic signs, especially speed limits, to keep the pueblo safe for children and the elderly.

• Keep children nearby and make sure they are respectful.

Photo: Chris Corrie

At the Eight Northern Indian Pueblos Arts and Crafts Show, visitors are welcome to photograph the dancers. But the individual pueblos have strict rules about photographing at other times.

— continued on next page

• Do not bring in pets.
• Alcohol, weapons and drugs are strictly forbidden.

Photography:
• Permits, fees and restrictions vary from pueblo to pueblo.
• Any photographs you take must be for private use only and may not be reproduced or used for commercial purposes without written permission.
• Please do not photograph any individuals without their express permission.
• Do not attempt to take a photo or make sketches or recordings if you are forbidden to do so.
• A photo permit does not give anyone license to disrupt dances by getting in front of the dancers or spectators.

---

30 in Española, turn left and continue southwest for about 2 miles southwest on N.M. 30.

Taos Pueblo
P.O. Box 1846, Taos 87571 • 758-1028 (tourism office), 758-9593 (governor's office)

Patron saint is San Geronimo (St. Jerome). Feast day is September 30 with pre-feast ceremonies on September 29.

The oldest and most well-known of all the existing northern pueblos, Taos (rhymes with "house") is also the most striking primarily because of its multistoried, tiered adobe buildings with jutting *vigas* and ladders still used to reach the upper floors. Taos has inspired countless artists in every imaginable medium to try to capture the drama of the pueblo at dusk, when it sometimes appears golden. In winter, its graceful, snow-lined walls, rooftops and *hornos* (round, outdoor mud ovens pronounced "OR-nose") provide a striking contrast to the deep purple of the Sangre de Cristo Mountains that watch over it.

Called Tu-tah — "Our Village" — in its native Tiwa, Taos Pueblo sits on 95,343 acres in the foothills of the northern Sangre de Cristos. Except for some modern housing, the pueblo probably looks much like it did 450 years ago, when Spain made its first foray into New Mexico — this despite a turbulent history that includes the Pueblo Revolt of 1680 and the Taos Rebellion against the United States in 1847, in which 150 tribal members died. Its unchanged appearance may be due to its northern location, which made it more inaccessible than the other pueblos. It's surely a result of the Taos people's fierce independence and a strict taboo on intermarriage, both of which have helped preserve the pueblo's traditions and culture. Plumbing and electricity are still forbidden in some of the oldest structures.

The Taos people have lived on the pueblo for 1,000 years, but little is known about their background because the pueblo forbids excavations. Anthropologists believe they could be related to the extinct Chaco culture. Because it's the northernmost pueblo, Taos was probably influenced by the Plains Indians, especially the Kiowa and Apache with whom the pueblo traded. The pueblo's economy was based on farming, raising cattle and horses and hunting bear, buffalo, deer, elk and birds. As a result, the Taos people became skilled in leather craft. Their boots, moccasins, clothing and drums are justly famous.

INSIDERS' TIP

In New Mexico, you will more often hear indigenous people refer to themselves as "Indians" than "Native Americans," though the latter is perfectly acceptable.

Pueblo Annual Events

New Mexico's pueblos hold numerous feasts, dances and other celebrations throughout the year that are open to non-Indians. We've included below a tentative schedule for 1998. Please call the pueblo before attending any event, as schedules can — and often do — change with little advance notice. Feast days remain the same from year to year. So do the celebrations for the Transfer of Canes and All King's Day celebrations, which fall respectively on New Years Day and January 6, as do the dances on Christmas Eve and Christmas Day. Be sure to check with the individual pueblo, however, to ascertain that the celebrations are open to the public. Please refer to our close-up on pueblo etiquette before your visit.

Close-up

January

January 1: Transfer of canes (inauguration of new tribal officials). Various dances. Most pueblos.

January 6: All King's Day celebration in honor of new tribal officials. Most northern pueblos.

January 22-23: San Ildefonso feast day. Various dances. San Ildefonso Pueblo.

January 25: St. Paul feast day. Various dances. Picurís Pueblo.
January 28: Cloud Dance or Basket Dance. San Juan Pueblo.

February

February 2: Various dances. Picuris Pueblo.

February 18: Deer dance. San Juan Pueblo.

March

March 30: Bow and arrow dances. Nambé Pueblo.

April

April 12: Easter dances. Most pueblos.

May

TBA: Corn dances. Tesuque Pueblo.
May 3: Santa Cruz feast day. Various dances. Cochití Pueblo.
May 4: Corn dances, footraces. Taos Pueblo.

June

June 1: St. Anthony's feast day. Various dances. Picurís Pueblo.
June 23-24: San Juan feast day. Various dances. San Juan Pueblo.
June 24: Corn dances. Taos Pueblo.

Photo:Don Strel/Southwest Assignments

Pueblo dances offer visitors insight into pueblo culture.

— continued on next page

July

First weekend: Weekend High Country Arts & Crafts Festival. Picurís Pueblo.
July 4: Nambé Falls celebration. Nambé Pueblo.
Second weekend: Taos Pueblo Pow-Wow. Taos Pueblo.
Mid-July: Annual Northern Pueblo Artist & Craftsman Show. At a northern pueblo.
July 25: Santiago feast day. Corn dances. Taos Pueblo.

August

August 9-10: San Lorenzo feast day. Various dances. Picurís Pueblo.
August 12: Santa Clara feast day. Various dances. Santa Clara Pueblo.
Late August/Early September: Corn dances. San Ildefonso Pueblo.

September

TBA: Harvest dance. San Juan Pueblo.
September 29-30: San Geronimo feast day. Taos Pueblo.

October

October 3-4: St. Francis of Assisi feast day. Various dances. Nambé Pueblo.

November

November 12: San Diego feast day. Various dances. Tesuque Pueblo.

December

December 12: Guadalupe feast day. Pojoaque Pueblo.
December 24: Vespers. Various dances. Nambé, Picurís, San Juan and Taos pueblos.
December 25: Matachine dance (Spanish). Various native dances. Most pueblos.
December 26: Turtle dance. San Juan Pueblo.
December 28: Holy Innocents Day. Children's dances. Picurís, Santa Clara pueblos.

Although the pueblo still shrouds itself in secrecy, visitors are welcome to enjoy the architecture on almost any day and to observe some of its ceremonies and rituals on selected dates. These include traditional footraces in May and the Taos Pueblo Pow-Wow the second weekend in July. The pueblo closes to non-Indians for about six weeks starting in February or March for religious activities. Taos has an estimated 1,166 residents.

Directions from Santa Fe: Take U.S. 84/285 N. 24.3 miles to the junction with N.M. 68 in Española; go 48 miles north on N.M. 68 to the junction with U.S. 64 in Taos; head 1 mile north on U.S. 64.

Tesuque Pueblo
Rt. 5, Box 360-T • 983-2667

Patron saint is San Diego (St. James). Feast day is November 12.

Tesuque (teh-SOO-keh) Pueblo — *Te-tsu-geh*, or "The Cottonwood Tree Place," in Tewa — encompasses approximately 17,000 acres in the lush foothills of the Sangre de Cristo Mountains, including forest land adjacent to the Santa Fe National Forest and farm land near the Rio Grande. The Tesuque people settled in this area, located just 9 miles north of Santa Fe, 14 years after the 1680 Pueblo Revolt in which Tesuque Indians literally struck the first blows against the Spanish and suffered the first casualties. Two members of the pueblo also served as messengers to the other tribes, spreading word of the revolt. An earlier Pueblo existed before the 12th century but was abandoned after the revolt.

A relatively small pueblo, Tesuque today is among the most traditional of the Tewa speaking people. Only a very few of its celebrations are open to the public, and the pueblo sometimes closes to outsiders with little or no notice. The pueblo owns and operates Camel Rock Casino, 984-8414, (800) GO-CAMEL, named for the centuries-old, distinctive sandstone formation near the entrance to the pueblo. Visitors may also buy permits to camp and fish at the lake or in the mountains. Among the pueblo's newest businesses is Tesuque Natural Farms, an organic produce company that sells at local farmers' markets and to upscale restaurants. Its oldest businesses include sales of arts and crafts such as the brightly colored pottery for which the pueblo has become known, figurines, sculpture, painting, jewelry and traditional clothing.

Directions from Santa Fe: Take U.S. 84/285 N. 9 miles.

A Footnote on "Anglos"

Anglo culture? What's that? If you've seen Woody Allen's 1986 film, *Hannah and Her Sisters*, you might think it's turkey sandwiches on white bread with mayonnaise. In much of the country, it's the short form for "WASP" — white Anglo-Saxon Protestant. In Santa Fe, however, "Anglo" takes on a variety of shades, from African American to Asian, Arab to Jew. As we've mentioned elsewhere in this guide, the term as generally used in New Mexico refers to anyone who's not Hispanic or Native American, regardless of race or heritage. Because that embraces so many cultures, it's difficult to define. But it's fun exploring the stereotypes. They include wealthy retirees or celebrities, perhaps buying their second or third home; trust-fund babies — age is unimportant — who come here to "find themselves;" New Age adherents in search of a mystical experience and hoping to find one by sheer proximity to Native Americans; hippies who arrived in the '60s and never left — some of them still hippies, others successful professionals or entrepreneurs; artists and writers looking for their muse; ski bums who work three seasons a year to play on the slopes all winter. We're sure everyone in Santa Fe could come up with a few stereotypes of its own.

Outside the cultural cliches are the "Anglos" who have lived here all their lives, some with roots going back 150 years to the Santa Fe Trail. Others are regular working stiffs who personally, or whose parents, chose Santa Fe as their home because of its physical beauty and fascinating blend of cultures. In the mix are pockets of ethnic communities including Tibetans, who have strong political support here in their fight to reclaim their homeland from China; Chinese, many of whom arrived here in the 19th century with the railroad; African-Americans, who account for 0.6 percent of the population; Ashkenazy Jews, whose ancestors helped blaze the Santa Fe Trail; scientists of all backgrounds who work at Los Alamos National Laboratory; and people of literally dozens of other ancestries from Afghanistan to Zimbabwe. Santa Fe is its own melting pot and becoming more so every year as people from one end of the country to the other, one end of the world to the other, discover all it has to offer.

Santa Fe is the only state capital in the country that doesn't have its own commercial airport — another reason it deserves its reputation as The City Different.

Getting Around

Four hundred years ago there was only one way into Santa Fe — *El Camino Real* (the "Royal Road" or "King's Highway"), an arduous and, for some, fatal network of roads and trails that began in Mexico City. This *camino de tierra adentro*, or "road to the interior," started out as Indian trails and slowly extended northward, segment by segment, throughout the 16th century, as *conquistadores*, settlers, missionaries, merchants and seekers of fame, fortune and adventure all made their way to New Mexico.

More than two centuries later, on September 1, 1821, William Becknell left Franklin, Missouri, with a wagon load of goods to trade with Indians. He never got farther than Santa Fe where, despite Spain's restrictions against Anglo Americans and trade with the eastern United States, colonists eagerly bought all his goods, which were scarce and highly coveted in the territory. This was in November. The following month — on December 26, 1821 — word reached Santa Fe that Mexico, and therefore New Mexico, had won independence from Spain. With that news the frontier opened and, with it, so did the Santa Fe Trail. For the next six decades, until the first locomotive steamed through northeastern New Mexico, the 900-mile stretch from Independence, Missouri, to Santa Fe, New Mexico, remained a bustling, if hazardous, trade route that represented profits to businessmen, adventure to mountain men and conversions for Protestant missionaries — all of them willing to risk disease, starvation or hostile Indians to achieve their goals.

Traces of the original Santa Fe Trail remain in the city, most notably behind the Museum of Indian Arts and Culture, where some claim you can still see the indentation of wagon wheels in the hard, dry dirt. Much of the original trail is now beneath the pavement and dirt of a newer well-traveled road called Old Santa Fe Trail — a scenic, narrow road wending its way from County Road 67 south of the city to its terminus at the Santa Fe Plaza. *El Camino Real*, however, is still a vital Santa Fe thoroughfare — at least the part now called Agua Fría ("Cold Water") Street, which begins in the Guadalupe District west of the Plaza and meanders parallel to the Santa Fe River through the west-side *barrio* and the Historic Village of Agua Fría.

Today, of course, there are a number of ways to get into and out of Santa Fe as well as around and through it — though never enough for some people and far too many for others. Additional roads naturally translate into more traffic and all its accoutrements: congestion, noise and the threat of polluting our pristine skies. So far, however, city and county governments and a population painfully aware of this particular downside of growth are trying to find a happy medium that allows for expansion of our highways and byways without destroying the aesthetic, cultural and historic integrity of Santa Fe. Here's what we've got thus far.

By Air

Santa Fe is the only state capital in the country that doesn't have its own commercial airport — another reason it deserves its reputation as The City Different. The city has a municipal airport for commuter and private jets, with scheduled flights daily to and from Denver and Dallas. To get to Santa Fe, most people fly into Albuquerque on a commercial jet and take ground transportation here or fly on a commuter flight to the Santa Fe Municipal Airport. The trip on land from Albuquerque will take between one and one and a half hours, depending on the mode of travel and the weight on the gas pedal.

Albuquerque International Sunport
2200 Sunport Blvd. SE, Albuquerque
• 842-4366

Located 60 miles south of Santa Fe, the Albuquerque International Sunport is the only airport in New Mexico with jet airline service. Regardless of your specific destination in the state, if you plan to get there via a commercial flight, your visit to the Land of Enchantment will begin in Albuquerque, the state's largest city. The airport, which the city shares with Kirtland Air Force Base, lies at the southern end of Albuquerque, approximately 4 miles south of the central business district. From the moment you set foot inside its cool, pink and turquoise, adobe-style interior, you know you're in the Southwest. Albuquerque architect William Emmett Burk Jr. (1909-1988) designed the 20 laminated ceiling beams, each about 84 feet long and carved with decorative motifs used by Pueblo and Navajo Indians. The airport's art collection comprises original paintings, weavings, sculpture, photography and other media — all by New Mexico artists, many of them with national and international reputations.

The terminal houses seven eateries ranging from a full-service restaurant and lounge to delis and snack bars. You'll find gift and news shops; cart vendors selling T-shirts, balloons, key chains and other *tchotchkies*; a bank and ATM; a barber shop; and a shoeshine stand.

Albuquerque International Sunport's 574,000-square-foot terminal has come a long

FYI

Unless otherwise noted, the area code for all phone numbers listed in this guide is 505.

way since 1928, when the entire airport was little more than a small adobe building and a dirt runway a few miles southwest of its present location. The first aircraft to land there was a Stearman piloted by Ross Hadley, who was chauffeuring "air tourists" from Hollywood to New Mexico. Other cross-country pilots quickly followed suit, including Charles Lindbergh; Arthur S. Goebel, winner of the 1927 Dole Prize for the first flight to Honolulu from the mainland; and air speedster Frank Hawk. The little Albuquerque airport saw its first commercial flights in 1929, when Western Air Express operated one eastbound and one westbound flight per day with radio equipment installed by the U.S. president's son, Herbert Hoover Jr. Two months later Trans-Continental Air Transport began operating a fleet of 10 Ford tri-motored transports, each accommodating up to 18 passengers.

The airport underwent a major remodeling in 1985, added another wing in 1992, put in a new traffic control tower two years later and, in 1996, underwent a small-scale expansion.

Today, Albuquerque International Sunport has 23 gates in two concourses. Eleven commercial carriers offer nonstop service to 28 cities including Atlanta, Chicago, Dallas, Denver, Houston, Los Angeles, Minneapolis, Phoenix, Pittsburgh, St. Louis, Salt Lake City, San Diego, San Francisco and Tucson. A four-level parking structure and adjacent surface lot accommodate 3,700 vehicles. Short-term parking rates start at $1 per half-hour with a maximum of $5 per day. Long-term parking costs $4 per day.

AIS is home to two fixed-base operators — Cutter Flying Service, 842-4184 or (800) 627-2887, and Executive Aviation Center, 842-4990 or (800) 593-4990. Other companies that provide services to business and private fliers include Four Seasons Aviation, 842-4955; Robertson Aircraft, 842-4999; Seven Bar Flying Service, 842-4949 or (800) 793-7227; and South Aero, 842-4337.

INSIDERS' TIP

Santa Fe Trails was the first bus system in the nation to use only natural gas-burning coaches and vans.

• **Car Rental at the Albuquerque International Sunport.** To get from AIS to Santa Fe, follow the signs to exit the airport, which will put you northbound on Yale Boulevard. From Yale, turn left on Gibson Boulevard heading west. Get into the right lane and take the on-ramp to U.S. Highway 25 N. to Santa Fe. Take the St. Francis Drive Exit to get downtown. The following rental-car companies serve AIS.

> Advantage Rent a Car, 247-1066
> Airport Car Rental, 247-4699
> Alamo Rent-A-Car, 842-4057
> Avis Rent-A-Car, 842-4080
> Budget Car Rental, 768-5900
> Dollar Rent-A-Car, 842-4224
> General Rent-A-Car, 843-9386
> Hertz Rent-A-Car, 842-4235
> National Car Rental, (800) 227-7368
> Payless Car Rental, (800) 729-5377
> Thrifty Car Rental, 842-8733

• **Bus Service from AIS to Santa Fe.** Greyhound and TNM&O coaches, 242-4998, provide bus service between the Albuquerque airport and the Santa Fe Bus Depot on St. Michael's Drive. Call for times and prices.

Shuttlejack Inc., 243-3244, provides nonstop service 10 to 12 times daily between the Albuquerque airport and most Santa Fe hotels, motels and bed and breakfast inns. It also provides service to a number of other locations in and around the capital city including retirement homes, the College of Santa Fe, Fort Marcy Compound and Glorieta Conference Center. Riders can make special pick-up and drop-off arrangements. The fare for the 70-minute ride is $20 — in cash or travelers checks on the bus or by credit card at the time you make your reservation.

Santa Fe Municipal Airport
443 Airport Rd. • 995-4708, 473-7243

Santa Fe's own municipal airport, at the southwest corner of the city, provides commuter service from Albuquerque, Denver and Dallas and handles all types of private aircraft. The 2,100-acre airport was established in 1941 as a military airfield during World War II. It became a "commercial" airport — technically a "non-hub primary" airport — in the 1950s and replaced its tiny terminal with the larger one you see today. Inside you'll find the Santa Fe Airport Grill, 471-5225, open 10:30 AM to 5:30 PM, though it plans to expand its hours to include breakfast and, when its get a liquor license, dinner. Airport parking is in an outdoor lot and costs $2 per day.

The airport handles 250 takeoffs and landings a day, most of them private corporate aircraft. Commercial commuter airlines, all limited to 30-seat planes, comprise about 5 percent of all flights. As a result, you'll rarely have to wait for a flight unless it has been delayed elsewhere. Two airlines service SFMA: United Express between Santa Fe and Denver, 473-4118, and Aspen Mountain Airlines between Santa Fe and Dallas, 471-3437 or (800) 877-3932. For hourly recorded weather information, call 438-3150. Three commuter lines operate at SFMA. The air-traffic-control tower, 471-3810, is open between 7 AM and 9 PM, though flights can take off and land 24 hours a day. Both the New Mexico State Police and Army National Guard keep aircraft at the SFMA. The airport has two fixed-base operators that fuel and service private, government and commuter aircraft: Santa Fe Jet Center, 471-2525, and Zia Aviation, 471-2700. Zia also provides air taxi and charter service. Santa Fe Airport plans to resurface its runways in 1998.

For ground transportation, you have a number of choices. Avis, 471-5892, and Hertz, 471-7189, have rental cars at the airport. To get to the downtown area, head east on Airport Road for about 3 miles. Turn left on Cerrillos Road, which will turn into Galisteo Road as you near downtown and dead-end at San Francisco Street exactly one block west of the Plaza. The drive will take about 20 minutes. Or you

---

INSIDERS' TIP

Be prepared for a shock when you fill up your car's gas tank in Santa Fe. Gas prices here are among the highest in the nation. Last year prices were more than 13¢ per gallon higher than the national average and 20¢ per gallon higher than in Albuquerque.

can take the Roadrunner Shuttle, 424-3367, to or from any hotel in town for $11. Roadrunner also shuttles passengers to casinos and Los Alamos.

By Land

Maybe things in Santa Fe haven't changed all that much since the days of *El Camino Real* and the Santa Fe Trail. Here we are, centuries later, and there still are only two direct overland routes to the state capital: U.S. Highway 25 northbound from Las Cruces, near New Mexico's southern border, and southbound from Buffalo in north-central Wyoming; and N.M. Highway 84/285 S. from Taos and Chama. The closest east-west route is U.S. Highway 40, which intersects U.S. 25 in Albuquerque at what's popularly called "The Big I."

Getting to Santa Fe is the easy part. It's getting around that's hard, especially in an old downtown filled with narrow, winding, one-way streets that seem to lead everywhere but where you want to go or continually lead you right back from where you came. Even if you manage to navigate the downtown area, at some point you're going to have to find a place to leave your car. And you thought parking was difficult in Manhattan! It's also at a premium in Santa Fe, especially in summer — so much so that a former municipal judge decided it just wasn't cricket to fine locals who parked illegally when legal parking spots were so hard to find. Every year at Thanksgiving, he offered amnesty to parking scofflaws who donated a turkey or two to one of the local homeless shelters in lieu of paying their fines. This wound up costing the city tens of thousands of dollars in lost revenue and eventually cost the judge his robes.

www.insiders.com

See this and many other **Insiders' Guide®** destinations online — in their entirety.

Visit us today!

Walking

All this is to suggest that if your digs are within walking distance of downtown, use shank's pony — your legs — to get there. Not only will you work off that extra sopaipilla you had for lunch, but you'll also see a lot more of Santa Fe. Beware, however, that Santa Fe is not particularly pedestrian friendly once you leave downtown. Sidewalks are rare; traffic lights on main drags often don't allow enough time to cross the street without making a run for it; and in wider, more heavily trafficked roads where the speed limits are higher, drivers may not be as aware of pedestrians as they might be in areas with more foot traffic.

Parking

If you're too far from the Plaza or just too tired to walk, the downtown area has nine municipal parking lots, including one parking garage and eight surface lots, several of which will accommodate RVs. They charge either 50¢ or 60¢ per half-hour with a maximum of $5 and $6 respectively per day (more for RVs). There are also six reasonably priced private lots within walking distance of the Plaza.

Street parking downtown comes in two forms: metered at an average cost of 25¢ for 20 to 30 minutes Monday through Saturday (free on Sunday); and permit parking for residents. While you may get away with an extra 20 minutes on the meter (but don't count on it), residents closely guard the parking rights they fought so hard to get. When all else fails, try the meters in front of the main post office on S. Federal Place, behind City Hall and just two blocks from the Plaza. You may have to drive around the block a few times, but with a little persistence your chances of landing a

---

INSIDERS' TIP

Some Santa Fe streets bear the names of their ultimate destinations: Galisteo, Agua Fría, Pecos Trail, Old Taos Highway and Cerrillos Road, for instance. Other names such as Water Street, Alto Street and Canyon Road reflect physical locations.

The Santa Fe Trails Transit System serves the city with
full-size buses and small vans like this one.

spot there are pretty good. On weekends —
except during Indian Market, Spanish Market
and Fiestas (see our Annual Events chapter),
you're almost guaranteed a spot in front of the
State Capitol building, affectionately called the
Roundhouse for reasons that will become obvious once you've seen it.

Of course, you can avoid both walking and
parking by using public transportation (see
the subsequent entries) or cycling (see our
Parks and Recreation chapter.)

Bus and Shuttle Service

Greyhound/TNM&O
858 St. Michael's Dr. • 471-0008

Greyhound and TNM&O — Texas, New
Mexico and Oklahoma — coaches provide bus
service between the Albuquerque airport and

the Santa Fe bus station on St. Michael's Drive
with coaches leaving for the airport and Albuquerque bus station at 7:30 AM, 3:50 PM and
8:05 PM. There's an additional 1:45 AM coach
to the Albuquerque bus station. Buses also
run between Santa Fe and Alamogordo,
Carlsbad, Clovis, Gallup, Grants, Las Cruces,
Las Vegas, Roswell and Taos in New Mexico;
Alamosa, Colorado Springs, Denver and
Pueblo in Colorado; Amarillo, Dallas and El
Paso in Texas; Flagstaff and Phoenix in Arizona; and New Orleans in Louisiana. Call the
bus station for times and fares.

Lamy Shuttle and Tours
1476 Miracerros Loop • 982-8829

The Lamy shuttle takes reservations to
meet the Amtrak trains that arrive once a day
at the Lamy Depot from Chicago and Los Angeles. For $14 per person — which works out

to $1 a mile — the shuttle provides door-to-door service from the depot to your hotel or residence. As its name implies, the company also offers custom tours. Call for details and prices.

Santa Fe Trails Transit System
1050 Siler Park Ln. • 438-1464

Not even 10 years old, the city bus system can take you nearly anywhere you want to go within the city limits on any of nine different routes. Buses run Monday through Friday from 6:30 AM to 10:30 PM and Saturday from 8 AM to 8 PM (times may vary, depending on the route). Santa Fe Trails does not run on Sunday or holidays. You can pick up a bus schedule and information book on board any Santa Fe Trails bus and at more than 75 locations throughout the city, including most public buildings and many stores. At 50¢ per ride for adults, including free transfers, Santa Fe Trails is one of the best buys in town. Plus, you can buy your newspaper on the bus or even stow your wheels on a bike rack if you get caught cycling in the rain or just can't bear to ride that last stretch. Seniors 60 and older and students from 6 to 17 years pay only 25¢ per ride, including transfers. Children younger than 6 ride free when accompanied by an adult. Santa Fe Trails also offers one-day passes for $1 and monthly passes for only $10. You can't beat it. For help planning a trip or for answers to any questions, call the customer assistance center at 438-1463 between 7 AM and 7 PM.

Shuttlejack Inc.
1600 Lena St. • 982-4311

Shuttlejack not only provides nonstop service between Santa Fe and the Albuquerque airport (see our listing for the Albuquerque International Sunport), but also offers scenic tours, nightly shuttles to the Santa Fe Opera (see our Arts chapter), daily shuttles to the Santa Fe Ski Area and charter buses and scheduled service to Glorieta, Taos and the Taos Ski Valley.

Train Service

Amtrak
CR 33, Lamy • 466-4511, (800) 872-7245

Amtrak's Southwest Chief trains, which run eastbound from Los Angeles and westbound from Chicago, meet each afternoon at the train depot in Lamy, 14 miles southwest of Santa Fe. Call Lamy Shuttle and Tours, 982-8829, (see previous entry) to arrange transportation to downtown Santa Fe or area hotels. To get to the Lamy Depot from Santa Fe, take U.S. 25 N. to Exit 290 (N.M. 285). Go south on N.M. 285 approximately 10 miles to the Lamy turn-off on the left. The railroad station is in the center of the village, easily seen on your right.

Santa Fe Southern Railway
410 S. Guadalupe St. • 989-8600

Santa Fe Southern Railway runs on tracks originally laid by the Atchison Topeka & Santa Fe Railway in 1880. AT&SF ended passenger service to its namesake city in 1960. When the line itself became threatened in 1992, Santa Fe Southern came into existence to preserve the historic piece of railroad. Today, SFSR delivers freight to Santa Fe and once again offers passenger service, however limited. The train travels only between Santa Fe and Lamy, some 14 miles away. But the ride is a delightful one in which passengers can watch the high-desert scenery through the windows of a restored 1920s coach. The train leaves the Santa Fe Depot at 10:30 AM Tuesday, Thursday, Saturday and Sunday and returns by 4 PM. Passengers can bring a picnic lunch or dine at the historic Legal Tender, a 19th-century saloon-turned-steakhouse. Fares are $21 for passengers 14 and older, $16 for ages 7 to 13 or 60 and older, $5 for children 3 to 6 years and free for children younger than 2, with a limit of two toddlers per adult. Santa Fe Southern also offers sunset rides every Friday from May to December. The $28 fare includes hors d'oeuvres and soft drinks. A cash bar is available.

Charter Vans

Charter vans are private buses or vans that offer individual and group rentals and prearranged or custom tours complete with tour guides. Some companies provide luxury vans and buses with private catering and special touches like blankets and gourmet chocolates. Others offer your basic driver, seats and wheels. Prices are commensurate with the services you choose.

Custom Tours by Clarice, 3201 Calle de Molina, 438-7116

Grayline Tours of Santa Fe, 1330 Hickox Street, 983-9491

Santa Fe Transportation, 1201 Cerrillos Road, 982-3504

Shuttlejack Inc., 1600 Lena Street, 982-4311

Limousine Service

Limotion VIP Limousine Service, 471-1265

Santa Fe HoteLimo, Santa Fe Municipal Airport, 443 Airport Road, 438-0202, (800) 927-3536

Rental Car Companies

Advantage Rent-A-Car, 309 W. San Francisco Street, 983-9470, (800) 777-5500

Avis Rent-A-Car, Garrett's Desert Inn, 311 Old Santa Fe Trail, 982-4361

Santa Fe Municipal Airport, 443 Airport Road, 471-5892, (800) 831-2847

Budget/Sears Rent A Car, 1946 Cerrillos Road, 984-8028, (800) 527-0700

Enterprise Rent-A-Car, 2641A Cerrillos Rd., 473-3600; 4450 Cerrillos Road, 474-3234; Hilton of Santa Fe, 100 Sandoval Street, 989-8859, (800) 325-8007

Hertz Rent A Car, Santa Fe Municipal Airport, 443 Airport Road, 471-7189, (800) 654-3131

Thrifty Car Rental, 3347 Cerrillos Road, 474-3365, (800) 367-2277

Taxi Service

Capital City Cab Co.
Industrial Rd. • 438-000

When it comes to taxi service, Capital City is the only game in town. As such, you'll see few of its cabs cruising for fares. Instead the company and its customers rely on a 24-hour computerized dispatch service. For those of you accustomed to hailing a cab from the curb, don't bother. Chances are, any cab you see in the street is already occupied or is on its way to a caller. Capital City charges a $2 flag fee the moment you step foot in the cab and $1.50 per mile. Each additional passenger costs $1 as does any piece of luggage that sits on the seat instead of in the trunk. Capital City participates in the city-sponsored Santa Fe Ride program, which allows disabled passengers to ride anywhere in the city limits for $1. Elderly passengers also get a discount. Call 438-1463 for details.

Pedi-Cabs

Feel like something out of the ordinary? Head for the Plaza and hail a pedi-cab — a three-wheeled rickshaw in which you sit back in the comfort of a shaded seat built for two while a driver cycles you around town. It's like riding on a covered bicycle, except someone else is doing all the work. You can use pedi-cabs as you would a taxi, though only for the downtown area. If you're feeling romantic, you might charter a pedi-cab to carry you and your love along the banks of the Santa Fe River on

INSIDERS' TIP

Perhaps the most important piece of advice to anyone visiting Santa Fe's downtown is to leave your car at home or in the hotel parking lot. Not only is downtown parking hard to come by, but the streets, some of which are 400 years old, are narrow and winding and often congested with cars and sightseers. So put on your walking shoes and stretch those muscles. It's the best way to see the downtown anyway.

Photo: Don Strel/Southwest Assignments

Although no major airlines serve Santa Fe, you will see
all sorts of aircraft during the Santa Fe Air Show.

E. Alameda Avenue or some equally lovely ride.

Ponyman Pedal-Cabs Inc.
2442 Cerrillos Rd., Ste. 266 • 440-9309

Ponyman Pedal-Cabs offer downtown taxi service and three prearranged tours of the downtown area. The company's $15 historical tour pedals past the Palace of the Governors, St. Francis Cathedral, San Miguel Mission, Loretto Chapel and other historic sites over the course of an hour. Or take the half-hour downtown tour which, for $8, explores restaurants, shops and nightlife spots. The $7 Canyon Road tour takes you through the heart of Santa Fe's artist community, dropping you off at the top of Canyon Road for a leisurely downhill stroll past the galleries, shops and restaurants. Ponyman also arranges custom tours for weddings, parties or other special events.

Make your reservations well in advance if you plan to be here during peak times — summertime and the holiday season.

Hotels and Motels

Santa Fe has an amazing number and variety of hotels and motels ranging from ultra-luxurious and very expensive to basic and cheap. In this chapter we've presented a cross-section of the area's hotels and motels in three geographic categories: Downtown, which is usually most desirable because of its proximity to the historic districts and the Plaza; Cerrillos Road and Environs, which primarily encompasses a 6-mile-long commercial strip that runs south from downtown Santa Fe directly into the beautiful Turquoise Trail; and the county, which takes in rural areas both north and south of town. For other types of accommodations, see our Bed and Breakfast Inns and Vacation Rentals chapter.

Perhaps the single-most important warning for visitors to Santa Fe is this: Make your reservations well in advance if you plan to be here during peak times — summertime and the ski season during Christmas and spring break — when rooms, especially on weekends, are at or near capacity. Lodgings often are booked up to a year in advance for Indian Market (see our Annual Events chapter) in late August and even during Christmas — a very special time in Santa Fe when the nights literally glow from thousands of *farolitos* burning on balconies and rooftops and pathways throughout the city. These times can, and usually do, command higher prices than the rest of the year. During Indian Market some establishments may add a surcharge even to their peak-season prices. Some hotels divide the year up into as many as a half-dozen seasons, with prices on a single room fluctuating as much as $50 in some cases.

While pricing can be tricky in Santa Fe —

rooms range anywhere from $34 a night (for a hotel not included in this chapter) to $1,500 for the Presidential Suite at Hotel Loretto — the general rule of thumb is, the closer to the Plaza, the more you'll pay. There are a few exceptions, however, which we've noted in this chapter. Most lodgings fall in the $50 to $200 range, and many hotels offer discounts for extended stays. Keep in mind that prices quoted here or elsewhere do not include taxes. Within the city limits, be prepared to pay 6.25 percent in gross receipts taxes as well as a 4 percent lodgers tax, a special levy whose proceeds are used in part to promote Santa Fe. You'll save money by staying in the county, where lodgers tax is only 3 percent and the gross tax receipt varies, though it's invariably cheaper than in Santa Fe proper.

Price Code

Our legend is based on the lowest rate per night for double occupancy during peak season. Price ratings don't reflect taxes or other surcharges and are subject to change.

$	less than $55
$$	$55-$89
$$$	$90-$139
$$$$	$140-$199
$$$$$	$200 and more

Unless otherwise indicated, all lodgings listed below have nonsmoking and handicapped accessible rooms, the latter to a lesser extent in some places than others. If you or a traveling companion use a wheelchair, be sure to confirm specifics — i.e., whether the bathroom doors are wide enough — before you make your reservation. You're probably safe if you simply ask whether the facilities are ADA (Americans with Disabilities Act) approved. People with physical disabilities can obtain a special guide called *Access Santa Fe* by writing or stopping by the State of New Mexico's Welcome Center or the Governor's Committee on Concerns for the Handicapped, both located at 491 Old Santa Fe Trail, 827-6465.

Amenities vary from place to place, but you can generally assume that all but the cheapest lodgings have telephones in the room, many with free local calls. If you're bringing your laptop and plan to spend time sending or receiving e-mail or surfing the Internet, confirm that the phones have dataports or are modem-friendly. You can also expect to find remote-control color cable televisions, though the channel selection may differ from place to place. Some also have VCRs, though this is more common in suites — guest rooms with a separate living room or sitting area, sometimes separated by a door, other times by no more than a partial wall divider or an arch. For descriptions of the Santa Fe-style embellishments you're likely to encounter in our lodgings — *kivas*, *vigas*, *latillas* and *nichos*, for example — refer to our Santa Fe Style close-up in our Real Estate chapter.

With very few exceptions — and they're all noted — establishments listed in this section accept most major credit cards. While we're on the subject, you might consider guaranteeing your reservation with a credit card during peak season, even if you don't regularly make a practice of doing this. Also be sure to check on cancellation policies, minimum stays and surcharges, especially for heavily trafficked weekends like the Indian and Spanish Markets or the opening week of the Santa Fe Opera.

One last caveat before you begin fantasizing about hot toddies and hors d'ouevres in front of a crackling fire on a snowy northern New Mexico night. Most lodgings do not allow pets. Some may be willing to break their own rules depending on the animal or the circumstances. Do be sure to check in advance before you plan on taking Duke the dog, Fluffy the cat or Alisssss, your pet boa constrictor, with you on your Santa Fe vacation.

In or Near Downtown

Eldorado Hotel
$$$$$ • 309 W. San Francisco St.
• 988-4455, (800) 955-4455

A favorite of visiting celebrities, the Eldorado is an enormous luxury hotel in the heart of downtown Santa Fe, just one block from the Plaza. The hotel boasts 227 elegant rooms and suites, many featuring *kiva* fireplaces and balconies or terraces overlooking the Sangre de Cristo Mountains. The Eldorado pampers guests with plush terrycloth robes, nightly turndown services, extended room service and valet parking. It even provides private, English-style butler service with deluxe rooms and suites. The Eldorado features a rooftop swimming pool and whirlpool along with a fully equipped fitness center, saunas and professional masseuses.

The Eldorado's Old House Restaurant offers fine dining six nights a week with creative gourmet dishes that have a definite Southwestern touch (see our Restaurants chapter). Less formal dining is available in the Eldorado Courts, which on Sunday serves a lavish prix fixe champagne brunch, buffet style, with prime rib and other meats carved to your liking; bottomless bowls of fresh shrimp,; smoked meats and fish; gourmet salads; omelette and waffle stations; standards like eggs Benedict; and a decadent dessert table. For live nightly entertainment, guests need go no further than the lobby lounge, which adjoins the Eldorado Courts.

The Eldorado offers a number of packages, including a one-day "Ski Escape" with complimentary lift tickets for the Santa Fe or Taos slopes or a three-night "Powder Ski Vacation" that includes discounts on massages. The hotel's three-night "New Mexico Romance"

FYI

Unless otherwise noted, the area code for all phone numbers listed in this guide is 505.

package welcomes guests with a bottle of chilled champagne in the room, a candlelight dinner at the Old House (you pay for the booze), breakfast in bed each morning, a massage or other spa treatment and monogrammed robes to take home with you. There's also a Santa Fe shopping package that features discounts at many of the city's boutiques, a "Holiday Enchantment" package for Thanksgiving and pre-Christmas and even a "Weekday Bargain" package for stays from Sunday through Thursday night.

Fort Marcy Hotel Suites
$$$ • 320 Artist Rd. • 982-6636, (800) 745-9910

Named for an 1846 military outpost, Fort Marcy Hotel Suites opened in 1983 as an alternative to hotel rooms in downtown Santa Fe. On 10 landscaped acres in a quiet residential neighborhood only four blocks from the Santa Fe Plaza — and directly on the road that leads to the Santa Fe Ski Area — the hotel features 100 one-, two- and three-bedroom suites with fireplaces, full kitchens, air-conditioning, VCRs and cable color television with Showtime and the Disney Channel. There's also a hot tub for guests. Rooms come with a complimentary continental breakfast, free laundry facilities and free, unlimited access to Santa Fe's largest public sports facility, Fort Marcy/Mager's Field Sports Complex, located two blocks away.

Garrett's Desert Inn
$$ • 311 Old Santa Tr. • 982-1851, (800) 888-2145

Garrett's offers very affordable rates in downtown Santa Fe. You won't find *vigas*, *kiva* fireplaces or *saltillo* tile at Garrett's. What you will find are basic but pleasant rooms and location, location, location. If you're looking for luxury, you can walk across the street to the Hotel Loretto. But be prepared to pay from three to 10 times as much, depending on the room. Either way, you're three blocks from the Plaza and just footsteps from some of the city's historic landmarks. Garrett's has both a restaurant and lounge on the premises and a seasonal outdoor heated swimming pool. It offers 76 standard rooms and six suites with small living rooms and kitchenettes furnished with microwaves and small refrigerators. The motel has limited handicapped access and no rooms designated as nonsmoking. There is a restaurant on site.

Hilton of Santa Fe
$$$$$ • 100 Sandoval St. • 988-2811, (800) 336-3676

Although it looks rather ordinary from the outside, the 21-year-old Hilton of Santa Fe is in fact quite extraordinary in that it was built around a *hacienda* that's more than 300 years old — Casa de Ortiz, which belonged to one of Santa Fe's early prominent families. Several years ago, the hotel opened its Casa Ortiz de Santa Fe, luxurious *casitas* built into and around what used to be the coach houses for Nicholas Ortiz III's horses. The builders maintained the integrity of the original structure by framing it before beginning construction. They placed "windows" in the walls of the *casitas* so guests can view the original thick adobe walls. Two of the spacious *casitas* are one-bedroom suites, and a third has two bedrooms. The decor is modern Southwestern with traditional touches like *kiva* fireplaces, *viga* ceilings and four-poster beds. In a total departure from tradition, one of the *casitas* has a heart-shaped tub.

Just a few blocks from the Plaza right across the street from the Eldorado, the hotel has a total of 158 rooms and suites, including the Casa Ortiz. It boasts Santa Fe's largest outdoor pool, which has a 6-foot tile bear fetish on the bottom. Other amenities include an outdoor Jacuzzi, a new health club and three restaurants. The award-winning Piñon Grill was built on the site of the Ortiz bedroom, and the hotel's 6,000-square-foot meeting space was the Ortiz family's private sanctuary.

Homewood Suites
$$$$ • 400 Griffin St. • 988-3000, (800) 225-5466

Homewood Suites looks more like an upscale garden apartment complex than a hotel. Designed with the business traveler in mind, the hotel offers one- and two-bedroom suites in a downtown location just five blocks northwest of the Plaza and two blocks from Sweeney Convention Center. It commonly hosts film crews shooting for two weeks or more and offers discounts for extended stay. Each of Homewood's 105 apartment-style suites features a comfortable bedroom, separate living room and a fully-equipped kitchen. Some also have fireplaces. The hotel offers a complimentary grocery shopping service. For those who prefer to squeeze their own tomatoes, Albertson's supermarket in the DeVargas Center is just a five-minute drive to the west, while Kaune's gourmet supermarket is about the same distance to the east. If you don't feel like venturing off the premises, the hotel operates a 24-hour convenience store. Among the hotel's other amenities are a complimentary continental breakfast and newspaper; an evening social hour; an exercise center, outdoor swimming pool and hot tubs; color cable television and VCR in every room; personalized voice mail; a free 24-hour business center with a personal computer, typewriter, fax machine, copier and business supplies. Homewood also offers meeting rooms that can accommodate up to 65 people; business equipment, including audio/video, computers, pagers, cellular phones and even technicians; and catering. Ask for its price list.

www.insiders.com

See this and many other **Insiders' Guide®** destinations online — in their entirety.

Visit us today!

Hotel Loretto

$$$$$ • 211 Old Santa Fe Tr. • 988-5531, (800) 727-5531 (except Sunday)

Named for the nearby historic Loretto Chapel whose "miraculous" spiral staircase has no central support, Hotel Loretto (formerly Inn at Loretto) is near the end of Old Santa Fe Trail, just one block from the Plaza. Its faux-adobe, pueblo-style architecture is complemented by furniture, doors, windows, corbels and light fixtures that are 13th-century replicas hand-crafted by local artisans. Even the interior wall mural incorporates designs and symbols found in New Mexico's pueblo and Spanish artistry as well as in ancient petroglyphs and weavings. Hotel Loretto is among the most photographed buildings in Santa Fe during the winter months, when its rooftops and balconies light up with electric *farolitos* — a version of the traditional candle-in-a-paper-bag Christmas decoration that has become an internationally recognized symbol of Santa Fe.

The 141 newly renovated guest rooms and suites feature individual climate control, refrigerators, in-room coffee service, speaker phones with data jacks, an outdoor pool and private balconies with spectacular sunset and mountain views. The Presidential Suite, which goes for $1,500 a night, provides a panoramic view of the city and a custom billiard table. The hotel restaurant, Nellie's, features primarily Southwestern-American cuisine, though guests with a yen for Asian food may find what they're looking for on Nellie's menu. The concierge can direct guests to other fine restaurants as well as arrange for golf, rafting, fly fishing, skiing, horseback riding or any number of other activities.

Hotel Plaza Real

$$$$ • 125 Washington Ave. • 988-4900

Hotel Plaza Real is a charming, territorial-style hotel whose 56 rooms feature hand-crafted furnishings, fireplaces, original artwork and private patios overlooking a very pretty courtyard. The Santa Fe Plaza is literally just steps away and visible from the hotel's sidewalk cafe, La Piazza, which offers pastries, cappuccino, sandwiches, homemade desserts, spirits and great people-watching. Or you can mingle among the masses on one of the concierge's complimentary walking tours of the city. The concierge will also make your restaurant reservations and suggest other outside activities. Rooms come with a compli-

INSIDERS' TIP

Like commercial strips everywhere, Cerrillos Road attracts a fair share of burglaries and robberies. Please take all common-sense precautions such as bringing your belongings from your car into your room at night and locking your vehicle at all times.

Photo: Hotel St. Francis

Santa Fe lodging ranges from quaint adobe rooms to deluxe mainstream American accommodations with a variety of choices in between.

mentary continental breakfast served in the Santa Clara Room, on the patio or delivered to your room.

Hotel St. Francis
$$$ • 210 Don Gaspar Ave. • 983-5700, (800) 529-5700

Built in 1923, the Hotel St. Francis combines 1920s style with distinctly Southwestern elements. Renovations in the lobby and rooms, each of which is unique, include refurbished antique and period reproduction furnishings that add to the historic ambiance of the European-style hotel. In keeping with European tradition, the St. Francis offers a locally popular high tea, which features an array of pastries, scones, finger sandwiches and, of course, plenty of fine, freshly brewed tea. The hotel restaurant is open daily and offers seasonal outdoor dining as well as room service. The front verandah, with its old-fashioned but comfortable iron tables and chairs, is a favorite spot for people-watching. The hotel, just a block from the Plaza, is on the National Register of Historic Places.

Hotel Santa Fe
$$$$ • 1501 Paseo de Peralta • 982-1200, (800) 825-9876

Unique is a word used so often in Santa Fe that it sometimes loses its meaning. But Hotel Santa Fe is indeed unique in that it's the city's only American Indian-owned hotel. The Picurís Pueblo is the majority owner with a 51 percent share, an arrangement that's reflected in more than just finances. The influence of the Picurís (pronounced pick-kuh-REES) is captured throughout the hotel — in the Pueblo-Revival architecture; the decor; the artwork, which includes three garden sculptures by renowned American Indian artist Allan Houser; native foods; and hospitality from a staff that is 25 percent Indian. Hotel guests and the public enjoy entertainment that includes Indian dancers, Hispanic and Indian musicians, lectures by local historians and native storytellers who weave tales in front of the lobby's majestic *kiva* fireplace. There's also an outdoor heated pool and Jacuzzi and an on-site masseuse. Although there are no sports facilities on the premises, guests may get complimentary passes to the Santa Fe Spa, located a few miles away.

The seven-year-old, 131-room hotel takes up a whole block at the corner of Cerrillos Road and Paseo de Peralta — just a few blocks from the heart of the historic Guadalupe district and a 10-minute stroll to the Santa Fe Plaza. If you prefer, you can take the complimentary hotel shuttle to the Plaza, which operates daily until 10 PM. Hotel Santa Fe, as all are downtown hotels, is near a variety of fine restaurants, though you needn't leave the premises to eat well. The in-house Corn Dance Cafe offers nouvelle American Indian cuisine that features a creative blending of traditional Indian foods and spices. Ask about hotel packages for skiing, romance, Native Americans and senior citizens.

Inn of the Anasazi

$$$$$ • 113 Washington Ave.
• 988-3030, (800) 688-8100

Just steps from the Plaza stands Inn of the Anasazi, an intimate, elegant luxury hotel named for the ancestors of today's Pueblo Indians. These ancient settlers of the Four Corners Region inhabited the cliff dwellings of Chaco Canyon and Mesa Verde, which served as inspiration for the hotel's architecture and design. The Inn's 51 guest rooms and eight suites have gas-lit *kiva* fireplaces, four-poster beds and traditional ceilings with *vigas* and *latillas*. Authentic regional artwork, including antique Indian rugs and hand-woven fabrics, grace the floors and walls. Sheets and towels are pure cotton; organic toiletries are local creations made with native cedar extract. Every room has a coffee maker, stereo and VCR. Guests may borrow videotapes from the hotel's extensive collection.

The inn's award-winning, world-class restaurant serves gourmet American Indian, northern New Mexican and American cowboy cuisine using locally grown organic produce whenever possible. Guests who want a more intimate setting can reserve the wine cellar for up to 12 people. The hotel also rents out its library/board room for private dinners of up to 40 guests as well as for corporate retreats and board meetings. When it's not rented out, the library is open to guests who may peruse the books on regional indigenous cultures. Those who want a closer look can request an escort to the Anasazi ruins at Chaco Canyon or Bandelier National Park or to any of the Eight Northern Indian Pueblos.

Inn of the Governors

$$$$ • 234 Don Gaspar Ave. • 982-4333,
(800) 234-4534

Inn of the Governors is a midsize, deluxe hotel just two blocks from the Santa Fe Plaza. Its 94 rooms and six suites are decorated in a light, airy Southwestern style with handmade furniture, local art work and special touches such as hand-painted tin mirrors, turquoise-washed writing desks, wrought-iron wall lamps, headboards and Mexican *trasteros* (cupboards). Some rooms also have wood-burning *kiva* fireplaces and/or private balconies overlooking the mountains or downtown. Amenities include a heated outdoor swimming pool open year round, complimentary newspaper and coffee, cable television with in-room movies and a restaurant/piano bar where guests can eat indoors or on the hotel's private patio.

Inn on the Alameda

$$$$ • 303 E. Alameda St. • 984-2121,
(800) 289-2122

Just a five-minute walk from the Plaza, this small luxury hotel is near the foot of Canyon Road, a historic and artistic center filled with galleries, boutiques and fine restaurants. Each of its 67 rooms and suites is individually designed to reflect classic Southwest design including Spanish tile, *vigas* and native woods; hand-crafted armoires, chairs, beds and lamps; and unusual wall hangings and fixtures. The inn's eight suites offer private patios or balconies, open courtyards and *kiva* fireplaces.

Although the hotel has no restaurant on the premises, it does provide a complimentary "Breakfast of Enchantment" — a continental breakfast of fresh fruit and juices, pastries and other baked goods, granolas, cereals, Kona coffee and more served buffet style in the hotel's lounge or for delivery to your room. Other amenities include massage and

---

INSIDERS' TIP

The double "L" in Spanish is pronounced like "Y" in English. So Cerrillos Road is pronounced Seh-REE-yose Road and villa (as in Villa Linda Mall) is pronounced VEE-yah.

Photo: La Fonda

Many local hotels have pools that offer a refreshing break in summer.

fitness facilities, two open-air Jacuzzi spas, same-day dry cleaning, cable and HBO. Some rooms also come with luxurious robes, wet bars and refrigerators.

La Fonda Hotel
$$$ • 100 E. San Francisco St.
• 982-5511, (800) 523-5002

Legend has it that an inn, or a fonda, has existed at the southeast corner of the Plaza since 1610. Since 1922, that corner has been home to La Fonda Hotel, renowned for its award-winning Spanish Pueblo-style architecture and its Southwestern hospitality. Its award-winning Spanish pueblo-style architecture makes it a beacon not only for tourists, but also for locals who meet in the summer, weather permitting, at the rooftop Bell Tower bar to watch incredible sunsets over Margaritas or who gather in La Fiesta Lounge to two-step to the country tunes of now-famous Bill and Bonnie Hearne or listen to other popular local musicians who perform nightly.

This vibrant, historic landmark is filled with colorful, hand-painted and handcarved wooden furniture, *vigas* and corbels as well as unique paintings and other original artwork. Many of its 153 rooms and suites, each uniquely decorated, have balconies and fireplaces. La Fonda also has a heated outdoor pool, hot tubs, massage service and a multilingual concierge. La Plazuela is an enclosed courtyard restaurant that's open daily.

La Posada de Santa Fe
$$$ • 330 E. Palace Ave. • 986-0000, (800) 727-5276

La Posada is Santa Fe's only hotel with a resident ghost. Both employees and guests swear they've seen or at least felt the presence of Julia Schuster Staab, who died on May 15, 1896, in her upstairs bedroom, now simply called Room 256. Julia was married to wealthy Santa Fe merchant Abraham Staab, who in 1882 built his German wife the Victorian mansion that is now the main building of La Posada. Although Julia is not the only ghost in Santa Fe, she's certainly the most famous. But her presence, at least in principle, doesn't seem to scare away either tourists or locals, who come in droves to this lovely, serene hotel set among 6 acres of lawns, trees and flowers.

Many of the 119 adobe accommodations come with *kiva* fireplaces, and each comes with its own unique decor. Five rooms, including Room 256, are in the original Victorian mansion. The rest are spread throughout the rambling grounds that are a favorite for weddings. La Posada's romantic Victorian bar is popular among locals, who come to socialize and listen to Chris Calloway, daughter of jazz legend Cab Calloway, belt out the tunes that made her father famous. Diners who eat on the patio of the hotel's Staab House Restaurant — which serves a variety of foods, many with Southwestern accents can also enjoy Chris through a sliding glass door kept open in the summer.

Radisson Santa Fe Hotel
$$$ • 750 N. St. Francis Dr. • 982-5591, (800) 333-3333

While not exactly downtown, this hotel is close enough — a five-minute drive to the Plaza in the hotel's free shuttle — to warrant a listing in this section. On a hilltop immediately north of Paseo de Peralta, which forms a U around the downtown area, the Radisson offers views of the mountains and sunsets from its rooms as well as its restaurant and bar. The hotel features 160 nicely furnished guest rooms, suites, and condominium units with fireplaces and full kitchens. The Santa Fe Salsa Company Restaurant and Bar, which specializes in specialty homemade salsas, serves Southwestern and traditional American cuisine with room service available from 6:30 AM to 10 PM. Guests may work out for free in the 20,000-square-foot Santa Fe Spa, which is practically next door, or relax poolside in the hotel's landscaped courtyard.

Rio Vista Suites
$$ • 527 E. Alameda St. • 982-6636, (800) 745-9910

Located along the Santa Fe River in a quiet residential neighborhood on the city's east side, Rio Vista Suites are the closest accommodations in Santa Fe to gallery- and boutique-lined Canyon Road. Only six blocks from the Plaza, the 12 one-bedroom suites are decorated with Southwestern furniture, Mexican *saltillo* tile and brick sidewalks and include such amenities as fully furnished kitchens, color cable television with free premium channels and VCRs, CD players and free parking outside your door. Suites come with a complimentary continental breakfast and unlimited use of Santa Fe's largest public sports facility.

Santa Fe Budget Inn
$$ • 725 Cerrillos Rd. • 982-5952, (800) 288-7600

Santa Fe Budget Inn is your basic, no-frills motel whose primary assets are location and price. Situated at the corner of Cerrillos Road and Guadalupe Street — the very beginning of Santa Fe's commercial strip — the motel is just six blocks from the Santa Fe Plaza and a short walk to the Guadalupe district, which is filled with restaurants and stores. Budget Inn offers clean, generic rooms with phones, color satellite television, a heated, outdoor swimming pool open during the spring and summer and plenty of on-site parking. For those without a car, or who can't walk another step, a Santa Fe Trails city bus stops in front of the motel to take you to areas hither and yon. Immediately adjacent is a family-style New Mexican restaurant with a McDonald's one building over.

Santa Fe Motel
$$ • 510 Cerrillos Rd. • 982-1039, (800) 999-1039

The closest motel to the Plaza, the Santa Fe Motel has 22 moderately priced, newly remodeled rooms with color televisions and HBO, direct-dial telephones and a message service. Five standard rooms have kitchenettes equipped with dishes and utensils. Eight rooms are in two renovated adobe houses with *viga* ceilings and patio entrances. One of these rooms has a fireplace, another a skylight. The motel also rents out the 75-year-old Thomas House, a two-bedroom, one-bath adobe home with *vigas*, a fireplace in the living room, a dining room, a fully equipped kitchen and a private garden. The motel serves a complimentary continental breakfast from May through September and free coffee all day — and all year — long.

Santa Fe Plaza Travelodge
$$ • 646 Cerrillos Rd. • 982-3551, (800) 578-7878

The rooms here are basic with a few Southwestern touches, but what you're paying for is convenience, not ambiance: You're just five blocks from the Plaza. You'll get a clean, pleasant chamber with cable television, a coffee maker and a small refrigerator stocked with coffee and tea. These rooms go fast so be sure to book long in advance of your trip, especially during peak season.

Seret's 1001 Nights
$$$ • 145 E. DeVargas St. • 982-6636, (800) 745-9910

Just two blocks from the Plaza and across the street from a church reputed to be the oldest in the United States, Seret's 1001 Nights is amidst some of Santa Fe's most celebrated restaurants and the narrow, rambling historic streets for which the city is famous. The hotel's 12 suites, which date back to the 19th century, have restored wooden floors and hand-trowelled, diamond-finished walls. Each has been fitted with centuries-old Spanish Colonial hand-crafted doors and shutters and furnished by Ira Seret, an internationally-known importer, with custom-made furniture and vintage weavings. All the suites have fireplaces, full kitchens, cable television with free premium channels and VCRs, CD players and access to a private central courtyard.

Cerrillos Road and Environs

Best Western Lamplighter Inn
$$ • 2405 Cerrillos Rd. • 471-8000, (800) 767-5267

The popular Lamplighter Inn is located a just few blocks from one of the busiest intersections in Santa Fe — Cerrillos Road and St. Michael's Drive. In the heart of the commercial district, the Lamplighter is surrounded by dozens of restaurants, from fast food to fine dining in a variety of ethnicities, and literally hundreds of businesses offering just about anything a body or soul could need or desire. You can hop in your vehicle and be downtown in 10 or 15 minutes, depending on traffic, or catch a Santa Fe Trails bus (see our Getting Around chapter), which stops one block from the hotel.

The Lamplighter Inn bows to Santa Fe style with a large *portal*, complete with wooden pillars, beams and carved corbels, attached to the swimming pool area. In addition, some of its 80 units — all recently remodeled — have high, beamed ceilings. Most of its rooms, however, are generic but pleasant, each with a refrigerator and coffee maker. Sixteen rooms have kitchenettes; the suites each have a VCR and a fold-out couch in addition to one or two beds. All guests have access to a coin-operated laundry. Among the most popular features of the Lamplighter is its 25-yard heated indoor/outdoor lap pool. Andrea's Mexican Restaurant and Lounge, which is part of the hotel, serves local New Mexican food from 7 AM to 9 PM. The lounge stays open until 10 or 10:30 PM.

Cactus Lodge
$ • 2864 Cerrillos Rd. • 471-7699

Cactus Lodge offers clean, inexpensive rooms by the day and, in ski season only, by the week. Each room at the lodge is different. Most have *vigas*, a pleasant surprise in digs this cheap. All have individual air-conditioning controls, televisions, phones and microwaves and/or refrigerators upon request. The motel also has a number of suites that sleep up to eight people. While none of the rooms are ADA approved, the motel's new owner says there are a few in which people with physical disabilities might feel comfortable. There was no eatery on the premises at the time this book went to press, but there's a Chinese restaurant called The Golden Dragon across the street.

Comfort Inn
$$ • 4312 Cerrillos Rd. • 474-7330, (800) 653-3396

At 4 years old, the 83-room Comfort Inn is a relatively new neighbor on the Cerrillos Road strip but has earned a reputation for comfort (as its name implies) and good service at a good price. Located south of the intersection at Cerrillos and Rodeo roads — approximately 6 miles from the Plaza — the hotel is within walking distance of Villa Linda Mall, Santa Fe's largest indoor shopping center. And while there's no restaurant in the hotel, there are a number of eateries nearby including several chains and a privately owned, down-home New Mexican restaurant called the Horseman's Haven. For breakfast, however, guests needn't leave the inn because an expanded continental breakfast

comes with their rooms. The hotel serves a buffet of hot and cold cereals, fruit, juice, hot beverages, Danish or muffins in a small dining room adjacent to its high-ceilinged lobby, which has a large *kiva*-style fireplace, tiled floor and a variety of attractive Southwestern decorations. The inn features a heated indoor pool and hot tub, a small exercise room, coin-operated laundry and free local calls in the rooms. Some rooms have whirlpool baths, microwaves and/or refrigerators.

Comfort Suites of Santa Fe
$$$ • 1435 Avenida de Las Americas (off Cerrillos Rd.) • 473-9004, (800) 228-5150

The 2-year-old Comfort Suites offers many of the same features and amenities as its (barely) older sister, Comfort Inn (see our entry in this chapter). The primary difference between the two establishments is the size of the rooms, which is reflected in the price, and the distance to downtown Santa Fe. Located 3 miles north of the inn — and 3 miles closer to the Plaza — Comfort Suites offers larger rooms with a divider separating the bedroom from a sitting area that comes furnished with a small refrigerator, microwave, sleeper sofa, VCR and, in some rooms, a dining table. Comfort Suites has a small exercise room featuring a stationary bicycle and a stair stepper, a heated indoor pool and two hot tubs, one indoors, the other outside. It serves a complimentary continental breakfast buffet and offers views of the entire city from its top floor. The lobby has a *kiva*-style fireplace, tall ceilings, bleached pine furniture and Native American details such as pottery, rugs and Kokopelli, the fun-loving flute player.

DoubleTree Hotel
$$$ • 3347 Cerrillos Rd. • 473-2800, (800) 777-3347

Although it's located toward the far end of Santa Fe's commercial strip, the DoubleTree has a distinctly "downtown" feel with its pueblo-style architecture, handsome Southwestern interiors and a spacious, meandering lobby that offers a number of attractive and comfortable sitting areas, including one with a large *kiva* fireplace graced on both sides by neat stacks

of logs. The hotel's 213 rooms and suites are also done up in Southwestern style with touches such as natural pine furniture, adobe-like textured wallpaper and earth-toned colors. All rooms have refrigerators, coffee makers, hair dryers, irons and ironing boards, at least two telephones with dataports and voice mail and cable color television with free and pay-per-view movie channels. Guests also have access to coin-operated laundry facilities.

The three-story hotel has an attractive outdoor courtyard, interior and exterior corridors, a heated indoor pool, two indoor hot tubs and an exercise room. In-house massages are extra. The hotel also provides a shuttle service to downtown Santa Fe that runs from 8 AM to 9 PM. The hotel restaurant, Cafe Santa Fe, is open from 7 AM to 10 PM. The hotel's signature greeting — fresh chocolate chip cookies at check-in — should sustain new guests arriving after hours. The hotel has a business center with a PC, phone, fax, copier, printer and access to the Internet.

El Rey Inn
$$$ • 1862 Cerrillos Rd. • 982-1931, (800) 521-1349

Don't be fooled by its location. El Rey Inn is one of Santa Fe's best kept secrets. Tucked into a busy street about 10 minutes by car from the Plaza, El Rey (The King) offers comfort, surprising tranquillity and Santa Fe style at affordable rates. Each of its 86 rooms, including 10 suites, is unique and blends traditional Southwestern decor — historic Spanish, Pueblo Indian or Victorian — with modern comforts including cable television with HBO and direct-dial phones with message service. Rooms open onto spacious gardens, patios, tiled walkways, fountains and tall elms that cover much of the 4-acre property. A heated pool for seasonal use and two year-round hot tubs — one indoors, the other outside — occupy one corner of the grounds while a playground occupies another.

El Rey's overall motif is traditional New Mexican Spanish architecture with wrought iron and whitewashed adobe and stucco. Rooms contain any combination of decorative touches that might include *latillas* held up by rough-hewn *vigas*, *kiva* fireplaces, *nichos* and murals as well as tile, wood and polished brass accents. A number of rooms also have complete kitchens. Rooms come with a complimentary continental breakfast of coffee and rolls or sweet breads in the inn's spacious, European-style breakfast room, and guests can help themselves to coffee throughout the day. El Rey also has laundry facilities for guests.

FYI

Unless otherwise noted, the area code for all phone numbers listed in this guide is 505.

Fairfield Inn-Marriott
$$ • 4150 Cerrillos Rd. • 474-4442, (800) 758-1128

Part of Marriott's economy line, the Fairfield Inn provides guests with reasonable prices and a little Santa Fe style. The lobby and entrance have *vigas, saltillo* tile and a *kiva* fireplace. Its 55 rooms have Southwestern touches and come with a continental breakfast as well as use of the year-round heated indoor pool. They also have dataports for laptop users and cable color television with free HBO. Valet laundry is available for a fee.

Located at the south end of town, about 6 miles from the Plaza, the inn is contiguous with the Villa Linda Mall — the largest indoor shopping mall in Santa Fe — and across the street from an upscale new strip mall. There's no restaurant on premises, but the inn is within walking distance of several eateries in and around both malls or a 15-minute drive from downtown Santa Fe, where the choices are greater.

Hostel International de Santa Fe
$, no credit cards • 1412 Cerrillos Rd. • 988-1153

"If they talk funny and have a backpack, they're ours." That's the overriding philosophy of the Hostel International de Santa Fe. The 80-bed hostel was founded in 1983 to make Santa Fe financially viable primarily for students or young workers who have saved for years to see the world. But there's no re-

striction on age at the hostel, just on attitude. If you feel like you're being sized up when you walk through the door, you're right. Staff members look for any indications that the person in front of them can live communally with strangers.

The hostel caters primarily to people traveling for personal development and self-education. A member of the American Association of International Youth Hostels, it naturally leans toward members of youth hosteling associations, though any brand of international youth travel card almost guarantees admission. Still, the management reserves the right to refuse anyone and is not shy about doing it.

The hostel has five single-sex dorms, each with enough bunk beds to sleep up to 15 people. There are also 15 private rooms for individuals, couples or families. And there's a fully-equipped cook's kitchen that rivals those in many restaurants with bread, cereals, pasta, rice, beans, coffee, tea, sugar, spices and other staples for use by lodgers. And, indeed, they are lodgers and not guests. This is a traditional hostel. That means no maid service. Hostelers not only clean up after themselves, but also must complete a 15-minute chore they choose themselves every morning. The earlier you get up, the better your choices.

If you call to make reservations, don't be put off if no one answers the phone immediately. In this case, persistence pays off. The hostel offers many amenities you won't find in other places — guitars and other musical instruments; games; pleasant, noninstitutional rooms; and lots of information about Santa Fe and the environs. The population tends to be primarily French in August and British in September. The rest of the year, you're likely to bump into anyone from anywhere.

King's Rest Court
$ • 1452 Cerrillos Rd. • 983-8879

This is a no-frills motel that provides the basics — bed, bath and cable television in a clean if unremarkable room. King's Rest Court does have a claim to fame, however, at least according to the previous owner, who says Roy Rogers and Dale Evans supposedly stayed there years ago. Among the motel's eccentricities is that it accepts no reservations; all business is on a drop-in basis only — a curse or a blessing, depending on your perspective. King's Rest Court could just be the only place in town with an available room during Indian Market, if you arrive at a propitious moment. Be warned, however, the rooms have no telephones. There's a public phone outside the office.

La Quinta Inn
$$ • 4298 Cerrillos Rd. • 471-1142, (800) 531-5900

People like La Quinta Inns because they know exactly what to expect. Santa Fe's won't disappoint, unless you're hoping for a touch of Santa Fe in the rooms. The only thing Southwestern about La Quinta is its name. But the 130-room hotel offers the same quality here as in its other hotels across the country, including "Gold Medal" rooms with floor-length draperies, built-in closets and vanities, ceiling moldings, bigger-than-a-breadbox bathrooms and color cable television with HBO and pay-per-view movies. Some rooms also have refrigerators. All rooms come with a continental breakfast with cereal, fresh fruit, pastries, bagels, muffin tops, juice, milk, coffee and tea. Other amenities include a heated outdoor swimming pool, same-day laundry and dry-cleaning, fax service, free local calls and a coin-operated laundry.

Luxury Inn
$$ • 3752 Cerrillos Rd. • 473-0567, (800) 647-1346

Despite its name, this privately owned hotel prides itself on providing a homey atmosphere and reasonable rates rather than Santa Fe style, which tends to cost more. Its 51 rooms come with color cable television and free HBO; some also have refrigerators and microwaves. Still, there's a bit of luxury here in the seasonal outdoor heated pool and hot tub. The hotel is near dozens of restaurants, some within walking distance, many a short way by car.

Pecos Trail Inn
$$ • 2239 Old Pecos Tr. • 982-1943, (800) 304-4187

A former speakeasy decades ago, the Pecos Trail Inn is a family-owned and family-friendly hotel on Santa Fe's southeast side at the crossroads of two historic trade routes — the Old Santa Fe Trail and the Old Pecos Trail, close to the scenic Old Las Vegas Highway. Situated on 5 acres of piñon trees about 10 minutes by car to the Santa Fe Plaza, the hotel is the only one in the area, which consists mostly of off-street residential developments rather than strip malls and gas stations. There's still a touch of the rustic here, despite the fast-moving traffic on Old Pecos Trail. There's also a park next door with a playground, jogging path and exercise equipment. The hotel itself has an outdoor heated pool open from May through September and offers its guests workout privileges at a local health club for $2.50 a visit.

Of the inn's 22 rooms, four are two-bedroom suites with living rooms and fully equipped kitchens and four units have kitchenettes. It's unlikely that many guests will want to bother cooking breakfast when they can eat anything on the hotel restaurant's breakfast menu for half-price. Pepper's Restaurant and Cantina is a family-style restaurant open for breakfast, lunch and dinner with eclectic offerings ranging from traditional New Mexican and American cuisine to calamari, build-your-own pizzas and a decent selection of low-fat, fat-free and vegetarian dishes.

Santa Fe Lodge Complex
$ • 6800 Cerrillos Rd. • 471-2727

Built 65 years ago as the Turf Club, the Santa Fe Lodge Complex is one of the oldest of the small motels on the outskirts of the city. It's the very last inn as you're heading south of town toward the interstate or the Turquoise Trail, a.k.a. N.M. Highway 14. This part of Santa Fe feels like another world, but it's only 8 miles — or a 15-minute drive — to the Plaza. Still, it proves you don't have to be downtown to sleep in a room with Mexican tile inlaid on the headboards and *vigas* on the ceiling. Of the motel's 17 rooms, 15 have kitchens. There's a gas station/convenience store on the premises where you can buy groceries and other supplies, if you plan to do your own cooking. But do take the opportunity to sample the food at the nearby Horseman's Haven. This blink-and-you'll-miss-it eatery attached to a Texaco station serves up enormous portions of home-cooked carne adovada, enchiladas and other New Mexican dishes at very reasonable prices.

Silver Saddle Motel
$ • 2810 Cerrillos Rd. • 471-7663

Independent film fans may already be familiar with the Silver Saddle from a 1988 German documentary called *Motel*. Filmmaker Christian Blackwood accurately portrayed the motel as an old-fashioned, authentically funky, cowboy-style inn with a Western motif provided primarily by the color scheme and the pictures on the wall. As the owner puts it, "We try to keep it simple and rustic." That may mean a few rough edges on this decidedly different "Cerrillos Road joint." But that's all part of the charm. That's not to say the Silver Saddle has no amenities. Ten of its 25 rooms have kitchenettes, and all of them have queen beds, color cable television with HBO, air conditioning and free local calls. Only 3 miles from the Plaza, the Silver Saddle has great shopping right next door at Jackalope (see our Shopping chapter). You can call for reservations or just ride up on your horse.

Stage Coach Motor Inn
$ • 3360 Cerrillos Rd. • 471-0707

A brothel in the 1940s, the newly renovated Stage Coach Motor Inn attracts a different sort of clientele these days — many of them low-budget but sophisticated travelers looking for what's different in The City Different. All the rooms are done up in Santa Fe style, some of them with *vigas*, many with *saltillo* tile, most with lots of woodwork and a fireplace in one of the two suites. The hotel is proud of its gardens, to which the new resident owners have been paying plenty of attention. They've designated the entire motel as nonsmoking and don't as yet have an official handicapped-accessible room.

County

The Bishop's Lodge
$$$$$ • Bishop's Lodge Rd. • 983-6377, (800) 860-9257

Once the private retreat of frontier Bishop Jean Baptiste Lamy, The Bishop's Lodge had been owned and operated as a resort since 1918 by the family of James R. Thorpe, who bought the property from the Pulitzer publishing family of St. Louis and sold it this year to an Austrailian firm. Today, the Bishop's original garden and chapel sit amid fruit trees planted by 16th-century Franciscan priests. Listed on the National Register of Historic Places, the chapel is a popular site for weddings. The lodge itself sits in the lush foothills of the Sangre de Cristo Mountains and, though only 3 miles from the Santa Fe Plaza, feels like another world entirely. That's because the resort is secluded in a private valley covering nearly 1,000 acres of both landscaped property and natural piñon-juniper forest.

The hotel comprises 88 rooms, including 20 suites, in 11 distinctive "lodges." The North and South lodges are the oldest and were once grand summer homes before World War I. The most recent addition is the Chamisa Lodge, which contains 14 deluxe accommodations above the banks of the little Tesuque Creek. All accommodations include voice-mail telephone with modem jacks, cable color television with HBO, private heat and air-conditioning controls, morning local paper delivery, plush bathrobes, hair dryers, evening turn-down service and an in-room safe. Deluxe rooms and suites have *kiva* fireplaces, refrigerator, irons and ironing boards and a private balcony or patio. Guests can choose between the European Plan, which includes only the room, or the Modified American Plan, which includes a full breakfast and a choice of either

FYI
Unless otherwise noted, the area code for all phone numbers listed in this guide is 505.

Staying in a pueblo-style structure will enhance your appreciation of local architecture.

lunch or dinner at The Bishop's Lodge Restaurant. The Bishop's Lodge Restaurant serves a prix-fixe Sunday brunch that's popular among locals as well as hotel guests.

The American plan also features a summertime program for children younger than 12. The hotel offers other special family packages throughout the year such as "Winter Firesides" and "Springtime Splendor." The lodge offers a variety of activities including horseback riding, hiking, nature walks, tennis, skeetshooting, an outdoor pool, indoor jacuzzi and an exercise area. Off-site, but still nearby, are golf, rafting, fishing and skiing.

Rancho Encantado
$$$$$ • N.M. Hwy. 592, Tesuque
• 982-3537, (800) 722-9339

Recently rated by *Condé Nast Traveler* as one of the top-500 places to stay in the world, Rancho Encantado is celebrating its 66th anniversary as a guest ranch. This rustic but elegant hideaway is 8 miles north of Santa Fe near the beautiful village of Tesuque. Its guest list reads like a *Who's Who*: Princess Anne of Great Britain, the Rainiers of Monaco, the Rockefellers, and many, many celebrities including Robert Redford, who is a frequent guest; Gene Hackman, a Santa Fe resident; Johnny Cash; Whoopi Goldberg; and a passel of Western movie stars including John Wayne, Jimmy Stewart, Gregory Peck, Henry Fonda and Kirk Douglas. The ranch itself has been the star of two books, a television series and a made-for-television movie.

The attraction is a combination of Spanish and American Indian influences as well as the Western cowboy spirit. The architecture is a blending of Pueblo and Territorial styles with multiple outdoor terraces, garden patios and artifacts of all three cultures throughout the ranch. The main lobby contains a collection of original paintings, photography, sculpture and wood carvings by renowned local artists. The 87 guest rooms and villas have a variety of special touches and amenities that might include private balconies, terraces or patios; *kiva* fireplaces; wet bars; refrigerators; fully equipped kitchens or any combination of the above.

Also available is the spectacular Egan House, a 5,000-square-foot, trilevel pueblo-style home with four bedrooms, each with a private bath, three fireplaces, a large dining room, fully equipped kitchen and private balconies and terraces with breathtaking views of the Jémez Mountains. The house is named for Betty Egan, a World War II captain in the Women's Army Corps and a widowed mother of three children who in 1968 bought the 188-acre Rancho del Monte Guest Ranch (made famous in the best-selling 1956 novel, *Guestward Ho*) and turned it into the very successful Rancho Encantado.

Today Rancho Encantado is run by Michael Cerletti, a former New Mexico tourism secretary, who recently introduced weekly barbecues and hoedowns to a long list of scheduled activities that includes tennis tournaments and instruction, a swim club, water aerobics, adult day camp, a children's recreation program, horseback riding and special culinary events throughout the year supervised by ranch chef Jeff Pufal, an instructor at the renowned Santa Fe School of Cooking whose specialties include contemporary Southwestern and continental cuisine. Among the resorts' many amenities are two heated swimming pools, an outdoor hot tub, a new exercise room, two tennis courts, sand volleyball, basketball, bocci ball, archery, hiking and horseback trails, horseshoes, pool tables and table tennis. The ranch also offers horse boarding year round.

Ten Thousand Waves
$$$ • 3451 Ski Basin Rd. • 982-9304

Ten Thousand Waves is a Japanese-style health spa built into the Sangre de Cristo Mountains. It recently added lodgings to its list of offerings, which includes chlorine-free hot tubs with saunas and cold plunges; numerous styles of professional massage; herbal wraps; salt glows; water therapy; and dry brush and aromatherapy — all in a magnificent alpine setting.

The Houses of the Moon are the closest luxury accommodations to the Santa Fe Ski Area. They consist of eight guest suites — Gemini Moon, Full Moon, Rising Moon, Blue Moon, New Moon, Luna, High Moon and Eclipse — located at the end of a path through a grove of piñon trees. The suites range in size

from a 1,000-square-foot space with a Japanese courtyard garden, separate bedroom, living room and dining room, full kitchen and a fireplace as well as a woodburning stove to a cozy, rustic studio *casita* with a *kiva* fireplace and a small private courtyard. All have private phones with voice messaging, mini-refrigerators or full kitchens, coffee makers with a supply of gourmet coffees and teas, and access to laundry facilities. Rooms are all nonsmoking.

Lodging guests receive complimentary access to the communal, clothing-optional tub and sauna; a 10 percent discount on all other services, including packages; and preferential treatment for private tub reservations, which often are booked a week in advance. Lodging is discounted 20 percent Monday through Thursday if the confirmation is sent to a New Mexico address or if you show a Santa Fe driver's license.

Most bed and breakfast inns prefer an adult-only clientele to ensure a peaceful stay for their guests. Some, however, will allow children above a certain age.

Bed and Breakfast Inns

Unlike hotels, which are fairly predictable in their offerings, bed and breakfasts, inns and guest houses tend to be as individual — and often as idiosyncratic — as their owners. That's certainly not a bad thing. In fact it's usually downright pleasant, and it's why guests choose to stay in these more personal lodgings. But it also means guests should confirm beforehand the rules of each house. For example, a number of Santa Fe inns have resident dogs and/or cats. People with allergies or who share W.C. Fields' philosophy — "Anyone who hates children and dogs can't be all bad" — should make a point of asking about pets on the premises and to which areas they have access. If their pets are particularly territorial, it may mean you can't bring little Fifi with you.

As for W.C.'s other bane — children — most bed and breakfast inns prefer an adult-only clientele to ensure a peaceful stay for their guests. Some, however, will allow children above a certain age — usually 10 years old. Check with the individual establishment for their policies regarding children and additional charges if you bring them. Most inns add $15 or $20 per night for an extra person in the room. Also be aware that some bed and breakfasts require a two-night stay on weekends, though that rule is usually bendable during the off-season. Unless we note otherwise, all inns in this chapter accept major credit cards.

The majority of Santa Fe inns boast smoke-free environments, though a rare few may offer a smoking room or two. Be sure to check with your hosts in advance if you absolutely cannot be within 100 yards of cigarette smoke or if you've got to take that last puff 30 seconds before hopping into bed. While your hosts will go out of their way to accommodate you on most things, the no-smoking rule is generally one to which they firmly adhere.

Around Downtown

Adobe Abode Bed and Breakfast
$$$ • 202 Chapelle St. • 983-3133

In a residential neighborhood just a few blocks from the Santa Fe Plaza, Adobe Abode is an early 19th-century adobe home-turned-inn with an eclectic charm. Details include antiques from France and England, a mahogany planter's chair from the Philippines, Spanish Colonial turn-of-the-century pieces, handmade Aspen pole beds, puppets from Java and folk-art animals from Oaxaca. Amenities include custom soaps and shampoos, fine designer linens, thick terrycloth robes, private phone lines in each room and color cable television. The inn also offers fax service, off-street parking and sherry and cookies all day long. Breakfasts are hearty and imaginative and feature a different Southwestern-style entree every day.

Like the breakfasts, no two rooms at Adobe Abode are the same. Bloomsbury, for example, is done in rose and celadon with an *Out of Africa* feeling, while English Garden was recently redecorated in Adirondack lodge style with plaids and stars. There's also Bronco, which looks exactly as it sounds — a rustic, Western-style room with cowboy hats on the wall, a saddle and *riatas* (lassos) on the bedposts and a private covered porch and brick patio with twig furniture. Cactus has a distinctly south-of-the-border flavor with hand-loomed fabrics from Oaxaca, whitewashed *vigas* and a *kiva* fireplace, while *Casita de Corazon*, or "Little House of the Heart," features Santa Fe-style decor, including custom-designed twin bed finished with aspen poles lashed together. Provence Suite contains a full-living room and separate bedroom with a queen whitewashed lodgepole bed and French designer linens that highlight the blue and yellow color scheme so reminiscent of southern France.

Alexander's Inn
$$ • 529 E. Palace Ave. • 986-1431, (888) 321-5123

This 1903 Craftsman-style home has been lovingly decorated with hand-stenciling, dried flowers and family antiques to create a warm, relaxing and nurturing atmosphere. The country cottage feel is enhanced by dormer windows, antiques and carefully restored architectural details. Sunlight streams through stained-glass windows or lace curtains onto gleaming hardwood floors. Fresh flowers grace every room in the house.

Accommodations include seven guest rooms, five named for flowers and a couple of two-storied units called the Casita and the Cottage. Most rooms are furnished with four-poster or brass and iron beds. The Peony and

Wildflower rooms share a bathroom, the Lavender Room has a private bath across the hall, the Rose Room has a private bath and a porch, while the Lilac Room has a private bath with a claw-foot tub, a fireplace and stained glass. The Casita (little house) and the Cottage both have upstairs bedrooms. The living rooms with *kiva* fireplaces are downstairs, as are the private baths. The Casita has a refrigerator and microwave, and the Cottage has a private Jacuzzi. In addition, Alexander's offers two remodeled adobe *casitas* located just up the lane from the inn. Both feature a Southwestern motif including *kiva* fireplaces, Mexican tile, full kitchens and patios. Casa de las Flores has two bedrooms, each with a queen-size bed, while the Madeleine, a 600-square-foot historic adobe, has one bedroom with a four-poster queen-size bed. The inn is in the process of remodeling an old hacienda with more rooms, each with a private bath.

Rooms at the Alexander are spacious and furnished with televisions and telephones as well as thick, fluffy bathrobes. A little basket of chocolates waits for you on the doorknob at the end of the day, before you snuggle under a down comforter. Mornings greet you with the aroma of freshly brewed gourmet coffee and homemade muffins. Other breakfast choices include homemade granola, whole-grain breads, yogurt and seasonal fruit salad. Winter breakfasts are served in the cozy kitchen warmed by a roaring wood stove. In warmer weather, guests can eat breakfast on the verandah overlooking a grassy lawn shaded by lilacs, wisteria and apricot trees in spring; roses, peonies, lavender and cosmos in summer. You can while away hours on the front porch's old-fashioned swing, sipping lemonade or iced tea and munching from the ever-present plate of homemade cookies and brownies or soak under the stars in a backyard hot tub. Guests have full privileges at upscale El Gancho Health Club.

Camas de Santa Fe
$$ • 323 E. Palace Ave. • 984-1337, (800) 632-2627

Close to the historic Santa Fe Plaza, Ca-

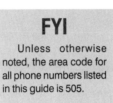

FYI

Unless otherwise noted, the area code for all phone numbers listed in this guide is 505.

mas de Santa Fe offers the charm and intimacy of a small European inn, yet has both the convenience and the accessibility of a downtown hotel. Designed in the Territorial style popular at the turn of the century, most of Camas' 15 guest rooms feature *viga* (beamed) ceilings, hardwood floors and private baths tiled in a Mexican motif. Some rooms have private entrances, *kiva* or gas fireplaces, refrigerators and even a Jacuzzi. All have air-conditioning, telephones and cable television. An interesting note: Camas de Santa Fe used to be the office of artist Georgia O'Keeffe's eye surgeon, Dr. John Gundzik, who converted it to a bed and breakfast. Guests in rooms No. 2 and No. 6 might even feel her presence. Those are the ones O'Keeffe used.

The inn offers a buffet of juices, fresh brewed teas and coffee, breads and cereals every morning between 8 and 10 AM. This is a good time to trade experiences with other guests or to ask staff for suggestions.

Casa de la Cuma Bed & Breakfast
$$ • 105 Paseo de la Cuma • 983-1717, (888) 366-1717

Located on a narrow, winding street just north of Paseo de Peralta — near the original Cross of the Martyrs (see our Attractions chapter) and its magnificent sunset views — Casa de la Cuma is a pleasant stroll to downtown Santa Fe and the Plaza. This Southwestern-style inn offers three rooms and a suite that share an outdoor patio with mountain views. The largest room contains a handcrafted king-size bed, a turn-of-the-century Navajo rug on the wall, an enamel, open-faced woodburning stove and a private entrance to the patio. Rooms No. 2 and 3 share a bath as well as views of the mountains, and the inn's garden, which is redolent with lilac bushes and shaded by a peach tree. The suite has its own living room with a queen sleeper couch, a wet bar, Mexican tiles in the bath and a queen bed in the separate bedroom. All rooms have air conditioning and televisions.

The common room has a cozy fireplace in front of which guests can browse through books and magazines scattered on several coffee tables. There's off-street parking for guests, a blessing on the narrow street, and an expanded continental breakfast that includes breads and pastries baked on premises or at one of Santa Fe's fine bakeries, along with homemade jam from the inn's peach tree, cereals, a selection of seasonal fruit, juice, freshly brewed coffee and a variety of teas.

Casa del Toro
$$$ • 229 McKenzie St. • 995-9689, (888) 995-9689

One of Santa Fe's newest bed and breakfasts, Casa del Toro sits at the corner of two of downtown Santa Fe's quietest streets — Chapelle and McKenzie — and right around the corner from the new Georgia O'Keeffe Museum. The adobe-style house features *viga* ceilings, *kiva* fireplaces, Mexican tile, skylights, and Southwestern art and knickknacks throughout. All rooms are furnished with down pillows and comforters and thick terrycloth robes. Each of the inn's four rooms has its own bathroom. The largest has a Jacuzzi as well as a fireplace and a walk-in closet. The smallest is connected by a foyer to another small room suitable for a child — available for an additional charge — with a private bathroom accessible from the foyer. These rooms share a private entrance from a communal garden patio and are closest to the kitchen for midnight snacking on home-baked goodies available 24-hours a day. There's a large color television in the common room, which conveniently abuts the counter with the snacks. Guests can also help themselves to tea, coffee and lemonade

Guests rave about Casa del Toro's gourmet breakfasts, which always include a hot entree such as a quiche or souffle with artichoke hearts, spinach and chiles; posole (hominy) with a purée made from white chile, cream, butter and crushed hot peppers. Sometimes there's more traditional fare — breakfast burritos, huevos rancheros, waffles with fruit from the local farmers market or pancakes with homemade chorizo. Breakfast also includes fresh fruit and juice, homemade breads and muffins (chile cheese corn muffins are a favorite), fresh coffee and a variety of dark and herbal teas. The host will accommodate special diets.

Castillo Inn

$$$ • 622 Castillo Pl. • 982-1212, (800) 405-2949

Just two and a half blocks from the Santa Fe Plaza, the charming Castillo Inn offers five unique rooms that give guests a taste of the various cultures that make Santa Fe unique. The Kachina room, named for the Indian statues that represent friendly messengers from the spirit world, has earth-toned textured walls on which hang dreamcatchers, peace pipes and other Native American decorations. The Santa Fe room features a handcarved bed and furniture with soothing, faux-adobe walls; the Western room has teak floors and paneling; the Mexican Fiesta room has a wrought-iron bed, authentic sombreros and bold, fanciful colors; and the English Rose room, with its roses and lace, antique furniture and claw-foot bathtub, is reminiscent of the Victorian era. Each room has a private entrance, patio, bath with glycerin soap made on the premises and a telephone. The inn serves a sit-down breakfast at 8:30 AM that includes homemade granola, quick breads and some mornings a quiche, fruit plates, juice, freshly ground coffees and tea. Upon request, and with enough advance notice, the hosts will prepare an afternoon tea with homemade scones, crème fraîche and jam, all on English bone china and at no extra charge.

Dancing Ground of the Sun Bed and Breakfast

$$ • 711 Paseo de Peralta • 986-9797, (800) 645-5673

Long ago the Pueblo Indians christened this region of northern New Mexico the "Dancing Ground of the Sun." This delightful downtown inn has taken this vision as its namesake. Only two blocks from the historic Santa Fe Plaza, Dancing Ground of the Sun's five *casitas* and two bedrooms are a celebration of light, tradition, color and design. The theme of Native American spirit dancers plays throughout the suites and is reflected in murals by Taos artist Katherine Henry.

Each suite is named for a colorful figure from Native American lore — Buffalo Dancer, Clown Dancer, Corn Dancer, Deer Dancer, Rainbow Dancer, Spirit Dancer and Kokopelli, the oft-recognized mythical flute player who represents good fortune and abundance. Suites feature *kiva* fireplaces, *vigas*, Southwestern-style furniture made by local craftspeople, hand-painted tiles and numerous other special touches. All *casitas* have fully equipped kitchens, dining rooms, living rooms, bedrooms and private baths; some also have balconies, patios and/or washers and dryers. Rooms come with a continental breakfast that includes homemade muffins or bread, fresh fruit, juice, coffee and tea.

www.insiders.com

See this and many other
Insiders' Guide® destinations
online — in their entirety.

Visit us today!

Don Gaspar Compound

$$$ • 623 Don Gaspar Ave. • 986-8664, (888) 986-8664

In the lovely and peaceful South Capital section of Santa Fe, Don Gaspar Compound welcomes you with the spreading arms of an old peach tree and a tranquil, adobe-walled garden courtyard where heirloom flowers and the trickle of water from a central fountain soothe the soul. The 86-year-old inn is a classic example of mission and adobe architecture with brick paths and distressed wooden gates.

Don Gaspar Compound offers six private suites for long- or short-terms stays, including the Main House — a sunny, beautifully appointed bungalow overlooking the gardens and that features two woodburning fireplaces, two bedrooms, two baths, a small room with a double futon and a fully-equipped kitchen. Also containing fireplaces and fully-equipped kitchens are the one-bedroom, one-bath Fountain Casita, named for the courtyard fountain visible through the living room's French doors, and the Courtyard Casita, which has its own private courtyard and garden, stained-glass windows above a king-size bed and a whirlpool bath.

The Southwest Suite's decor is true to its name with an adobe woodburning fireplace and fine Southwest furnishings; the Aspen Suite takes its name from the trees in the garden,

Photo: Preston House

Bed and breakfasts offer splendid accommodations
in a comfortable, homelike atmosphere.

which are in full view from the kitchenette and the window seat in the bedroom; and the Western-style Colorado Room, with French doors opening onto its own patio, could easily be called "home on the range" with its cowboy motif. In addition, the owners make available a charming home located in a quiet residential neighborhood about 2 miles southwest of Don Gaspar Compound. San Juan House is a small two-bedroom, one-bath adobe with French doors in each bedroom that open onto a deck.

All accommodations have private bathrooms, television and private phones. Those without fully equipped kitchens have kitchenettes with refrigerators, microwaves, coffee makers, toasters and some utensils. The refrigerators are stocked with fresh coffee beans, spring water and Blue Sky natural sodas. Guests, including those at San Juan House, generally take their morning meal in Don Gaspar Compound's breakfast room, where they can choose from a variety of gourmet coffees and teas, fresh-squeezed orange juice, pastries, cereals, fresh fruit and a different regional specialty daily.

Dos Casa Viejas
$$$$ • 610 Agua Fría St. • 983-1636
Situated in the heart of the historic Guadalupe District, near Sanbusco Market and the Railyard and only 10 minutes by foot to the Plaza, Dos Casas Viejas ("Two Old Houses") provides guests with the quintessential Southwestern bed and breakfast experience. Housed within a walled and gated adobe compound on a half-acre of land, this intimate and sophisticated collection of charming adobe buildings offers the character, charm and tradition found in Santa Fe during the 1860s.

Each *casita* provides the utmost in privacy with individual entry gates leading to bricked, landscaped patios, complete with custom-built willow furniture, behind adobe walls. French doors lead into the *casitas*, which are decorated with period furnishings as well as state-of-the-art amenities. All have *kiva* fireplaces, *vigas*, cable television, private telephones, answering machines and bar refrigerators with complimentary beverages and snacks. The inn also provides fresh flowers; custom soaps, shampoos and lotions; luxurious personal robes; and hair dryers.

Guests can breakfast in the dining room, in the main building adjacent to a lobby/library, take their food back to their quarters or, if they prefer, dine *al fresco* on the patio of the compound's 40-foot heated lap pool. Dos Casas Viejas can accommodate up to 40 people for weddings, private parties, banquets or meetings.

Dunshee's

$$$ • 986 Acequia Madre • 982-0988

With only two units — a large suite in the main house and a two-bedroom guest house next door — Dunshee's is among Santa Fe's smallest inns, though that's not a reflection on the size of the rooms, which are quite spacious. Traditional New Mexican-style furniture, *kiva* fireplaces, Mexican tile, folk art and well-placed antiques along with the owner's personal touches — fresh flowers, home-baked cookies, good books and quiet breakfasts — create an intimate, homey, old-fashioned atmosphere without sacrificing the convenience and pleasure of modern amenities like phones and televisions.

The bed and breakfast is in a restored adobe home that hosts only one party at a time with accommodations for the exclusive use of guests. They include a private entrance; a large living room with a cozy sitting area and a *kiva* fireplace; a queen-size bed in the bedroom, which also has a *kiva* fireplace; a sheltered, flower-filled patio; a *portal* (roofed porch) overlooking a large backyard; an eclectic library; and a refrigerator and microwave. Breakfast, served on the patio or *portal* in summer or by the fire during crisper weather, includes fresh-squeezed juice, freshly ground coffee, home-baked goods, seasonal fruit and various entrees such as omelettes with herbs from the garden, sour cream pancakes or green chile soufflé.

Located next door is Dunshee's *casita*, a two-bedroom, one-bath pueblo-style adobe guest house with a private patio, a living room supplied with books and a stereo system and a complete kitchen that even includes a dishwasher. You'll arrive to a full cookie jar and a refrigerator stocked for breakfast: gourmet coffee, fresh juice, seasonal fruit and home-made muffins. Guests can help themselves to herbs and tomatoes from the garden. The *casita* is available for long-term rentals. Ask for prices.

In a quiet, historic and charming neighborhood named for the *Acequia Madre* ("mother ditch") that runs through it, Dunshee's is a pleasant mile from the Plaza and only three blocks from the galleries and shops, cafes and restaurants of elegant Canyon Road.

El Farolito Bed & Breakfast Inn

$$$ • 514 Galisteo St. • 988-1631, (888) 634-8782

A few short blocks from the Plaza and around the corner from the State Capitol building, El Farolito welcomes guests to its off-street compound in one of the city's historic districts. The inn features five guest rooms in two buildings, two private *casitas* and a main building with a dining room and lounge/library. A number of the buildings are adobe, and all have been decorated in traditional Southwestern style ranging from Native American to Mexican folk art. The owners have displayed paintings, pottery, *kachinas*, weavings and other items from their private art collection throughout the inn.

Each room has a private entrance and outdoor patio as well as a private, hand-tiled bath, brick or tile floors, wood-beamed ceiling, handcarved furniture and a *kiva* fireplace as well as color cable television and a private phone. Some rooms also have wet bars with small refrigerators. The inn's rooms reflect Santa Fe's tricultural heritage of Pueblo Indian, Spanish Colonial and pioneer Anglo settlers.

The breakfast room is a sunny, brightly colored affair with a fireplace and tables for two, four and eight, so guests can eat in privacy or company, according to their mood. El Farolito serves an expanded continental breakfast that includes a fresh fruit plate, pastries brought in fresh each morning, yogurt, cereals, bagels, toast, English muffins, coffee, tea and juice. Those craving a hot breakfast can venture into the retro-1960s Cafe Oasis next

---

INSIDERS' TIP

If you're counting your pennies, staying in the county could save you some money — up to 1.5 percent in taxes alone. Santa Fe County charges only 5.75 percent in gross receipts tax and 3 percent in lodgers tax compared to the city, where you'll pay a 6.25 percent gross receipts plus 4 percent lodgers tax.

door (but not until 9 AM) or to any number of more traditional restaurants downtown.

El Paradero Bed & Breakfast Inn
$$ • 220 W. Manhattan Ave. • 988-1177

Built between 1800 and 1820, El Paradero was originally a Spanish farmhouse to which territorial touches such as pillars were added in the late-19th century. In 1912, the main house underwent a complete remodeling that included Victorian doors and windows. The current innkeepers bought the house 17 years ago and turned it into Santa Fe's second bed and breakfast inn. They have since remodeled it, adding some modern architectural touches while maintaining the eccentric, rambling character of the old farmhouse — from its thick adobe walls to its high ceilings, *kiva* fireplaces, *vigas*, *bancos*, (benches built into the walls) and *nichos* (small niches in the wall to place religious icons or decorations).

El Paradero has 14 rooms: nine around the courtyard, three upstairs and two suites in an adjacent 1912 brick coachman's house — a plaqued New Mexico historic structure. Ten of the rooms have private baths, four less expensive rooms share two bathrooms along a short hallway. Each room is furnished with Southwestern-style furniture, handwoven textiles and folk art; many have fireplaces and skylights or mountain-view balconies. Breakfasts are hearty. They include a gourmet entree, home-baked bread, fresh fruit and juice. Sundays bring lighter-than-air pancakes, a tradition of the innkeepers, who will meet special dietary needs. They serve tea — either hot or iced — hot cider and homemade baked goods and chips and salsa every afternoon. A warning for those with allergies: The inn has a cat and dog on premises.

Four Kachinas Inn
Bed and Breakfast
$$$ • 512 Webber St. • 982-2550, (800) 397-2564

Four Kachinas Inn takes its name from the ancestral spirits of the Pueblo Indians, in this case four Hopi spirits who reside in the San Francisco Peaks of the Four Corners region. *Kachinas* take three forms: pure spirit; a masked dancer believed to embody a particular spirit during a religious ceremony; or a carved doll in the costume of the spirit. It is the latter that appears in each of four correspondingly named rooms at the inn — Koyemsi, a fun-loving, mudhead clown *kachina*; Poko, a dog *kachina* that represents the spirits of domestic animals; Hon, a powerful and healing bear *kachina*; and Tawa, the sun god.

The inn features two additional rooms — Digneo and Cradleboard — in the main house, a landmark Victorian-style cottage with its own private guest lounge and library. Digneo Cottage is named for the man who built the house in the early 1900s, a stonemason who worked on St. Francis Cathedral. Both rooms are decorated in the Native-American motif seen throughout the inn.

Four Kachinas Inn is on a quiet residential street in view of the State Capitol and just a few short blocks up the Old Santa Fe Trail to the historic downtown Plaza. Ground-floor rooms have individual garden patios, while an upstairs room offers views of the Sangre de Cristo Mountains. All are decorated with Southwestern art and handiwork, including handmade wooden furniture, *saltillo* tile, antique Navajo rugs and, of course, *kachina* dolls. Each room has a private telephone and color cable television.

The heart of the inn is its sunny, bricked courtyard, which was built alongside the historic *Acequia Madre* — the "Mother Ditch" watercourse that meanders through Santa Fe — and the adobe lounge. Built of adobe bricks made on the property years ago, the lounge looks like an old Southwestern trading post and indeed sells fine arts and crafts made by native artisans along with guide books and maps. Guests are invited to peruse the hosts' personal library of art and travel books while they enjoy complimentary beverages and snacks all day long. The baked goods are always a special treat because one of the owners is an award-winning baker. Breakfast, delivered to your room each morning, include delicious breads or pastries, freshly brewed coffee or tea, juice, milk, yogurt and fresh fruit.

Grant Corner Inn
$$ • 122 Grant Ave. • 983-6678, (800) 964-9003

Surrounded by graceful weeping willow trees and a trim white picket fence, Grant Corner Inn, a 1905 Colonial manor home, maintains a country elegance in the heart of downtown Santa Fe. Just two blocks from the Santa Fe Plaza, the inn offers both comfort and convenience as well as justly famous breakfasts that feature entrees such as creative breakfast burritos, cinnamon raisin French toast, blue corn blueberry pancakes and a variety of freshly baked breads, pastries, coffee cakes, muffins and cookies from the inn's bakery. Breakfasts come with homemade jams, fresh-fruit frappés, freshly squeezed juice and seasonal fruit. The inn is open to the public for breakfast and lunch Wednesday through Saturday and on Sunday for brunch.

The inn has 12 charming guest rooms — 10 on the main premises and two in a hacienda located six blocks away — most with private baths. Rooms are beautifully appointed with antiques, handmade quilts, vintage photographs and rabbits in every medium (and every corner) imaginable from the collection of the innkeeper, who is also a decorator.

Guadalupe Inn
$$$ • 604 Agua Fría St. • 989-7422

On the historic Camino Real, an ancient route used first by American Indians and then by Hispanic traders to get from Mexico to northern New Mexico, the Guadalupe Inn is owned and operated by three members of the Quintana family. They built the bed and breakfast six years ago on the site of their grandfather's small grocery store — a halfmile from the Plaza on Santa Fe's west side.

The inn's 11 guest rooms and two-bedroom suite are uniquely decorated in Southwestern-style with furniture and fixtures handcrafted by members of the Quintana family and other artisans. Guadalupe Inn serves as a gallery for local artists, whose work is displayed throughout the inn and is for sale. All rooms contain private baths, queen-size beds, televisions, telephones and air conditioning. Seven rooms have fireplaces, four feature whirlpool baths, while the Celebration Room has a large porcelain tub with brass claw feet. The suite offers a private balcony with views of the Jemez Mountains to the west and the Sangre de Cristo

Mountains to the east. Guests share an indoor tiled hot tub surrounded by plants, planked walls and plenty of windows.

Guadalupe Inn serves a hearty breakfast with an entree that includes choice of huevos rancheros, breakfast burrito, pancakes or a chile relleno souffle. Breakfasts always come with homemade pastries or turnovers, cereal, fruit, juice and coffee or tea.

Inn of the Animal Tracks
$$$ • 707 Paseo de Peralta • 988-1546

Inn of the Animal Tracks is a whimsical little bed and breakfast that takes its animal theme seriously. The five guest rooms — all with queen-size platform beds, feather mattresses, hardwood floors, *vigas*, private baths, phones and cable television — and the two common rooms reflect the critters for which they're named.

"Rabbits," as the innkeepers call their guests in Sign of the Whimsical Rabbit, are provided with big fluffy bathrobes to tiptoe to their bathroom across the hall. Rabbits get the first whiffs of the inn's home-baked breads and pastries from the kitchen next door and have first dibs on the pantry for midnight snacking. Sign of the Soaring Eagle is an airy room overlooking apple, pear and honey locust trees as well as its own private patio. It has a *kiva* fireplace, soft colors to contrast with the blue sky that pours into the six large windows and photographs of eagles. Sign of the Gentle Deer is a serene room tucked next to a hazelnut thicket where resident squirrels gather nuts just outside the window. It has a handicapped-equipped private bath.

"Otters" in Sign of the Playful Otter can stare for hours at the inn's garden from a birch rocker and sleep under *vigas* and loomed throws on the bed. Its private bath has both a shower and tub. Sign of the Loyal Wolf is decorated with vibrant colors that mimic Santa Fe's sunsets and enjoys the fragrance of lilacs, juniper and a rare ginkgo tree outside the room. It has both a twin and queen-size platform bed.

With its life-size toy bear, the living room couldn't be called anything but Sign of the Bear, which signifies introspection. Here guests can

FYI

Unless otherwise noted, the area code for all phone numbers listed in this guide is 505.

relax in front of a *kiva* fireplace to the sounds of classical music or sink into an overstuffed sofa with a book from the inn's library. The dining room is appropriately named Sign of the Buffalo, an animal that symbolizes abundance, though guests can breakfast outside on the private patio, if they prefer. The inn serves hearty, calorie-laden breakfasts featuring innovative entrees, homemade muffins, fresh fruits and juices and, of course, coffee and tea. Guests can help themselves to home-baked cookies, cakes, pies and snacks all day long.

Inn of the Animal Tracks occupies a 110-year-old adobe that underwent a complete renovation in 1989. In addition to its spiritual namesakes, the inn is home to a number of live pets. So if you tend to be allergic or can't bear (no pun intended) the occasional stray animal hair, you might want to consider another inn. If you choose to stay here, you'll find yourself three pretty blocks east of the Plaza and north of Canyon Road.

Inn of the Turquoise Bear (Poet's House)

$$$ • 342 E. Buena Vista St. • 983-0798, (800) 396-4104

This historic bed and breakfast inn on the Old Santa Fe Trail occupies the home of poet Witter Bynner (1881-1968), for decades a prominent citizen of Santa Fe whose work in recent years has slipped into obscurity. During his day, Bynner was a leading figure of Santa Fe's flourishing writer's colony — a noted poet, translator and essayist who staunchly advocated equal rights for women, Native Americans, gays and other minorities. Bynner also loved a good party, hosting with Robert Hunt, his companion of more than 30 years, many a "Bynner's bash," as photographer Ansel Adams described their riotous soirees. Their home was a gathering place for the literati and glitterati, Santa Fe's answer to Mabel Dodge Luhan's home in Taos. Among Bynner's and Hunt's guests were D.H. Lawrence, who spent his first night in an American home here and who eventually settled near Taos; Willa Cather, whose classic novel, *Death Comes for the Archbishop*, has been for many readers their first introduction to Santa Fe; Aldous Huxley; Christopher Isherwood; Thornton Wilder; Mary Hunter Austin; Ansel

Adams; composer Igor Stravinsky; poets Edna St. Vincent Millay, Robert Frost, W.H. Auden and Stephen Spender; Hollywood stars Clara Bow, Errol Flynn and Rita Hayworth; music critic Carl Van Vechten; dancer and choreographer Martha Graham; Georgia O'Keeffe; and even Robert Oppenheimer, under whose leadership Los Alamos Scientific Laboratory built the world's first atomic bomb.

The new resident owners of the Bynner estate, Ralph Bolton and Robert Frost (no relation to the *other* Robert Frost), are dedicated to rekindling the spirit of excitement and creativity that thrived there when Bynner was alive as well as restoring and even extending the poet's legacy. To that end they give readings of Bynner's work and, in the process, provide their guests with a unique setting that captures the essence of traditional and literary Santa Fe.

Bynner's rambling adobe is built in the Spanish Pueblo Revival style around a core of rooms that date to the mid-1800s. The grounds are truly magnificent with soaring ponderosa pines, rock terraces, stone benches, meandering flagstone paths and gardens filled with lilac, wild roses and other flowers — all enclosed by adobe walls and coyote fences. The interior contains 11 Southwestern guest rooms, 10 of them with *kiva* fireplaces, *viga* ceilings, *saltillo* tile, private entrances, and brick or wooden floors. Most have private baths and sitting areas; all have phones, cable televisions and VCRs. The inn has an impressive video library and, as you might expect, an extensive book collection.

Among the little luxuries that make Inn of the Turquoise Bear so special are the robes in the rooms and flowers and fruit throughout the house. The hosts also serve wine and cheese at sunset and an expanded continental breakfast that includes fresh-squeezed orange juice, cereals, seasonal fruit, a variety of pastries, and coffee from a roaster down the street. The inn is six blocks from the Plaza and a pleasant stroll to Canyon Road. There are also a number of galleries, shops and restaurants in the vicinity.

Inn on the Paseo

$$ • 630 Paseo de Peralta • 984-8200, (800) 457-9045

The Inn on the Paseo comprises two historic homes joined by a central wing. The relatively large bed and breakfast inn with 16 rooms and two suites was renovated eight years ago in contemporary Southwestern style. Each room has a private bath, a down comforter and, in most cases, a patchwork quilt handmade by one of the innkeepers, a third generation quiltmaker. The decor is country style with washed pine furniture and pastel-colored walls, though no two rooms are alike. One might include a four-poster bed, while another has a fireplace, a sloped ceiling or, in the Honeymoon suite, a whirlpool bath. Some have hardwood floors, others are carpeted. Many feature original works of art, which, like the quilts, are for sale. All have private heat and air conditioning controls, telephones and cable color television with HBO.

Breakfast is made on premises and usually consists of at least one hot entree — frittata, French toast or breakfast burritos, for example — along with homemade breads, fresh fruit, yogurt, hot and cold cereals, juice and gourmet coffee. Guests can eat indoors or on the back deck. The inn serves homemade cookies and cakes every afternoon along with hot or cold drinks in a living room with a large fireplace, a skylight and lots of windows overlooking a sunken patio and gardens.

Just a few blocks northeast of the Plaza, Inn on the Paseo is across the street from Cross of the Martyrs (see our Attractions chapter) and a short stroll to nearby Canyon Road. The inn offers free parking for guests.

La Tienda Inn
$$$ • 445-447 W. San Francisco St.
• 989-8259, (800) 889-7611

This out-of-the-way bed and breakfast and its resident cat, Adolfo, are both named to honor the history of one of its buildings — a small adobe built in the 1930s by Adolfo Montoya, who operated a little neighborhood store (*tienda*) behind its thick mud walls and beneath the unpeeled log *vigas* that support its earthen roof. The market remained open under a number of shopkeepers until the 1960s. Now, it's the Old Store Common Room, which has been renovated without sacrificing the traditional architecture or ambiance.

La Tienda has seven individual guest rooms, each with a private bath and entrance and all named for neighbors past and present. The owners discuss the namesakes in their newsletter, which comes out several times a year. Three rooms — Romero, Montoya and Mascarell — are in the air-conditioned Territorial House, which is nearly 100 years old and is listed in the state Historical Register. The Romero Room features a sun porch and its own picket-fenced garden, while the Montoya and Mascarell rooms overlook the front gar-

Photo: Don Strel/Southwest Assignments

Local inns offer a charming change of pace for a night's stay.

den and fountain. The remaining rooms are in the "old store adobe," whose thick mud walls keep the rooms cool in summer and warm in winter, though a swamp cooler adds to the comfort in summer. The wheelchair-accessible Trujillo Room has a fireplace, as do the Ortiz and Duran rooms. Duran also has a *viga* ceiling while the Conklin Room opens on to a quiet courtyard. All rooms have telephones and color cable television.

Guests are served a generous continental breakfast of warm breads, fresh fruit and juices served in the room or in the garden when the weather allows. Guests can take afternoon tea in the Common Room, where a large fireplace beckons when there's a chill in the air.

Las Palomas
$$$ • 119 Park Ave. • 988-4455, (800) 955-4455

In a tree-covered compound with rambling courtyards only three blocks from the Plaza, Las Palomas offers the charm, elegance and ambiance of a country inn in the heart of the city. And because of its affiliation with the elegant Eldorado Hotel two blocks away, Las Palomas can provide its guests with the best of both worlds — the intimacy of a small bed and breakfast and the amenities of a world-class resort.

Las Palomas was built sometime around the turn of the century. In restoring these 21 *casitas*, the owners strove to keep the style and feel of the adobe structures while adding the comforts of modern life. The odd-size doorways, uneven adobe walls and individual *kiva* fireplaces combine with air-conditioning, cable television, VCRs, stereos with CD players and modern kitchens to strike this aesthetic balance. Each of the fully restored adobe *casitas* has a living room, dining area, kitchen and private bath. The inn serves a full continental breakfast each morning.

Preston House
$$ • 106 Faithway St. • 982-3465, (888) 877-7622

Tucked at the end of a street that even many Santa Feans don't know exists is the elegant Preston House, the city's first bed and breakfast inn. Obscured by ancient elms in summer and open to the sun in winter, this lovely Queen Anne-style house, built in 1886, now bears a historical plaque. A charming garden winds its way throughout the property, offering guests a colorful display of seasonal blooms and an inviting patio on which to enjoy reading and afternoon tea and pastries.

The Victorian-style guest rooms are fantasies in linen and lace, stained glass, antique armoires, delicate floral wall coverings and ornately carved fireplaces. The Southwestern rooms in the adobe compound next door contain original artwork and hand-crafted furniture. All but the smallest room have a telephone and television. All but two have private baths. Guests breakfast in a big country kitchen on freshly squeezed orange juice, coffee or tea, and breads and pastries baked daily in the Preston House kitchen and are likely to be joined by the resident cat, Smokey, and dog, Griffith.

Pueblo Bonito Bed & Breakfast Inn
$$$ • 138 W. Manhattan St. • 984-8001, (800) 461-4599

Secluded behind thick adobe walls, Pueblo Bonito Bed & Breakfast Inn occupies an adobe built around the turn of the century. The newly renovated inn is in the midst of Santa Fe's historic downtown and a five-minute walk from the Plaza. The compound was once a private estate with its own stable and landscaped grounds. Today it still boasts beautiful private courtyards, narrow brick paths, adobe archways to the street and shady gardens sheltered by huge trees. The second-floor balcony overlooks Santa Fe's winding streets and the Sangre de Cristo Mountains to the east.

Eighteen cozy guest rooms, each with its own corner fireplace and private bath, provide intimacy, hospitality and traditional Santa Fe ambiance. They're named for area Indian tribes and furnished with Navajo rugs, baskets and sand paintings; Pueblo and Mexican pottery; antiques; *santos* and other work by local artisans. The inn offers many modern conveniences, such as on-site laundry facilities, color cable television and ample private parking within the compound.

Continental breakfast is served buffet style with a variety of fresh fruits, juices, Danish, muffins, croissants and cereals along with fresh-brewed coffee and an assortment of different teas. Guests can eat on the outside patio or in the newly renovated communal dining room. The innkeepers also serve an afternoon tea.

Territorial Inn Bed & Breakfast
$$ • 215 Washington Ave. • 989-7737, (800) 745-9910

In the heart of downtown Santa Fe, just one block from the Plaza, Territorial Inn is the last of the private homes along tree-lined Washington Avenue. The inn, built in the 1890s, is a charming blend of New Mexico's various architectural styles, mixing stone and adobe with a pitched roof and territorial-style pillars. The interior is furnished in a turn-of-the-century Victorian/Territorial style with rooms that range in size from large and luxurious to cozy and quaint. Two of the inn's 10 rooms have fireplaces, eight have private baths and all are elegantly decorated. The grounds feature lawns — a rarity in Santa Fe — as well as large cottonwood trees and a private rose garden. The inn serves a generous complimentary continental breakfast that includes a selection of freshly baked pastries, breads, bagels and other baked goods from the nearby Plaza Bakery; cereals; fruit; juice; and coffee and tea. Guests can dine in their rooms, on the patio, in the lounge or go to the inn's new coffee shop where, for an extra charge, they can get a hot breakfast. The coffee shop is also open for lunch and serves an eclectic choice of inexpensive foods including Frito pies and New Orleans style po-boy sandwiches. To work off your meals, ask the management for a free pass to a nearby health club. The inn hosts a social hour in the late afternoon that includes brandy, tea and homemade cookies.

Water Street Inn Bed & Breakfast
$$$ • 427 W. Water St. • 984-1193, (800) 646-6752

An award-winning adobe restoration has earned Water Street Inn a rightful place among Santa Fe's more luxurious bed and breakfasts. Its eight spacious rooms all have private baths, *kiva* and/or antique fireplaces (yes, some of the rooms have more than one) and/or wood stoves. The decor is refined Southwestern and varies from room to room with details such as brick floors, beamed ceilings and built-in sleeping *bancos* in addition to beds of various styles— sleigh, pediment, four-poster and New Mexico pine — depending on the room. One room has a spiral staircase and a private deck, another has a private patio with a *portal*. The Tesuque Suite has a private landscaped patio and enough room to sleep a family of five. A number of the rooms open onto a fountained courtyard. One room is handicapped accessible.

Breakfast includes fresh pastries, cereals, fruit, juices, coffees and a morning paper. The inn also hosts an evening happy hour when it serves New Mexican wines and hot hors d'oeuvres. Many fine restaurants are nearby, and the Plaza is just two blocks away.

FYI

Unless otherwise noted, the area code for all phone numbers listed in this guide is 505.

County

Crystal Mesa Farm Bed and Breakfast
$$ • 3547 S.R. 14, Bldg. B • 474-5224

Unlike many bed and breakfasts, Crystal Mesa Farm welcomes children. Its collection of miniature critters — potbellied pigs, African pygmy hedgehogs, pygmy goats and a very stubborn miniature donkey called Duke — is always a delight for youngsters. Newborns are a constant occurrence so be sure to ask your hosts about any new arrivals. The inn also provides such child-friendly amenities as cribs, room-to-room intercoms, a sandbox and easy trails peppered with rocks that draw children like magnets. You and your kids can explore *arroyos* (natural rain ditches) and mesas, stare endlessly at hawks and falcons and watch for prairie dogs and coyotes. Crystal Mesa Farm is also an exotic bird rescue station with an aviary/sun room that is home to a number of permanent feathered residents and a few visitors taking temporary refuge. You can even have one of the birds "room" with you during your stay.

Built on the ancient site of the San Marcos Pueblo on the historic Turquoise Trail, this charming bed and breakfast inn offers a lovely alternative to staying in town. Each guest room has a private bath and entrance, cable television, a VCR and a phone. The San Marcos Suite features a king-size bed flanked by antique columns from an Indian palace, a woodburning stove and private access to the inn's library and hot tub. The Sunset Room has a west-facing terrace and queen-size bed. An Apache ladder leads to a meditation loft with breathtaking views of the sunset and starry night skies. The Lookout Room boasts a bed designed by Santa Fe "cowboy artist" L.D. Burke, a kitchen and a private deck with its own panoramic view. The more adventurous can follow the Tipi Trail to the inn's Sioux tipi, which contains a platform futon, flagstone floor, sheepskins and central fire pit which makes for cozy nights in winter.

The Farm's decor is an eclectic blend of Southwestern, cowboy and Far Eastern antiques along with many contemporary pieces. The inn is filled with stained-glass windows, including one called the "star of summer," which focuses the light of sunset during the summer solstice through a central prism onto a *nicho* across the room, bathing it and the statue it holds in a rainbow of light.

The inn serves a continental breakfast of homemade cinnamon toast, French toast or other sweet breads with freshly squeezed orange juice, fresh fruits, coffee, tea and milk. It hosts a cocktail hour in a common area with a cozy conversation pit with a *kiva* fireplace and antique wood-burning cook stove. Guests are welcome to peruse the extensive library for information on local wildlife, history, ancient and modern Indian sites and the magic that draws so many to this area. There's also a collection of videotapes on the wildlife, plants, indigenous peoples, history and lore of the land.

Galisteo Inn
$$ • H.C. 75, Box 4 (No. 9 La Vega), Galisteo • 466-4000

About 20 miles southeast of Santa Fe,

Galisteo was once a Spanish Colonial outpost built on the ruins of an ancient Indian pueblo. Today, it's home to artists, writers, healers and a native community that retains a strong sense of its Indian and Spanish traditions. It's also home to Galisteo Inn, a 252-year-old hacienda that belonged to one of the original Spanish settlers of the area.

The inn itself is an 8,000-square-foot Territorial-style adobe building on eight secluded acres. It features large, missionary-style carved wooden doors; wood-planked floors covered with antique rugs; white-washed walls and fireplaces with built-in *bancos*; beamed and *latilla*-ed ceilings; hand-crafted period furniture and fixtures; a lounge filled with sofas and books; and an ambiance of genteel country antiquity.

Each of the inn's 13 rooms is named for a native tree — in descending order by price: cottonwood, spruce, birch, piñon, poplar, juniper, ponderosa, elm, aspen, willow, cedar, sycamore and oak. Most of the rooms have private baths; some have fireplaces and televisions. All include a full buffet breakfast by a chef who has earned raves both locally and nationally, though primarily for her creative, nouvelle Southwestern dinners (Wednesday through Sunday only, prix fixe). Breakfasts are imaginative, with a main dish that could be chile frittata one morning or breakfast burritos the next, along with such standards as home-baked breads, fruit salad, yogurt, smoothies and freshly brewed coffee and tea.

Among the amenities at Galisteo Inn are a 50-foot, outdoor heated lap pool, open May through October; an outdoor hot tub guests can use all year long; an indoor sauna; and mountain bikes. For additional charges, guests can also enjoy massages, horseback riding, picnic lunches and, of course, the inn's famous dinners.

Heart Seed B&B and Spa
$$ • 516B C. R. 55, Cerrillos • 471-7026

Heart Seed is both an inn and a spa located 25 miles south of Santa Fe on the scenic Turquoise Trail. The inn's four guest rooms

---

INSIDERS' TIP

The City of Santa Fe has more than 4,850 rooms in hotels, motels and bed and breakfast inns.

and separate three-bedroom chalet are situated on 100 spectacular acres in the Ortiz Mountains with breathtaking views that let you see for 80 miles. Also on the grounds is a day spa offering a variety of massage techniques, facials, salt glows and herbal or cellulite wraps with treatments ranging in price from $55 an hour to $75 for an hour and a half. The spa also offers discount packages by the day or by the week.

Rooms at the Heart Seed are spacious and attractive with private baths; two rooms have fully equipped kitchenettes. The Adobe Room has a natural adobe wall with a *nicho*, an antique, full-size bed, marble and cherry antique furnishings and a view of the Sangre de Cristo Mountains. The Desert Hearts Room is decorated in a 1950s cowboy/cowgirl motif with two queen-size beds, a camp kitchen with a hot plate and cooking supplies, rustic antique furnishings and a small patio with great views of the Ortiz Mountains. The Piñon and Juniper rooms are studio-apartment-style suites in the separate Retreat House, a short walk from the main house. Each includes a fully equipped kitchenette, a queen-size bed, futon couch, table and chairs, refrigerator and cooking facilities. Both afford fine views of the Sangre de Cristos and Jemez mountains. The chalet is a three-bedroom log cabin with two baths, two upstairs decks providing 360 degree views, a stone fireplace, wood floors, hand-crafted banisters and a fully equipped kitchen.

All accommodations include a full breakfast — gourmet entrees, homemade breads and freshly ground coffee — at the main house and unlimited use of all facilities except the spa, which is charged separately. The property features a large shaded deck, hot tub, meditation garden, goldfish pond, labyrinth, common room/library, hiking trails, a telescope for stargazing and plenty of bird watching.

Open Sky Bed and Breakfast
$$ • 134 Turquoise Tr. • 471-3475, (800) 244-3475

This is a true country bed and breakfast, located 20 minutes south of downtown Santa Fe off the historic Turquoise Trail. The inn offers spectacular 360 degree views and Southwest elegance from its adobe architecture to its brick floors and high *viga* ceilings. Guests can choose from three rooms. The largest is 540 square feet with a king-size bed, private shower and bath, fireplace, sitting area and patio. The next largest is half the size with a king bed and a full private bath that has both a tub and a shower as well as double sinks. The smallest room has a queen bed and a large private bath next door with a shower and an antique tub. The two smaller rooms offer northern views that show the Santa Fe skyline to advantage at night. The largest room faces the Ortiz Mountains to the south.

Open Sky serves a continental breakfast of fresh breads, cereals, fruit, juice and a hot beverage of your choice at private tables facing a garden courtyard. The inn also has an outdoor Jacuzzi, a large lounge with a fireplace and a number of private patios.

The Triangle Inn
$$ • Rt. 11, Box 5T • 455-3375

The Triangle Inn is a beautifully rustic country bed and breakfast that caters to the lesbian and gay community. Located on an old abode compound surrounded by Tesuque, Nambé and Pojoaque pueblos, the inn is just 15 minutes north of downtown Santa Fe and convenient to all that northern New Mexico has to offer. Guests stay in their own private *casitas*, which range in size from a cozy studio to a large, two-bedroom house. Each is unique and features rustic Southwestern decor and attention to detail complemented by

INSIDERS' TIP

Prices in Santa Fe hotels, motels and inns are often negotiable — especially during the off-season, which may vary from one establishment to another. Be prepared, however, to meet with some surprise, if not downright indignation, in some quarters if you try to bargain. After all, this isn't Mexico. Still, it doesn't hurt to ask and you just might score a good-natured success.

Mexican and hand-crafted furnishings, fireplaces, *viga* ceilings and private courtyards. All have kitchenettes and either king or queen-size beds with down bedding. Additional amenities include stereos with CD players, color televisions and VCRs, telephones, hair dryers and gourmet coffees and teas in the room. The hosts even provide you with terry robes and spa towels for use in the bath or the 24-hour hot tub in the Main Courtyard, which also has a large deck and sunbathing area. The Hacienda Courtyard has extensive gardens, an orchard and a large freestanding *portal* with an outdoor fireplace. Your hosts serve refreshments here in warmer months. All rooms include a heavy continental breakfast of muffins, a fruit platter, yogurt, oatmeal, juice, coffee and tea.

Vacation rentals come
in several flavors:
apartments,
condominiums, *casitas*
and private houses.

Vacation Rentals

Visitors looking to stay in Santa Fe for more than a few days, especially those who don't want to dine out every meal, might consider a vacation rental instead of a hotel, motel or bed and breakfast. Vacation rentals come in several flavors: apartments, condominiums, *casitas* ("little houses") or private homes. They're usually only available for short-term leases, though that can mean several months in some instances, especially in timeshares. Many require a minimum stay of two to three days. Some of these facilities are pedestrian, others elegant. You can be sure that the style will be reflected in the price.

Vacation rentals are ideal for skiers who would rather spend money on the slopes than on their digs. Even cushy rentals can turn out to be downright reasonable for families or groups of friends. Ditto for opera buffs who don't mind digging into their pockets for season tickets but cringe at paying hundreds, if not thousands, of dollars on their accommodations.

Some people prefer to do their own cooking, whether it's to save money or to accommodate special diets. Either way, you can easily recoup some of the cost of your chi-chi accommodations (if that's what you choose) by cooking at home. For those of you who fit into this category, please, eat at least a few meals out. Visiting Santa Fe without tasting the local cuisine is like going to New York without catching a Broadway play. You could do it, of course. But why would you want to?

If smoking, pets, children or handicapped access are important issues for you, be sure to ask about them before you make a reservation. Unless we note otherwise, all the accommodations listed here accept major credit cards.

Price Code

Our legend is based on the lowest rate per night during peak season. Price ratings don't reflect lodgers tax or other surcharges.

$	less than $55
$$	$55-$89
$$$	$90-$139
$$$$	$140-$199
$$$$$	$200 and more

Downtown

Chapelle Street Casitas
$$ • 209 and 211 Chapelle St.
• 988-2883, (888) 366-1717

Like its sister business, Casa de la Cuma Bed & Breakfast (see our Bed and Breakfasts chapter), Chapelle Street Casitas are Southwestern in atmosphere and character. Located downtown, in a tranquil, tree-lined residential neighborhood a few blocks northwest of the Plaza — and right around the corner from the new Georgia O'Keeffe Museum — the inn offers four attached *casitas*, three of them with fully equipped kitchens that include coffee makers and dishwashers. Each is decorated differently with antiques and Navajo rugs, authentic Mexican sombreros, serapes and saddles. One has a claw-foot bathtub, another an enamel wood-burning stove that opens up like a fireplace. All *casitas* include an expanded continental breakfast that includes a fruit plate, home-baked yeast and quick breads, fresh bagels and croissants, cold cereals, freshly ground coffee, a variety of teas, milk and juice. The corner building is a turn-of-the-century structure with wooden floors, tall windows and high ceilings with ceiling fans. Guests share a patio in a garden that features a 100-year-old apricot tree. Although there's no innkeeper on site, the owners — longtime New Mexico residents and avid skiers, hikers and mountain bikers — are always just a phone call away and happy to share their knowledge of local trails.

FYI

Unless otherwise noted, the area code for all phone numbers listed in this guide is 505.

Cielo Grande Condominiums
$$$$ • 442 Greg Ave. • 982-5591, (800) 333-3333

Cielo Grande is a luxury condominium complex owned and operated by the Radisson Hotel, located one street away. It features 33 one-bedroom, one-bath and two-bedroom, two-bath furnished apartments with *kiva* fireplaces, *bancos*, large dining areas, private balconies with city and mountain views and attractive Santa Fe-style furniture and decor. Cielo Grande guests have access to all the amenities and privileges of the Radisson except room service. This includes free shuttle service to the downtown area and passes to the 20,000-square-foot Santa Fe Spa next to the hotel.

Las Brisas de Santa Fe
$$$ • 624 Galisteo St. • 982-5795

Las Brisas is a compound of 29 one-, two- and three-bedroom condominiums. Ten are timeshares, the rest owner-occupied or rentals, and all of them are pure Santa Fe: exposed adobe walls, *saltillo* tile floors, *viga* ceilings, *kiva* fireplaces, enclosed courtyards or patios, punched tin decorations and other Southwestern touches. For the truly decadent, there's even one with a whirlpool bath and an enclosed atrium with a skylight. All units are fully furnished and include dishwashers, microwaves, cooking and eating utensils, linens,

stackable washers and dryers and a queen sleeper sofa in the living room. They do not include daily maid service. Las Brisas is around the corner from the State Capitol and six blocks from the Plaza. Guests can rent by the night, the week or the month, based on availability.

Otra Vez en Santa Fe
$$$ • 202 Galisteo St. • 988-2244, (800) 536-6488

At the corner of Galisteo and Water streets, above two narrow intersecting streets in the heart of historic downtown Santa Fe, sits an elegant timeshare that few locals even know exist. Otra Vez occupies the second and third floors of a relatively "new" Santa Fe building, circa 1923, above Harry's, a chic men's store, and Foreign Traders, which sells high quality Mexican furniture, collectibles and accessories.

Otra Vez doesn't have to advertise. It fills up its 18 one- and two-bedroom units by word-of-mouth. Among the attractions are a sun terrace with a year-round, outdoor hot tub and barbecues. The apartments are elegantly decorated in modern Southwestern style with hand-crafted furniture. Each has a full kitchen with microwave, dishwasher and cooking and eating utensils. The rates include daily maid service, access to free laundry facilities and parking in a lot behind the building.

San Ysidro Inn
$$, no credit cards • 509 Grant Ave. • 989-7964

San Ysidro (pronounced ee-SEE-dro) is among the more recent additions to Santa Fe's choice vacation rental list. Just a five-minute walk from the Plaza, the inn consists of two attached one-bedroom suites behind an adobe-walled entrance. Each has its own private garden patio, one with a fireplace. Both have a living/dining room with a *kiva* fireplaces; a full bath with Mexican tile and clawfoot tub; well-equipped kitchens that include microwaves and coffee makers; cable television and VCR; and fax facilities upon request. Also upon request, the owner will stock your refrigerator and handle other arrangements including dinner reservations, horseback riding or tours —

all before you arrive. After check-in, you'll find fresh fruit, chilled wine and soft drinks waiting for you.

Zona Rosa

$$$ • 429 W. San Francisco St.
• 988-4455, (800) 955-4455

Just one block from the luxurious Eldorado Hotel, the Zona Rosa Suites is an independently owned complex of nine luxury condominiums managed by the same company that runs the hotel. Each one-, two- and three-bedroom suite features Southwestern furnishings, an authentic *kiva* fireplace, *saltillo* tile floors, rustic *viga* ceilings and Native American artwork. All contain a full kitchen, living room, a balcony or patio, separate entrance and off-street parking. The two- and three-bedroom units have two full bathrooms. Guests at Zona Rosa may use all the Eldorado Hotel facilities including the rooftop swimming pool, fitness center and sauna.

County

Rancho Elisa

$$ • 1027-B Canyon Rd. (office address)
• 982-0383

On Hyde Park Road next to a Japanese-style bathhouse (see Ten Thousand Waves in our Health and Wellness chapter), Rancho Elisa was originally a hacienda built in the 1920s that has since been divided into eight privately owned homes. Two of them are available for short-term rentals by the day (with a minimum of two days) or by the week. One is a tri-level, three-bedroom, two-bath house that can be rented in its entirety or

divided into two units — a two-bedroom, one-bath suite on the upper level and a one-bedroom, one-bath suite below. The house is made of adobe and features traditional New Mexico architecture including *saltillo* tile floors, *viga* ceilings and three *kiva* fireplaces. The second house is a secluded, rustic one-bedroom, three-quarter bath (a shower but no tub) with wood plank ceilings; wood, brick and tile floors; and a deep *kiva* fireplace.

The owners also offer a couple of vacation rentals right in the city, one on upscale Canyon Road (the office address) and another on Agua Fría Street in the historic Guadalupe District. The Canyon Road rental is a bright one-bedroom, one-bath home with skylights throughout and a rooftop patio with a small *kiva* fireplace and views of the mountains and a park. It's fitted with Mexican tile and wooden floors. The house on Agua Fría is a sunny one-bedroom, three-quarter-bath home with a private yard and patio. It has an adjoining living room and kitchen, a woodburning stove and floors with wood, tile and carpet (in the bedroom). Additional rentals may also be available.

Rancho Jacona

$$$ • Rt. 5, Box 250, Pojoaque
• 455-7948

The name of this vacation rental/farm comes from the Tewa Indian word *Saconai* — "the cliffs where the tobacco grows." Wild Indian tobacco still grows here, along with lots of critters — rabbits, sheep, goats, pigs and birds. Kids love it. This is without a doubt a child-friendly place with lots to offer adults, too, including beauty, quiet, relaxation and

---

INSIDERS' TIP

Dogs are welcome in Santa Fe. In fact, they're about as ubiquitous as the kitschy bandana-clad, howling coyote you'll see everywhere. Keep in mind, however, that a city ordinance requires all dogs to be leashed in public, even in parks and on trails. In the county, your pooch must be within voice command. For energetic canines, this could present a real hardship. Please consider this before deciding to take Rufus with you to see — and, of course, smell — The City Different. He may be happier at home with a dog-sitter or staying with a neighbor.

Photo: Don Strel/Southwest Assignments

Vacation rentals are ideal for skiers who want homelike accommodations after a day on the slopes.

proximity to the Santa Fe Opera (see our Arts and Culture chapter), Bandelier National Monument and a number of Indian pueblos, all within a half-hour of town.

The farm's six self-catering *casitas* — Rabbit, Parrot, Piglet, Raccoon, Coyote and Rooster — are cheerfully furnished pueblo-style adobe houses with one bathroom and one, two and three bedrooms, each with a queen bed. All the *casitas* have fireplaces in addition to central heating; portals or patios for sitting, sunning or barbecuing; fully equipped kitchens, including garbage disposals; washers and dryers; cable television; and private phones. The grounds feature a 60-foot heated outdoor pool set among lawns and trees, a pond, a barn and lots of pasture land. Rancho Jacona requires a three-day minimum stay. Prices drop be-

tween $10 and $20 per night for stays of one week or more.

Rental Agencies

In addition to these listings, many real estate companies also offer rental services. See our Real Estate chapter.

Cyrano's Inc.
1300 Luisa Street, No. 2 • 982-6800, (800) 722-0099

Cyrano's can match you up with a condo, *casita*, private home or guest house with Santa Fe charm and modern conveniences. Homes, many built of adobe and featuring patios or decks, come with fully equipped kitchens, laundry facilities, linens, televisions and VCRs. The agency will even provide wood for the fireplace.

The Management Group
320 Paseo de Peralta, Ste. G • 982-2823, (800) 283-2211

The Management Group handles one-, two-, three- and four-bedroom homes and condominiums throughout Santa Fe with prices ranging from $100 to $500 a night, depending on the season and length of stay.

Both *Playboy* and *Money* magazines selected Santa Fe in the top-25 culinary destinations in the United States.

Restaurants

People who live in Santa Fe are spoiled when it comes good food. This community of some 65,000 residents has more than 200 restaurants. And among them are many that have received national acclaim — The Coyote Cafe, Santacafe, La Casa Sena, Il Piatto, Anasazi, Geronimo's, The Compound and others. Santa Fe ranks in the top-25 culinary destinations in the United States as selected by both *Playboy* and *Money* magazines.

Variety marks Santa Fe's restaurant scene. You'll find many places that specialize in the tasty regional cuisine, ranging from elegant, like La Tertulia, to charming and informal, like Tomasita's and Maria's. If you decide you'd like to eat something that doesn't have chile in it, Santa Fe can accommodate you with first-rate American cuisine from deluxe dining at places like The Old House to laid-back spots such as the Zia Diner and the Cowgirl Hall of Fame. Santa Fe is also blessed with a nice assortment of Italian and Asian restaurants.

"Santa Fe is fortunate to have the most fine restaurants per capita of any city in the world," said the president of the Santa Fe Restaurant Association, Al Lucero. "In a study done about five years ago, we learned that the primary reason people come to Santa Fe is for the culture and the natural beauty. But upon leaving, they say one of the things they like best was the selection of cuisine."

Santa Fe's luster as a food town is reflected in the city's many food-centered benefits and special events. The Wine and Chile Fiesta, a city-wide celebration each September, brings nationally and internationally acclaimed chefs to town along with thousands of eager gourmands (see our Annual Events chapter). The city has a long-established, well-regarded cooking school, the Santa Fe School of Cooking, which frequently hosts guest chefs from around the country.

This chapter offers some suggestions on where to eat. Although Santa Fe has its share of chain restaurants, we mention only places unique to the area. We've organized the listings by style of food served. If you're unfamiliar with the New Mexican style of cuisine, see our close-up in this chapter, which explains and defines many of the foods and terms you'll encounter when dining out in Santa Fe.

Our advice on reservations is simple — make them whenever you can. There are some places that don't take reservations or that take them only for large parties. Call these places ahead of time, though, and they will gladly give you an idea of when to come to minimize your wait. After all, it's their business to make you happy.

Dress is casual here, although diners tend to dress better when they go to more expensive places. Nowhere in Santa Fe, however, requires a coat and/or tie for men.

Unless otherwise noted, the restaurants listed in this chapter accept major credit cards and are open daily. However, many restaurants close for Christmas, Thanksgiving, New Year's Day and other holidays — if you want to dine out on those days, please call ahead. Keep in mind that some places expand their hours during the summer or cut back during the winter.

Although there is no city policy on smoking in restaurants, the many members of the Santa Fe Restaurant Association agreed to voluntarily establish smoking and nonsmoking sections in their restaurants. Some 95 percent either limit smoking to certain sections of their restaurants or ban it altogether. Unless we note otherwise, the restaurants listed here allow smoking in a special section, in the bar or on an outdoor patio.

Price Code

The dollar signs after each restaurant's name refer to the average price of dinner entrees for two — excluding appetizers, desserts, side orders, wine, even a Diet Coke. We also did not factor in tax or gratuity. If a restaurant is open only for breakfast and lunch, we made adjustments accordingly. Because of the range of prices available in many restaurants, you probably can spend more or less than our ranking — the key offers a rough guide. And, of course, prices can change. If you're concerned, call to verify.

$	less than $15
$$	$15 to $25
$$$	$26 to $40
$$$$	$41 and more

American Food, Fine Dining

The Anasazi Restaurant

$$$$ • Inn of the Anasazi, 113 Washington Ave. • 988-3236

This award-winning restaurant prides itself on food that is a feast for the eyes as well as the palate. The menu changes frequently but includes fresh fish, game and a wonderful, eclectic assortment of appetizers and desserts. Prix-fixe meals and à la carte dining are available. Organic produce and free-range meats are used. The staff knows wine and can competently suggest a selection to complement your food. The Anasazi serves breakfast, lunch and dinner and also has a bar menu served after the dining room closes.

Bishop's Lodge

$$$ • Bishops Lodge Rd. • 983-6377

Have a summer lunch on the deck here, and you'll be seated beneath umbrellas and ancient cottonwood trees, watching the hummingbirds buzz at the feeders and looking out on the resort's lovely grounds. The indoor dining room is pleasant, too, with plenty of room for private conversations and attentive but unobtrusive service. The food holds its own despite the irresistible ambiance. The restaurant serves breakfast, lunch and dinner and has a full bar. The Sunday brunch here is rightfully famous.

La Casa Sena

$$$$ • Sena Plaza, 125 E. Palace Ave. • 988-9232

Wonderful old Santa Fe ambiance combined with a creative approach to food makes La Casa Sena a longtime favorite place to celebrate special occasions. Try the trout cooked in adobe for a succulent and different dish. The patio is one of Santa Fe's nicest. For less formal and less expensive dining, visit the Cantina, where you'll hear waiters and waitresses present excerpts from Broadway shows. The restaurant has a full bar and a nice wine selection. It is open daily for lunch and dinner.

The Club

$$$ • Hotel St. Francis, 210 Don Gaspar Ave. • 992-6312

The Club dining room is decidedly un-Santa Fe, and that's part of its charm. Decorated to resemble a hunt club, complete with deep colors and heavy tables, The Club offers some of the city's most professional service, and the food is fine. Breakfasts include huevos rancheros and French toast stuffed with cream cheese. Lunch might feature soft pork tacos or a great Caesar salad. Dinners may spotlight grilled salmon with special sauces, apricot-glazed pheasant or pumpkin ravioli. Don't miss afternoon high tea. A pub menu is available until midnight. The Club has a full bar and a lovely enclosed patio.

Coyote Cafe

$$$ • 132 W. Water St. • 983-1615

The legendary Coyote Cafe helped put and keep Santa Fe on the gourmet map. Owner Mark Miller's food is an interesting and tasty mix of Tex-Mex, Pueblo Indian, Hispanic-New Mexican and his own innovations — nouvelle Southwestern cuisine. The menu changes often, and the wait staff is always well informed. Even without the excellent food, the whimsical decor would capture your attention. Among the Coyote's trademark dishes are its griddled buttermilk corn cakes and the amazing 24-ounce New Mexico Cowboy Rib Chop — come hungry for this one, pardner! Both have been on the menu since the Coyote opened more than 10 years ago. Be sure to note the genuine cowhide chairs. This is a great place for celebrity watching. The Coyote is open for lunch Monday through Friday and dinner every night. From mid-April until mid-October, you can eat at the Coyote Cantina, a rooftop restaurant that offers more casual dining, cocktails and appetizers. You can order lunch and at the cantina à la carte. In the dining room, service is exclusively prix fixe, three courses for about $40. The Coyote has a full bar.

Geronimo
$$$ • 724 Canyon Rd. • 982-1500

Housed in a landmark adobe built in 1756, Geronimo carries on a fine tradition of good restaurants in this lovely site. The front room has a large fireplace, and shiny, brass-plated tables give it a festive air. The eclectic food makes some references to New Mexican cuisine, but you won't find the standard enchilada here. Instead, look for unusual salads, burgers with toppings such as a chile-pineapple salsa and gruyère cheese, and good meat and chicken dishes. Geronimo is open for dinner daily and for lunch daily except Sunday. It has a full bar and offers a patio.

Nellie's
$$$-$$$$ • Loretto Hotel, 211 Old Santa Fe Tr. • 984-7915

Nellie's takes a fresh approach to food. The menu features old favorites, such as barbecue ribs with garlic potatoes, and more exotic offerings, such as wild-boar quesadillas and lobster won tons. The dining room is arranged for quiet and privacy and offers a view of the historic Loretto Chapel. Nellie's has a full bar and is open for breakfast, lunch and dinner. There's outdoor seating when weather permits.

The Old House
$$$ • Eldorado Hotel, 309 W. San Francisco St. • 988-4455

The food here is both beautiful and original. You'll find variations on New Mexican cooking such as a venison burrito and veal chop in a red chile glaze. Or try the grilled pesto halibut with honey-braised artichokes. Desserts not only taste great, but they're also beautiful. The restaurant does not allow smoking. The Old House, which offers a full bar, is open for dinner only and is closed on Monday. You can also eat at the Eldorado Court, which serves breakfast, lunch and dinner and offers a less-gourmet, less-expensive menu. The Eldorado Court seating adjoins a sometimes-lively cocktail lounge.

Paul's
$$$ • 72 W. Marcy St. • 982-8738

This intimate bistro isn't afraid to try something new, and you'll find food with Southwestern influences as well as Provencal French inspirations. Lunches feature Caesar or Niçoise salads and sandwiches — with fresh Ahi tuna — that you probably wouldn't fix at home. In the evening, the food gets fancier with entrees such as baked salmon in pecan-herb crust or ginger-sesame filet mignon. Desserts get rave reviews here too. Paul's chocolate ganache, a rich and irresistible blend of white and bittersweet chocolate in a pecan crust, won the dessert category in the 1994 Taste of Santa Fe competition. The cheese cake brulee, a pudding/custard-type creation, the crystalized ginger custard and the fresh berry cobbler also get rave reviews. Paul's serves lunch and dinner Monday through Saturday. No smoking is allowed. Beer and wine are available.

Rancho Encantado
$$$-$$$$ • Rancho Encantado Resort, N.M. Hwy. 592 • 982-3537

This is one of the few restaurants in the Santa Fe area with a view, and it's just 10 miles from the Plaza. The dining room and the patio face west, and the sunsets can be magnificent. The signature dish here is Jack's Tenderloin of Beef, an 8-ounce, pan seared, oven-finished steak cooked to your specifications and topped with the chef's special Jack Daniels sauce and Tumbleweed Onions. For brunch, try the Fritatta Florentine, an oven-baked omelet with spinach, goat cheese, pesto and roasted pine nuts. The food and service are good, and the restaurant is open for breakfast, lunch and dinner. There's a full bar.

Santacafe

$$$$ • 231 Washington Ave. • 984-1788

This is one of Santa Fe's "don't miss" places, a well-established restaurant with a creative approach to food and fine service. The cuisine frequently blends Asian and Southwestern flavors with wonderful results. Food critics, including those who write for *Condé Nast Traveler, Gourmet Magazine* and *The New York Times,* praise the offerings and presentation. The grilled filet mignon with roasted garlic-green chile mashed potatoes and blackened tomato-oregano sauce took the cover of *Bon Appetit* magazine. The Santacafe occupies part of a restored hacienda, and its white walls, fresh flowers and warming fireplaces add to the dining experience. It also has a lovely patio. Santacafe serves lunch Monday through Friday and dinner daily. The restaurant has a full bar.

Willie's on Water

$$$ • 402 W. Water St. • 982-0008

Located in an old home, Willie's has a pleasant patio for summer dining and simple, white rooms where you can enjoy eclectic food and good service. The food includes pasta, sandwiches and salads for lunch, dinner specials such as chicken Kiev and clam linguine and good desserts. Willie's is open for breakfast, lunch and dinner daily except Tuesday. You can order beer and wine with your meals.

American Food, Casual Dining

Atalaya Restaurant-Bakery

$$ • 320 S. Guadalupe St. • 982-2709

A tempting bakery case greets you as you walk into this restaurant, and you can take home a loaf of freshly baked bread or get some pastry and coffee to go. Atalaya makes all kinds of great coffee drinks and can do so with soy milk. Among the specialties here is Low-Country-style shrimp and grits, with bacon, mushrooms, green onions and hot sauce. Atalaya is probably best known for breakfast, which it serves all day. The migas — eggs with corn strips and salsa — are a favorite here. And expect excellent toast, no matter

what bread you select. This is a bakery, after all. The lunch/dinner menu is served after 11 AM, but you can order breakfast all day.

Friendly service marks this small, well-managed place. In the summer, Atalaya expands its seating by offering meals on the pleasant covered patio. Beer and wine are available.

Atomic Grill

$ • 103 E. Water St. • 820-2866

This casual place has a fine selection of beers to accompany its meals. You can dine outdoors in the summer. The menu is an eclectic mix of cuisines and flavors and includes wood-fired pizzas, fish tacos, burgers, quesadillas and homemade desserts. Patrons include vegetarians who've just got to have an Earth Mama Garden Burger (they're *delicious*), a meatless Frito pie or any number of other vegetarian delights. Carnivores might crave the Atomic Grill's half-pound All Terrain Burger, a catfish sandwich or any of the restaurant's other eclectic American specialties, including breakfasts served all day and fresh pastries and desserts from the Plaza Bakery next door. The Atomic stays open until 3 AM and is a popular late-night gathering spot. It sometimes offers live entertainment. No smoking is allowed.

Back Street Bistro

$, no credit cards • 513 Camino de los Marques • 982-3500

Just off the beaten track, this informal cafe serves first-rate soup, with 10 choices featured daily. The chef consistently wins Best Soup and Best Presentation at the Annual Souper Bowl Fundraiser. Try the sweet pepper bisque or the Santa Fe onion soup. The sandwiches, including New York corned beef, can be ordered by the half so you'll have room for the topnotch pies and desserts. Daily specials are posted on white boards. The restaurant does not allow smoking. The menu is mainly lunch food, but Back Street opens early enough for breakfast, if you're interested in, say, quiche and a good cup of coffee.

Carlos' Gosp'l Cafe

$, no credit cards • in the Plaza at the Interstate Bank Building, 125 Lincoln Ave. • 983-1841

The consistently good soup and sandwiches here make this one of the favorite lunch spots for folks who work downtown. The patio provides a pleasant place to enjoy lunch and conversation in the summer; inside the aromas that surround you are sure to make you hungry. Carlos' is famous for its Hangover Stew, a savory assembly of potatoes, corn and green chile with Monterey Jack cheese. Don't get too full for dessert — the freshly baked lemon-meringue pie is worth loosening your belt a notch. The cafe lives up to its name by continuously playing gospel music. Seating includes shared community tables, and the place is usually crowded. The cafe is closed on Sunday.

Celebrations
$$-$$$ • 613 Canyon Rd. • 989-8904

As you're visiting Canyon Road, stop at Celebrations for lunch or dinner daily year round or breakfast in the summer and on the weekends. Celebrations occupies an old house on this arty street. Meals are served indoors and on the enclosed patio, which has a fireplace and heaters for use year round. The menu changes frequently and might include butternut squash soup, lamb stew, sauteed sea scallops, crawfish etouffee and New Mexican specialties. The restaurant has a full bar and doesn't allow smoking.

Cowgirl Hall of Fame
$$ • 319 S. Guadalupe St. • 982-2565

The cowgirl theme of this restaurant comes through in the funky Old-West decor and includes some great old photos of real cowgirls. The focus of many of the dishes is barbecue and meat, although you can find fish and veggie offerings here too. Cowgirl's patio is busy in the summer, and the crowd often includes families with kids. Among the favorites, besides the barbecue, are fried catfish fingers, a nice catfish po' boy and Cowgirl chicken fajitas. The menu also offers chicken fried steak, barbecued brisket and ribs, burgers, jerked chicken, gumbo and other Louisiana specialties. The fine dining room, which should be open by the time this book goes to print, will specialize in wild game of the Rocky Mountains and in creative dishes inspired by the American West. This room will be open Friday, Saturday and Sunday. The Cowgirl serves lunch and dinner daily and breakfast on weekends. The restaurant has a full bar including a nice beer menu.

Harry's Roadhouse
$$ • Rt. 9, Box 52 D, Old Las Vegas Hwy. • 989-4629

This restaurant is a bit out of town, but worth the drive. It's a comfortable, casual little place for breakfast, lunch or dinner. You may have to wait, but the service tends to be quick once you're seated. The menu has something for just about everyone, including some excellent choices for vegetarians. Harry's always includes a vegetarian choice among its five or six weekly specials. The roasted eggplant sandwich with goat cheese and olive paste, linguine with greens, tamale vegetarian plate and roasted vegetable salad with feta cheese are local favorites. For breakfast, don't overlook the blueberry buckwheat pancakes.

The freshly made soups are a good way to start — or can be paired with a salad or appetizer for a meal. For dinner try the turkey meat loaf, the pecan-coated chicken breast with peaches, New Mexican specialties or perhaps dishes with Asian influences. The desserts are good, and the servings are generous. The restaurant is smoke-free.

Plaza Restaurant
$$ • 54 Lincoln Ave. • 982-1664

Location gives this diner a definite edge on the competition. You'll find big, Santa Fe-style breakfasts as well as lunch and dinner. The menu includes burgers and salads, enchiladas and tacos and some Greek dishes. The atmosphere is reminiscent of the '50s, complete with some interesting old photos on the walls. Beer and wine are available with meals. If you're lucky enough to get a window seat, you can watch life on the Plaza as you enjoy your food. This is a favorite spot of many longtime Santa Feans.

San Francisco Street Bar and Grill
$$ • Plaza Mercado, 114 W. San Francisco St. • 982-2044

People who work downtown and value good food at a good price eat here often, enjoying the famous green chile cheeseburger. The menu features a huge Greek salad, fresh grilled seafood, daily pastas, steak, chicken and sandwiches. The restaurant offers daily specials and a nice selection of wine by the glass. There's also a full bar. Although the restaurant is indoors, the tables in Mercado's open space have a patio feeling to them. The restaurant is smoke-free.

Zia Diner
$$ • 326 S. Guadalupe St. • 988-7008

Locals eat here for the same reason that visitors are willing to stand in line to try it: The Zia offers generous portions of good food at fair prices. This is comfort food — potatoes and gravy, fish and chips, piñon meat loaf, cherry and other home-made pies and ice cream drinks. The eclectic menu also offers hummus with pita, Greek salads, spaghetti, enchiladas and, on some days, Asian specials. The Zia serves lunch and dinner daily and offers patio dining in the summer. You can also eat in the bar.

FYI

Unless otherwise noted, the area code for all phone numbers listed in this guide is 505.

Asian

Chow's
$$$ • 720 St. Michael's Dr. • 471-7120

Even though it looks like a shopping center storefront, Chow's offers gourmet Chinese food in a calm, upscale setting. The contemporary, eclectic Chinese cuisine is a long way from steam-tray chow mein. Appetizers include firecracker dumplings filled with vegetables, ground turkey and chile served with a pesto dipping sauce and wonderful barbecued ribs. The noodle dishes satisfy the appetite and the eye, and interesting vegetarian choices are available. Chow's makes everything without MSG. It's open Monday through Saturday for lunch and dinner. Beer and wine are available with meals in this smoke-free restaurant. Credit cards are accepted for meals that cost more than $20.

Dynasty
$$ • 500 Cerrillos Rd. • 983-2011

You can order from the menu, but what's fun at Dynasty is the Mongolian Barbecue Buffet. This isn't Texas-style ribs with sauce by any

means. You'll find a spread of noodles, fresh veggies of all kinds, meat and a wide range of sauces. Select what you'd like, and the chef will cook it for you. Soup, salad bar and egg roll come with the buffet at lunch and dinner. You can even go back for more. The restaurant is smoke free and offers wine and beer with meals.

Hunan Chinese Restaurant
2440 Cerrillos Rd. • 474-6688

Red and gold are the color scheme here, and you're greeted by a dragon in the entry way. This is one of Santa Fe's largest Chinese restaurants and a popular place for locals. The daily luncheon buffet captures your attention with its multitude of choices, including seafood, chicken, beef, pork and vegetarian offerings. No MSG is used. The menu includes family dinners and a combination plate. On the other end of the spectrum, Hunan will create Peking Duck for you with 24 hours advance notice. Service is usually prompt and efficient. You can order beer or wine with your food in this nonsmoking restaurant, located in a large shopping center on the south side of town.

Sakura
$$ • 321 W. San Francisco St. • 983-5353

At Sakura you can eat in a private screened room, squeeze into a place at the sushi bar or pick a table in the adjoining dining room. Sakura offers patio dining when the weather allows. Entrees include Yakiniku, thick slices of beef sauteed with a special sauce, and King Hirame Kawarayaki, a halibut steak with a hint of spiciness in the sauce. Sushi and sashimi, tempura and teriyaki add to the mix. Beer and wine are available with meals in this nonsmoking restaurant. It's open for dinner daily and for lunch Monday through Friday.

Shohko-Cafe
$$ • 321 Johnson St. • 983-7288

A nice selection of Chinese entrees is available at Shohko-Cafe, but the Japanese food is the house specialty. Look on the board for the daily appetizer specials, which may include wonderful steamed dumplings. The sushi bar includes a half-dozen tables in addition to the

Photo: Chris Corrie

Santa Fe offers a fine assortment of restaurants for fine dining.

counter where you can watch chefs roll your sushi. There are two other dining rooms where you can order yakitori, superb sukiyaki or even sushi made with green chile or green chile tempura. Beer and wine are available with meals in this nonsmoking restaurant. Shohko is open weekdays for lunch and daily except Sunday for dinner.

Star of Siam
$$$ • 2860 Cerrillos Rd. • 438-8644

It's an unimposing shopping center storefront on the outside, but inside Star of Siam transports you to the Orient with its decor and cuisine. This is the only Thai restaurant in Santa Fe. The extensive menu includes Thai salads, curries, beef, pork, chicken and seafood dishes, vegetarian selections and much more. You can ask for whatever degree of spiciness you prefer. The restaurant has an extensive selection of beer and wine. Star of Siam is smoke free and open for dinner daily except Sunday.

Yin Yang Chinese Restaurant
$$ • 418 Cerrillos Rd. • 986-9279

At Yin Yang you'll find a fresh and varied lunch buffet as well as an extensive menu. In addition to hot items, the buffet includes a salad bar with several kinds of fruit and, some days, cold shrimp. Our favorite dinner entree is the Crispy Orange Scallops. The atmosphere is Oriental, especially during the day when sunlight from the large bank of windows facing Cerrillos Road adds to the restaurant's charm. You can order beer or wine with your meal.

Breakfast

Cafe Pasqual's
$$ • 121 Don Gaspar Ave. • 983-9340

Pasqual's serves great lunches and dinners, but breakfast is its signature meal. Pasqual's is well-known for its freshly baked bread and freshly concocted chile sauces. Try the chorizo burritos or the breakfast quesadillas for a dining experience you won't get in Topeka. And just looking at this place, decorated with Mexican garlands and homages to San Pasqual, the patron of the kitchen, lifts your spirits. Expect a wait. Pasqual's has a community table where you're welcome to sit and join the conversation. The smoke-free restaurant serves three meals daily. You can order beer and wine too.

Cloud Cliff Bakery-Cafe-Artspace
$ • 1805 Second St. • 983-6254

If breakfast in a bakery strikes you as the right thing to do, Cloud Cliff can fill the bill. You can sit at the long bar and watch as your food is prepared or pick a table with a view of the art. Frequently changing exhibits of local paintings, collages and other creations fill the walls. Portions are generous. Try waffles and eggs Benedict on weekends, potatoes topped with chile and cheese, and granola made on the premises. You can buy a wide variety of whole grain breads, rolls, muffins, cakes, pies and cookies to take with you. Cloud Cliff also serves lunch. Beer and wine are available. The restaurant is smoke-free and has a patio.

www.insiders.com

See this and many other **Insiders' Guide®** destinations online — in their entirety.

Visit us today!

Grant Corner Inn
$$ • 122 Grant Ave. • 983-6678

This charming bed and breakfast inn, known for its creative cuisine, welcomes the public (with reservations) for breakfast or lunch. In the summer, you can dine outside beneath the shaded porch of this old brick home — one of the few of its kind in Santa Fe. Breakfast includes granola, juice or fruit, pastries and hot specials — eggs, potatoes, meats or a breakfast burrito. You might find orange-granola pancakes or some version of eggs Benedict on Sunday. The inn offers a special menu for children. Breakfast is served daily, and the restaurant is nonsmoking.

Guadalupe Cafe
$ • 422 Old Santa Fe Tr. • 982-9762

The Guadalupe Cafe is famous for its great breakfasts, beginning with good coffee and friendly service. The restaurant bakes it own muffins and serves a variety of unusual offerings including migas, a combination of eggs, chile, cheese and corn chips, and sausage and cheese enchiladas. The huevos rancheros are excellent. Lunch and dinner here are good too — tasty soup, chile

dishes plus sandwiches heaped with meat. Desserts are made on the premises and are worth saving room for. The patio faces Old Santa Fe Trail; you can eat outside and watch Santa Fe go by. The Guadalupe is open for breakfast, lunch and dinner daily except Monday. Beer and wine are served with meals on request.

Santa Fe Baking Company
$ • 504 W. Cordova Rd. • 988-4292

You won't mind standing in line to place your order here because you get to see all the fresh-baked goodies in the display counter. Muffins, Danish pastry, croissants and fruit-filled turnovers may tempt you, but you can also get eggs, breakfast burritos and other hot specials. Coffee drinks are a specialty. The Baking Company also serves lunch and dinner. The restaurant is nonsmoking except for the patio.

Tecolote Cafe
$ • 1203 Cerrillos Rd. • 988-1362

If you like French toast, this is definitely your place. Tecolote — it means "owl" — lists the variety of breads available on the board, along with the fresh fruit you can add to your breakfast order. The chile is wonderful but not for the faint of heart. Pancakes, including the Tollhouse with walnuts and chocolate chips, are another specialty. A basket of homemade sweet breads comes with your meal. You can also order any of the sandwiches, burgers or other lunch items throughout the day — and vice versa for breakfast. The restaurant is smoke-free on Sunday.

Continental/French

Bistro 315
$$$-$$$$ • 315 Old Santa Fe Tr. • 986-9190

This small French restaurant is big on imagination and service. The specials change daily and seasonally with usually eight to 10 entrees offered at lunch and dinner. Bistro 315 offers creative soups, frequently with a nice touch of garlic, salads, unusual appetizers and entrees that might include grilled smoked chicken, Seafood Papillote or stuffed Portobello mushrooms. Delicious desserts complement the food so save room. It's open for lunch and dinner. The dining room is smoke-free, but you can dine and smoke on the patio in summer.

The Compound
$$$-$$$$, American Express only
• 653 Canyon Rd. • 982-4353

After 30 years of serving Santa Fe residents and their visitors, The Compound has perfected dining to an art. Part of the pleasure of eating here comes from the building itself, a stunning adobe beautifully designed and appointed by architect Alexander Girard. Another part of the pleasure comes from the service, unquestionably among the very best in the region. And, of course, there's the food. The menu is limited to a few wonderful choices — no matter what you order you won't be disappointed. The mushroom soup is a signature dish, and you'll usually find a special appetizer. Entrees, which arrive beneath beautiful silver domes, include trout, salmon, scallops, lamb and beef. The Compound is open Tuesday through Saturday and has a full bar. Smoking is prohibited.

The Pink Adobe
$$$ • 406 Old Santa Fe Tr. • 983-7712

This restaurant has become a local tradition because of its beautiful Santa Fe-style dining room and the consistent quality of its food and service. Housed in a centuries-old building with 36-inch-thick walls and six fireplaces, the restaurant gets it name from its characteristic pink stucco exterior. The Creole Salad Bowl, with egg slices and velvety avocado, is a luncheon star. At dinner, try the combination of juicy beef and the pep of green chile in Steak Dunnigan, one of the Pink's signature dishes. Save a little room to share a piece of apple pie with hot brandy sauce. The Pink Adobe is open for lunch Monday through Friday and dinner daily. The restaurant's bar, The Dragon Room, serves a limited menu and is frequently standing room only. Smoking is permitted in the bar, but the dining rooms are smoke-free.

In a Class of Their Own

Corn Dance Cafe
at the Hotel Santa Fe
$$$ • 1501 Paseo de Peralta • 982-1200

Come to the Corn Dance Cafe for cuisine with an American Indian focus served in a lovely dining room. The menu includes lighter dishes and hearty entrees. The chef's several nightly specials include unusual offerings such as rabbit stew or venison shanks simmered in a sauce with juniper berries. You'll find a roasted ear of fresh corn among the appetizers, and dinner starts with corn bread sticks richly flavored with jalapeños. Don't miss the Kick Ass Chili — a Texas-style dish rich with meat. Try the Little Big Pies, a sort of pizza with toppings including caramelized onion and goat cheese or spicy shrimp. They make a nice light dinner if matched with a salad or a cup of the squash soup or the soup of the day, which might be red pepper bisque. The names on the menu reflect some of the tribes that have influenced the menu — Potowatomi Prairie chicken or Tlingit salmon. Among the desserts you may find pumpkin cheesecake with piñon nut crust and a lovely strawberry-cranberry-rhubarb cobbler that's large enough for two. Corn Dance has a full bar and does not allow smoking. You may find music, including an American Indian flute player/guitarist, in the evenings.

El Farol
$$$ • 808 Canyon Rd. • 983-9912

If you're looking for tapas, El Farol can fill the bill. You'll find cooking from many regions of Spain, with paellas as well as fresh seafood and El Farol's signature garlic soup. El Farol also has an extensive list of wines, sherries, ports and brandies from the Iberian peninsula and elsewhere. The atmosphere here is that of an old Western bar inside a rustic, plank floor adobe building. You can listen to live music and dance most nights. El Farol is open daily for lunch and dinner. Patio dining is available in season.

India House
$$ • 2501 Cerrillos Rd. • 471-2651

India House's luncheon buffet, complete

with tandoori chicken, vegetarian specials, salad and dessert, is both elegant and satisfying. For dinner, take your choice of many entrees including seafood and vegetarian choices. The mango lassi and rice pudding are recommended as good dishes for the little ones to enjoy. The restaurant is nicely appointed with fresh flowers, table cloths and well-dressed and well-trained waiters. Beer and wine are available. Lunch and dinner are served daily except Sunday, when only dinner is served.

India Palace
$$ • 227 Don Gaspar Ave. • 986-5859

This may be the only East Indian restaurant in the country to be housed in an adobe building with Santa Fe charm inside and a mural of India on the outside. India Palace sits on the edge of a city parking lot across from the Hotel St. Francis. From certain tables, you can watch what's happening in the kitchen through a window. The food includes all the Indian specialties you'd expect and well-prepared tandoori meats. You can get succulent lamb as well as vegetarian choices. The hearty luncheon buffet is a good value. Beer and wine are available with lunch and dinner, and you can dine on the patio in the summer.

Whistling Moon Cafe
$$$ • 402 N. Guadalupe St. • 983-3093

In this comfortable, casual restaurant, you'll find Mediterranean fare inspired by the cuisines of Morocco, Egypt, Turkey, Greece and elsewhere. If you're curious, a salad sampler plate offers a nice variety of flavors and textures. The soft pitas filled with grilled lamb, falafel or lemon-marinated chicken, and the pizzas, calzones and pastas are all first-rate. Whistling Moon serves lunch and dinner daily, with beer or wine available, in a casual but nicely appointed smoke-free dining room.

Italian

Andiamo!
$$$ • 322 Garfield St. • 995-9595

Andiamo!, which means "let's go!," offers good, fresh food. The menu changes daily and may include an antipasto such as freshly made mozzarella with appropriate accompaniments or crispy polenta set off with a topping of rosemary and gorgonzola. Each evening features a pasta special, and desserts are beautiful as well as flavor packed. The restaurant operates from an old bungalow redone in rich yellows and reds. No smoking is allowed inside. Andiamo! is open for dinner daily except Tuesday. Beer and wine are available.

Julian's
$$$ • 221 Shelby St. • 988-2355

When Santa Fe folks are asked to name the city's most romantic restaurants, Julian's always makes the list. The beauty of the surroundings adds to the dining experience — soft jazz, stained glass, twinkling lights, enormous mirrors, large bouquets of fresh flowers and, in the winter, warming fireplaces. The menu is filled with good choices, and you can finish with an unusual dolce and steaming espresso. Julian's is open for dinner daily. The restaurant has a full bar and is smoke-free except for the patio.

Osteria D'Assisi
$$$ • 58 S. Federal Pl. • 986-5858

The Osteria specializes in northern Italian cuisine, and you'll find good pasta here as well as nicely presented grilled dishes and pleasing desserts. The restaurant has a bright, open feeling to it and offers patio dining when the weather permits. You can order beer or wine to go with your lunch or dinner. Osteria is closed Sundays and is nonsmoking except for the patio.

INSIDERS' TIP

For Santa Fe dining, make a reservation whenever possible. While during the off-season you may be able to slip into a popular place, don't count on it. If you want to eat somewhere that doesn't take reservations, you can call and ask when you're likely to have the shortest wait.

Photo: Chris Corrie

Known as *ristras*, these strings of red chile aren't just for decoration.
The chile can be ground and used in cooking.

The Palace
$$$ • 142 W. Palace Ave. • 982-9891

This plush restaurant is another leading contender for a romantic rendezvous as well as a hot spot for the Santa Fe equivalent of a power lunch. Red leather booths, white linens and a well-trained staff complement the good food you'll find here. Luncheons include homemade pastas, fresh fish, sandwiches, prime rib and a nice assortment of salads. For dinner, start with the Caesar salad prepared at your table. And save room for dessert, which you can select from a cart of temptations rolled to your table. Our favorite is the tiramisu. The Palace is open Monday through Saturday for lunch and dinner and also serves dinner on Sunday. The Palace has a popular bar that offers live music on the weekends and a lovely patio.

Pastability
$$ • 418 Cerrillos Rd. • 988-2856

Casual is the tone for dining here. This friendly little restaurant inside the Design Center, has the ambiance of a sidewalk cafe, but it's indoors. As you'd assume from the name, pasta is the specialty. You'll find penne, rigatoni, linguine and more. Sauces include game hen and puttanesca — a combination of capers, olives and anchovies. The menu also features antipasto selections and some desserts. The restaurant is smoke-free and serves dinner Tuesday through Saturday.

Il Piatto
$$$ • 95 W. Marcy St. • 984-1091

This downtown storefront makes the most of its available space to create a lively coziness. The tables, covered with white cloths topped with white paper and trimmed with fresh flowers, add a nice touch to the low-key decor. The menu is limited and excellent, and the values are especially good for dinner. You can choose from appetizers, soup, salads, pastas and entrees or pick a special. The minestrone is packed with chunks of vegetables. Try the zabaglione or the panettone bread pudding for dessert. Smoking is not allowed. Il Piatto is open for dinner nightly and lunch Monday through Friday.

Pranzo Italian Grill
$$$ • Sanbusco Ctr., 540 Montezuma Ave. • 984-2645

Service at Pranzo is consistently professional, a skillful blend of friendliness and knowledge. The menu offers a nice selection of starters, delicious pasta and original entrees to keep locals and visitors happy. A good opener is the Antipasto Misto, a sampler plate that includes a head of roasted garlic, a grilled Portobello mushroom, salmon, prosciutto, fontina cheese and more. Salads are served with entrees at no extra charge; we recommend the gorgonzola dressing. The restaurant is nicely appointed, comfortable and classy. The staff happily accommodates special food requests. Pranzo is open for lunch Monday through Saturday and for dinner every night of the week. You can get light food at the bar. Smoking is allowed in the bar and upstairs on the terrace.

Mexican

Old Mexico Grill
$$ • College Plaza South Shopping Ctr., 2434 Cerrillos Rd. • 473-0338

You'll find the true cuisine of Mexico here, not New Mexico's adaptations. Start with a classic ceviche — fish cooked in a lime-juice marinade. Arracheras — also known as fajitas — come to the table sizzling with fresh tortillas and all the accompaniments. You'll find Mexican moles, spicy and slightly sweet, along with an assortment of salsas. Watch the board for daily specials. You can sit at a booth, a table or at the bar, which offers several flavors of Margaritas and an assortment of cold Mexican cervezas. Old Mexico Grill serves lunch Monday through Friday and dinner nightly.

Mariscos "La Playa"
$$ • 537 Cordova Rd. • 982-2790.

This simple little eatery has an authentic, south-of-the-border feel. You can imagine you're on the beach as you look at the mural of white sand, waves and para-sailers as you wait for your meal. Chances are the wait will be a quick one — the kitchen runs efficiently. You can choose cold selections, such as seafood cocktails or ceviche, or hot fish and shellfish entrees fixed many ways. The soups are filled with fish and vegetables, and the grilled platters are served hot and well-seasoned. You can get fish tacos and shrimp burritos, along with soft, fresh corn tortillas. The restaurant serves lunch and dinner daily except Tuesdays. You can order beer, Mexican or from the good ol' USA, with your meal.

New Mexican

Blue Corn Cafe
$$ • 133 Water St. • 984-1800
Blue Corn Cafe and Brewery
$$ • 4065 Cerrillos Rd. • 438-1800

Start your meal with fresh chips and salsa, then, if you want New Mexican food, create your own combination plate or choose from those on the menu. The grilled corn and chipotle soup will spice up your day, and the

FYI

Unless otherwise noted, the area code for all phone numbers listed in this guide is 505.

INSIDERS' TIP

Don't be shy about asking your waiter or waitress for recommendations. If you don't understand the menu, seek their advice, especially when it comes to New Mexican food. For example, they can tell you if the red or green chile is hotter.

A Beginner's Guide to Santa Fe Dining

Does a menu listing enchiladas, flautas and chalupas tantalize your appetite? Or leave you in confusion?

Traditional New Mexican cuisine grows from simple, delicious ingredients. First come the chiles, then pinto beans, both corn and flour tortillas, cheese, beef, chicken, pork and often onions. From the mouth-watering aromas of steaming green chile to the sultry velvet texture of guacamole and the dollop of sour cream that blends and soothes the fiery red, traditional New Mexican food leaves few indifferent. Many crave it with such enthusiasm that they take recipes and ingredients home with them.

As you embark on this culinary adventure, take note that dairy products will quench the peppery fires of chile dishes: cheese, a glass of milk and a dish of ice cream are your palate's best coolants. Restaurants that specialize in this spicy cuisine serve many chile dishes topped with chopped lettuce and tomato to help calm the heat. Bread, either flour tortillas or the puffy sopaipillas served with the meal, will also help. And if you're afraid the chile may be too hot, you can ask for a sample or have it served on the side.

Venture forth with good appetite; the rewards come in the eating!

What's What in New Mexican Food

Biscochito: An anise-flavored cookie.

Burrito: A flour tortilla rolled to enclose meats, beans, cheese or a combination of these and often served smothered with chile sauce and melted cheese. Breakfast burritos may be filled with scrambled eggs, potatoes and bacon.

Carne adovada: Cubes of marinated meat, usually pork, cooked in red chile, garlic and oregano.

Chalupas: Corn tortillas fried into a bowl shape, filled with shredded chicken, beef and/or beans, usually topped with guacamole and salsa.

Chile: The vegetable that puts the fire in traditional New Mexican cooking. Green chile is the fresh vegetable, which is roasted, chopped and thickened to produce a sauce. Red chiles are mature green chiles, which are dried and used as seasoning or for a sauce. While red may look hotter, the spiciness depends not on the color, but on where the chile was grown and the weather conditions during the growing season.

Chile con queso: Green chile and melted cheese mixed together into a dip.

Chile relleno: A whole green chile roasted, peeled and stuffed (usually with cheese), then dipped in a batter and fried.

Chorizo: A spicy pork sausage seasoned with garlic and red chile.

Christmas: The phrase that means you'd like to try both red and green chile on your dish.

Empanada: A turnover usually filled with a sweetened meat mixture or fruit.

Enchiladas: Corn tortillas filled with chicken, ground meat or cheese and covered with chile sauce and cheese, often topped with shredded lettuce and tomato. The tortillas may be rolled with the filling inside or stacked with the filling in between. Either yellow-corn or blue-corn tortillas — made from a special variety of corn with blue kernels — is used. Enchiladas may be served topped with a fried egg and/or sour cream.

Fajitas: Strips of grilled steak, chicken or sometimes shrimp with sauteed peppers and onions, often served still sizzling in a metal fry pan. Warm tortillas and side dishes

— continued on next page

of salsa, cheese, sour cream and guacamole are served alongside so you can make your own burritos.

Flan: Caramel custard dessert similar to crème caramel.

Flauta: Tightly rolled corn tortillas filled with meat and fried to a crunch, usually served with salsa and guacamole for dipping.

Frijoles: Beans, usually pinto beans; frijoles negros are black beans.

Guacamole: Mashed avocado, usually seasoned with chopped onion, garlic, lime juice and chile powder. Served as a dip, a topping for some dishes or even a filling for tacos.

Huevos rancheros: Eggs, usually fried, served atop corn tortillas and smothered with chile and cheese. A popular Santa Fe breakfast.

Menudo: A soup made with tripe and chiles. (It's known as the "breakfast of champions.")

Nachos: Corn chips topped with refried beans, melted cheese and sliced jalapeños. If served "grande" they will probably include ground beef or shred-

Photo: Don Strel/Southwest Assignments

Northern New Mexican cooking gets its integrity from ingredients that are grown locally — chile, corn and beans. Dried chile, which turns red, also has wonderful decorative potential.

ded chicken, guacamole and sour cream. Olives, fresh tomatoes and onions may be added.

Natilla: Soft custard dessert.

Pico de gallo: Salsa with chopped fresh chiles, tomatoes, onions and cilantro. It's usually spicier than traditional salsa.

Posole: Hominy stew, usually made with pork, onions and oregano, usually served with chile sauce on top or on the side.

Quesadilla: A turnover made of a flour tortilla filled with cheese and sometimes beef, chicken or other ingredients, then toasted, fried or baked.

Refritos: Beans, usually pintos, that have been mashed and fried.

Ristra: A bunch of chiles, usually red, hung to dry or for decoration.

Salsa: An uncooked mixture of chile, tomatoes, onions, cilantro and other spices. Usually eaten as a dip.

Sopaipilla: Puffed, fried yeast bread served hot with honey or honey-butter and eaten with the meal.

Taco: A folded corn tortilla either fried crisp or soft and usually filled with meat or chicken and garnished with cheese, fresh chopped lettuce, onions and tomatoes.

Tostadas: Corn tortilla chips. This term also means a open-face fried corn tortilla covered with refried beans, salsa, cheese and chopped lettuce and tomato.

Tortilla: A flat bread made of corn or wheat. Flour tortillas may be served with the meal in New Mexican cooking; corn tortillas tend to be incorporated in dishes and baked with sauce.

blue corn posole is a nice touch. The Water Street location is downtown and offers wonderful window tables where you can watch the world walk by below you. The Cerrillos Road restaurant, which includes the brewery, is newer and has a larger bar where they make their own beer. The brewery offers daily beer specials. Lunch and dinner are served daily.

The Burrito Company
$ • 111 Washington Ave. • 982-4453

This casual place, where you stand in line to place your order, is the bargain of downtown and a good spot to take kids. Not only is the food good, but also you can get in and out quickly and have money left to buy your Santa Fe T-shirts. But don't let the casual atmosphere fool you — the chile is the real thing, with enough spark to get your attention. In addition to New Mexican favorites, you can order pastries, coffee drinks and hot dogs. It's open for breakfast, lunch and early dinner. The Burrito Company does not allow smoking or serve alcohol.

La Choza
$$ • 905 Alarid St. • 982-0909

Well-prepared simple food is the hallmark of La Choza. Operated by the same folks who run The Shed (choza means "shed"), this place has the same good food but a little more space for its diners. It's off the beaten path and, perhaps because of that, a favorite among locals. The carne adovada is one of the house dishes to die for. La Choza is open for lunch and dinner daily except Sunday. Specials are posted on the blackboard. The restaurant is smoke-free. When weather permits dining outside, the patio is lovely.

Diego's Cafe and Bar
$$ • DeVargas Center, 193 Paso de Peralta • 983-5101

You'll find first-rate New Mexican food in this comfortable, unpretentious restaurant. The burritos are huge, the chile well-seasoned and the sopaipillas mouth-watering. The restaurant offers "light lunch" specials, which provide ample food for the average appetite. You may have to wait to get in, but it's worth it. Diego's serves lunch and dinner daily and has a full bar.

Gabriel's
$$$ • U.S. Hwy. 285., 15 miles north of Santa Fe • 455-7000

Getting to Gabriel's require a quick drive, but it's worth it. Start with the ice-cold Margaritas and guacamole prepared at your table from a cart with avocados, fresh garlic, onions, cilantro, salt, lime juice, tomatoes and jalapeños. In addition to New Mexican food, you can get a good steak and other non-ethnic dishes. The patio is gorgeous in the summer with abundant fresh flowers, a bubbling fountain and plenty of shade. Inside, Gabriel's has the spacious feel of an old home. This is a great place to linger. It's open for lunch and dinner daily except Monday.

La Plazuela Restaurant
$$$ • La Fonda Hotel, 100 E. San Francisco St. • 982-5511

If a contest were held for Santa Fe's most charming dining room, La Plazuela would definitely be a finalist. Diners — among them hotel guests, visitors and locals who work downtown — have a sense of timelessness as they relax in this bright space and enjoy the colorful painted windows, the mural of New Mexico pueblo life and the welcoming fireplace. The bright table settings and waitresses attractively dressed in flowing skirts and Santa Fe-style blouses add to the ambiance. Most diners favor the restaurant's New Mexican offerings, including a hearty combination plate and first-rate chile rellenos. You can order pork or vegetarian tamales topped with red or green chile. Or, for a change, how about wild boar carnitas? You'll get a hearty offering of nicely seasoned pork wrapped in soft flour tortillas and served with colorful gently cooked vegetables that you can add to the meat or enjoy on their own. For vegetarians, the eggplant sandwich gets a gold star — grilled eggplant and a hint of pesto. La Plazuela is open for breakfast, lunch and dinner and offers a full bar. You can also have cocktails at the Bell Tower, a full bar upstairs on a patio that overlooks the city, or in La Fonda's lounge.

Maria's New Mexican Kitchen
$$ • 555 W. Cordova Rd. • 983-7929

Maria's is known for a lot of things — great

luncheon specials, one of Santa Fe's best Margarita menus and murals in the cantina by artist Alfred Morang, which the artist traded for food and drink. There's a lot of history in this place — it's been in business in the same location for 50 years. You can order dozens of types of Margaritas, made with different tequilas and complementary liquors, each served with panache. The food is tasty and affordable, and Maria's uses local chile and produce whenever possible. You can watch the tortillas being made so you know they're fresh. Strolling musicians add to the ambiance in the evenings. Reservations are welcome — and a good idea. Lunch and dinner are served every day.

PC's Restaurant and Lounge
$ • 4220 Airport Rd. • 473-7164

If you're shopping or visiting on the south side of town, this place can be a welcome oasis in a sea of fast food chains. PC's has a bar with a TV for watching sports and a pleasant dining room with your choice of booths or tables. Ask about the daily specials, but keep in mind that the generous burritos are a perennial favorite. PC's is open daily except Monday for lunch and dinner and serves breakfast on the weekends.

Pepper's
$ • 2239 Old Pecos Tr. • 984-2272

This cheerful place, which serves breakfast, lunch and dinner, is a boon to Santa Fe's growing neighborhoods in the Old Pecos Trail area as well as to people in Arroyo Hondo, Eldorado and other points beyond. Peppers offers well-priced, good food, a festive setting and efficient service. The bar has a TV and a nice view of the city lights.

Rancho de Chimayó
$$ • 3 miles from the N.M. Hwy. 76 intersection with N.M. Hwy. 520, 32 miles north of Santa Fe, Chimayó • 351-4444

The drive is part of the pleasure of dining in this long-established New Mexican restaurant. Allow yourself at least 45 minutes from Santa Fe. Plan your reservations just after sunset, and you'll have a chance to see the Jémez Mountains against a wonderful golden, crimson or peach-colored sky. Rancho de Chimayó gets an "A" for ambiance. The restaurant, a sprawling old hacienda, sits near apple orchards and offers patio dining and a lovely bar with a fireplace. Try one of the house special drinks, a Chimayó cocktail. You'll find strolling musicians here most weekends. The fare is New Mexican with a few other choices for non-chile eaters. From mid-May through mid-November the restaurant is open daily for lunch and dinner; otherwise it's closed Mondays. It's nonsmoking except for the terraces.

The Shed
$$ • 113½ E. Palace Ave. • 982-9030

The Shed is housed in a part of Sena Plaza, a historic hacienda a block off the Plaza. The small rooms give you a feeling of Santa Fe ambiance, and the food will kindle your inner fire. Established in 1954, The Shed's signature dish is red chile enchiladas, served with a piece of garlic bread. Save room for the mocha cake. The Shed is open for lunch and dinner daily except Sunday. The restaurant is smoke-free.

La Tertulia
$$ • 416 Agua Fría • 988-2769

Based in an old Dominican convent, La Tertulia is definitely a class act, with lace cloths on the tables and a well-dressed wait staff who

INSIDERS' TIP

Chile sparks New Mexico's regional cuisine. Some are harvested green — usually beginning in September — roasted until the skin blisters, then peeled. Chile enthusiasts claim that chopped green chile, sometimes thickened with a bit of flour to make a sauce, goes well with meat, fish, fowl, eggs, cheese and vegetables. No one will think it unusual if you ask for a side of green chile with just about anything — even hash browns.

know the menu. Be sure to notice the Spanish Colonial art that is on display throughout the restaurant and the mural in the back room of life at the convent. The food is fine, from the chips and salsa and the black bean jalapeño soup that could start your meal to the flan and other delectable desserts that could close it. The restaurant serves lunch and dinner daily except Monday and takes reservations. You can sit on a lovely patio in the summer if you plan ahead.

Tia Sophia's
$ • 210 W. San Francisco St. • 983-9880

Come to Tia Sophia's for breakfast or lunch and experience good well-priced food in nonpretentious atmosphere. You may have a short wait to get seated at one of the old wooden booths or a table. The green chile stew and daily Blue Plate Specials are ever popular, and the sopaipillas are some of Santa Fe's best. Service is good natured and efficient. No alcohol is available.

Tiny's Restaurant & Lounge
$$ • 1015 Pen Rd. • 983-9817

Tiny's fajitas are a good choice but so are the baked chicken flautas with blue corn tortillas. And be sure to check the daily specials. Tiny's has a full bar and a cozy patio. You'll find entertainment most weekends in this lively place, which is open for lunch weekdays and dinner daily except Sunday, when its closed.

Tomasita's Santa Fe Station
$$ • 500 S. Guadalupe St. • 983-5721

Expect to wait if you decide to eat here, but you won't be disappointed. The red and green chile are both excellent, the sopaipillas light and tender, and the sangria tempts you to linger. The daily specials make ordering easy, and in addition to New Mexican food you'll find stuffed grape leaves. Located in a restored train station, Tomasita's serves lunch and dinner every day except Sunday. There's a full bar, which also serves as the smokers' dining room, and patio service when the weather permits.

Tortilla Flats
$$ • 3139 Cerrillos Rd. • 471-8685

This is the place to go if you want to grab a bite without making a big production out of it. Generous portions rule. You'll find great offerings for breakfast, including a hefty breakfast burrito and tender pancakes. For lunch or dinner the vegetable quesadilla with fresh carrots, broccoli and two cheeses is a winner, as are the brisket burrito and the carne adovada. The atmosphere is casual, and the service is good. Children are made to feel welcome. Tortilla Flats is open for breakfast, lunch and dinner and offers a full bar.

Pizza

Pizza Etc.
$ • DeVargas Ctr., 564 N. Guadalupe St. • 986-1500

You could enjoy several hearty salads and delicious calzones in this shopping mall cafe, but pizza is the house specialty, just as you'd expect. You'll find unusual toppings including smoked oysters and chile-chicken sausage. This little place does a good carry-out business and has some tables for dining in. It's open for lunch and dinner daily and is smoke-free.

Upper Crust Pizza
$ • 329 Old Santa Fe Tr. • 982-0000

Open daily for lunch and dinner, Upper Crust is a Santa Fe tradition. The food is served hot and fresh, and you can order pizza with whole-wheat crust. In addition to pizza, Upper Crust serves meal-like salads, several sandwiches and three types of calzones. In the summer, after you order at the counter, you can eat on the front porch and watch the crowds stroll by. The restaurant is smoke-free except for outdoors.

Il Vicino
$ • 321 W. San Francisco St. • 986-8700

When you've had enough chile or too many fancy dinners, the casual, comfortable Il Vicino will fill the bill. Order at the counter, choosing among wood-fired pizzas, salads, soups, calzones, sandwiches and maybe lasagna. You can select a beer — including their own microbrew — or wine from their extensive list. Smoking is allowed on the patio only.

Many Santa Fe restaurants combine upscale ambiance with a menu that includes traditional New Mexican offerings and American favorites.

Pubs

The Green Onion

$ • 1851 St. Michael's Dr. • 983-5198

This is one of Santa Fe's most popular watering holes. With TVs that offer all the games and nightly food and drink specials, the Onion is a popular hangout for local recreation league teams. The chile dishes are good and so is the pizza. Ask about the nightly specials. The Green Onion is open for lunch and dinner daily.

Second Street Brewery
$$ • 1814 Second St. • 982-3030

Off the beaten track, the Second Street Brewery recently won a gold medal in a state competition for microbrews. In addition to beer made on the premises, you can get sandwiches, desserts and hot entrees at this neighborhood restaurant. The atmosphere is casual, complete with a dart board. Lunch and dinner are served daily, and the restaurant is smoke-free. You may find live music in the evenings.

Wolf Canyon Brewing Company
$$ • 9885 Cerrillos Rd. (N.M. Hwy 14 frontage road) • 438-7000

This large, nicely appointed restaurant offers its own home brews as well as a full bar. The servings are generous and, in addition to the standard sandwich-burger-salad-nachos fare, Wolf Canyon serves homemade sausage, prime rib and a nice roasted spiced chicken. But try to save room for dessert, which includes a first-rate root beer float and chocolate eclair.

Steaks

El Nido
$$$ • C.R. 73 at Bishops Lodge Rd., Tesuque • 988-4340

Good meat, fresh fish and good service mark this getaway, a long-established Santa Fe favorite. It's 2.5 miles from the U.S. 84/285 Tesuque exit and 7 miles from the Santa Fe Plaza. Consistency throughout the years has given El Nido a cadre of loyal customers. The small, lively bar adds to the restaurant's ambiance, as does the adobe building, complete with fireplaces. The menu is built on meat — prime rib, sirloin, lamb chops — fresh seafood and some other choices, such as duck breast with a blueberry-chile glaze. You'll also find several nightly specials — braised lamb shanks, perhaps — and some new Asian fusion touches. Start with the onion soup — they're famous for it. El Nido is open for dinner every day except Monday.

Piñon Grill
$$$-$$$$ • Hilton, 100 Sandoval St. • 986-6400

If you're looking for meat, fish or interesting salads, the Piñon Grill is the place to come. The guacamole, freshly made at your table and served with a basket of tricolored chips, is a great starter. The menu offers plenty of choices for meat eaters, including a chile-wrapped and -rubbed filet. Try the beef stuffed with wild mushrooms, blue cheese and green chile. If you book ahead, you can ask to sit in front of the welcoming fireplace in the winter. The grill is open for lunch and dinner daily. The restaurant is nonsmoking.

Steaksmith at El Gancho
$$$ • Old Las Vegas Hwy., 1 mile from I-25 Exit 387 • 988-3333

This spacious restaurant, a Santa Fe standby since 1973, is well-known for its appetizers including spinach-cheese balls and deep-fried avocado. The bar with a fireplace and TVs is a lovely spot to relax. Steaks and seafood are the rule here, and dinners are served with a choice of salads and homemade soup. You can order green chile, piñon chile or other sauces on the side. For dessert, try the sour cream apple walnut pie. The Steaksmith is open for dinner every night. The view, which you'll notice from the parking lot, is one of Santa Fe's nicest vistas with the sparkling lights of the city on display each evening.

Vanessie
$$$-$$$$ • 434 W. San Francisco St. • 982-9966

There's not another place like this in town. With its soaringly high ceilings, huge fireplaces and stylized antlers, Vanessie reminds some of an update on the medieval hunting lodge. The lounge features piano music and warming fireplaces, and winter or summer it's usually packed. The adjoining restaurant offers beef, lamb, fish, roasted chicken, salads and vegetables à la carte and a delectable onion appetizer that resembles a huge basket of onion rings cooked into a loaf-like shape. Desserts are good here too — and most things are big enough to share.

Thanks to Santa Fe's magnetic attraction for artists, musicians and celebrities of all ilk and notoriety, local talent is excellent and plentiful here.

Nightlife

If you're in search of nonstop, highly varied nightlife, may we suggest you catch the next flight to Los Angeles, Miami or New York? It's not that commercial nighttime entertainment doesn't exist in Santa Fe. In fact, The City Different boasts a thriving nightlife. You just have to look a little harder for it than you would in larger cities, and it's somewhat limited in scope, especially as evening turns into night and night turns into morning. Except for bars, a few dancing locales and a handful of cafes, Santa Fe rolls up the sidewalks after 10 PM. Many bars close at 11:30 PM or midnight during the week, some even on weekends.

Locals are resourceful, however. They create their own nightlife, much of which consists of meeting friends at favorite restaurants or bars, which, like their denizens, have distinct personalities. For those who live to dance, there's one honest-to-goodness "disco" in town, several country-and-western venues and a few Latino clubs. Many hotels also offer live entertainment, much of it home-grown — though that by no means rules out the occasional big-name act. Thanks to Santa Fe's magnetic attraction for artists, musicians and celebrities of all ilk and notoriety, local talent is excellent and plentiful here.

For detailed information about how to fill your evenings in Santa Fe, check the "Comings and goings" section of "Pasatiempo," the Friday arts and entertainment section of the local daily newspaper *The Santa Fe New Mexican*. The section lists nightly entertainment and events and contains a special jazz section as well as family-oriented nightlife ideas. *Journal North* and *The Santa Fe Reporter* also publicize entertainment information. (See our Media chapter.)

Coffeehouses, Restaurants and Late-Night Haunts

Atomic Grill
105 E. Water St. • 820-2866

Located one block south of the Plaza and open until 3 AM Monday through Saturday, the Atomic Grill attracts a cross section of Santa Fe residents and tourists, especially in the wee hours of the morning. The restaurant is a popular after-hours spot for people spilling out of the bars at the 2 AM witching hour; some folks need to sop up the booze with a meal, others are just plain hungry, and many simply aren't ready to stop partying. You can't drink here after 11 PM, but before then you can choose from a selection of up to 96 beers and a half-dozen wines. Or try a hot drink — a cappuccino, perhaps, or maybe an eggnog latte during the holiday season. The arty, warehouse-style restaurant offers live, mostly acoustic music on summer weekends. The Atomic Grill is open Monday through Friday from 11 AM to 3 AM, Saturday from 7 AM to 3 AM and Sunday from 7 AM until midnight. (See our Restaurants chapter.)

Aztec Street Coffee House
317 Aztec St. • 983-9464

The Aztec Street Coffee House is about as close as you can get to an old-fashioned, European-style cafe. It's one of those increasingly rare places where you can buy a single cup of coffee, get your one free refill and spend the rest of the day reading, writing, composing, consulting, ciphering or contemplating your navel without pressure to buy more, eat more, drink more, say more, do more or leave. The minimalist, unpretentious — some call it downright funky — atmosphere attracts a clientele that runs the gamut from working and starving artists, musicians, filmmakers and writers to students, local business people, New Agers, conspiracy theorists, tubthumpers, gadflies, barflies or anyone looking for what many patrons claim is the best cup of coffee in town. You can even buy the house blend by the pound.

FYI

Unless otherwise noted, the area code for all phone numbers listed in this guide is 505.

The Aztec also serves a wide variety of food, including homemade oatmeal with real maple syrup, fresh breakfast burritos, bagels, scones and pastries (many of them homemade) starting at 7:30 AM Monday through Friday and 8 AM on weekends. In the afternoon it's homemade soups, stews, bruschette (open-faced grilled sandwiches), hummus and tabbouleh, fresh tamales, hot entrees and daily specials until closing at 9 PM Sunday through Thursday and 10 PM on Fridays and Saturdays. This is a place where vegans and meat eaters can rendezvous without compromising their principles or their palates.

It's also a happy meeting ground for smokers and nonsmokers, though not necessarily in the same rooms. The patio, however, is the equivalent of international air space and is open to both camps. Evenings at the Aztec feature a Sunday open-mike session called "Open Unplugged" for music, poetry, performance or any other variation of the spoken — or nonspoken — word. Monday nights bring classical music, and Thursday is reserved for live acoustic sounds. The cafe also runs an art show on its adobe walls, showing the work of local artists and changing the exhibit monthly.

Cafe Oasis
526 Galisteo St. • 983-9599

Stepping into the ultra-eclectic Oasis is like stepping into a time warp. Is it the psychedelic '60s? Or is it fin-de-siècle Paris? Well, it all depends which room you're visiting. The "Mystic Room," an opium den without the opium, is for bare feet only with old Turkish rugs on the floor and not a chair in sight. You sit on pillows, eat at low tables and ought to be listening to Ravi Shankar or perhaps some bellydancing music. If you prefer, you can climb in or sit under the loft and eat, drink, meditate or write your memoirs. Down a hot pink hallway decorated with painted flames you'll find the intimate "Victorian" or "Romantic Room," whose persimmon walls are decorated with turn-of-the-century John Waterhouse prints set off by antique furniture of that and other periods. You can sit at a clawfoot table, a 1950s booth or on a comfortable couch with a low-lying table, perfect for a tête-à-tête over tea.

Tobacco users should head directly for the "Smoking Room," whose mosaic and wood-paneled walls are reminiscent of an old-fashioned pub. Or go no further than the "Social Room," the large, bright, fauna-filled room at the entrance where live music — blues, cowboy, flamenco, folk, jazz, Middle Eastern and other genres — plays Wednesday though Sunday starting at 8:30 PM. You won't pay a cover charge for the entertainment, though there is a $6 minimum you won't mind spending on the cafe's natural food. If you prefer, you can dine outdoors in the restaurant's spacious patio, which is encircled by plants of the Southwest and lighted with Tiki torches and candles. There's also a lovely garden up front with flagstone and mosaic benches and tables and a mosaic floor. Cafe Oasis is open 365 days a year. It stays open until midnight Sunday through Wednesday and until 2 AM Thursday through Saturday.

Casa Sena Cantina
Sena Plaza, 125 E. Palace Ave.
• 988-9232

You're just about to bite into your almond-crusted salmon while your partner is slicing into honey-glazed New Mexico pork loin. Suddenly, your waiter breaks into song. If it's Broadway, it must be Casa Sena Cantina. No, that's not the number he's singing. It's a dinner club where the wait staff also entertains — and we don't mean by spilling soup in (other) diners' laps. Adjacent to Casa Sena (see our Restaurants chapter) in peaceful and pretty Sena Plaza, the Cantina is a dinner club whose wait staff doubles as musical comedy performers usually after, though sometimes during, your meal. There are two seatings nightly — at 5:30 PM and again at 8 PM. The 5:30 seating is usually a condensed Broadway musical such as *Sunset Boulevard*, *Phantom of the Opera*, *Little Shop of Horrors* or *Follies*, while the late show is always *The Best of Broadway* — a selection of songs from a variety of Broadway shows.

The performance begins about an hour after you arrive, probably around the time you're having dessert and coffee, and lasts approximately one hour. Prior to the show, piano music plays in the background as you dine on any of a variety of innovative New Mexican and Southwestern entrees, which range in price from $12 to $18 à la carte. There's no additional charge for the entertainment; it's included with your dinner. But do leave some extra cash in the tip bowl for the performers in addition to a gratuity for serving your dinner — in view of their talents and effort, it's more than fair to supplement their nightly income. Casa Sena Cantina is open seven nights a week, 364 days a year, closing only on Christmas Day. Walk-ins are welcome, but we strongly recommend you make reservations, especially during the summer and on holidays. For Indian Market weekend (see our Annual Events chapter), people often book months in advance.

Dana's Afterdark
222 N. Guadalupe St. • 982-5225

The owners of this fairly new late-night cafe describe their popular establishment as an "alternative coffeehouse for the uninhibited." To understand what that means, you need only show up one evening (but not on Mondays, when it's closed) anywhere from, say, 10 PM to 4 AM. You may well find yourself playing Battleship, Monopoly, Trivial Pursuit, even Chutes and Ladders next to, or possibly with, gay couples, health gurus, movie stars, operatic sopranos, prolific authors, purple-haired and tongue-pierced high school students,

wealthy matrons, willing patrons and — well, I'm sure we've left someone out. Dana's is in a quaint, early 20th-century adobe house in which each parlor has its own distinct ambiance. The main room is bright and cheerful and features a glass case displaying such goodies as Snickers pie, Milky Way mousse pie, Black Forest cake and other rich, gooey desserts. This room also has a large (and loud) espresso machine, where Dana's many coffee drinks begin, and more than 40 varieties of tea that the owners will blend to taste (yours, not theirs) and suspend in a porous bag on a long toothpick in cups big enough for a swim.

Another room has several couches, a huge coffee table, the previously alluded to game corner and an 80-year-old piano that patrons are welcome to play. A third room has low lighting and distressed Mexican furniture and is a great place to watch who's coming and going from the cover of relative darkness. There's a large patio in back, a small porch in front that is often crowded with smokers, and a resident dog, Sissy, who likes to investigate but can be somewhat aloof — don't take it personally. Located throughout the cafe are strategically placed works of art, many of them for sale.

The cafe undoubtedly caters to the gay community, but as you'll note from our description above — or simply from a visual sweep of the premises — the clientele is diverse and eclectic, drawing night birds of all species. Dana and his partner, Rody, take pride in serving "comfort food" including a wide variety of sandwiches (roast beef, ham or turkey and Swiss cheese, mozzarella and red bell pepper, for example), Frito pies, soups and other simple entrees as well as the desserts mentioned above. The cafe is open in warm weather from sunset to 4 AM and in cooler weather from 6:30 PM until about 1 AM on Sunday, Tuesday and Thursday and to 4 AM on Wednesday, Friday and Saturday. The owners may expand their hours to include Sunday brunch starting in 1998.

Downtown Subscription
376 Garcia St. • 983-3085

Though Downtown Subscription is primarily a daytime establishment, the coffeehouse/international newsstand stays open an extra hour and a half or so every other Wednesday evening for poetry readings sponsored by a Santa Fe-based cultural education /literary organization called Recursos de Santa Fe. Poets are chosen based on work they have submitted. Most are local, though some come from other cities and occasionally even other states. Readings start at 7 PM and last until approximately 8:30 PM. You might want to show up early because the readings get crowded — sometimes with up to 80 people, many of them sipping cappuccino, hot Mexican mocha made with ground Ibarra chocolate, tea or any number of other hot or cold nonalcoholic drinks, perhaps accompanied by a lime bar, rugelach, Aunt Helen's sour cream coffeecake or maybe even a sandwich. There is no cover charge for poetry readings. Downtown Subscription's regular hours are from 7:30 AM to 7 PM daily. The cafe, which is extremely popular among locals, sells magazines and newspapers from around the world with up to 2,500 titles in stock at any one time.

Java Joe's
College Plaza, 2430 Cerrillos Rd.
• 471-5637
Rodeo Plaza, Rodeo Rd. • 474-JAVA
There are two Java Joe's — they have the same owners, but their ambiances are as different as day and night. In fact, it's the nights that set them apart. The Cerrillos Road location stays open some evenings until 9 PM — two hours later than its Rodeo Road sister — for open-mike sessions, poetry readings and occasional live music. Check the calendar in the local papers for details. Located just south of the intersection at St. Michael's Drive, behind Austin's Steaks and Saloon at the southern end of a large strip mall called College Plaza, Java Joe's on Cerrillos Road is an odd mixture of coffeehouse, coffee store and seller of handmade clothing and assorted knick-knacks. Somehow, the combination and location work, probably because it's outside the downtown area and attracts mostly locals who live, work, shop or attend school nearby. They can choose from any of four different blends of coffee daily or a wide variety of black, green

and herbal teas. Java Joe's also offers juices, Italian sodas and soft drinks, fresh panini sandwiches on focaccia bread and a selection of homemade muffins, scones, cookies and desserts, including to-die-for tiramisu. The lighting is conducive to reading, socializing or simply sitting back and people-watching through the cafe's glass facade. Java Joe's on Cerrillos Road opens daily at 7 AM and generally closes at 7 PM Monday through Thursday and Saturday — except for special events (check the newspapers) when it stays open until 9 PM. On Fridays, the cafe stays open until 9 PM for open mike. Java Joe's closes Sundays at 5 PM.

www.insiders.com
See this and many other **Insiders' Guide®** destinations online — in their entirety.
Visit us today!

Tribes Coffee House
139 W. San Francisco St. • 982-7948
You might call Tribes Coffee House the Superman of Santa Fe cafes. By day, it's like mild-mannered Clark Kent — a clean, well-lighted and extremely tame place for downtown workers and tourists to have lunch or a long, lingering cuppa. Come nighttime, it dives into a metaphorical phone booth and emerges in tights and a cape, ready to kick butt with live music ranging from bluegrass, country, folk and jazz to Celtic, Middle Eastern (including belly dancing), Native American, reggae and other ethnic sounds. Situated in a narrow covered walkway between San Francisco Street and Palace Avenue in downtown Santa Fe, Tribes is a hidden treasure that even many locals might not know exists because of its discreet location. But word of mouth travels quickly in this town, and Tribes is earning a reputation as a hip and increasingly popular nighttime venue for an interesting cross-section of Santa Fe — everyone from adults looking for an alcohol-and largely smoke-free place to dance to the under-21 set because it's one of the few happening night spots in Santa Fe available to them.

On nights when there's live entertainment, a $5 cover charge will get you in the door. The rest of the time, the price of a cup of coffee, tea, chai — or a dish of authentic hummus, falafel or homemade soup — is your ticket to a five-minute or five-hour sky-lighted escape from the world. You may feel a bit exposed in the daytime because of all the windows, so if you're truly looking to escape, bring a newspaper to hide behind or wear dark glasses. Tribes is open 8:30 AM to 6 PM Sunday through Thursday and 8:30 AM to 11 PM Friday and Saturday.

Comedy Clubs

Ramada Inn Comedy Club
Ramada Inn, 2907 Cerrillos Rd.
• 471-3000

It's not the Improv or San Francisco's Holy City Zoo. But if you're looking for laughs and can forgive the basement ambiance, the Ramada Inn Comedy Club is a good bet. No, you're not likely to see Robin Williams or Whoopi Goldberg on the marquis (though Whoopi spottings are frequent all around Santa Fe as the comedienne-turned-actress often visits for pleasure rather than work). But the Comedy Club has featured such well-known comics as Gabe Kaplan of "Welcome Back, Kotter" fame and Chris "Crazy Legs" Fonseca, who has appeared on MTV, HBO and "The Tonight Show with Jay Leno", as well as plenty of local comics.

Located in the Ramada Inn toward the southern end of Santa Fe's commercial strip, the Comedy Club is a dinner theater that serves American and New Mexican foods — everything from steak and ribs to enchiladas and tacos. There's a two-drink minimum and a $3 cover charge, though some acts may cost up to $7. Doors open at 8 PM, and the show starts at 9. Reservations are recommended on weekends. Dress is relaxed, but not overly casual — you're likely to be turned away if you show up in cut-off shorts and a T-shirt. The club has a nonsmoking section.

Country-and-Western Clubs

Fiesta Barn
Rancho Encantado, N.M. Hwy. 592,
Tesuque • 982-3537

The Fiesta Barn at luxurious Rancho Encantado (see our Accommodations chapter) is an honest-to-goodness barn that features live country-and-western music by popular local bands on Sunday nights from April through October. Erected about 20 years ago, the unheated Fiesta Barn is rustic and earthy yet cozy and comfortable with Mexican blankets adorning the beams, haystacks around the perimeter and picnic tables for chowing down on fresh barbecue. Beer seems to be the most popular item from the small, full-service bar — especially the ever-popular, all-American Budweiser — though some local microbrews give the Clydesdales a run for their money. But it's the dance that's the draw. Literally hundreds of people show up to two-step, waltz, polka and swing the night away to the sounds of South by Southwest or Hired Hands, both enormously talented bands.

You'll see some darned good dancers here, but don't let that intimidate you. The wooden dance floor is big enough for everyone, and the ambiance is friendly and fun not to mention energetic and downright electric. In the end, it's pure country, right down to the fashions, which include lots of cowboy hats and boots and women in swinging skirts. Five bucks will get you into the Fiesta Barn, which is a separate building complete with nearby outhouses in a wooded area close to the main lodge. The faint of heart may use the bathrooms in the lobby, just a short stroll away along attractive, lighted paths. While you're in the lobby, do take a minute to absorb its curious but attractive blend of northern New Mexican and European charm complete with huge log *vigas* on the ceiling, a couple of large fireplaces, overstuffed couches and an eclectic mix of period furniture. You might want to show up some Friday at the Main Lodge between 5:30 and 7:30 PM to hear talented wranglers from the luxury resort's own stables read original poetry and sing songs.

On Sundays in the winter and Wednesdays in the spring and summer, Rancho Encantado features dinner dancing in its top-rated restaurant. The resort literally rolls up the carpet to expose the dance floor so diners can cut a rug to Big Band sounds. You'll see everything from swing and samba to the bossa nova and cha-cha. Casual elegance is the dress code for these nights, which tend to attract a somewhat older audience, say 40 and up. The dinner dance goes from 5:30 to 9:30 PM and is open to the public as well as hotel guests. There is no cover charge. Check the newspapers for special events.

Rodeo Nites
2911 Cerrillos Rd. • 473-4138

Rodeo Nites is almost two nightclubs in one. It starts out nearly every evening as a straight-ahead country-and-western club that attracts a loyal group of fairly genteel dancers who really know their way around the dance floor. They two-step, swing, line-dance, polka and waltz until about 10 or 10:30 PM. Then the music gets louder and harder and younger — and so does the crowd. Between sets by almost invariably a country-and-western band, the later crowd also dances to ranchero, salsa, Tejano and rock spun by two deejays on the brigs. The live music starts nightly at 8 PM. Rodeo Nites has brought in such national luminaries as Freddie Fender, Perfect Stranger, Neal McCoy and Sammy Kershaw as well as local and regional favorites like South By Southwest, Ricochet, Midnight Fire and Wild West Band. The club charges $2.50 to get in the door on Thursdays and $3 on Fridays and Saturdays. The rest of the week there's no cover. Wednesday night is ladies' night, but don't get your hackles up, fellas. The perks — mainly discounts on special drinks — apply to you, too. And every night is discount night at the shot bar, where you pay less for beers and shots by getting them yourself instead of waiting for table service. The atmosphere at Rodeo Nites is strictly saloon with a brass rail separating the 90-foot oval dance floor from the raised platforms with tables and chairs. Rodeo Nites opens nightly at 5:30 PM and closes at 2 AM (midnight on Sundays).

Sports Bars

Green Onion Sports Bar
1851 St. Michael's Dr. • 983-5198

The Green Onion is exactly what you'd expect in a sports bar: lots of beer and other booze, lots of smoke, lots of rowdy sports fans and, of major importance, lots of televisions — 11 to be exact, including a 60-inch set used during parties for the Superbowl, the World Series, NBA playoffs and other major televised sports events. Two of the sets are hooked up to the National Trivia Network, which runs half-hour trivia games of 15 questions in which players compete at no charge against other bars around the country.

A staple in Santa Fe, the Green Onion is where sports fans of all sorts gather to watch games and where local sports teams meet after their own games. The Green Onion is truly a local bar, even a neighborhood bar. Founded 25 years ago by an Irishman, the Green Onion is considered the only traditional Irish bar in Santa Fe where St. Patrick's Day is treated like a national holiday with a huge party featuring bagpipes and other live music and the usual culinary suspects — corned beef and cabbage and Irish stew. The rest of the year, the Green Onion serves classic pub food including hot and cold sandwiches, pizza and excellent hamburgers as well as pretty darned good New Mexican dishes. The Green Onion is open Monday through Saturday until 2 AM and Sundays until midnight. The kitchen stays open until 9:30 PM on weeknights and 8:30 PM Saturday and Sunday.

Pizzazz
100 N. Guadalupe St. • 820-0002

Located in downtown Santa Fe, Pizzazz is a somewhat upscale sports bar and restaurant that attracts an assortment of locals and visitors. You'll find lawyers and librarians, CPAs and construction workers, painters and politicians, businesspeople and barflies — anyone, in other words, who likes to watch televised sports in a crowd. The lounge boasts six televisions, including one large-screen set and five 32-inchers. Pizzazz has a definite downtown feel to it, right down to the food, which includes wood oven-fired pizzas, homemade soups, salads, appetizers and daily specials as well as more traditional pub fare.

Unlike many downtown establishments, Pizzazz has ample free parking, which locals especially appreciate. Visitors will like its proximity to many downtown hotels. The atmosphere at Pizzazz is relaxed, including its smoking policy — it's a cigar-friendly saloon. The bar gets mighty crowded during major sports

Photo: Don Strel/Southwest Assignments

Farolitos decorate Santa Fe at Christmas.

events such as the Superbowl, World Series, pro basketball and the Olympics, so get there early or you'll have to elbow your way to the bar. Pizzazz is open until 11 PM (and often later) seven days a week.

Rocky's Bar & Grill
1201 Cerrillos Rd. • 986-1992

Rocky's is a family-owned lounge that is part sports bar, part dance bar. Its four television sets are tuned to sports channels at all times and are visible from most corners of the saloon, even by the pool tables, which rent out for $1 per person per game. The owners host parties during big sporting events with food and drink specials such as $1.99 super nachos and $2 pitchers of beer for parties of six or more.

On Wednesday, Friday and Saturday nights, the bar turns into a cabaret with live local bands playing rock, blues or R&B for a $2 to $3 cover charge, depending on who's performing. The crowd changes with the music — younger people for alternative rock, baby boomers for blues. Sporting events draw all age groups. Rocky's tends to attract more locals than tourists because it's not downtown. As a result, it has the feel of a neighborhood bar with lots of regulars. As the name implies,

Rocky's Bar & Grill also serves food, specializing in burgers and New Mexican dishes. Rocky's is open Monday through Thursday until midnight and Friday and Saturday until 2 AM. It's closed on Sunday.

Everything Else

A Bar
331 Sandoval St. • 982-8808

Walking into the ultra-sophisticated A Bar is like taking a step back in time. You almost expect to see Nick and Nora Charles sipping martinis and swapping repartees with each other or with one of the suspendered bartenders at the small, curved bar, whose lighting from below gives it an other-worldly quality. Indeed, everything about the A Bar screams the '30s and '40s, from the stylish, art deco chandeliers and faux leopardskin chairs and barstools to the understatedly elegant little black boxes of wooden matches on every table.

The entertainment fills the bill, too, with live music, usually jazz. One or two nights a week you'll find singer Chris Calloway, one of Santa Fe's many resident luminaries, belting out many of the tunes her legendary father,

Cab Calloway, made famous at the Cotton Club in Harlem and in the movies. Jazz flutist Herbie Mann, another famous Santa Fe resident, also performs occasionally at the A Bar.

Keeping to the retro mood, you might try one of the A Bar's oh-so-refined mixed drinks, such as a Vesper Martini — Stolichnaya vodka and Bombay gin à la James Bond, i.e., shaken not stirred — a Manhattan served with pre-served sweet bing cherries or perhaps a Nob Creek old fashioned. And don't be afraid to ask for your favorite brand of liquor; the lounge takes pride in its extensive premium bar. A Bar is open Tuesday through Saturday until 2 AM. Live music generally starts at 8 or 9 PM with a cover charge from $3 and $20, depending on who's playing.

Blue Corn Cafe & Brewery
133 W. Water St. • 984-1800

The Blue Corn attracts primarily a younger crowd, the majority of them locals, who come to sample the half-dozen microbrews and nightly drink specials and to listen to contemporary music — usually one person or a duo on acoustic guitar and vocals. The tiny, cheerful lounge is near the entrance to the restaurant, which serves reasonably priced New Mexican food with a mild nouvelle twist (see our Restaurants chapter). The bar stays open until 2 AM Monday through Saturday and until midnight on Sunday. Thus far, the Blue Corn has never demanded a cover charge for music, though that may change in 1998. There's another Blue Corn Cafe & Brewery at 4056 Cerrillos Road, Suite 6, 438-1800.

Bull Ring
150 Washington Ave. • 983-3328

The Bull Ring steakhouse and lounge is *the* place to go if you like rubbing elbows with politicians. It's the "other" State Capitol, a second office of sorts for lawmakers when the state legislature is in session during January and February and, every other year, in March as well. New Mexico legislators and lobbyists head to The Bull Ring at the end of the legislative day to hang out, chill out and sometimes strike political deals. The upscale restaurant

and lounge with its elegant dark green and wood decor attracts a variety of professionals, many of whom mingle at the oaken and brass-railed bar. The Bull Ring serves USDA prime, corn-fed steak from Chicago in its smoke-free dining room. The bar — where you not only can smoke cigars, but also buy them — remains open until 10:30 or 11 PM.

Catamount Bar & Grill
125 E. Water St. • 988-7222; Catamount Bar Billiards Room, 988-7299

The popular Catamount Bar & Grill is a literal stomping ground for the 20- to 30-year-old set who come to dance, dine and maybe meet the love of their lives in a dark, Irish tavern-like atmosphere. The Catamount features live music on weekends — primarily rock, blues and jazz, mostly by local talent (from Santa Fe, Albuquerque or Taos) and occasionally a national band on tour. A cover charge, generally between $2 to $5, will get you in the door. Then it's up to you to find space on the packed tile dance floor. The grill offers standard bar fare, including chicken breasts, hamburgers, buffalo wings and nachos, while the bar bills its Margaritas as a specialty and carries locally made microbrews from Wolf Canyon Brewing Company (see subsequent entry). Upstairs is a billiards room with six 9-foot Brunswick pool tables that rent for $8 to $10 an hour, depending on the time of day, plus $2 for each additional person. Smoking is allowed throughout the establishment, including cigars, which are for sale in the billiards room. The Catamount stays open until 2 AM Monday through Saturday and midnight on Sunday.

Club Alegría
2791 Agua Fría St. • 471-2324

Club Alegría is a live music and dance club. Beyond that, it's impossible to categorize. The club, on lower Agua Fría Street, is probably most famous, at least locally, for its Friday night salsa show starring Pretto y Parranda featuring Father Frank Pretto — the Peruvian-born, piano-playing, singing priest of San Isidro Catholic Church. The minute the music starts, the dance floor fills to the edges with men and

---

FYI

Unless otherwise noted, the area code for all phone numbers listed in this guide is 505.

women swaying their hips — some subtly, others wildly — to salsa, cumbia, merengue and other Latin rhythms. This is tropical music, and when you're dancing to it, there's definitely a heat wave. Some couples actually know what they're doing. Many don't, but nobody cares. And everyone has fun. If you want to know how it's really done, show up an hour before the show for free dance lessons from 8 to 9 PM. Saturdays and Sundays at Club Alegría often feature Mexican *norteño* music, best described as Mexican cowboy music.

During the week, the club books popular national acts, everything from rock, blues and rhythm and blues to alternative, New Age and country-and-western. Past performers have included Marcia Ball, Beausoleil, Bo Diddley (who lives in Albuquerque), Joe Ely, Beau Jocque and the Zydeco High-Rollers, Leon Redbone, Michelle Shocked, the Marshall Tucker Band and many others. Show prices range from $5 to $25, depending on the act. Pretto y Parranda will cost you five bucks. It's a steal, and you'll probably even lose weight in the bargain by shaking it up on the dance floor. For those who'd rather shoot pool than dance, there are two $1 tables at the back of the club, conveniently located right next to the bar. There's plenty of free parking behind the club in a well-lighted lot with security. Club Alegría is open daily from 8 PM to 1:30 AM on Wednesday, Friday and Saturday and on nights when a national act plays. Sunday hours are from 8 PM to midnight.

Cowgirl Hall of Fame Bar BQ & Western Grill
319 S. Guadalupe St. • 982-2565

The Cowgirl Hall of Fame is a highly popular restaurant, bar and mini-museum as well as an entertainment space for music, live theater and comedy. As you might expect from its name, the theme is Western with a capital W. The walls and mantels of the front room are filled about to capacity with all sorts of Western knickknacks and memorabilia including rodeo crowns, covered wagon lamps, graphic old calendars, ads and magazine covers, early movie posters, new and used cowboy boots, spurs and even a certified aerosol can of "Bullshit Repellent" behind the bar. The bar itself is a copper-topped half-rectangle made from barn-board planking with barstools constructed from tractor seats or covered with faux Holstein cowhide. Resting their boots on the iron footrest are real cowboys, urban cowboys, artists, bankers, cooks, doctors, EMTs, farriers, furriers, good ol' boys and just plain folks. This room also serves as the smokers' dining room as well as the stage for free live music that might be blues, folk, country-and-western or rock 'n' roll. The music can also be heard in the large nonsmoking dining room in the back, whose glittered walls feature dozens of black and white archive photos of honorees inducted into the original Cowgirl Hall of Fame, now located in Fort Worth, Texas. The Cowgirl in Santa Fe and its sister establishment in New York pay the museum — recently in transit from Hereford to Ft. Worth, Texas, and due to open there soon — royalties to use the name. In summertime, musicians often play on the spacious, attractive front patio from 9 PM to 1 AM. Foodwise, the Cowgirl specializes in "deep Southwestern barbecue with a twist." A fine dining room, which should be open by the time this book goes to print, will specialize in wild game of the Rocky Mountains and creative dishes inspired by the American West. Monday through Thursday the fine dining room will revert back to its current status as the "Opry Room," featuring comedy, theatrical performances and concerts showcasing primarily local bands that sometimes record a "Live at the Cowgirl" CD. Ticket prices range from $5 to $10. The Cowgirl Hall of Fame stays open Monday through Saturday until 2 AM and Sunday until midnight. (See our Restaurants chapter.)

Drama Club
125 N. Guadalupe St. • 988-4374

This is Santa Fe's only true "disco," where men and women put on their spandex and dance, dance, dance. The Drama Club — which tied for the best nightclub and the best place to meet singles in the *Santa Fe Reporter*'s "Best of Santa Fe, 1997" — caters primarily to gays and lesbians, but everyone is welcome provided they have a healthy attitude. You'll see everything here from dreadlocks to drag queens and lawyers to lipstick lesbians. Some come to strut their stuff — perhaps in a G-string or something equally scanty, and even on stage if they so desire — others play the voyeur. Whichever end of the spectrum you find comfortable, the Drama Club is definitely not for the peevish.

Every night of the week brings a different brand of entertainment and often a different crowd. Mondays feature a dance party called "Post," while Tuesday is "Poetry Allowed" night for local bards. Wednesday is one of the hottest nights of the week starting at 8 PM with comedy by the Improvertz followed by "Trash Disco," a retro chic dance party featuring music from the '70s and '80s and fashions to match. Thursdays are a revolving showcase mostly for local bands, though the club occa-

sionally brings in national acts. Weekends are also big nights at the Drama Club, as you might expect, with Access Party on Friday nights featuring high-energy dance music with a harder edge and "Diva" on Saturday night when various DJs, both local and out-of-state, spin whatever grabs them. Sundays calm down somewhat with country-and-western music and dance from 5 to 10 PM, though when the clock strikes 10, DJ Jimme Chiocci takes over with dance tunes of the '80s and '90s.

The cover charge at the Drama Club normally falls in the $3 to $5 range, though some acts might command up to $15. An Access Pass allows bearers to get in most nights for free and entitles them to drink specials. The club has a couple of $1 pool tables and a resident rock theater group, Live Without a Net, that stages condensed versions of musical productions including *Rent* and *The Rocky Horror Picture Show* for a cover of $7. Drama Club is open daily from 4 PM to 2 AM (midnight on Sundays).

El Farol
808 Canyon Rd. • 983-9912

Located on chic Canyon Road, El Farol is as much a fixture in Santa Fe's nightlife as the Plaza is in the city's daylife, though the 400-year-old Plaza has a few years on El Farol. Established in 1968 in what was previously La Cantina del Cañon, El Farol is in a beautiful old adobe building that dates back to 1835. Look closely at the wooden floor, and you'll see spots worn down by four decades of flamenco dancing. The front of the building is framed by an old porch with pillars and *vigas*. The inside is dominated by the paintings of Alfred Morang, who traded paintings for drinks at La Cantina del Cañon and other Santa Fe bars. Many artists frequented La Cantina, and then El Farol, largely because of its location in the midst of one of Santa Fe's most well-known artistic enclaves. As a result, it has always been a hip establishment, attracting an eclectic clientele, even today. You'll find well-known artists and actors drinking with carpenters and farriers, secretaries and CEOs as well as all variety of wannabes.

Famed for its inviting atmosphere, El Farol tied with the Pink Adobe Dragon Room Bar as the friendliest bar in the *Santa Fe Reporter*'s "Best of Santa Fe, 1997." Some people come to drink and socialize, others to listen to music — blues, country, flamenco, folk, jazz, klezmer, you name it. The bar is relatively small, but that has never stopped patrons from wearing out the floor yet another millimeter or two with dancing. Live entertainment commands a cover charge of $2 to $7, depending on who's playing. The sounds tend to spill into El Farol's adjacent restaurant, famous for its tapas and Spanish cuisine (see our Restaurants chapter). The bar is open daily until 2 AM every day except Sunday, when it closes at midnight.

El Paseo Bar & Grill
208 Galisteo St. • 992-2848

In the heart of downtown Santa Fe, El Paseo Bar & Grill beckons strollers to wander in and relax over a few brews and free live music — especially in summer when its front window are open, and the music and laughter and clinking of glasses sifts out into Galisteo Street. Although El Paseo is a relatively new saloon with only a couple of years under its belt, it already has that worn-in feel of a neighborhood bar. Its clientele is a mixture of ages and backgrounds including service-industry workers and older, well-heeled professionals who like to come in for a drink and some socializing after work. During the week, El Paseo offers various drink specials to go with the variety of sounds: $1 Tecate beers on Tuesday, which is open-mike night for singers and songwriters; $2 drafts on Wednesday when KBAC radio (see our Media chapter) tapes New Mexico rock 'n' roll, R&B or blues bands for playback on the air; just jazz on Thursday, with $3 gin drinks to set the mood; and rhythm and blues on Friday and Saturday with dancing, despite the small space.

El Paseo has a wide selection of microbrews on tap from throughout the Southwest, including some brewed locally and quite a few from Colorado. It also serves daily food specials from a full menu with traditional pub fare as well as northern New Mexican dishes. For those of you who like to smoke your Havanas in the comfort of a warm room instead of being banished to the outdoors, this is a cigar-friendly saloon. In fact, there are plans afoot to sell cigars behind the bar. El Paseo is stays open until 1:30 AM Monday through Saturday and until midnight on Sunday.

Evangelo's Cocktail Lounge
200 W. San Francisco St. • 982-9014

Don't let the Harleys in front intimidate you. Evangelo's Cocktail Lounge is a friendly neighborhood bar with a mixed, youngish clientele that runs the gamut from bikers to bankers. Only one block west of the Plaza, Evangelo's practically owns the corner of W. San Francisco and Galisteo streets, attracting scores of tourists in summer who find themselves drawn to the lounge's wall of windows and the crowd spilling out into the street, day and night. Interestingly enough, the boisterous bar coexists happily with several bookstores in the immediate vicinity and some rather pricey jewelry and clothing boutiques. During winter, Evangelo's belongs to the locals, who appreciate the $2 domestic beers, $2.50 imports (of which there are more than 30), the selection of Greek drinks including Metaxa and Ouzo, and the downstairs pool tables at 50¢ a game.

Regardless of season, weekends at Evangelo's are always fun, happening times with live rock 'n' roll and rarely a cover. On New Year's, Fiestas and other special events, you'll have to cough up $5 or so to get in the door, a small price indeed to behold the odd mixture of Polynesian, Greek and Santa Fe decor. But the blend works, lending a unique personality to the bar, which has been featured in *The New York Times* and other national dailies as well as in newspapers and magazines in Sweden, Norway and Japan.

Evangelo's first opened its doors in 1971 when Evangelo Klonis, a Greek immigrant and American World War II hero, decided to branch out from his restaurant business on the Plaza. Today his son, Nick Klonis, runs both the bar and Evangelo's Mediterranean Cafe farther down Galisteo Street. Nick attributes the popularity of Evangelo's to its being "the only bar left in Santa Fe where you can go have a drink, meet friends, have a good time and not be pretentious." A number of Santa Fe bars would surely dispute the "only" in that sentence, though the rest is undoubtedly true. Evangelo's is open until 2 AM Monday through Saturday and until midnight on Sundays.

La Fiesta Lounge
La Fonda Hotel, 100 E. San Francisco St. • 982-5511

Located in the attractive Spanish/New Mexican-style lobby of Santa Fe's most historic hotel — legend has it that a *fonda*, or inn, has existed on that same corner since 1610 — La Fiesta Lounge is a welcome haven for both the weary and the wired, a place to relax over a beer or a Margarita or to dance 'til you drop. Whether you lean toward country-and-western, ranchero or Latin jazz, La Fiesta offers top-quality live entertainment nightly, most at no charge. Only South By Southwest, a hugely popular C&W band that plays on occasional Sunday nights, commands an entrance fee — $7 at last reckoning. That covers the cost of opening the hotel ballroom or the New Mexico room, which can accommodate the group's legions of loyal fans. They arrive dressed to kill — the men in jeans, Western-style jackets, cowboy boots and hats and even the occasional neckerchief. Women also wear boots and "country chic" dresses or skirts, sometimes adorned at the waist with *concha* belts. What you wear is less important than your enthusiasm for the dance, whether it's the two-step or the Western waltz. It's truly a sight to behold such a dandied-up crowd genteelly gliding around the dance floor.

Also popular are Bill and Bonnie Hearne, a local country-and-western duo transplanted from Austin who have achieved national prominence of late. They usually play La Fiesta Lounge on Wednesday and Thursday nights. The lounge also attracts a crowd of regulars on Monday and Tuesday nights when Yoboso — a four-piece band with congas, keyboard, drums, bass and vocals — plays salsa, merengue, cumbias and other Latin sounds. Friday, Saturday and Sunday nights in the lounge

feature Sierra, which plays country-and-western, Tex-Mex, ranchero and a variety of other Western and Southwestern music. For mellower sounds, visit the lounge during happy hour when Ramon Bermudez and Tim Valentine play Spanish classical guitar. La Fiesta Lounge is open Monday through Thursday until 11:30 PM, Friday and Saturday until 12:30 AM and Sunday from until 11:30 PM. From May to October, take time to sip a summer cocktail and view incredible sunsets in the La Fonda's outdoor Bell Tower Bar on the hotel's fifth-floor roof. The views more than make up for drinking from a plastic cup.

Legal Tender Saloon and Restaurant
Main St., Lamy • 466-1223

The Legal Tender describes itself as "the real Old West where gunfighters, gamblers and beautiful ladies have dined, danced and dallied." People still dine, dance and dally in the Victorian-era saloon, but there's no more gunfighting or gambling — except, perhaps, in the memory of ghosts said to inhabit the 107-year-old building. Among them are the "Man in Black," who, legend has it, got in the way of a stray bullet during a gambling dispute. Some claim to have seen the "Lady in White," dressed in a lovely white Victorian gown, pass through a room. Others have noted a child in a long dress sitting on the balcony steps. The balcony contains far more tangible evidence of the period, notably two paintings depicting the coming of the railroad to the West, both used as studies for murals that would eventually wind up in the 1916 Pan Pacific Exposition in San Diego. You'll also see on the balcony two chromolithographs of the Grand Canyon by noted landscape artist Thomas Moran, whose large paintings, *The Grand Canyon of the Yellowstone* and *Chasm of the Colorado*, grace the U.S. Capitol in Washington, D.C. Take note, too, of the hand-carved cherry-wood bar, imported from Germany in 1894 by John Flueger, who took over the operation of his father-in-law's general store and added a saloon that's said to have hosted a chained Billy the Kid when lawmen brought him there after his famed escape from the Lincoln County Jail.

Some 60 years later, the bar would again

achieve notoriety, this time as the Pink Garter Saloon, whose vaudeville and cancan performances drew audiences from miles around. Country singer Glen Campbell got his start at the Pink Garter playing in his uncle Dick Bills' country-and-western band. Renamed the Legal Tender in 1969, the saloon added its Americana Room, which contains bits and pieces of architectural and decorative Americana from around the country, including a tin ceiling from the original Hilton Hotel in San Francisco, large windows from the first train station in Albuquerque, drapes and chandeliers from the presidential suite of Chicago's Sherman Hotel and many of the saloon's original oak tables and chairs. Today the Legal Tender is a relatively tame country-and-western dinner/dance club featuring popular local musicians such as South By Southwest, Hired Hands, Bill and Bonnie Hearne and a Native American jazz-country band called Firecats of Discord. This is early evening fun: It closes at 9 PM Tuesday through Thursday (except in winter when it's closed on Tuesdays and Wednesdays), 10 PM on Friday and Saturday and 5 PM on Sunday. Cigars are allowed in the bar.

LobbyBar
Hotel Loretto, 211 Old Santa Fe Tr. • 988-5531

The LobbyBar in the casual, upscale Hotel Loretto has two faces. Monday Night Football is a sacred event in the cozy lounge, a time when locals and guests sit back in overstuffed sofas and chairs, eyes glued to a 60-inch television tuned in to the game. Anyone who tampers with the dial does so at great personal risk. The rest of the time, the plush, comfortable LobbyBar offers free entertainment, including a solo guitar player and vocalist for Friday and Saturday happy hour, (5 to 8 PM), and contemporary Latin dance music on Thursday, Friday and Saturday night from 9 PM to midnight. The LobbyBar attracts primarily locals on weekends and a mixture of residents and visitors the rest of the week. Among the attractions is a large fireplace, a ceiling decorated with hand-painted wood carvings and a track-lighting system that patrons are welcome to adjust. The bar serves sandwiches, salads and appetizers as well as seasonal drink specialties such as hot toddies and alcohol-infused coffee drinks in winter and iced drinks in summer. The LobbyBar is open nightly until midnight.

Mañana Bar
Inn of the Governors, 234 Don Gaspar Ave. • 982-4333

Located off the lobby of the Inn of the Governors, on the corner of Don Gaspar and Alameda avenues a few blocks south of the Plaza, Mañana Bar is popular among locals, tourists and hotel guests because of its nightly "piano bar" — in quotes because you can't actually sit around the grand piano, though you can still hum along to all your old favorites — and giant picture windows that open up to the world outside. Its horseshoe-shape bar, copper-topped tables and Southwestern-style decor create a warm ambiance enhanced in winter with a crackling fire in a large *kiva* fireplace, perfect after a day on the slopes, especially with a hot toddy or coffee drink. You could enjoy a full dinner from the adjacent restaurant without ever leaving the bar. Or you can choose from a large selection of appetizers while you're waiting for your table. Mañana attracts primarily the over-30 set, including lots of professionals and a fair share of lawmakers during the legislative session. The atmosphere is smoke-friendly, though not for cigars. Sports fans can watch games on the bar's 32-inch television when there's no entertainment. Mañana Bar is open 11:30 AM to 1 AM Monday through Saturday and midnight on Sundays.

Mine Shaft Tavern
2846 N.M. Hwy. 14, Madrid • 473-0743

For a taste of a real honest-to-goodness mining town bar, don't miss the Mine Shaft Tavern in Madrid, once a booming coal mining village that turned into a ghost town after it fell on hard times in the 1950s. Two decades later, Madrid (pronounced MA-drid) began enjoying a renaissance with the arrival of artists and craftspeople who converted many of the old buildings into galleries and shops and turned it into a sightseeing mecca. The Mine Shaft, however, remains today pretty much as it was in 1946 when Oscar Huber, who owned the mining comany that literally owned Madrid, built a tavern for the coal miners who worked for him. Perhaps the biggest change in the intervening half-century is the absence of the rail cars that used to travel directly between the mine and the bar.

The tavern is a cavernous rustic room with a 50-foot lodge pole pine bar — the longest stand-up bar in New Mexico, the owners claim. On the wall above the fireplace is a buffalo's head. Above the bar are paintings depicting Madrid's history. Gracing the wooden walls throughout the tavern are an eclectic collection of cowboy paraphernalia, Native American items, railroad memorabilia and mining accoutrements. The clientele is as eclectic as the decor. You'll find everyone from artists and old hippies to cowboys and Indians, Vietnam vets and yuppies, tourists and commuters, skiers and couch potatoes and even a few ghosts. Except for the ghosts, they come to drink, eat what the owners claim is the best burger west of the Mississippi or authentic Cajun food (one of the owners is from Louisiana), and dance to live music on the weekends. The Mine Shaft is open daily, closing at 11 PM on weeknights and midnight or thereabouts on the weekend.

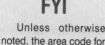

Ore House on the Plaza
50 Lincoln Ave. • 983-8687

The Ore House bar and restaurant has both tourist and local appeal, not only because of its location, but also because of its large, heated balcony overlooking the Plaza. Inside, the decor is strictly Southwestern, with *vigas* on the ceiling, *saltillo* tile on the floor and a *kiva* fireplace in the restaurant. Ore House offers free live music Friday and Saturday with classical guitarist Gerard Moreno from 4 to 6 PM and rock, jazz, blues, country-and-western or any of a number of other genres from 8 PM until closing. There's no dance floor, however, so you'll have to be satisfied tapping your feet or playing drums with your fingers on the table.

Bar patrons can order from an appetizer menu or from the restaurant's main menu, which features steak, seafood and Southwestern specialties. If you have a favorite wine, it's a good bet you'll find it among the Ore House's award-winning wine selection. For those of you who like your liquor hot and sweet with a jolt of caffeine, try some of the Ore House's specialty coffee drinks such as Choc' Full O' Nuts with Godiva chocolate liqueur and Amaretto; Downtown Mexican Coffee with tequila and Kahlua; or Ore House Mocha with Godiva chocolate liqueur, Bailey's Irish cream and either coffee or espresso — all topped with whipped cream. If those aren't enough to get your sweet tooth aching, there's the Balcony Snuggler with peppermint Schnapps, dark Crème de Cacao, hot chocolate and whipped cream. The bar also makes its own hot buttered rum, which appeals to the après ski crowd. The Ore House stays closes at 11 PM Sunday through Thursday and midnight or 12:30 AM on Friday and Saturday.

Palace Restaurant and Saloon
142 W. Palace Ave. • 982-9893

The Palace is a Santa Fe institution. Around since 1835, the restaurant and bar got its start under the proprietorship of Doña Gertrudis Barcelo — a.k.a Doña Tules ("Miss Trudy") or La Tules — who opened a gambling saloon that remained popular until her death in 1853. The details about what happened to the saloon after La Tules' died are sketchy, but popular myth has it that it was a bordello at some point in its post-Tules history. Fueling that legend was the discovery in 1959 — the year the owners broke ground for the present establishment — of a horseshoe-shaped doorknocker whose left side had been fashioned into a high-heeled, fishnet- stockinged leg in profile, complete with bare buttocks, and containing the inscription, "Burro Alley — 1873." Burro Alley is a historic lane at the west entrance to the Palace that once housed a burro pen along with the old saloon.

Today, the Palace is widely popular among locals — though it certainly gets its fair share of tourists — who appreciate the fine bartending of Alfonso Alderette, a Cuban national who has been tending bar at the Palace for years and who often wins the title of "Best Bartender" in the *Santa Fe Reporter*'s annual "Best of Santa Fe" poll. When he gets to know you, he'll often surprise you with a drink he feels suits your taste or your personality. But it's not just Alfonso's drinks that are so good, it's his contagious laugh. Patrons also appreciate the bar's atmosphere, which is unapologetically dark and, well, bordello-like, complete with red flock paper and pictures of reclining nudes.

Many regulars, including state legislators when they're in session, hold court in the saloon, which features a 140-year-old mahogany bar with a brass foot rail. There's often live background music — either someone playing the piano in the back of the room or perhaps a duet in front. Drinks are generous, and there's always a dish of mixed nuts handy. If you need something more substantive, you can order upscale pub fare off the bar menu — a superb prime rib sandwich au jus, perhaps, or maybe some truffle duck mousse pâté, escargot in garlic ragout or a truly delicious burger. You may also choose from the restaurant menu (see our Restaurants chapter). The Palace is open until midnight and sometimes until 1 AM.

Paolo Soleri
Santa Fe Indian School, 1501 Cerrillos Rd. • 989-7489

This open-air amphitheater is as popular among performers — B.B King, k.d. lang, Lyle Lovett and James Taylor, to name just a few — as it is among audience members, who get to listen to world-class music under the Santa Fe stars. It's also the only venue in town that gets such big-name acts. For obvious reasons, shows are limited to summertime only. Tickets can be pricey, though, we've rarely heard anyone grumble that their money was ill-spent after a concert here. Call the theater or check *Pasatiempo*, the entertainment section of *The New Mexican* for scheduled performances. (See our Arts chapter.)

Pink Adobe Dragon Room Bar
406 Old Santa Fe Tr. • 983-7712

Attached by a driveway to the Pink Adobe,

a fine New Mexican restaurant that's been a staple in Santa Fe since 1944, the Dragon Room is an extremely popular bar among locals, especially the 30-and-older crowd who enjoy its informal atmosphere and warm camaraderie — not to mention the help-yourself popcorn from the movie theater-style popper near the door. Just a few doors down from the State Capitol building, the Dragon Room also packs in state lawmakers during the legislative session. It's no wonder *Newsweek*'s 1988 international edition named the Dragon Room one of the top 10 bars in the world. The lounge also tied with El Farol (see entry this chapter) for Friendliest Bar as well as with the Drama Club (see entry this chapter) for Best Place to Meet Singles, in the *Santa Fe Reporter*'s "Best of Santa Fe, 1997."

Regardless of why you're here, you'll find service with a smile from a professional wait staff that keeps regulars coming back and welcomes newcomers. But the warmth is not merely metaphorical. During winter, the bar keeps two fireplaces burning, one each in the front and back rooms, making it a truly cozy place for a beer or a bourbon. There are often so many bodies here, however, that the fireplaces can be superfluous heat-wise, though they're always a welcome addition to the atmosphere. There's still more fire on Christmas Eve when a traditional *luminaria* (bonfire) burns on the sidewalk in front of the bar for *farolito* viewers and passersby to warm themselves. The Dragon Room even burns its own effigy of Zozobra during Fiestas (see our Annual Events chapter).

The rest of the year, the primary entertainment is David Salazar, who plays Spanish folk music Tuesdays and Thursdays from 8 to 10 PM and Saturdays from 7 to 9 PM. While you're listening to the music, glance around the room at the paintings by owner Rosalea Murphy, who also hand-painted the tables. And do try some of the food from the bar menu which, while admittedly limited, is creative with such

---

INSIDERS' TIP

Too tipsy to drive home from a restaurant or bar? Ask the manager or bartender about SafeRide Home. He or she will summon a taxi, which will deliver you safely anywhere in Santa Fe County at no charge.

offerings as green chile stew, onion soup or a gypsy stew made with chicken, tomatoes, onions and pepper. And by all means, do try the Pink Adobe restaurant, which serves superb New Mexican-style food (see our Restaurants chapter). The Pink Adobe Dragon Room Bar is open Monday through Saturday until anywhere between midnight and 2 AM and Sundays until midnight. Parking is at a premium in the lot behind the bar. We recommend you park in the state office building lot across the street.

Second Street Brewery
1814 Second St. • 982-3030

A relatively new addition to Santa Fe's food, drink and night scene, Second Street Brewery is a nonchain brew pub with some of the best beer in Santa Fe. But don't take our word for it. The brewmaster, originally from Oregon, won several awards last year at the Great American Beer Festival in Denver — the Superbowl of beer festivals in the United States — including a bronze medal for the cream stout. The food is darned good, too, with such traditional English pub fare as fish and chips (the real thing, served with malt vinegar), shepherd's pie, chicken pot pie and London broil as well as classic American dishes including burgers, Philadelphia cheese steaks, Reuben sandwiches and a number of creative vegetarian offerings. (See our Restaurants chapter.) Second Street offers live entertainment — anything from folk and Celtic music to good old rock 'n' roll — throughout the week in an attractive yet unpretentious setting. The crowd ranges in age from college students to septuagenarians. While it's located a bit off the beaten path — in other words, neither downtown nor on one of Santa Fe's main drags — Second Street Brewery is nonetheless well worth visiting. The pub is open until midnight every night. The kitchen stays open until 10 PM.

Shooters Saloon & Grill
1196 Harrison Rd. • 438-7777

Shooters Saloon & Grill is a nightclub catering primarily to an older Mexican clientele and anyone else who appreciates Mexican *norteño* music. One of that country's favorite types of dance music, *norteño* is Mexican cow-

boy music featuring accordion, saxophone and an elaborate 12-string bass guitar called *bajo sexto*. Here you'll see couples doing the *quebradita*, a very popular Mexican dance similar to the two-step, as well as polka, *cumbia* and *banda*. Dancers have plenty of room to maneuver on the 40-foot by 25-foot dance floor, one of the largest in Santa Fe. The walls are decorated with murals by local artists, Mexican flags, *sombreros* and Mexican instruments. Shooters has live entertainment Thursday through Sunday featuring both local musicians and well-known bands from Mexico such as Banda Zeta, Polo Urias and Los Rieleros. Most nights feature two groups. Bands command a cover charge of $6 to $12. There's no cover the rest of the week..

Adjacent to the dance hall is a sunken 70-foot by 35-foot billiards room with its own bar and 10 pool tables. Games cost 50¢ each. In addition, the club has two 10-foot projection screens that are one of the city's main sources for pay-per-view boxing matches. The bar offers an appetizer menu that includes onion rings, french fries, barbecued wings, Frito pies and nachos. Shooters is open until 2 AM Monday through Saturday and until midnight on Sunday. The music starts at 7 PM and ends at 1:30 AM.

The Staab House Lounge
La Posada de Santa Fe, 330 E. Palace Ave. • 986-0000

The Staab House Lounge is an oh-so-genteel and very Victorian drinking establishment that's extremely popular among locals, in part because it's remarkably unpretentious despite its rarefied decor. That's because the lounge doesn't pretend to be anything more than it is — a lovely, aging grouping of old-fashioned parlors that include a graceful Victorian cherrywood bar with a brass foot rail, elegant old crystal chandeliers, well-worn leather and upholstered chairs, faded brocade loveseats and settees, solid square fireplaces, brass mirrors everywhere and lots of low tables with little lamps on them. Some of the parlors feel like smoking rooms, others like a maiden aunt's sitting room. In any room you'd feel just as comfortable drinking tea as tequila or even just talking. You'll want to cease all conversation, however, when Chris Calloway picks up the microphone. The daughter of legendary jazz singer and dancer Cab Calloway, Chris croons or caresses or belts out song after song with a voice that is alternately honey and hard whiskey. Don't miss her on weekends, when she sings to an appreciative audience in the lounge's back room from 9 PM to midnight.

The building is under new ownership, and the new owners are talking about refurbishing the entire lounge to include new paint, some new fixtures, new local artwork and different furniture, both antiques and copies. Perhaps they ought to check first with Julia Staab, whose ghost manifests itself fairly frequently in and around the bar with flying glasses, swinging chandeliers, banging in the lounge bathroom and even a curl of smoke by a particular chair, as if someone were sitting there holding a lighted cigarette. She can't object much to an expanded liquor selection to include up to 30 tequilas, a larger collection of single malt scotches and extensive collection of cordials, ports, brandies and cognacs. Nor is it likely she'd be upset with an upscale bar menu to include the likes of smoked trout-and shrimp-stuffed rellenos or chips with avocado salsa. But one can only wonder if glasses will fly when the old Staab library becomes a piano lounge, or the Rose Room — the original Staab family dining room — turns into a private dining room and wine cellar, or the Mason Room transforms into a cigar lounge complete with humidor. The Staab House Lounge is open daily from 11 AM until at least 11 PM or midnight and, except for Sundays, possibly later if business warrants remaining open.

Summerscene
Santa Fe Plaza

During the summer, some of Santa Fe's most popular and accessible nightlife is right on the Plaza — and it's free. It's called Santa Fe Summerscene, a community program partially funded by the City of Santa Fe Arts Commission and staged by a nonprofit group of the same name. Summerscene is an outdoor nightclub without walls or alcohol. People of all ages are welcome to dance under the stars to everything from bluegrass to opera. Very occasionally, Summerscene brings in a dance troupe to perform. Summerscene takes place on Tuesdays and Thursdays from noon to 1:30 PM and again from 6 to 8 PM beginning the first week in June and continuing through the last week in August for a total of 40 concerts in all. We recommend you dine al fresco with a picnic lunch or supper.

Tiny's Restaurant & Lounge
1015 Pen Rd. • 983-9817, 983-1100

As Insiders, we would be remiss if we didn't include Tiny's Restaurant & Lounge in our Nightlife chapter. Located in an unassuming little strip mall that also houses Domino's Pizza and Bonanza City discount store, Tiny's isn't merely a dining and drinking establishment, it's an experience — especially in the lounge. Let's get one thing out of the way first. The New Mexican food at Tiny's is authentic, and it's good. But we've dealt with that in our Restaurants chapter. Here we're concerned with only two things: drinking and dancing — and we don't mean Coca Cola and rock 'n' roll.

As the restaurant nears closing, the lounge takes on a life of its own with an older crowd that really knows how to cut a rug, whether they're listening to country-and-western or old standards. They put their younger brethren to shame, dancing nonstop, arm-in-arm, with honest-to-goodness certified dance steps from swing to salsa to two-step. The atmosphere is, well, kind of bare bones, with bright lighting, Formica tables and a television set over the bar and the dance floor. But when the musicians play, nothing else matters. The performers and the audience have a ball! And it's contagious, even if neither the music nor the dancing is your normal style. While you're sitting one out, take a gander at the hundreds of decanters around the bar and the restaurant. The barkeep, a professional who has been tending bar for more than 20 years, will tell you they belonged to the original owner, Tiny Moore, who opened the restaurant and nightclub in 1950 and began collecting the bottles in the late '50s. Tiny's son-in-law, Jimmy Palermo, has been running the restaurant since 1959, which is why you'll hear many old-timers call the place Jimmy and Tiny's. But he's kept the restaurant in Tiny's name — and kept the decanters, too — as a tribute to his father-in-law, who died 13 years ago. Tiny's stays open until 2 AM Monday through Saturday. Sunday hours are from 11 AM to 6 PM. You can hear live music Thursday, Friday and Saturday nights.

Vanessie of Santa Fe Restaurant and Piano Bar
434 W. San Francisco St. • 982-9966

Vanessie is a very sophisticated, very elegant and, surprisingly, very comfortable place to have a cocktail, whether you're sitting at the bar watching the bartender mix magic or sitting around the grand piano singing to the timeless standards Doug Montgomery has been performing there since 1982. *Esquire* magazine named Vanessie one of the best piano bars in America several years ago. It's a perennial favorite in Santa Fe among largely well-heeled professionals of all ages, though older locals who have been following Montgomery for the past 15 years have claimed Sunday as "their" night.

While every night is special at Vanessie — this is a place where you truly feel you're stepping out in style — New Year's Eve is a gala affair for which people fly in from around the world to listen to music, drink champagne and dine on Texas-size servings of prime rib. All of Vanessie's classic American cuisine — steak and seafood, salads, baked potatoes, its famous onion loaf, cheesecake, etc. — come in obscenely large portions, beautifully presented (see our Restaurants chapter). Vanessie keeps a computer file behind the bar with hundreds of drink recipes, many with creative — and occasionally risqué — names like a "slippery nipple," for example, (a.k.a. a Butterbaby) made from Baileys Irish cream and butterscotch liqueur. While you're sipping your drink or digging into your 16-ounce steak, you're likely to spot actor Jack Palance or perhaps Harry Connick Jr., Gene Hackman, Barbara Hershey, Neil Sedaka, Tom Selleck or any number of stars who either live in Santa Fe or frequent the restaurant when they're in town. Vanessie is open nightly until 2 AM except Sundays and winter weekdays, when it closes at midnight.

Wolf Canyon Brewing Company
9885 Cerrillos Rd. • 438-7000

The largest and oldest microbrewery in Santa Fe, Wolf Canyon Brewing Company has been around only since 1996, but it's already making a name for itself as serving brews worthy of driving several miles south of town. Located at the start of the Turquoise Trail, a scenic stretch of road that meanders south of the city through old mining villages like Madrid and Cerrillos, Wolf Canyon is primarily a restaurant that serves classic pub food with a Southwestern twist. But the brew pub is attracting a growing number of regulars who come to socialize and drink. Most live in the "neighborhood" — a sprawling stretch of county that includes ranches, rural estates, art galleries, mobile homes and even the Penitentiary of New Mexico, though the inmates don't get out much for brews. Some come for happy hour, when the lounge offers drink specials, free pizza and, on Fridays, live entertainment. Others come in the evening, when the pizza/appetizer bar remains open long after the main kitchen closes. Friday and Saturday nights feature live music. Wolf Canyon serves four classic brews daily plus two "brewer's choices," which might include a Scottish ale, a double bock or perhaps something more exotic like black cherry beer in the winter or raspberry ale in summer. Wolf Canyon stays open until 11 PM during the week and midnight on weekends. The kitchen stays open until 9 PM on weekdays and 10 PM on Friday and Saturday.

Teen Scene

Santa Fe doesn't have much to offer in the way of nightlife for teenagers. The younger-than-21 set is pretty much left to its own devices to create evening entertainment. For

---

INSIDERS' TIP

Santa Fe restaurants and bars that participate in the county's Designated Driver Program will provide soft drinks on the house to a table's designated driver(s). Some establishments even offer the entire table free snacks.

many, that means skateboarding until curfew in the summertime (see our Parks and Recreation chapter) and movies the rest of the year. There are the occasional raves— all-night warehouse teen parties with nonstop dancing to electronic music spun by talented deejays in the dazzle high-tech lights, video images and special effects. Raves are a word-of-mouth phenomenon. Occasionally, flyers will appear on bulletin boards, and that is all the invitation you need. Here are a few other suggestions.

Harambe
Trades West Rd. • 424-9044

Harambe is a performing arts and cultural education center that specializes in outreach for at-risk teens. It's housed in a 5,000-square-foot refurbished warehouse with two dance studios and performance areas. Harambe, which means "we shall pull together" in Swahili, organizes evening and all-night dances and performances primarily for individuals between 13 and 25 years old. One of the aims is to expose teens and young adults to the music and dance of other cultures in addition to the hip-hop and electronic music to which they're more accustomed. Harambe tries to stage twice-monthly all-night functions starting at 11 PM on a weekend night and continuing until 8 AM the next morning. Other weekends feature musical, theater or dance events. During the day and early evening, Harambe offers free classes in the afternoon and early evenings that might include urban, free-style or modern dancing, drumming, mar-

tial arts, computers and languages. The organization is in the process of building a recording studio for vinyl, tapes and CDs. Hours of business are 11 AM to 10 PM. Anyone is welcome to stop by and hang out.

Silva Lanes Bowling Center
1352 Rufina Circle • 471-7250

Silva Lanes is great evening entertainment for all ages, and many teens like to go here on weekend nights or week nights when school is out. And the price is right, too, starting at $1.20 to $2.75 a game plus $1 to $1.75 to rent shoes. See our Recreation chapter for more information.

Warehouse 21
1614 Paseo de Peralta • 989-4423

Founded in 1990 as CCA (Center for Contemporary Arts) Teen Warehouse, Warehouse 21 helps fill the void of youth-oriented activities in Santa Fe for 10- to 21-year-olds. During the day, the organization sponsors free after-school workshops and seminars in the arts — from knitting and puppetry to acting, deejaying, guitar, photography, silkscreening and tai chi. It also forges apprenticeships, internships and mentorships. At night Warehouse 21 produces music shows and dances every couple of weeks featuring live local bands on Friday nights and deejayed rock dances on Saturdays followed by swing dancing. During the summer, the organization stages outdoor screenings of monster flicks, 3D films and other movies of interest to teenagers.

Albertsons®

FOOD & DRUG

Santa Fe

- 199 Paseo De Peralta

- 2006 Cerrillos Road

Shopping

The most difficult decision about shopping in Santa Fe is where to start. The clusters of stores and the shopping plazas in the downtown area can lure even the most shopping-resistant travelers. The city's unique shops delight visitors and draw return local business. Often located in former homes, many of the specialty shops downtown and on Canyon Road are built around pleasant courtyards with fountains and well-tended gardens. Of course, like Any Town, U.S.A., Santa Fe has malls, chain stores, a flea market and outlets to fill all kinds of shopping needs.

In this chapter we describe Santa Fe's main shopping areas, followed by a listing of specialty stores. We couldn't possibly list all of the fine places to shop, but we've done our best to include a representative sample. Santa Fe has such an eclectic and plentiful arts and crafts market that we've included those types of stores in their own chapter, Regional Arts and Crafts, and in the "Galleries" section of our Arts chapter. Retail businesses can change quickly so don't be shy about checking out a shop or boutique that may have opened since we finished this guide.

Cash, credit cards and traveler's checks are welcome in most of the area's specialty shops, malls, plazas, boutiques and shopping centers. Most shops are open from 9 or 10 AM until 5 or 6 PM Monday through Saturday, and some are open Sunday afternoons.

Santa Fe is a great place to find items you might not be able to buy at home — locally made crafts, chile-based products or cookbooks that specialize in the cuisine of the region. The city has an active arts community, and many shops carry handmade work at affordable prices. And, of course, there's no reason to go home without a Santa Fe T-shirt.

Shopping Areas

Downtown/The Plaza

The Plaza sits between San Francisco Street, Old Santa Fe Trail, Palace Avenue and Lincoln Avenue, and the Downtown area stretches two or three blocks from the Plaza in all directions. You'll find city-owned parking lots on Water, San Francisco and Marcy streets. There's limited on-street parking, and some private lots are available for shoppers.

As the last stop along both *El Camino Real* and the better-known Santa Fe Trail, the Plaza has been a shopping paradise since the days when wagons unloaded their imported treasures here. If you time your visit right, you can still shop there on days when the city hosts outdoor arts and crafts shows or during Spanish or Indian Market (see our Annual Events chapter). The Plaza pulses with activity, especially in the summer. On special occasions, parades march around and music pours from the bandstand. The Plaza's shady benches offer an ideal place to take a break while shopping.

We think the best guide for shopping in the Plaza area is to follow your nose. So stroll along the streets just off the Plaza: Marcy Street, Galisteo Street, Don Gaspar Avenue, Water Street, Shelby Street and others. It's easy to stumble into the most delightful places and find just what you weren't looking for sweetly beckoning. The nooks and crannies in this easily walked area can provide days of just-poking-around entertainment.

In this central location you won't find many "deep discounts." Downtown shops pay steep rent for the privilege of high accessibility to visitors.

The overall tenor of Santa Fe's downtown area is galleries, American Indian goods and tourist souvenirs such as T-shirts and coffee mugs, but you'll discover an interesting variety of upscale merchandise here.

The most intriguing spot for buying Indian wares is under the *portal* of the Palace of the Governors on Palace Avenue (see our Attractions chapter). Another first-rate place for Indian merchandise is Packard's Indian Trading Co., on the corner of Old Santa Fe Trail and San Francisco.

If you're in the market for souvenirs, visit Dressman's Gifts, 58 Lincoln Avenue, just across the Plaza. This longtime business is geared for the tourist who wants to take back some inexpensive reminders of Santa Fe. You'll find Indian jewelry, other crafts and gifts and a large selection of T-shirts.

Just down the street, across from a Häagen Dazs ice cream shop and bakery, Ortega's on the Plaza has sold fine Indian jewelry for 25 years. You may find a pot by the famous San Ildefonso Pueblo potter María Martínez here. Other downtown shops with Indian goods are the Eagle Dancer, Virginia Trading Post, Desert Blossom, Pueblo Trading Company and the Santa Fe Indian Trading Company.

Plaza Galeria on San Francisco Street is an arcade of shops selling T-shirts, prints, *kachinas*, sculptures, *concha* belts and sports clothes.

Down the street is a Christmas shop, called The Shop, 116 E. Palace, selling the most ornaments this side of the North Pole, many in the Pueblo Indian style. The Shop has a second downtown location at 114 Old Santa Fe Trail.

You'll find the Plaza Mercado Shopping Plaza at 112 W. San Francisco Street. This complex spans a solid half-block and includes an interesting variety of shops and restaurants arranged over three stories. Nambé Foundry has a shop here selling the beautiful, silver-colored metalware they've been designing and manufacturing since 1951. You'll find every-thing from heavy baking dishes to Christmas ornaments, and you can also buy seconds. The Mercado complex includes the Santa Fe School of Cooking, with its shop of all you need to make your own New Mexican recipes.

Around the corner on Don Gaspar Avenue you'll find more shops including Spirit of the Earth, which features jewelry by Tony Malmed, clothing and collectibles.

FYI

Unless otherwise noted, the area code for all phone numbers listed in this guide is 505.

Need a chocolate break? Head for the Rocky Mountain Chocolate Factory on San Francisco Street. The wafting aroma of freshly made candy flows all the way out to the sidewalk. What an enticement!

Origins, 135 W. San Francisco Street, has been around for 25 years and feels a little like a folk art/textile museum, showing dolls, puppets, jewelry and wearable art from around the world. You'll find clothing from Africa, Pakistan, India and Thailand as well as creations by local designers. Just walking in makes you feel elegant.

Intermixed with downtown's Indian focus, you'll find many chic and original clothing stores such as Chico's, 328 Guadalupe Street; Char of Santa Fe, 101 W. Marcy Street; and Susan K's, 135 W. Palace Avenue.

The White House, 112 W. San Francisco Street, is a small, intimate women's shop with sleek dresses, blazers and slacks all in white or light beige. Santa Fe Dry Goods, 53 Old Santa Fe Trail, a steady fixture in downtown merchandizing, features tasteful shoes and scarves and clothing for men and women.

A few nationally known stores usually found in malls add to the Plaza mix. You'll find places like Banana Republic, 123 W. San Francisco Street, for the casual look; The Gap, 78 E. San Francisco Street, for the young look; Talbots for the stylish look; J.Crew for the sporty look; Eddie Bauer for the outdoor look and Ann Taylor for the professional look. (Talbots, J.Crew, Eddie Bauer and Ann Taylor are all in Lincoln Place, a shopping complex at 130 Lincoln Avenue.) But keep looking — Santa Fe's downtown/Plaza area has much more shopping ahead.

At 101 W. Marcy Street, the Design Warehouse has been around 16 years, offering comfortable and affordable home furnishings and kitchenware. Gloriana's, 55 W. Marcy Street, delights bead lovers with jars and bags and strands of every shape, size and color. Next door at the Marcy Street Card Shop, 75 W. Marcy Street, you can choose from more than 500 postcards and then move on to cards for birthdays, anniversaries, getting well, first communions, retirements and more. For a look at wonderful handcarved folk-art animals, take a step into Davis Mather's Folk Art Gallery on at 141 Lincoln Avenue. Be cautious: The fanciful wooden snakes beg to go home with you!

At 223 Galisteo Street you'll find Lucille's, a store packed full of those long flowing skirts you see Santa Fe women wearing, with blouses, vests, jackets and more to mix and match. The Sheepskin Overland Company, 215 Galisteo Street, a mainstay in the area, carries the most luscious coats and bags and rugs out of sheepskin and many different leathers. Artesanos Import Co., 222 Galisteo Street, displays an intriguing pottery selection and other items for home decorating and remodeling in Mexican and Southwestern style. Next door, Harry's, 202 Galisteo, carries fine men's clothing as well as some great items for the ladies.

Sena Plaza
121-135 Palace Ave. • no central phone

Although it's downtown, Sena Plaza deserves mention all its own because of its special shopping ambiance. This former family home, one block east of the Plaza on Palace Avenue, offers a variety of shops as well as a first-class restaurant. You can park behind the building. It's easy to find Sena Plaza: The sidewalk running in front is covered by a low wooden *portal*. Originally part of a 1697 land grant, the place still has that old Spanish ambiance. The two-story building was once the gracious home of the Senas, a prominent family. Myriad rooms run under long *portals*, all facing an enclosed patio.

The original adobe rooms now house galleries and specialty shops with a diversity that can keep you browsing for hours. Goler Fine Imported Shoes tempts the most sophisticated feet with snazzy shoe styles, and Taos Mountain Candles De Santa Fe offers an array of shaped, colored and scented candles. The

cleverly named Soap Opera carries a wide range of fragrances, lotions, massage oils and items for the bath. Gusterman Silversmith shows a fine collection of original affordable jewelry. The African Trader takes you instantly to a continent of deep jungles and mysterious traditions.

Susan's Christmas Shop gets the prize for best use of a tiny space. You'll find ornaments from around the world with a nice selection of handmade Southwestern items. Zephyr offers unusually handsome women's clothing.

Canyon Road

Best known for its galleries, this scenic, narrow street is worth a visit. Canyon Road begins just east of Paseo de Peralta and runs roughly parallel to Alameda Street. You can walk from downtown hotels. Historically important and currently quaint, the road began as a trail down from the mountains. People would lead their burros this way into town to sell or trade their wares.

The area teems with Santa Fe charm: thick adobe walls draped with vines, sidewalks shaded from large cottonwood trees, lovely gardens and a mix of residential and commercial uses — shops, restaurants and galleries. You can easily spend a day moseying along the road, taking your time, learning how to slow down Southwestern style.

Canyon Road is famous for its galleries that line the street for blocks and blocks (see our Arts chapter). Interspersed, you'll discover clothing, jewelry, leather and crafts stores. Most of the retail shops cluster near the intersection of Camino del Monte Sol. A walk of just a few blocks on either side of this corner will take you to most of the shops.

Gypsy Alley, 708 Canyon Road, can lure even the most leg-weary tourist. This once dusty place, now lined with flower beds brimming with color in summer, has been renovated into a row of shops (and of course more galleries). Nestor's Universe: Outsider Art, 708 Canyon Road, is a unique craft shop selling necklaces, folk art, tiles, stained-glass suncatchers, scarves and rugs. The owners will explain that everything in their store is made by "people marginalized," a growing phenomenon in the country. It means crafts by prisoners, the mentally impaired or the institutionalized. Take a look.

Judy's Unique Apparel, 714 Canyon Road, with offerings for both men and women, is worth an excursion in itself. The colors and textures of the clothes will make you want to linger, touch and try things on.

At Artisan/Santa Fe, 717 Canyon Road, an art-supply store packed to the gills, you'll find what you need for that creative urge. The owners boast that Georgia O'Keeffe used to come here for all her paints and brushes. They've been in the same location for 23 years. A small parking lot for patrons is on the west side of the building.

www.insiders.com

See this and many other **Insiders' Guide®** destinations online — in their entirety.

Visit us today!

Desert Son, 725 Canyon Road, another old-timer on this street, has been selling belts, buckles, hats and silver buttons for 20 years. Its custom boots are snazzy to say the least. Wind down a path and find Canyon Road Pottery, 821 Canyon Road, a store filled with handsome glazed and originally designed contemporary pots.

Visitors know the Canyon Trading Post, 670 Canyon Road, as "the belt place." In business at this location for 20 years, the store welcomes shoppers with the distinctive scent of rich leather. In addition to a selection of 18,000 belts, you can buy tin ornaments, cactus lamps and antler chandeliers.

If you are a quilt aficionado, take a look at Quilts Ltd., 652 Canyon Road. Some 200 quilters from around the United States work for this distinctive shop, the only store of its kind in Santa Fe. It's been on Canyon Road 10 years and reminds some customers of a quilt museums as much as a shop. The beautiful one-of-a-kind quilts attract celebrity customers as well as regular buyers. You'll also find leather, tapestry and quilted clothing designed by the owner in her own local workshop.

To shop Canyon Road, park along the main road and side streets. A few stores have small lots for patrons, and a public lot is available at the intersection of Canyon Road and Camino del Monte Sol.

Guadalupe Street
Between Agua Fría and Garfield Sts.

This shopping area, also an easy walk from downtown, attracts locals and visitors.

In the '70s, Guadalupe Street was the place where several hippies tried their hand at retail — often selling their own arts and crafts — fitting their shops in among the garages and upholstery shops. Renovation has been extensive, and Guadalupe is now a street of the modern commercial age. You'll find restaurants, a movie theater, a historic church, a train station and, during the summer, the Farmers' Market (see our Attractions chapter). You'll also find a variety of original shops selling everything from furniture to fancy underwear.

One of the area's trademark businesses is Cookworks, 316 Guadalupe Street. Here, you'll find all those new gadgets no cook can be without. The buyers keep up with the latest trends — if it's 'in' they've got it. The store has been so successful, it's expanded to two other outlets on the same street. Cookworks Gourmet, 318 Guadalupe Street, sells coffees, bagel mixes, jellies, special cooking oils and pastas. Cookworks Tableware and Gifts, 322 Guadalupe, offers a great selection of high-end dinnerware and flatware. Exquisite salad bowls, soup tureens and pitchers in deep colors and rich styles imported from Italy, France, Morocco, Mexico and Peru will take your breath away.

Another landmark business is The Flower Market, at Guadalupe and Manhattan streets. Wonderful fresh-cut flowers by the stem are the speciality here. The market shares its building, an old house, with Cardrageous, a place to find unusual greeting cards of all kinds as well as wrapping paper, journals and gifts.

On the corner of Guadalupe and Read streets at 435 S. Guadalupe is Placita Guadalupe, where the High Desert Angler sells everything an angler needs. Kicks, right next door, sells everything a dancer needs. Street Feet carries everything a woman needs — shoes, clothing and accessories. (Well, not quite everything . . .)

For eight years the Rio Bravo Trading Co., 411 S. Guadalupe, has specialized in "American Indian and Western relics — collectible cowboy stuff," to use the words of the owner. Saddles, spurs, hats, chaps, Indian jewelry and Old West posters abound.

When strolling along Guadalupe Street, be sure to take a slight detour up Garfield Street to Wild Things, 316 Garfield Street. This is the place where dresses hang from the porch. Inside is stuffed with goodies. The owner, Tobi, says her place is "totally hip — with antique, vintage, ethnic, trippy clothing." She's been in business in Santa Fe for 10 years, and customers come here for the best of period pieces.

Santa Fe Pottery, 323 S. Guadalupe Street, had a Guadalupe address before the street was a shoppers' paradise. The shop has been around 26 years, specializing in dinnerware and one-of-a-kind ceramics by local potters. You'll find colorful, whimsical pieces here, and they will gladly take special orders.

Found a painting or a poster you want framed? Take it to the Frame Crafters, 321 S. Guadalupe, reliable framers with an extensive choice of mats and frames.

Another fun place is the old Santa Fe Train Station, 410 S. Guadalupe, now with a blown-glass shop and a designer-clothing store in the old depot.

At the corner of Guadalupe and Montezuma Avenue is a shopping plaza at 328 S. Guadalupe Street. Inside the Plaza are several stores, including Southwest Spanish Craftsman a stylish furniture store that has been in the area since 1927. Shoppers with a longing to live in Santa Fe will find everything they need in Southwestern carved furniture. Next thing you know, you'll have to buy a house to put it in! Next door, Paper Unlimited offers a rich supply of cards, ribbons, gift boxes and bags. Horizons, a nature-discovery store that's been around nearly 15 years, has telescopes, compasses, nature kits, bird feeders and toys, all with a scientific bent. Locals shop here for unusual, practical gifts for the nature lovers. And be sure to be lured into Allure, a high-end lingerie shop with an interesting variety of the feminine and sensuous. On the north side of Southwest Spanish Craftsman, Form and Function has sold lights and an impressive

variety of lamp shades for 12 years. Le Bon Voyage, whose owners advertise themselves as "the Bag Ladies," has a great assortment of travel accessories — portable alarm clocks and coffee warmers and the like in addition to luggage. A bookstore specializing in travel guides, The Travel Bug, adjoins them.

The shopping plaza across the street at the northeast corner of Montezuma Avenue and Guadalupe Street is a center with practical services, such as shipping and photo processing and copies, and Captain Kid's Toys, 333 Montezuma Avenue, where you'll find something tempting for the little travelers on your list. The store has a great assortment of durable toys that spark a child's imagination. You'll also find a variety of prices here.

About a half-block east of Guadalupe on Montezuma Avenue is the Base Camp, a well-stocked place to buy wilderness gear, fishing gear and books. It has been in Santa Fe nearly 18 years and is a good place to gather information.

Metered parking is available along the street. Some of the stores have free parking in very small lots.

Sanbusco Market Center
500 Montezuma Ave. • 983-9136

From Guadalupe Street, the Sanbusco Market Center is just a block to the west. The building that now houses these shops originated in 1882 as part of Santa Fe's warehouse district. Renovation in the 1980s made it a bright addition to Santa Fe's shopping options. Complete with restaurants and a spacious across-the-street parking lot, Sanbusco wins the locals' affection for agreement to host the Farmers' Market several times a week during the summer. While some of the small, upscale shops come and go here, Bodhi Bazaar is a longstanding tenant. This women's store offers linen and cotton clothing, which attracts a strong local clientele. You could walk out with something that ascends current style — fashion that will last for years.

Another local favorite is Teca Tu, a store for pets. The owner is fond of both cats and dogs, and her array of bowls and brushes, beds, collars, fancy dog blankets and leashes gives you plenty of choice for your pet. There's also a small collection of books and cards and soft, cuddly stuffed animals and cute dog vests.

On Your Feet (and On Your Feet, Too — also in Sanbusco) are fun places to shop for shoes. They carry Wolky and Sebago and other name-brand footwear. The tasteful displays feature shoes on slatted willow crates or set on old Spanish tables. Shoppers can pass directly on to the adjoining Get It Together, a woman's delight for everything drapey like scarves and dresses that give that dramatic slinky look and feel. The New Territory Leather shop carries an amazing selection of fine leather bags, Western jackets and vests. Its tapestry coats definitely say "original." The merchandise changes with the seasons.

Malls

While some longtime locals may complain that malls lack Santa Fe style, they have to acknowledge the convenience malls offer. Where else can you use your JCPenney, Sears and Dillard's cards? And you'll find specialty shops in the malls as well as national chains. At all three of Santa Fe's malls, you can buy New Mexican foods, spices and other treats as well as Indian arts and crafts to remind you of your Santa Fe vacation.

DeVargas Center
564 N. Guadalupe St. • 982-2655

At the corner of Guadalupe Street and Paseo de Peralta, DeVargas Center is Santa Fe's oldest mall. Small and easy to negotiate, DeVargas is anchored by Albertson's Food Center on the northeast side and Western Warehouse on the southeast side. Among the roughly 40 shops you'll find a post office, movie theaters, a candy shop, restaurants, antique stores, pharmacies, shoe stores, jewelry stores and several women's clothing boutiques.

Stag Tobacconist, one of the mall's longest-established merchants, sells pipes, canes, postcards and, of course, special kinds of to-

bacco. Las Cosas Kitchen Shop offers a great variety of pots and pans and many nifty gadgets for the cook. Radio Shack, Ross Dress for Less and Christine's bridal and tuxedo shop are here, along with Roberto's, a small shop that sells delightful imported dresses with exotic flavors. She Said, a bookstore for women, carries some unusual selections. Gameco offers a place for people, mostly teens, to play "Magic" and other games and to buy cards and supplies. A large Hastings has a wide selection of music, magazines, books and videos and a coffee bar. On the north end of the mall, the Mail and Parcel Center will ship your packages home. DeVargas Center is surrounded by a large parking lot, which is regularly patrolled by security officers.

Villa Linda Mall
4250 Cerrillos Rd. • 473-4253

With more than 80 shops, this is Santa Fe's largest mall, the place where teens hang with their friends and folks buy their back-to-school clothes. South of town at the corner of Rodeo and Cerrillos roads, Villa Linda is a great central place to get all those normal, necessary things. Of course some fun, unnecessary things can be found here too. Villa Linda has a food court, two six-screen movie theaters and a video arcade.

Anchors include Sears on the southwest end, JCPenney on the east, Dillard's on the north and Mervyn's on the west. Between the big department stores, scores of shops offer clothing, accessories, jewelry, shoes, sports equipment, software, home furnishings, gifts and books.

Small clothing stores are scattered throughout the mall. Deb caters to teenage girls. Lerner New York carries women's styles at reasonable prices. You can walk into Victoria's Secret and fulfill that slinky fantasy. Lane Bryant, Vanity, The Closet, Northern Reflections and Jay Jacobs offer women's casual apparel. Para Niños is exclusively for

---

INSIDERS' TIP

Santa Fe Village, a collection of shops at 227 Don Gaspar Avenue, includes some unusual offerings such as Keshi, a store that specializes in fetishes, or small carved animals, from Zuni Pueblo.

young children and carries some hard-to-resist dressy outfits. Miller's Outpost and County Seat carry clothing with a cowboy touch for men and women, as does the Western Warehouse, a store to help you dude up with pearl-button vests, jeans, shirts with fringe, fancy skirts and boots. Sports Mania has sports caps galore, jackets, T-shirts and jerseys — all with your favorite team's name. Walk into Gadzooks and feel like you've stepped out of Santa Fe and into a shop on some big-city block. The clothing here is designed for the fast lane. The front end of a VW bug in the center of the store sets the tone. Teens will love this place!

Villa Linda shoe stores include Payless ShoeSource, Kinney Shoes, Lady Foot Locker, Athletic Express, Foot Locker and Footaction USA.

Two interesting accessories shops in the mall are Afterthoughts and Claire's Boutique. Both carry a delightful array of inexpensive things for the hair and ears. For more jewelry, try Zales and Jewel Time.

In the center of the promenade running the length of the mall are booths, carts and islands, those pagodas that offer everything from seasonal specialities like Christmas ornaments or Halloween costumes to fancy reading glasses, lighters, knives and specialty foods. At Southwest Expressions, you can pick up Indian *kachinas*, Christian angels and Spanish *concha* belts.

For gifts, Trevors has country throw pillows and silk flowers. Chili Pepper Emporium sells Southwestern *ristras*, wreaths and jars of cactus jellies and jams. The Coach House offers candles, beads, T-shirts and gift bags. At Joni's Hallmark store you'll find cards, photo albums, pens and more. Need to get your glasses adjusted? Lenscrafters has a large store here.

The post office has a substation in the mall that makes mailing all your packages easy. A Walgreen Drug Store is on the northwest side. The General Nutrition Center, for all your health needs, sells supplements and supplies. You'll also find a branch of the Santa Fe Public Library here. Because the storefront space is small, the library calls it a Bookstop or even a "twig."

A large parking lot surrounds the entire mall, and security officers are always on duty.

Santa Fe Premium Outlets
I-25 at Cerrillos Rd. • 474-4000

A relatively new addition to Santa Fe, this shopping center offers about 40 factory stores selling a wide variety of name-brand merchandise at a discount. You'll find clothing, shoes, luggage, gifts and housewares. There also are also some purely local shops. The stores all open onto a central outdoor patio, and are all on one level. You can get a bite to eat here too.

In clothing, some of the name stores are Boston Traders, Brooks Brothers, London Fog, Van Heusen, Jockey and Jones New York. The range runs from casual to professional to conservative for both men and women. Tastefully displayed items make it hard to resist the deals.

Sissel's — Fine Indian Jewelry, Pottery and Kachinas carries just what the sign says and lots of it. With a sharp eye you can get some good buys. The Peruvian Connection sells textiles from that South American country.

For home furnishings, among the stores you'll find are Dansk, Royal Doulton and Villeroy and Boch. Shopping for shoes? Try on styles from Cole Haan, Joan and David, Famous Footwear and Etienne Aigner. Top-quality luggage and leather goods are available at Bruce Alan, Coach and Sharif Collection. There's plenty of parking here, and the views of the mountains are marvelous.

Specialty Shops

Here's a brief introduction to some of Santa Fe's more interesting shops.

Antiques and Home-Decorator Items

Antique Warehouse
530 S. Guadalupe St., #B at the railyard • 984-1159

This store's name isn't trendy; it really is a warehouse in Santa Fe's original warehouse district. You'll find more than 300 sets of doors and shutters, along with gates and windows from Mexico. Telephone inquiries are welcome,

Fresh seasonal produce is available at the Santa Fe Farmers' Market and roadside stands.

Photo: Don Strel/Southwest Assignments

but it's fun to come and look. It's closed on Sunday.

Artesanos Imports Co.
222 Galisteo St. • 983-1743

Mexican imports are the specialty in this store, which has been in the same location for 31 years. The quantity and variety are dazzling. Artesanos has lights, tile, glass and pottery items, some stored in a large outdoor lot. You'll find genuine pigskin furniture as well as hundreds of types of tile for the floor, bath or countertop. Artesanos says it is the largest distributor of Mexican tile in the United States. It's closed on Sunday.

Foreign Traders
202 Galisteo St. • 983-6441

Heavy carved tables and other furniture, glassware of all sorts and other items imported from Mexico are in abundance at Foreign Traders. This shop was originally established in 1927, just across the street from its present location, by Tony Taylor, Lady Bird Johnson's brother.

Jackalope Pottery
2820 Cerrillos Rd. • 471-8539

You can spend several hours here poking around and looking at all the imported pots, figurines, weavings, clothing and decorations. Jackalope's international collection of goodies occupies several large buildings, including one that looks like an old church. Don't miss the prairie dog village. You may find music on the patio in the summer. This company, which began in Santa Fe in 1975, now has several other outlets and a catalog business.

El Paso Imports
Design Ctr., 418 Cerrillos Rd. • 982-5698
• 320 Sandoval St. • 986-0037

This business has been around many years, carrying an extensive selection of old and new furniture shipped in from Mexico. Tables, wardrobes, bedframes and other large items are a specialty.

Christopher Selser, American Indian and New Mexican Antiques
830 Canyon Rd. • 984-1481

You can pick up some good deals here among the top-quality wares. The collection is well-displayed to show the antiques and art to optimum advantage. Selser, a national expert on Indian antiques, was recently featured on a PBS special.

Southwest Spanish Craftsman
328 S. Guadalupe St. • 982-1767

In business since 1927, this store specializes in heavy Southwestern carved chairs, tables, beds and sofas. The look that characterizes the selection is one of carefully constructed solidity. You'll also find Southwestern tinwork here. It's closed on Sunday.

The Santa Fe Look — Women's Apparel

The following list of shops, by no means complete, provides a few places where you can find the items you might need to complete your Santa Fe look — boots, flowing skirts, *concha* belts, velvet or satin blouses and turquoise jewelry. Also included are some places that sell wearable art. If your favorite

isn't here, just let us know, and we'll try to include it the next time.

Judy's Unique Apparel
714 Canyon Rd. • 988-5746

A fire in the fireplace welcomes visitors to Judy's on winter days. The lovely clothing — from casual to evening wear, from practical to romantic, from pampering silks to linens to cozy jackets —occupies several rooms. You'll find hats, belts and unique jewelry patterned after antiques. The prices are such that locals remain among Judy's longtime clientele and recommend this place to friends and visitors. There's also a menswear section and plenty of places for non-shoppers to wait comfortably. The staff is helpful and will let you wander through the store at your own speed. Judy Broughten started the business in 1978 as a painted-T-shirt shop in one of the rooms Judy's now so nicely occupies.

Lucille's
223 Galisteo St. • 983-6331

A front-porch sale rack welcomes shoppers here. Lucille's specializes in Santa Fe style and its creative variations, with plenty of flowing skirts, dresses, silk T-shirts, blouses and tops. Natural fibers are the rule, with merchandise imported from India and elsewhere. Shoppers like the ranges of styles, colors and sizes — including clothing that looks great on full-figured women. Lucille's also has a tempting collection of earrings at $20 or less and fanciful necklaces from Africa and India. The shop carries sweaters all year long.

Maya
108 Galisteo St. • 989-7590

If you're shopping for something different, the fashions hanging outside this downtown store are sure to catch your eye. Indoors, you'll discover two stories packed with folk art and fashion. In addition to easy-to-wear blouses, pants, skirts, dresses and vests imported from around the world, you'll find all sorts of jewelry, belts and hats. This eclectic shop also offers international folk art including carvings from India, *milagros* — charms from Latin America that are said to aid in healing — and a wonderful assortment of Day of the Dead figures from Mexico.

Origins
135 W. San Francisco St. • 988-4626

This is one of those stores that compels you to go inside — even if there's absolutely nothing you think you need. For starters, the windows skillfully combine art and marketing, displaying the clothing and accessories in combination with folk art for eye-catching results. Among the plentiful merchandise are creations especially designed for this shop, wearable art by local and world-renowned artists from elsewhere in the United States and Europe. Evening wear and the more casual fashions include styles and sizes that look great on every woman, not just the size 2s. The jewelry, including 18 and 24 karat gold, and objects from around the world will demand your attention.

FYI

Unless otherwise noted, the area code for all phone numbers listed in this guide is 505.

Pat Peterson's Blue Rose
131 W. San Francisco St. • 989-9594

It's easy to miss this shopping treasure chest because it doesn't have a street-front show window. But if you're looking for handmade, one-of-a-kind fashions, seek it out. Blue Rose represents 25 New Mexico fabric artists on consignment, with creations ranging from handwoven vests and shape-flattering jackets to lacy, flowing skirts that make you want to dance flamenco. Examples of Blue Rose fashions greet you from the hallway, and this shoe-box-shape store uses overhead space to great advantage. Peterson has been in business since 1990 and planned to add a catalog to her marketing tools for 1998.

Purple Sage
110 Don Gaspar Ave. • 984-0600

Handwoven clothing is a specialty here, and you'll find styles from Santa Fe chic to elegant silks. Ask about the sueded rayons, designed and handmade by a local fabric artist. Be sure to take a look at the nice assortment of handbags. Contemporary handwoven jackets and shawls in rayon chenille are one of Purple Sage's trademarks. Another is the colorful handblown glass that makes this store not just another fashion shop. More than 35 glassblowers show their wares, including many perfume bottles, platters and vases. You'll also find gift items along with an impressive assortment of kaleidoscopes. For non-shoppers, Purple Sage has couches, magazines, TV and candy. Can't decide? Take home a catalog for phone orders.

Sign of the Pampered Maiden
123 W. Water St. • 982-5948

In business since 1968, this tasteful women's clothing and accessory store specializes in what the owner aptly describes as comfortable, beautiful clothing you can wear every day. You'll find her inventory on the romantic side, with plenty of velvet, lace and silk. Granddaughters, moms and grandmothers can shop together here — and take home something they'll like. In addition to clothing, this downtown shop also offers a variety of accessories to complement the fashions.

Spirit of the Earth
108 Don Gaspar Ave. • 988-9558

In business in Santa Fe for more than a decade, Spirit of the Earth sells clothing that could be described as wearable art and jewelry by designer Tony Malmed in gold with precious stones and festive opals. Malmed's bracelets, rings, necklaces, earrings and the like are one-of-a-kind pieces, which means if you like it and it fits your budget, take it home because you'll never find it again. The fashions are soft and sensual in cut velvets, lace and sueded rayons with a feminine flowing look. You'll find an abundance of color and luscious tactile fabrics. The sales staff knows how to be helpful without being pushy and are happy to help you make the right choice to complement your figure and coloring.

Styles de Santa Fe
112 W. San Francisco St. • 982-5675
128 W. Water St. • 982-5100

What we have here is big-time, quintessential Santa Fe style. Nearly all the clothing is especially made for these two stores with design and fabric changes based on conversations between the owner and her customers. The approach works; Styles de Santa Fe has been in business for nearly two decades in a town where many retailers quickly fail. This is the perfect place to buy the characteristic broomstick skirt — so called because the pleats were once made by wrapping yards of material tightly around a broomstick. You'll find several styles of blouses to go with your skirt, two types of dresses and a variety of belts to finish off your Santa Fe look. Cotton, rayon suede, silks and other fabrics are available in a rainbow of colors that the shop adjusts according to season. Styles de Santa Fe also carries some fashions by other labels, including Route 66 designers of Albuquerque. Styles de Santa Fe offers a catalog so you can order what you like in between visits to Santa Fe. The staff will treat you well too.

Bargain Shopping

Act 2
410-B Old Santa Fe Tr. • 983-8585

At Act 2 you'll discover vintage and modern clothing, jewelry and accessories. You might have to hunt for this shop — it's slightly off the beaten path near the Pink Adobe Restaurant — but it's worth the search.

Double Take
320 Aztec St. • 989-8836

This shop, on Aztec Street just off Guadalupe Street, labels itself "eclectic," with styles for men, women and children. The items are carefully chosen and well-displayed — you don't have to wade through junk. The management mixes a few new items with the old, and the layout makes going through the racks exciting. If you're interested in furniture, ask to see theirs.

Encore 505
505 Old Santa Fe Tr. • 983-5055

This upscale consignment shop is in the Kaune's Market Center. You'll find nice women's clothing and colorful and unusual accessories to make you feel like a million dollars.

Goodwill Industries Store
927 Baca St. • 983-7156

Careful shoppers can discover old favorites or something they've always wanted to read in the book racks at Goodwill. The sales are hard to beat. This store, unlike many thrift stores in Santa Fe, tends to have furniture. Proceeds benefit Goodwill and its rehabilitation work.

Photo: Don Strel/Southwest Assignments

The White House offers a unique shopping alternative — all white clothing.

Hospice Center Thrift Store
3961 Cerrillos Rd. • 471-6857

You can stop at the Hospice store on your way to Villa Linda Mall and find all sorts of secondhand treasures — some of the nicest things you'll find in the recycled world. Items for sale have been appraised, so you know you're getting your money's worth. The funds raised help the nonprofit Hospice Center continue its highly respected work with the dying and their families.

La Luz de Santa Fe
2325 Cerrillos Rd. • 438-0877

This is your basic thrift store with "sack sales" — all you can load up in a grocery bag for a dollar or two. Prices may not be posted — feel free to make an offer. Proceeds from the clothing and other items purchased help this nonprofit Christian group continue its work with homeless families.

Open Hands Thrift Stores
3965 Cerrillos Rd. • 438-9290
851 W. San Mateo Rd. • 986-1077
905 W. Alameda St. • 989-7209

Open Hands outlets serve Santa Fe residents throughout the city. The well-stocked stores have lots of choices in clothing and household goods at good prices. The donations and sales receipts go for a worthy cause — operation of their adult day care and other programs for the elderly.

St. Vincent De Paul Thrift Store
1088 Early St. • 988-4308

You'll find racks and racks of goodies in this store, all at low prices. Operated by a Catholic auxiliary, money raised through this business benefits Santa Fe's poor.

Salvation Army Thrift Store
1202 Camino Carlos Rey • 473-7735

This is Santa Fe's largest thrift store. You'll find everything from furniture to wedding dresses and racks of clothing for the whole family. The Salvation Army's programs provide crucial help to Santa Fe's children and poor families. In addition to holiday meals, one popular project provides back-to-school clothing for children.

Trader Jack's Flea Market
U.S. Hwy. 84/285 • no phone

This huge flea market sits on Tesuque Pueblo land (16 miles northwest of Santa Fe) right next to the Santa Fe Opera in one of those wonderful Santa Fe juxtapositions. Open Friday, Saturday and Sunday from 8 AM to 5 PM, connoisseurs say this is one of the best markets of its kind around. You'll find whole sections of antiques, imports from Africa, Bali, South and Central America, vintage and handmade clothing and more. Depending on the season, you might be able to take home watermelons, apples from northern New Mexico orchards or fresh flowers. You'll see tables by commercial dealers who specialize in Indian jewelry, rainsticks or collectible fishing tackle as well as neighbors who've pooled their junk and brought it here rather than having a yard sale. Nonprofit agencies rent space to sell donated treasures and raise a few bucks. It's easy to spend hours and money as you amble among the stalls. If you get hungry or thirsty, you can buy what you need from the concession stand. Parking and admission are free.

Yard Sales

Santa Fe residents love their yard sales. If you read *The New Mexican* any weekend during the summer, you're likely to find scores of yard sales, estate sales, multifamily sales, garage sales — junk and treasure recycling opportunities by any name you can think of. Clothing, toys, furniture, books, treats and necessities for baby, exercise bikes, antiques, plants, knickknacks and all those things you don't know how you managed to live without await you. Saturday is the big sale day, but some folks extend buyers the opportunity to visit Sunday as well.

The best selection goes to those who arrive early, but please respect the "no early birds" advisory. Real bargains can come to those who shop late, waiting until the seller would rather make a sweet deal than repack his or her items to save them for another sale or donate them to Salvation Army or Open Hands. While May through September is Santa Fe's prime yard sale season, you'll find a sprinkling of sales sooner and later in the year, depending on the weather. Take small bills and change; the seller will smile at you. Be sure to poke through boxes and bags — while families tend to display their best stuff, taste varies. And if you see something you like that you think is overpriced, make an offer. If the seller refuses, you can leave your phone number for him or her to call later if the item hasn't sold.

Bookstores — New Books and Magazines

Ark Books
133 Romero St. • 988-3709

Ark Books is a mainstay for New Age books and tapes, but the store has a good selection of material on self-improvement, anthropology, cultural studies, women's issues and more. You'll find nice jewelry and stones as well as drums and tarot cards. Authors sometimes come here to speak and sign. The Ark, operating out of a converted home in a largely residential area, opened in 1980, survived a fire and came back bigger than ever.

Book Warehouse
Santa Fe Premium Outlets, I-25 at Cerrillos Rd. • 473-5508

You'll find discounts on already discounted books at the Book Warehouse. Good deals await in children's books, former bestsellers, big photo books, cookbooks and more!

The Collected Works Bookstore
208-B San Francisco St. • 988-4226

This store gets the prize for Santa Fe bookstore longevity; it's been in the same downtown location since 1978. You'll find healthy Southwestern and Indian sections as well as a good selection of nature, travel and children's books in this easy-to-browse store. Local and regional authors sometimes sign here. The staff is great with special orders, and they will ship your orders.

Downtown Subscription
376 Garcia St. • 983-3085

This place has one of the best selections of magazines in Santa Fe. The atmosphere is always lively, and you can get a good latte and a pastry to keep up your energy while you read. Locals love this hangout. Don't miss the back garden.

Garcia Street Books
376 Garcia St. • 986-0151

This locally owned and operated bookstore has a wide variety of books and a great computer system that helps you find what you need. Book people work here, and it's an easy stroll from Canyon Road. Garcia sometimes hosts autograph parties.

Hastings Books and Music & Video
2414 Cerrillos Rd. in College Plaza • 473-5775
542 N. Guadalupe St. in DeVargas Ctr. • 988-3973

In addition to the bestsellers and selections for kids, these stores carry good representations of books about the Southwest. You can rent videos, buy cards and magazines and shop for CDs and tapes here too.

Horizons — The Discovery Store
328 S. Guadalupe St. • 983-1554

Peruse an outstanding collection of nature books for children and adults in this science store. You'll find guide books galore, along with a nice assortment of globes, atlases, binoculars and gifts for children and adults with an interest in the natural world around them.

La Fonda Newsstand
La Fonda Hotel, 100 E. San Francisco St.
• 988-1404

How do they pack so much interesting stuff into such a small space? Especially designed for tourists, La Fonda has a collection of Southwestern books covering the most often requested titles. You'll also discover some unusual magazines as well as old favorites.

Good Books
526 W. Cordavas Rd. • 992-1900

This store advertises itself as a "general bookstore with a Christian specialty." In addition to a large collection of books, it carries cards and tapes.

Palace Avenue Books
209 E. Palace Ave. • 986-0536

Look here for scholarly, hard-to-find books and Southwestern titles. The store features museum art books, volumes on American Indians, Western history and more. They'll gladly ship your purchase home.

Railyard Books
340 Read St. • 995-0533

In this comfortable bookstore you can nestle into a sofa and spend a while discovering which book you can't put down. The small coffee shop on the premises adds to the ambiance. Railyard carries sheet music too. This is a popular spot for book signings. Check out the staff-recommended titles.

Spirit Flight Bookstore and Psychic/Healing Center
924 Paseo de Peralta • 983-4495

This place has everything you need to transport you to other realms. It carries a good selection of spiritual reading material, from bestsellers to more esoteric volumes.

St. John's College Bookstore
1160 Camino de la Cruz Blanca
• 984-6056

This store is a wonderful place to browse. As one would expect from a college which focuses on the "great books," you'll discover an excellent selection of the classics here as well as mainstream titles and more experimental literary offerings. While you're here, take a look at the attractive campus.

Travel Bug
328 Montezuma Ave. • 992-0418

A sister store to the popular Garcia Street Books, this outlet specializes in travel books, maps, guides, travel journals and what they call "airplane books" — easy-to-read fiction you don't mind leaving at the airport.

Waldenbooks
Villa Linda Mall, 4250 Cerrillos Rd.
• 473-4050

At Waldenbooks you'll find a nice section of regional books and an extensive travel section as well as all the bestsellers you'd expect from one of America's biggest book retailers. The convenient mall location makes this a popular weekend spot.

Books — Used, Rare and Hard to Find

Blue Moon Books and Video
329 Garfield St. • 982-3035

In an old house turned bookstore, Blue Moon's books and rooms seem to go on and on — it's easy to lose yourself in the stacks. Not only will you find your way out again, but you'll also discover a great selection of videos to rent or buy, and a staff that knows the inventory.

INSIDERS' TIP

Don't miss the museum shops if you're looking for an unusual gift or a present for yourself to remind you of your trip to Santa Fe. In addition to the Museum of New Mexico, the Santa Fe Children's Museum, El Rancho de las Golondrinas and the Wheelwright Museum all have well-stocked shops with unusual, top-quality merchandise.

Books and More Books
1341 Cerrillos Rd. • 983-5438

A well-stocked, well-organized bookstore, Books and More Books offers pre-owned treasures in categories ranging from art to science. Ask the owner, a poet, for his recommendations on a specific topic.

Book Mountain
Used Paperback Exchange
2101 Cerrillos Rd. • 471-2625.

The owners know the merchandise, and this storefront space is crammed with books of all kinds. You'll find a good selection of mysteries and romances as well as bestsellers, Westerns and even comic books. You can pick up some inexpensive vacation reading and trade them in when you're done for something else.

Margolis and Moss
129 W. San Francisco St. • 982-1028

This fine store carries rare books and prints, photographs and ephemera. It has been a fond fixture of Santa Fe's book world for many years. You'll find things here you didn't even know you needed!

Nicholas Potter Bookseller
211 E. Palace Ave. • 983-5434

Now located in an old house on historic Palace Avenue, Potter has made use of all the available space — and then some — to the delight of his established customers and newcomers who might chance on the store. A selective and savvy book dealer, Potters has been in the book business for 28 years. He knows his trade.

Specialty Foods
and Health Products

Alfalfa's Market
333 W. Cordova Rd. • 986-8667

This supermarket-size food store also has an extensive restaurant/deli and one of Santa Fe's best salad bars. Besides organic meat and veggies and wonderful freshly baked bread, you can get vitamins, hair products, dairy products and dairy alternatives.

Herbs Etc.
1345 Cerrillos Rd. • 982-1265

Jars of dried leaves, stems and flowers cover the shelves at Herbs Etc. You can find tinctures, oils and infusions as well as herbs packed in capsules just like Tylenol. The people who work here can answer health questions from an alternative perspective.

Kaune Food Town
511 Old Santa Fe Tr. • 982-2629

This is a great place for the gourmet shopper. You'll find out-of-the-ordinary sauces and mustards, imported crackers and caviar to spread on them. Kaune's carries jars and cans of everything you need to fix that unique Asian, Italian or otherwise one-of-a-kind meal. This locally owned grocery is packed with the unusual and exotic, but you can also buy milk, eggs and, if you must, sliced white bread. It carries a fine selection of fresh meat and welcomes holiday orders.

Kaune's Grocery Co.
208 Washington Ave. • 983-7378

This store always offers some excellent buys on wines and spirits. It also has all the basics, fresh meat and a nice assortment of fancy food. It's within walking distance to several downtown accommodations — a blessing for visitors staying downtown. Despite the names, the two Kaune's are not under the same management or owners.

Kokoman Circus
301 Garfield St. • 983-7770

A relatively new deli, bar and restaurant, Kokoman has uncommon wines and spirits as well as fresh breads and fine chocolates. You

INSIDERS' TIP

For a special reminder of Santa Fe, take home coffee from Las Civas Coffee Roasters. They've come up with a special Barkin' Brew blend, whose proceeds benefit the Santa Fe Humane Society.

The Santa Fe Flea Market is a popular shopping attraction.

can get a sandwich, a cup of soup and a latte as well as everything you need to fix them on your own. Save room for dessert — they usually have at least a half-dozen tasty things to choose from.

The Market Place Natural Grocery
627 W. Alameda St. • 984-2852

Santa Fe's oldest health-food store, The Market Place and its local ownership and management helps it fill an important niche. This small alternative grocery stocks an amazing array of food, including an interesting section of prepared carry-home items.

Vitality!
513 Camino De Los Marquez • 983-5557

This shop is one of the old standbys of Santa Fe's alternative health community. Not just another health-food store, Vitality! bills itself as an alternative-health center (see our Healthcare and Wellness chapter). Staff consultants are ready to answer questions about homeopathy, vitamin therapies, herbs and supplements. They also have offered urine and saliva testing to speed diagnosis and get one on a personal health plan.

Wild Oats Community Market
1090 St. Francis Dr. • 983-5333
1708 Llano St. • 474-4943

These big, clean, well-lit stores are a cross between a mainstream supermarket and a health-food store. Everything exotic you need, like those little Chinese roots called for in some esoteric recipe, can be found here. Both stores have great carry-out food sections and place to eat in the store. The St. Francis Drive store is the larger of the two and frequently hosts workshops on various aspects of health and nutrition. Wild Oats is a quickly growing national enterprise that began in Colorado.

Oriental Rugs

Guadalupe Fine Oriental Rug Gallery
314 Guadalupe St. • 988-2181

These importers carry kilims and somaks — old styles and new designs, antique and contemporary. They've been in the same location 16 years and will ship anywhere in the United States.

Santa Fe Oriental Rugs
212 Galisteo St. • 982-5152

In business 18 years, the owner says this shop carries "the largest inventory of anyone in town both in quantity and quality." Its fine display room will make you want to take home a whole truck load.

Santa Kilim
401 Guadalupe St. • 986-0340

In Santa Kilim, you'll feel like you've walked into a sheik's tent with wall-to-wall tribal rugs and antiques. The colors and textures are luscious, and outdoor displays lure visitors strolling along Guadalupe Street.

Seret and Sons Rugs and Furnishings
232 Galisteo St. • 983-5008
148 E. Alameda St. • 988-9151

This long-established rug dealership offers tremendous variety. The Galisteo showroom covers 65,000 square feet, and the space displays not only rugs but also other exotic imports, including life-sized carved horses. The Alameda location offers an outdoor display area that's like an Eastern rug bazaar. Seret custom-makes its own furniture.

Among the pueblo people, the Hopi are the best-known basket-makers, with different colors and designs reflecting the artistry of each village.

Regional Arts and Crafts

In addition to its deserved reputation as one of the best cities in the nation to buy fine art, Santa Fe also offers a host of wonderful places to purchase arts and crafts by American Indian and Hispanic artisans. There are many ways to approach this kind of shopping, and they're all fun.

Some visitors spend time learning as much as they can about such things as traditional Indian jewelry, pottery, baskets and weaving. Others, fascinated by the city's Spanish heritage, gravitate toward the Hispanic artisans' *santos*, tinwork and straw inlay. These savvy shoppers try to find out who are the best among the modern practitioners of these indigenous crafts and then search Santa Fe's shops for their work.

Other shoppers just follow their eyes to bracelets, earrings, bolo ties, pots of all sizes, shapes and design, and masterful handwoven rugs. They discover a wealth of other American Indian arts and crafts and Hispanic treasures.

Whatever method you pick, you'll find that Santa Fe offers dozens of attractive options. There's no problem finding beautiful shops that sell first-quality Indian-made items; places to buy traditional Hispanic arts and crafts are harder to come by but worth the search.

Among the good places to shop for American Indian items are the **Plaza Vendors Market** beneath the *portal* of the Palace of the Governors, 107 W. Palace Avenue, and the shop operated by the Museum of New Mexico at the Palace — where you may also find some Hispanic art as well. You can see and buy interesting Indian jewelry, pottery and weavings as well as a fine selection of books at the shop at the **Museum of Indian Arts and Culture**, 710 Camino Lejo. The shops at the **Institute of American Indian Arts Museum**, 108 Cathedral Place, and the **Wheelwright Museum**, 704 Camino Lejo, also offer authentic handmade Indian items. You'll find Hispanic arts and crafts and other interesting items at the shop at **El Rancho de las Golondrinas** a few miles out of town in La Cienega. A percentage of the sales at all these interesting little stores benefits the respective museums. The volunteers on staff know about the artists and their works. (See our Attractions and Arts chapters for more about these museums.)

If your timing is right, you'll enjoy shopping at **Indian Market** in August or at the **Spanish Market** and the **Eight Northern Pueblos Arts and Crafts Show** in July (see our Annual Events chapter). At any of these shows, you can get an education while you make a purchase. Ask the artists about their work; the more you understand, the more you'll appreciate these longstanding traditional art forms.

You can see excellent examples of early New Mexican Spanish handicrafts at the **Museum of International Folk Art**. Indian arts and artifacts are exhibited and explained at the Museum of Indian Arts and Culture and elsewhere. (See our Attractions chapter.) Scholars have written shelves full of books about Indian arts and crafts — their origins, the interconnectedness of themes and materials, the evolution of certain designs, family heritage in various arts and crafts, use of native or commercial materials, innovation in design and much more. If you're seriously interested, bookstores around Santa Fe offer wonderful resources. Although less has been written on the traditional Spanish Colonial art forms, there are several fine published sources of information available. Our purpose in this chapter is to provide a basic overview of the local arts and crafts to help visitors encountering them for the first time.

American Indian Art

Jewelry

When you think of Indian jewelry, do you expect turquoise and silver, feather designs and strands of beads? Well, you'll find that — but that's only the beginning. How about a butterfly pendant with a pearl head and diamond-edged wings? Or a sophisticated bracelet with a finely crafted miniature ear of corn with coral kernels in a golden husk?

Even a quick look at Santa Fe's shops and galleries or a walk along the Vendors Market at the *portal* of the Palace of the Governors will help orient you to the vast and varied world of American Indian jewelry, a kingdom in which traditional designs and materials share their popularity with innovative approaches building on long-established traditions of craftsmanship.

Much of the jewelry you'll see for sale in Santa Fe comes from the surrounding pueblos, including Santo Domingo, San Felipe, Cochití and San Juan. You'll also find work by Navajo and Hopi artists. The Navajo learned to work silver from Mexican silversmiths in the second half of the 19th century. The *concha* belt, named after the Spanish word for shell, is among their best-known designs. The belts are a collection of silver discs, sometimes with inset stones, connected on a leather belt.

While American Indian jewelry can be made from many different materials and in a huge spectrum of styles, authentic pieces are crafted by hand and usually one of a kind. The jeweler normally begins with metal. While silver is the most common metal used, you'll also see American Indians working in gold.

Jewelers create through cutting, shaping, hammering, soldering, texturing and stamping, roller printing and embossing metal. Stamping involves using a steel tool to press a decoration into the surfaces of metal. Casting is a metalsmithing method that gives jewelry both surface texture and shape. Molten metal is poured into a mold and hardened to make a jewelry form. Jewelers use both tufa casting, which employs porous rock made of volcanic ash, and the lost-wax method to make their creations.

Turquoise and coral are traditional Indian jewelry stones. Turquoise, reminding us of our clear blue sky, has been New Mexico's official gem for 30 years. According to some, turquoise is the creator's way of telling us that earth and sky are one, inseparably linked. Indian jewelers have used this wonderful stone for centuries. During an early exploration of Chaco Canyon's Pueblo Bonito — one of the world's most extensive Anasazi ruins — workers found 56,000 pieces of turquoise, mostly beads and pendants. The turquoise found at Chaco may have come from the mines in Cerrillos just outside of Santa Fe. The Pueblo Indians mined turquoise long before the Spanish arrived. They used the stone as currency, as a valuable trade item and in all sorts of jewelry. Because New Mexico's native supplies of turquoise were largely depleted in the 1980s, most jewelers now get their stones from traders who buy it in Arizona, Colorado, Nevada or even China. Turquoise comes in a variety of colors, from intense blue to pale green.

But you'll find more than turquoise in Indian jewelry. During your exploration of Santa Fe you're likely to see Indian jewelry made with lapis, diamonds, rubies, ironwood, opal and about any other stone you can think of.

In addition to setting them in metal, jewelers may use turquoise, coral and shell as the basis for lapidary work, shaping the raw materials into beads, some so delicate they seem fragile. Beads may be formed and smoothed using a hand drill; other jewelers tool them on machines. Indian jewelers also incorporate stones, coral and shell for inlay work, setting a decorative pattern of various colors into a base of silver or other material.

Silver overlay, a technique developed in the 1940s, is a distinctive Southwestern procedure used by the Hopi people of Arizona and other American Indians. The jeweler cuts a design into a sheet of silver, then places the design over a solid layer of silver. The jeweler then solders the pieces together and allows oxidation to darken the bottom layer that shows through to make the design more pronounced.

Here are a few tips for jewelry shopping:

• Look at the craftsmanship. Check to see that the edges are smooth and the stones securely fastened, that the stamp work is deep, sharp and even and that the finish is consistent.

• Try on the bracelet, necklace or bolo before you buy it. Make sure it's comfortable to wear and of the appropriate size and weight for you. Look at it in a mirror; get a friend to give you an opinion.

• Ask about the materials and techniques the jeweler used.

• Fine jewelry will have the stamp or signature of its creator.

Pottery

New Mexico's Pueblo Indians were skilled potters for generations before the Spanish arrived. Today, collectors the world over prize pueblo pottery for its craftsmanship, design and intrinsic beauty and because of the continuity with its traditional roots each piece represents.

A generation ago, it was easy to tell where a potter came from because the pottery from one pueblo differed sometimes markedly from another in color and design. Today, the definitions are less rigid, but pueblo potters still follow their ancestors' traditions in the type of clay they use, the symbols incorporated in the design and in many other ways. But each potter also is an individual, and the final work reflects this artist's creativity, inspiration and even sense of humor.

Picurís, Isleta and Taos pueblos specialize in micaceous ware. They make it using clay that has bits of mica in it, which gives the finished pots a lovely sparkle. Potters may add relief bands, handles and lids. They commonly make large jars and pots, along with animal figures. These tribes also make storytellers — ceramics that feature a central character such as a grandmother covered with smaller characters, like grandchildren, listening to a story.

These pueblos also make undecorated ceramics.

Acoma, Cochití, Laguna, Santo Domingo, Santa Ana and Zia pueblos traditionally make white or buff slipped vessels with black and brick colored motifs, usually with a reddish-brown base. Black and white fine-line pots, storytellers and animal figurines are among these tribes' specialties. Larger, earth-tone vessels are also popular. Their design elements may include stylized rain, lightning and clouds, humans and animals as well as crosshatching and geometric patterns.

Nambé, Pojoaque, San Ildefonso, San Juan, Santa Clara and Tesuque traditionally make black or red polished jars, wedding vases — tall pots with two spouts — water and storage jars, nativity scenes and bowls. They carve, etch or paint the finished pot, which tends to be black, red or a combination of both colors. These pueblos also make some micaceous ware.

Jémez, a pueblo in the Jémez Mountains between Santa Fe and Albuquerque, is known for buff or red-slipped wares with buff, white or red designs. Storytellers, clowns and animals figures are among the pueblo's specialties.

Hopi pottery, made by the Pueblo people of the Arizona mesa land, tends to be warm amber colored with designs that include stylized birds, *kiva* steps and rain symbols.

Zuni Pueblo traditionally makes large bowls and jars with brownish, black and red designs painted on a white or buff slip. The rain bird, plants and animals form the basic designs. Owl effigies and designs created by adding clay relief figures to the surface of the vessel are also common.

Although best known for their weaving and jewelry, the Navajo also make some pottery. It tends to be dark with a shiny finish and is usually unpainted.

Just like jewelers, potters approach their craft with tremendous variation and innovation within their tribal tradition. You'll find vessels inlaid with turquoise, exquisite miniatures, and carved and etched pots. Indian artists make all sorts of animals and figures and decorate their work, large and small, with everything from geometric designs to *kachina* figures to acrobats. The innovative artist who made a pot on display at the Museum of Indian Arts and Culture in Santa Fe, for example, decorated it with dinosaurs.

Traditional artists fire their pots in shallow pits. After they place the pots inside and cover them with wood bark and animal dung, they ignite the fuels, and the vessels smolder. Some set the pottery on a metal crate atop stones or old cans rather than in a fire pit. Fire clouds, or dark spots on the surface, are a result of these firing methods. In traditional firings as much as 25 percent of the pottery can break. Other potters use kiln firing, a sometimes controversial innovation, which reduces the breakage but also changes the finish of the pot.

www.insiders.com

See this and many other
Insiders' Guide® destinations
online — in their entirety.

Visit us today!

Basketry

Basket-making is the oldest and most widespread of all the American Indian crafts. Archaeologists have found evidence that Indians were making baskets as early as 9,000 B.C. Baskets traditionally had many functions, and the variety of the modern craft reflects this heritage.

Indians coiled or twined large cylindrical baskets for carrying food and fuel. They used broad, shallow trays to help winnow seeds. Basket bowls of many depths and shapes were used for food preparation and eating. Large, lidded baskets stored food; open baskets were used for washing corn. Tribes also made basket cradles to carry their babies. Other baskets had special ceremonial uses.

Baskets can be woven from many different materials, but American Indian baskets are usually crafted from plant stems, either whole or split. The materials produce an interesting range of natural color, and some basket-makers also use dyes, both commercial and vegetable, to enhance their work. Basket-makers

use three basic techniques to make their art: twining, plaiting and coiling. Because of the hundreds of hours involved in creating the basket — a good one can take five months — a beautiful, well-made piece will demand a high price.

Among the Pueblo people, the Hopi are the best-known basketmakers, with different colors and designs reflecting the artistry of each village. Flat plaques and shallow bowls as well as deep containers characterize this work. The coiling is done from right to left. The Hopi also make some plaited wicker baskets. The design may include *kachina* or spirit figures, traditional abstractions or birds.

Navajo basket-making underwent a renaissance in the 1970s, with more practitioners taking up the craft and more commercial-quality baskets created. Navajo baskets come in many sizes and shapes in both new, original designs and in the historic tradition.

The Jicarilla Apaches, whose reservation is in northern New Mexico near Chama, have been known for their superbly crafted baskets for centuries. The term "jicarilla" means finely made baskets. Their cylindrical and hamper-shaped baskets, which they tend to decorate with geometric forms, catch collectors' eyes and get top dollar.

Weaving

While most people think "Navajo" when they think of American Indian weaving, the Pueblo people, including the Hopi of Arizona, also create fine textiles. Early evidence of pueblo weaving dates to turkey feather and fur blankets and to items of clothing made from the native cotton that grew in the Rio Grande Valley and in irrigated fields in Arizona. An early account of the Spanish encounters with the Hopi mentions their cotton dresses.

INSIDERS' TIP

January is a great month for sales in Santa Fe. In addition to major savings on clothing, many shops selling Indian arts and crafts also reduce their prices with sales following the holiday buying madness.

Photo: Miguel Gandert

Stamped tin, used in frames, switch plates and elsewhere, is a popular and beautiful Hispanic folk art you'll discover at the Spanish Market and in area shops.

The arrival of the Spanish meant the arrival of sheep's wool, looms and a new approach to an old craft. By the 18th century, wool weaving was an established pueblo tradition. When commercial cloth became available with the opening of the Santa Fe Trail, the pueblos near Santa Fe de-emphasized weaving, but in the more isolated Hopi country the tradition continued. The Hopi helped supply the woven articles other pueblo people needed.

Pueblo men traditionally are the weavers, although women also weave. Handwoven clothing is used in pueblo dances and is also sold commercially.

When the Navajo people migrated into the Southwest, they learned weaving from the agricultural Pueblo Indians. The Navajo soon became sheep herders, a livelihood ideally adapted to their traditional nomadic way of life. They transformed the skills they had acquired with cotton to the working and weaving

of wool. By 1800 they were masters of the craft and had moved away from the pueblo tradition to create their own patterns and designs. They made blankets, rugs, sashes and even bridles for their horses. Weavers created items for their family's own use and for trade. The weavers, who were usually women, dyed the wool with natural dyes as well as chemicals. Their work utilized traditional designs and colors, creating textile styles that were influential in the development of weaving in the American Southwest.

By the early 20th century, Navajo weaving had become so famous and important that museums were collecting samples. Designs range from geometric patterns of all styles to depiction of Navajo figures or Yeis, to pictorial weaving, which might have trains, trucks or whatever else catches the weaver's fancy. There are no machine-made Navajo or pueblo weavings — all the work is done by hand.

Kachinas

Kachinas, or ceremonially costumed dolls, were originally an element used in the Pueblo peoples' complex and private religion. They are most common among the Hopi people. Although they were not part of the Navajo tradition, the Navajos make some *kachinas* today.

The *kachinas* were a way to represent forces outside of human control, to maintain the balance between the natural world and human world. They help the people learn about a hierarchy of power and responsibility but are not similar to Christian icons.

Some represent creation and life; death and war; lightning and storms; stars and planets; water and air; mountain peaks; the important foods of corn, squash and beans; other tribes; and animals birds and insects. There may be various depictions of the same *kachina*. Carvers generally craft *kachinas* from cottonwood roots. Men are the traditional carvers, but women also make *kachinas*. Traditionally children were encouraged to believe that the dolls are made by *kachinas* spirits.

The oldest dolls were simple with painted faces and uncomplicated bodies. Hopi and Zuni *kachinas* were known for the most figurative detail. Earliest *kachinas* hung on walls, but after World War II, collectors sought figures that showed more action, and the carvers responded with *kachinas* that could stand on flat surfaces. The figures passed from religious icons to fine art.

Each *kachina* is unique; buyers should make sure they know who the artist is and that the work is guaranteed as Indian-made and made by hand. The name of the artist and the *kachina* should be on the piece. In buying *kachinas*, look for graceful positioning of the body, attention to details in the carving and skilled use of paint and costuming. The price, as with all American Indian art, depends on the age and quality of the piece and the renown of the artist.

Pricing

As you shop for jewelry, pottery, textiles, baskets, *kachinas* and other American Indian arts and crafts, you'll probably notice a tremendous variety of prices. Some of the differences may be due to the quality of materials used, the artist's skill in design or his or her reputation and popularity. If a piece seems too inexpensive to be authentic, ask where it came from and how it was made. Likewise, if the price seems excessive, ask why. A reputable dealer or legitimate artist will be delighted to tell you.

Traditional Spanish Arts

Although not as well-known as American Indian arts and crafts, the northern New Mexico Hispanic tradition of handmade items, many of them religious, is honored in Santa Fe.

In the centuries before New Mexico became part of the United States, the settlers here had to use their own resourcefulness and creativity to produce what they needed for daily life. In addition to useful items, this included images of Jesus and the saints to help bring them closer to their god. The traditions of wood carving, straw inlay, embroidery and weaving that began from these modest, utilitarian roots grew into a unique indigenous art form. The Museum of International Folk Art, 706 Camino Lejo, has one of the most important collections of Spanish Colonial art, with pieces dating from the late 1500s to the present.

Among the Spanish Colonial arts you may find in Santa Fe or elsewhere in northern New Mexico are religious figures carved from wood or painted on wooden panels; loom weavings from hand-spun vegetable-dyed yarn; decorative and utilitarian furniture usually made from pine; wheat-straw and corn-husk appliqué applied to wood in intricate designs; tin that the artist has cut, punched and worked into useful and/or decorative objects; forged iron used for tools and household objects; and gold and silver filigree jewelry.

As you shop for traditional northern New Mexican Spanish items, you may come across these terms:

Bulto — A statue or three-dimensional image of a saint

Colcha — A distinctive embroidery style

Reredos — An altar screen

Retablo — A painting of a saint on a wooden panel

Santo — A saint

Photo: Chris Corrie

Santa Fe has a rich diversity of shops that specialize in American Indian arts and crafts.

A final word of advice: Follow your heart. If you love it and can afford it, buy it. If you don't, someone else probably will and chances are you may never see its likes again.

Santa Fe has dozens of wonderful commercial shops in addition to the nonprofit museum shops mentioned in the introduction to this chapter. The following selection, which also includes places to buy Hispanic arts and crafts, is provided for your convenience. Unless otherwise noted, these places accept credit cards. Most shops are open from 9 or 10 AM until 5 or 6 PM Monday through Saturday. Some may be open on Sunday, especially during the summer.

Shopping Guide

Andrea Fisher Fine Pottery
211 W. San Francisco St. • 986-1234
This classy shop specializes in just one thing: Southwestern Indian pottery. You'll see fine examples from New Mexico's pueblos, including historic work by María Martínez. You'll also find exquisite work by New Mexico's contemporary potters. Fisher, the owner, arranges her contemporary and historic pieces by area, to give the viewer a sense of place. They're also grouped according to age and then by families, sometimes showing seven generations of pots by one family. The owner says a visit is an educational experience — we wish all education was this much fun!

Arrowsmith's Relics of the Old West
402 Old Santa Fe Tr. • 989-7663
In business since 1959, this shop carries top-quality antique American Indian art and sells baskets, rugs and other items to collectors and museums. It also carries Spanish Colonial items as well as Egyptian, Greek and Roman treasures.

INSIDERS' TIP

If you travel from Santa Fe to Taos in the summer or fall, you'll notice roadside produce vendors selling farm-grown fruits and vegetables from the backs of their trucks or fruit stands. Stop and see what's for sale. You might find *ristras* (bunches of chiles strung together), honey and other treats too.

The Clay Angel
125 Lincoln Ave. • 988-4800

This downtown shop presents work by New Mexico Hispanic artists along with imports from around the world. You'll find aspen, pine and cottonwood *bultos*, painted *retablos* and altar screens by Anita Romero-Jones. Just a short walk from the Plaza, the store specializes in ceramics, but you'll find a variety of other fine crafts here too. Ask to see work done by New Mexicans.

Cristof's
106 W. San Francisco St. • 988-9881

This downtown shop is known for its first-rate Navajo weavings, collected from throughout the reservation. The staff can help you understand what you're looking at — and look-

Photo: Don Strel/Southwest Assignments

Robert Dale Tsosie's *War Spirits* illustrates some of the stunning diversity of material, styles and technique in American Indian art. Prices vary widely too.

ers are welcome. You'll also find a nice selection of jewelry, pottery, sculpture, *kachinas*, storytellers and sandpaintings.

Dewey Galleries Ltd.
53 Old Santa Fe Tr. • 982-8632

Dewey Galleries is one of Santa Fe's best-known places to buy Indian pottery, jewelry and artifacts, and it has a fine collection of Navajo rugs. It will do appraisals and handle estates and collections. You'll also find Pendleton blankets here. Dewey Galleries is on the second floor of the building.

Eagle Dancer
57 Old Santa Fe Tr. • 986-2055

If you can't spend hundreds or thousands of dollars on Indian art, you may find something to suit your pocketbook here. This store carries a fascinating range of merchandise, from lovely storyteller dolls and fine Hopi *kachinas* to Santa Fe kitsch. It's open daily.

La Fonda Indian Shop and Gallery
La Fonda Hotel, 100 E. San Francisco St. • 988-2488

This gallery features fine art by American Indians from throughout the Southwest. La Fonda acquires private estates and collections on a consignment basis. You may find beautiful etched miniature pots or Indian jewelry made from gold and opals as well as silver and turquoise.

Helen Hardin Estate/Silver Sun
656 Canyon Rd. • 983-8743

Santa Clara Pueblo artist Helen Hardin, who died in 1984, left a wonderful legacy of artwork, which is featured in this gallery along with small Navajo sculpture and delicate Acoma pottery. You'll also find a wide range of Indian jewelry at a wide range of prices.

The shop's jewelry specialty is natural American turquoise stones in custom-designed silver settings, created by their own Navajo silversmiths. It also sells pottery, rugs, fetishes and carvings.

Indian Trader West
204 W. San Francisco St. • 988-5776

This place feels like an old-time trading post, with items available in many price ranges. You'll find everything that will say Indian and Southwest when you get back home — top-quality merchandise as well as souvenirs.

Davis Mather Folk Art Gallery
141 Lincoln Ave. • 983-1660

This tiny gallery is packed full of wonderful animal woodcarvings by New Mexican Hispanic artists and American Indians from in-state and elsewhere. Among the craftspeople featured are Josefina Aguilar, Ron Rodriguez and Lula and Wilfred Yazzie. The gallery has been in business since 1975 and is open daily.

Montez
125 E. Palace Ave., Stes. 33 and 34 • 982-1828

Traditional-style arts and crafts by New Mexico's leading Hispanic artists are on display in this gallery. The owner, from a family of *santeros* himself, knows his business. You'll find wood carvings of the saints, tin work, *santos* and other lovely and unusual items. The shop is in Sena Plaza near the northwest corner. It's closed on Sunday.

Morning Star Gallery
513 Canyon Rd. • 982-8187

Morning Star promotes itself as the largest gallery in the country devoted exclusively to antique Native American art. In business 13 years, the gallery occupies an old Canyon

INSIDERS' TIP

For unique candy, visit Senior Murphy Candymaker in three locations. The piñon concoctions, including piñon brittle, piñon fudge and a piñon log, are hard to find outside of Santa Fe. The candy is made at the Santa Fe factory, but the candymaker will gladly ship it for you as long as the weather isn't too hot. For a special, nonmelting treat, try the red chile peanut brittle or the chile jelly.

Photo: Don Strel/Southwest Assignments

Helen Tafoya Henderson displayed these pots at the annual Eight Northern Indian Pueblos Arts and Crafts Show. The show is held at one of the pueblos just outside of Santa Fe each July.

Road hacienda. The inventory includes a variety of material from the major cultural areas of North America. The emphasis is on Plains beadwork, quill work, ledger drawings and parfleche, Southwestern pottery, baskets, textiles and jewelry.

Ortega's On The Plaza
101 W. San Francisco St. • 988-1866.

In business for 25 years, Ortega's sells fine Indian jewelry from all the pueblos. You'll also find old Navajo rugs, baskets and even a pot by the famous San Ildefonso Pueblo potter María Martínez. The merchandise is beautifully presented, and the staff is knowledgeable.

Packard's Indian Trading Co.
61 Old Santa Fe Tr. • 983-9241

This business has been in the same location and owned by the same American Indian family for 76 years. You'll find top-quality Indian goods from pottery and *kachinas* to exquisite silver and turquoise necklaces. Fine contemporary designs are included along with traditional styles. Packard's is open daily.

The Rainbow Man
107 E. Palace Ave. • 982-8706

At The Rainbow Man you'll find works by regional Hispanic folk artists, including some of the people who show at Santa Fe's annual Spanish Markets. Don't miss the wood carvings with nice touches of fantasy. The shop also has an interesting selection of early Chimayó and Rio Grande Weavings as well as an extensive collection of Native American arts and crafts — including miniature *kachinas*. The store is open daily.

As you explore Santa Fe, you'll find many superlatives: the biggest adobe office building, the oldest bell, the largest sculpture garden in New Mexico, the largest collection of contemporary American Indian art . . . and that's just for starters!

Attractions

We're the first to admit it. Santa Fe thrives on its contradictions, and one of the most basic is this: Why is it that a town that prides itself on its *mañana* attitude offers more things to do than a place three or four times its size? Don't worry if Santa Fe's many options to spend your time seem overwhelming — they are!

The diversity of attractions here, coupled with the community's natural beauty, bring visitors back year after year. The most recent figures place Santa Fe's visitors at 3 million annually — or 50 tourists for every resident!

As you explore Santa Fe, you'll find many superlatives: the biggest adobe office building, the oldest bell, the largest sculpture garden in New Mexico, the oldest Indian boarding school, the largest collection of contemporary American Indian art, the only museum dedicated to a woman artist of international stature . . . and that's just for starters.

Santa Fe offers so much, that if you're making your first trip, we recommend that you take a city tour. You can take walking tours of all sorts, ride an open-air tram or climb aboard a big bus. A few hours with a well-trained guide will not only give you a better appreciation for the tremendous historic and cultural riches you'll find here, but it can also help you avoid spending any of your precious vacation time getting lost or searching for a parking place.

In this chapter you'll find the attractions divided into logical categories for Santa Fe: churches, museums, historic buildings and districts, other attractions, tours and visitor information. In addition to information here, please take a look at our Arts, Recreation and Kidstuff chapters for more ideas.

We've done our best to include up-to-the-minute information about hours and admission fees of the attractions we list, but if you're on a tight budget or a tight schedule, please call to see if anything has changed since our book was published.

Historic Buildings

Lamy Building
491 Old Santa Fe Tr. • 827-7336 (State of New Mexico Santa Fe Welcome Center)

Visitors who stop here for information are literally stepping into history. Named after Archbishop Jean Lamy, the building was erected in 1878 as part of St. Michael's College, the oldest private school in New Mexico. (See our Education and Child Care chapter.) The three-story structure had classrooms and community rooms on the first two floors and a dormitory for the boys who came from throughout northern New Mexico on the third floor. With its tower, portico, galleries, veranda and mansard roof, the building is typical of many 19th-century New Mexico buildings, most of which have now disappeared. In 1926, fire almost completely destroyed it, but the students saved the day by forming a fire brigade. The Lamy Building's graceful two-story *portal* is one of the few remaining in Santa Fe. The visitors center is open from 8 AM to 5 PM daily with very few exceptions, but your best view of the building is from outside.

National Park Service Southwest Office
1100 Old Santa Fe Tr. • 988-6100

Curious about what lies behind Santa Fe's pervasive adobe walls? This attractive building, a National Historic Landmark, can help satisfy your curiosity. Not only is it beautiful, but also it's the largest known adobe, or mud brick, office building and one of the largest secular adobe buildings in the United States.

The Park Service building derives its significance from its architecture, art collections, and association with the federal relief programs of the New Deal era. The sculptural, massive quality of the adobe walls, the lovely patios and the hand-worked wooden beams and corbels reflect some of the characteristic elements of "Santa Fe Style," a type of architecture that began here around 1910 and continues to be popular today. To do the construction, the Public Works Administration provided the materials and skilled labor, and the Civilian Conservation Corps provided unskilled workers, a crew of unmarried men ages 17 to 23. They earned about $1 a day for their work and had to send home at least $22 a month. The men made the structure's 280,000 adobe bricks by hand. From the artisans they worked with they learned woodwork, stone and foundation masonry and traditional tinwork to decorate and enhance the building. The government completed the job by acquiring paintings by local artists, Navajo rugs and Pueblo pottery. That collection remains on display.

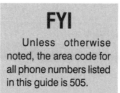

FYI

Unless otherwise noted, the area code for all phone numbers listed in this guide is 505.

Although the offices are closed to visitors — after all, people are working there — the patio, lobby and conference room give you a fine feeling for the building's wonderful architecture and skillful finishing touches. You can visit between 8 AM and 4:30 PM Monday through Friday. There's no charge, and you'll find a brochure for a self-guided tour in the lobby.

New Mexico State Capitol
Paseo Peralta at Old Santa Fe Tr.
• 986-4589

Visit the New Mexico State Capitol and in the process learn a lot about New Mexico's history, politics and its rich artistic community. The Capitol, nicknamed the Roundhouse for its circular shape, was built in 1966 and remodeled at a cost of $34 million in 1992. The architectural design comes from the Zia Pueblo sun sign or circle of life, the same symbol you'll notice on New Mexico's red and yellow state flag. The current Capitol is New Mexico's fourth, following the Palace of the Governors and a downtown building constructed in 1887 and reconstructed in 1890 after it burned in a fire.

The Capitol has four levels, three above ground. In the basement (which is not open to the public) are the House and Senate chambers. The second floor, at ground level, con-

tains a visitor information office and the rotunda where visitors find changing art exhibits. The floor of the rotunda displays the state seal. All the semiprecious stones decorating the seal and the marble of the surrounding walls and floor were mined in New Mexico. Old photographs of past legislators line the walls of the third floor House and Senate galleries, the area where visitors may watch laws being made. During the legislative sessions — the 30-day financial session and 60-day general session in alternating years — the Roundhouse is filled with students on field trips, lobbyists and interested residents who come from around the state to observe their elected representatives in action. Recent hot topics have included Indian gaming, prison construction and highway funding. The Legislature convenes beginning at noon on the second Tuesday in January.

On the fourth floor, the Governor's Gallery features art by New Mexicans in exhibits that rotate often. Walls elsewhere in the building display paintings, photographs, weaving and mixed media work by some of New Mexico's best known artists. On the Capitol grounds, you'll find monumental sculptures by Allan Houser, Glenna Goodacre and others. Docents offer free guided tours at 10 AM and 2 PM Monday through Friday. The Capitol building is open from 8 AM to 5 PM Monday through Friday.

Randall Davey Audubon Center
1800 Upper Canyon Rd. • 983-4609

You might see a bobcat track in the snow at this quiet sanctuary, only a 10-minute drive from the Plaza. In 1847, at the beginning of the U.S. occupation, the first sawmill in the territory was built here, providing planks for the construction of Santa Fe's Fort Marcy, where U.S. troops were garrisoned. At the turn of the century, Candelario Martinez farmed this land until he sold the property to artist Randall Davey in 1920. Davey converted the mill into a two-story home and used the Martinez hacienda for his studio. The house still contains a representative sample of Davey's work and his furnishings. You can tour the Davey home on Mondays in the summer (please call for times) and otherwise by appointment.

The Audubon Society acquired this property in the mid-1980s and operates it as a nature center and the group's New Mexico headquarters. Included is land along the Santa Fe River. The center's trails begin in the piñon and juniper woodlands and meadows and climb up to cool ponderosa pine forest. More than 100 species of birds have been observed here, along with coyote, black bear, mountain lion and mule deer. In addition to the do-it-yourself nature trails, the center offers guided hikes, wildlife interpretive programs and summer activities for children. The center's gift shop sells bird seed, books and other items of interest to naturalists.

To reach the center, follow Canyon Road past the intersection of Camino Cabra at Cristo Rey Church to Upper Canyon Road. The center is the very last structure on Canyon Road. The center is open from 9 AM to 5 PM daily. The trail fee is $1 for nonmembers.

St. Catherine Indian School
801 Griffin St. • 982-6258

Founded in 1887, St. Catherine Indian School is the oldest Native American boarding high school in New Mexico. More than 25 different American Indian cultures have been represented here including Navajo, Apache, Hopi, Zuni, all the Pueblo Indians of New Mexico and other tribes of the Southwest (see our Education and Child Care chapter).

You can tour the grounds, visiting the Pueblo-style chapel with traditional Native American prayer symbols and the original convent and school building erected in 1887. Murals throughout the campus celebrate American Indian spirituality. The mural of Our Lady of Guadalupe, for example, details 10 major events in the Americas, blending mainstream, religious and American Indian historic figures into the design. In the Historical Room you can look through vintage photos from the late 1800s. The campus also has a gift shop and a gallery that displays traditional American In-

dian pottery, jewelry, weaving and painting, including student work. All proceeds from sales benefit the school. Call to arrange a free tour.

Sena Plaza
100 Block of E. Palace Ave. • no phone

One of the city's most popular courtyards, this beautiful place gives you a feel for the old Territorial days when Santa Fe was still a village. With its beautifully landscaped patio and fountain, this spot entices you to sit and relax, smell the flowers or watch the snow fall and enjoy the day. From the Palace Avenue *portal*, you won't know this oasis is here unless you come through the narrow entranceway and take a few steps inside.

The property was originally part of a land grant from Don Diego de Vargas, the man who brought the Spanish back to New Mexico after the 1680 Indian revolt, to one of his captains, Arias de Quiros. In 1844, the property, which included a small house and patio, was bequeathed to the mother of José D. Sena, a major in the U.S. Civil War who was later to inherit it. Sena expanded the living quarters into a 33-room house, which he eventually occupied with his family. The second story was added to the east and north portions of the estate in 1927 when the building was sold and remodeled into shops and offices. (See our Shopping chapter.) Visitors are welcome, free of charge, from 10 AM to 10 PM.

El Zaguan
545 Canyon Rd. • 983-2567 (Historic Santa Fe Foundation)

This long, rambling Territorial-style house has long been regarded as one of New Mexico's showplaces. The old hacienda with its lovely garden was named El Zaguan, "the passageway," because of the long hall running from the patio to the garden. James Johnson, one of the first Yankee merchants to settle permanently in Santa Fe, purchased the property, which included a small house, in 1849. In the Santa Fe pattern, the building was enlarged and remodeled several times.

INSIDERS' TIP

If you don't want to sound like a tourist, please call the Plaza, "The Plaza," not "The Town Square."

Early floor plans showed two patios, a central patio that served as the entry from the street with larger, more formal rooms opening onto it and an east patio, which was the center of household activities. The house, today with 14 rooms, once had 24 rooms, including a chapel, a "chocolate room," and a library that once housed the largest collection of books in the territory. Servants' quarters were across the street. The garden was reportedly laid out by Adolph Bandelier — the writer and archaeologist for whom Bandelier National Monument is named — with peony bushes from China and two large horse chestnut trees brought from the Midwest.

In 1962 the property was purchased for preservation by El Zaguan Inc., and today one of its apartments is an office shared by the Historic Santa Fe Foundation and the Old Santa Fe Association. The Foundation, incorporated in 1961 to receive tax-exempt donations for historic preservation, conducts research to identify worthy buildings and preserves and maintain landmarks in Santa Fe and the nearby communities. The foundation office is open from 8 AM to noon Monday through Friday. Visitors are welcome to El Zaguan during business hours.

Historic Churches

Archbishop Lamy's Chapel
Bishop's Lodge Resort
1292 Bishop's Lodge Rd. N. • 983-6377

Santa Fe's remarkable Archbishop Jean Baptiste Lamy prayed in this lovely little chapel that he built as a retreat beginning in the late 1860s. The building, about 3 miles from the Santa Fe Plaza, reflects both European and traditional Hispanic New Mexico architectural styles. The walls are adobe, or mud brick, but the spire looks like something from New England. Changes over the years included replacing the rafters with white-washed *vigas* and covering the floor with cement. But the wooden entry doors and their hardware are original.

In addition to his role as religious leader and promoter of education (see our Educa-

tion and Child Care chapter), Lamy attempted to transform Santa Fe from an adobe village to a more European-looking city. He contracted stone masons and artisans from France and Italy who in 1869 began to build the St. Francis Cathedral. He also guided the construction of Loretto Chapel.

Today, the Bishop's chapel is virtually surrounded by Bishop's Lodge Resort. The chapel is open to visitors during daylight hours free of charge. Visitors can arrange for weddings, baptisms and other religious ceremonies in the chapel.

Cristo Rey Church
1120 Canyon Rd. • 983-8528

The parish of Cristo Rey uses this church, America's largest adobe building, for regular worship, but visitors are welcome. A classic example of New Mexico mission architecture, Cristo Rey was built of 200,000 adobe bricks made from soil at the church's site. The 1940 construction commemorated the 400th anniversary of Coronado's exploration of the Southwest, which led, of course, to the founding of Santa Fe. In addition to the architecture, notice the restored painted stone *reredos*, a sculpted Spanish Colonial-style altar screen with images of the saints. Crafted in 1760, the 18- by 40-foot screen originally was commissioned for an old military chapel situated near the Plaza. Admission is free. The church is open to visitors from 7 AM to 7 PM daily.

Loretto Chapel
207 Old Santa Fe Tr. • 984-7971

This chapel, dedicated to Our Lady of Light, was the first Gothic structure west of the Mississippi. Today, the chapel is one of Santa Fe's top visitor attractions and a popular place for weddings and concerts.

Built for the Sisters of Loretto, the style of this jewel-like chapel testifies to the influence of Santa Fe's first bishop, Frenchman Jean Baptiste Lamy. The Sisters came to Santa Fe at the request of Lamy to establish a school for young women downtown. Their Loretto Academy occupied the site upon which the Loretto Hotel now stands.

The French influence includes the white altar, beautifully adorned sanctuary, rose windows and architectural beauty modeled after Paris' Sainte Chapelle. The chapel's claim to fame, however, is a graceful spiral staircase that winds to the choir loft with no center support and not a single nail. Legend has it that work on the chapel was nearly done when the sisters realized no room remained for a traditional staircase. They prayed to St. Joseph for guidance, and believed he answered their novena when a carpenter arrived. He agreed to build the staircase. Using only a saw, a carpenter's square and tubs of hot water to soften and shape the wood, he crafted a beautiful circular staircase. He then disappeared before he could be paid. The story recently captured the attention of the producers of *Unsolved Mysteries* and got national television exposure.

The chapel is administered by the Sisters of Loretto but maintained by the Historic Santa Fe Foundation. Admission is $2; children younger than 6 get in free. The chapel is open from 9 AM to 6 PM daily and from 10:30 AM to 5 PM Sunday.

San Miguel Mission
401 Old Santa Fe Tr. • 983-3974

Many people believe this mission is the oldest church in the United States. Construction began in 1610 by the Tlaxcalan Indians who came from Mexico as servants of the Spanish soldiers and missionaries. The job was completed in 1625. When the Pueblo Indians drove the Spanish from New Mexico in 1680, they nearly destroyed the mission and burned all records of its early history. The sturdy adobe walls remained unharmed, however. When the Spanish returned, they ordered the church rebuilt and construction was finished in 1710. For many years it served the surrounding Barrio Analco, one of Santa Fe's most historic neighborhoods.

Inside you can see traditional religious im-

ages crafted by Hispanic artists. The wooden *reredos*, or altar screen, dates to 1798 and holds paintings from the early 18th century. You'll see rare and ancient images of Jesus on buffalo and deer hides, testimony to the faith and ingenuity of frontier artists. Among the chapel's drawing cards is the San Jose bell, cast of silver, copper, iron and gold. Touted as the oldest bell in America, some historians date its fabrication to 1356. Spanish churches used it before it was shipped to Mexico and then hauled to Santa Fe by oxcart in the 19th century.

A helpful staff of Christian brothers and a six-minute audio presentation that runs continuously as a recorded tour will help orient you to the mission. It's open Monday through Saturday from 9 AM to 4:30 PM and Sunday from 1:30 to 4:30 PM. Admission is free. Mass is celebrated here Sunday at 5 PM.

Santuario de Guadalupe
100 Guadalupe St. • 988-2027

At one time this Santa Fe-style building resembled something straight out of Colonial New England. In another incarnation, it was California mission-style. Today, the unassuming adobe church looks much like it did when it was first built, between 1776-96. It is the oldest shrine to Our Lady of Guadalupe in the United States. Our Lady of Guadalupe is a name given by the Catholic Church to the apparition of the Virgin to an Indian outside of Mexico City in the 16th century. This Madonna speaks of the Virgin's love for native people of the Americas. You'll find her representations throughout New Mexico, on everything from T-shirts to the hoods of lowrider cars.

Franciscan missionaries oversaw the construction of the original church, which had a dirt floor, no pews and a simple ladder leading to the choir loft. In the 1880s, Archbishop Jean Lamy assigned a French priest to the little church and made it a regular parish. Father James DeFouri (for whom nearby DeFouri Street

INSIDERS' TIP

Among the questions tour guides frequently get: Does it ever snow? At what elevation do deer turn into elk? Why did Indians build ruins? Why are all the houses brown? Do Indians still live here?

El Rancho de las Golondrinas, a museum just south of Santa Fe,
offers a variety of festivals and self-guided tours.

is named) supervised extensive remodeling, the first of many for the structure. It took on a pitched roof, steeple and a white picket fence. The church was modified again in the 1920s following a fire, this time redone in California mission-style. In the 1960s, the growing Guadalupe parish built a new church next to the mission. The old church retained its California look until 1976, when a restoration brought the building back to its simple mission origins — but this time with a floor and seats. The restoration covered the original adobe walls, which ranged from 3- to 5-feet thick, with two layers of hand-plastered adobe finish. The lintels above the windows and the front door are original. The ceiling includes some original beams, but the building's roof, brick parapets and bell are new. You can see pictures of the Santuario in its incarnations in the history room.

Among the Santuario's art is an 1783 oil-on-canvas altar painting of Our Lady of Guadalupe by Mexican baroque artist José de Alzibar, a renowned Mexican painter. It is one of the finest and largest oil paintings of the Spanish Southwest. It came to Santa Fe in

pieces and was reassembled on site. The non-profit, nonsectarian Guadalupe Historic Foundation operates the Santuario as museum, performing arts center and occasional art gallery. The Santa Fe Desert Chorale has performed most of its summer and Christmas concerts here since 1982. You can visit the Santuario Monday through Saturday from 9 AM to 4 PM. It's closed weekends from November through April. Admission is free. Mass is celebrated here once a month.

St. Francis Cathedral
213 Cathedral Pl. • 982-5619

In this city of flat-roofed adobe buildings, the towering cathedral stands out from the crowd. Constructed from New Mexico's golden brown sandstone, St. Francis Cathedral was the first church between Durango, Mexico, and St. Louis, Missouri, to be designated a cathedral. Archbishop Jean Lamy supervised its construction, recruiting artisans from Europe and working on the plans himself. Lamy died before the workers finished. (He is buried beneath the cathedral's altar.)

Built beginning in 1869, the cathedral arose around an earlier mission church on the same site. The cathedral's Romanesque-style stained glass imported from Clermont, France, and dual bell towers stand in sharp contrast to New Mexico's simple adobe churches. The exterior was completed in 1884, but work went on inside for many years after that.

The builders erected Corinthian columns leading to a ribbed vaulted ceiling. Frosted glass chandeliers illuminate the sanctuary. The windows depict the 12 apostles; today, painted stations of the cross in the New Mexican folk art *santero* style hang on the wall beneath them, a fitting reminder that this is Santa Fe, after all.

In a small chapel — all that remains of the original church on this site — the cathedral shelters a religious icon greatly revered by New Mexico's Hispanic Catholics and others who treasure the state's religious history. This small wooden statue of the Virgin Mary was for years known as La Conquistadora and now is also called Nuestra Señora de la Paz, or Our Lady of Peace. It is the oldest representation of the Madonna in the United States. Spanish friars brought the image from Mexico City to Santa Fe and carefully took it out of New Mexico again when they fled during the Pueblo Revolt. La Conquistadora returned to Santa Fe with Don Diego de Vargas during the reconquest and is carried in procession as part of the religious commemorations of the Santa Fe Fiesta.

When you visit the cathedral, it's hard to overlook the massive bronze double doors out front. They chronicle more than four centuries of the Roman Catholic religion in New Mexico. Each panel weighs 25 pounds. Notice La Conquistadora in the "1680" panel. The cathedral is open to visitors from 6 AM to 5:45 PM. Admission is free. Mass is celebrated daily.

Historic Districts

Barrio Analco
E. De Vargas St. between Don Gaspar Ave. and Old Santa Fe Tr.

Believed to have been one of the first parts of Santa Fe to be settled by the Spanish, this area was named "*analco*" or "other side of the river" because it sits across the Santa Fe River from the Palace of the Governors. The early residents were the Mexican Indians who came to Santa Fe in the early 1600s with the Spanish settlers, missionaries and soldiers. The Spanish lived closer to the thick-walled haven of the Palace. Because of its vulnerability, angry Pueblo Indians were able to totally destroy this area during the revolt of 1680. The neighborhood was rebuilt when the Spanish returned and as years went by became a more class-inclusive kind of place. Today state buildings dominate this area, but some of the old charm remains. The homes are privately owned and not open to visitors, but a stroll along E. DeVargas Street gives you a sense of Santa Fe in its early days.

Canyon Road
From Paseo De Peralta to Camino Cabra, roughly parallel to E. Alameda and Acequia Madre

If you only have a weekend in Santa Fe, you ought to spend at least part of it walking along Canyon Road, exploring some of the many shops and galleries, observing the historic homes that still dot the area and getting a feel for old Santa Fe. The best way to explore Canyon Road is on foot; wear your walking shoes. Don't worry if you get hungry, there are restaurants here too. If art interests you, you'll discover a variety of styles, media and prices here. Many of the road's galleries and shops occupy former homes.

Several nearby streets — Camino del Monte Sol, Garcia Street and Acequia Madre — are also worth a look. Primarily residential, they offer another glimpse of Santa Fe's classic beauty. In the spring and early summer, the lilacs and fruit trees here are spectacular. Acequia Madre means "mother ditch," a name that comes from the irrigation ditch which runs along the street. In pre-Spanish times, Indians used this footpath to travel between the Santa Fe River valley and Pecos Pueblo. Later it was the conduit for haulers bringing their loads of firewood from the mountains to sell in town. Farmers grew chile, beans and peaches, drawing the water for irrigation from *acequias*, or communal ditches. Sheep and goats grazed on the nearby hillsides.

Canyon Road owes part of its fame to a

group of artists who came to Santa Fe in the 1920s. They called themselves "Los Cinco Pintores" (The Five Painters) and built homes along Camino del Monte Sol, just off Canyon Road. Their paintings often reflected a romantic Santa Fe. (See our Arts chapter.) The artists became neighbors of Canyon Road's long-established Hispanic families. The cultures intermixed, and the area saw little visible change until recent years, when some longtime residents began selling their land, in part because of rising taxes. Today, this area, known as the East Side, is one of Santa Fe's most desirable and pricey neighborhoods. (See our Real Estate and Neighborhoods chapter.)

Artist Olive Rush, said to be the first female Anglo artist to move to Santa Fe, lived and worked in a studio at 630 Canyon Road for 40 years. A Quaker, Rush left her home to the Santa Fe Society of Friends at her death, and it is still used for Quaker Meetings. El Zaguan, 545 Canyon Road, is among the street's historic buildings. (See separate write-up in this chapter).

Parking in the Canyon Road area can be a challenge, especially in the summer. You can look for parking places along the street or in the city lot, 225 Canyon Road, near the corner of Canyon Road and Camino del Monte Sol.

The Plaza/Downtown

Directly across from the Palace of the Governors, the Plaza is bordered by Lincoln Avenue to the west, Washington Avenue to the east, San Francisco Street to the south and Palace Avenue to the north. The downtown area extends several blocks from the Plaza in all directions.

The Plaza, a shady expanse of trees, grass, benches and monuments, is the core of old Santa Fe, the city's "Central Park." It's one of four sites in Santa Fe listed on the National Register of Historic Places. (The others are the Palace of the Governors, the National Park Service Southwest Headquarters and the Barrio Analco near the San Miguel mission.) To many residents, despite all the changes over the past decades, the Plaza is still the community's sentimental place of the heart. A recent city-sponsored program of free entertainment on the Plaza was appropriately called "El Corazon de Santa Fe" (The Heart of Santa Fe).

For many visitors, time spent exploring the Plaza and downtown Santa Fe with its museums, shops, restaurants and historic attractions, forms one of their most vivid memories of this unusual city. The Plaza is Santa Fe's favorite place for festivals and fairs. You'll find Spanish Market, Indian Market, Fiesta de Santa Fe, the Christmas drama *Las Posadas* and many other events here. They fill the Plaza and spread into the surrounding streets, bringing Santa Fe residents and visitors downtown. In the summer the city traditionally blocks traffic on San Francisco Street and Lincoln Avenue to make the area more pedestrian friendly.

The Plaza has several monuments that present pieces of its long, rich history:

• The small stone marker on the north side, just across the street from the Palace of the Governors, notes the arrival of Gen. Stephen Watts Kearny with the Army of the West in 1846 during the war between Mexico and the United States. Kearny claimed Santa Fe for the U.S. government without firing a shot; Santa Fe's Mexican governor may have believed the resistance was useless.

• The monument on the south side of the Plaza marks the end of the Old Santa Fe Trail and provides an idea of the historic route from Missouri to Santa Fe. The Santa Fe Trail brought wagons filled with tons of goods to New Mexico between 1822 and 1870. The wagons' bounty was sold or traded for furs and pelts, gold and silver. Interstate 25 follows the same route from Santa Fe to Denver. The old trail brought contact with the United States that ultimately led to New Mexico becoming a state. The Plaza also marks the end of an older commercially important trail, *El Camino Real*, the trade route to Santa Fe from Mexico.

• At the center of the Plaza, the obelisk commemorates Civil War battles in the area. Although most visitors may not realize it, the Civil War reached New Mexico in 1861. The Confederacy, in an effort to take the West, sent soldiers from Texas up the Rio Grande to capture New Mexico's Fort Union, the garrison established by the U.S. Army to protect wagons along the Santa Fe Trail from Indian marauders. The Confederacy controlled both Albuquerque and Santa Fe by 1862, setting up headquarters in the Palace of the Governors. The rebel plan would have succeeded except for the pivotal Battle of Glorieta on March 28. Maj. John Chivington took some Union soldiers and destroyed the Confederates' central supply base, leaving them with no support and no choice except to abandon the area.

Surrounding the Plaza are narrow streets and distinctive buildings that represent three and a half centuries of continuous civilization beginning with the 1610 establishment of the city as the seat of the government of Spain's northern frontier. Architectural styles range from Spanish Pueblo to Territorial and European. Strict building codes govern what you can design, erect or demolish. Rents are high, and as a result, in addition to museums, you'll find shops that handle exclusive and expensive merchandise and shops that make their money on heavy sales of less expensive items. The Häagen-Dazs ice cream store on San Francisco Street, for example, is reputed to be the busiest such outlet in the United States.

Parking in the Plaza area can be difficult. The city operates several downtown lots (see our Getting Around chapter), and some private businesses offer limited parking. There also are a few spaces along the street. Your best bet, if you're staying downtown, is to walk from your hotel. If you're outside the downtown area, you can take a city bus, hotel shuttle or a taxi.

Museums

Archdiocese of Santa Fe Museum
223 Cathedral Pl. • 983-3811

Because the Spanish government wanted converts as well as gold from New Mexico, the Catholic faith played a vital role in the area's history (see our Worship and Spirituality chapter). This unimposing little museum features historic documents, photographs and artifacts that trace the development and role of the Catholic Church in New Mexico.

You can see the beautiful chalice used by Archbishop Jean Lamy when he said mass more than a century ago and the proclamation formally re-establishing the Spanish presence and Catholicism in Santa Fe, dated June 20, 1692, and signed by Don Diego de Vargas. The museum is open from 9 AM to 4:30 PM Monday through Saturday. Admission is by donation.

Bataan Memorial Military Museum and Library
1050 Old Pecos Tr. • 474-1670

Organized through the efforts of the New Mexico National Guard, the Bataan Veterans Organization and many other interested parties, this museum displays artifacts collected by the state's military veterans and honors all New Mexicans who have done military service. The museum occupies an old armory and displays items dating from World War I through Desert Storm. The highlight is a tribute to the Bataan veterans, the 200th Coast Artillery Regiment that was sent to the Philippine Islands to furnish anti-aircraft support. The regiment was later divided to form the 515th Coast Artillery Regiment. The men saw enemy action on Bataan when the Japanese overran the Philippines in 1942. The 200th is officially credited with firing the first shot and being the last to surrender to the Armies of Japan. The 200th consisted of 1,800 men when deployed. After three and a half years of brutal captivity, less than 900 men returned to their families in New Mexico. The state has a government office building named in honor of these brave fighters, and a perpetual flame burns for them just outside it.

The museum has 30,000 artifacts, an extensive research library and an archive of military documents relating to New Mexico's history. It's usually open Tuesday through Saturday from 7:30 AM to 3:30 PM, but hours can change with seasonal visitors and tour groups. There is no admission charge.

Institute of American Indian Arts Museum
108 Cathedral Pl. • 988-6281

If you're interested in contemporary American Indian art, be sure to visit this downtown attraction. The museum is affiliated with the Institute of American Indian Arts, which has long been one of America's leading schools for Indian arts. Among the teachers and students whose work has put the IAIA on the

Photo: Don Strel/Southwest Assignments

The aspens' brilliant fall colors are an awesome sight.

national map are Allan Houser, Fritz Scholder, Linda Lomahaftewa and T.C. Cannon. With more than 6,500 pieces in the collection representing 3,000 artists, the museum is the largest repository of contemporary Indian art in the world. Painting and sculpture, traditional crafts such as beadwork, pottery, weaving and basketry are displayed in the museum's five galleries. The museum offers educational programming and the outdoor Allan Houser Art Park for large sculpture. The IAIA Museum is open from 10 AM to 5 PM Monday through Saturday and noon to 5 PM on Sunday. Admission is $4 for adults, $2 for seniors and students with an ID and free for children younger than 16.

El Rancho de las Golondrinas
334 Los Pinos Rd., La Cienega
• 471-2261

It's easy to imagine the relief of the tired travelers along the famous *Camino Real*, the main trade route connecting New Mexico to Mexico, when they reached this shady oasis. The ranch was the last stop before Santa Fe on the grueling journey from Mexico City to the northern province of New Spain. Centuries later, the natural beauty remains.

Approximately 15 miles southwest of Santa Fe, El Rancho de las Golondrinas, "the ranch of the swallows," offers a vivid re-creation of the area's 18th- and 19th-century history. The restored buildings — built on original foundations — have been furnished as appropriate to the period. You can visit an 18th-century *placita* house, a home built around a patio with thick walls and defensive towers. You can see a water-powered mill, feel the heat in a blacksmith shop, visit a school house, hike through the mountain village and notice the solemnity in the *morada*, a chapel/meeting house used by an influential religious society.

Santa Fe residents like to bring their out-of-town visitors to the museum for its popular festivals and Civil War weekend. During these lively events, volunteers dress in traditional costumes, chat with visitors and demonstrate many of the skills early settlers needed to survive on the frontier. The museum comes alive with dancing, music, sales of food and crafts and activities of all sorts. You can see, taste, smell, hear and touch the life of Spanish Colonial and Territorial New Mexico. El Rancho de las Golondrinas also presents theme weekends throughout the summer, focusing on topics such as arts, oral history and storytelling, Colonial traditions, the

Catholic faith as it shaped the area's arts and the animals the Spanish brought with them.

From June through September, you can tour the ranch on your own. Admission is $4 for adults; $3 for seniors (62 and older) and teens and military personnel; and $1.50 for ages 5 through 12. Children younger than 5 get in free. The museum's self-guided tour involves about a 1.5-mile walk over roads and trails that are sometimes steep and rocky. You should allow at least an hour and a half for the tour. During the festivals or Civil War Weekend, admission is $6 for adults; $4 for seniors (62 and older), teens and military; $2.50 for children ages 5 to 12 and free for children younger than 5. To reach the ranch from Santa Fe, take I-25 S. to Exit 246 and bear right on N.M. Highway 599. Turn left at the first intersection on the frontage road and right just before the race track on Los Pinos Road. The museum is 3 miles from this intersection.

School of American Research Indian Arts Research Center
660 Garcia St. • 982-3584

Although not, strictly speaking, a public museum, the public can view this extensive collection of American Indian textiles, pottery, basketry and jewelry once a week on a special tour. Docents will explain the SAR's fascinating history and role in American archaeology in addition to offering insights into the beautiful objects you'll see. Tours, by reservation only, are $10 and are normally held Fridays at 2 PM.

Wheelwright Museum of the American Indian
704 Camino Lejo • 982-4636, (800) 607-4636

The story of the Wheelwright Museum is a tale of amazing transition, one which testifies to this institution's ability to adapt to the times. Mary Cabot Wheelwright, who founded the museum as the Museum of Navajo Ceremonial Arts in 1937, came to the Southwest from New England, bringing with her an outsider's appreciation for what she found and the economic and social connections to create a new institution. Her collaborator in the establishment of the museum was Hastiin Klah, an esteemed and influential Navajo singer or "medicine man." Klah was born in 1867 when most of the Navajo people were held as prisoners of war by the United States government. Klah had witnessed the decades of relentless efforts by the government and missionaries to assimilate the Navajo people into mainstream society. To Klah, the future of traditional Navajo religious practices appeared bleak.

Traders Frances "Franc" and Arthur Newcomb introduced Wheelwright and Klah, and the two became close friends. They were determined to create a permanent record of Klah's and other singers' ritual knowledge. Klah dictated, and Wheelwright recorded, the Navajo Creation Story and other great narratives that form the basis of Navajo religion. While Wheelwright concentrated on the spoken word in Navajo ritual, Franc Newcomb focused on the sandpaintings the singers create and destroy during the healing ceremonies. She re-created versions of them in tempera on paper. Klah, who was also a skilled weaver, recorded the sandpaintings in tapestry.

By the early 1930s it was clear to Wheelwright and Klah that a museum would be needed, not just as a repository for the manuscripts, recordings, paintings and sandpainting tapestries but also to offer the public an opportunity to sense the beauty, dignity and profound logic of the Navajo religion. The architect they

INSIDERS' TIP

Except for the annual Spanish Market, you won't find any Hispanic crafts or work by any other ethnic groups under the portal of the Palace of the Governors. Only American Indians can sell under the portal, a policy that was challenged as discriminatory several years ago but upheld by the courts. The Indian vendors are part of the museum's official program tied to historic preservation.

chose, William Penhallow Henderson, based his design for the building on the hogan — the traditional eight-sided Navajo home and the setting for Navajo ceremonies. The museum's earliest names were the Navajo House of Prayer and House of Navajo Religion, but soon after it opened its official name became the Museum of Navajo Ceremonial Art.

Times changed, and, far from becoming assimilated, the Navajo people became one of the most powerful Indian groups in the United States. The resilient Navajo culture proved that the apprehension Wheelwright and Klah shared about the death of the Navajo religion was unfounded. In the 1960s and 1970s, the Navajo Nation exerted its independence in a number of ways, including the establishment of its own community college system. Also at that time, Navajo singers founded the Navajo Medicine Men's Association. The teaching of traditional Navajo religion enjoyed a revival, and its practitioners began to express their concerns about the sacred items and information in museums throughout the country.

In 1977, the Navajo Museum's board of trustees acknowledged the wisdom and authority of the Navajo Medicine Men's Association by voting to repatriate several Navajo medicine bundles and other items sacred to the Navajo people. The Navajo Nation now maintains them at the Ned A. Hatathli Cultural Center Museum at Navajo Community College in Tsaile, Arizona. With the repatriation in 1977, the museum changed its name to the Wheelwright Museum of the American Indian and now showcases art by contemporary American Indian artists.

Although it is no longer actively involved in the study of Navajo religion, the Wheelwright Museum maintains world-renowned collections and archives that document Navajo art and culture from 1850 to the present.

(Scholars may view the collections through special arrangements with the museum director.) Exhibitions in the main gallery include contemporary and traditional American Indian art with an emphasis on the Southwest. The exhibits rotate every four months. A second gallery presents one-person exhibitions. The entrance displays outdoor sculptures by Allan Houser and others. Special activities include storyteller Joe Hayes on Saturday and Sunday evenings in July and August. Hayes entertains in a tipi; visitors sit on blankets and listen to tales that reflect Santa Fe's Indian, Hispanic and Wild West heritage. The museum also hosts a children's powwow in the fall. The Case Trading Post sells art work, jewelry, pottery, books and unusual items. The museum is open from 10 AM to 5 PM Monday through Saturday and 1 to 5 PM on Sunday. Admission is free.

The Museum of New Mexico
Administrative offices, 113 Lincoln Ave.
• 827-6451

Headquartered in Santa Fe, the state's museum system includes research libraries, artifact conservation, archaeological research, education programs and traveling exhibits, the American Indian *portal* vendors "living exhibit," the Museum Press and *El Palacio* magazine. Operated with state funding, private grants and money earned though admission fees, the museum system is managed as part of the New Mexico Office of Cultural Affairs. The four Santa Fe-based museums are the Palace of the Governors, Museum of Fine Arts, Museum of International Folk Art, Museum of Indian Arts and Culture/Laboratory of Anthropology. The Palace and the Fine Arts Museum are downtown. Museum of Indian Arts and Culture and the Museum of International Folk Art are about 2 miles from the Plaza on Camino

INSIDERS' TIP

Santa Fe is host to many historic districts and neighborhoods that contain more than 100 individual sites which are recognized on the National Register of Historic Places and the State Register of Cultural Properties. These buildings, streets, bridges and archaeological digs — many of which are included in this guide — receive this designation because they help people understand the history and culture of the nation, the state and Santa Fe.

Lejo, just off the Old Santa Fe Trail. The Georgia O'Keeffe Museum is a private institution that operates in close association with the Museum of New Mexico, sharing programming, admissions, collections and membership. Members of the Museum of New Mexico are automatically members of the Georgia O'Keeffe Museum.

Museum of New Mexico/ Georgia O'Keeffe Museum: Hours and Prices

The four museums operated by the Museum of New Mexico — Palace of the Governors, Museum of Fine Arts, Museum of International Folk Art, Museum of Indian Arts and Culture/Laboratory of Anthropology — and the privately funded Georgia O'Keeffe Museum follow the same pricing schedule and hours. Instead of repeating this information in each entry, we've put it here for your convenience.

Daily admission for all museums is $5 for one day, $1 on Sunday for New Mexico residents with ID; $10 for a four-day pass that provides unlimited admissions to The Georgia O'Keeffe Museum and to all branches of The Museum of New Mexico. Free admission is offered daily to people age 17 and younger. Those 60 and older with ID get in free on Wednesdays. From 5 to 8 PM on Fridays all patrons get in free at The Georgia O'Keeffe Museum, The Museum of Fine Arts and The Palace of the Governors. Annual passes are available for $25.

All branches of the Museum of New Mexico and the Georgia O'Keeffe Museum are open from 10 AM to 5 PM Tuesday through Sunday. The Museum of Fine Arts, Palace of the Governors and The Georgia O'Keeffe Museum are also open from 5 to 8 PM on Fridays. The museums are closed Mondays, New Year's Day, Easter, Thanksgiving and Christmas. For information about the Museum of New Mexico's events and attractions call the 24-hour information line, 827-6463.

Museum of Fine Arts
107 W. Palace Ave. • 827-4468

The Museum of Fine Arts is easy to find once you're on the Plaza. It's right across the street from the Palace of the Governors at the corner of Lincoln and Palace avenues. Its classic Santa Fe style makes it one of the city's most-photographed buildings. The collections focus mainly on art from the Southwest and New Mexico and include both traditional and contemporary work in a variety of media. The museum owns and displays creations by many well-known artists, including the Santa Fe and Taos master painters who first brought the art world's attention to New Mexico as well as Georgia O'Keeffe and Peter Hurd. (See our Arts chapter.) The museum's galleries change exhibits fairly frequently and usually include cutting-edge work by living artists as well as shows that draw on the collections.

Like its sister, the Palace of the Governors, this museum attracts attention for its architecture as well as its archives. Completed in 1917, the museum is a beautiful example of the Pueblo Revival style of construction, complete with split cedar *latillas* (roof supporters), hand-hewn *vigas* (log roof beams) and corbels. The gracious style reflected in the thick walls, pleasantly landscaped central courtyard, smooth interior plaster and other finishing touches became synonymous with "Santa Fe Style."

The Museum of Fine Arts offers art classes for kids, an extensive program of lectures and gallery talks. The Santa Fe Chamber Music Festival makes its home in the museum's St. Francis Auditorium during the summer.

Museum of Indian Arts and Culture
710 Camino Lejo • 827-6344

This museum's pride and joy is its newest permanent exhibit, "Here, Now and Always," which opened with tremendous fanfare and blessings from Indian leaders in August 1997. The exhibit goes on the must-see list for anyone interested in American Indians and their arts, culture and history. Housed in a large new wing, "Here, Now and Always" tells the story of the Native American presence in the Southwest with more than 1,300 objects and a multimedia production created during the eight-year period the museum spent in collaboration with Native American elders, artists, scholars, teachers, builders and writers. These consultants worked with a team of Indian and non-Indian museum curators and designers to develop an exhibit that combines the actual voices of contemporary American Indians with ancient artifacts. The architectural design helps bring centuries of culture and tradition to life.

The exhibit uses stone and silver, clay and wool, feast days, fairs and family stories to tell of the enduring communities of the Southwest. To orient visitors, it incorporates the landscape itself, mesas and settlements, plazas and sacred peaks. Visitors proceed by theme through the galleries. You can visit a pueblo kitchen, an Apache wickiup, a Navajo hogan, a 1930s trading post and a contemporary vendor's booth at a tribal feast day celebration. The stories in "Here, Now and Always" are told on video tape by 24 American Indians.

The Museum of Indian Arts and Culture was established in 1987 next to its adjoining research facility, the Laboratory of Anthropology. In addition to exhibits, the museum has a resource center with looms, magazines, books, maps and other useful tools. The museum is noted for its prehistoric and historic pottery, basketry, woven fabrics and jewelry. The museum offers a "Breakfast With the Curators" program, daytrips and other special events.

Museum of International Folk Art
706 Camino Lejo • 827-6350

Just as the Museum of Indian Arts and Culture provides a fascinating and informative orientation to the American Indian cultures of the Southwest, the Folk Art Museum does the same for the New Mexico's Hispanic culture. And that's just one of its exhibits! The Hispanic Heritage Wing features Spanish Colonial folk art and an interactive computer program in its "*Familia y Fe*/Family and Faith" exhibit. The finely crafted displays delineate the central position of extended family relationships and the Catholic faith in northern New Mexico's Hispanic culture. The exhibit also underlines the resourcefulness of the pioneer families who lived for more than a century in tremendous isolation from manufactured goods, European medicine and formal education.

In addition to insight into New Mexico's Hispanic past, museum visitors can come away with a better sense of the world as a whole. This museum is the repository for the world's largest collection of international folk art. In the "Multiple Visions: A Common Bond" exhibit, for example, you'll find objects from more than 100 countries displayed in fascinating dioramas. Toys from 19th-century Europe, Chinese prints, embroidered Indian mandalas, Mexican Day of the Dead mementos and examples of early 20th-century Americana are among the treasures. This exhibit alone displays more than 10,000 pieces of folk art, all donated by the Girard Foundation Collection.

The museum hosts changing exhibits and a variety of special events, some ready-made for children and families. Check with the museum about docent-guided tours, which are free with admission.

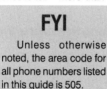

FYI

Unless otherwise noted, the area code for all phone numbers listed in this guide is 505.

Palace of the Governors
105 E. Palace Ave. • 827-6483

With its chronicle of more than 450 years of European presence in the Southwest, the Palace presents a first-class historic introduction to Santa Fe and northern New Mexico. Built in 1610, this massive adobe building sits as simple testimony to New Mexico's long, rich and fascinating history. It's the oldest public building in the United States and has been in continual use since shortly after the day its builders, probably Indian slaves, laid the last adobe or mud brick.

Despite the name, don't be surprised that this building doesn't look much like a storybook palace or the grand structures of Europe. Santa Fe's Palace, a single-storied, earth-colored building with a long front *portal* and a shady interior courtyard, suited the place and the time of its construction. It speaks more of early New Mexico's entrepreneurial, frontier style than the glory of mother Spain. The Spanish used the Palace until the Pueblo Revolt of 1680, when consolidated forces of Pueblo Indians seized the building and drove the Europeans out of New Mexico. (See our

History chapter.) The Indians remained in control for 12 years, then the Spanish returned and the Palace again became their Territorial headquarters. When Mexico won its independence, taking New Mexico with it, the Mexican flag flew here. The U.S. government seized control during the Mexican-American War. Confederate forces occupied the Palace during their attempt to win the West. Territorial Gov. Lew Wallace wrote part of *Ben Hur* here.

The building was replaced as a governmental seat in 1909 after it had housed 60 New Mexico governors. It then became Santa Fe's first museum. Apart from any of the displays, the building itself is rich with history because of the many events and decisions crucial to the history of New Mexico that were born inside these thick mud walls. Whenever changes to the building that are more than superficial are made, archaeologists discover more treasures and historic tidbits beneath its floors. The rooms display thousands of treasures including Indian pottery made before the Spanish "discovered" this place, written accounts of the Coronado Expedition, a reconstruction of a 17th-century Spanish cart, maps of 18th-century Spanish America, horse-drawn hearses, a full-scale reproduction of a mountain village chapel, a chuck wagon dating to the mid-19th century and a book bindery and presses from an old print shop.

Period rooms, including the 1846 New Mexico Governor's Office and a much more ornate parlor used in 1893 by Gov. L. Bradford Prince, re-create the Palace of the past. The American Indians who sit in front of the museum along the *portal* are an attraction that draws international attentions. (See our close-up in this chapter.) The museum also has a fine shop that offers unusual merchandise and a good selection of books. The Palace hosts lectures and book signings with pleasant frequency and offers a variety of special programs including Christmas at the Palace and the Mountain Man Rendezvous (see our Annual Events chapter).

Georgia O'Keeffe Museum
217 Johnson St. • 995-0785

Georgia O'Keeffe is New Mexico's best-known artist — even people who don't know a pastel from a poster have heard of O'Keeffe and seen reproductions of her famous paintings of skulls or giant flowers. The museum, Santa Fe's newest, celebrated its opening in July 1997 with parties, a flurry of national and international publicity and free admission. It hosted about 3,300 visitors daily for its first four days.

The Georgia O'Keeffe Museum is America's first museum dedicated to the work of a woman artist of international stature. O'Keeffe visited New Mexico in 1917 and came here permanently in 1949, settling in an old adobe home in the small village of Abiquiu (see our close-up in the Arts chapter). She lived there, inspired by the landscape and the light, for nearly 40 years before moving to Santa Fe a few years before her death in 1986 at age 98.

The Georgia O'Keeffe Museum houses the world's largest permanent collection of her work, including many pieces the artist kept for herself that have never exhibited previously. At the museum, you'll see drawings, paintings, pastels, sculptures and watercolors O'Keeffe produced between 1916 and 1980. Flowers and bleached desert bones, abstractions, nudes, landscapes, city-scapes and still lifes are all here. The museum's galleries trace O'Keeffe's artistic evolution in a wide range of media and follow the depth and breadth of her long, productive career.

As a secondary goal, the museum collects works by contemporaries of O'Keeffe who were part of her artistic community. Anne and John Marion, philanthropists who also funded the new visual arts center at the College of Santa

---

INSIDERS' TIP

In the Plaza area you'll find artists who'll do your portrait as a souvenir of your visit to Santa Fe. You can also buy carnitas, tortilla sandwiches made from roasted meat, from another vendor. These entrepreneurs and others who sell on the Plaza are licensed by the city.

Fe, endowed the 13,000-square foot museum. The building itself allows plenty of room for the paintings. The display throughout the museum's 10 galleries is simple and unpretentious, just as O'Keeffe would have liked. The museum offers guided tours, educational programming and special events. You can watch a short video about O'Keeffe's life and learn about her contribution to American art.

Other Attractions

The Cross of the Martyrs and Commemorative Walkway
Paseo de Peralta at Otero St. • no phone

You feel like you're walking through history as you climb the winding brick path that takes you to the Cross of the Martyrs. Informative plaques line the walkway, summarizing the city's early history and the events that led to the deaths of the Franciscan missionaries who are commemorated by a 20-foot white metal cross at the path's end. From the top of the hill, you get a lovely view of the city and a panorama of the Sangre de Cristo, Jémez and Sandia mountains — a reward for your energetic effort. Santa Fe's annual Fiesta ends with a candlelight procession from the cathedral to the cross. And on Christmas Eve, bright bonfires, or *luminarias*, surround it. There are no official visiting hours, and no fees are charged.

The Planetarium
Santa Fe Community College, 6401 Richards Ave. • 438-1777, 438-1677

The Planetarium, one of the city's newer, out-of-the-way attractions, offers a changing schedule of productions intended to give the audience a better feeling for the night sky. The Celestial Highlights program the first Thursday of each month provides an introduction to the stars and constellations that will be visible for the next 30 days. Showtime is 7 PM. The planetarium, on the upper level in the west wing of the Community College, also offers family programs each Saturday at 10:30 AM and a different program on Fridays, usually with showings at 6:30 and 8 PM. Recent

productions included Sesame Street characters and a report on the findings of the *Magellan* spacecraft, one of NASA's greatest success stories. Tickets are $3.50 for adults, $2 for children 12 and younger and for seniors 65 and older and for SFCC students with a current ID. Tickets go on sale a half-hour before showtime.

Santa Fe Botanical Garden
Santa Fe Community College, 6401 Richards Ave. • 438-1684

Santa Fe Botanical Garden doesn't have a full-fledged garden open to the public quite yet, but visitors can take a look at the demonstration plantings the group has done on the community college campus. The four Geobotany Beds near the school's main entrance offer a glimpse at the creative use of native plants and drought-tolerant horticulture. The college has leased 25 acres to the gardeners. The land will be developed into a place for research and education as well as natural beauty. Santa Fe Botanical Garden also offers regular programs about different aspects of gardening for members and the public and presents popular tours (see our Annual Events chapter). You can visit for free during daylight hours.

Santa Fe Farmers' Market
Sanbusco Market Center Parking Lot, 500 Montezuma St. • 983-4098

Farmers' Market brings fresh area produce along with homemade salsa, baked goods, herbal remedies, cheeses, organic meat, fragrant cut flowers, plants for landscaping and more. What you discover in the farmers' booths depends on the season and how early you show up. But you can be assured that you'll find a crowd of Santa Fe residents and curious visitors. The vendors come from throughout northern New Mexico and as far east as Ft. Sumner, nearly 200 miles away. When you buy here, you not only get delicious food, you're supporting small business. Music, free samples, coffee and baked goods for sale mark most morning markets. The market is open from 7:30 to 11 AM on Tuesday and Saturday and from 9:30 AM to 1:30 PM on Sunday. Those who come early find the best

FYI

Unless otherwise noted, the area code for all phone numbers listed in this guide is 505.

selection. The market usually runs from mid-May until sometime in October depending on the weather. Potential buyers and their children are admitted free.

Shidoni Foundry and Gallery
P.O. Box 250, Bishops Lodge Rd.,
Tesuque • 988-8001

Established in 1971, Shidoni is one of the world's leading fine-art casting facilities and showplaces. Sculpture produced here represents leading artists from throughout the world. Shidoni has done work for Allan Houser and cast Glenna Goodacre's Washington, D.C., memorial for women who served in the Vietnam War. On Saturday (times vary, please call), you can watch 2,000-degree molten bronze as it's poured into ceramic shell molds for casting. The foundry is open to walk-through visitors from noon to 1 PM Monday through Friday and from 9 AM to 5 PM on Saturday. The self-guided tours are free. Shidoni also offers an 8-acre sculpture garden with 500 works, the largest outdoor sculpture display in New Mexico. You can stroll among monumental sculptures in a variety of styles and media year round from 8 AM to sunset. Shidoni makes its grounds available for private parties and fund-raising ventures. A contemporary art gallery elsewhere on the property features changing exhibits of painting and sculpture. The free gallery is open from 9 AM to 5 PM Monday through Saturday. Shidoni is in Tesuque, about 5 miles north of Santa Fe

Ski Santa Fe Chairlift Rides
Santa Fe Ski Area, 16 miles northeast of
Santa Fe on N.M. Hwy. 475 • 983-9155,
982-4429

The Super Chief Quad, a four-person chairlift, takes sightseers to the top of Aspen Peak at an elevation of 11,000 feet. The stunning view from this part of the Santa Fe National Forest includes the Jémez and Sandia mountains, Mount Taylor, San Antonio Peak and the Rio Grande valley. A descriptive sign with tubes you can look through helps identify major landmarks. Even in the summer, it's a good idea to bring a sweater or jacket — the air can be cool up here in God's country. If you're feeling energetic, you can continue hiking through the spruce, fir and ponderosa pine. You may see marmots, dozens of different wildflowers and colorful mushrooms. Afterwards you can buy lunch, a snack or a cold drink at the ski area's La Casa Cafe Grill near the base of the chairlift.

The chairlift operates weekends and holidays from 10 AM to 3 PM July 4 through Labor Day and again in the fall for aspen viewing, with the dates determined annually based on the weather. Rates are $6 for adults and $4 for children 12 and younger. Those shorter than 46 inches may ride for free accompanied by a paying adult. Tickets for seniors are $4, and one-way trips for hikers are $4.

Pueblo Casinos

Camel Rock Casino
Tesuque Pueblo, U.S. Hwy. 84-285, 10
miles north of Santa Fe • 984-8414,
(800) GO-CAMEL

Named for the distinctive rock formation just across the highway, this casino has one of the nicest locations in northern New Mexico. The attractive, 60,000-square-foot building includes a large bingo hall, dining area, gift shop and plenty of slot machines and gaming tables. Minors can eat at the buffet but otherwise are not allowed in the casino. The casino is open 24 hours a day, seven days a week. In addi-

---

INSIDERS' TIP

As you walk in the Plaza area and in other older neighborhoods, you may notice plaques installed by the Historic Santa Fe Foundation. The Foundation has placed bronze plaques on more than 50 Santa Fe buildings the group judges to be worthy of preservation. Most of these structures are included in the New Mexico State Register of Cultural Properties.

tion to a huge lot for free parking, valet parking is available.

Cities of Gold Casino
Pojoaque Pueblo, U.S. Hwy. 84-285, 15 miles north of Santa Fe • 455-3313, (800) 455-3313

The early Spanish explorers sought the legendary cities of gold when they came to the Southwest. Gamblers here hope to have better luck. In addition to the usual attractions, this casino includes a sports bar with more than 700 slot machines and a free shuttle with several daily pickups at downtown and Cerrillos Road motels. The casino, which is open 24 hours a day, seven days a week, does not allow minors.

San Felipe's Casino Hollywood
I-25, Exit 253, 30 miles south of Santa Fe • 867-6700

The most Las Vegas-like of Santa Fe area casinos, Casino Hollywood has all the flashing lights, bells and whistles a person could want. The casino promotes giveaways such as cars and a trip on a private charter yacht. You may find some big-name entertainment here. Casino Hollywood will let you try your luck 24 hours a day, seven days a week. The establishment is owned by San Felipe Indian Pueblo.

Tours

Afoot in Santa Fe Walking Tours and The Loretto Line Tram Tours
211 Old Santa Fe Tr. at the Loretto Hotel • 983-3701

In business since 1990, this tour company prides itself on hiring guides who know their history and have a good sense of humor. Owner Charles Porter has conducted tours for groups from the National Parks Foundation and the Smithsonian. The walking tours involve more history; the driving tours on the Loretto Line trolley cover more sightseeing territory. The walking tour, which encompasses about 2 miles of the city's nooks and crannies, leaves daily March through November at

9:30 AM and 1:30 PM. From December through February, the company offers only the morning tour. Fee is $10 per adult and free for children younger than 16 with a parent.

The open-air trams leave at 10 AM, noon, 2 and 4 PM, with additional tours added during the busiest summer weeks. The one hour and 15-minute tour costs $9 for adults and $4 for children 12 and younger and lasts about 75 minutes. The trolleys normally run from April through October depending on the weather. No reservations are needed for either tour. All tours depart from the Loretto Hotel. Pay parking for tour guests is usually available at the hotel.

FYI

Unless otherwise noted, the area code for all phone numbers listed in this guide is 505.

Outback Tours
P.O. Box 961, Santa Fe 87504 • 820-6101, (800) 800-JEEP

These jeep tours focus on the natural history, ecology and archaeology of the Santa Fe area. All guides have advanced degrees in fields such as botany, geology and archaeology. The tours are fully insured and the company has been in business for seven years. Regularly scheduled trips, such as into the Jémez Mountains, to Taos or into the national forest above Santa Fe, are offered from March through October, with custom tours available other months. Prices begin at $55, and reservations are necessary. They'll pick you up at your hotel.

Randal Walker's Excellent Adventures
201 Galisteo St. • 984-2559

Customized outdoor excursions featuring four-wheel-drive vehicles will pick you up and take you outside the city to explore petroglyphs, cliff dwellings, river valleys or alpine country. The company offers hiking and biking excursions and other adventures for up to seven guests. Water, snacks, lunch, sunscreen and even a day pack to carry them in come with the tours. Guides design the trips to suit the ages, abilities and interests of the visitors. The company also offers "An Excellent Adventure for the Physically Challenged." Reservations at least a day in advance are necessary. Half-day excursions begin at $65 per person; full-day trips start at $125.

Rojo Tours
P.O. Box 15744, Santa Fe 87506
• 474-8333

Rojo offers a variety of customized tours and arranges packages for convention and meeting planners. In addition to Santa Fe driving and walking tours, they will take visitors to cave dwellings and Indian pueblos. Rojo offers an O'Keeffe country tour and a tour of fine-art studios and sculpture gardens. They'll also drive you to Taos, to Hispanic and Indian villages along the Rio Grande and even to Chaco Canyon in a 12-hour extravaganza. Balloon rides, whitewater rafting, backpacking excursions and more are available. Prices range from $50 to $350, depending on the trip. Please call to find out where to join a specific tour.

Santa Fe Detours
54½ E. San Francisco St. • 983-6565, (800) DETOURS

In town or out of town, by foot, raft or railroad, Santa Fe Detours has served visitors and residents for more than 15 years. This locally owned and operated company handles the bookings for the *Roadrunner*, the open-air yellow trolley that cruises Santa Fe's historic neighborhoods. This company will also arrange horseback riding, private guides for hiking and biking, Grayline bus tours and even help find tickets to popular performances. Prices depend on the services selected; they offer a comprehensive package that includes a ride on the *Roadrunner* and a walking tour for $17.

Santa Fe Soaring
535 Cordova Rd., No. 436 • 424-1928

Departing from the Santa Fe Airport, Santa Fe Soaring presents scenic glider rides over the city and above the surrounding mountains on the STEMME S10 glider. The pilot and a single passenger quietly fly alongside birds on the plane's 75-foot wings. You can take pictures through the large canopy; the glorious view of mountain ranges, valleys and the Santa Fe countryside is unobstructed. Flight time is about an hour, and the fee is $125. Reservations are recommended; usually flights can be arranged the same day.

Santa Fe Southern Railway
410 S. Guadalupe St. • 989-8600

Take a trip from the city to the neighboring community of Lamy, about 20 miles away, on the comfortable vintage coaches of a working freight train. The train leaves from the Santa Fe Depot in the Guadalupe Street area — a great place for shopping — and travels south over the old Atchison Topeka & Santa Fe line. You'll see the northern New Mexico high desert ringed by the blue Jémez, Sandia and Sangre de Cristo mountains. The train stops in the village of Lamy, home of the Lamy Depot that is used by the Amtrak line and the Victorian-style Legal Tender Saloon & Restaurant. Passengers spend 90 minutes in Lamy enjoying a picnic they've brought with them or dining at the Legal Tender, then make the ride back. Trains depart for the four-and-a-half-hour ride at 10:30 AM. Trips are on Thursday and Saturday every week of the year, with additional Tuesday trips March through April and additional Tuesday and Sunday trips April through October. From May through October the train offers Sunset/Starlight rides on Friday evenings with departure one hour before sunset; call for specific times. Tickets are $21 for ages 14 to 59; $16 for ages 7 to 13 and those older than 60; $5 for ages 3 to 6. Children 2 and younger ride free, with a limit of two per adult. Group rates, charters, private cars and school rates are available.

Santa Fe Walks
624 Galisteo, No. 32 • 988-2774

Also known as Aboot About, this company

INSIDERS' TIP

The New Mexico Office of Cultural Affairs, Historic Preservation Division at 228 E. Palace Avenue, 827-6320, can give you detailed information about historic buildings in Santa Fe and northern New Mexico.

Photo: Don Strel/Southwest Assignments

San Miguel Mission, Santa Fe's oldest church, sits next to another historic building, the original home of St. Michael's High School, now a state office building.

offers walking tours with guides who are archaeologists, artists and anthropologists. In addition to the popular Santa Fe orientation tour, the company offers ghost and mystery walks, literary walking tours, artist and gallery tours and many more walking and driving trips. The basic historic walking tour is a two-and-a-half-hour stroll to Santa Fe's significant sites. Tours leave daily at 9:30 AM and 1:30 PM from the Hotel St. Francis, 210 Don Gaspar Avenue, and at 9:45 AM and 1:45 PM from the Eldorado Hotel, 309 W. San Francisco Street, with morning-only tours from January through March. Fee is $10 per person, and people younger than 16 go along free if accompanied by an adult. You can parking in city lots across the street from both hotels.

Second Wind Tours
P.O. Box 1314, Santa Fe 87504
• 690-4550

This company, in business a year, offers pedicab tours when the weather is nice and walking tours year round, rain, snow or shine. The walks are led by guides, whom the management describes as "interested in showing off the town." Strollers leave from Häagen Dazs Bakery, just off the Plaza at 56 E. San Francisco Street. The two-and-a-half-hour exploration is offered every day but Monday at 9:30 AM. Price is $8 a person. Trips take about two and a half hours, and no reservations are needed.

Southwest Safaris
P.O. Box 945, Santa Fe 87501
• 988-4246, (800) 842-4246

These unique air/land tours take visitors to some of the Southwest's most magnificent country and provide a fine look at the area's geology and archaeology. The one-day expedition to Canyon de Chelly flies over the Rio Grande, Jémez Mountains, Chaco Canyon, the Bisti Badlands and the Chuska Mountains, then heads down the full length of Canyon de Chelly to land on the Navajo reservation. A Navajo guide meets the travelers for a jeep tour of the famous canyon with its pictographs and ruins. Fee for the tour is $349 per person, and the trip leaves Santa Fe at 7 AM and returns by 3:30 PM.

The Mesa Verde expedition flies over colorful plateaus, mesas, buttes, canyons and pueblos. The plane lands in Cortez, Colorado, and visitors proceed by car to Mesa Verde National Park to hike through selected Anasazi cliff houses. Fee is $399 per person and the trip leaves Santa Fe at 7 AM and returns by 4 PM. Pilot/guide Bruce Adams will also arrange custom trips. All trips are by reservation.

Wings West
2599 Camino Chueco • 473-2780

You can enjoy the wonders of bird-watching with an Audubon Society tour leader on full- and half-day trips or custom adventures to your liking. Company founder Bill West has worked with live raptors at the Wildlife Center in Española for many years. Popular tours include walks along the Nambé and Pecos rivers and

the Rio Grande, or visits to Las Vegas National Wildlife Refuge, Maxwell National Wildlife Refuge or the Bosque del Apache Wildlife Refuge. Fees are $150 for a full-day trip for one or two visitors, including lunch, or $90 for a half-day trip. All trips are customized by reservation.

Visitor Information

La Bajada Visitor Center
I-25 at the La Bajada exit, 17 miles south of Santa Fe • 690-6610

La Bajada, Spanish for "the descent," was clearly named by travelers heading south to Rio Abajo or the lower Rio Grande country — rather than those making the arduous climb up hill from Albuquerque. La Bajada Visitor Center offers a wide assortment of free publications about Santa Fe and northern New Mexico and the state of New Mexico's comprehensive free vacation guide. It's a logical first stop for travelers arriving from Albuquerque. For added comfort, the center has public restrooms and telephones maintained by the state highway department. Take an extra minute here and enjoy the view of glittering Santa Fe below you with the blue Sangre de Cristo mountains towering in the background. The center is open from 8 AM to 5 PM daily except Christmas and New Year's Day.

Plaza Information Booth
62 Lincoln Ave. in the portal window of the First National Bank on the Plaza
• no phone

Volunteers from the Santa Fe Chamber of Commerce staff the Plaza Information Booth as a service to Santa Fe's multitude of visitors during the peak of the tourist season. You'll find brochures of all kinds and free copies of locally published visitor guides. They can give you a list of restaurants and lodging possibilities. Even better, you'll find people who live here and can answer your questions. Mid-May through mid-September, the booth is open from 9 AM to 4 PM Monday through Friday, .

New Mexico Public Lands Information Center
1474 Rodeo Rd. • 438-7542

This interagency program offers a full line

Indian Portal Sales Continue Long Tradition

What's Santa Fe's most popular visitor attraction? The American Indian vendors under the portal at the Palace of the Governors win the contest.

The Museum of New Mexico estimates that 2.4 million people spend some time each year looking at the jewelry, pottery and other wares on display and for sale here. Pictures of this colorful bazaar have run in thousands of national and international publications. The portal program is the only operation of its kind in the country. The market, officially known as the Native American Vendors Program, is the oldest, the largest and the most visible program of the entire Museum of New Mexico system.

The tradition of trade on the Palace porch predates the museum by centuries, but the museum happily encouraged the practice when it became caretaker of the historic building. The sales fit in nicely with the museum's goal of protecting and advancing Southwestern American Indian arts. The program also allows the museum to provide information about the vitality and diversity of Indian arts and crafts to the public. Visitors can talk directly to the artists and craftspeople about their work and their lives in an historically relevant setting. For some people, this may be the first conversation they've ever had with an American Indian. For the vendors, it's an opportunity to meet people from throughout the world and to sell their work on a schedule that allows them to take time for the social and ceremonial duties living on a pueblo or reservation may require.

The American Indians you see selling on any given day come from a group of 800 approved vendors representing more than 300 households. The vendors elect a 10-person committee each year to monitor the program, making sure all merchandize is handmade and of the highest quality and screening new participants. Many of the American Indians who sell here also have been selected to participate at the annual Indian Market sponsored by the Southwestern Association for Indian Arts and at the Eight Northern Pueblos Arts and Crafts Show.

Among the artists are American Indians from all 19 of New Mexico Pueblos, the Hopi, the Navajo Nation and the Jicarilla and Mescalero Apache tribes. Although some of the artists are descendants of people who sold here centuries ago, no one is guaranteed a space.

The program is remarkable for its egalitarian nature. Each morning numbers are put along the portal's thick adobe walls designating each sales space. When the vendors arrive, they put their

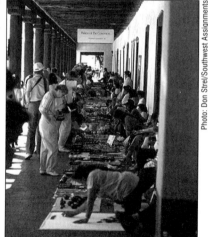

The American Indian vendors under the portal at the Palace of the Governors are one of our most popular attractions.

— continued on next page

blanket beneath the number of the space they want. If 69 or fewer vendors come for the day, everyone get his or her selected space. If more than 69 artists want to sell, a lottery is held. Each vendor draws a chip. Those who get chips with numbers win spaces; those who get blanks . . . well, they may still get spaces.

"If a person draws a blank, he can go home but usually he can still sell," museum program coordinator Sarah Laughlin said. "Usually a friend will share, will give up half his space. There are some spaces along curves on the wall which can't be easily shared, but the portal can accommodate up to 120 people. Fair is the main value among the vendors."

The prices here are also fair. They may be a little lower than in the nearby shops, but because all the jewelry and pottery is created with labor intensive methods, it isn't inexpensive. Each piece must bear the artist's stamp or signature. Some vendors may bargain a little on prices. The artists welcome questions about their work, even if you're "just looking." The more you know about a piece, the more you will appreciate its beauty.

The Portal Program is in every sense a "living exhibit," and it operates 360 days a year from 8 AM to dusk. Even in the dead of winter at least a dozen artists can be found selling here, sometimes wrapped in several colorful blankets. Although there is no provision for taking credit cards along the portal, some of the vendors accept personal checks and travelers checks. The museum also sells gift certificates, which any vendor will welcome.

of books, maps, permits and licenses for people interested in outdoor activities and audiovisual information about recreational opportunities on all of the state's public lands. A partnership between the Bureau of Land Management and the Southwest Natural and Cultural Heritage Association established and maintains the center. In addition to first-rate materials you can buy, you'll find all sorts of free publications. The staff knows the area well. The center is open from 8 AM to 4:30 PM Monday through Friday, and there's plenty of parking.

Santa Fe Chamber of Commerce Information Center
510 N. Guadalupe St. at DeVargas Center North • 983-7317

If you're considering a move to Santa Fe, stop here for information about real estate, taxes, the business climate and more. The Chamber of Commerce has a separate room devoted to all kinds of free material provided by members. It sells, for $35, an annual publication that offers considerable insight into Santa Fe County from a statistical standpoint.

Santa Fe Convention and Visitors Bureau
Sweeney Center, 201 W. Marcy St.
• 984-6760, (800) 777-2489

You'll find a variety of information about Santa Fe here along with a schedule of events for Sweeney Center, one of Santa Fe's most popular spots for conferences, conventions, trade shows and public events. If luck is with you, you'll be able to get a parking place in the city-owned lot right next door. The bureau is an easy walk from the Plaza and downtown hotels. You can pick up information between 8 AM and 5 PM Monday through Friday.

State of New Mexico Santa Fe Welcome Center
491 Old Santa Fe Tr. • 827-7336

Conveniently located near the corner of Old Santa Fe Trail and Paseo de Peralta, right across the street from the State Capitol, this is one of Santa Fe and New Mexico's most comprehensive sources for visitor information. The free maps, brochures and visitor guides are arranged by county. The friendly and knowledgeable staff can answer your questions, or at the very least, refer you to someone else

Photo: Don Strel/Southwest Assignments

The Plaza welcomes the community and visitors during the year.

who can. And if you time it right, you might be able to find a shady parking place for your RV while you gather the information you need. Best of all, this center is open from 8 AM to 5 PM seven days a week! The center occupies the historic Lamy Building (see the listing in this chapter).

Worth the Trip

The Georgia O'Keeffe House
C.R. 165, No. 13, Abiquiu • 685-4539

If homes reflect the personalities of their owners, you won't find a better example than the Abiquiu house of the late Georgia O'Keeffe. Like the artist herself, the 7,000-square-foot adobe is strikingly beautiful yet austere and even aloof. Despite its cool, almost disengaging personality, the residence reveals magnitudes about O'Keeffe and her work. Once off-limits to the public, the mesa-top home and its magnificent views are now available by appointment only.

No doubt O'Keeffe, who treasured her privacy nearly as much as the stones and skulls she collected on her countless high-desert hikes, would be appalled at gawking strangers traipsing by the dozen through her home to glean some small nugget of information about the enigmatic artist.

The public, however, apparently does not share that opinion. Literally thousands of O'Keeffe admirers have visited the artist's house and studio since the Santa Fe-based Georgia O'Keeffe Foundation began giving tours in 1994. Few are disappointed with the four-bedroom, three-bath residence, which remains essentially as O'Keeffe left it in 1984 when she moved to Santa Fe — and nearer to medical care — for the last two years of her life. One certainly comes away from the house understanding O'Keeffe's keen sense of simplicity, balance and focus. Her home inspires a soothing, inviting calm with clean, simple lines and muted colors that draw in and celebrate the glorious Southwestern panorama that so captivated O'Keeffe.

Tours of O'Keeffe's home and studio are by reservation only. Make reservations well in advance as the waiting list sometimes tops 100. To schedule a tour and get directions, contact the Georgia O'Keeffe Foundation, P.O. Box 40, Abiquiu, NM 87510, 685-4539. The foundation usually limits tours to 12 people at a time, but it may accommodate larger groups with advance notice. Tours take place Tuesdays, Thursdays and Fridays from April through November and possibly through December. The hour-long tour costs $20 per person. Proceeds benefit the Georgia O'Keeffe Foundation and are tax deductible. Abiquiu is approximately one hour northwest of Santa Fe — out of our normal coverage area but well-worth the trip.

Despite its reputation as a cultural mecca and sophisticated town, Santa Fe also welcomes kids with all sorts of fun things to do.

Kidstuff

Keep them busy! Every parent knows that activity is a key to sibling peace and parental sanity. If children are playing, reading, exploring and discovering new things, they don't have the time or energy to fight with each other or argue with you.

In this chapter, you'll find a variety of events, attractions, camps, excursions and programs for children in the Santa Fe area. Despite its reputation as a cultural mecca and sophisticated town, Santa Fe also welcomes kids with all sorts of fun things to do. Not only will they be busy, but they'll also learn something here, too!

Like adult visitors, children have two basic sets of options: things to see and to do in town and attractions and adventures in the big outdoors surrounding Santa Fe. The city has a museum designed and constructed just for kids, complete with a special child-size door. Santa Fe has a river to walk along, parks to explore, an Audubon Center, swimming pools, places to skate and a bowling alley. The mountains and foothills surrounding Santa Fe are rich with opportunities for family picnics, hiking, skiing and mountain biking. If you didn't bring bikes, you can rent them in town. And don't forget the sunscreen!

In the spring and summer, parents and kids can take a raft trip, spending a day on the Rio Grande or Rio Chama having fun and getting wet. Many commercial rafting companies are based in Santa Fe and offer a variety of options from gentle floats to white-water excitement. Please call first and ask if there are age requirements; some trips don't accept the youngest children. (See our Recreation chapter for more on rafting.) Horseback riding is another popular option. Trail rides through a variety of terrain, breakfast trips and campfire rides are available from several businesses and resorts in the area. Many stables also offer riding lessons for children.

Fishing, surprisingly to some people, is as much a part of summer here as it is anywhere in the USA. Children younger than age 12 can fish for free in New Mexico. In the Santa Fe area, opportunities for lake fishing — which is often easier for young children — include the Cochití, Abiquiú, Santa Cruz and Monastery lakes. Nambé, Santa Clara and San Juan pueblos have public fishing lakes (see our regional map in the front of this book). If you want your kids to try stream or river fishing, the Rio Grande between Santa Fe and Taos off N.M. Highway 68 — especially near Pilar — is worth a visit. Or cast your lines into the Pecos River and streams that flow into it in the Santa Fe National Forest outside the community of Pecos, off Interstate 25 on N.M. Highway 63 about 30 miles east of Santa Fe.

In the winter, you and your kids can have fun together at the Santa Fe Ski Area, which offers an extensive program of classes for children, or along cross-country trails in the Santa Fe National Forest and elsewhere. You can go sledding or tubing in Hyde Park, north of Santa Fe on N.M. Highway 475. Take a look at our Recreation chapter for other activities and destinations that are ideal for children.

Because Santa Fe boasts one of the country's most vibrant arts communities, our children benefit. Kids can study everything from painting and pottery to drama and dance. We've mentioned a few of these schools in this chapter, but be sure to check the phone book or specialized publications for children for more suggestions. Santa Fe children can put on their own shows or go to professional theater, opera and music productions. Some groups offer special free concerts just for children. Many of the city's events include children in wonderful ways. The Fiesta de Santa Fe, a community celebration each September, invites kids to walk in their own parade. Both the Spanish and Indian Markets, major summer arts and crafts shows, have exhibitor spaces dedicated to children who are also artists.

And, if Santa Fe seems a little too different at times, please realize that our community has the comfortable old standbys — franchised and independent video rental outlets, movie theaters, video arcades and a mall where teens can meet their friends. For more information, *The Santa Fe New Mexican*, 995-3839, offers a "Family Attractions" category in its "Pasatiempo" calendar each Friday and "Best Bets for Kids," on Thursdays. Two specialized free publications, *Tumbleweeds*, 984-3171, and *New Mexico Kids!*, 820-7773, present pages of ideas, suggestions and insights into services and activities for children in the Santa Fe areas.

FYI

Unless otherwise noted, the area code for all phone numbers listed in this guide is 505.

We've done our best to make sure all information in this chapter is current, but the phone numbers are listed for your convenience if you wish to double check on any information. In addition to the information here and in our Recreation chapter, you'll find more suggestions in our Attractions and Arts chapters. Have a good time and remember: Before you know it, your little ones will be all grown up.

Be A Happy Camper

Brush Ranch Camp
Brush Ranch, P.O. Box 5759, Santa Fe 87502 • 757-8821, (800) 722-2843

This long-established camp along the Pecos River in the Sangre de Cristo Mountains east and north of Santa Fe offers an assortment of programs: all sorts of kids' camps for ages 6 to 16 and parent/child camps. You'll find traditional camp and adventure camp for older children, Mountaineers sessions for 9- and 10-year-olds, Trailblazers for 6- to 8-year-old first-time campers and family camp for all ages from grandparents on down. The setting amid the ponderosa pines is beautiful and convenient to Santa Fe. Sessions run one to eight weeks from mid-June through mid-August. Prices range from about $150 to $4,250.

Children's Adventure Company
P.O. Box 146, Tesuque 87574 • 984-8870

This popular program offers an extensive summer camp, overnight camping and after-school programs for children ages 5 up through the 9th grade. Summer day camps include nature trips, cooking, swimming and art with field trips to Albuquerque. The fee for 1997 was $170 a week. Overnights include locations such as Carlsbad Caverns, Abiquiú Lake, Lake Powell and Mesa Verde. Prices began at $180 for a three-day trip. The company also offers enriched after-school programs for kindergartners through 6th graders at $230 per week, with price adjustments for children who don't attend every day.

College of Santa Fe Day Camp
College of Santa Fe, Driscoll Fitness Center, 1600 St. Michael's Dr. • 473-6370

Kids ages 5 to 12 can spend as much as eight weeks here enjoying aerobics, art, basketball, creative dance, field trips, gymnastics, racquetball, rock climbing, soccer, volleyball, swimming, field trips, tennis and theater games. Each two-week session runs from 8 AM to 5 PM Monday through Friday. Fee for the program is $300 per session and includes snacks, hot lunches and a T-shirt. Campers are grouped by age in two-year spreads, and each group contains no more than 20 children. The camp director recommends reservations; programs fill up fast.

Kids College
Santa Fe Community College, 6401 Richards Ave. • 438-1251

Why wait until you're big to go to college? Santa Fe Community College invites children ages 5 to 10 to come on campus and take courses especially designed for them. In the past, programs have included explorations of the cultures of Latin America, Africa and Japan through music, toy-making and food. Another component teaches science using games, magic tricks and rocket building. In other years, programs have combined physical activities such as dance and aikido with the arts, including theater and studio art, in inventive ways. The Kids College is offered in two different four-day sessions in late July and early August. The fee in 1997 was $65 per session.

Southwest Basketball Camp
5555 Zumi Ave. SE, Ste. 280,
Albuquerque • 265-6673

For children who enjoy dunking, layups and the excitement of basketball, Southwest Basketball Camp is a dream come true. Camp director Marvin Johnson works with boys and girls ages 6 to 16, focusing on fun, skill improvement and making new friends. Johnson, a former Chicago Bull and University of New Mexico Lobo, brings the camp to Santa Fe each summer and during school breaks. The program, which draws kids from throughout the city, includes conditioning, skills work, drills and tournaments with prizes to the top players. Participants are divided into groups according to age and ability. Camps usually run five days and cost about $100. The camp is frequently held at New Mexico School for the Deaf, 1060 Cerrillos Road.

SWAIA Youth Art Camp
P.O. Box 15353, Santa Fe 87506
• 983-5220

The Southwestern Association for Indian Arts Inc. welcomes students from kindergarten through the 9th grade to apply for this four-week, half-day camp that usually begins in mid-June. The children work with American Indian artists and counselors and concentrate on a different cultural subject each week. Areas of focus include painting, beadwork, pottery, drawing and music. The camp is open to Indian and non-Indian students, and space is limited. The fee in 1997 was $185.

Youth Leadership Camp
Santa Fe Community College, 6401
Richards Ave. • 438-1618

Designed to teach self-confidence as well as outdoor skills, this camp welcomes boys and girls from ages 11 to 16. The programs include a ropes course, orienteering, environmental awareness, team building and collaborative skills. In addition to outdoor skills, the leaders help the participants learn to trust themselves and each other and to make their own good decisions. Fee in 1997 was $250, and camps were held in two five-day sessions in June and July. The camp is part of the Santa Fe Community College Intercultural Community Leadership Program.

Be Dramatic/Get Arty!
Classes and Workshops

Art Academy de los Niños
2504 Calle de los Niños • 473-3003

The summer camp and after-school programs here focus on many different art media. Private sessions can also be arranged. The teacher is a longtime art educator who works with students to help develop and release their innate creativity. Media range from drawing and painting to sculpture and pottery. Camps runs for a week for $75 including all materials; after-school classes are $45 a month for weekly 90-minute sessions.

Art and Clay Studio
851 W. San Mateo Rd., Ste. 4 • 989-4278

This comprehensive art school offers programs for ages 6 through adults and has separate classes for teens. All arts and crafts activities are taught by professional artists. Students may work with a potter's wheel or try sculpture, painting, printmaking, tie-dying, silkscreening, puppet making, paper making, bookbinding and more. The studio offers after-school, holiday and summer programs. The fee for seven weeks of class is about $100.

Art is Fine
Museum of Fine Arts, 107 W. Palace Ave.
• 827-4472

Fourth through 8th graders can take classes in various forms of the fine arts here. A recent session offered 10 Saturday mornings of painting with acrylics, beginning with stretching and priming canvases and culminating with an exhibit at the museum. Fee is $100 for the 10-week session.

The Children's Dance Program
Railyard Performance Center, 430 W.
Manhattan Ave. • 982-1662

Ballet, modern dance, tap, jazz, hip-hop, flamenco, Asian and Persian dance, programs for mothers and daughters and more are offered here for children ages 3 to 15. Kids can go to class after school or on weekends, with special summer workshops available.

Santa Fe Dance Foundation
1504 Cerrillos Rd. • 983-5591

Children ages 3 through their teens can study ballet, modern dance, creative movement and jazz here. Adult classes are also available. The students dance in at least one annual public performance. A single class costs $10; the rate goes down depending on the number of classes taken. An annual performance of the *Nutcracker* and a spring recital gave the students on-stage experience.

Movement Arts of Santa Fe
3662 Cerrillos Rd., Ste. A5 • 438-4440

This school of contemporary dance offers classes for boys and girls, children and teens. Programs include creative dance for 3-and 4-year-olds, movement for boys ages 5 to 7 and ballet, modern dance, tap, jazz and Spanish dance for several different ages. Class size is limited. Scholarships and discounts for multifamily members are available.

National Dance Institute of New Mexico
P.O. Box 831, Tesuque 87547 • 983-7646

This exceptional program works with several Santa Fe Public elementary schools each year to offer the students an introduction to movement and dance. Lessons culminate with a public performance. A recent show, *El Arbol de Familia* brought together a cast of 400 children from schools throughout the city — most of whom had never been on stage before — to present an original musical at Greer Garson Theater for parents, friends and the community in general. The National Dance Institute of New Mexico was founded to help children develop discipline, a standard of excellence and a belief in themselves that will carry over to other aspects of their lives. Participation is free thanks to grants and volunteers.

Catch Some Culture

Santa Fe Opera Youth Night and Backstage Tours
Santa Fe Opera Theater, 7 miles north of Santa Fe on U.S. Hwy. 84/285
• 986-5900, (800) 280-4654

Youth Night at the Opera provides children and young adults an opportunity to attend dress rehearsals of the opera productions at low cost. A special adjunct, the Pueblo Opera Program, brings pueblo children and their parents to the opera. (For more information on the Opera, see our Arts chapter.) The kids see a real opera — not a watered-down production. Tickets in 1997 were $25 for one adult chaperone and three children or $40 for two adults and four children. Each additional child's ticket is $5. Tickets for young adults who may come without chaperones (ages 15 to 22) are $5. Most youth night performances sell out early.

Children ages 7 to 15 can accompany a parent free of charge on the Opera's Monday through Saturday back stage tours. Docents show visitors costumes, sets, scenery and props and explain how the Opera makes them. Tours run from late June through the end of the Opera season, usually the third week in August, at 1 PM. People older than 15 pay $6.

Santa Fe Chamber Music Festival Youth Concerts
St. Francis Auditorium, Museum of Fine Arts, Santa Fe Children's Museum
• 983-2075

The festival's youth concerts, founded in 1993, bring music to children in free perfor-

INSIDERS' TIP

Altitude can have an effect on children too. Make sure that your kids get plenty of sleep — or at least rest — during your visit to Santa Fe. They'll need their energy to handle the 7,000-foot elevation, not to mention all the things you'll want to do.

The Santa Fe Children's Museum has a climbing wall, a table filled with magnets and a special day just for preschoolers. Kids even get their own child-sized door here.

mances during July and August. Past programs have included jazzy string music, a presentation about violin-making, a flamenco-inspired piece for chamber ensemble and dancers and a program that highlighted young musicians. The concerts are free thanks to private foundations and support from the City of Santa Fe and the state. The Festival's Passport project gives kids a free ice cream cone and a T-shirt if they attend the entire six-concert program.

Santa Fe Performing Arts School & Company
Armory for the Arts, 1050 Old Pecos Tr.
• 982-7992

These after-school and summer programs provide training in music, dance and drama for Santa Fe kids ages 3 to 18. Company members use the skills and techniques they learn in the workshops to present four annual productions, two designed for and acted by younger children and two for older company members. Past shows have included *Robin Hood*, *Guys and Dolls* and *Little Shop of Horrors*. Tickets for performances are $5 to $12; watch the newspapers for a schedule.

Southwest Children's Theatre
Santa Fe Playhouse, 142 E. DeVargas St.
• 984-3055

Quality children's plays and theater education are offered by this nonprofit group. Adult professionals join the students for final productions, and the classes welcome preschoolers through 8th graders. The children present public performances several times a year, and they build sets and design costumes in addition to acting. Each August, the company schedules a theatrical showcase written, produced and performed by students. This company has worked with children in after-school and summer programs since 1988. Tickets to the shows are usually $2 for adults and children.

Get Moving!

Santa Fe Climbing Gym
825 Early St. • 986-8944

This indoor, air-conditioned gym welcomes children as young as 5 as well as more experienced customers. The weekly Kids Climb program provides fully supervised instruction by climbers who are also trained teachers. The gym also presents outdoor climbing excursions in northwestern New Mexico. Summer programs include wilderness experiences, low-impact camping, ecological expeditions and more. Helmets, shoes, ropes and all other equipment are provided. Rates range from $15 for a Kids Climb session to $225 for a five-day camp. Normal operating hours are from 5 to 10 PM Monday through Friday, 9 AM to 8 PM on Saturday and 1 to 8 PM on Sunday.

DeVargas Skateboard Park
W. De Vargas St. at Sandoval • no phone

A 6-foot-deep bowl, ramps, a half-pipe and a smaller bowl for beginners are part of Santa Fe's downtown skate park, which opened in 1996. Due to its popularity, the city expanded the park in 1997, and it now includes 5,000 square feet of places to skate. This is a great place for middle-school kids, and you'll find older teens and adults here too. Skateboarders have to bring their own wheels. The park charges no fees and is open during daylight hours.

Rockin' Rollers Event Arena
2915 Agua Fría St. • 473-7755

Kids and their parents can rent skates here and roll on to the rhythms that roll out over the sound system. You can even skate to karaoke. All skating sessions include interactive games for skaters of all ages. Rink staff teach skating classes, and if you get tired of skating, you can play in the video arcade. On the weekends, the rink hosts free all-ages evening concerts presenting local bands or a live DJ with music and accompanying videos on what's advertised as Santa Fe's largest screen.

The arena is open for rollerskating on Wednesday from 3 to 5 PM, Friday, Saturday and Sunday afternoons from 1 to 3 PM and an additional Friday session from 3 to 5 PM. Hours are due to expand in 1998. Admission is $3 for one two-hour session or $4.50 for Friday's two-in-a-row with discounts available for groups of 10 and larger. Skaters can bring their own skates — in-line or four-wheelers — as long as they have rubber brakes instead of the plastic ones, which rip up the floor. Or they can rent a pair of quads for 50¢.

Friday and Saturday nights at Rockin' Rollers feature free, dances with an in-house DJ or live concerts featuring local bands. The own-

ers have thousands of music selections to suit every age group and taste — from rap, reggae and rhythm and blues to oldies, disco and easy listening. They also do karaoke and "roller-oke" — karaoke on wheels — and play rock videos and movies on a front projection screen the size of one of their enormous walls. Customers will be pleased to know that the rink's concession stand offers a large variety of reasonably priced snacks. Rockin' Rollers is also available for private parties at $75 for two hours, including a DJ.

Silva Lanes Bowling Center
1352 Rufina Cir. • 471-2110

The 32-lane Silva Lanes offers junior bowling programs including scholarship leagues and scholarship tournaments for competitors as young as 3. Small shoes and light balls make the sport easier for children. The youngest bowlers can try bumper bowling — and be assured of no frustrating gutter balls! This is also a popular spot for Santa Fe's younger set to hold birthday parties. You'll find a full service pro shop, snack bar and video games. The bowling alley is open from 10 AM to 2 AM daily. Fees are $2.25 per game per person for adults and $2 per child. Shoe rental is $1.75 for adults and $1 for kids.

City of Santa Fe
Public Swimming Pools
Fort Marcy Complex, 490 Washington Ave. • 984-6725
Salvador Perez Pool, 601 Alta Vista St. • 984-6755
Tino Griego Pool, 1730 Llano St. • 473-7270
Bicentennial Pool, 1121 Alto St. • 984-6773 (open summers only)

The city's pools score big with Santa Fe kids. Fort Marcy has a tot pool with warmer water and a shallow bottom for minnows 5 and younger. The pools all set aside special times for recreational swimming and family fun. Each pool has different hours for open swimming, and schedules vary seasonally; please call for information and to find out about classes. Swimming costs $1.25 for adults 18 and older, $1 for students with IDs, 50¢ for children 8 to 13 and free for children younger than 7 and seniors older than 60.

Santa Fe City Parks and Recreation Programs
Locations vary • 438-1485

The City of Santa Fe offers an extensive summer recreation program and an assortment of other events during the year. Children can learn to swim and play tennis or spend the day in a park with a program of sports, games and arts and crafts. All offerings are free or inexpensive — $20 for a month of daily half-hour swimming classes, for example. Kids also can compete in basketball and football contests, races and fun walks. The city sponsors summer gymnastics, cheerleading camps, a diaper bash, pumpkin-carving contests and an Easter egg hunt. Listing all the specifics would take the rest of this chapter, but if you call the city recreation office at the number above, you can get a free printed schedule — a booklet, actually — with all times, dates, prices and addresses.

When it comes to parks, Santa Fe had 49 at last count, and all of them welcomed kids. Many have swings, slides, tot equipment, tennis courts, basketball hoops and fields for sports. Salvador Perez, 610 Alta Vista Street, 984-6755, provides a fine fenced tot lot where toddlers can swing, slide, play in the sand and explore to their hearts content. The park, next to the Salvador Perez Pool, has a train locomotive engine (fenced for safety) as its centerpiece. The Villa Linda Park, 4250 Cerrillos Road, offers swings, slides and climbing bars as well as a picnic area and a multipurpose field that's perfect for Frisbees. The Monica Roybal Center, 737 Agua Fría Street, 984-6750, has lit outdoor basketball courts and offers programs for kids after school and during the summer. The Roybal Center stresses family involvement through many of its programs. At the Fort Marcy Complex, 490 Washington Avenue, 984-6725, you'll find a gym for basketball, fitness classes for kids, a weight room and outdoor fields for soccer, baseball and other sports in addition to a pool.

For a different kind of park, visit the Arroyo Chamisa Trail. The paved path stretches from Yucca Road to Villa Linda Mall and past the Monica Lucero Park with its ballfields, playground and tot lot at 2356 Avenida de la Campanas. The trail meanders along the Arroyo Chamisa, a major wash that is dry 99 percent of the year, and past a colorful mural painted by Santa Fe youth. The trail draws families from all over town. The route can be used by strollers and tricycles and is especially inviting at sunset. And don't forget the Frenchy's Field Park, Agua Fría Street and Osage Avenue, a passive park with walking trails, picnic areas and its own pond.

Join the Club

Santa Fe Boys and Girls Club
730 Alto St. • 983-6632

This longtime Santa Fe youth center finished an extensive remodeling job in 1997 and launched some new programs to help serve Santa Fe kids for decades to come. Established in 1942, the club now serves about 4,500 Santa Fe county children and teens with special events and activities. Programs include basketball, music, dancing, photography, boxing, computer labs, tutoring of all sorts and job training. The club staff also works with members on substance-abuse prevention and personal and social skills including conflict management. Children and teens can study for scholarships and college placement tests or prepare for their high school diplomas.

In addition to the main building on Alto Street, the Boys and Girls Club offers programs in other locations in Santa Fe county. The members are ages 6 to 17. The club is open after school until 6 PM and from 7:30 AM to 6 PM during spring and winter break and during the summer. Membership, on a sliding scale, ranges from $30 a week during the summer to $30 a year.

Girls Inc.
301 Hillside Ave. • 982-2042

Girls Inc. and its predecessor, the Santa Fe Girls Club, have served Santa Fe girls since 1957. Part of a national organization to help girls, Girls Inc. offers after-school programs, a summer camp and special camps during the schools' winter holidays and spring break. Programs are designed for girls ages 6 to 12 and include arts and crafts, sports, cooking, field trips, guest speakers, community service projects and more. The summer and holiday camps work with girls from 7:30 AM until 6 PM

Monday through Friday and are popular among parents who work at the State Capitol or City Hall because of the club's downtown location near Hillside Park. Membership fee is $10 annually. The camps are offered on a sliding fee scale; some girls attend at no cost.

Just for Fun

Engine House Theatre
Melodrama Engine House Theatre, 2846 N.M. Hwy. 14, Madrid • 438-3780

Kids and adults can have fun together at the Engine House Theatre. The company presents classic Victorian melodrama, inviting the audience to cheer the hero and hiss the villain. They pattern the plots after old-time shows: A sweet young thing in distress is threatened with loss of home and virtue by a sinister, black-hearted scoundrel, but in the nick of time, the handsome hero . . . you get the picture. The show runs weekends and holidays from Memorial Day through mid-October. Curtain time is 3 and 8 PM on Saturday and 3 PM on Sunday and holidays, with matinees only during October. Tickets are $9 for adults, $7 for seniors and $4 for children younger than 12. Allow at least a half-hour to get to the theater from Santa Fe. The drive, along what's known as the Turquoise Trail, will take you past the historic village of Cerrillos and into Madrid, an old mining town.

FYI

Unless otherwise noted, the area code for all phone numbers listed in this guide is 505.

Jets Arcade
Villa Linda Mall, 4250 Cerrillos Rd. • 471-2909

Santa Fe's largest video arcade, Jets offers a variety of games, including Laser Storm. Junior-high and high-school kids like to hang here, testing their skill against each other and the video geniuses who invent these games. Kids drop in quarters to play and win tickets, which they exchange for prizes. The arcade has a party room for birthday celebrations and nonviolent games suitable for younger children. The arcade is open from 9:30 AM to 10 PM on weekdays, from 9:30 AM to 11 PM on Friday and Saturday and from 11 AM to 10 PM on Sunday.

Santa Fe Southern Railway
410 S. Guadalupe St. • 989-8600

If your children are interested in trains, you can satisfy their curiosity here. The vintage coaches of this working freight train leave from the Guadalupe Street area, travel to the neighboring community of Lamy, stop 90 minutes for lunch and then come back. The railway also offers special rides, including some with Santa and clowns — call to find out if they have any scheduled. The trains leave at 10:30 AM and usually return by 3 PM. Trips are held on Thursdays and Saturdays every month, with additional Tuesday trips from March through October and additional Sunday trips from April through October. From May through October the train offers Sunset/Starlight rides on Friday evenings with departure one hour before sunset; call for specific times. Tickets are $21 for ages 14 to 59, $16 for age 7 to 13 and those older than 60, $5 for ages 3 to 6 and free for children two and younger (limit two per adult). Group rates, charters, private car facilities and school rates are available.

Stories at the Tipi
Wheelwright Museum, 704 Camino Lejo • 982-4636

Affable Joe Hayes entertains children and grownups with stories drawn from Hispanic and American Indian traditions and the Wild West. Join this professional writer and yarn-spinner on summer evenings for first-class entertainment. You can carry along a picnic, and be sure to bring a blanket or cushion to sit on. The program usually lasts about an hour, and even the youngest children stay attentive because of Hayes' skill at presenting the different accents and voices of the characters he's talking about. The audiences especially love stories about *La Llorona*, Santa Fe's legendary weeping woman, and funny tales of Coyote the Trickster. Hayes entertains on at 7 PM on Saturday and Sunday from July through August. Admission is free.

Toy Lending Center
Santa Fe Community College, Division of Early Childhood, 6401 Richards Ave.
• 438-1354

Parents can borrow toys and equipment free of charge here, selecting from among more than 2,000 items. The center offers a good assortment of toys for preschoolers with some choices for kindergartners and school-age children. Among the possibilities are blocks, riding toys, woodworking tools, easels, chalkboards and musical instruments. Best of all, the center will loan you the toys and equipment you want for free once you've completed the registration forms. The center is open weekdays from 8 AM to 5 PM.

Kid-Friendly Museums

El Rancho de las Golondrinas
334 Los Pinos Rd., La Cienega
• 471-2261

The geese, goats, sheep and burros are waiting for your kids here. Frogs croak and swim in the ponds, and lizards sun themselves on rocks nearby. Animals are a big attraction of this living ranch and museum, where no one says "don't touch." Kids may have a chance to sample bread freshly baked in an *horno*, an outdoor beehive-shape oven, and to grind corn with *mano* and *metate*, the stone tools used by the early settlers. They can also meet costumed villagers who will explain what it was like to live in New Mexico 200 years ago. "The ranch of the swallows" offers a vivid re-creation of the area's 18th- and 19th-century Hispanic history. The ranch wasn't built for tourists; this was the last stop on *El Camino Real* before Santa Fe on the grueling journey from Mexico City to the northern provinces of New Spain.

Children can walk inside the restored buildings — built on original foundations and furnished as appropriate to the period. They can sit in a Colonial school house and marvel at the lack of playground equipment and computers. The museum's self-guided tour involves about a 1.5-mile hike over roads and trails that are sometimes steep and rocky. There's plenty of shade, but it can still be a major expedition for a preschooler. You should allow at least an hour and a half. If you're in luck, you'll be able to bring your kids to Golondrinas on a festival day, when the museum buzzes with excitement. Volunteers chat with visitors and demonstrate many of the skills early settlers needed to survive on the frontier. Lively dancing, foot-stomping music and scrumptious food add to the fun.

El Rancho de las Golondrinas also presents theme weekends throughout the summer, including one that focuses on storytelling and another about the animals the Spanish brought with them to New Mexico — both fine events for children. (Check with the local papers or call the museum for the dates.) Admission fees vary depending on what's happening at the museum. From June through September, you can tour the ranch on your own and bring a picnic. Admission then is $4 adults, $3 seniors (62 and older), teens and military and $1.50 for ages 5 through 12. During the festivals or Civil War Weekend, admission is $6 adults, $4 seniors, teens and military and $2.50 for children 5 through 12. Children younger than 5 always get in free.

To reach the ranch from Santa Fe, take I-25 S. to Exit 246 and bear right on N.M. Highway 599. Turn left at the first intersection on the frontage road and right just before the race track on Los Pinos Road. The museum is 3 miles from this intersection.

Santa Fe Children's Museum
1050 Old Pecos Tr. • 989-8359

Children — especially those 12 and younger — get a chance to learn by doing here. The "exhibits" are hands-on activities that involve water, magnets, live snakes and giant cockroaches, bubbles you can stand inside, a climbing wall, microscopes, magnets, pulleys, beading and weaving looms and a place outside to garden and make adobes. Founded in

1989, Santa Fe Children's Museum was the first museum just for kids in the state. It receives more than 65,000 visitors a year. Children from all 50 states and 49 foreign countries have played inside these walls. Because it treasures toddlers, too, the museum has a special climbing structure for them and sets aside time each month when toddlers and their parents have the place all to themselves.

The Children's Museum complements its exhibits with a lively program of guest teachers and special evening performances for families. Saturday afternoons, the museum invites guest art teachers to work with children in a variety of media. Sundays, visiting scientists introduce astronomy, physics, electricity and biology in ways that can make kids giggle. Once a month, the museum invites children with special needs to a Very Special Arts Day. For parents, child development specialists are on hand on Saturdays to answer questions about how best to raise your son or daughter.

The museum is open from 10 AM to 5 PM Thursday through Saturday and noon to 5 PM on Sunday from September through May. June through August, it's also open on Wednesday. The museum is closed from Labor Day through the second Tuesday in September. Please call for special holiday hours and programs. Admission is $3 for adults and $2 for children younger than 12.

Museum of International Folk Art
706 Camino Lejo • 827-8350

Even kids who think they don't like museums will enjoy the treasures of "Multiple Visions: A Common Bond" in the Girard Wing. It's the largest collection of dolls, toys and miniatures ever assembled by a private citizen. Collector Alexander Girard's folk art gems shine even more brightly because the museum displays them in "environments" resembling miniature cities, village markets,

even Heaven and Hell. Windows cleverly placed at a child's eye level enable the smaller visitors to see on their own. The museum has juxtaposed the 106,000 objects from more than 100 countries to stress their connections through themes and imagery. For instance, a market scene unites objects from the Mediterranean and Latin America; African beadwork is exhibited with Native American beadwork.

The museum sometimes schedules special weekend programs and celebrations for children and their families. Events such as a Caribbean festival, complete with island music, and a chile festival in honor of northern New Mexico's harvest bring happy crowds of parents and children. See our Attractions chapter for information on hours and prices for the museums for the Museum of New Mexico system.

Museum of Indian Arts and Culture
710 Camino Lejo • 827-6344

You and your children can get a wonderful introduction to the richness of American Indian culture in the "Here Now and Always," exhibit. This multimedia presentation lets children hear Indians speaking their own languages and look at a pueblo kitchen, an Apache wickiup, a Navajo hogan, a 1930s trading post and a contemporary feast day vendor's booth. The museum is next to the Museum of International Folk Art; if you're judicious in your looking, you can easily take your children to both on the same day. See our Attractions chapter for more information.

The Palace of the Governors
105 E. Palace Ave. • 827-6483

Kids can see authentic armor like that worn by the conquistadors and Old West stage coaches that traveled the Santa Fe Trail. Among the museum's displays, you'll spot

INSIDERS' TIP

The Santa Fe Children's Museum hosts an annual birthday party each February, with free admission and a big birthday cake to thank everyone who makes it the city's most popular museum among the younger set. The night before the family party, the museum hosts a benefit dinner and auction to raise some of the money needed to keep its doors open.

tools used by the Spanish settlers, traps used by the early fur traders and fancy party dresses worn by Santa Fe *senoritas* centuries ago. The artifacts help bring the state's story to life. The collections here will be of interest to older children, especially those who know something about New Mexico's days as a Spanish territory or who are curious about the past. See our Attractions chapter for more details.

Kid-Style Events

May

Community Day in Santa Fe
On the Plaza • 984-6568

Face-painting, chalk-drawing, balloons, music, food and more add sparkle to this annual event, designed to bring local families back to the Plaza. The activities pack the Plaza with friendly folks, including children, grandparents and even some teenagers. The Santa Fe Public Schools may use the occasion to highlight special projects in the works in their buildings all over towns. Nonprofit agencies that help families and children use the festival to get the word out about their services.

Children's performing groups from local schools often add to the day's mix of live entertainment. The program varies from year to year, but the goal is the same: a day of relaxed, free fun. Watch for Community Day on a Saturday in early to mid-May.

El Corazon de Santa Fe
On the Plaza • 984-6568

Children are welcome at this series of family events, sponsored by the City of Santa Fe in conjunction with nonprofit and commercial sponsors. These free Saturday night performances may begin as early as mid-May and stretch into September. Among the specific themes in summers past have been Teen Night, organized by the Santa Fe Boys and Girls Club; a tribute to rock'n'roll complete with a '50s-style band with poodle skirts; community talent night, which featured Santa Fe's best amateur musicians, dancers and comedians; and Festival Santa Fe, with cameos from many of the city's performing arts groups. Bring the kids and don't dress up. You don't need a ticket because the events are free. The entertainment usually lasts from 6 until 10 PM, and you can arrive and depart at your convenience. The performance schedule runs in the newspapers beginning in late spring.

Photo: Don Strel/Southwest Assignments

The Santa Fe Airshow, held each Father's Day, gives kids a chance to climb inside planes and helicopters.

June

Santa Fe Air Show
Santa Fe Airport, Airport Rd. S.
• 471-5111

Children love this event because they can see the planes up close and even climb right inside some of them. Among the air show's drawing cards are flybys, stunt pilots doing aerobatics and a sizeable display of military aircraft. The event has simple objectives: family fun, promoting and educating people about aviation and raising money for local charities, including those that work with kids and families. The date is easy to remember: It's always on Father's Day weekend so kids can bring their dads. (Moms and grandparents are welcome too.) The show is ideal for strollers and wheelchairs — once you reach the airstrip, everything is paved and flat. Visitors can buy T-shirts and a variety of aviation memorabilia and nosh on hot dogs and other festival-type food. Bring a hat and wear your sunscreen: It can get hot on the tarmac! Tickets are $5; children younger than age 5 get in free. Parking fee is $1.

FYI

Unless otherwise noted, the area code for all phone numbers listed in this guide is 505.

July

Fourth of July Pancake Breakfast
On the Plaza • 983-7317

Santa Fe families often plan to meet their friends on the Plaza for this festival event. Food is the centerpiece of this day of community fun, a fund-raiser for United Way of Santa Fe County. Hundreds of community volunteers cook pancakes and ham, serve coffee, orange juice and milk and chat with the crowd. On the bandstand, continuous entertainment ranges from mariachi music to dancing grandmothers. Red, white and blue balloons make the Plaza look festive, and you can buy a commemorative T-shirt for yourself and your brood to mark the day. Breakfast tickets are $5 and can usually be purchased in advance from the Chamber of Commerce as well as on the

Fourth itself. Watch the papers for other sales locations.

Western Days
Various locations and prices • 471-4300

The Rodeo de Santa Fe is the centerpiece of this nine-day celebration that calls attention to an interesting part of Santa Fe's past — its role in the development of the American West. The rodeo has expanded in recent years to spotlight special events just for the little wranglers. In the calf scramble, kids grab for a ribbon tied to the tail of a calf; in mutton busting they try their skill at riding uncooperative sheep. Registration is free, but only a limited number of kids can join the fun: It's first-come, first-served. Tickets for rodeo performances range from $4 to $14, and parking is free. The Rodeo takes place at the Santa Fe Rodeo Grounds, Rodeo Road at Richards Avenue. You can buy food and beverages from vendors who stroll the stands or from booths on the rodeo grounds. Western Days begin the Wednesday after the Fourth of July with a community parade complete with clowns, horses and candy for the kids. In 1997 the celebration included other events and festivities, among them a free Western Days Dance on the Plaza, with music for the two-step and line dancing from 6 to 10 PM. Buckaroos of all ages are welcome. Rancho Encantado, on N.M. Highway 592 about eight miles from the Plaza, 982-3537, hosted a Western barn dance, ($5) and trail rides ($45 or $35 for resort guests). Watch the newspapers for a complete schedule of events.

Eight Northern Indian Pueblos Arts and Crafts Show
At a Northern Pueblo • (800) 793-4955

The largest Indian-run art show in the country, the annual Eight Northern Pueblos Arts and Crafts Fair doesn't leave kids out. Young American Indian artists have their own booth at this huge outdoor event and get to meet potential buyers and talk about their work. Children also share space in family booths throughout this huge outdoor show and sale. Usually held the third weekend in July, this show attracts top American Indian artists from throughout New Mexico, the Southwest and the nation. A variety of live performances of American Indian music and traditional dancing adds to the festival, and many of the dance groups include children. You can buy food and drinks here as well as jewelry, pottery, baskets, weavings, paintings, designer clothing and other arts and crafts. Various northern pueblos take turns hosting the show, but none is far from Santa Fe. Wear sunscreen, a hat and sturdy shoes — you may have to hike several blocks from the parking area to get to the show grounds.

Traditional Spanish Market/ Contemporary Hispanic Market
On the Plaza • 983-4038

Work by children and teens is included in the traditional market, both in conjunction with their families and at a table devoted exclusively to youth. *Santos* (painted images of the saints), *bultos* (carved religious images), tinwork, silver filigree jewelry, secular wood carving, weaving, straw inlay and embroidery are all here. The youths' creations are especially popular among market shoppers who may be looking to discover the next major *santero*. The traditional market celebrates Santa Fe's Spanish heritage; the contemporary market allows the artists more leeway to experiment with new materials and techniques. Both are juried. Children also enjoy the demonstrations of ancient craft techniques including rope making and blacksmithing. Traditional Hispanic dancing, music and food add to the fun. Admission is free.

August

Ice Cream Social
Santa Fe Children's Museum, 1050 Old Pecos Tr. • 989-8359

If there's any better way to sweeten a summer afternoon than with a bowl of ice cream, it involves adding the goodies you need to turn your vanilla into a sundae or even a banana split. The museum goes all out for this annual family-style fund raiser. The sticky fun begins at noon, traditionally on the first Sunday in August, and contin-

ues through early evening — or until the ice cream runs out. Santa Fe celebrities, including the mayor, the superintendent of schools and chief of police, have helped with the scooping. Some years, a big red fire truck is on hand, and the firefighters offer the little ones an up-close look. You'll also find music and performances by children here throughout the day. All the money goes directly for new exhibits at the museum, the only one in Santa Fe dedicated to kids. There's no admission fee, and ice cream is $2.50 a serving.

Mountain Man Trade Fair
Palace of the Governors, 105 E. Palace Ave. • 827-6483

The mountain men, traders and trappers who lived by their wits and spent long months of time in the backcountry, are a colorful part of northern New Mexico's history. The Palace of the Governors, once the center of New Mexico's political life and now a popular history museum, hosts this annual fair as tribute to Santa Fe's role as a trade center. Modern mountain men — and mountain women — come in costume to sell handmade items that are often reproductions of the tools, weapons and domestic items these traders would have sold a hundred years ago. Demonstrations of mountain-man skills, such as tomahawk tossing and musket firing, and a program on animals such as beaver, fox and mink are guaranteed kid pleasers. Please call for specific events and a schedule. The fair is usually held mid-month in the museum's central courtyard. Admission is free.

Santa Fe County Fair
Santa Fe County Fair Grounds, Rodeo Rd. at Richards Ave. • 471-4711

Santa Fe County 4-H plays a major role in this event, and youth exhibits are one of its major attractions. Children can see goats, rabbits, ducks and lambs. One of the highlights is the frog-jumping contest, open to participants of all ages. Kiddie rides, entertainment and concessions sold by bright-eyed 4-Hers add to the fun. Watch for it in early August. Admission is free, and parking is $1.

Indian Market
On and around the Plaza • 983-5220

Although this event is primarily aimed at adults with an interest in American Indian art, several features may appeal to kids. The tented area in Cathedral Park next to St. Francis Cathedral, 131 Cathedral Place, displays work produced by youth who participate in a special outreach and mentorship program though the Southwestern Association for Indian Arts, the group that presents Indian Market. SWAIA opens this area free of charge to talented young people who do not have family members exhibiting at Indian Market. (Those with family may share their booth.) Children also may be interested in the fashion show, usually held on Sunday afternoon of Market weekend, and the musical events on Friday and Saturday nights. The entertainment and its locations change annually — please call or check the local newspapers for detailed information.

Another kid-friendly facet of the market is the demonstrations that are offered continually both Saturday and Sunday of the show. Children can watch American Indian artists make pottery, do silverwork, weave a basket, create intricate beadwork or shape a sculpture from a chunk of stone. And kids love the food, which ranges from green chile cheeseburgers to Indian tacos — dinner-plate-size pieces of quickly fried yeast bread topped with ground beef, onions, chile, tomatoes, lettuce and cheese. You can also buy hot dogs and sodas. To make the market less overwhelming, SWAIA publishes a guide that lists every artist by name and category and includes a map of booth locations. You can get a free copy at the SWAIA office or at their booth on the Plaza during the event. Indian Market is always the weekend following the third Thursday of the month. Admission is free. (Please see our Events chapter for more information on Indian Market.)

September

New Mexico State Fair
State Fair Grounds, 300 San Pedro Blvd. N.E., between Central Ave. and Lomas Blvd., Albuquerque • 265-1791, (800) 867-FAIR

The fair is huge, block on block of displays and attractions. If you're bringing a toddler, don't forget the stroller! A favorite attraction is the midway with its rides and games. A special section, the Kid's Park midway, is dedicated to younger kids with less-intense attractions and two stages for performances, which usually include magic shows and puppet theater.

In addition to the rides, you can spend hours at the petting zoo and in the Spanish, Pioneer and Indian Villages where you'll find entertainment, exhibits and food. At the Youth Hall, young exhibitors have their own competitions in categories from model building to sewing. Don't miss the Insect Zoo in the Youth Hall, complete with giant Madagascar hissing cockroaches and the Central American stripe-legged tarantula. In the evenings, the 16 rodeo performances, complete with top-of-the-line country singers, are also great family fun.

And everyone likes the food, served by more than 100 vendors in virtually every corner of the fairgrounds. You'll find corn on the cob, all sorts of New Mexican treats, freshly baked pies, cool snow cones, cotton candy, hot dogs and burgers, Greek specialties, barbecue and more. The State Fair usually runs from early to mid-September. You can pick up a free schedules of each day's events and a map of the grounds at the information booth. Admission in 1997 was $1 for early birds Monday through Thursday; $4 after 2 PM and on Fridays and weekends. Parking fees are $4 to $8.

INSIDERS' TIP

You'll notice murals throughout the city created by the Santa Fe Youth Mural project. The program teaches teenagers the basics of art, teams them with professional artists and decorates walls and utility boxes with a variety of paintings. Buses and even garbage trucks have been painted as part of the project.

Fiesta De Santa Fe
On the Plaza and other locations
• 988-7575

Not only do kids have their own event at the Fiesta, the entire festival is kid-friendly. The Fiesta, held the weekend following Labor Day, commemorates the Spanish resettlement in Santa Fe after the Pueblo Revolt chased the conquistadors back to Mexico. (See our History chapter.) It's the oldest continuous community celebration in the United States. Children love Fiesta, partly because they get a much-appreciated half-day school holiday on Fiesta Friday. For most revelers, Fiesta begins with the burning of Zozobra and a fireworks show Friday evening. You'll pay $5 (kids get in free) to watch from the field, which is usually VERY crowded. Santa Fe artist Will Shuster created Zozobra, a 44-foot tall puppet with glowing eyes and a gravely voice, to personify the disappointments and mistakes of the year. (His nickname is Old Man Gloom.) Crews of volunteers build Zozobra the week before Fiesta and erect the giant puppet on a huge pole at Fort Marcy Park, 490 Washington Avenue. As the sky grows dark, the puppet comes to life, moaning, growling and waving his hands. (Very young children may be scared.) Finally, after a performance by the Fire Dancers and children dressed as Little Glooms, Zozobra disappears in flames to a rowdy chorus of cheers.

One of the Fiesta's most charming events, the Pet Parade, or *Desfile de los Niños*, "Parade of the Children," happens Saturday morning. Children, parents and pets ranging from cats and dogs to llamas, circle the Plaza and walk along downtown streets. Many of the humans wear costumes to be real or imaginary animals; many of the animals are also dressed up. Watch from the shade of the Plaza or in front of the Palace of the Governors, just across from the Plaza bandstand. Come early for a good seat. Watching and participating are both free.

Throughout Fiesta weekend, the Plaza is alive with free entertainment provided by a variety of local and area music and dance groups, including some composed only of children. A commercial carnival at the Rodeo Grounds adds to the weekend's merriment.

October

Albuquerque International Balloon Fiesta
Balloon Fiesta State Park, Osuna Rd.
near I-25, Albuquerque • 821-1000

Children love this festival, which fills the Albuquerque sky with hundreds of balloons of all colors, shapes and sizes, including some whimsical flying creatures. You can attend four mass ascensions, several evening balloon glows (in which the balloons are inflated but stay on the ground like giant light bulbs), contests that test pilots' skill and a special shape "rodeo." More than 100 of the special shape balloons can be found at the Fiesta; in the past participating pilots have brought giant macaws, flying tennis shoes, dragons and pink pigs. The Balloon Explorium, a tent at the launch site, gives kids a chance to learn about balloon operations from inflation through flight and landing. The history of the sport and safety aspects of ballooning also get attention here. The exhibit is open during ballooning events and there is no charge. About 1.5 million people attend this event over its nine-day run. In addition to the balloons, the Fiesta presents live music including jazz, country-western and mariachi. Food and shopping concessions await visitors. Admission is $4 for adults; kids younger than 12 get in free. (See our Spectator Sports chapter.)

Annual All Children's Powwow
Wheelwright Museum of the American Indian, 704 Camino Lejo • 982-4636

A visit to the powwow is a wonderful way to introduce non-Indian children to one small aspect of American Indian culture. Children can watch other children dance in this competition, which is also a social occasion for the American Indian families who participate. The oldest powwow in the country for children, this event attracts more than 100 young American Indians who perform intertribal, blanket and social dances on either the first or second Saturday of the month. Prizes go to the winners in different age groups, and spectators can take pictures. You'll also find Indian crafts and food sales. The event usually runs from late morning until dusk. The grand entry,

Dinosaur fans of all ages travel to the New Mexico Museum of Natural History in Albuquerque. It's worth the trip.

which opens the powwow, is especially colorful and photogenic. Admission is free.

December

Christmas at the Palace of the Governors
Palace of the Governors, 105 E. Palace Ave. · 827-6483

Musicians, carolers, storytellers and dancers carry the spirit of the holiday season to this big, free party. Christmas at the Palace draws hundreds of Santa Fe families and lucky visitors with good timing. It's an ideal event for children. The celebration includes a visit from Santa and activities that fill nearly every room of this sprawling old museum. Although the party is free, in keeping with the spirit of the season donations of nonperishable food for the poor are welcome. The event, funded in part by the city's arts commission, is usually held on a Thursday and Friday evening in mid-December.

Nature, Anyone?

Chairlift Rides Santa Fe Ski Area
16 miles northeast of Santa Fe on N.M. Hwy. 475 · 983-9155, 982-4429

Kids feel all grown up when they ride to the top of the mountain on this comfy, four-person chairlift. The lift, which is also great for anyone who might enjoy the chance to see a magnificent view without a big hike, takes passengers to the top of Aspen Peak at an elevation of 11,000 feet. If you're energetic, you can continue hiking through the spruce, fir and ponderosa pine. You may see marmots, bushy-tailed woodchuck-like creatures also known as "whistle pigs" for their high-pitched barks. You'll find dozens of different wildflowers and colorful mushrooms. When you're ready, you can ride the lift back down.

The chairlift operates from 10 AM to 3 PM on weekends and holidays from July 4 through Labor Day and again in the fall for aspen viewing, with the dates determined annually based on the weather. Rates are $6 for adults and $4 for children 12 and younger. Children shorter than 46 inches may ride for free accompanied by a paying adult. Tickets for seniors are $4, and one-way trips for hikers are $4.

The Planetarium
Santa Fe Community College, 6401 Richards Ave. • 438-1777, 438-1677

One of Santa Fe's newest attractions for children and families, the Planetarium offers a changing schedule of productions intended to give the audience a better knowledge of the night sky. The planetarium presents children's programs each Saturday at 10:30 AM. Big Bird and Oscar have been among the celebrities who help introduce the young audience to the wonders of astronomy. The planetarium schedules shows of interest to adults as well as children on the first Thursday of each month and on Fridays, usually at 6:30 PM and 8 PM. About 10,000 children visit the planetarium for free each year through a special arrangement with the Santa Fe Public Schools. Tickets are $3.50 for adults, $2 for children 12 and younger and for seniors 65 and older and for community college students with a current ID. Tickets go on sale a half-hour before showtime.

Randall Davey Audubon Center
1800 Upper Canyon Rd. • 983-4609

The popular summer nature programs here fill up quickly and rightly so. Kids get to spend time outside learning about such things as animal camouflage and disguises, nocturnal creatures, tracking and native birds. But you don't have to sign up for a workshop to enjoy this beautiful spot. Families take pleasure in walking along the nature trail — it's a nice stroll even for the youngest ones. You might see a coyote, and you'll probably spot several different varieties of birds. The center's trails begin in the piñon and juniper woodlands and meadows and climb up to the cool ponderosa pine forest. The gift shop sells bird seed, books and other items of interest to naturalists. One of the center's attractions is its convenience; it's only a 10-minute drive from the Plaza. Follow Canyon Road past the intersection of Camino Cabra at Cristo Rey Church to Upper Canyon Road. The center is the very last struc-

ture on Canyon Road. It is open from 9 AM to 5 PM daily. Trail fee is $1 per person.

Santa Fe Farmers' Market
Sanbusco Market Center Parking Lot, 500 Montezuma St. • 983-4098

If your kids think peas come from a can and carrots from a bag, a trip to Farmers' Market will open their eyes and please their taste buds. You can see and buy fresh area produce, colorful cut flowers and freshly baked treats here three days a week, usually from mid-May until sometime in October. You'll find live music at the market most mornings, sometimes with children as part of the performance. The market sometimes hosts special demonstrations and events and sponsors an annual tour to working farms. It's open from 7:30 to 11 AM on Tuesday and Saturday and 9:30 AM to 1:30 PM on Sunday, but those who come early find the best selection. Potential buyers and their children are admitted free.

On the Road

Abiquiú

Ghost Ranch Living Museum
14 miles north of Abiquiú on U.S. Hwy. 84 • 685-4312

This child-welcoming place provides a great introduction to northern New Mexico's animals and geology. Children can see many critters native to this part of the state including hawks and eagles, bears, coyotes, deer, mountain lions and bobcats. The museum houses the creatures, many of whom came to the museum as injured wildlife or abandoned pets, in habitats designed to resemble the animals' native environment. The beaver are big child-pleasers because kids can see inside a beaver den and watch the animals swim and play underwater. The museum also contains exhibits that tie the area's colorful geology to dinosaurs found here. Other exhibits re-create an aspen ecosystem and let children climb inside a fire lookout tower. The museum is open from 8 AM to 4:30 PM Tuesday through Sunday. Admission is by donation.

Albuquerque

Albuquerque Aquarium and Botanic Garden

2601 W. Central Ave. N.W. • 764-6200

The Albuquerque Aquarium, one of Albuquerque's most popular attractions, stands out as one of the few aquariums in the country that isn't located near the ocean. Kids flocked to the place when it opened in 1997, and they're still coming! Children and their parents can have an encounter of the most direct kind with whelks, sea urchins, sea stars and other invertebrates at a hands-on education station — the marine equivalent of a petting zoo. Kids get a kick out of the eel cave with its large population of scary-looking moray eels. The "Inside the Wreck" exhibit features a replica of a 16th-century Spanish ship. But the aquarium's most popular attraction among visitors of all ages is the 285,000-gallon shark tank, where about 20 sand, tiger, brown and nurse sharks circle and watch the people who've come to watch them. The aquarium was blessed with eight baby sandbar sharks in 1997, a rare instance of sharks being born in captivity. Children also enjoy the cool pond outside the building where cartoon-like iron fish, frogs and pelicans splash. The Rio Grande Botanic Garden is just across the plaza from the aquarium. The aquarium is open from 9 AM to 5 PM daily. Admission is $4.50 for adults ages 16 to 64, $2.50 for seniors and children ages 3 to 15. Kids younger than 3 are admitted for free.

Rio Grande Zoological Park

903 10th Street S.W. • 764-6200

The Rio Grande Zoo makes a nice daytrip for northern New Mexico families and for Santa Fe visitors. The zoo offers everything you'd expect and more. The beautifully landscaped grounds include an aviary, elephants, petting departments and a reptile house with 6-foot cobras, 20-foot pythons and Komodo dragons. The zoo recently moved its polar bears to a new $2.2 million exhibit where they cavort in a 14-foot-deep pool, lounge by a stream, play under four waterfalls, slip down a water slide and enjoy an air-conditioned ice cave. Austra-lian animals, Mexican wolves, an exhibit that replicates the African plains and a primate area add to the zoo's attraction. Free bird shows, story hours, animal discovery demonstrations, concerts and other summer programs are part of the zoo's regular events. Call for a schedule.

The zoo has won praise from wildlife specialists for its innovative design techniques that help ensure the animals' physical and psychological well being. The zoo invites children and their parents to become foster parents by sponsoring or "adopting" certain animals as zoo parents. The zoo raises money with special events, including "Saturday Night Wild," in mid-June, which welcomes visitors in the cool of the evening to see the animals when some of them are most active. Contests, face-painting, international food, magicians, puppets, clowns and music add to the fun. Admission to the event is $7. If seeing all the animals makes you hungry, you can buy food at the mid-park Cottonwood restaurant/snack bar or enjoy a brought-from-home picnic. The zoo is open from 9 AM to 4:30 PM Monday through Friday and from 9 AM to 5:30 PM holidays and weekends. Zoo admission is free to children younger than 2, $2.25 for seniors and ages 3 to 15 and $4.25 for ages 16 to 64. Children 12 and younger must be accompanied by an adult.

Explora Science Center and Children's Museum of Albuquerque

Sheraton Old Town Mercado, 800 Rio Grande Blvd. N.W. • 842-5525

Once separate museums, these two programs moved to a shared space in late 1997. Children enjoy the hands-on exhibits, which are especially designed for ages 2 to 12. Weekends bring storytellers, musical performances, science and art workshops, dance concerts and more. Kids are welcome to have birthday parties here. The museum is open 9 AM to 4 PM on Thursday and Friday, 9 AM until 8 PM on Wednesday, 9 AM to 5 PM on Saturday and noon to 5 PM on Sunday. It is closed Mondays and Tuesdays. Admission is $2 for ages 2 to 12 and for visitors older than 62; it's $4 for ages 13 to 62 and free for children younger than 2.

New Mexico Museum of Natural History and Science
1801 Mountain Rd. N.W. • 841-2878

This may be New Mexico kids' all-time favorite museum. It certainly gets the vote of all little tykes fascinated by dinosaurs. From the life-size sculptures of Spike the Pentaceratops and Alberta the Albertosaurus to the FossilWorks Laboratory where kids can watch scientists extract real dinosaur bones from rock, the museum is full of dinosaurs. Children can stand next to the skeletons of real dinosaurs that actually lived in what is now New Mexico and see casts of their footprints. The museum's other attractions include a habitat of New Mexico's ancient seashore, a walk through a simulated volcano and ride in an "Evolator" that takes you back to the days when arid Albuquerque was a rain forest.

The museum's hands-on learning center gives kids a chance to look through microscopes, test their sensory perception and ask science questions. Dynamax theater presents movies every hour on the hour from 10 AM until 5 PM. Recent topics included whales and their migrations and the rain forest. The museum is open from 9 AM to 5 PM daily except Christmas and non-holiday Mondays in January and September. Admission is $4 for adults, $3 for seniors and students and $1 for ages 3 to 11. Tickets to Dynamax theater are the same price as admission except $2 for ages 3 to 11. Combination admission/Dynamax tickets are $7 for adults, $5 for seniors and students and $3 for ages 3 to 11.

Los Alamos

Bradbury Science Museum
15th St. at Central Ave., Los Alamos
• 667-4444

Children with curiosity about science en-

joy this museum for its hands-on displays and lively demonstrations and shows. The museum offers visitors the opportunity to play with a laser, see Fat Man and Little Boy atomic bombs, learn about DNA fingerprinting, work with computers and interactive video and watch a 20-minute movie about the development of the atomic bomb. Operated by Los Alamos National Laboratories, the museum shows the role Los Alamos played in the atomic bomb's creation and offers interactive exhibits explaining the scope of its nuclear research today. The museum is open daily except Thanksgiving, Christmas and New Year's Day. Hours are 1 to 5 PM Saturday, Sunday and Monday and 9 AM to 5 PM Tuesday through Friday. Admission is free.

Bandelier National Monument
5 miles south of Los Alamos on N.M.
Hwy. 4 (45 miles northwest of Santa Fe)
• 672-3861

Kids will find ladders to climb and caves to crawl inside at this popular National Park, all the while getting a firsthand look at the way an ancient people lived. The monument encompasses more than 1,000 Indian dwellings, homes to people who may have been the ancestors of some of the modern Pueblo Indians. A good place to start is with a walk through the visitors center, where displays introduce this prehistoric Anasazi culture. Then head out along the self-guided ruins trail that begins in back of the museum. Children enjoy walking on the narrow paths formed by Indian feet hundreds of years ago. They can climb ladders to reach the upper cliff dwellings and step inside caves where Indian families slept or stored their food and belongings many hundreds of years ago. They'll see how smoke from the ancient fires blackened the cave ceil-

INSIDERS' TIP

Santa Fe will someday have an ice rink where kids can learn to skate and play hockey. It will be part of a major new city recreation center planned for the south side of town. The Santa Fe Skaters Association worked hard to persuade the Santa Fe City Council to authorize and fund the rink, which will be the city's first major public ice rink.

The Santa Fe Ski Area and other northern New Mexico ski areas offer special classes and programs for children. During Santa Fe's Winterfiesta, children have their own events.

ings and notice petroglyphs carved along the cliffs.

One of New Mexico's most famous and popular attractions, the area now known as Bandelier was occupied as early as A.D. 1100. The people who lived here were farmers and hunters. Since they had no written language, much of their culture remains a mystery. The monument preserves a wealth of archaeologi-

cal ruins covering about 450 years of human history. Large pueblos, medium-sized house clusters, single-room shelters and cave dwellings are all here; Bandelier National Monument was established to protect and preserve this priceless heritage.

The monument is named for Adolph Bandelier, an explorer, historian and author who visited here on five different occasions.

Bandelier's novel *The Delight Makers* used one of these ancient pueblos as its setting.

When you've seen enough ruins, you can picnic along the stream or hike to a waterfall — most of the park is wilderness. Overnight camping is allowed, and summer campfire programs explain the wildlife, plants and people of the area. (Please call for a schedule.) The park is about an hour's drive from Santa Fe through some of northern New Mexico's most interesting geologic country. The monument is open from dawn to dusk. Entry fee is $10 per vehicle.

Pecos

Pecos National Historical Park
25 miles southeast of Santa Fe on I-25, Exit 299 then 2 miles east on N.M. Hwy. 63 • 757-6032

In this park, children and their parents will get a fascinating introduction to the life of the Pueblo people prior to and after the Spanish arrived. Before touring the ruins, stop at the museum for displays that explain the 15th-century pueblo and its mission church, built under the guidance of Spanish friars. In the museum, kids can touch ancient Indian artifacts and watch a short, exciting film about the Spanish exploration of New Mexico. Then walk the trail through the ruins, which begins just outside the museum. Don't miss the *kiva*, the Pueblo's ceremonial center, where you can push a button to fill the room with American Indian music. The mission, now reduced to only low mud walls, was once described as "the most magnificent church north of Mexico City." During the summer, the park often has demonstrations of Indian or Hispanic arts and crafts. (Call for a schedule.) The park is open daily from 8 AM to 6 PM Memorial Day through Labor Day and until 5 PM the rest of the year. Admission is $2 for adults (children get in free) or $4 per car load, whichever is less.

Near Santa Fe

Hyde Memorial State Park
7.5 miles northeast of Santa Fe on N.M. Hwy. 475 • 983-7175

With its hiking opportunities and cross-country ski trails, a cold stream to splash in and plenty of picnic tables, Hyde Park draws a nice crowd of Santa Fe residents and visitors into the Sangre de Cristo Mountains year round. Backpackers and Nordic skiers use Hyde Park to begin their explorations of the adjoining Santa Fe National Forest. Campsites, including areas for large groups, and the park's playgrounds are popular in the summer. In the winter, there's a sledding slope and tubing run. The road from Santa Fe to Hyde Park and beyond is designated as a National Scenic Byway, and the trip to takes you through beautiful mountain country over a paved, two-lane highway that is steep and twisty in some places. Day use is free; the fee for camping is $7 per day for a tent site or $11 for a site with electricity.

Santa Fe National Forest
Headquarters, 1220 S. Francis Dr. • 438-7840

This sprawling forest has five ranger districts throughout northern New Mexico, but the area closest to Santa Fe is among the most scenic and popular. This section of the Santa Fe National Forest begins at the northern border of Hyde Park, 7.5 miles northeast of Santa Fe and stretches for miles into the Pecos Wilderness. You might see a deer or even a black bear. You'll find campgrounds and cross-country ski trails here as well as the Santa Fe Ski Area, which operates on a forest service lease. Campgrounds include Aspen Basin, Aspen Vista and Big Tesuque. Camping fee is $10 per night in most campgrounds.

While Indian Market draws the most visitors, Fiesta wins hands-down as Santa Fe's oldest celebration and takes the honors as a favorite with residents.

Annual Events and Festivals

Arts festivals, celebrations deeply rooted in the area's history and traditions, family events and even a dog show just for mutts: Santa Fe's schedule of special events is unmatched in communities twice its size.

As is true in most places, summer means more activities. But there's something to do year round. Many events here are benefits for one good cause or another, a testament to Santa Fe's generosity.

August brings Santa Fe's most popular event, Indian Market. The market, a two-day show and sale, highlights the best in American Indian arts from throughout the country, packs Santa Fe's hotels and restaurants and sends some locals packing too! Galleries around town honor their best and best-selling artists on market weekend with exhibits and gala openings. Indian Market includes a growing performing arts component, offering a chance for Native American musicians, storytellers and dancers to perform before an appreciative audience.

While Indian Market draws the most visitors, Fiesta wins hands-down as Santa Fe's oldest celebration and takes the honors as a favorite with residents. Held the weekend following Labor Day, Fiesta commemorates Santa Fe's Spanish heritage with parades and pageants, music, dancing and food galore. Fiesta also has a strong religious element, celebrating the contribution of the Franciscan missionaries and the city's deeply rooted Catholic heritage.

Christmas in Santa Fe also showcases the community's rich traditions. *Farolitos* — little bags filled with sand and lit with a small candle — and *luminarias*, or bonfires, line the streets and light the way for the Christ child and for neighbors and churchgoers on Christmas Eve. A troupe of Spanish-speaking actors present an ancient Christmas pageant, *Las Posadas*, each December on the Santa Fe Plaza.

The Santa Fe Ski Area hosts special winter events, including the Celebrity Ski Classic, which draws actors, singers and other Hollywood types to town to raise money for United Way of Santa Fe. In 1998, Santa Fe celebrated its first community WinterFiesta.

Spring brings the annual Easter pilgrimage to the historic church at Chimayó, about 40 miles north of Santa Fe. Pilgrims from throughout New Mexico walk to the shrine on Good Friday as a testimony to their faith or to ask for divine blessings.

Summer offers a full schedule of performing and visual arts events to Santa Fe, too many to list separately in this chapter. From June through August, the city buzzes with choices ranging from Shakespeare to modern theater, from storytelling in a tipi to lectures on culture and history and from ballet to flamenco performances. The visual arts scene sparkles with gallery openings and outdoor art shows and fairs. Summerscene brings free music to the Plaza during the week. Please see our chapter on Arts and Galleries for more specific insights and phone numbers. And check the local papers to see if a big-name jazz artist, a reggae concert or who-knows-what-else has arrived for the weekend.

We've organized this list of the year's highlights based on when the event occurs. Unless otherwise noted, prices are per adult ticket, and parking is free. (During Indian Market and Fiesta, some entrepreneurs and nonprofit groups may set up lots and charge for parking. If you don't want to pay, you can park elsewhere for free, but you'll have a longer walk.)

You'll notice that many events happen on the Plaza. You'll find the Plaza, Santa Fe's town square, downtown at the northern end of Old Santa Fe Trail, at the corner of Lincoln and Palace avenues.

In addition to this calendar, don't forget the public events at the Indian pueblos near Santa Fe, which are listed in the Pueblo Culture section of our Local Cultures chapter.

Unless otherwise noted, the area code for all phone numbers listed in this guide is 505.

January

Winterfiesta
The Plaza and various other locations
• 984-6760, (800) 777-2489

Billed as a tribute to the city's arts, cultures and cuisine, Winterfiesta is designed to put a little sparkle into one of Santa Fe's quiet months. The idea here is simple: to help locals and their guests enjoy the winter. This weeklong celebration, beginning the last Friday of the month, includes a Plaza balloon glow, gallery openings and receptions, music and drama performances, a chile cookoff and activities for both visitors and residents. Events are staged at the Santa Fe Ski Area, in galleries downtown and on Canyon Road, in the city's performing arts venues and in major hotels. The first Winterfiesta, held in 1998, was created with the enthusiastic support of the city's Convention and Visitors Bureau and the Santa Fe City Council. Many events, except the plays, concerts and Gold and Silver Ball, are free.

Celebrity Ski Classic
Various locations • 982-4429, 982-2002

You can have fun and help a good cause at this star-studded four-day event, usually held in late January or early February. The Classic opens with a benefit concert (which costs about $20 to $30) on Thursday at the Lensic Theater, 211 W. San Francisco Street. In the past, the event has featured Toni Childs, the

Nitty Gritty Dirt Band, Kim Carnes, Rita Coolidge and Karla Bonoff. On Friday, the public is invited to a free autograph session at the Eldorado Hotel, 309 W. San Francisco Street, followed by an evening Auction Party with the Stars ($20 in 1997) at Sweeney Center, 201 W. Marcy Street. In addition to the art, collectibles, furniture, jewelry, ski apparel and travel packages up for bid, auction guests enjoy impromptu quips of comics and comic actors who work as emcees.

On Saturday, the television celebrities, music personalities and movie stars team up with local and area skiers for a day of racing. In the past, luminaries have included Kenny Loggins, Melissa Etheridge, Hal Ketchum, Jay Thomas and Kevin Meaney to name just a few. Ski teams are limited to sponsors, with sponsorships starting at $2,000. The public is welcome to watch the ski race Saturday, but you need skis and a lift ticket to reach the course at the Santa Fe Ski Area. (See our Winter Sports chapter.) Some years, the Classic offers you a chance to race one-on-one against willing celebrities for a fee of $20 or so. Money raised helps United Way of Santa Fe County fund the many agencies it supports — groups which work with children, the elderly and others in need.

February

Jimmie Heuga Ski Express
Santa Fe Ski Area, 16 miles northeast of Santa Fe on N.M. Hwy. 475 • 982-4429

This event raises money for scholarships to send New Mexicans with multiple sclerosis to the Jimmie Heuga Center in Colorado. At the center, people with MS learn about diet, exercise and attitude adjustments that can make their lives more pleasant. Jimmie Heuga, an Olympic medalist who has MS, founded and directs the program. Santa Fe hosts New Mexico's oldest Express.

Skiers compete on three-person teams for prizes that include a trip to Vail to represent the Santa Fe Ski Area in the finals. Santa Fe's Express usually includes a race through the gates and an endurance event. Santa Fe skiers have

Rodeo de Santa Fe brings professional riders and visitors to the city.

placed among the top 10 teams at the finals. The date of the event varies according to snow conditions; call the number above to find out the year's date. To enter, each three-member team must contribute a minimum of $1,000. Spectators and volunteers are welcome but must be able to ski and purchase ski lift tickets.

March

Gladfelter Bump Contest/ Southwest Snowboard Championships
Santa Fe Ski Area, 16 miles northeast of Santa Fe on N.M. Hwy. 475 • 982-4429

The area's best mogul skiers and snowboarders compete for glory and prizes in the annual Gladfelter competition. The Snowboard Championships include jumps, half-pipes and a slalom course and draw snowboarders from throughout the region. Both events are held in late March or early April, depending on snow conditions. Spectators are welcome, but you have to be able to ski or snowboard to get to the course, and you'll need a lift ticket. Registration for the competition is $10 plus the cost of a lift ticket.

Oscar Night Gala
Location varies • 473-6400

Sip champagne, enjoy a generous buffet and watch the Academy Awards presentation in style. This black-tie party benefits the scholarship fund for the College of Santa Fe's Moving Image Arts Department. (For more information on CSF, see our Education chapter.) Santa Fe residents love this party; tickets go fast, and it's usually sold out. This is always held on the Tuesday night of the Academy Awards, usually late in the month or in early April, so mark your calendar. Tickets cost $65 per person. The event is usually held at a downtown hotel; call ahead to find out the location.

April

Closing Day at the Santa Fe Ski Area
Santa Fe Ski Area, 16 miles northeast of Santa Fe on N.M. Hwy. 475 • 982-4429

The end of the ski season usually brings a celebration. The Santa Fe Ski Area hosts free ski races, events for kids, a bike-in-the-snow event, a contest for dummies (and we don't mean the human kind) on skis and live music on the deck at Totemoff's Grill, usually on a Sunday in mid-month. Each closing day's program is a little different. Skiers get in the spirit by coming in Hawaiian costumes. Some years you can ski in shorts if you're brave enough; other times the end of the season has brought a spring blizzard. In 1997, the prices were $18 per ticket.

Chimayó Pilgrimage
Santuario de Chimayó, Chimayó
• **no phone**

Every Holy Week beginning on Thursday, thousands of pilgrims walk to the Santuario de Chimayó, about 40 miles from Santa Fe. Christians, a few of them carrying wooden crosses, walk to this beautiful adobe church to repay a solemn vow or to ask for Christ's blessings. Pilgrims travel along U.S. Highway 84-285 through Santa Fe to the Nambé junction at N.M. Highway 503 and then on to Chimayó on N.M. Highway 76. The majority of the devout walk late on Holy Thursday and on Good Friday. Area law enforcement pays close attention to traffic to keep the pilgrims safe. If you're driving this route, please slow down and be careful. If you'd like to join the pilgrims for your own spiritual reasons, by all means do so. This is not a spectator event. It is free.

People walking at night should bring a flashlight and wear light-colored clothes. Day or night, carry plenty of water, wear sturdy shoes and watch for cars.

May

Superintendent's Ball
Sweeney Center, 201 W. Marcy St.
• **474-0240**

You can get dressed up, schmooze with the city's other movers and shakers, enjoy a good meal and dance the night away — all for a fine cause. The Ball, inaugurated in 1997, raises money for the Santa Fe Public Schools and promotes community awareness of and involvement in the work the schools do. High

school volunteers serve as greeters, ushers and servers and provide the music. The event, usually held the first Saturday in May, is sponsored by Partners in Education, a nonprofit group dedicated to helping teachers and students succeed in the classroom. The cost is $75 per person.

Taste of Santa Fe
Sweeney Center, 201 W. Marcy St.
• **983-4823**

On the first Tuesday in May each year, more than two dozen Santa Fe restaurants strut their stuff, competing for attractive plaques and the bragging rights that go to the winners. But the real winners are the 900 or so hungry people who attend and the Museum of New Mexico's Palace of the Governors, which receives the proceeds. Ticket holders get to taste and vote on everything from appetizers to desserts. Chefs go all out for this event, and the food ranges from relatively simple New Mexican dishes — Santa Fe's comfort food — to the fancy, exotic and sublime. Last year winners included Paul's Restaurant for appetizers — red chile duck wontons in a soy ginger sauce. A no-host bar, where you can buy your favorite libation, and a coffee booth are part of the evening's festivities. A "nonessential auction," which usually includes trips and meals in private homes, is part of the evening's fun. Tickets cost $25 per person.

Community Day in Santa Fe
The Plaza • **984-6568**

Designed to bring local families back to the Plaza, Community Day features entertainment, activities for kids, a car show, food booths and information about dozens of nonprofit agencies that make Santa Fe a better place to live. The activities pack the Plaza with friendly folks. City officials use the opportunity to mingle with residents, especially during an election year. Newcomers will get an excellent orientation to the community here; longtime residents get a kick out of seeing old friends and reminiscing about the days when the Plaza truly was the city's center. Watch for

www.insiders.com

See this and many other **Insiders' Guide®** destinations online — in their entirety.

Visit us today!

Community Day on a Saturday in early to mid-May. The event is free.

The Santa Fe Century Ride
Ride begins at Capshaw Junior High, 351 E. Zia Rd. • 982-1282

Bicyclists, more than 2,000 of them, come from throughout New Mexico and elsewhere to ride 100 miles of history on this trip. Cyclists who are in for the "century" ride down the Turquoise Trail, through the old mining towns of Madrid and Golden, across the Estancia Valley to the villages of Cedar Grove, Stanley and Galisteo and back into Santa Fe. You can also sign on for 25-, 50-, or 75-mile loops. The idea here is to have fun, and to that end organizers offer detailed maps, sag wagons (vans to pick tired riders) and a van with a bike mechanic. You can stop for snacks and food and water along the route and purchase a hearty pancake breakfast or an organic pasta lunch at the beginning and end of the trail. The ride traditionally happens on a Sunday mid-month. The cost to enter is $10 to $13. A strong rider completes the trip in four or five hours, to the cheers of friends and family who may be waiting at the finish line.

A Day at the Opera Ranch
Santa Fe Opera, U.S. Hwy. 84/285, 7 miles north of Santa Fe • 986-5955

Continuous entertainment showcasing talented children and teens from Santa Fe and elsewhere in New Mexico is one of the attractions for this event. The entertainment, which lasts from 10 AM until 3 PM, includes performances by Celebrate Youth!, a statewide mentorship program of children performing music, dancing and excerpts from plays. Visitors can tour a gallery of Santa Fe Opera costumes and watch various opera performances including student-produced operas and a concert performance by Opera Mosaic, a group of professional players who present opera in the schools. But the biggest drawing card is the beautiful opera grounds, a grassy oasis in the arid foothills of Santa Fe. The opera's administrative offices and training studios are known as the "ranch," and visitors can picnic on the grounds as part of the fun. Backstage tours at the theater itself, just up the hill, draw opera buffs interested in seeing exactly how the nonmusical magic is made. The Guilds of The Santa Fe Opera Inc. have hosted this event for years, usually on a Saturday in mid- to late May. You can buy drinks and picnic food such as hot dogs and Frito pies. Be sure to bring a hat and sunscreen. The event is free.

Civil War Weekend
El Rancho de las Golondrinas, 334 Los Pinos Rd., La Cienega • 471-2261

Families can step back in time to the days of the Civil War and New Mexico's Battle of Glorieta at the annual Civil War Weekend festival at this living history museum just south of Santa Fe. (See our Attractions chapter for more information on the museum.) In addition to the demonstrations and information, visitors can stroll the lovely grounds and visit the historic buildings on this old ranch, a stop on El Camino Real, the main trail from Santa Fe to Mexico City. Admission is $6 for adults; $4 for seniors (62 and older), teens and military; and $2.50 for children 5 to 12. Children younger than 5 always get in free. To reach the ranch from Santa Fe, take I-25 S. to Exit 246 and bear right on N.M. Highway 599. Turn left at the first intersection on the frontage road and right just before the race track on Los Pinos Road. The museum is 3 miles from this intersection.

El Corazon de Santa Fe
The Plaza • 984-6568

The City of Santa Fe joins with nonprofit and commercial sponsors to present a series of free evening performances. These "In the Heart of Santa Fe" productions are a summer party honoring the community's heritage and its happy tradition of live entertainment. On most Saturday evenings from mid-May through September, the Plaza comes alive with dancers, actors, music and fun. Among the spe-

INSIDERS' TIP

At Spanish Market and Indian Market award-winning work tends to sell quickly. If you want to see the winners, come early.

cific themes in summers past are Teen Night, organized by the Santa Fe Boys and Girls Club; a tribute to rock'n'roll; community talent night; and Festival Santa Fe, presented by the city's finest performing arts groups. Bring everyone, even the kids and grandma; visitors and residents are all cordially welcome. (El Corazon is preempted by major events such as Indian and Spanish market and the Fiesta.) The entertainment is free and runs from 6 to 10 PM. Check the newspaper for a schedule.

June

Santa Fe Botanical Garden's Garden Tours
Various locations • 438-1684

Beginning in early June, Santa Fe's nonprofit Botanical Garden offers you a glimpse at some of Santa Fe's most interesting and beautiful gardens. Tours might include artists' gardens and xeric gardens, which use drought-resistant plants to great advantage. Trips leave from a central location, so participants can carpool, and are held on Sunday afternoons. You can visit one garden or enjoy the whole series, which normally lasts through August. A guide leads the six-tour series. The cost per tour is $10 for members and $15 for nonmembers.

Spring Festival
El Rancho de las Golondrinas, 334 Los Pinos Rd., La Cienega • 471-2261

During this two-day celebration on a weekend in early June, the old ranch comes to life with dancing, music and demonstrations of the skills necessary for successful living in early New Mexico. Among the things you'll see with are hand-shearing of the curly-horned churro sheep; a procession honoring San Isidro, the patron of New Mexico farmers; a working blacksmith shop; and bread baking in traditional outdoor ovens. Music, dance, art and entertainment add to the fun. Admission is $6 for adults; $4 for seniors (62 and older), teens and military; and $2.50 for children 5 to 12. Children younger than 5 always get in free. To reach the ranch from Santa Fe, take I-25 S. to Exit 246 and bear right on N.M. Highway 599. Turn left at the first intersection on the front-

age road and right just before the race track on Los Pinos Road. The museum is 3 miles from this intersection.

Santa Fe Air Show
Santa Fe Airport, Airport Rd. S.
• 471-5111

On Father's Day weekend, kids can bring their dads (moms and grandparents are welcome too) to the airport for a day of demonstrations and ground exhibits. Among the air show's drawing cards are flybys, stunt pilots doing aerobatics and a sizeable display of military aircraft. Visitors can even walk through some of the planes and helicopters. Rotary del Sur came up with the idea for the show in 1989, and it's now run by a private, nonprofit group. This is a first-rate volunteer effort, with a crew of about 100 doing most of the work. The event has simple goals: family fun, promoting and educating people about aviation and raising money for local charities. In addition to seeing planes, visitors can buy T-shirts and a variety of aviation memorabilia and nosh on hot dogs and other festival-type food. Bring a hat and wear sunscreen: It can get hot on the tarmac! Admission costs $5 and is free for children younger than 5. Parking costs $1.

Santa Fe Furniture Expo
Sweeney Center, 201 W. Marcy St.
• 984-9144, (800) 823-0163

One-of-a-kind home furnishings and accessories fill Sweeney Center for this three-day show and sale, usually held in mid-June. More than 100 exhibitors present a host of styles from Spanish Colonial to Shaker. Founded in 1993, the expo has expanded to include all types of modern, eclectic and traditional artisans. In addition to a strong showing from New Mexico, the expo draws craftspeople from throughout the country. Seminars on how to care for furniture, selecting antique pieces and other topics are usually part of this popular event. Admission is $5.

Buckaroo Ball
El Rancho de las Golondrinas, Los Pinos Rd., La Cienega • 982-6363

Founded in 1993, the Buckaroo Ball takes the honors as Santa Fe's singlemost profit-

The Pancake Breakfast, held annually on the Fourth of July,
brings out the community in support of United Way.

able fund-raising event. Loosely modeled after the Cattle Baron's Ball in Dallas, the Buckaroo Ball is an upscale gala evening with first-rate food, exotic auction items and stunning entertainment. The 1997 event, for example, featured singer Patty Loveless, a casually glitzy crowd of about 1,200 and raised $700,000. A committee disperses the money as grants to nonprofit groups working with children. Despite the price ($300 to $700), tickets sell quickly and usually disappear long before party night.

Annual West Muttster Dog Show
Alto Park, 1043 Alto St. • 983-4309

Dogs don't need a pedigree for this show, but they might need a costume! The Santa Fe Animal Shelter and Humane Society sponsors a day of fun, usually a Saturday in mid-June, as a reunion for the dogs that have gone to good homes thanks to the shelter's work. Contests include dog and owner lookalikes, "old dog, new trick/new dog, old trick," "most extraordinary tail," "most spots" and "stands out in a crowd." Dog obedience demonstrations, music, food and face painting add to the mix. Admission is free.

Arts and Crafts Show
The Plaza • 988-7621

Challenge New Mexico, a group that works with people with disabilities and sponsors a popular and a successful horseback therapy program, benefits from this show. You'll find arts and crafts from all disciplines. Everything is handmade by professional artists. You can chat with the artisans, and food and live music add to the weekend's festivities. The mid-month event attracts artists from throughout the region. Admission is free.

Opening Night, Santa Fe Opera
Santa Fe Opera Theater, U.S. Hwy. 84-285, 7 miles north of Santa Fe • 986-5900, (800) 280-4654

Opening night at the Santa Fe Opera means tails and tailgate parties, black ties and caviar. For the most part, Santa Fe isn't a dress-up town, but you'd never know it tonight. Denim with diamond studs, velvet capes, lace and satin, cowboy boots shined to a high polish, the latest New York fashions and thousands of pounds of turquoise come out for the occasion. Sometimes the glimmer of the audience rivals that on stage. A variety of public and private parties precede the night's operatic performance — watch the papers or call the opera to find out what's on the schedule. After the opening night soiree, (which is either the last Friday in June or the first Friday in July), the opera season continues through late August with five productions in repertory and some special concerts by apprentice artists. (See our Arts chapter.)

July

Fourth of July Pancake Breakfast
The Plaza • 983-7317

Food is the centerpiece of this day of community fun, a fund-raiser for United Way of Santa Fe County. Hundreds of community volunteers cook pancakes and ham, serve coffee, orange juice and milk and chat with the crowd. On the bandstand, entertainment ranges from mariachi music to dancing grand-

mothers. An antique car show presented by Santa Fe Vintage Car Club lines the streets. You can even sleep late if you want; the grills stay hot, and the pancakes keep coming until noon, or as long as the batter lasts. The price is $5 per person.

ASID Designer Showhouse
Location varies annually • 988-4640, 984-1040

The American Society of Interior Designers transform a Santa Fe home into a work of art for about two weeks each July. The public is welcome to take a look and get some ideas for spiffing up bedrooms, living rooms, kitchens and gardens. In addition to daily open houses, the event includes lectures from the artists and designers involved in the project. Proceeds benefit Santa Fe Pro Musica and the design society. Tours cost $15.

Western Days
Various locations • 471-4300

The Rodeo de Santa Fe is the centerpiece of this nine-day celebration, which calls attention to a part of Santa Fe's past and its role as part of the American West. (See our Spectator Sports chapter for more on this event.) But you'll also find a wine festival, walking tours of a movie ranch, dances and dance lessons, scenic train rides and special events for children as part of the fun. In addition to the Santa Fe Rodeo Grounds, venues include El Rancho de Las Golondrinas, 334 Los Pinos Road, La Cienega, 471-2261, and the Santa Fe Southern Railroad, 410 S. Guadalupe Street, 989-8600. The community inaugurated Western Days in 1997. Prices vary, and some events are free. In 1997, the celebration included El Corazon de Santa Fe Western Days Dance, with free music for two-step and line dancing on the Plaza from 6 to 10 PM. Rancho Encantado, on N.M. Highway 592 about 8 miles from the Plaza, hosted a Western barn dance, ($5) and trail rides ($45, or $35 for resort guests).

Eight Northern Indian Pueblos Arts and Crafts Show
At a Northern Pueblo • (800) 793-4955

Held the third weekend in July, this show

attracts 1,500 top Native American artists from throughout New Mexico, the Southwest and the nation. It's the largest Indian-run art show in the country. Every piece here is made by the artist or someone in his or her family. Entries are juried for quality, and awards are given for best work. During the two-day event, visitors and artists can pause from their shopping to watch a variety of dancing with music by flute players and drummers. Various northern Indian pueblos take turns hosting the show, but none are far from Santa Fe, and the outdoor setting on pueblo land makes this show special. Photography is allowed with a permit, but please ask permission before taking a picture of an artist's work. You can also buy food and drinks. Wear sunscreen, a hat and sturdy shoes — you may have to hike several blocks from the parking area to get to the show grounds.

Behind Adobe Walls House Tours
Various dates and locations • 983-6565, (800) DETOURS

The Santa Fe Garden Club presents this annual event, which offers visitors and residents an up-close look at some of the city's finest homes and gardens. A recent tour, for example, visited a historic Canyon Road property with mature landscaping beautifully designed to complement the home's architecture and location. Participants enjoyed the soothing sound of the *acequia*, which watered the flowers, trees, shrubs and colorful groundcover plants, and marveled at the showpiece apple tree, the largest of its kind in Santa Fe county. Buses take visitors to four different homes each day of the tour, which usually runs for four consecutive Tuesdays beginning in mid-July. Money from ticket sales goes to community beautification projects. The cost is $35 per tour.

Live at the Lensic
Lensic Theater, 211 W. San Francisco St. • 986-3820

A galaxy of stars assemble for this variety presentation, which benefits Santa Fe Cares and its work with people with AIDS. The event features performances of music, theater and comedy. Lauren Bacall emceed the event in 1997, and participating entertainers have included actors Carol Burnett, Tim Curry and Michael York. Local celebrities join in, and the result is a Sunday afternoon in late July jammed with music, comedy, dance and fun. Tickets cost $35.

Traditional Spanish Market/ Contemporary Hispanic Market
The Plaza • 983-4038

Unique work in the Spanish Colonial tradition fills the Plaza for a weekend in late July, while on adjoining Lincoln Avenue, Hispanic artists display contemporary adaptations. Much of the traditional work is religious — carved and painted images of the saints that reflect New Mexico's long isolation from the religious art of Mexico and Spain. Some 300 artists also display handsome tin work, silver filigree jewelry, wood carvings, weaving, straw inlay and embroidery. Many of the artists featured here don't show in galleries; the Spanish Market and the Winter Market in December offer two of the few opportunities to see and purchase their work. Prizes go to the best entries in each medium. Music, dance, food and pageantry add to the fun. Artists' demonstrations continue throughout both days.

The contemporary show, sponsored by the Santa Fe Council for the Arts, varies in content considerably more than the traditional market. Some of the pieces you'll see are cousins of the traditional works but built from more contemporary materials. A recent show, for instance, featured refrigerator magnets of traditional religious images crafted from bottle caps. Both markets are free — unless you decide to buy something.

Santa Fe Opera
Community Concerts
St. Francis Cathedral, 131 Cathedral Pl. • 986-5924

Each summer, the Santa Fe Opera and cooperating sponsors present free public concerts in town featuring apprentice artists from the Santa Fe Opera. The concerts, about an hour of arias, duets and ensemble music, offer a no-risk introduction to operatic music, and you don't even have to drive to the theater. The project started as a way to reach the elderly, disadvantaged and children. Everyone is welcome, and the cathedral is usually filled. Admission is free. Usually two performances, one in late morning and the other in early afternoon of the same day, are held on a weekday late in the month.

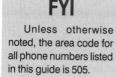

FYI

Unless otherwise noted, the area code for all phone numbers listed in this guide is 505.

August

Arts and Crafts Fair
The Plaza • 982-2042

From early morning to dusk, usually on the first weekend in August, the Plaza is filled with all sorts of arts and crafts from exhibitors who come to Santa Fe from throughout the country. Girls Incorporated of Santa Fe, a nonprofit organization that offers programs for girls during the school year and over the summer, benefits from the booth fees. Santa Fe residents and visitors can see and buy paintings, handmade clothing, original toys, jewelry of all sorts, stained glass and more. Admission is free.

Santa Fe County Fair
Santa Fe County Fair Grounds, Rodeo Rd. at Richards Ave. • 471-4711

Santa Fe County 4-H plays a major role in this event, which draws produce, livestock and other entries from throughout rural Santa Fe County. Among the highlights are the frog-jumping contest, a llama show, a herding-dog

exhibition and, of course, the livestock auction. Kiddie rides, entertainment and concessions sold by bright-eyed 4-Hers add to the fun. Watch for it in early August. Admission is free, but parking costs $1.

Ice Cream Social
Santa Fe Children's Museum, 1050 Old Pecos Tr. • 989-8359

This annual family-style fund-raiser, traditionally held the first Sunday in August, begins at noon and continues through early evening — or until the ice cream runs out. Santa Fe celebrities, including the mayor, the superintendent of schools and the chief of police, have helped with the scooping. Visitors can make their own sundaes or banana splits. All the money goes for new exhibits at the museum, the only one in Santa Fe dedicated to kids (see our Kidstuff chapter). Besides the ice cream, the museum serves up free demonstrations and entertainment. There might even be a visiting fire truck for the little ones to explore. The cost is $2.50 per serving of ice cream.

Mountain Man Trade Fair
Palace of the Governors, 105 E. Palace Ave. • 827-6483

The Palace of the Governors, once the center of New Mexico's political life and now a popular history museum, hosts this colorful fair as a tribute to Santa Fe's history as a trade center. Demonstrations of mountain man skills, a Santa Fe Trail film festival, book signings, "Critters in the Courtyard" and more are traditional parts of this colorful event. In 1997, for example, the two-day film festival featured movies about the Old Santa Fe Trail with showings from 1 to 5 PM Thursday and again from 3 to 8 PM on Friday. Ghost Ranch Living Museum in Abiquiu brought Wally the Beaver, Rocky Raccoon and other animals in a tour-and-learn program that explained how important wild animals were to mountain men. And historian Marc Simmons lectured on his recent book, *The Old Santa Fe Trail*, and signed copies of it for interested readers. The Mountain Men — contemporary versions of the original mountain men who lived off their wits and the bounty of the Western mountains as trappers, guides, hunters and traders — display a variety of handmade items. You'll find examples of the goods their counterparts traded a century ago. .

Haciendas — A Parade of Homes
Various locations • 982-1774

The Santa Fe Area Home Builders Association offers this tour of more than a dozen new homes to showcase their members' most professional and creative work. A map guides visitors to the homes, built in various Santa Fe neighborhoods, from working-class to millionaire territory. The showcase includes juried competitions for Best Floor Plan, Best Kitchen, Best Craftsmanship and other categories in each price range. The association also awards a "Best of Show" prize in each price category and an overall winner, the "Grand Hacienda." After you've seen the homes, you can vote for your favorite. You might even want to buy it! Tours are free.

Wheelwright Museum Auction
Wheelwright Museum, 704 Camino Lejo • 982-4636

Jewelry, paintings and pottery by contemporary Native American artists will be on the auction block here, along with dinners donated by some of Santa Fe's finest restaurants. Other services, such as art appraisals, spa treatments or tax advice, are also offered. But the real reason this event attracts a crowd is the high-quality Indian art sold to benefit the museum, one of Santa Fe's favorite institutions. The Wheelwright is a small, private museum devoted to contemporary Indian art, and the auction is its main money-making event. The sale opens around 10 AM with a preview. Patrons can enjoy lunch while they prepare to bid. The sale usually runs from 1 to 5 PM. The auction audience gathers in a big tent on the museum grounds, usually the Thursday before Indian Market. Admission is $10.

Indian Market
On and around the Plaza • 983-5220

Serious collectors and the curious flock to Santa Fe for this show and sale, always held the weekend following the third Thursday of the month. One of Santa Fe's most famous and popular events, the market features a wide selection of the finest American Indian art from 1,200 exhibitors. Dancing, food sales (including favorites such as mutton stew) and demonstrations of various craft techniques add to the market's attraction. In 1997, Indian Market began a Fashion Showcase, a juried clothing show open to artists working in wearable art, sewing, weaving and beadwork. A youth market occupies nearby Cathedral Park. Admission to the market is free.

The Southwestern Association for Indian Arts Inc. has presented Indian Market since 1922. It is the largest contemporary American Indian art event in the world, generating some $130 million in revenue for artists, galleries and the tourism industry. (The average amount spent on Indian arts and crafts during the market is $734 per visitor, organizers say.) The market has become a driving force in setting prices and standards for first-class American Indian art. Indian Market's awards program distributes more than $60,000 in prizes in 350 categories. Artists cherish the awards for the prestige they carry. There's a long waiting list of artists to join the market; these folks may have a chance if the artists first chosen sell out early during the market.

To make the market less overwhelming, SWAIA publishes a guide that lists every artist by name and category and includes a map of booth locations. You can pick them up at the SWAIA office, 142 W. Palace Avenue. Since the market draws about 80,000 visitors, expect crowds.

Serious collectors become members of SWAIA for a chance to preview the prize-winning works before they go on sale the next morning. Memberships, which begin at $50, can be purchased at Sweeney Center, 210 W. Marcy Street, on Friday night before the preview. Having seen what they want, collectors line up long before the booths open for a chance to purchase the winning pieces.

During Indian Market, parking downtown is at a premium, and the city runs shuttles from outlying lots to reduce downtown congestion and frustration.

Special shows and gala openings in most of Santa Fe's galleries and exhibits in Sweeney

Vintage cars are on display at the annual Fourth of July Pancake Breakfast.

Center and many area hotels also are part of Indian Market weekend. Speaking of hotels, make reservations early — some 70 percent of those in attendance come from outside New Mexico; the majority of these visitors say that Indian Market was the primary reason for their visit.

Fiesta Melodrama
Santa Fe Playhouse, 142 E. DeVargas St. • 988-4262

This funny, spunky show has a different plot each year but always features the same theme — poking fun at Santa Fe's foibles. An anonymous committee puts together an original script about contemporary Santa Fe, structuring the show to resemble an old-time melodrama. The villain is always terrible, the heroine always in big trouble, and the good guys always win. The story itself draws on the city's freshest controversies and might include contentiousness among city, county and state officials, Santa Fe's ongoing saga of street repair and crazy traffic, the water situation, the latest uproar in the arts, school politics or New Age hype as subjects of its comic ridicule. The Fiesta Melodrama is a beloved Santa Fe tradition. The show usually opens in late August and runs through the Santa Fe Fiesta weekend in mid-September. Although some of the jokes might be rated PG, children are welcome. Tickets cost $12 for adults and $10 for children, students and seniors.

Santa Fe Bluegrass and Old Timey Music Festival
Santa Fe Rodeo Grounds, Rodeo Rd. at Richards Ave. • 438-6230, 298-3080

For more than 20 years, folks who enjoy banjo and fiddle music and other traditional fare have gathered at the Rodeo Grounds for a long weekend in late August or early September. Concerts, workshops, events and contests run throughout the day. Among the highlights are original song-writing performances and concerts by the prior year's winners in the Bluegrass Band and Old Timey Band contests. Don't miss the children's fiddle contest, which is usually held on Saturday morning. As part of the event, the grounds are open to campers. Tickets in 1997 were $6 for the Friday concert and $8 for general admission Satur-

day and Sunday. The Saturday evening concert costs $8. People younger than 12 or older than 65 receive free daily admission. You can buy food and beverages outside the stadium.

September

Labor Day Arts and Crafts Show
The Plaza • 988-7575

Jewelry of all styles and materials — from delicate silver earrings to bolo ties like the ones cowboys wear — is one of the highlights at this end-of-summer show. You'll also find oil and watercolor paintings, sculptures, ceramics both useful and decorative, one-of-a-kind clothing and more. Proceeds from the Plaza booth rentals benefit the Santa Fe Fiesta Council, the volunteer group who present the community's biggest party, La Fiesta de Santa Fe. As with all Plaza shows, artists have to submit their work to a jury and may sit on the waiting list before they get one of the coveted spaces to show and sell their creations. Since Labor Day brings a fresh wave of visitors to town, this show is especially popular. It's held on Labor Day and the Saturday and Sunday immediately preceding it. It's free.

New Mexico State Fair
State Fair Grounds, 300 San Pedro Blvd. N.E. between Central and Lomas Aves., Albuquerque • 265-1791, (800) 867-FAIR.

The New Mexico State Fair is one of the state's most popular events, and the fair's attendance records usually top all but two other shows in the West. (It's exceeded by the Texas State Fair and the Houston Livestock Show and Rodeo.)

The State Fair runs from early to mid-September. You'll find free schedules of each day's events and a map of the grounds at the information booth. Kids flock to the midway; the cowboy crowd loves the 16 nights of rodeo and its accompanying concerts in Tingley Coliseum; and the cultured set is drawn to several galleries. Everyone likes the food, served by more than 100 vendors in virtually every corner of the fair grounds. Don't miss Indian Village, Villa Hispana and Pioneer Village, all of which serve up tasty ethnic dishes and pleasing entertainment. The fair also offers a day of bull-riding competition and daily horse shows.

Animal exhibits include a large petting farm for the little ones. At the Creative and Home Arts exhibits, you'll find everything from dolls to homemade donuts. The Kid's Park midway for ages 12 and younger features its own rides and two stages for performances, including a magic show and puppet theater. Admission costs $4 after 2 PM and on Fridays and weekends. Early bird admission before 2 PM Monday through Thursday is $1. Parking fees range from $4 to $8.

Fiesta De Santa Fe
The Plaza and other locations • 988-7575

Fiesta is one of Santa Fe's favorite parties. Held the weekend following Labor Day, Fiesta commemorates the Spanish resettlement in Santa Fe after the Pueblo Revolt chased the conquistadors back to Mexico (see our History chapter). It's the oldest continuous community celebration in the United States. Schools and state and city employees usually get a much-appreciated half-day holiday on Fiesta Friday.

Each year at the Santa Fe Fiesta, the city remembers the contribution of Don Diego de Vargas and the Catholic Church to the community's survival. The Fiesta began as a religious commemoration, but parties, parades, a fashion show and Zozobra, a giant puppet that is burned with great fanfare, were added as the community changed and grew.

Even before Fiesta officially begins, Santa Fe starts celebrating. The Fiesta Melodrama (see August), appearances by the Fiesta Queen and the Caballeros de Vargas, pre-Fiesta shows and mariachi concerts are part of the fun. Throughout Fiesta weekend, the Plaza is alive with free entertainment provided by a variety of local and area music and dance groups. The Gran Baile de la Fiesta, or Fiesta Ball, a show of historic fashions and a commercially operated carnival at the Rodeo Grounds add to the merriment. Admission to the ball is $10; the fashion show costs $5.

For most revelers, Fiesta begins with the burning of Zozobra and a fireworks show Friday evening. You'll pay $5 to watch from the field, which is usually VERY crowded. Santa Fe artist Will Shuster created Zozobra, a 44-foot tall puppet with glowing eyes and a gravely voice, to personify the disappointments and mistakes of the year. (His nickname is Old Man Gloom.) Crews of volunteers build Zozobra the week before Fiesta and erect the big white puppet on a huge pole at Fort Marcy Park, 490 Washington Avenue. As the sky grows dark, the puppet comes to life, moaning, growling and waving his hands. (Very young children may be scared.) Finally, after a performance by the Fire Dancers and children dressed as Little Glooms, Zozobra disappears in flames to a rowdy chorus of cheers. Afterwards, many in the crowd head down the hill to the Plaza to dance, eat and socialize.

One of Fiesta's most charming events, the Pet Parade, or Desfile de los Ninos, begins around 10 AM on Saturday. Children, parents and pets ranging from cats and dogs to llamas and snakes circle the Plaza and walk along downtown streets. Many of the humans wear costumes to be real or imaginary animals, and many of the animals are dressed up too. Watch from the shade of the Plaza or from in front of the Palace of the Governors, 105 E. Palace Avenue, just across from the Plaza bandstand. Arrive early for a good curbside seat.

Among Sunday's highlights is the Historical/Hysterical parade. The parade, which features floats, marching bands, horses and politicians, begins at 2 PM. It starts in the parking lots at DeVargas Mall, North Guadalupe at Paseo de Peralta, continues to the Plaza and returns using a different downtown route.

A final review of Fiesta celebrities — Don Diego de Vargas, his court and the Fiesta Queen — follows the parade. At 7 PM comes the Fiesta Mass of Thanksgiving at St. Francis Cathedral, 213 Cathedral Place, followed by a candlelight procession from the church to Cross of the Martyrs, north of Palace Avenue off of Paseo de Peralta. The soft light of hundreds of candles as the procession makes its way up the hill is a beautiful sight and an appropriate ending to the weekend's events.

Viva la Fiesta!

FYI

Unless otherwise noted, the area code for all phone numbers listed in this guide is 505.

Aspen Viewing
Santa Fe Ski Area, 16 miles northeast of Santa Fe on N.M. Hwy. 475 • 982-4429, 983-9155

Ride the chairlift to enjoy shimmering golden aspen, fall wildflowers and a stunning view. The aspen schedule depends on the weather; some years the viewing lasts from the mid-September through mid-October. You can, of course, also see the aspen from your car and from other spots along N.M. 475, including the well-named Aspen Vista hiking and picnic area. From the chairlift, however, you get an eagle's-eye look at the trees and panoramic views of mountains as far away as the Colorado border. You can purchase a one-way ticket and hike down through the spruce, aspen and wildflowers or ride both ways. Lunch and snacks are served at the outdoor grill on the Ski Area deck near the chairlift. Bring a jacket — it's cool up here at 12,000 feet! Rates are $6 for adults and $4 for children 12 and younger. Children shorter than 46 inches will ride for free if accompanied by a paying adult. Tickets for seniors are $4, and one-way trips for hikers are $4.

Wine and Chile Fiesta
Various locations • 982-8686

Food and wine tastings featuring Santa Fe's finest restaurants and dozens of the world's best vineyards, cooking demonstrations, a wine auction, tours, seminars and even golf — what more could you want in a gastronomic extravaganza? The annual Santa Fe Wine and Chile Fiesta has grown in size and stature since its founding in 1990. The Big Event, the Grand Food and Wine Tasting at the Hilton of Santa Fe, 100 Sandoval Street, costs $60 and includes more than 200 varietals to compliment the chile-inspired cuisine prepared by about 60 of Santa Fe's best restaurants. Usually held over a four-day weekend in late September, the festival also features area tours that have included artist Georgia O'Keeffe's house in Abiquiu. This costs $95.

Prices for the 21 separate events hosted by many of Santa Fe's finest restaurants range from $125 for a lunch with guest chef Patricia Quintana and a tour of the village of Chimayó to $95 for a cooking demonstration and lunch with chef Mark Miller of the Coyote Cafe to $45 for food and wine seminars at the Hilton. Some 1,500 people usually attend celebration so the organizers encourage reservations.

October

Harvest Festival
El Rancho de las Golondrinas, 334 Los Pinos Rd., La Cienega • 471-2261

The Harvest Festival gives modern visitors a chance to see what the harvest season of the Spanish Colonial era was like. Harvest meant hard work in early New Mexico, but the visitors at this re-enactment get to have fun. Special events for this weekend in late September or early October depict life on an old ranch using volunteers in the costumes of the time. Music and dancing, artists and craftspeople selling their work and the baking and sampling of bread and *bizcochitos,* New Mexico's famous anise and sugar cookies, add to the fun. Visitors can see a wheelwright at work, attend outdoor mass and join a procession in honor of San Ysidro. Adding to the harvest ambiance, volunteers demonstrate techniques for stringing chiles into *ristras,* preparing fruits and vegetables for drying, making sorghum molasses, shelling corn and making *chicos* (dried corn to last the winter) and threshing wheat. The farm's animals — burros, horses, goats, sheep, turkeys, geese, ducks and chickens — are always popular with children. During the festival, admission is $6 for adults; $4 for seniors (62 and older), teens and military; $2.50 for children 5 to 12. Children younger than 5 always get in free. To reach the ranch from Santa Fe, take I-25 S. to Exit 246 and bear right on N.M. Highway 599. Turn left at the first intersection on the frontage road and right just before the race track on Los Pinos Road. The museum is 3 miles from this intersection.

Albuquerque International Balloon Fiesta
Balloon Fiesta State Park, Osuna Rd. near I-25, Albuquerque • 821-1000

If you're anywhere near New Mexico during the first two weeks of October, make it a point to visit this spectacular event. Not only is the Albuquerque International Balloon Fiesta worth the 60-mile drive from Santa Fe, but it's also worth getting up before dawn to get there! The world's largest ballooning event, the Balloon Fiesta usually draws more than 800 balloons from around the world and plenty of eager spectators. Pilots compete for prizes in precision events and fly for fun.

The nine-day festival includes mass ascensions held on the four weekend mornings, filling the sky with balloons of every shape, size and color. The ascension begins at dawn — other attractions are even earlier. Festival vendors peddle coffee, hot chocolate, breakfast burritos and other morning treats to help you enjoy the show wide-eyed. The mass ascensions are the festival's most popular events and draw more than a million spectators.

If dawn is too early for you, don't despair. You can get a taste of the Fiesta at the evening balloon glows. The enormous colorful balloons lit by the flame of their propane burners against the dark sky resemble oversized light bulbs lined up on the launch field.

Everyone loves the special-shape balloons so much that the balloons have been given events all their own — a special shape mass ascension and a balloon glow "rodeo." Dinosaurs and dragons, flying shoes and bottles, fantasy castles and a cow jumping over the moon delight the audience during each Fiesta.

Albuquerque hosts the Balloon Fiesta from the first Saturday through the second Sunday of October at the Balloon Fiesta Grounds near Osuna Road and I-25. Don't worry about getting lost if you're coming from Santa Fe — signs, the steady flow of vehicles, and traffic cops will help you find the field. Admission is $4 for adults and free for children younger than 12. Parking is free.

Annual All Children's Powwow
Wheelwright Museum, 704 Camino Lejo • 982-4636

The oldest children's powwow in the country, this event attracts more than a hundred young American Indians who perform intertribal, blanket and social dances on either the first or second Saturday of the month. Prizes go to the winners in different age groups, and spectators are welcome to take pictures. You'll also find American Indian crafts and food sales. The event usually runs from late morning until dusk. If you can't stay the whole time, the grand entry that opens the powwow is especially colorful and photogenic. An all-volunteer staff does the organizing and recently enlarged the powwow area and added bleachers and a new tipi. The event is free.

AIDS Walk Santa Fe
Begins on the Plaza • 989-WALK

If you live in Santa Fe long enough, chances are you'll be asked either to join this AIDS walk or to sponsor someone who's walking. Santa Fe has a high percentage of people with AIDS and HIV, and the community offers a variety of services for them (see our Healthcare chapter). The AIDS Walk, usually held in early October, assembles hundreds of walkers, including children, babies in strollers, teens from area churches, people with AIDS and those who care about them. After warmup exercises and a blessing, the walkers start off on a 5-mile loop, which bring them back to the Plaza for lunch and music. Participants not only have fun, but they also raise money to help Santa Fe Cares continue its support of AIDS services throughout northern New Mexico. Contributions are required to walk.

November

Ski Swap
Sweeney Center, 210 W. Marcy St.
• 982-9958

The Santa Fe Ski Team, kids who like to ski race, sponsors this event to raise the money they need to travel from Santa Fe for races during the year. You'll find great buys on used, and some new, equipment here. You can re-cycle your outgrown, unneeded skis, boots and whatever else in the sports equipment category and help a good cause. Volunteers include people who work in the ski business. They can give you advice on how to buy boots and skis that suit your style. This is also a good place to find children's equipment. Ad-mission is $1.50 during regular hours Satur-day and Sunday or $25 and $5 for each addi-tional family member for the preview on Fri-day evening before the sale officially begins..

Opening Day at the Santa Fe Ski Area
Santa Fe Ski Area, 16 miles northeast of Santa Fe on N.M. Hwy. 475 • 982-4429

If the snow gods smile on us, the ski area opens on Thanksgiving Day. In good years, the lifts might start a little sooner; in snow-free seasons the opening is delayed. Sometimes just the beginner slopes are in good shape; some years the whole mountain is gloriously covered in sweet powder. Santa Fe's snow pattern differs from that of Colorado or Taos Ski Valley. The skiers usually frolic through mid-April. (See our Winter Sports chapter.) Adult all-day all-lift tickets are $39; half-day tickets, morning or afternoon, are $26. The beginner chair is $20. Children age 12 and younger and skiers between the ages of 62 and 71 pay $24 for an all-day, all-lift ticket. Children shorter than 46 inches tall in their ski boots and super seniors 72 and older ski for free.

AID and Comfort Gala
ElDorado Hotel, 309 W. San Francisco St. • 989-3399

Santa Fe gets into the holiday spirit with this festive, big-hearted event, always held the Saturday after Thanksgiving. In addition to fabu-lous buffets of tasty finger foods, AID and Com-fort features a glittering assortment of enter-tainment, an auction of Christmas wreaths and other wonderful things, and a sale of Christmas trees decorated for the occasion by students from Santa Fe's schools. This is one of the few occasions when Santa Fe folks dress up grandly, and it's one of the favorite social events of the season. The proceeds benefit those with AIDS. Tickets cost $45 per person.

December

Winter Spanish Market
Sweeney Center, 201 W. Marcy St. • 983-4038

Like its sister event, the Traditional Spanish Market in July, Winter Market showcases work in the Spanish Colonial tradition by artisans from throughout New Mexico and southern Colorado. You'll find holiday gifts you can't buy anywhere else and a special booth of work by children. When they're not making sales, most of the artists are happy to explain the history behind their art. The Spanish Colonial Arts Society spon-sors this event, which is usually held the first weekend of the month. Admission is free.

Christmas at the Palace of the Governors
Palace of the Governors, 105 E. Palace Ave. • 827-6483

Usually held on a Thursday and Friday evening in mid-December, Christmas at the Palace draws hundreds of Santa Fe families and lucky visitors. This annual community cel-ebration brings the museum to life with music, dance, puppet shows, a visit from Santa and more. Volunteers serve hot cider and *biscochitos*, New Mexico's traditional anise sugar cookies. The museum sparkles with *farolitos* and other decorations. Although the party is free, donations of nonperishable food for the poor are welcome.

The annual Albuquerque Balloon Fiesta, held in early October, is attended by hundreds of thousands of visitors from around the world.

Las Posadas
The Plaza • 827-6483

Wear your hat and gloves when you come to see this traditional New Mexican folk drama, which presents the story of Joseph and Mary and their search for shelter. (*La posada* means "the inn" in Spanish.) A troupe of actors perform this ancient play in original archaic Spanish beneath the stars, or amid falling snowflakes, usually on the second Sunday of December. The pageant concludes in the courtyard of the Palace of the Governors with hot chocolate for everyone. Spectators are asked to bring a candle or a flashlight. No flash photography is allowed. The event is free.

12 Days of Christmas
Inn of the Anasazi, 113 Washington Ave. • 988-3030

This series, which concludes on Christmas Eve, features daily activities at one of Santa Fe's most luxurious downtown hotels. You'll find music, storytelling, crafts demonstrations, slide presentations and other events that reflect holiday traditions of the region. The programs culminate with a lighting ceremony and caroling on Christmas Eve. From here it's an easy stroll to the Plaza to see the city's Christmas decorations. The events are free.

Farolito Walk
Hillside Ave., Acequia Madre, Cross of the Martyrs and elsewhere in the downtown/Canyon Rd. area • no phone

On Christmas Eve, old Santa Fe twinkles with the light of thousands of tiny candles. The city's ancient neighborhoods are decorated with *farolitos*, little paper bags weighted with sand and lit with a candle. They line sidewalks and the tops of adobe walls. Neighbors and neighborhoods join to create this subtle, beautiful reminder of the days when Santa Fe was primarily a Catholic town where residents lit the way for Baby Jesus. *Luminarias*, or bonfires, stand on corners to warm the walkers. Because of the number of pedestrians along Garcia Street and Acequia Madre, the city often closes roads in this area to all but resident traffic. The closure means that you don't have to walk through gasoline fumes and suffer bright car lights to enjoy the sights — but be sure to dress warmly. Some households or merchants along the way serve hot cider to passersby. Strangers often congregate to sing Christmas carols.

The Cross of the Martyrs, at the top of the hill just off Paseo Peralta near Marcy Street, is another fine place to see *luminarias* and *farolitos*. In addition, many churches decorate with *farolitos* for the Christmas Eve services, and private homes throughout the city keep the tradition alive.

While you're cruising, don't forget to take a look at the Plaza, which sometimes has holiday ice sculptures in addition to its decorations. And the Loretto Hotel, a downtown hotel designed to resemble an Indian Pueblo, does Christmas up right with electric *farolitos* to highlight its many levels. All of the sights are free.

Santa Fe's blue skies,
incredible light and
diverse landscape
began to draw painters
and photographers from
the east at the start of
the 20th century.

The Arts

Long before "cultural tourism" became a catch phrase, the arts and culture drew tourists to Santa Fe. Although the city is best known for its visual arts, as reflected in its nationally known museums and some 200 galleries, you'll also find opera, chamber music of all sorts and vocal music. You'll discover theater, both homegrown and imported, and a smattering of dance, including world-famous flamenco by María Benítez. Santa Fe has everything from free performances to $100-a-ticket extravaganzas.

The arts here encompass the traditional and the modern. The petroglyphs in the Galisteo area and along the rock canyons of the Santa Fe River south of the city testify to the antiquity of Santa Fe's attraction as an arts center. The descendants of the city's founding families set the stage for Santa Fe's development as an art mecca with their indigenous arts — the *colcha* embroidery, delicate straw inlay, painting and carving. The Spanish brought the arts of silversmithing, ironsmithing and weaving to New Mexico. The early Europeans, who used their skills to create religious images and beautiful, practical items for the home and ranch, must have been inspired, as visitors are today, by the pottery and jewelry created at the nearby Indian pueblos.

Santa Fe's blue skies, incredible light and diverse landscape began to draw painters and photographers from the east at the start of the 20th century. The artists found plenty to inspire them — buildings that seemed to grow from the earth itself, narrow twisting streets, the blue bulk of the mountains and foothills framing the city to the east and the fiery sunsets against the Jémez Mountains to the west.

Many of the earliest artists came seeking better health. The same sunshine and dry air that made them feel better also captured their eyes and imaginations. Carlos Vierra, for example, came for his health and made Santa Fe his permanent home. Vierra, a painter and photographer, worked with the School of American Archaeology (now the School of American Research) and helped develop a unique style of architecture drawn from Santa Fe's antiquity and practical use of available materials. Vierra and other artists also pushed for the restoration of historical buildings. He painted some of the murals that you can still see on the walls of St. Francis Auditorium at the Museum of Fine Arts. Before World War I, Sheldon Parsons, Victor Higgins, Gerald Cassidy, William Penhallow Henderson and his poet wife, Alice Corbin Henderson, B.J.O Nordfeldt and many more artists came to Santa Fe, enriching the city with their art and energy.

The establishment of the Museum of Fine Arts in 1907 gave Santa Fe artists a boost, helping them financially by making studios available and professionally by displaying their work. The new museum opened with an exhibit of art by Santa Fe and Taos painters. The artists donated paintings to the museum, forming the basis of its now expansive permanent collection. Many of those featured are regarded as the most important U.S. artists of their time.

In the 1920s, Will Shuster — now best known for creating Zozobra, a giant puppet that is burned as part of the Santa Fe Fiesta — and four other Santa Fe painters became known as *Los Cinco Pintores* (The Five Painters) and spread the glory of Santa Fe's scenery and people with their art. Even earlier, John Sloan, George Bellows and Leon Kroll — important names in 20th-century American art — had visited and painted in Santa Fe. Edward Hopper and Marsden Hartley lived here in the 1920s and '30s, as did Robert Henri and Andrew Dausburg. Writers "discovered" Santa Fe too. Mary Austin, Willa Cather, Jack London, H.L. Mencken, Ezra Pound, Witter Brynner and many others either lived here or were frequent visitors.

The Santa Fe Concert Band, which traces its founding to 1869, is the community's oldest performing organization still in existence. The all-volunteer band includes amateurs and some retired professional performers who still get a kick out of playing before an audience. The group performs several times a year, usually in public parks or on the Plaza, and all concerts are free. (Call 471-4865 for information.) Santa Fe Playhouse, formerly Santa Fe Community Theater, is another long-established amateur company, founded 10 years after statehood in 1912. The Santa Fe Concert Association has brought classical music to Santa Fe audiences for more than 60 years.

Santa Fe's arts community took a step into the national spotlight in 1957, when the Santa Fe Opera staged its first performances. The Santa Fe Opera, with its commitment to nurturing American talent and offering a venue for new works, is a major player in the operatic world and draws opera fans and the curious from throughout the world for its summer season. Composer Igor Stravinsky spent more than 10 summers here, in part because of his affection for the outdoor Santa Fe Opera. The Opera's success inspired other performance companies, with the Santa Fe Chamber Music Festival, the Santa Fe Desert Chorale and, in recent years, Santa Fe Stages, adding to Santa Fe's artistic reputation. María Benítez, one of the nation's best known flamenco dancers and choreographers, spends summers here dancing with her company and has also performed and choreographed for the Santa Fe Opera.

St. Francis Auditorium, an attractive, shoebox-shaped hall, is a popular venue for musical groups. Acoustics are good here, but some audience members may have trouble seeing. The same is true for the beautiful but small Loretto Chapel and the Santuario de Guadalupe, an old church that has been graciously rented out for music and theater as well as some visual art shows. Sweeney Center, the city's all-purpose public space, can seat large crowds and offers convenient parking. The James A. Little Theater at the New Mexico School for the Deaf, the Armory for the Arts Theater and Greer Garson Theater are among Santa Fe's most frequently used venues, in part because they were actually built to be theaters!

New Mexico's best-known painter, Georgia O'Keeffe, lived in Santa Fe in the years immediately preceding her death in 1986 and is honored with the city's newest museum. O'Keeffe followed a long tradition of artists from the east migrating to Santa Fe, Taos and nearby communities. Now, by some estimates, more than a thousand artists — some famous, some unknown but hopeful — live in Santa Fe and the surrounding area.

The Museum of Fine Arts, The Georgia O'Keeffe Museum and the exhibits at SITE Santa Fe add to the city's standing as a visual-arts center. The city estimates there are between 200 and 300 art galleries here, making Santa Fe one of the nation's leading places to buy and sell art. Among the galleries are those that show work by well-known national and international artists, those that look for emerging artists and cutting-edge work and some that strive to display paintings and drawings that average buyers can afford. From traditional cowboy paintings and sculpture to work by Santa Fe and Taos painters of the 1920s and '30s to contemporary art and even some avant garde creations, if it calls itself art, you probably can buy it here.

But galleries don't have a monopoly on art. The long-established Indian Market brings

FYI

Unless otherwise noted, the area code for all phone numbers listed in this guide is 505.

INSIDERS' TIP

Art is among the clues archaeologists used in their search for evidence of prehistoric trade routes stretching from Chiapas, Mexico, into New Mexico. Macaw feathers from Mexico have been uncovered in pueblo ruins near Santa Fe, and New Mexico turquoise, possibly from mines near Cerrillos, decorated ceremonial masks in Oaxaca.

leading American Indian artists and craftspeople from throughout the country to Santa Fe each summer. Spanish Market, held in July and December, offers a rare occasion to see work patterned after traditional Spanish Colonial arts created with fresh inspiration by living Hispanic artists. Santa Fe's Plaza hosts a parade of summer arts and crafts shows, which make shopping for art — or just looking — accessible to the whole family. (See our Annual Events chapter.)

The city of Santa Fe's mural program has resulted in murals at City Hall, on street corner signal boxes, municipal buses and even on garbage trucks. Today, arts of all sorts intermingle as part of the fabric of contemporary Santa Fe. From subtle chamber music to lively bilingual theater, it's hard to find a weekend without a concert, lecture, film or recital to entice you. Enjoy!

The following listings offer a look at some Santa Fe arts organizations. For logical use, it is arranged alphabetically. Where possible we've given addresses for performance locations.

Community Arts Centers

Plan B Evolving Arts
Armory for the Arts, 1050 Old Pecos Tr.
• 982-1338

Plan B provides space for film, workshops and performance — and plenty of parking. Live performances by local, regional and national artists may include modern dance or pieces that combine music, video, theater and movement in unusual and creative ways. Plan B also serves as an alternative space for visual arts. You'll find cutting-edge and experimental work from nationally known talent and emerging and progressive New Mexico artists. A recent Plan B art exhibit, *Rise Overrun*, was an interactive sculpture that rose from the floor toward the roof complete with a stairway, suspension bridge and a ladder. Participants had to sign a liability release before they could see the show.

Plan B offers a variety of classes and workshops including jewelry making, figure drawing, assemblages and preparing and utilizing organic materials. The Arts Parts store on the premises recycles leftovers from businesses to school art programs and private artists. The center publishes a highly informative monthly calendar with detailed descriptions of the events as well as times and prices. Its Cinematheque program has long been a favorite for Santa Fe moviegoers and is one of the few places in town you can see top-flight foreign films (see more information in our Film section in this chapter). The center is usually open from noon to 7 PM daily.

Dance

María Benítez Teatro Flamenco/ Institute for Spanish Arts
Radisson Hotel, 750 N. St. Francis Dr.
• 983-8477, (800) 905-3315 Protix

Talented and passionate about her art, María Benítez has brought flamenco dance to Santa Fe each summer for many years. Benítez performs with a company of dancers, guitarists and a singer or two from July until early September. In addition to engagements with the company, Benítez frequently appears as a guest artist and choreographer with the Santa Fe Opera and has performed with Santa Fe Stages. Teatro Flamenco has been broadcast in all 50 states and internationally and has appeared on PBS-TV. The Institute for Spanish Arts is the educational part of the company and presents classes and workshops. For the past several seasons, Teatro Flamenco has danced in the María Benítez Theatre at the Radisson Hotel.

Daystar
Performance locations vary • 471-4822

This national American Indian contemporary dance company is based in Santa Fe but appears throughout the country. Performances draw on Native American oral tradition within a modern dance context. Daystar offers workshops for students and professional dancers in storytelling and Native American dance and song. Rosalie Jones, founder and artistic director, established Daystar in 1980. The company recently finished a collaboration with Bulgarian folk dancers. The group offers at least one Santa Fe concert a year, usually in the spring.

New Mexico Dance Coalition
Performance locations vary • 820-2636

Organized by the state's leading dance companies and based in Santa Fe, the Dance Coalition was formed as an advocacy group to help arrange performance opportunities and provide other services for New Mexico dancers. Among the group's activities have been a benefit Dance Bash with eclectic performances; an evening of choreography by solo dance artists; a free global dance and music festival on the Santa Fe Plaza and an annual choreographers' showcase each fall at the Armory for the Arts, 1050 Old Pecos Trail. The coalition also publishes a newsletter and acts as fiscal agent for small companies.

www.insiders.com

See this and many other
Insiders' Guide® destinations
online — in their entirety.

Visit us today!

Santa Fe Dance Foundation
Performance locations vary • 983-5591

Gisela Genschow, a dancer born and trained in Germany who arrived in Santa Fe via New York and Pittsburgh, founded this dance school in 1992. In addition to ballet classes for children and adults, the company presents an annual holiday performance of *The Nutcracker*, which brings in professional dancers for the leading roles. The 1997 show, at Greer Garson Theater, opened with a gala reception for the artists and ran for three performances over two days. Adult tickets were $25 for the gala and $15 for the other performances, with lower-priced admission for children and seniors.

Santa Fe Festival Ballet
James A. Little Theater, New Mexico
School for the Deaf, 1060 Cerrillos Rd.
• 989-8898, (800) 905-3315 (ProTix)

A new kid on the performing arts scene, Festival Ballet presented its inaugural season in the summer of 1997, featuring guest artists from the New York City Ballet and music by Santa Fe Pro Musica. After their well-received debut, the company planned to build future seasons to again include guest dancers from a major professional company and live music. Tickets range from $15 to $45.

Film

Cinematheque Program
Plan B Evolving Arts, 1050 Old Pecos Tr.
• 982-1338

Plan B's Cinematheque is one of Santa Fe's most reliable sources for unusual films, including some of classic vintage and some beautiful, seldom-seen foreign movies. Recent offerings included Antonioni's *Blow-Up*, documentaries by ethnographer John Cohen, Japanese erotic film and a series of films from Hong Kong. Most films open on Friday and run for six days. Alternative films are shown every day. Tickets are $6 for adults with discounts for children, students and seniors. Please call for a schedule and show times. Plan B has plenty of parking.

Grand Illusion
St. Michael's Village West Shopping Ctr.,
1614 St. Michael's Dr. at Llano St.
• 471-8935

During the summer, Grand Illusion becomes Santa Fe's family theater with a continuous long run of a Disney feature or otherwise appropriate movie for kids and their parents. *Pocahontas* and *Hercules* were big hits. Evenings and during the rest of the year, Grand Illusion offers foreign-language films and some mainstream movies. You'll find convenient parking in the shopping center lot.

Jean Cocteau Cinema and Coffee House
418 Montezuma St. • 988-2711

A Sunday movie, discussion brunches and a first-rate coffeehouse set this downtown art theater apart from the crowd. This cozy, classy little theater isn't your usual movie palace. You'll find foreign films, alternative American productions and mainstream classics here. Jean Cocteau Cinema uses a customer wish list to help with its programming. The coffeehouse is open from 3 PM until midnight and offers live music before the midnight movies.

You can park along the street or in nearby lots.

The Movies/DeVargas Center
6 DeVargas Ctr., 564 N. Guadalupe St. (Guadalupe St. at Paseo de Peralta) • 988-2775

This six-screen theater shows smaller, less commercial films, some with mainstream audience appeal and others you'd expect to find at art cinemas rather than at a mall movie house. Santa Fe is a hot market for art films — some studies have shown that the percentage of Santa Fe residents who attend these movies is the highest in the country. Many of those featured are regarded as the most important U.S. films of their time. Art films usually cost theaters less and build an audience over several weeks through word of mouth; blockbusters, in contrast, peak in the their first week. Some 90 percent of films that are nationally distributed eventually come to Santa Fe, and many of them here to The Movies. Abundant parking in the DeVargas Center awaits.

St. John's College Film Society
St. John's College Great Hall, Peterson Student Center, 1160 Camino Cruz Blanca • 984-6000

Varied programming of classic films marks this series, which draws students as well as film buffs from the community. A recent Wednesday featured a slate of modern French films including *The City of Lost Children* about a sleepless monster who kidnaps children to steal their dreams. The weekend series runs on Saturday nights with a film at 7 PM and sometimes a second feature at 9:15 PM. Admission is only $3, $4 if a double feature is on the program — one of the biggest movie bargains in town.

United Artists Theaters
Lensic Theater, 211 W. San Francisco St. • 982-0301
United Artists North, 4250 Cerrillos Rd. • 471-3377
United Artists South, 4250 Cerrillos Rd. • 471-6066

United Artists is the central force in Santa Fe commercial cinema, with 19 screens that show Hollywood products, the movies that get the expensive TV commercials and whose stars are interviewed on talk shows and profiled in *People*. But unlike most multiplex cinema extravaganzas, one of these places — the Lensic — is an old-fashioned theater with just one big screen and the classic look of a turn-of-the-century movie palace. United Artists North and South are on the appropriate sides of Villa Linda Mall. You'll find lines of teens here most weekends. Parking at Villa Linda is easy in the mall's sprawling lots, and there's a city parking garage across the street from the Lensic.

Literature

Book Signings

Santa Fe is a literary center and has played host to such writers as Willa Cather, Carl Sandburg, Tony Hillerman, Vachel Lindsay, Robinson Jeffers, Thornton Wilder, Evan Connell, Robert Frost and many more. Some only visited, some stayed for years, others live here still. Most weekends at least one author, either local or imported, is celebrating the long-awaited arrival of a new book with an autograph party at any one of the local bookstores. All three Santa Fe newspapers publish author interviews and information about signings. Sometimes in addition to signings, authors will also read from their new works. Please see our Shopping chapter for the addresses and phone numbers of the bookstores.

Recursos de Santa Fe Southwest Literary Center
826 Camino de Monte Rey • 982-9301

Founded in 1984, Recursos is a nonprofit educational organization that includes among its missions the encouragement of good writing. To this end, Recursos Southwest Literary Center presents seminars, conferences, expositions, study tours and academic and artistic projects. The Writers Reading Series gives Santa Fe its only regular opportunity to hear poets, novelists and nonfiction writers read from their works. Sponsored by grants including support from the Witter Brynner Foundation for Poetry, a national organization based here, the free programs bring writers and read-

The New Mexico Film Office

If you've never been to Santa Fe but have deja vu when you get here because everything looks so darn familiar, you can credit Santa Fe's long-standing popularity among filmmakers. The state's film office works with movie companies to attract their business to New Mexico, help them find the right location and arrange for the necessary support services.

Nearly 300 feature films have been shot in New Mexico, starting with silent pictures in 1898. The diverse landscape, incredible light and rich blue skies top the list of why the state was chosen for such films as *Salt of the Earth*, *The Grapes of Wrath*, *Wyatt Earp* and *Contact*. Santa Fe and northern New Mexico have long been popular with movie-makers — more than half of the state's movies have been shot within the city's mountain and mesa vistas. The early movies here were Westerns, but the area soon became a popular location for a variety of films. In the video classic *The Man Who Fell to Earth*, David Bowie dropped to an old mine site in Madrid, a vintage coal town south of Santa Fe. Much of *Easy Rider* was shot in Santa Fe and Taos. Cult favorite *Billie Jack* was shot at the Eaves Ranch just south of Santa Fe — a movie set that is occasionally open to the public — and at Santa Clara Pueblo and Bandelier National Monument. Another underground favorite *Pow Wow Highway*, an American Indian Western of sorts produced by George Harrison, was shot around Santa Fe.

Some of Hollywood's best-known stars have been here. John Wayne made *The Cowboys* at San Cristobal Ranch near Galisteo and at Chama. Lee Marvin and Paul Newman filmed *Pocket Money* in Santa Fe and Truchas, a scenic village north of Santa Fe. Danny De Vito and Arnold Schwarzenegger gathered considerable attention during their stay in Santa Fe for *Twins*, and Schwarzenegger and family have been frequent visitors ever since. Robert Redford's *Milagro Beanfield War* was filmed in Truchas and resulted in numerous Redford sightings at Santa Fe shops and restaurants. Kevin Costner came for *Wyatt Earp*, and Kenny Rogers filmed *The Gambler III* in Santa Fe and at Rancho de las Golondrinas near La Cienega. Woody Harrelson, Patricia Arquette and Nicholas Cage were in town in the fall of 1997 for *The Hi Lo Country*. Many commercials, television productions and music videos are shot here also.

Contact the film office at P.O. Box 2003, Santa Fe, NM 87504, 827-9810, (800) 545-9871.

Photo: Don Strel/Southwest Assignments

Santa Fe has long been a favorite location for making commercial movies. The makers of *Wishbone*, with a talking dog as the central character, hired locals when they shot at the J.W Eaves movie ranch.

ers together twice a month. The series has included Paula Gunn Allen. A Discovery Reading presents less-familiar voices, winners of the national Discovery Writing Competition that Recursos sponsors annually.

Each year the nonprofit organization conducts about six writers' workshops, which have drawn attendees from throughout the country. Recent topics have included Writing Women's Lives with Western States Book Award novelist Demetria Martinez and Pam Houston, who won the same award for her short-story collection. George Johnson, former editor of the *New York Times News of the Week in Review* joined other top writers for Writing Science Today, a seminar for professional science writers. Recursos also brings many major writers to Santa Fe each summer for its annual Santa Fe Writers Conference. Student participants are selected based on written submissions; attendance is limited to allow for more individual attention at this popular and successful series. Faculty members have included E. Annie Proulx, Tony Hillerman, John Nichols and many other published writers of national and international reputation. Fee for conferences is approximately $450 for a five-day program.

New Mexico Book Association
P.O. Box 1285, Santa Fe, NM 87504
• 983-1412

This Santa Fe-based organization works to nurture the growing literary scene throughout New Mexico. In recent years many small presses publishing fine works by local writers have emerged, tested their dreams against reality and survived in pleasingly strong numbers. NMBA publishes a lively newsletter, "Libro Monthly," with plenty of news from writers and publishers in Santa Fe, New Mexico and even out of state. The group hosts monthly luncheons for publishers, writers and readers. They also publish *New Mexico's Book World: A Resource Guide*, a directory of book people and services in the state.

PEN New Mexico
2860 Plaza Verde • 473-4813

Chartered under the U.S.A. PEN Los Angeles Chapter, this group started in 1991. A nonprofit professional organization, PEN sponsors local readings, seminars, regional conferences and other events relevant to writers and the literary world. A recent state conference dealt with Censorship in Cyberspace and featured a day of programs and lunch — all for $15. Although attendance at any one workshop or seminar may fluctuate from a handful to a roomful, PEN knows that published authors and the would-be-published like to schmooze, and to that end hosts social as well as professional events.

SITE Santa Fe
1606 Paseo de Peralta • 989-1199

Although most of the attention here is devoted to visual art, SITE Santa Fe also offers a fine literary series featuring internationally recognized authors and emerging poets and writers. Among the guests have been Pulitzer Prize winner Charles Simac and Nobel Prize winner Derek Walcott. Tickets are $5 for the readings. Check the newspapers for upcoming events. SITE Santa Fe also presents Writing in the Galleries, a workshop led by New Mexico poets and writers, on Wednesdays and Sundays at noon, usually at mid-month. Admission is free.

Music

Collaborations College of Santa Fe
Greer Garson Theatre Center, 1600 St. Michael's Dr. • 473-6511

This music series features an eclectic mix of contemporary performances in the intimate space of the Weckesser Studio Theater inside the Greer Garson Theater Center. Performers may be New Mexicans or visitors from out of state. Ticket prices range from $8 to $12. Performances are scheduled during the school year; call for a schedule of events.

St. John's College Concert Series
St. John's College Peterson Student Center, 1160 Camino Cruz Blanca
• 984-6104

Concerts here tend to stress piano music. Musician-in-residence Peter Pesic offers informal noon performances in the spring and fall in the Junior Commons Room with commentary about the music. The programs are free.

The college also hosts visiting musicians in evening programs, to which admission may be charged. Among recent guests have been Paul Hillier, founder and director of Theatre of Voices, a medieval music ensemble.

Paolo Soleri Amphitheater
Santa Fe Indian School campus, 1501 Cerrillos Rd. • 989-6318

This open-air theater, designed by the renowned architect Paolo Soleri, hosts popular concerts during the warmer months, usually beginning about May and extending to early October. Among the singers who've performed here are k.d. lang, B.B. King, Dan Fogelberg, Ziggy Marley and James Taylor. The theater is frequently the venue for native Roots & Rhythms Festival, a performance component that accompanies Santa Fe's annual Indian Market. Most concerts start with warm-up groups around dusk. Food, drinks, tapes, CDs, T-shirts and other concessions may be sold outside the theater.

Santa Fe Chamber Music Festival
St. Francis Auditorium, Museum of Fine Arts, 107 W. Palace Ave. • 983-2075, 982-1890 in summer

The Chamber Music Festival began in the summer of 1973 and has grown into an event with an international following. The Festival draws consistent critical acclaim for the depth of its programming and its vision in commissioning new pieces and presenting seldom-heard works. The Festival celebrated its Silver Jubilee — 25 years of festival music — in 1997 with a series of special concerts, including many works by Brahms on the centennial of his death. That same season, the festival recorded 11,500 concert-goers and a 38 percent increase in group ticket sales. In honor of its anniversary, the Festival's Board of Directors hosted a community party on the Plaza, complete with Latin American music, a string player on a skateboard and a giant birthday cake — all for free.

Festival musicians, renowned players from major ensembles throughout the world, played in honor of the opening of the O'Keeffe Museum just as the Festival had performed for O'Keeffe at her Abiquiú home in gratitude for the artist's willingness to let the organization reproduce her paintings as their season posters for many years. Each summer, performers at the Festival include established musicians and up-and-comers. A typical season includes more than 30 concerts, a composer-in-residence, emphasis on American music and attention to masterworks. Jazz may continue to play a major role. But the classics, performed by such musicians as Ani Kavafian, Daniel Phillips, Nathaniel Rosen and Andre-Michel Schub, form the festival's life blood. Repertoire ranges from the works of J.S. Bach to the world premiere of Bright Sheng's Festival commission, *The Silver Ring*. The programming is arranged in separate series to make it easier for patrons to hear the music they like best. The music is taped and frequently broadcast over public radio and on classical stations.

To help inform the audience, the Festival presents a series of previews about the music and artists before the season begins at $10 per lecture. Immediately before the concerts, free discussions feature guest composers, artists and musicologists reviewing the day's repertoire. Festival musicians often give free concerts to senior citizens, residents of rehabilitation centers and hospitals. The Chamber Music Festival offers a special series for children, also for free. Concerts are rehearsed and performed in St. Francis Auditorium. The public can sit in on selected daytime rehearsals free of charge. The season runs from the second weekend in July through mid-August. Seating is reserved, and individual tickets cost from $24 to $36.

Santa Fe Concert Association
Performance locations vary, usually St. Francis Auditorium, Museum of Fine Arts, 107 W. Palace Ave. • 984-8759, (800) 905-3315 (ProTix)

Since 1936 Santa Fe Concert Association has made Santa Fe a more cultured place to live by bringing in nationally known artists. Before the Opera and the Chamber Music Festival, the top-quality musicians who came to town under this nonprofit group's sponsorship offered city residents their only chance to hear national artists without a road trip. This group's impressive performance list draws the best musicians and singers from around the world. The association arranges a dozen or more

Santa Fe's more than 200 art galleries range from contemporary to traditional, from experimental to realistic. You'll see work by newcomers along with established professionals.

events from September to May with performances ranging from soloists to string quartets, trios to chamber orchestras. Past guests have include pianist Leon Fleisher, the Prague Chamber Orchestra, Czech violinist Josef Suk and flutist James Gallway. The Concert Association's Christmas Eve and New Year's Eve concerts presented by local and visiting musicians have been a regular and very popular addition to Santa Fe's musical life since 1981. Ticket prices range from $25 to $60.

Santa Fe Desert Chorale
Santuario de Guadalupe, 100 Guadalupe St., and the Loretto Chapel, 207 Old Santa Fe Tr. • 988-7505 (box office), (800) 905-3315 (ProTix)

The Chorale is the only professional vocal ensemble in New Mexico and remains one of the few groups presenting music of early Mexico as well as vocal music from Mozart, Debussy, Copland and many others. Established in 1982, the chorale usually performs five separate programs in its summer season with concerts in both Santa Fe and Albuquerque. Among the voices of the chorale are singers recruited from throughout the country and

local talent. Like the Opera, the chorale presents world-premiere pieces, sometimes inviting the composers to work with the singers for the debuts. Among the concert themes have been Spiritual Inspiration, Songs of the Feminine and music in the glee club/barbershop quartet tradition. For its 1997 anniversary season, the chorus commissioned *Archbishop Latour Dreams the Future* by Lori Westmoreland Schoenfeld, based on Willa Cather's novel *Death Comes for the Archbishop*. At other concerts, traditional African-American songs, Sephardic music and Gregorian chants share the program with Renaissance works. To add to the audience's enjoyment of the music, the chorale offers a preconcert lecture an hour before the performance. If you can't make it to a Santa Fe concert, you can hear the Santa Fe Desert Chorale on National Public Radio's *Performance Today*. The chorus has many recordings, including numerous American and world premieres. The group released its 10th recording *Music from Loretto Chapel*, in 1997.

The chorale performs in two venues, both historic churches — the Santuario de Guadalupe, built between 1776 and 1795, and the Loretto Chapel, the town's Gothic-Revival landmark, famous for its "miraculous" staircase (see our Attractions chapter). In December, the chorale presents festive holiday concerts. The program combines a variety of new and seldom-heard music along with a few old favorites. The holiday concerts sell out; book your tickets early. Tickets range from $18 to $25.

The Santa Fe Opera
Santa Fe Opera Theater, 7 miles N.W. of Santa Fe on U.S. Hwy. 84-285
• 986-5955, (800) 280-4654

The Santa Fe Opera, a summer company that draws its talent from America's leading operas, reached international stature soon after its inception. The fame is due mainly to the high-quality performances and the company's sense of adventure in tackling new or rare works. The Opera continues to present a combination of classics, rarely heard works and an American or world premiere in beautiful productions that attract opera lovers from around the world. The Opera opened on July 3, 1957, in a 480-seat theater. Its founder, John Crosby, continues as general director — the longest-tenured operative in that role in America — and also serves as a conductor for several performances during the season. The original theater burned in 1967 and was replaced with a 1,889-seat open-air theater by the start of the next season. That theater served the company through the 1997 season.

The Opera operated on a budget of $110,000 its first season; the 1997 budget was approximately $9 million. The Santa Fe Opera remodeled its theater beginning in the fall of 1997 to preserve the open-air ambiance while offering the audience more protection from the elements and adding about 200 seats. The redesign completely roofed the audience seating area and extended the roof line farther on the sides in a design tested in a wind tunnel and refined to keep out wind-driven rain. The new theater seats 2,126 patrons — all of them under cover. Unlike the old fiberglass seats, the new seats are fully upholstered and can be removed at wheelchair stations in three locations in the theater. The remodeling added 37 lavatory fixtures, five drinking fountains and three public telephones. The reconstruction, an $18 million project, also included better handicapped accessibility. New in-seat text displays will provide simultaneous English translations beginning in 1999, using a system similar to New York's Metropolitan Opera's.

Behind the scenes, the new theater has a wetlands sewage treatment and water reclamation system to harvest rain water from summer thunderstorms. The newly expanded and renovated theater, which was set to open with parties and other festivities in 1998, sits in the long-established location atop a hillside in the Sangre de Cristo Mountains with a stunning view of the Jémez Mountain range. As with the old theater, performances begin just after sunset in this outdoor theater, so you can enjoy the natural light show first.

The Santa Fe Opera makes its musical magic with the assistance of more than 600 company members at the height of its summer season. The company has presented more than 100 different operas including more than three dozen American and world premieres. Friday and Saturday performances frequently sell out weeks in advance. Although the theater has been renovated, the Santa Fe

---

INSIDERS' TIP

Although it's based out of Albuquerque, Southwest Writers Workshop is important enough — and, indeed, close enough (only an hour away) — to merit mention in a book about Santa Fe. Its goal is to help writers, especially beginners, learn their craft and become professionally competent authors. SWW presents numerous workshops throughout the year, some of them in Santa Fe, that feature well-known writers and instructors. For more information, write Southwest Writers Workshop, 1338-B Wyoming Blvd. NE, Albuquerque, NM 87112, or call 293-0303.

Opera doesn't plan to tinker with the performance formula that has made it successful for more than 40 years. Normal repertoire includes a familiar opera such as Verdi's *La Traviata*; a work by Mozart; a Richard Strauss opera; an older, seldom-heard work, such as Handel's *Semele*, which was included in the 1997 season; and an American or world premiere.

In addition to its willingness to take a chance on a new work, the Santa Fe Opera also takes a chance on new talent with its extensive apprentice singer and technician programs. Apprentices, chosen by audition, appear in the productions as chorus members and understudies for major roles. They learn the many facets of opera from some of the world's best conductors, directors and coaches. Well-known singers including Samuel Ramey, Ashley Putnam and James Morris are among the program's graduates. Kiri te Kanawa made her American debut here. Each August the Opera gives the apprentices the stage on their own, in two concerts that showcase their talents with a variety of opera vignettes. Other apprentices learn technical aspects of opera — lighting, costumes, sets, wigs, makeup and more.

To help patrons enjoy the performances even more, the Opera hosts a series of free, in-town lectures. Some programs feature musicologists who offer background and insight into the works on the program; others introduce cast members, directors or conductors who talk about their experience on the Santa Fe stage. The Santa Fe Opera reaches out to young people and children through its Opera for Youth and Pueblo Opera programs. Children and teenagers can attend the final dress rehearsals of several season productions and have the theater much to themselves; adult tickets are restricted on those nights. Opera Day at the Ranch, an annual free preseason open house, takes place in May.

Backstage tours through the costume shop and production area continue throughout the season, Monday through Saturday at 1 PM, and reservations are not required. Since the company makes most of its own sets, props and costumes, there's plenty to see. The opera offers elegant pre-performance picnic suppers, buffets with guest speakers and a full bar for libations between the acts. At the gift shop you can buy tote bags, sweat shirts and other merchandise with the Opera's distinctive SFO logo, and a portion of the sales benefit the company.

Tickets for the Santa Fe Opera performances range from $20 to $110 Monday through Thursday and from $28 to $118 on Friday and Saturday. Standing room is $6 to $8. The season runs from late June or early July through the third week in August.

Santa Fe Pro Musica Chamber Orchestra and Ensemble
Performance locations vary • 988-4640

This group consists of a 35-member chamber orchestra and smaller chamber ensembles. The orchestra performs without a conductor in a long-standing tradition of chamber music. Pro Musica presents orchestral concerts in October, November, December, February, March and April. The ensembles, drawn from the main group, perform an additional five concerts a season. Pro Musica also offers a popular Christmas concert and a Holy Week Baroque Festival. The musicians perform the baroque music on period instruments — wooden rather than metal flutes, violins with lower bridges and less taut bows — which leads to a general softening and mellowness of sound. Pro Musica's soloists, who often come from leading ensembles throughout the country, have included Allan Vogel, an oboist of national stature who appeared with the Chamber Ensemble in 1997. The group covers an impressive repertoire, with works from Mozart, Beethoven, Haydn, Bach, Vivaldi and contemporary masters who celebrate the concerto and symphonic forms. Santa Fe Pro Musica performs in the James A. Little Theater on the grounds of the School for the Deaf, 1060 Cerrillos Road; at the Loretto Chapel, 207 Old Santa Fe Trail; and at the St. Francis Auditorium, 107 W. Palace Avenue. Tickets range from $15 to $30.

Santa Fe Symphony and Chorus
Performance locations vary • 983-1414 (box office), (800) 480-1319

The Santa Fe Symphony started in 1984 and despite some financial and artistic adjustments seems to be going strong. One of the group's proud claims is that all of its musi-

At the height of the summer season, the Santa Fe Opera makes its musical magic with the assistance of more than 600 company members.

Photo: Paul Slaughter

cians are New Mexicans. Many studied at the Julliard School of Music and the Manhattan School of Music and came to Santa Fe to join this growing group. Four years after it began, the symphony combined with the Santa Fe Chorus and began operating under joint management. The two consistently perform together. Among the repertoire have been Bach's *Christmas Oratorio*, the Mozart's *Requiem* and Resphigi's *The Birds*. Concerts have included Haydn symphonies, jazz with Eddie Daniels playing clarinet, a spring pops concert and the Bach Passions. *Messiah* following Thanksgiving and a Beethoven Festival scheduled around the composer's birthday in December have become traditions. The Symphony's season runs from October through April with nine concerts. Tickets range from $8 to $30, and student tickets are available at a discount.

Santa Fe Women's Ensemble
Loretto Chapel, 207 Old Santa Fe Tr.
• 983-2137

This 12-voice group has delighted Santa Fe audiences since 1980 and attracts an en-thusiastic audience. The women sing two concerts a year, their Spring Offering and a Christmas Offering. Past concerts have included the world premiere of Michael Mauldin's *We Are One* and Dean Roush's *Stabat Mater*. Performances are held in the jewellike Loretto Chapel, which sets off the voices in splendor. The ensemble is sponsored by the Santa Fe Concert Association.

Serenata of Santa Fe
Santuario de Guadalupe, 100 Agua Fría
• 989-7988

Another of Santa Fe's long-established musical groups, the Serenata has two goals: To present chamber music to audiences of all economic resources in an informal, friendly way and to provide an opportunity for musicians to get together to perform pieces they love. The programs range from solo music to octets. Ensemble members may chat with the audience about the music and composer prior to concerts. The ensemble's players change, and guest performers may be added depending on the pieces in rehearsal for any of their three or four annual concerts. But the group prides itself on not compromising on rehearsal time and not shying away from challenging works. Tickets are $15 by phone or $12 at the door (an incentive to be spontaneous!).

Summerscene
The Plaza • 438-8834

Summerscene concerts bring free music to the Santa Fe Plaza each summer. Recent series have run on Tuesdays and Thursdays at noon and 6 PM from June through August. Programs feature a range of music from folk to jazz. Many locals who work downtown bring their lunch and find a shady Plaza bench where they can relax and enjoy the melodies while they watch the city's visitors marvel at the sights. The early evening shows are ideal family events — the perfect environment for a young child who might grow restless in a concert hall.

20th Century Unlimited
Performance locations vary • 820-6401

In addition to its focus exclusively on 20th-century music, two other things separate this group from the crowd: All tickets are $5, and the group does no local fund-raising. The organization presented its inaugural season in 1997 and offered four concerts for its 1997-98 season, including a complete staged performance of Stravinsky's A Soldier's Tale. The group brought on Yehuda Gilad as conductor for that presentation with actors from Theaterwork. Works by Ginastera, Bartok, Rachmaninoff and others will also be presented by this new Santa Fe group, which bills itself as "A different music series for the City Different."

The ensemble is composed of resident musicians and visiting artists. In addition to affordable concerts, 20th Century Unlimited plans programs in the public elementary schools and intends to use radio to help inform the public about 20th-century music and entice an audience. Concerts will be presented in St. Francis Auditorium, 107 W. Palace, the Santuario de Guadalupe, 100 Agua Fría, and the James A. Little Theater, New Mexico School for the Deaf, 1060 Cerrillos Road.

Theater

Engine House Theater Melodrama Company
2846 N.M. Hwy. 14, Madrid • 438-3780

For unadulterated fun, it's hard to top the Madrid melodrama. Since 1982, the company based in the old theater next to the MineShaft Tavern has drawn enthusiastic crowds to cheer for the heroes and hiss at the bad guys. Bags of marshmallows to toss at the villain are included with admission. The plays are 1800s-style melodramas that fit in well with this old one-time mining town. The season runs weekends from Memorial Day through mid-October. Tickets in 1997 were $9 adults, $7 seniors and $4 for kids younger than 12.

Greer Garson Theatre
Center College of Santa Fe, 1600 St. Michael's Dr. • 473-6511

The 500-seat Greer Garson Theatre is the venue for four yearly stage productions by the College of Santa Fe's nationally recognized Performing Arts Department. The shows, including a musical, feature student casts and usually have faculty members as directors. (The college offers majors in contemporary music, theater, acting, design/theatre technol-

---

INSIDERS' TIP

Artist Georgia O'Keeffe offered to paint a mural for the stairwell of the Museum of Fine Arts while visiting from New York in 1936. Edgar Lee Hewett, the first director of the museum — and better known as an ethnologist than an art historian — turned down the offer. He said he wasn't interested in having "that bone painter" in his museum. Outraged, O'Keeffe resolved not to sell or donate to the museum. Subsequent museum directors for decades tried to patch up the institution's relationship with the state's most famous artist.

ogy and music theater.) Recent seasons have included *Lend Me a Tenor, Dracula, A Midsummer Night's Dream, Dames at Sea, The Diary of Anne Frank* and *Once Upon a Mattress.* Tickets range from $7 to $15. Greer Garson — the actress whose generosity is recognized with buildings in her and her husband, Buddy Fogelson, names throughout the campus — once joined the student company for a production or two. The college is generous about allowing other performance companies access to the theater and to the smaller Weckesser Studio.

FYI

Unless otherwise noted, the area code for all phone numbers listed in this guide is 505.

Santa Fe Performing Arts School and Company
Armory for the Arts Theater, 1050 Old Pecos Tr. • 982-7992, 984-1370 (box office)

The "school" part of this company is probably its better-known activity, especially among Santa Fe parents. But Santa Fe Performing Arts has an adult component that presents performances as well. Shows for kids, using child actors, have included *Tom Sawyer* and *Charlie and the Chocolate Factory.* Among the company's other work is *Jesus Christ Superstar* and *Zoot Suit*, a play based on the Los Angeles riots of the 1940s. Tickets range from $5 to $10.

Santa Fe Stages
Greer Garson Theatre, 1600 St. Michael's Dr. • 982-6683 (box office), 982-6680

Founded in 1995 with the idea of bringing the best theater and dance to Santa Fe, Santa Fe Stages has grown tremendously in terms of quality of productions, audience and critical response. Repertoire has included the North American premiere of an English comedy about the Brontë sisters, flamenco dancer María Benítez, *Tartuffe* and other classics and European clown/buffoon theater. Santa Fe Stages also has experimented with mixed media, layering video and movement. Santa Fe Stages presented more than 65 performances on two stages of the Greer Garson Theatre Center in 1997, bringing productions from London, Quebec, Hungary and France to Santa

Fe. The company offers "Meeting the Artists" matinees, which give audience members a chance to interact with the actors, writers, directors and stage crew in pre- and/or post-show discussions. Stages also hopes to co-produce work with other companies. The season runs from June through August. Tickets range from $25 to $40.

In 1997, the company began selling less expensive tickets the morning of performance.

Santa Fe Playhouse
142 E. DeVargas St. • 984-3055, 988-4262 (box office)

This amateur company, founded in 1922, gets the honors as New Mexico's longest established theater group. The Playhouse presents its own shows, opens its downtown space for use by other theater companies and serves as a venue for other performance arts. Known for many years as Santa Fe Community Theater, the nonprofit company became Playhouse in 1997 but kept its focus of allowing the community access to a stage as both actors, directors, playwrights and audience. Recent productions included *The Kindness of Strangers: Tennessee's Women* and *The Secret Affairs of Mildred Wild*, a comedy by Pulitzer Prize winner Paul Zindel. The Santa Fe Fiesta Melodrama, which pokes fun at the city's events, politicians, celebrities and quirks in the guise of an old-time melodrama, is the group's best-known production. Southwest Children's Theater uses Santa Fe Playhouse for its shows, which offer local children a chance to write their own scripts. The theater also hosts a five-day spring Poetry Festival. Tickets for most shows are $15 or $7 for those younger than 12. Admission is $5 on Thursdays, and Sundays are "pay what you wish" performances.

Shakespeare in Santa Fe
Outdoors near the John Gaw Meem Library, St. John's College, 1160 Camino de la Cruz Blanca • 982-2910

Shakespeare in Santa Fe adds to the city's cultural scene with summertime outdoor performances of a selection from the English language's most famous playwright. The company presents a different show each summer with weekend presentations from early July through mid-August. Since the company's beginning in 1987 as Shakespeare in the Park, the professional actors and directors have created mostly comedies with a sprinkling of tragedy and romance. Original music and Southwestern settings add to the fun. The company estimates that 120,000 patrons have watched its shows. Shakespeare in the Schools, another venture of this company, has offered five programs specifically designed to introduce local students to Shakespeare in an entertaining, nonintimidating way. More than 50,000 children have been exposed to Shakespeare's work through the in-the-schools winter tour and workshops. The company's Tea and Shakespeare lecture-demonstration-conversation is a pre-season fund-raiser and educational outreach program. The company hosts an intern program that welcomes select high school and college students to work with the cast on both performance and technical aspects of the productions.

After years of free admission, entry by donation and encouraging patrons to pay for reserved seating, Shakespeare in Santa Fe began charging all viewers in 1997. Tickets start at just $5; you can buy advance seating for $15 and $25. The performances are preceded with Elizabethan-style gathering music. You can buy dinner, drinks and dessert on the grounds or bring your own picnic. Performances are Friday, Saturday and Sunday evenings.

Theaterwork
1336 Rufina Cir. • 471-1799
This small group, relatively new to Santa Fe, offers a season from September through May. The company's core consists of veteran actors who started performances as

Theaterwork in Minnesota in 1979. Productions, held in the 70-seat Rufina Circle studio — a converted warehouse — range from *King Lear* to plays by local playwrights. The company also hosts acting and music theater workshops and a playwright's lab. Other projects have included *Bataan: The Journey Home*, an original drama based on stories from the survivors of the World War II Bataan Death March. Tickets for most performances are about $10.

Visual Arts

Noncommercial Galleries and Museums

For more information about Santa Fe museums that include art in their collections see our Attractions chapter.

College of Santa Fe Fine Arts Gallery
1600 St. Michael's Dr. • 473-6555
You'll find exhibits by students as well as local, regional and nationally known artists in this space in the college's Southwest Annex, just across from the Fogelson Library. Among the annual highlights is the February Monothon exhibit, featuring the best work produced during a weeklong printmaking marathon. In October, the gallery features smaller indoor sculptures that are part of the college's annual Sculpture Festival. Outside, the campus displays monumental and abstract sculpture for an entire year. Most exhibits begin with an artist's reception and hang for about two weeks. The gallery is normally open Tuesday through Friday from 1 to 5 PM, but extended hours are offered for some exhibits. Admission is free.

INSIDERS' TIP

Los Amigos de El Museo Cultural de Santa Fe hope to build a cultural center here to preserve, promote, protect and encourage the Hispanic culture of northern New Mexico. The group is raising money and hopes to have an interactive, hands-on museum in the future. For information, you can write the organization at P.O. Box 6424, Santa Fe, NM 87502-6424.

CSF will become even more of a visual arts center with the opening of the Anne and John Marion Center for the Photographic Arts, a new $11 million art building scheduled to open in the fall 1998. The Marion Center will house an art history building, a 100-seat lecture hall and a studio art building and will be the new home of the Santa Fe Art Institute.

The Governor's Gallery
New Mexico State Capitol, Fourth Floor, Old Santa Fe Tr. at Paseo de Peralta • 827-3028

Exhibits here feature New Mexico artists and change with some frequency. Receptions, always open to the public, bring people to the State Capitol and introduce the many Roundhouse visitors and state workers to a wide assortment of visual art. The gallery also hosts an annual exhibit of work by the winners of the Governor's Awards for Excellence in the Arts, a program to recognize New Mexican painters, writers, musicians, dancers and others whose creative work makes the state a better place to live. The gallery, an outreach of the Museum of Fine Arts, is open 8 AM to 5 PM Monday through Friday. Admission is free.

Institute of American Indian Arts Museum
108 Cathedral Pl. • 988-6281

American Indian art as an expression of contemporary life — that's one of the underlying themes you'll find in the art displayed here. Or, as the curator of exhibits once said, the museum shows Indian art through Indian eyes. The museum designs its exhibits to give viewers a sense of the appreciation the artists and their communities feel for the works created. With more than 6,500 pieces in the collection representing 3,000 artists, the museum is the largest repository of contemporary Indian art in the world. Paintings, sculpture and traditional crafts such as beadwork, pottery, weaving and basketry are displayed in the museum's five galleries. The museum also offers educational programming and the outdoor Allan Houser Art Park for large sculpture.

The museum is in an attractive adobe, or mud brick, building that formerly housed Santa Fe's main post office. It is part of the Institute of American Indian Arts. The IAIA shares campus space with the College of Santa Fe on the south side of town and has worked with American Indians and Alaskan Natives here since 1971. (See our Education and Child Care chapter.) Among the teachers and students whose work has put the IAIA on the national map are Houser, Fritz Scholder, Linda Lomahaftewa and T.C. Cannon.

The IAIA Museum is open from 10 AM to 5 PM Monday through Saturday and noon to 5 PM on Sunday. Admission is $4 for adults, $2 for seniors and students with ID and free for children younger than 16.

The Museum of Fine Arts
107 W. Palace Ave. • 827-4468

Stately and beautiful in classic Pueblo-Revival style, the Museum of Fine Arts isn't just another pretty adobe. The institution played a pivotal role in helping establish Santa Fe as an arts center. Its open-door exhibition policy in the 1920s gave Santa Fe and Taos artists, many of whom had moved here from the Eastern United States, a convenient place to show their work. The collections focus mainly on art from the Southwest and New Mexico and include both traditional and contemporary work in a variety of media. The museum owns and displays creations by many well-known artists including the Santa Fe and Taos master painters who first brought the art world's attention to New Mexico. You'll also discover work by Georgia O'Keeffe and Peter Hurd.

The museum's galleries change exhibits fairly frequently and usually include provocative work by living artists as well as shows that draw on the collections. Adult admission to the museum and the Georgia O'Keeffe Museum (see the following listing) is $5 for one day or $10 for a four-day pass that provides unlimited admissions to all branches of The Museum of New Mexico. On Sundays adult admission for New Mexico residents with an ID is $1. From 5 to 8 PM on Fridays, admission is free at the Georgia O'Keeffe Museum and The Museum of Fine Arts. The museum and the Georgia O'Keeffe Museum are open from 10 AM to 5 PM Tuesday through Sunday and on Friday evenings. The museums are closed Mondays, New Year's Day, Easter, Thanksgiving and Christmas.

The Museum of Fine Arts' St. Francis Au-

Photo: Courtesy of Robert Bluestone

Guitarist Robert Bluestone is one of a number of professional musicians who live and work in Santa Fe.

ditorium, with its lovely murals and church-like atmosphere, provides one of the city's most popular venues for musical performances and other productions.

The Georgia O'Keeffe Museum
217 Johnson St. • 995-0785

The newest star in Santa Fe's visual arts galaxy, The Georgia O'Keeffe Museum opened in the summer of 1997 with tremendous fanfare and crowds to match. The crowds continued — on nice fall days three months later you could still find a line of art lovers waiting outside the museum doors. They came to see the world's largest permanent collection of O'Keeffe's work, including many pieces the artist kept for herself that have never been exhibited previously. O'Keeffe, a transplant from New York, became New Mexico's best known artist and brought national attention to northern New Mexico's austere and colorful landscapes. You can see her famous paintings of skulls and giant flowers, along with less familiar works, at this museum. The mu-

seum displays O'Keeffe's drawings, paintings, pastels, sculptures and watercolors produced between 1916 and 1980 with simplicity and elegance. Abstractions, nudes, landscapes, city scenes and still lifes are all here. The museum's galleries trace O'Keeffe's artistic evolution and follow the depth and breadth of her long productive career. The museum also collects and exhibits works by contemporaries of O'Keeffe who were part of her artistic community in New Mexico and throughout the nation. The museum offers guided tours, educational programming and special events. You can watch a short video about O'Keeffe's life and a presentation on her contribution to American art. (See the Fine Arts Museum write-up for fees and hours.)

St. John's College Gallery
Second Floor, Peterson Student Ctr,
1160 Camino de la Cruz Blanca
• 984-6099

This small exhibit space hosts shows from faculty members and artists of national reputation. There's an annual student show, judged by members of the college's Fine Arts Guild. The hours fluctuate, but the gallery is normally open from 5 to 8 PM Friday and Saturday and from 1 to 5 PM on Sunday and by appointment. Admission is free.

SITE Santa Fe
1606 Paseo de Peralta • 989-1199

Established in 1995, SITE Santa Fe occupies a former warehouse on the edge of the Guadalupe Street neighborhood — a walkable distance from the downtown museums. This non-profit visual arts organization displays work by regional, national and international contemporary artists in an 18,000-square-foot warehouse. Major exhibits may be accompanied by lectures, films, performances and symposia on similar topics. You may find interactive art including work that uses cameras and projections, interdisciplinary presentations, focused-theme exhibits and one-person shows. Among the exhibits have been *Longing and Belonging*, which featured 31 artists from 13 countries who created work depicting a sense of place especially for the SITE Santa Fe space. *Now Eleanor's Idea* a four-part opera with lowriders, was also produced here.

SITE Santa Fe has an international mission and national affiliations as well as strong connections with private galleries and public museums. The Venice Biennale international art show, for example, will be featured here in the year 2000 as its final tour stop. Opening receptions for artists are usually held on Friday evenings. The gallery is open Wednesday through Sunday from 10 AM to 5 PM. Admission is $2.50 for adults and $1 for seniors and students. It's free on Sunday.

Wheelwright Museum of the American Indian
704 Camino Lejo • 982-4636, (800) 607-4636

You'll find work by living American Indian artists showcased here. Exhibitions in the main gallery include contemporary and traditional art with an emphasis on the Southwest. The exhib-

its rotate every four months. A second gallery presents one-person shows, usually with opening receptions where the public can meet the exhibitor. The entrance displays outdoor sculptures by Allan Houser and others. The museum is open Monday through Saturday from 10 AM to 5 PM and Sunday from 1 to 5 PM. Admission is free. (See our Attractions chapter.)

Private Galleries

Santa Fe has many private galleries where you'll discover an exciting variety of visual arts. What we offer here is just a small sampling of them. Many of the galleries listed here are members of the Santa Fe Gallery Association.

Michael Atkinson Gallery
120 W. San Francisco St. • 820-0411

This gallery, one block west of the Plaza, showcases nationally known watercolorist and sculptor Michael Atkinson. Also displayed are life-size bronzes, landscapes, colorful abstracts on canvas, carved-wood sculptures, turned-wood vessels and a large variety of graphics and posters. The gallery is open daily from 10 AM to 5 PM.

Cline Fine Art Gallery
526 Canyon Rd. • 982-5328

A haven for serious or beginning art collectors, this gallery occupies a 200-year-old landmark adobe and has been in business since 1991. The contemporary painters and sculptors represented include Keith Crown, William Lumpkins, Bill Barrett, Tony Abeyta, Evelyne Boren, Jonathan Sobol and Francisco Benitez. Deceased regional artists with works hanging in the gallery are Alexandre Hogue, Ben Messick and Louis Ribak. The gallery is open Monday through Saturday from 10 AM to 5 PM and from noon to 4 PM on Sunday.

Cline LewAllen Contemporary
129 W. Palace Ave. • 988-8997

The largest contemporary gallery in the

INSIDERS' TIP

Santa Fe Winterfiesta includes many arts and cultural events. Watch for special gallery openings and community art exhibits as well as festive performances.

Southwest with more than 10,000 square feet of exhibit space, Cline LewAllen hosts monthly rotating exhibitions of contemporary artworks in all media by regionally, nationally and internationally celebrated artists. You'll see are works by Forest Moses, John Fischer, Emmi Whitehorse, Donald Roller Wilson and Elaine deKooning. The gallery has been in Santa Fe since 1977. It's open Monday through Saturday from 9:30 AM to 5:30 PM. In July and August the gallery is open on Sunday.

Dreamtime Gallery
223½ Canyon Rd. • 986-0344

In business since 1995, this is the only gallery in the United States to exclusively represent Australian Aboriginal Art. The exhibits change monthly and represent more than 100 Australian artists. You can park in front of the gallery. Dreamtime is open Monday through Saturday from 10 AM to 5 PM and Sunday from 11 AM to 4 PM.

Linda Durham Contemporary Art
Across from the Galisteo Inn, Galisteo • 466-6600

Recently relocated from Santa Fe to the picturesque village of Galisteo, about a half-hour drive away, this gallery shows contemporary, serious, exciting, emerging New Mexico-based artists. The owner has been in business since 1977 and knows her stuff. The gallery is open Tuesday through Saturday from 10 AM to 5 PM.

Nedra Matteucci Galleries
1075 Paseo de Peralta • 982-4631

You'll discover contemporary and historic art in this sprawling gallery, along with a wonderful variety of American Indian antiquities and Spanish Colonial furniture. The gallery features paintings from California regionalists and work by the Hudson River, Ashcan and Brandywine schools. And New Mexico isn't ignored; you'll find first-rate, museum-quality bronzes and paintings by the Santa Fe and Taos artists who put New Mexico on the cultural map more than 50 years ago. The gallery displays work by Joseph H. Sharp, E. Martin Hennings, Walter Ufer, Victor Higgins, Nicolai Fechin, Leon Gaspard and Fremont Ellis. Outside, monumental sculpture by George

Carlson, Glenna Goodacre and many others is featured in the gallery's beautifully landscaped garden, complete with a large pond. The gallery is open Monday through Saturday from 8:30 AM to 5 PM (5:15 PM in the summer). The Nedra Matteucci Gallery, formerly Fenn Galleries, has been in business for more than 25 years. You can park in front of the gallery.

The Allan Houser Compound
P.O. Box 5217, Santa Fe, NM 87502 • 471-1528

Apache artist Allan Houser, one of the best known American Indian artists in the world, envisioned this compound as a permanent place to share his work with friends and visitors. In collaboration with his son, Phillip Haozous, he acquired the original 50 acres and constructed a sculpture studio, visitors center and sculpture garden. Since Houser's death in 1994, the project has grown and the studio expanded into a complete bronze foundry. The sculpture garden now displays both the family collection of Houser's work and available bronze editions. The 104-acre compound is open by appointment Monday through Saturday. The owners prefer that you get directions when you call to make an appointment. Tours of the gardens and show rooms are available at $10 or by group rate.

Charlotte Jackson Fine Art
123 E. Marcy St., Ste. 108 • 989-8688

Carving its own niche in Santa Fe's diverse art market, Charlotte Jackson represents "concrete" and radical painters from the United States and Europe. These large monochromatic works are seldom seen in the United States. Sculpture and paintings that focus on the exploration of light and surface are also in the collection. Exhibits rotate throughout the year. The gallery also hosts lectures and sponsors publications. The gallery is open Monday through Friday from 10 AM to 5 PM and Saturday from 11 AM to 4 PM.

The Marcus Gallery
213 Galisteo St. • 982-9363

In business since 1983, this gallery offers a carefully chosen selection of contemporary and traditional art. The business, which sits in

Photo: Neil Jacobs

Movie theaters show a wide diversity of films, including those shot in Santa Fe.

a historic brick-paved interior courtyard off the Plaza, exhibits 20 recognized and emerging artists who work in a wide variety of media from watercolor and oil to bronze, clay and wood. The gallery represents Nelson Boren, James Roybal, Mikki Senkarik and Walker Moore. It's open Monday through Saturday from 10 AM to 5:30 PM and on Sunday from 11 AM to 4 PM during the summer.

Meredith-Kelly Latin American Art
135 W. Palace Ave. • 986-8699

This gallery exclusively represents Latin American contemporary artists, all of museum quality. There's no other like it in Santa Fe. It's open Tuesday through Saturday from 10 AM to 5 PM and Sunday and Monday from 11 AM to 4 PM.

Morning Star Gallery
513 Canyon Rd. • 982-8187

Morning Star promotes itself as the largest gallery in the country devoted exclusively to antique Native-American art. In business 13 years, the gallery occupies an old Canyon Road hacienda. The inventory includes a variety of material from the major cultural areas of North America. The emphasis is on Plains beadwork, quillwork, ledger drawings and parfleche, Southwest pottery, baskets, textiles and jewelry. Featured is pottery by María Martínez and her family, jewelry by Charles Loloma and Hostien Goodluck and engravings by Karl Bodmer. Parking is available in a lot adjacent to the gallery. The gallery is open Monday through Saturday from 9 AM to 5 PM. Visitors are also welcome on Sundays from 9 AM to 5 PM during the month of August.

Leslie Muth Gallery
131 W. Palace Ave. • 989-4620

In business since 1980, this gallery represents outsider, visionary and self-taught con-temporary American artists with an emphasis on Southwest artists such as Nicholas Herrera and Jim Wagner. The owners say they were the first to exhibit Navajo folk art. The building that houses the gallery was originally a general store. The gallery is open Monday through Saturday from 10 AM to 5 PM and Sunday by appointment.

Gerald Peters Gallery
439 Camino Del Monte Sol • 988-8961

Fine American and European art, including classic works of the 19th century and selections by prominent artists of the American West and the Taos Society, are featured here. The gallery also has a fine collection of works by New Mexico modernists and Georgia O'Keeffe as well as contemporary paintings, drawings and sculptures by leading New Mexico and national artists. The old home that houses the gallery formerly belonged to writer Mary Austin. Peters has been in business for 25 years and operates other galleries throughout the country. He plans to open a 32,000-square-foot gallery on Paseo de Peralta in the summer of 1998. The gallery is open Monday through Friday from 9 AM to 5 PM and Saturday from 10 AM to 5 PM. Parking is available in front of the gallery.

Peyton Wright Gallery
131 Nusbaum St. • 989-9888

Peyton Wright Gallery has two main departments — contemporary and historic. With rooms especially designed for showing art, the gallery represents approximately 15 contemporary painters and sculptors. Their work ranges from figurative expressionism to organic abstraction and nonobjective traditions. Artists represented include Darren Vigil Gray, Orlando Leyba, Miguel Zapata, Suki Bergeron, Peter Opheim, Kellogg Johnson, Larry Fodor, Jim Amaral and Jeff Bertoncino. The historic

---

INSIDERS' TIP

A partial list of arts celebrities who have lived in the Santa Fe and Taos area includes Willa Cather, D.H. Lawrence, Georgia O'Keeffe, Ansel Adams, Mary Austin, Robert Creeley, John Denver, Judy Chicago, Randall Davey, Ernest Thompson Seton, Wallace Stegner, Eliot Porter, Greer Garson, Errol Flynn, Burl Ives and John Nichols.

department includes Russian icons from the 17th to 19th centuries, Spanish Colonial paintings, silver and religious objects, paintings from the Cuzco School in Peru, textiles from North and South America and the Middle East, and many other antiquities of beauty and fine aesthetic quality. Established in 1989, the gallery is open Monday through Saturday from 9 AM to 5 PM and Sunday by appointment.

Reflection Gallery
201 Canyon Rd. • 995-9795

This gallery is at the base of Canyon Road in a 75-year-old adobe home. It features traditional, realist and impressionist works by artists such as Dalhart Windberg, Vladimir Nasonov, Robert Cook, Jan Saia, Yuri Novikov and Dennis Perrin. Patrons can park in the rear. The galley is open daily from 10 AM to 5:30 PM.

Running Ridge Gallery
640 Canyon Rd. • 988-2515

A contemporary fine crafts and fine-art gallery, Running Ridge exhibits art works in ceramics, fiber, glass, metal and wood as well as paintings, prints, sculpture, jewelry and lovely handcrafted vessels. Of the 120 artists represented in the gallery, James Lovera, Edwin Scheier and Henry Isaacs are included. Fabric-collage artist Amanda Richardson is shown along with the original characters of Laidman Dogs by Roberta Laidman. In an adobe building more than a century old, the gallery has had the same owners since 1979. Special arrangements can be made for parking on premises; call in advance. There's a handicapped parking space in front of the gallery. Running Ridge is open Monday through Saturday from 10 AM to 5 PM. The gallery is also open Friday nights until 7 PM in the summer and fall and for special holidays. Sunday hours are noon to 5 PM.

Laurel Seth Gallery
1121 Paseo de Peralta • 988-7349

Laurel Seth Gallery continues a 20-year tradition of presenting outstanding Southwestern art. Featured artists include Vallerie Graves, Geoffrey Landis, Angie Coleman, Teresa Archuleta-Sagel and many more. The intimate gallery also specializes in the work of early Taos and Santa Fe artists. Parking is available behind the gallery. It's open from 1 to 5 PM Tuesday through Saturday.

Shidoni
Bishop's Lodge Rd., Tesuque • 988-8001

Set in an old apple orchard 5 miles north of Santa Fe, Shidoni is New Mexico's largest sculpture garden. Open since 1971, it's also the oldest gallery in Santa Fe to be continuously owned and operated by the same individuals. More than 100 artists are represented here including Nina Akamu, William Allen, Joan Andrew, Harry Caesar, Leonda Finke, Michael Pavlovsky, Una Hanbury, Bruce Niemi, Kevin Robb, Betty Sabo and Frank Morbillo. Shidoni's outdoor sculpture display, beautifully arranged on the sprawling grounds, can be viewed from dawn to dusk year round. In addition to the expansive outdoor display, Shidoni has a Bronze Gallery adjacent to the foundry and a 5,000-square-foot Corporate Gallery near the entrance to the grounds. Abundant parking is available. The galleries are open Monday through Saturday from 9 AM to 5 PM. The foundry, where many of the works were made, is open for visitors Monday through Friday from noon to 1 PM and on Saturday from 9 AM to 5 PM.

Andrew Smith Gallery Inc.
203 W. San Francisco St. • 984-1234

Andrew Smith Gallery has an exclusive focus on fine American photography and has been in business for 25 years. You'll discover a broad and deep selection of work by the

---

INSIDERS' TIP

One of Santa Fe's finest theaters, the Santa Fe Opera theater is very rarely used for other performances because the Opera's intensive practice and production schedule keeps the building fully booked for most of the time that the weather is clement enough for outdoor performance.

Artist Gerald Cassidy was one of Santa Fe's early painters who put the community on the map as a good place for artists to live and work. This painting is part of the collection of the Museum of Fine Arts.

major photographers of the 19th and 20th centuries. The gallery carries original classic photography of the American West by E.S. Curtis, Charles Lummis and others along with work by Ansel Adams, Eliot Porter, Edward Weston and more. The gallery is open Monday through Saturday from 10 AM to 5:30 PM and Sunday from noon to 4 PM.

Support Organizations

New Mexico Arts
La Villa Rivera Building, 228 E. Palace Ave. • 827-6490

New Mexico Arts, an arm of state government, offers many resources for artists, from grants to tips on networking and other types of technical assistance. The division supports programs throughout New Mexico and has been zealous in its determination to spread the state's artistic wealth among smaller communities. Major programs include Arts in Public Places, which encourages municipalities

to allocate 1 percent of building funds for public art in public buildings, and programs that use artists, musicians, writers and actors to teach art, music, writing and drama in New Mexico schools. The agency also administers The Governors Awards for Excellence in the Arts, a tradition since 1974. Awards have gone to New Mexico artists working in all media and honorees include Georgia O'Keeffe, potter María Martínez, playwright Mark Medoff, author Tony Hillerman and visual artists Fritz Scholder, Luis Jimenez and Allan Houser. New Mexico Arts is part of the state's Office of Cultural Affairs.

Santa Fe Arts Commission
120 S. Federal Pl. • 984-6707

This arm of city bureaucracy administers grants to local arts and cultural groups, produces a directory of the arts and offers technical assistance to visitors and residents. The commission also publishes an annual arts calendar and a good list of arts and crafts shows.

Photo: George Ancona

Shakespeare in Santa Fe has performances at St. John's College each summer.

Santa Fe Council for the Arts
P.O. Box 8921, Santa Fe, NM 87504
• 988-1878

A grassroots organization composed mainly of visual artists, the Santa Fe Council for the Arts organizes summer art shows in Cathedral Park, an annual Our Lady of Guadalupe exhibit and the Contemporary Hispanic Market exhibit. The group also produces workshops and lectures as the need arises on such topics as taxes, building a portfolio and the business of art. The nonprofit organization began in 1978 and has about 400 members.

Santa Fe Gallery Association
P.O. Box 9248, Santa Fe, NM 87504
• 982-1648

The Santa Fe Gallery Association is dedicated to supporting the artistic and cultural heritage of the greater Santa Fe area by striving to improve the business conditions for Santa Fe galleries and art dealers, by providing a forum for communication between galleries and art dealers and by supporting charitable organizations and causes directly related to the arts. Among its activities, the association raises funds for art supplies for Santa Fe's elementary school children.

Santa Fe is colder in the winter and the summer than one might expect because of the influence of elevation on temperature.

The Natural Environment

Santa Fe's charm begins with the sky. On a July afternoon, for instance, you can watch the thunderheads build, a symphony of towering clouds sometimes accompanied by a wispy chorus of higher, drier formations.

The billowing clouds that create Santa Fe's summer thunderstorms also mean incredibly rich sunsets. It's not unusual to see cars pulled to the side of U.S. Highway 84-285 near the Old Taos Highway or along Artist Road. People park, climb out and look westward, watching the sky change minute by minute. Sunsets confound the eyes with a palette of color — pinks and oranges, magentas and golds, lilacs and vivid reds.

Winter skies can be equally startling. After a February snowstorm, for instance, the brilliant blue of the heavens is as intense as the turquoise the Indians sell under the *portal* along the Plaza. The snow glistens like spun glass in the intensity of the sun's light. To the east, the frosted Sangre de Cristos shine a brilliant white against a cloudless blue backdrop.

The night sky weaves its own magic. Go outside on a moonless evening and look up. When your eyes adjust, you'll see layer on layer of sparkling stars, planets and constellations. If you watch a little longer, you may see meteors, passing satellites and the blinking red lights of planes on their way to Los Angeles or Denver. Some nights the sky looks black; other times it's a deep indigo.

In addition to centuries of history, a unique architectural style and a wealth of arts and culture, the natural environment makes Santa Fe special. The sky, the mountains, the beauty of the place, take people by surprise.

Climate and Weather

At an elevation of 7,000 feet, Santa Fe is the highest state capital in the United States. The air is clear here, thanks to the economic base of tourism and government, and the sun shines at least part of the day 300 days a year.

Average temperatures range from a low of 4 degrees in January to a high of 91 in July and August. It's not uncommon for evening temperatures to drop below zero in the winter and for the heat to soar into the mid 90s in the summer, but such extremes tend to last only a day or two. Few traditional Santa Fe homes have air conditioning. If you keep the windows closed during the heat of the day and let the cool evening air come in, you'll be comfortable. Even in summer, nighttime temperatures may dip into the 40s. And the dryness makes summer's warm days easier to take. Humidity usually registers at 50 percent or less.

Most summers, the thunderstorms begin around the Fourth of July and continue through August. This isn't constant rain. The clouds start to build in late morning, clumps of thunderheads piling like cotton candy atop the Sangre de Cristos and Jémez mountains. By late afternoon, lightning may bounce from one cloud to the next, making them glow as if under strobe lights. Great spear-shaped flashes or slender slivers of energy crack toward the ground. The show can go on for hours. New Mexico and Florida lead the nation as lightning centers, but this is a dangerous beauty. Lightning strikes start several forest fires near Santa Fe each summer and occasionally kill hikers.

In an average summer, Santa Fe gets

about 14 inches of rain — as much as might fall in Houston in a single stormy weekend. The rest of Santa Fe's precipitation comes in six or eight major winter snowstorms. Average total snowfall in town is 2½ to 3 feet. The snow usually melts after a few days, (10 inches of snow equals abut 1 inch of water) but accumulates to greater depths in the mountains. The Santa Fe Ski Area reports an average snowfall of 210 inches a year. Much to the delight of skiers, snow here tends to be light powder (see our chapter on Winter Sports).

New Mexico is one of the nation's driest states because of its inland location. In the summer, storms born over the Pacific Ocean or in the Gulf of Mexico have a long trajectory across dry land areas before they reach Santa Fe. In the winter, most Pacific storms that head eastward across the United States pass too far north to have much impact here.

Despite its southerly latitude — about the same as that of Casablanca and Baghdad — Santa Fe is colder in the winter and the summer than one might expect because of the influence of elevation on temperature. Hotel concierges tell stories of January visitors who come with shorts and tennis rackets instead of skis and parkas. Sometimes by late February, however, you could enjoy both sports in the same day.

As the snow melts in the mountains, the Santa Fe River, usually gently or barely flowing, is transformed to a rushing creek. Some years, it's stocked with fish for a weekend or two. The acequias, a system of irrigation ditches that date to Spanish times, flow with springtime water, which some residents divert to their gardens.

evation and temperature. Each zone has distinctive plants and animals. New Mexico has six of the seven recognized life zones, missing only the lowest tropical zone. This means the variety of plants and animals that can live in the state is virtually unsurpassed.

The Sangre de Cristo Mountain Range, which rises from Santa Fe's backyard, is the southernmost portion of the Rocky Mountains. The mountains lie to the northeast of town, providing a good point of orientation. The name Sangre de Cristo means "Blood of Christ."

First-time visitors, especially those who expected Santa Fe to resemble the prairie, find the mountains something to write home about. The collection at the Museum of Fine Arts includes many paintings that depict the Sangre de Cristos and their gentle foothills.

If you drive up into the Sangres and ride the chairlift to the top of Aspen Peak, you'll look out on a panoramic view with the town of Santa Fe far below. The Sandia Mountains near Albuquerque, the Ortiz Range with their gold-mining scars and the gentle Cerrillos Hills rise to the southwest. To the north, you can see San Antonio Peak, a rounded blue mass on the Colorado border.

To the west on a clear day you can see the ancient volcanic Mount Taylor rising to 11,300 feet. This place plays a major role in the origin stories of the Navajo Indians. Closer lies another volcanic range, the Jémez Mountains, which were home to the ancestors of some of New Mexico's Pueblo Indians. Black Mesa, a formation beloved by many of the Rio Grande Pueblo people, stands in dark contrast to the reddish hues of the Rio Grande Valley.

The Landscape

Technically, Santa Fe sits on the edge of the Transition or Mountain life zone and the Upper Sonoran life zone. "Life zones" describe variations in living conditions caused by el-

Vegetation

At the ski area, besides the stunning views, you'll notice ponderosa pine, spruce, aspen, columbine, wild strawberries and other plants suited to the cooler, damper climate at 12,000

Photo: Don Strel/Southwest Assignments

A gentle stream offers the perfect spot for an afternoon
of picnicking, fishing, hiking or sketching.

Photo: Don Strel/Southwest assignments

Springtime brings a profusion of blossoming plants throughout Santa Fe.

feet. As you head down toward Santa Fe through the Santa Fe National Forest and Hyde State Park, the vegetation changes. In less than 20 minutes, you're in the warmer, drier piñon/juniper zone. Natural vegetation throughout most of the county includes ricegrass, sagebrush and western wheatgrass. You don't have to be a botanist to notice that all the plants here are not cactus!

Piñon, a small pine tree, produces edible nuts popular among both animals and humans. Junipers have purple berries that attract birds. Both common in the Santa Fe area, they are tough, slow-growing evergreens. They tolerate heat and below-freezing temperatures and once established survive in a climate where rain is always a blessing. A 12-foot piñon tree may be 100 years old; mature trees are 200 to 250 years old and piñon can live up to 400 years. Piñon trees alive today were growing when the Spanish occupied the city of Santa Fe. Some people use juniper in their fireplaces; it's a slow-burning wood with a wonderful, crisp aroma.

Because of the elevation, wildflowers of the Santa Fe area have more in common with those of southern Colorado than with their Albuquerque cousins just 60 miles south. You'll

INSIDERS' TIP

Don't forget to take down your hummingbird feeders in the fall. The little birds can't winter here, and a steady supply of nectar may delay their migration.

Don't Let Altitude and Allergies Get You Down

When some people talk about how Santa Fe takes their breath away, they mean it literally.

Because Santa Fe is perched at 7,000 feet, the air is thinner here. Your lungs and heart have to work harder to do their jobs, and the result can be headaches, lack of energy, nausea, nosebleeds and other uncomfortable  symptoms. People with chronic illnesses such as heart disease or high blood pressure need to pay close attention to how they feel here; if you have any questions about the effect altitude may have on your health, ask your doctor.

Another thing that may leave you breathless is allergies. While Santa Fe ranks low in visible air pollution, the pollen from native plants such as juniper, elms, sage and cottonwood can make your throat scratch, your eyes itch and your nose run.

Since more visitors are likely to notice the altitude, we'll talk about that first.

Altitude

Altitude sickness is odd in its unpredictability. A healthy 20-something person may be slowed down here for a few days; another who might be older and not in the best of shape could notice nothing. Travelers who live at an elevation of 3,000 feet or lower may be listless and headachy, dizzy or light-headed and have trouble falling asleep or staying that way. More serious symptoms of altitude sickness include appetite loss, nausea, vomiting, heart palpitations or a pounding pulse, congested lungs and trouble breathing. All this signifies that your body hasn't adjusted to life in the high country.

There are some things you can do.

• Before you come, try to get enough rest, drink plenty of fluids and eat a diet higher in protein.

• Give your body extra time to adjust. If you're flying to New Mexico from Los Angeles or Houston, you might consider spending a night in Albuquerque. At roughly 5,000 feet, Albuquerque treats you a little more gently. It's a good place to let your system begin to adapt.

• Take it easy. Don't exercise vigorously until you've adjusted to the altitude. If you feel like a nap in the afternoon, indulge yourself.

• Drink plenty of water. Beside being thin, the air here is dry. Dehydration will only add to your discomfort.

• Stay at this elevation until you feel better instead of going higher. If you leave Santa Fe for a drive to see the aspens or go skiing, expect the symptoms to worsen.

In addition to altitude sickness, higher altitudes also mean more solar radiation and a decreased tolerance for alcohol. People who study these things say one drink at 7,000 feet is the equivalent of three at sea level. So remember your hat and sunscreen when you sit on the patio, and slowly sip your afternoon Margarita.

Most people adjust to the altitude in a few days. If you stay in Santa Fe long enough you'll notice a pleasant side-effect when you return to sea level. You may have more energy for a day or two.

Allergies

The body's reaction to pollen is just as unpredictable as its response to altitude.

— continued on next page

Photo: Don Strel/Southwest Assignments

Even though it's high and dry in Santa Fe, many flowers thrive here. Most people don't have to worry about pollen from flowers like these, but trees such as juniper and elms cause itchy eyes and stuffy noses in allergy sufferers.

About 1 in 20 people is allergic to pollen of some sort. If you move to a different climate, doctors say it usually takes about two years to develop new sensitivity to native plants. Many people who are not initially allergic find they develop allergies after living here a while — sometimes after 20 or 25 years.

A person who's allergic responds to pollen by acting as if the pollen were a virus. Juniper, one of the area's most annoying pollens, usually begins to bother people in February and continues for several weeks. Other pollens that aggravate come from elm and cottonwood trees, ragweed and native grass. The good news? Most people are not allergic to the flowers here. And Santa Fe usually ranks low in mold spores because of our dry climate.

If pollen here catches you off guard, there are things you can do besides reach for the antihistamines:

• Most pollen is released in the morning. If you can plan your activities so you aren't outside early you'll lessen your exposure. What a great excuse to sleep late!

• Wind is the enemy. Stay out of it.

• Besides giving you shade from Santa Fe's intense sun, sunglasses help keep pollen out of your eyes.

• A change in elevation may help. The plants that grow near the ski area differ from those you'll find at the rodeo grounds.

find the vivid blue of delicate-looking flax, the deep purple, scarlet and pale pink penstamon, the white blooms and feathery seeds of Apache plume and cheery orange and red blanket flowers. In the fall, watch for the brilliant yellow of the chamiso framed by pale purple wild asters. And the aspen trees in the Sangres and the Jémez mountains put on a wonderful golden show beginning in mid- to late September.

Santa Fe is a four-season city. You can feel the stirring of spring as early as February, even though the last snowstorm often comes in May, burying the daffodils and covering the apricot blossoms. If the snow has been deep or the city gets spring rain, tulips and hyacinth, fruit trees and iris bloom in abundance. New Mexico's state flower, the yucca, grows in and around Santa Fe. Yuccas generally begin to bloom in May. The large, bell-shaped flowers rise in magnificent showy overstatement. You may notice the cream-colored display as you drive along Interstate 25 between Santa Fe and Albuquerque.

Just before summer hits in full force comes the sweet smell of Russian olive blossoms, tiny yellow flowers among greenish-gray leaves. Wisteria and lilacs flourish, and migrating hummingbirds return. Native grasses turn green. The cholla cactus explodes with magenta blossoms.

Santa Fe does have big trees like cities elsewhere. Walk along the Santa Fe River, for instance, and you'll see towering cottonwoods, trees so big it takes two adults holding hands to encircle their trunks. Fruit trees, especially those bred to bloom late, thrive in backyards and in orchards where they can be watered. Water always makes the difference.

Landscaping designed to conserve water is called xeriscaping, and you'll see many lovely examples of it in Santa Fe. While gardeners may not be able to grow the same things they did in Topeka or San Diego, hundreds of plants thrive in cultivation despite low rainfall and the city's restrictions on watering.

If you're interested in native plants and how to grow them, visit a Santa Fe nursery. Most sell attractive and hardy flowers, shrubs, trees and grasses that survive just fine without much water. You can also take a look at the public xeriscape demonstration gardens at Santa Fe Greenhouses, 2904 Rufina Street, 473-2700, or at the "Geobotany Beds" at Santa Fe Community College, 6401 Richards Avenue. Santa Fe Botanical Gardens at the Community College, 438-1684, offers tours of established gardens and workshops for gardeners from beginners to experts.

Birds and Animals

One of your best resources for learning about the birds and animals that live here is the Randall Davey Audubon Center, less than 4 miles from the Plaza (see our Attractions chapter). While hiking along the center's trails, bird-watchers have identified more than 140 species of birds, ranging from hawks to hummingbirds.

The big birds with iridescent blue wings that you'll see commonly in Santa Fe are piñon jays. In the fall, they scout the foothills in noisy flocks, looking for their favorite meal, the rich nuts of the piñon trees. Colorful northern flickers, several types of swallows, ravens, mountain chickadees and robins all are common here. You'll find cottontail rabbits, jack rabbits, coyotes, squirrels, skunks and several kinds of lizards here too. You probably won't see a rattlesnake, unless you're hiking outside of town in rocky areas. Despite their reputation, rattlers tend to be shy creatures. If you leave them alone, they'll return the favor.

You won't have to look far to find one animal you may not be used to seeing — the prairie dog. Related to ground squirrels and marmots, prairie dogs eat roots and seeds and live in burrows underground in vacant lots around Santa Fe. The sentry dogs stand on their hind feet at the edge of the burrows, watching for danger or, maybe, enjoying the

Photo: Don Strel/Southwest Assignments

The geologic contrasts between formations at 6,000 feet and
the high country at 12,000 feet are stunning.

view. Prairie dogs communicate with different barks and warn each other of an advancing owl or a coyote. When a person approaches, the little tan creatures disappear with a flick of their short black tails.

A large colony of prairie dogs lives on the city-owned railyard property, and you may spot them near the railroad tracks just west of Cerrillos Road between Guadalupe Street and St. Francis Drive. The Jackalope store, 2820 Cerillos Road, 471-8539, has a Prairie Dog Village on its grounds (see our Shopping chapter). A few years ago, the animals claimed squatters rights to the DeVargas Junior High School athletic field. Volunteers from Prairie Dog Rescue relocated as many of the critters as they could catch and the holes were filled, saving students from the possibility of broken legs.

New Mexico is a veritable outdoor paradise with stunningly beautiful public lands, many of them wild and woolly, some of them tame and comfortable.

Parks and Recreation

From birding to whitewater rafting, baseball to volleyball, disc golf to ultimate Frisbee, The City Different either has it or can get you to it with little fuss. Santa Fe and the county that shares its name are veritable playgrounds for the young and old, the rich and the poor, the active and the sedentary. You'll find an abundance of city parks here, many with athletic fields, some just for sitting back and taking in the sunshine. We have a national forest in our backyard with literally dozens of hiking trails ranging from easy to strenuous and biking galore, each hairpin turn yielding magnificent vistas. Santa Fe is a gateway to world-class hunting and trout-filled streams that draw anglers like magnets to iron.

From A to Z — well, okay, B to W — we've included in this chapter a good-sized sampling of what Santa Fe and the surrounding country has to offer in the way of public lands as well as indoor and outdoor recreation. A mere glance through this chapter ought to convince even the most die-hard couch potatoes to put down the remote control and explore Santa Fe's recreational bounty.

Parks

City Parks

The City of Santa Fe maintains 54 parks on 326 acres, including 235 acres of manicured grounds. Some city parks offer extensive facilities and organized activities such as sports, community events and holiday festivities. Others offer little more than a bench or two, some grass, perhaps a sculpture and a quiet, restful place to eat lunch, paint a picture or contemplate your navel. Whatever your fancy, there's a park in town to meet your needs and desires. For a list of all city parks, call the City of Santa Fe Parks and Recreation Department at 473-7236.

The Plaza
63 Lincoln Ave.

Without a doubt, the most popular of all city parks is the Plaza, the heart of downtown Santa Fe. Adult readers of the *Santa Fe Reporter* in 1997 voted the Plaza the best place to take visitors, walk dogs, people-watch, spot celebrities or simply hang out. It's also the choice spot to begin and/or end parades, make speeches, hold community festivals and dances, play Hacky Sack or take a noontime snooze, if you can wrangle one of the white-painted wrought-iron benches for yourself.

Salvador Perez Park
601 Alta Vista St. • 984-6755

Kids, who have different priorities, voted Salvador Perez their favorite city park in the *Santa Fe Reporter's* survey. What makes this one a favorite? Maybe it's the imposing, authentic locomotive car on the large, centrally located property. Perhaps it's the recently renovated indoor heated pool. Or it could be the park's cool new playground with lots of equipment made from recyclables. There's also a Little League field with tons of room to run and jump — enough even for grown-ups, who borrow the field in summer for mushball. With several tennis courts, volleyball courts barbecue grills and lots of picnic tables, Salvador Perez is an ideal spot for a family outing.

Alto Park and Bicentennial Pool
1121 Alto St. • 984-6773

Located next door to the City of Santa Fe Division of Senior Services and the Mary Esther Gonzales Senior Center, Alto Bicentennial Park and Pool has something for everyone: Little League; Young American Football for kids 13 and younger; noontime mushball for city, county and state employees; tennis courts for whomever gets there first; and, of course, the pool. Open Monday through Friday from 7 AM to 8 PM and weekends from 10 AM to 6 PM, the Bicentennial Pool features lap swims and, during the week only, Seals in the morning and recreational swimming in the afternoons. There's also an all-day tot pool, which gets cleaned after each recreational swim.

FYI

Unless otherwise noted, the area code for all phone numbers listed in this guide is 505.

Fort Marcy Ballpark/ Mager's Field Sports Complex
490 Washington Ave. • 984-6725

Perhaps the most used park in Santa Fe — after the Plaza, of course — is Fort Marcy Ballpark/Mager's Field Sports Complex because of its enormous indoor/outdoor recreation center. In addition to the ballpark, Fort Marcy features other outdoor fields and tracks, an indoor heated pool, a gym and weight room, and a wide variety of classes from swimming to country dancing. Fort Marcy is also the site of the burning of Zozobra — "Old Man Gloom" — at the end of Fiesta in September. (See our Annual Events chapter for details.)

Franklin E. Miles Park
1027 Camino Carlos Rey at Siringo Rd.

The city's largest park, Franklin E. Miles offers a variety of facilities including softball fields, soccer fields, basketball and volleyball courts, one of the largest playgrounds in Santa Fe, barbecue grills, plenty of picnic tables and good lighting at night.

Herb Martinez Park
2240 Camino Carlos Rey

Another well-used park with good sports facilities is Herb Martinez, a large park with soccer fields that serve school and youth leagues from March through November as well

as softball fields, tennis courts, basketball courts, a small playground, barbecue grills and tables.

Cornell Park (Rose Garden)
1203 Galisteo Pkwy.

While you can find an appropriate spot in any park to celebrate a quiet moment, some are more conducive than others to meditation and aloneness. Among them is Cornell Park, a lovely refuge from the world located a couple of miles south of the downtown area. A small park — it's about as wide and as long as a city block — in a residential neighborhood, the "Rose Garden," as most Santa Feans know it, is aptly named for the rose bushes that come to life in spring and summer, scenting the air with their fragrant blossoms. The promenade is lined with old trees, making it a favorite among dogs as well as their owners.

Amelia E. White Park
900 Old Santa Fe Tr.

At Amelia E. White Park — just a few blocks from the Wheelwright Museum, Museum of Indian Arts and Culture, Museum of International Folk Art and the Laboratory of Anthropology — you might catch a painter in action as you sit under a grape arbor admiring the sky. This is a park for relaxing and just enjoying the day.

Tom Macaione Park
301 E. Marcy St.

Just a few blocks east of the Plaza, you're likely to have this park, which is also called Hillside Park, all to yourself — or nearly so if you visit any time except summer. Then, it's put to good use by the school-age girls at Girls Inc. You'll share it with a bronze sculpture of the much-loved, eccentric impressionist painter for whom the park is named. Macaione died a few years ago, and the town is still mourning his passing.

Ragle Park
Zia Rd. and Yucca St.

Ragle Park, in a residential area near Santa Fe High School, has the largest adult softball complex in Santa Fe. See our Softball section for details. The park also contains a decent playground, perfect for softball players with little ones in tow.

East Santa Fe River Park
700 E. Alameda St. • 827-7173

Located only a few blocks south of the Plaza, East Santa Fe River Park is a lovely, narrow stretch of land that begins in front of the Supreme Court Building at Don Gaspar Avenue and continues for about a mile to the intersection with Palace Avenue. The park offers shaded, tree-lined walkways and picnic tables along the Santa Fe River, attracting local and visiting brown-bag diners when the weather permits.

State Parks

Hyde Memorial State Park
Hyde Park Rd. • 983-7175

Located 12 miles northeast of Santa Fe and a mere 3 miles below the Santa Fe Ski Area, Hyde Memorial State Park contains 350 beautiful acres filled with Ponderosa pine, aspen and meadows at an elevation of 8,500 feet. It's a favorite among locals for hiking and picnicking and a popular base for backpackers heading into the Pecos Wilderness. The park's campground has drinking water but not showers. However, for $1.25, you can shower at Fort Marcy (see entry later in this chapter) and even get in a swim, if you're so inclined. Pool rules require that you shower before you swim, but there's no rule requiring you to swim after you shower.

National Forests and Parks

New Mexico is a veritable outdoor paradise with stunningly beautiful public lands, many of them wild and woolly, some of them tame and comfortable. Santa Fe, which is surrounded by more than 3 million acres of national forest, is a doorway to many of these. In fact, nearly half the state's national wilderness areas are in north central New Mexico. These include the popular Pecos Wilderness, which contains some of the state's highest peaks along with glacial lakes and 150 miles of rivers and streams, and the lesser-known Dome Wilderness area next to Bandelier National Monument near Los Alamos. The Dome Wilderness is recovering from a severe 1996 forest fire. Call the Jémez Ranger district, 829-3535, for current conditions and access. If the Dome Wilderness isn't accessible, check out the lesser known — and lesser used — San Pedro Parks northeast of Cuba, New Mexico. San Pedro contains 41,000 spectacular acres of aspen, evergreen forest and meadows and reaches altitudes in the 10,000-feet range. All three wilderness areas are part of the Santa Fe National Forest, headquarters at 1474 Rodeo Road, 438-7840, whose 1.5 million acres comprise some of the finest mountain scenery in the Southwest. The forest is divided into two sections: the Jémez Mountains west of the Rio Grande, with elevations ranging from 5,300 feet in White Rock Canyon to 12,000 feet at the summit of Chicoma Peak, and Valle Grande, the oldest volcanic caldera in the United States. Also within these mountains are the ancient Indian ruins at Bandelier National Monument and the ultramodern Los Alamos National Laboratory.

East of the river, and much closer to home, the Sangre de Cristo Mountains watch over Santa Fe. Truchas Peak reaches a magnificent 13,101 feet at the summit. Scattered among the Alpine peaks are large, aspen-bordered meadows, splendid canyons, trout-filled streams and rivers, crystal clear glacial lakes, a huge variety of wildlife and recreational opportunities galore. Santa Fe National Forest offers 1,000 miles of mapped trails, 400 miles of fishing streams, hunting, 26 campsites, 12 picnic areas, ski runs, scenic drives and mile after mile of breathtaking beauty.

Bandelier National Monument
HCR1, Box 1, Ste. 15, Los Alamos 87544 • 672-3861 ext. 517 (visitors center), 672-0343 (24-hour information)

Located along N.M. 4 on the Pajarito Plateau of the Jémez Mountains, near the towns of Los Alamos and White Rock, Bandelier National Monument encompasses 32,737 acres of scenic wilderness and striking land formations that contain cliff houses and what once were multistoried pueblo-style dwellings inhabited between the 12th and 16th centuries by the ancestors of today's Pueblo Indians.

Allow two hours to explore the main trail, which includes *kivas* (round, underground, ceremonial rooms) and the Ceremonial Cave, accessible only by ladder. In addition to the archeological sites, Bandelier offers 75 miles of no-pets-allowed hiking trails and beautiful scenery as far as the eye can see. The trails begin at the visitors center at the bottom of Frijoles Canyon, where a creek by the same name provided water to the ancient Indians who lived and farmed there. Backpackers are required to carry a wilderness permit, available at the visitors center.

Open year round except for Christmas and New Years days, the visitors center features exhibits on prehistoric and historic Pueblo culture as well as information on the monument and nearby attractions. The park also offers regularly scheduled guided walks, evening programs and interpretive talks in summer months. The visitors center is open from 8 AM to 6 PM in summer, 9 AM to 5:30 PM in fall and spring and 8 AM to 4:30 PM in winter. The campground is open from March through November. Fees run $10 a week for private vehicles and $10 per night to camp. Call for group rates. To get to Bandelier from Santa Fe, take I-25 north to N.M. 84/285, head west in Pojoaque to N.M. 502, and cross the Rio Grande to N.M. 4. Then follow signs to Bandelier.

Pecos National Historical Park
P.O. Box 418, Pecos 87552 • 757-6032
visitors center, 757-6414 administrative offices

The 6,000-acre Pecos National Historical

Park, 25 miles southeast of Santa Fe on N.M. 63, embraces 12,000 years of history including the ancient Pecos Pueblo, two Spanish Colonial missions, parts of the original Santa Fe Trail and the site of the Civil War battle of Glorieta Pass. Visitors may take a 1.25-mile self-guided tour through the old Pecos Pueblo and the mission ruins. Groups can arrange guided tours in advance. The visitors center contains exhibits in both English and Spanish, including a 10-minute introductory film. The park offers special summer programs including weekend cultural demonstrations and night tours. It also holds an annual Feast Day Mass the first Sunday in August. You can picnic in the park but you can't spend the night. However, the U.S. Forest Service operates six campgrounds, and private companies run three, all within a 20-mile radius of the park. Pecos National Historical Park is open all year except Christmas and New Years days. Hours are 8 AM until 6 PM Memorial Day to Labor Day and 8 AM until 5 PM from Labor Day to Memorial Day. Entrance to the park is $4 per car or $2 per person, whichever is less. To get there from Santa Fe, take I-25 to Exit 299 (Pecos Village) and continue south for 2 miles.

Recreation

What Santa Fe lacks in spectator sports, it more than makes up for in recreation and participatory sports. You could come to Santa Fe and do nothing but play — outdoors, indoors, solo or on teams. For league sports such as baseball, basketball, football, mushball, soccer, softball, volleyball, etc., the City of Santa Fe Parks and Recreation Department, 1142 Siler Road, 473-7228, is your best single information

INSIDERS' TIP

Remember, this is high desert, and the climate is extremely dry. Make sure you build fires only in designated fire pits and thoroughly douse them before you leave with water or a combination of water and dirt. In an emergency, build fires away from trees and shrubbery that could easily ignite.

source. The department can provide details about nearly all adult and youth sports and recreational activities in Santa Fe, even those it doesn't sponsor, because chances are any non-city leagues play in city parks or other facilities. You can pick up the department's annual *Activity Guide* or call for details.

In addition to participatory sports, this section will also deal with a host of other recreational activities, from hiking and biking and horseback riding to flying, rock climbing and scuba.

Recreational Facilities

Municipal Recreation Complex
205 Caja del Rio Rd. • 986-6931
This long-awaited outdoor sports complex so far contains five soccer fields, four softball fields, one baseball field, a special events area, a 2-mile asphalt running and pedestrian trail and both a nine-hole and 18-hole golf course. There are also plans in the works for volleyball, tennis and basketball courts; rugby fields; a BMX (bicycle/motocross) trail; and even an equestrian center. The 1,260-acre city-owned complex will also feature a playground, restrooms and concession stands. To get there from downtown Santa Fe, drive south on Cerrillos Road, turn right on Airport Road, right again on U.S. 599 and left at Caja del Rio. The sports complex is about 1.5 miles from the turn on the east side of the road.

Baseball

Santa Fe Parks and Recreation Department
1142 Siler Rd. • 473-7228
Although Santa Fe has no city-sponsored baseball teams, its recreation division can point you in the right direction for little league, semi-pro and seniors baseball, though you may have to do a little legwork on your own to find a team. For little league, 983-4186, team placement depends on where the child lives. Eastside children play on American Little League, west-siders on Metropolitan and south-central kids play with the National Little League team. Teens play in the Santa Fe Amateur

Baseball Congress, 983-4643, comprising three divisions that play at Fort Marcy Ballpark, Franklin E. Miles Park and Ashbaugh Park, 1703 Cerrillos Road. They occasionally use the public high schools (Capital and Santa Fe) as backup fields.

For adults, Santa Fe is home to two semi-professional teams, the Expos, 983-7839, and a non-sanctioned team called the Rielleros, with the Northern Rio Grande Baseball League, 471-0663, which also includes teams from a number of Indian pueblos north of Santa Fe. Some Santa Feans play for the Los Alamos Bombers, 672-0262, an appropriate name for a team located in the birthplace of the atomic bomb. Both the Expos and the Bombers belong to the Greater Albuquerque Baseball League, which means lots of commuting between Santa Fe and Albuquerque.

Santa Fe also has two seniors teams for players older than 30: the Santa Fe Cubs, 827-3954, and the Santa Fe Pirates, 473-2690, both part of the Men's Senior Baseball League, 989-8261, also based in Albuquerque. The senior leagues play away games at University of New Mexico Lobo Field, an NCAA-quality ballpark. All Santa Fe teams generally play home games at Fort Marcy Ballpark (Fort Marcy/Mager's Field Sports Complex, 490 Washington Avenue, 984-6725).

Basketball
Thirteen of the city's 54 parks have outdoor basketball courts. You can get a list from the city by dropping into the Siler Road location or calling 473-7236.

City of Santa Fe Parks and Recreation Department
1142 Siler Rd. • 473-7228
The City of Santa Fe sponsors a number of basketball-related activities throughout the year, including men's and women's summer and winter basketball leagues; girls' and boys' basketball clinics; Lobo basketball camp; and such special events as the Hot-Shot competition, in which participants ages 7 to 12 try to make as many baskets as possible from various hot spots on the court, and Free-Throw, in which throwers ages 7 to 12 attempt 25 shots in each of two rounds. The city also

sponsors several adult basketball tournaments, including three-on-three and five-on five competitions.

Biking

Talk about cycling in the Southwest, and zealots will tell you it can only mean one thing: mountain biking. Indeed, northern New Mexico is among the best places in the world to pedal in the mountains and along back-country trails. Ranked as one of the most popular sports nationwide, mountain biking is especially suited to this area because of our beautiful and varied terrain, ranging from high-desert plateaus and stark mesas to alpine forests and flower-filled meadows. The region contains thousands of acres of public land and thousands of miles of trails, many open to mountain bikers.

It's important that mountain bikers follow certain understood rules of the trails, i.e., yield to hikers, horseback riders and uphill traffic; practice low-impact cycling by treading lightly and remembering that "skids are for squids;" and avoid getting so lost that search and rescue teams have to find you. As long as cyclists continue to respect these rules, New Mexico will likely continue bucking the national trend of closing trails to mountain bikes. Do note, however, that all designated wilderness areas — the Pecos near Santa Fe, Taos County's Wheeler Peak or Sandia Peak east of Albuquerque, for example — and the trails leading to them are always off limits to mountain bikes. If you violate the rules, you risk losing your wheels. For more information on New Mexico bicycle laws, contact the state Highway and Transportation Department, 1120 Cerrillos Road, 827-5100 or (800) 827-5514.

A locally popular and scenic route for both mountain and touring bikes goes straight up N.M. Highway 475 — variously called Artist, Hyde Park or Ski Basin Road, depending on the particular section — to the Santa Fe Ski Area. Starting at the Fort Marcy/Mager's Field Sports Complex, 490 Washington Avenue, it's a 15-mile uphill ride to the ski basin, or 8 miles to Black Canyon, a nice midway stopping point. The road gets quite narrow and practically shoulderless as you near the ski slopes, and you'll encounter numerous hairpin turns and sometimes heavy traffic. But the stunning views are worth every whiff of carbon monoxide, not to mention the trail of impatient cars at your back. Take warm clothing, as it can get

Photo: Don Strel/Southwest Assignments

Summertime offers visitors rare opportunities to experience uncrowded forests and wilderness areas.

quite chilly in the higher elevations. Also bring rain gear, in case of a sudden thunderstorm, and plenty of water, especially if you're unaccustomed to an arid climate.

A comfortable ride for beginners that's popular even among experienced mountain bikers is the Santa Fe Rail Trail between Santa Fe and Lamy. It became legal to use the trail in November 1997 after its illicit use for years by bikers, hikers and equestrians. The 11.5-mile dirt trail runs alongside the train tracks originally laid by the Atchison, Topeka & Santa Fe Railway in 1880, used today by the Santa Fe Southern Railway that runs between the downtown Santa Fe and Lamy depots. Make your way to S. St. Francis Drive and head south until it turns into Frontage Road. Continue southbound until you see the train tracks and follow them to Lamy. Along the way, you'll pass over a trestle bridge that one devotee happily describes as "pretty scary." If you're lucky, or you plan it right, you might even meet up with a train. Once in Lamy, you can have a drink or a meal at the historic Legal Tender, a 19th-century saloon, and either bike back into town or catch the Santa Fe Southern Railway and ride back in style in a restored 1920s passenger coach.

If you're looking to explore the hinterlands, the Jémez Mountains provide spectacular scenery for both on- and off-road cyclists. One of the more popular loops begins at N.M. Highway 501 about 35 miles northwest of Santa Fe in the parking lot of Los Alamos National Laboratory. Continue south along N.M. Highway 4 to the Los Alamos "Truck Route," — an otherwise unnamed road belonging to LANL'S overseer, the U.S. Department of Energy — and finally back to the lab. The 26-mile trek takes you past the ancient pueblo ruins at Bandelier National Monument and Tsankawi and opens up to remarkable vistas.

If you choose to go south, the Turquoise Trail to Albuquerque via the Sandia Crest Scenic Byway offers a route as rich in history as it is in scenery. The 52-mile journey begins on N.M. Highway 14, called the Turquoise Trail because of the turquoise mined in the mountains there. You'll pass through a number of old mining villages, some of which are long-deserted ghost towns while others, like Madrid and Cerrillos, are thriving artistic communi-ties. Once in Albuquerque, go the extra 12 miles to Sandia Crest, a 3,700-foot climb along N.M. Highway 536, a scenic byway, to an elevation of 10,678 feet at the summit. On the way up, be sure to observe how the desert vegetation changes to ponderosa pine forests because you'll be too busy catching your breath on the way down to notice. If you're here in May, you might want to try your hand — er, feet — at the 100-mile Santa Fe Century Ride, a challenging but scenic ride beginning at St. Francis Drive and Zia Road, continuing along the lovely Turquoise Trail in the shadow of the Ortiz Mountains to Madrid and Cerrillos and back to Santa Fe again via I-25 — but not before hitting "Heartbreak Hill," a half-mile killer climb steep enough to force the majority of cyclists to walk their bikes. The Century will take you anywhere from 4.5 to nine hours, depending on your strength and skill. For more information call 982-1282 or ask around at any of the bike rental shops in town.

The competitive-minded might want to participate in La Tierra Torture Bike Race, a 10-, 20- and 30-mile course in September with a women's open category and men's beginning, intermediate and pro categories. Registration fees last year were $15 for early registration, $20 on the day of the race. For more information, contact the Santa Fe Parks and Recreation Department, 1142 Siler Road, 438-1491, or New Mexico Bike-N-Sport, 521 N. St. Francis Drive, 820-9390 (see the write-up in this section).

Many of the outings we've suggested here are for off-road bikes. If you're looking for information regarding on-road biking, call Sangre de Cristo Cycling Club at 982-0664. Otherwise, you can get information on trails and tours as well as rent bikes and other equipment from most bike rental shops in town. Some specialize in guided tours, including the following:

Known World Guide Service
825 Early St. • 988-9609, (800) 983-7756

Known World offers a variety of mountain-bike adventures from single-day trips to multiday excursions throughout northern New Mexico. You can bring your own bike or rent one of Known World's lightweight Kona Hahanna bikes. The company will arrange trips for all ages and skill levels, from gradual climbs on logging or ranch roads for beginners to steep, gnarly trails for experts. Full-day trips cost $50 with your own bike, $65 with a rental, and include a high-energy lunch and knowledgeable guides and mechanics. Multiple-day trips range from simple overnights to truck-supported adventures and cost $100 per night with a 10 percent discount for three- to four-day trips and 15 percent off for five or more days, including food.

New Mexico Mountain Bike Adventures
49 Main St., Cerrillos • 474-0074

In artistic Cerrillos in the Ortiz Mountains south of Santa Fe, New Mexico Mountain Bike Adventures offers a variety of scenic and historic rides throughout New Mexico. It specializes in custom bike tours exploring Indian prehistory, ancient turquoise mines, *El Camino Real* and 19th-century railroads in and around Santa Fe County. It will also arrange tours in the Jémez Mountains as well as the Apache and Gila national forests. Customers can choose from half-, full- and multiple-day bike trips for all riding abilities. Half-day trips, including bike rentals, start at $45. Full-day trips start at $90, including bike rental and lunch. Multiple-day trips run about $110 per day, including meals but not bike rentals. Ask about group discounts.

New Mexico Bike-N-Sport
521 N. St. Francis Dr. • 820-9390

New Mexico Bike-N-Sport offers mountain-bike tours starting at about $30 a day plus the rental fee, which can range from $14 to $30, depending on the bike. You have your choice of either front or full-suspension. Tours are usually brown-bag, but can include a prepared lunch if you arrange for it ahead of time. The staff is closed-mouthed about its favorite trails, no doubt in hopes of keeping them from becoming overpopulated for as long as possible. Perhaps that's why lots of hard-core mountain bikers frequent the store, which has its own 10-person racing team sponsored by local businesses as well as national bike manufacturers. In September Bike-N-Sport and the City of Santa Fe cosponsor La Tierra Torture Bike Race, a 10-, 20- and 30-mile course with a

women's open category and men's beginning, intermediate and pro categories. Registration fees last year were $15 for early registration and $20 on the day of the race. For more information, contact the Santa Fe Parks and Recreation Department, 1142 Siler Road, 438-1491.

rob & charlie's
St. Michael's Village West, 1632 St. Michael's Dr. • 471-9119

A trusted locals' favorite, rob & charlie's is Santa Fe's longest-reigning bike shop and skateboard shop (see our Skateboarding section in this chapter). In business 19 years, rob & charlie's has earned a reputation for being friendly, helpful and, most importantly, knowledgeable about all aspects of bicycles — from buying one to riding one and, inevitably, repairing one. The store carries a large selection of mountain bikes, road bikes, BMX bikes and kid's bikes from Giant, Raleigh, Schwinn, Litespeed, Redline and S E Racing, to name just a few brands. It also sells roof racks, parts and all manner of accessories and accouterments from clothing, shoes and water bottles to books, magazines and maps. Priceless to those who don't have it, yet free for the asking at rob & charlie's, is the skinny on bitchin' biking trails from the most popular to the lesser known. rob & charlie's is open Monday through Saturday from 9:30 AM to 6 PM.

Birding

New Mexico is home to a number of bird sanctuaries, including one right in Santa Fe and several a few hours away. But you need only venture outside the city limits to observe hawks soaring in search of prey or even the occasional bald eagle, which is always a special sight. In spring and autumn, Santa Fe hosts an astounding number of migrating birds because of its location along a major migratory pathway.

Bosque del Apache National Wildlife Refuge
N.M. Hwy. 1 S., San Antonio, N.M. • 835-1828

One of the top birding sites in the United States, Bosque del Apache ("woods of the

Apache") is well-worth the two-and a-half-hour drive from Santa Fe, even if you're not a card-carrying birder. Within the 57,191-acre Bosque, as New Mexicans familiarly call this gorgeous wildlife refuge, are 13,000 acres of moist bottomland at a wide spot of the Rio Grande. There, tens of thousands of birds gather each autumn and stay through the winter. At dusk you can witness flocks of snow geese and Arctic geese, eagles, sandhill cranes and even whooping cranes — one of a number of endangered species that winter at Bosque del Apache — returning to roost in the marshes. During the spring and fall you'll see migrant warblers, flycatchers, and shorebirds. In summer, the season for nesting songbirds, waders, shorebirds and ducks, the Bosque returns to its quiet existence as an oasis of ponds, marsh, riparian cottonwood, willow and tamarisk on the northern edge of the Chihuahuan desert. Year-round residents include mule deer, coyote, porcupine, muskrat, Canada geese, coot, pheasant, turkey, quail and New Mexico's state bird, the roadrunner.

To get to Bosque del Apache from Santa Fe, take I-25 S. to Exit 139. Go east on U.S. Highway 380 for a half-mile, then take N.M. Highway 1 S. another 8 miles to refuge.

Las Vegas National Wildlife Refuge
Rt. 1, Box 399, Las Vegas • 425-3581
Located about 70 miles east of Santa Fe off N.M. 104, Las Vegas National Wildlife Refuge consists of 8,672 acres of marsh and water, native grasslands, cropland, timbered canyons and streams providing habitat for a wide variety of plant and animal life. Up to 271 species have been observed since 1966, when the refuge had only been in official existence for a year. Among its feathered visitors are Neotropical migrants, a type of bird that nests in the United States or Canada, spending the winter primarily south in Mexico, Central or South America or the Caribbean. These include colorful hawks, hummingbirds, warblers and orioles as well as shorebirds, flycatchers

and thrushes. The existence of the refuge, which preserves their habitat, is essential to the survival of many of these birds.

Maxwell National Wildlife Refuge
P.O. Box 276, Maxwell • 375-2331
With 200 species of birds observed over the years around its largest compound, the Maxwell National Wildlife Refuge is home to large concentrations of ducks and geese in winter and to the burrowing owl in summer. Migrating birds are attracted to the many irrigation impoundments that serve this primarily agricultural area in the northeastern corner of the state. To get to the refuge, take U.S. Highway 25 due north for about 150 miles and get off at the Maxwell exit, between the towns of Springer and Raton.

Boating and Canoeing

New Mexico may be desert, but there's still plenty of water on which to play. Getting to the water from Santa Fe, however, will take a bit of traveling. Nearest to Santa Fe are Cochití Lake, 465-0307, alongside a beautiful, winding road some 20 to 25 miles south of the city, and Abiquiú Lake, 685-4371, some 45 miles northwest of Santa Fe. Both are managed by the U.S. Army Corps of Engineers. Cochití is a no-charge, no-wake lake with paved boat ramps and a no-frills slip-rental marina managed by Cochití Pueblo, 465-2219. There are no boat rentals at the lake itself, but you can rent a craft in Santa Fe and take it with you. Among the most popular watersports at Cochití are sailing, windsurfing and, in summer, swimming. To get there, take I-25 south to the turnoff for N.M. 16, which is near the bottom of a long and infamously steep hill called La Bajada ("the descent"). From N.M. 16, turn right on N.M. 22, which will take you directly to the lake.

Abiquiú Lake, about 7 miles northwest of the village of Abiquiú, provides a stunning sight from U.S. 84. Its shimmering aqua color makes

---

INSIDERS' TIP

It's unlawful and disrespectful to remove pottery shards, arrowheads or other artifacts from public lands. You can look at them, but don't pocket them.

a lovely contrast to the red hills that surround it. The lake, which has two paved boat ramps on its north side, is a popular site for water-skiing, Jet Skiing and simply cruising. Swimmers also take advantage of the lake in summer, despite its lack of developed swimming areas. From Santa Fe, take U.S. 84/285 north to Española. Turn left at Dandy Burger, where the highway splits. Follow U.S. 84 for 18 miles to Abiquiú and another 7 miles to the turnoff for Abiquiú Dam, which is on your left. To rent canoes or kayaks, call Wild River Sports, 1303 Cerrillos Road, 982-7040. It's open 9 AM to 7 PM with longer, flexible hours in summer.

Bowling

Silva Lanes
1352 Rufina Cir. • 471-7250

With 32 lanes, Silva's is larger than your average bowling alley. That's because it's the only one in town and, as such, is always buzzing with activity. Silva Lanes is home to literally dozens of sanctioned leagues for kids from age 3 and older, who earn money for college with every game they play. There are adult leagues, too, including men's, women's, coed and even nonsmoking leagues. Silva Lanes is open from 10 AM to midnight five nights a week and until 1 AM on Friday and Saturday. Prices range from $1.20 to $2.75 a game plus $1 to $1.75 to rent shoes. Hourly rates for groups of up to six people start at $13.50 and include shoe rentals. Silva's has a snack bar and a fully licensed, glassed-in lounge with hosted karaoke every night.

Camping

Most of New Mexico's parks, national monuments and forests have campsites ranging from primitive to developed sites with running water and restrooms. Some also have RV hookups, occasionally even with cable television. Public campsites are usually open from May through October on a first-come, first-served basis and cost just a few dollars. You don't need a permit to camp in national forest wilderness areas, but you do in national parks and monuments. They're available for free from the visitors centers so make sure you stop in

to register. Check with the National Park Service, P.O. Box 728, 988-6012, for additional information about permits.

In Town

Los Campos RV Resort
3574 Cerrillos Rd. • 473-1949

Five miles south of the Plaza on Cerrillos Road, Los Campos caters strictly to motor homes. The 11-acre, year-round trailer park has 93 sites, a coin laundry, groceries, a heated pool and a playground. Costs are $20.75 per night for two people plus $2.50 for each additional person. Weekly and monthly rates are available.

Trailer Ranch
3471 Cerrillos Rd. • 471-9970

This is a combination RV and mobile-home park, with the first third of the park reserved for up to 45 RVs with full hookups. Amenities include cable television as well as public showers, coin laundry, a heated, seasonal swimming pool and a community house with a pool table, library and card tables. The back two-thirds of Trailer Ranch is a seniors-only mobile-home park with a minimum age of 55. Daily rates range from $22 to $26 with discounts for senior citizens.

Out of Town

Rancheros de Santa Fe
Frontage Rd., 10.5 miles east of the Plaza • 466-3482

With 131 campsites on 22 acres, including 28 sites for tents only, Rancheros de Santa Fe is the largest camping facility in the Santa Fe area. Amenities include a pool, a recreation room, coin laundry and a playground. Guests can buy groceries and propane on site. Rates run from $2.50 to $17.50 for up to two people plus $1.50 to $2 for each additional person. The campgrounds are open March through November.

Santa Fe KOA
934 Old Las Vegas Hwy. • 466-1419

This KOA offers 25 tent sites and 65 RV

Photo: Chris Corrie

Santa Fe's five golf courses offer varied terrain and spectacular scenery.

hookups on 30 acres in lovely Apache Canyon, about 14 miles southeast of Santa Fe off the Old Las Vegas Highway. Rates run $13.50 for up to two people with a $2 surcharge for each additional person. "Kamping Kabins" cost $24.95 each. Ask about weekly rates. Campers have access to a coin laundry, a recreation room and a playground. Groceries and propane are available on site. The camp is open March through November.

Tesuque Pueblo RV Campground
U.S. Hwy. 84-285, 10 miles north of Santa Fe • 455-2661

Despite the name, Tesuque Pueblo RV Campground accommodates tents as well as RVs in 83 sites on 17 acres. The campground has a heated pool, a whirlpool, coin laundry and a grocery store. Camping costs $15 for up to two people and $2 for each additional person. Weekly and monthly rates are available.

Santa Fe National Forest
Hyde Park Rd. • 753-7331

The Santa Fe National Forest has three campsites close to Santa Fe, all located off N.M. 475 on the way to the Santa Fe Ski Basin. From the lowest elevation to the highest — which, of course, is the order in which you'll encounter them — they are:

Black Canyon, 8,400 feet. Open May through October, Black Canyon has 42 campsites, restrooms, drinking water and trailer parking. Fees are $5 per night for a maximum of 14 days.

Big Tesuque, 9,700 feet. With no drinking water or trailer parking, Big Tesuque has seven free campsites open for 14-day maximum stays between May and October.

Aspen Basin, 10,300 feet. For the truly hardy, Aspen Basin has six free campsites open year round with restrooms, drinking water and picnic tables. Maximum stay is 14 days.

Hyde Memorial State Park
Hyde Park Rd. • 983-7175

Located 12 miles northeast of Santa Fe on N.M. 475, Hyde Memorial State Park campground has both primitive campsites and developed ones with electric hookups. The camp offers drinking water, restrooms and a dump station.

Disc Golf

Dead Plastic Society
Ashbaugh Park, Cerrillos Rd. and Fourth St. • 982-8079

The Dead Plastic Society is a loose organization of people of all ages, genders and skill levels who play golf with a Frisbee-like disc. The tee boxes and stationary metal baskets were provided by the City of Santa Fe and configured by a course pro. Santa Fe's disc golf course is one of about 800 around the world. The sport, which originated in California (of course), has gained tremendous popularity over the last few decades and is still growing. You can catch the Dead Plastic Society in action in the city's Ashbaugh Park, usually on Sunday starting between 10 and 11 AM. Members (and we use that term loosely) also play doubles on Wednesday night starting at about 5 PM. The times fluctuate with the season — and that includes winter, when players put on Sorels instead of sneakers. During those times, you'll find anywhere from 10 to 40 people tossing around little grey discs that cost about $8 each. Some people cart around bags of them, just like traditional golfers do with their clubs. In fact, many golfers also play disc golf, though being good at golf doesn't necessarily mean you'll be good at disc golf, which requires an athletic throwing arm. But don't be intimidated. The Dead Plastic Society welcomes all players, including first-timers who will get a handicap commensurate with their experience. Who knows, after some practice you might find yourself competing in tournaments against teams from Albuquerque.

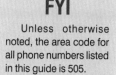

FYI

Unless otherwise noted, the area code for all phone numbers listed in this guide is 505.

Fishing

New Mexico is an angler's paradise. The waters in the state offer a variety of coveted freshwater game fish, including Rio Grande cutthroat trout — the state fish, and one for which New Mexico is rightly famous — as well as brown trout, rainbow trout, brook trout and lake trout. You can also fish for Kokanee salmon, black bass, white bass and striped bass; largemouth, smallmouth and spotted bass; panfish, catfish, walleye, bluegill, black crappie and carp.

There's little fishing to speak of in Santa Fe County, though it's not unheard of to catch a stocker or two in the pretty-but-piddling Santa Fe River. But Santa Fe is a gateway to some superb fishing. The nearest place to Santa Fe to fish for trout is the Pecos River in San Miguel County, about 35 miles southeast of Santa Fe. An especially good area is upstream from the Village of Pecos and in Villanueva State Park south of I-25. If you're willing to hike, the Pecos Wilderness, where the Pecos River originates, is filled with trout streams such as the Rio Del Medio near Pecos Baldy, where native cutthroat and rainbow trout thrive. If you plan to fish in this area after September, be prepared for severe winter weather, which can hit with little warning at any time.

The Rio Grande, which starts in Colorado and heads south to the Gulf of Mexico, is your other choice if you want to stick close to Santa Fe. Take note, however, that it's a temperamental river where fishing is a delight one day and impossible the next. We don't recommend you even try to fish the Rio Grande during spring runoff, when the water is far too swift and muddy.

On a good day, the Orilla Verde Recreation Area north of Pilar, off of N.M. 68 which heads to Taos, offers some fine fishing. So does the Taos Box of the Rio Grande, about two hours north of Santa Fe along N.M. 68, but you're likely to find yourself competing with whitewater rafters. You might also try the Rio Santa Barbara, a medium-size river that starts in the Pecos Wilderness near Truchas Peak and flows into Peñasco, between 52 and 67 miles northeast of Santa Fe, depending on which route you take.

If you're willing to travel a couple of hours or more, the northern part of the state has some of the best trout fishing in New Mexico. In the northwest, the San Juan River below Navajo Dam offers excellent trout fishing year round, often yielding trout longer than 20 inches. The most fished part of the San Juan is designated as "special trout" or "quality" (protected) water with restrictions that limit anglers to artificial flies and lures; single, barbless hooks; and bag and possession limits. In northeastern New Mexico near the Colorado border, the Valle Vidal unit of the Carson National Forest — open for fishing from July 1 through December 31 only — offers outstanding trout fishing, as does the Red River south of Questa. La Junta, the confluence of the Red River and the Rio Grande in the Upper Taos Box, has some of the best fishing on the Rio Grande, though its swift and wild waters are recommended for experienced anglers only. Be warned, however, that it will take some serious hiking to get down to the river and even more serious hiking to get back to your car. Part of the Red River is quality water with special restrictions.

Perhaps the single-most important piece of advice before tossing your line in the water is to get a copy of the state fishing proclamation wherever you buy your license. You can buy a license at the New Mexico Department of Game and Fish or at any one of more than 200 vendors statewide, including outfitters, some hardware and grocery stores and Wal-Mart. An annual fishing license costs $17.50 for residents, $39 for nonresidents. A one-day-only license is $8 for everyone, while a five-day permit costs $16. Seniors and juniors are eligible for discounts. We strongly recommend you pay the extra $5 for a wildlife habitat improvement stamp that allows you to fish on federal lands. Be prepared to pay a $1 vendor fee. If you have any questions about the rules and regulations, call or visit the New Mexico Department of Game and Fish, 408 Galisteo

Street, 827-7911. The department will provide you with a copy of *New Mexico Public Fishing Waters*, which includes a map as well as comprehensive descriptions of streams and lakes throughout New Mexico. You can also call the department's toll-free, 24-hour telephone number, (800) ASK-FISH, for up-to-date fishing and stocking reports and information on regulations, special waters, boat access, etc. For additional information on stocking, call 827-7905.

If you're interested in looking at fish but not catching them, the Game and Fish Department operates six fish hatcheries that are open for touring. They include Lisboa Springs at Pecos; Red River near Questa; Seven Springs near Jémez Springs and Parkview near Chama in the northern part of the state. South of Santa Fe, you can tour the Glenwood hatchery, near the Gila Wilderness, and Rock Lake in Santa Rosa, the nearer of the two. Call the Fisheries Division at 827-7905 for additional information.

The following local operators offer guided fishing trips and gear.

High Desert Angler
S. Guadalupe St. • 98-TROUT

In business for more than 10 years, High

A number of companies offer whitewater rafting trips in this area.

Photo: Chris Corrie

Desert Angler was Santa Fe's first full-service fly-fishing shop. It offers high-quality fly-fishing equipment and supplies, including popular area fly patterns. It also guides fly-fishing trips throughout northern New Mexico and rents all manner of fly-fishing gear, including Sage rods, reels, waders and pontoon boats. High Desert Angler supplies maps, guide books, licenses and the latest fishing reports, including some that are firsthand.

Known World Guide Service
825 Early St. • 988-9609, (800) 983-7756

Known World offers a variety of fly-fishing trips on many of northern New Mexico's best trout waters, including the Pecos, Rio Grande and Red rivers as well as high alpine lakes and smaller creeks. Guides try to avoid crowds and provide personalized service. Most trips last all day and sometimes into the night. Full-day trips include a light breakfast and hearty lunch. Known World also rents out equipment including rods, reels, waders and boots.

FYI

Unless otherwise noted, the area code for all phone numbers listed in this guide is 505.

The Reel Life
Sanbusco Ctr., 510 Montezuma St.
• 995-8114

The Reel Life, which has stores in Santa Fe and Albuquerque, is an outfitter endorsed by the Orvis Company to guide fishing trips and sell the company's high-quality fishing and outdoor gear. The Reel Life stocks hundreds of patterns and sizes of flies for freshwater and saltwater fishing as well as material and instruction to tie your own. The store also offers guided fishing trips to many of the fine waters of New Mexico including the San Juan River, the Rio Peñasco, Taos area streams and private lakes in Chama.

Fitness Centers/Gyms

Carl & Sandra's Physical Conditioning Center
DeVargas Ctr., 153-A Paseo de Peralta
• 982-6760

Under the direction of former U.S. and Olympic weightlifting coach Carl Miller, Carl & Sandra's

Physical Conditioning Center is the only gym in town that offers Olympic-style weightlifting in addition to aerobic and anaerobic weight-training programs for all ages, from children to senior citizens. Carl & Sandra's specializes in cardiovascular circuit training to build both strength and endurance with creative, individualized programs updated every six to seven weeks. Training and nutritional counseling focus on weight loss or gain, stress reduction, specific sports, flexibility, bone density, pregnancy, rehabilitation or Olympic-style weightlifting. Carl & Sandra's 7,000-square-foot gym is light on frills — it has a small coed sauna and separate dressing rooms with showers and lockers — but heavy on well-maintained equipment: free weights, weight stack pulley systems similar to Universal, hydraulic resistance machines, Concept II rowers, Schwinn Aerodyne stationary bikes, gymnastic rings and a host of other machines and gadgets designed to exercise every conceivable muscle and joint in the body along with the cardiovascular system. Staff members are dedicated and well-trained and work out regularly. Miller, a guru of sorts for many members, holds a master's degree in health, physical education and recreation with specialties in exercise physiology, biomechanics and nutrition. He has devised hundreds of exercises based on Olympic lifts and incorporates this into his clients' personalized programs. His wife, Sandra Thomas, an accredited teacher, has been a mountaineer for more than 30 years and is a former search and rescue team and EMT team member.

Memberships at Carl & Sandra's Physical Conditioning Center run about $1,100 a year. Ask about family, group and senior-citizen discounts. The daily rate is $10 for guests of members and $13 for walk-ins. The gym is open from 6 AM to 1:30 PM and 3:30 to 8 PM on Monday, Wednesday and Friday, 8 AM to 1:30 PM and 3:30 to 8 PM Tuesday and Thursday, 9 AM to 4 PM on Saturday and 11 AM to 4 PM on Sunday.

Club International Family Fitness Center
1931 Warner Ave. • 473-9807

Located off St. Michael's Drive, one of

Tent Rocks, located 35 miles south of Santa Fe, offers
hikers views of spectacular rock formations.

Santa Fe's major commercial strips, Club International is a 17,500-square foot-fitness center with four racquetball courts; a basketball court; free weights and a variety of resistance and electronic cardiovascular and weight machines including Nautilus, Concept II rowers, Stairmasters, Nordic Trak, Lifecycles and StarTrac; an indoor heated swimming pool, hot tub, steam room and dry sauna; and classes in aerobics, yoga and stretching. The center also offers, at additional cost, supervised child care, tanning beds, Shotokan karate instruction by a 5th-degree black belt who holds world and national records, and professional racquetball instruction. Memberships run from $55 for one month to $360 a year if prepaid. Daily guests pay $10. Call for corporate or group rates. Club International is open from 5:30 AM to 9 PM Monday through Friday, 9 AM to 5 PM on Saturday and 10 AM to 5 PM on Sunday.

El Gancho Fitness, Swim and Racquet Club
Old Las Vegas Hwy. • 988-5000

South of Santa Fe, adjacent to the Steaksmith restaurant on the scenic Old Las Vegas Highway, this beautiful 18,000-square-foot health club describes itself as a "complete health, tennis and sports activity center." The facilities include indoor and outdoor tennis courts with resident pros available for instruction and adult and junior tennis programs; squash, racquetball, basketball and volleyball courts; an outdoor running/walking track; a strength and conditioning center with free weights, Universal and a variety of cardiovascular machines including Stairmaster,

Cybex and Schwinn; aerobics classes, body toning and sports-conditioning classes; indoor and outdoor heated swimming pools with certified swimming instruction available; kiddie and wading pools; hot tubs, steam rooms and saunas. Among the services the club offers are personal fitness trainers, nutrition counseling, massage therapy, child care and a summer day camp for kids. Special programs include fitness evaluations, yoga, swim play, tango instruction, martial arts, a teen circuit and CPR. El Gancho memberships start at $70 a month for individuals with a onetime initiation fee of $300 with special rates and initiation fees for couples, families, single families, children and corporations. The club is open from 6 AM to 9:30 PM daily, except on Tuesday, when it opens at 2 PM.

Fitness Plus
1119 Calle del Cielo • 473-7315

The only all-women's gym in town, Fitness Plus describes its mission as providing women in Santa Fe with a "special place in which they can comfortably acquire better health and enhanced self esteem." The club has free weights, Nautilus, Universal, stretch-and-tone tables and something it calls a "cardio theater," in which you can hook up to any of six televisions or two radios while sweating on Versaclimbers, rowers, steppers, treadmills and other cardiovascular equipment. The gym also offers aerobics and yoga classes, personalized weight-management plans, massage, European body wraps, salt glows, tanning beds and child care for $1 an hour. Amenities include towels and daily lockers with locks.

FYI

Unless otherwise noted, the area code for all phone numbers listed in this guide is 505.

INSIDERS' TIP

Each year, a few people die of exposure in the mountains here. Don't be one of them. Take plenty of warm, waterproof clothing on the trail with you, even if you're just going out for a couple of hours. The mountains here are unpredictable and unforgiving. A few hundred feet could mean a sudden and unexpected snow storm — even in late spring and early fall — so be prepared. You should also take some sort of shelter (a space blanket), plenty of water, matches, some food and a topo map. This is not being alarmist — it's being safe.

Membership includes one free personal-training session, one four-week follow-up and an orientation to the equipment. Fitness Plus offers a 14-day free trial, after which membership is $39 a month with a one-year commitment plus a $75 initiation fee. If you enroll during the free trial period, the initiation fee is cut in half. Members can also join on a month-to-month basis for $49 and an $89 membership fee. Ask about discounts for full-time students, senior citizens older than 65 and families. Daily guest passes cost $9 per visit. Club hours are Monday through Friday from 6 AM to 8 PM, Saturday from 8 AM to 5 PM and Sunday from 10 AM to 3 PM. Owners Joe Oliaro and Barb Petkus are doctors of naprapathy, a offshoot of chiropractic. Oliaro is also a doctor of Oriental medicine, certified in acupuncture and herbology.

Fort Marcy Ballpark/
Mager's Field Sports Complex
490 Washington Ave. • 984-6725

The city-run Fort Marcy Ballpark/Mager's Field Sports Complex has an indoor pool; separate gym and weight rooms; a racquetball court; outdoor fields and tracks; dance and fitness classes; body sculpting and stretching classes; swimming classes for all ages from infants to seniors; and martial arts. The complex also hosts various onetime competitions throughout the year in a variety of sports, including basketball and football. Fort Marcy offers a variety of memberships to suit nearly every user, including a $25-a-year user fee card that allows partial use of the facility with per diem rates to use the pool or other facilities, depending on your age. An unlimited annual membership costs $294 per individual and $420 per family, while $126 a year will buy you use of the weight room, gym or racquetball court only. Nonmember users pay $4 per day if they're adults, $2 for ages 14 to 17 and $1 for ages 8 to 13. Senior citizens age 60 and older and children 7 and younger get in free. Fort Marcy is open Monday through Friday from 6 AM to 8:30 PM, Saturday from 8

AM to 6:30 PM and Sunday from noon to 5:30 PM.

Mandrill's Gym
708 W. San Mateo St. (at Pacheco)
• 988-2986

Formerly Gold's Gym, Mandrill's came under new ownership — and a new name — in 1991 when Martin Sanchez, a bodybuilder, decided he wanted to put his own stamp on the gym. Still big on body building — many members are competitive in the sport — Mandrill's is also a family gym for general fitness with free weights, Universal, resistance machines and cardiovascular equipment including steppers, climbers, treadmills and rowers. Personal trainers who work out of the gym charge private rates. Among the amenities at Mandrill's are a dry sauna, dressing rooms with showers, $1 towel rentals and a variety of drinks and supplements for sale. Membership prices range from $42 per month to $365 per year. Daily passes cost $5. Mandrill's is open Monday through Friday from 5:30 AM to 9 PM, Saturday from 8 AM to 5 PM and Sunday from 9 AM to 5 PM.

Quail Run Fitness Center
3101 Old Pecos Tr. • 986-2222

Quail Run Fitness Center is part of a luxury development in southeast Santa Fe, but the public is welcome to join. The center features a 65-foot heated indoor lap pool, a hydrotherapy pool, two hot tubs, two outdoor tennis courts, a weight room, cardiovascular equipment and a 1.75-mile jogging trail around the Quail Run Golf Course (see our Golf section in this chapter). The club offers ongoing classes in low-impact, step and water aerobics; stretching; tai chi; and yoga. Personal training runs $30 per hour, with special group rates available. Swimming lessons and tennis lessons cost $25 per half-hour, $40 per hour with discounts for groups. The club also offers massage, spa services, facials and manicures by special appointment.

Membership in Quail Run Fitness Center

INSIDERS' TIP

Get to your campsite early, especially during peak season, or you may find yourself sleeping in your car instead of a tent.

requires a onetime, $1,800 initiation fee for individuals and monthly dues of $95. Families pay a $3,500 initiation fee and $180 a month. Call for information on corporate memberships. To get on the membership waiting list, you will need to put down a $500 deposit. Once accepted, members have access to the billiards room, card room, banquet facilities and the bar and grill, where you will be charged a minimum of $35 a month, assessed quarterly. Per diem rates run $20 for members of the International Health, Racquet and Sports Club Association. The club does not accept drop-ins.

William C. Witter
Fitness Education Center
Santa Fe Community College, 6401 Richards Ave. • 438-1615

Named after the college's founding president, who died in 1993, the William C. Witter Fitness Education Center is the largest indoor physical-fitness center in Santa Fe and one of the best deals in town in that arena. For the price of a single physical-education course — a requirement to use any of the facilities — anyone can take advantage of the 25-meter lap pool, indoor and outdoor tracks, basketball and volleyball courts, four tennis courts, large resistance training center with hydraulic and free weights and cardiovascular equipment, and outdoor playing fields. Classes in the P.E. center cost $20 a credit — few are more than one-credit classes — plus a $55 lab fee. The college also sells five daily guest passes for $25, $15 for seniors. The fitness center offers instruction in a wide variety of classes including aerobics, badminton, basketball, martial arts, tennis, volleyball, walking and yoga. There are also many different swimming classes from which to choose, including water safety instructor certification classes. The center is open Monday through Friday from 6:30 AM to 9 PM and Saturday from 9 AM to 3 PM. It's closed on Sunday and when school is not in session.

Flying

Zia Aviation
405-A Airport Rd. • 471-2700

Zia Aviation provides flight training that will turn a beginner into a private pilot after an average of 60 hours in the air. The school's FAA-certified instructors charge $25 per hour to teach students in a Cessna 172, which rents for $58 an hour including fuel. Each flight lesson includes approximately one hour on the ground and an hour in the air. Zia recommends students fly at least twice a week for optimum learning and retention. The company offers an introductory flight over Santa Fe, in which students may take the controls, for $39.95. Zia is open seven days a week from 6 AM to 9 PM. Call ahead for an appointment.

Football

Santa Fe has no adult football leagues, though you're bound to find a group of players tossing a football around in some of the city parks. However, the Fort Marcy Ballpark/Mager's Field Sports Complex, 490 Washington Avenue, 984-6725, sponsors an annual Punt, Pass & Kick competition for kids in which participants get three tries at punting, passing and kicking a football, with each attempt measured for distance. The highest

INSIDERS' TIP

An abundance of crosswinds make hot-air ballooning in Santa Fe an iffy proposition at best. Your best bet for taking to the skies is in Albuquerque, and Santa Fe Detours will be happy to arrange the adventure. In summer, you'll probably be aloft by early morning when the air is still cool enough to ensure the balloon will rise. In cooler seasons, you're likely to be in the air by noon so pack a lunch if one isn't being provided for you. Contact Santa Fe Detours, 54½ E. San Francisco Street, 983-6565, (800) DE-TOURS.

scores in each category are added together. Contestants with the three highest total scores win trophies. The competition costs $5.

Young American Football League de Santa Fe
1750 Cerrillos Rd. • 820-0775

This 27-year-old private coed league is part of a statewide organization for young footballers from ages 6 to 13. Four hundred youths, the vast majority of them boys, participate in the Santa Fe league, which sponsors 14 teams that play in the city's Franklin E. Miles Park (Siringo Road and Camino Carlos Rey) and Ashbaugh Park (Cerrillos Road and Fourth Street) from August through October. The season starts with four weeks of rigorous conditioning and practice before players are allowed to play. After that, teams rotate practice Monday through Friday between 5:30 and 7 PM. Two games are played per night on Tuesday, Wednesday and Thursday from 6 to about 9 PM, and three games are played on Saturday between 9 AM and 1 PM. The league discourages stardom and a "winning is everything" mentality. Instead, it concentrates on teaching kids how to play the game and on sportsmanship.

Golf

Santa Fe golf courses offer lots of hills, varied terrain and spectacular scenery, but they also have a unique feature that golfers have to love: The high elevation drives the ball farther than the same effort would get them at sea level. Combine that with the high-quality bluegrass and bentgrass that local courses use on their greens and fairways — not to mention relatively mild weather that allows golfers to play their game somewhere nearby

all year long — and you can see why Santa Fe is attractive to golfers.

Sun Country Amateur Golf Association
100-35 Country Club Land NW, Ste. 5, Albuquerque • 897-0864

This is the governing body of amateur golf in New Mexico and can provide suggestions about where to play and how.

Pueblo de Cochití Golf Course
5200 Cochití Hwy., Cochití Lake • 465-2239

Located in the foothills of the Jémez Mountains, this 18-hole, par 72 course ranks in the top 50 nationwide among public golf courses. Golfers play roughly 50,000 rounds a year here on scenic bluegrass fairways and bentgrass greens and tees. Championship tees play at 6,541 yards, men's tees at 5,996 yards and ladies' tees at 5,292 yards. Guests pay a $15 greens fee on weekdays and $20 on weekends. Carts cost $10 per player. Pueblo de Cochití Golf Course is open sunup to sundown year-round, weather permitting. The premises feature a restaurant and full-service pro shop.

Quail Run Golf Course
3101 Old Pecos Tr. • 986-2255, (800) 548-6990

Quail Run is a luxury, gated community with a private nine-hole, par 32 golf course that's open year round, weather permitting, to guests from reciprocating country clubs with prior approval of the golf pro. The Arthur Jack Snyder-designed course, opened in 1986, features native grasses, bluegrass fairways, and tees measuring between 2600 and 1800 yards. Visitors pay $50 a day, including cart, to golf at Quail Run, where some 9,000 holes are

---

INSIDERS' TIP

For the latest and most accurate information about public lands in New Mexico, contact the New Mexico Public Lands Information Center at 1474 Rodeo Road, 438-7542. The center — a partnership between the Bureau of Land Management and Southwest Natural and Cultural Heritage Association — offers maps, books (including guidebooks), licenses and permits as well as talks, demonstrations and other monthly events.

played each year. The club has a pro shop that offers lessons as well as food and beverages. Hours are Tuesday through Sunday starting at 6 AM.

Santa Fe Country Club
Airport Rd. • 471-0601

Founded in 1946, this is a wide-open, 18-hole, par 72 public golf course. Golfers play about 45,000 rounds here each season, which runs from February through December. The course measures between 7098 yards from the championship tees to 5862 yards at the forward tees and offers a putting green, pitching green and practice range. Guests pay $40 per day plus a $9 cart fee. You can buy food and beverages at the club. It's closed on Monday.

Marty Sanchez Golf Course
Municipal Recreation Complex, 205 Caja del Rio Rd. • 986-6931

Named for a young Santa Fe golf champion who died of cancer at age 25, this brand-new golf course — construction finished in 1997 — is the first municipal green in Santa Fe. A nine-hole, par 28 course was planned to open in spring of 1998 with an 18-hole, par 72 course following in late summer or early fall. Call the Municipal Recreation Complex (see the entry in this chapter) for details.

Hiking

Santa Fe's backyard is a beautiful maze of trails, some forging deep into the mountains, others meandering easily in and around grassy, flower-filled meadows. Hyde Park is just minutes away from downtown Santa Fe and offers a variety of trails, some easy, others strenuous. Among the most popular is the Winsor Trail, above Hyde Park in the Santa Fe National Forest. It leads into the Pecos Wilderness, though you needn't take it that far. It shares its bottom trailhead with the Borrego Trail, a very easy 4-mile hike that takes you through rolling meadows and forested hills. Simply follow Hyde Park Road about 8.5 miles north to a parking lot where you'll find the trailhead.

If you're looking for a strenuous hike, the trail to Lake Katherine will give you spectacu-

lar views of Santa Fe Baldy, Penitente Peak, the upper Pecos Basin, the Rio Grande Valley and the Jémez Mountains. This is a 14.5-mile hike that requires seven to eight hours of hiking each way plus additional time to rest and eat. In that time, you will climb 3,200 feet. In about half the time, you can climb Atalaya Mountain, which literally is in Santa Fe's backyard. Starting off at St. John's College, park in the visitors parking lot, where you'll find the trailhead. Follow the signs, which will take you along an arroyo and eventually across a road. That's the point where you'll start climbing, gradually at first and then quite steeply in the middle and at the end of the trail. You'll be rewarded with magnificent, sweeping views of the entire city.

For more information on trails and conditions, call or visit the New Mexico Public Lands Information Center, 1474 Rodeo Road, 438-7542. Or call the Santa Fe chapter of the Sierra Club, Plaza Desira, 621 Old Santa Fe Trail #10, 983-2703, and leave a message on the answering machine. Someone really will get back to you. You might also check the "Outdoors" section of Thursday's Santa Fe New Mexican, which lists Sierra Club outings for the upcoming weekend and phone numbers of the group leaders. If you're a serious hiker, by all means buy a copy of the local Sierra Club's self-published Day Hikes in the Santa Fe Area. Now in its fourth printing, this 228-page paperback describes in delightful detail 45 hikes ranging from easy to strenuous, some in Santa Fe, others as far as 85 miles away. If you're not the do-it-yourself type, there are numerous guides in Santa Fe who will be happy to guide you on half-day to multiple-day hikes.

For more information about hikes in this area, see our Parks section of this chapter.

Horseback Riding

The Bishops Lodge
N. Bishops Lodge Rd. • 983-6377

Just 3 miles from Santa Fe Plaza, The Bishops Lodge was once the private retreat of Santa Fe's famed 19th-century bishop-turned-archbishop, Jean Baptiste Lamy — the father, as it were, of St. Francis Cathedral in the downtown area. Today the lodge is a resort on 1,000 acres of private land in a lush valley nestled into the foothills of the Sangre de Cristo Mountains. Its backyard is a natural piñon-juniper forest with a maze of scenic trails through which wranglers lead groups of up to 30 people, from beginners to experienced riders, on horseback for up to an hour and 45 minutes. You'll be riding along narrow mountain trails so you'll rarely go faster than a trot, though you may be able to canter on the roads leading to the trails.

The stables are open Tuesday through Saturday from 9:30 AM to 2 PM year round, though the lodge schedules fewer rides during the winter. Hotel guests pay $30 an hour, nonguests pay $40. If you're not staying at the lodge, be sure to call ahead — a day or two is best — to guarantee a spot. Don't plan on taking children younger than 9, unless they are big for their age. The stable keepers will not allow anyone who weighs more than 230 pounds to ride their quarterhorse mixes.

Broken Saddle Riding Company
Old Gravel Pit Rd., Cerrillos • 470-0074

South of Santa Fe, about 26 miles from the Plaza, Broken Saddle is the only stable in the state that offers smooth-riding gaited horses such as Tennessee Walkers and Missouri Fox Trotters that use all four legs for power. With horses like these, it goes without saying that, unlike many stables, Broken Saddle allows riders to trot, canter and even gallop. That's a big draw, especially for experienced riders who want to feel the wind in their face. With a lease on 19,000 acres in the Cerrillos Hills south of Santa Fe, Broken Saddle is intimately familiar with dozens of beautiful trails in juniper and piñon country you'll recognize from classic Western movies. Perhaps you'll ride to Devil's Canyon with its beautiful rock formations, to one of the 221 old mines in the Cerrillos Hills — maybe even to Old Grand Central Silver Mine, one of the bigger ones — or to the Madrid Overlook with 360-degree views of five mountain ranges. Guided rides average two hours and cost $45 per person for up to six people. Beginners are welcome, but riders shorter than 4'10" are not. The stable is open for business year round.

Summertime is especially busy, so call two to three days in advance. The stable is a quarter-mile past the railroad tracks on Old Gravel Pit Road.

Rancho Encantado
N.M. Hwy. 592, Tesuque • 982-3537, (800) 722-9339

Home to riders since its beginnings as Rancho del Monte in 1932, Rancho Encantado is a luxury Southwestern ranch resort on 200 acres in the Sangre de Cristo Mountains. Just 10 minutes north of Santa Fe, the ranch has long been a popular destination for such famed riders as rodeo legend Larry Mahan and Hollywood stars like John Wayne, Henry Fonda and Kirk Douglas, who rode in real life as well as the movies. The stables at Rancho Encantado are open year round to riders of all experience levels, including beginners. Depending on the wrangler's mood, you may take any of a dozen different trails through *arroyos*, piñon, juniper and ponderosa pine. The stable offers three to four scheduled rides per day, weather permitting, at 9:30 AM, 12:30 PM, 3:30 PM and sunset. Rides last up to an hour and a half and cost $35 for overnight hotel guests, $45 for day-use visitors. More experienced riders may prefer a private session in which they can ride faster and/or choose a specific, perhaps more adventurous, trail. These rides tend to be longer in duration and cost more. Call the stable for details. Rancho Encantado also offers group rides for eight or more people with special rates and pony rides for children. It's a good idea to schedule rides ahead of time rather than just showing up expecting to throw your leg over a horse. In summer, call at least a day ahead.

Rancho Las Palomas
Ojo de la Vaca Rd., Cañoncito • 466-3874

At the top of Glorieta Mesa southeast of Santa Fe, Rancho Las Palomas is the old homestead of owner/wrangler Bob Romero's grandfather. Romero will take up to six people, fewer with children, on scenic rides on any of a dozen trails in the Santa Fe National Forest — through wide-open valleys with up to 300 head of cattle grazing in the summer right on into the mountains. Rides run $35 for an hour,

$40 for an hour and a half and $45 for two hours. Children age 6 and older are welcome as long as they're accompanied by an adult. Experienced riders are welcome to run. The stables are open year round, seven days a week, with riders generally going out at 9:30 AM, 1:30 PM and, upon request, at sunset. You can show up and take your chances, but it's best to call ahead of time — up to a day or two in summer.

Makarios Ranch
198 Camino Querencia, Cerrillos
• 473-1038

In the old mining town of Cerrillos, Makarios caters primarily to experienced riders of all ages who are looking for adventure on the back of a horse. Be warned, this is not easy riding. You'll be traveling on rough, mountain terrain at high speeds, either on your own horse or on one belonging to the ranch. Your journey may take you into the lovely Galisteo Basin area or deep into the Cerrillos Hills or the Ortiz Mountains. This is wild country with Indian ruins and old mines, some of which you might want to stop and explore. Rides are by appointment only and cost $45 for two hours, more for half-day and day-long rides. The ranch also has a wagon and a team of horses for parties. Ask about prices.

Hunting

Northern New Mexico offers excellent trophy hunting for elk, deer, antelope and limited bighorn sheep on state, federal, Indian and private land. Any would-be hunter's first step should be to get a copy of the New Mexico Game and Fish Department's annual *Big Game Proclamation*, which comes out in midwinter. The proclamation outlines rules and regulations as well as license fees. Be sure to read the pamphlet carefully because it's extremely — some would say ridiculously — dense and complicated. Contact the New Mexico Department of Game and Fish at 408 Galisteo Street, 827-7911.

Hunters should be aware that the application deadline for special hunts, which include most big game, is in early spring. A special note for out-of-state hunters: You may have to hire a licensed guide to apply for any big-game permits issued through a lottery system. You'll find details in the proclamation. Ask the Game and Fish Department for its list of certified outfitters as well as its list of guides about whom complaints have been received or whose licenses have been revoked. Guides and outfitters must have permits from the appropriate agency if they will be guiding on federal (national forest, Bureau of Land Management or State Trust) lands. Prospective clients should insist that any outfitter provide names of prior customers and should follow up by checking all references. They may also get additional information from the New Mexico Council of Outfitters and Guides, 160 Washington Street SE #75, Albuquerque, N.M. 87108.

For elk, which is the top trophy animal in New Mexico, the Valle Vidal Unit of the Carson National Forest in northeastern New Mexico is about as good as it gets on public land anywhere in the United States. The Sargent and Humphries wildlife areas near Chama, in north central New Mexico, also offer record-book heads. Competition is fierce in both areas for limited slots, however. If you don't mind paying to hunt on private land, Vermejo Park Ranch, 445-3097, — adjacent to the Valle Vidal and recently purchased by media magnate Ted Turner — has one of the finest elk herds in the country, second perhaps only to the national elk refuge in Jackson, Wyoming. Vermejo Park's herd is a natural herd that has been managed for even age distribution, which allows elks to reach maturity. The ranch also offers world-class accommodations and is priced accordingly. Guided rifle hunts for mature bulls can cost up to $10,500, including lodging and food. That compares to $750 for nonresident hunters going after trophy elk on public land, such as the already mentioned Valle Vidal unit or, farther south (and much closer to Santa Fe), the Pecos Wilderness, which offers good hunting for those willing to hire a guide with the necessary horseback transportation. Please see the paragraph above regarding outfitters.

On the other side of the Rio Grande, hunters are finding increasing success in the Jémez Mountains, northwest of Santa Fe, as the state elk herd continues to expand. The private Baca Ranch in Valle Grande near Los Alamos, ensures an even better success rate, though you'll pay top dollar

— up to $8,600 for a guided bull elk hunt. Contact the Baca Land and Cattle Company, 662-2270, or Baca Outfitters, (800) 456-6620. On the same side of the Rio Grande, north to Dulce near the Colorado border, the Jicarilla Apache tribe, 759-3255, offers trophy animals and high success rates. The Jicarilla recently purchased a first-class lodge in Chama featuring some 30,000 acres of prime habitat for elk and deer. The tribe offers guided hunting trips as well as fishing trips on well-stocked private lakes.

Compared to elk, hunting mule deer on New Mexico's public lands is an iffy proposition. Many experts say increasing numbers of elk have pushed out their smaller brethren. Hunters seeking trophies can expect to work hard for them, climbing high, rough country far from paved roads. You may not come home with a trophy — or even a non-trophy animal, for that matter — but you'll see some stunning country. Farmington, in the northeast corner of the state, is among the better deer hunting areas in the state. The terrain may not be the only challenge deer hunters face in New Mexico. While hunters may still purchase licenses over the counter, New Mexico is increasingly going to a system requiring hunters to apply through a lottery system for a limited number of permits. Again, applications for drawings are due in early spring.

If it's bighorn sheep you're after, the odds of drawing a license are precipitously against you. If you manage to land a permit, do yourself a favor and hire a good outfitter to make the most of a rare opportunity. A handful of hunters each year are lucky enough to get licenses for bighorn sheep in the Pecos Wilderness. These animals, frequently so tame as to eat snacks from the hand of passing backpackers, may offer their biggest challenge in the drawing of the permit. Similarly, would-be antelope hunters have the option of facing long odds in public drawings or paying ranch-

ers, who often advertise in local newspaper, for the privilege of hunting their land. Eastern New Mexico on both sides of Interstate 40 offers trophy heads of the keen-sighted animals.

Small-game season in New Mexico is the entire month of September, a perfect time for those who want to combine a lovely hike in the autumn woods with bringing home supper — perhaps a squirrel or grouse. Turkey season is in spring and fall. Locals addicted to this challenging — some say impossible — pastime find some success in the lower hills of the Pecos Wilderness and in the northern mountains.

Mushball

Santa Fe Parks and Recreation Department, Recreation Division
1142 Siler Rd. • 438-1492

Don't let the name put you off. This is a very popular coed sport among Santa Fe adults, particularly women. It has similar rules to softball, but the ball is the size of a large grapefruit. There are city-sponsored leagues and private leagues, all of which play in city parks. The leagues run from May to August.

Racquetball

A number of gyms in town have racquetball courts and offer lessons. These include William C. Witter Fitness Education Center at Santa Fe Community College, 6401 Richards Avenue, 438-1615; Club International Family Fitness Center, 1931 Warner Avenue, 473-9807; and El Gancho Fitness, Swim and Racquet Club, Old Las Vegas Highway, 988-5000. See our Fitness Centers and Gyms section for additional information on these facilities.

INSIDERS' TIP

The unwritten code of the West is to leave things as you found them. If you open a gate, close it behind you. If the previous "tenant" left a pile of dead wood at your campsite, leave some for the next camper. Of course, if you find garbage or other unwanted remnants at your camp or on a trail, by all means tote it out along with your own.

Fort Marcy Ballpark/
Mager's Field Sports Complex
490 Washington Ave. • 984-6725

The City of Santa Fe sponsors summer and winter racquetball leagues based out of the Fort Marcy/Mager's Field Sports Complex, which features two racquetball courts. The leagues play a 12-game schedule and hold post-season tournaments in which first- second- and third-place winners receive awards and all participants get T-shirts — not bad for $30. The summer league begins in June, the winter league in December. Call Fort Marcy for specific dates.

Rock Climbing

While northern New Mexico is not exactly a mecca for rock climbers — rocks here tend to be sandstone and crumble easily — there are still enough challenges in the region to keep local climbers active and happy between trips to Yosemite or the Tetons. Closer to home, you can find excellent, frequently climbed local crags, especially in the Los Alamos/White Rock area in the Jémez Mountains northwest of Santa Fe.

Santa Fe Climbing Gym
825 Early St. • 986-8944

Before you head out climbing, you might want to spend some time in the Santa Fe Climbing Gym, the only place of its kind in Santa Fe. The Climbing Gym emphasizes sport climbing, which is less about discovery and the technical aspects of climbing than the athletic or gymnastics. The gym is located in a large, new warehouse with 3,500 square feet of artificial climbing walls. The main room has a 40-foot-wide wall that reaches 28 feet at its highest point and contains dozens of different holds as well as inclines and overhangs. Students practice climbing with their hands and with ropes, alone and in groups. The floor is padded with carpeting over rubber to cushion falls, which are inevitable.

The Santa Fe Climbing Gym holds weekly, three-hour introductory classes for $40 each, including gear, and intermediate classes for $50. It also offers advanced classes, which in the past have featured such renowned climbers as Timy Fairfield, ranked No. 1 in the United States, and Bobi Bensman, who is one of the

top women climbers in the country and among the best in the world. These seminars change every season so be sure to call the gym for descriptions, schedules and prices.

Adult climbers have a variety of membership options, including unlimited use of the facilities for $50 a month, three-month passes for $125, a 10-visit punch pass for $100 and day passes for $12 day, $6 for bouldering only (no ropes). Private instruction costs $25 an hour. The gym has open climbing Monday through Friday from 5 to 10 PM, Saturday from 2 to 8 PM and Sunday from 1 to 8 PM. Children younger than 14 can climb on Friday between 3:30 and 5 PM and Saturday from 9 to 11 AM. Weekdays at the Climbing Gym are reserved for public and private school classes and after-school programs. The gym also holds a weekly "kid climb" — a two-hour class for children age 7 and older at $15 per session, $75 for six visits or $120 for 10 visits. Parents and guardians need not be present. The Climbing Gym also offers summer programs. Ask for details.

Rollerskating

Rockin' Rollers Event Arena
2915 Agua Fría St. • 473-7755

Santa Fe youth have long complained that there's little or nothing for them to do in Santa Fe, especially at night. Rockin' Rollers Event Arena has come to the rescue. Located on Agua Fría Street, 50 feet south of Siler Road, Rockin' Rollers is a fantasy in purple that features a 3,500-square-foot tiled skating rink — yes, it's purple — with purple walls, including one featuring a mural of sea-green waves. Friday and Saturday nights at Rockin' Rollers feature dances with an in-house DJ or live local bands. All ages are welcome, but this place is a favorite of the younger set, so we've included a more extensive write-up in our Kidstuff chapter.

Rugby

Rio Grande Rugby Union,
Santa Fe Chapter
1216 Parkway Dr. • 988-2205

Santa Fe has a very active all-male rugby

club, the Santos, that celebrated its 25th anniversary in 1997. A member of the Rio Grande Rugby Union — which encompasses the area from El Paso, Texas, to Durango, Colorado, and takes in all of New Mexico — the Santos have hosted a number of international clubs and even toured England in 1986. It has another foreign jaunt in the works, possibly for 1998. They're considering Vancouver, the Carribbean or even New Zealand. The 23-man club boasts a number of high-profile members, including a state senator and an English coach. While it doesn't have the depth of many clubs — some of its members have only been playing rugby five years, though they have backgrounds in football, soccer, wrestling and other aggressive sports — the team's overall athleticism is on par with any rugby club in the country. Most teammates are 35 and younger. Older members are called the Anasazi, after an ancient tribe of Pueblo Indians.

The club's home field is in Ashbaugh Park, at Cerrillos Road and Fourth Street, with home games on Saturday starting at 1 PM. Members practice Tuesday and Thursday starting at 5:30 or 6 PM. The Santos play primarily in fall and spring, though the club won't say no to summer games in the Colorado Rockies, where the weather is still comfortably cool. The spring season starts in early March, weather permitting, and continues through mid-May. The fall season begins in September and goes through November. The club sponsors an annual Labor Day weekend rugby tournament, which begins 9 AM on Sunday with finals at about 5 PM. Santa Fe won 1997's tournament, the first featuring a women's bracket.

Running/Walking

The beauty of Santa Fe is that practically anywhere you live, you can step outside your door and within a few minutes find yourself away from cars and people and, depending on the part of town, even pavement. If you're lucky enough to be in a relatively undeveloped part of town, or if you don't mind driving to your run or your walk, Santa Fe offers umpteen unpaved roads and trails, some in town, others in the county; some with respectable inclines, others downright intimidating. And

practically anywhere you go, you'll find beautiful scenery and attractive architecture — unless, of course, you hate either real or faux adobe. In that case, go to Minneapolis.

Santa Fe also offers almost ideal weather for running and walking — even in the winter for fanatics who won't let a little snow or slush stop them. There's nothing quite as beautiful as getting out first thing in the morning after a night's snowfall when the trees and adobe walls are outlined in soft shelves of white snow that muffle all sounds, including that of your shoes hitting the ground. Do be careful about slipping, however. The snow may cushion the thud, but it might not provide an adequate cushion for your back or hips.

The downside of running or walking in Santa Fe is that it's not a particularly pedestrian-friendly town, except perhaps for the area in and around the Plaza. The city has a dearth of sidewalks so you'll find yourself sharing the road with cars and bicycles or treading on terribly uneven shoulders that threaten twisted ankles or worse. The best defense is a pair of off-road running or walking shoes that provide lots of ankle support. For runners and walkers both, it's always a good idea to run facing traffic, especially on Santa Fe's many curving roads. Ideally, you want to find a place that has very little car traffic. That way you avoid carbon monoxide as well as possible accidents. If you run or walk at night, wear something reflective and be sure to ask around to make sure the area you choose is safe. Running or walking in groups certainly lessens the odds of being a crime victim, though for some it defeats the purpose entirely. If you prefer to run or walk in company, we've included a few suggestions here.

Villa Linda Mallwalkers
Villa Linda Mall, 4250 Cerrillos Rd.
• 473-4253

Celebrating its 13th year in 1997, the Villa Linda Mallwalkers is a group of up to 100 people, most of them senior citizens, who walk laps around the interior of the Villa Linda Mall. The mall opens its doors at 7 AM Monday through Saturday to accommodate the walkers, and Luby's Cafeteria, 473-7084, provides 25¢ cups of coffee with free refills until 9:30 AM. On the first Friday of each month from

7:30 to 8 AM, Luby's also hosts a breakfast of biscuits, pancakes, eggs, bacon, ham, hot cereal, fruit salad, juice, coffee, tea and milk for $4.50 per person. Except in summer, breakfast is followed by an 8:15 AM by a speaker from St. Vincent Hospital or Lovelace Health Systems who leads a 45-minute discussion on a variety of health topics of particular interest to seniors.

In addition to being an exercise group, the Villa Linda Mallwalkers has also turned into an ad hoc support group, helping members get through illness and the deaths of loved ones. Many long-lasting friendships have been forged along the 0.6-mile course. Members organize parties and in 1997 even took a cruise together.

A smaller group meets at the opposite end of town in DeVargas Center at North Guadalupe Street and Paseo de Peralta. Call the mall at 982-2655 for more information.

Santa Fe Parks and Recreation Department
1142 Siler Rd. • 438-1491

The city sponsors a number of races throughout the year including the Santa Fe Run-Around in June, a 5K run and 1-mile walk it cosponsors with the Santa Fe Striders (see our next entry); the annual Sylvia Pulliam Memorial "Hot Chile Run" in August and a 5K and 10K run starting at Salvador Perez Park, 601 Alto Street.

Santa Fe Striders
P.O. Box 1818, Santa Fe 87504
• 983-2144

Affiliated with Road Runners Club of America, Santa Fe Striders is a local running club for everyone from the casual runner to 100-mile ultra-marathoners. The club has approximately 60 members of varying ages, from 20 to 70, who promote running, sponsor races and gather for informal runs open to anybody who's interested. Members meet at 6 PM every Wednesday at the Plaza for a 5- to 7-mile run followed by beer and a bite to eat. Anywhere from three to a score of runners show up, regardless of weather. Most are members, though anyone is welcome. These runs always start and finish around the Plaza. Competitive runners in the club meet Tuesday

nights at the Santa Fe High School track for speed workouts. Another group meets for occasional long-distance runs on weekends to prepare for marathons or just for the heck of it.

Members also like to meet at least once a year at La Bajada — a steep incline along U.S. Highway 25, about 20 miles south of Santa Fe — to run along the old *Camino Real*. Sometimes they hold informal races from Santa Fe to Lamy in which the first team of two runners and a cyclist to arrive, wins. The club organizes many other informal runs, sometimes followed by a picnic, a potluck or dinner at a restaurant.

The Santa Fe Striders put on several 5K and/or 10K races a year, including the Santa Fe Run-Around in June (see the previous entry); a charitable 5K run on the Saturday before Thanksgiving to benefit the Salvation Army; and the *Corrida de Los Locos* ("Run of the Crazies") in late January or early February, an unsanctioned 4.2K race for which contestants pray for the worst weather possible. For the truly *loco*, there's even a snowshoe race in mid-January. All races are advertised in the club's newsletter as well as in an annual calendar available from New Mexico USA Track and Field, 31 Sandhill Road, Los Lunas, NM 87031, 865-8612. You can also call the Santa Fe Striders directly for its schedule or for suggestions on where to run.

For visitors, the club often recommends running around St. John's College, which sits directly in the foothills of the Sangre de Cristo Mountains. It also sends runners up Artist/Hyde Park Road, the beginning of a long uphill stretch that winds up at the ski slopes; along winding, scenic Bishop's Lodge Road; or up Atalaya Mountain — a 3.5-mile run with an elevation increase of 1,780 — for some "light" spring, summer and autumn running. For endurance running, the Santa Fe Striders recommend running up and down Tesuque Peak, 11.6 miles round trip from the gate at the north end of the Aspen Vista parking lot to the radio towers at the top.

Scuba Diving

Believe it or not, Santa Fe has not one, but two scuba-diving centers. Why? Because even desert dwellers like to explore the underwater world. New Mexicans get practice here and then go to Belize or Cozumel where the water is warm and they can look at the reefs. What better thing to do in winter than go off to the tropics and play in 80-degree water? Between those times in the ocean, you can dive in open water at Blue Hole in Santa Rosa, New Mexico, about 115 miles southeast of Santa Fe. Blue Hole is a spring-fed sink hole with 64-degree water and 20 to 30 feet of visibility. It's popular among divers in New Mexico and neighboring states, and it fills up quickly because it's only 70 feet across. If you go during the week when few other divers are around, especially around noon or 1 PM when the sun is at a high angle, the water is so clear that you can stay on the surface and count pebbles on bottom.

Other popular diving spots in New Mexico include Navajo Lake, 130 miles northwest of Santa Fe; Conchas Lake, about 135 miles east of the capital city; and Elephant Butte Reservoir near Truth or Consequences, about 200 miles to the south. Avoid the Abiquiú Reservoir and Cochití Lake, which are cold and dark, and the Rio Grande, which is filled with dead trees, snags and all sorts of obstacles. Among the main draws in New Mexico for divers is that it's one of the few states that allow spearfishing for game fish. The rule here is: If you can angle for it, you can hunt for it. And remember, if you're wet, you're having fun.

Blue Water Dive and Travel Co.
855 Cerrillos Rd. • 988-5566,
(800) 357-2091

About a block from the intersection of Cerrillos Road and St. Francis Drive, Blue Water Dive and Travel has been selling equipment and certifying people for scuba diving since 1993. A member of the Professional Association of Dive Instructors, the company teaches beginning scuba diving all the way to instructor-level courses. Along with its sister store in Albuquerque, it's the only five-star IDC (Instructor Development Course) facility in New Mexico. It's a full-service store that also services and repairs diving equipment. It has a full rental department as well as a travel agency that specializes in scuba trips.

Blue Water Dive and Travel offers about 14 classes, including a beginners class costing $150 that includes use of a tank, wet suit, regulator and buoyancy compensator; a weekend of classroom and pool instruction; and a weekend at Blue Hole in Santa Rosa. Another $275 will buy you your mask, fins, snorkel and text book, complete with video. The owners recommend you register at least a week in advance to allow enough time to read the book and watch the video. Other classes cost around $100 for up to two weekends and include altitude diving, night diving, deep diving, photography, dry-suit diving, (ship)wreck diving and spear fishing. Blue Water is open from 10 AM to 6 PM every day except Sunday and Wednesday. Classes are held Friday evenings and weekends. Open-water classes occur every three weeks.

The Scuba Company
4350 Airport Rd., Ste. 6 • 438-3006

Open since the early 1990s, The Scuba Company offers recreational diving classes for rank beginners and instructors. The Scuba Company holds classes in its Airport Road store and uses two city pools — one at Salvador Perez Park, 601 Alta Vista Street, 984-6755, and another at the Tino Griego Center, 1730 Llano Street, 473-7270 — for practice before going into open water at Blue Hole in Santa Rosa, where the water is warm and visibility is good. For $500 students get about 30 hours of training including all fees (pool, open water, park, etc.), certification, reading material, use of the school's scuba equipment (or students can bring their own equipment, with the school's permission) and personal snorkel equipment to keep — a mask, fins, booties and snorkel. The Scuba Company is open Monday through Friday from 10 AM to 6 PM and Saturday from 10 AM to 3 PM. Classes are usually held on the weekends: Saturday from 9 AM to 3 PM and Sunday from noon to about 7 PM. Altogether, students will spend about 16 hours in the classroom and an equal amount of time in the pool. The last weekend is devoted to open-water diving at Blue Hole in Santa Rosa.

Although there's no law requiring scuba divers to be certified, The Scuba Company will not rent out equipment or fill tanks without a diver-certification card.

Skateboarding

It took some political finessing, but Santa Fe now has an "official" skateboard park on public land — an unusual gesture for any city to make and yet one more reason that Santa Fe deserves its nickname, The City Different. Located downtown in West De Vargas Park at De Vargas and Guadalupe streets, this park has concrete ramps and culverts galore, making it a popular destination for skaters who once practiced in and around the Plaza — to the consternation of many (evidently) and the fascination of a few. Bike riders and rollerskaters use the park too. Like all city parks, "Skateboard Park" has a 10 PM curfew. This seems to pose few hardships, except in summer, when avid skaters can never get enough of their favorite pastime.

Beyond Waves Mountain Surf Shop
333 Montezuma St. • 988-2240

When they're not in Skateboard Park, you're likely to find skaters in Beyond Waves Mountain Surf Shop. It's one of only two specialty stores in Santa Fe — and the only one located downtown — that sells skateboards and accessories, including apparel. On rainy days, you're likely to see groups of kids just hanging out at Beyond Waves, conveniently located down the street from Skateboard Park, some watching any of the store's more than 150 skating or snowboarding videos, others listening to music and exploring the wares. The store sponsors an annual summer skateboard contest in which participants in various age groups are judged for ability. Trophies are awarded, and the store donates skateboards, T-shirts and other goodies to winners. Everyone gets a free bumper sticker. The event usually gets some radio and television coverage. Beyond Waves is open seven days a week from 10 AM to 7 PM in summer with an 8 AM opening time in winter to rent snowboards. During the winter, the store closes at 6 PM on Sunday.

rob & charlie's
St. Michael's Village West, 1632 St. Michael's Dr. • 471-9119

Santa Fe's other skateboard headquarters is rob & charlie's, in St. Michael's Village West near Wild Oats and AAA. Although primarily a bicycle shop, rob & charlie's is also Santa Fe's oldest existing skateboard shop with 19 years in the business. It's not a skater's hangout like Beyond Waves, nor does it aim to be. Its goal is to sell a variety of high-quality decks, wheels and trucks, and it does that very well, thank you. rob & charlie's is open Monday through Saturday from 9:30 AM to 6 PM.

Soaring

Santa Fe Soaring
405 Airport Rd. • 424-1928

Santa Fe Soaring, which operates out of Zia Aviation, offers rides and instruction in motorized sail planes, tailwheel checkouts (airplanes with the wheel on the tail) and aerobatic airplanes. For $125, you can sail above the Sangre de Cristo or Jémez mountains for an hour and a half in a solar heated, glass-canopied Stemme S10, a German sail plane with a 23-meter wing. One of only 10 in the country — it was only the third when it arrived in 1993 — the Stemme S10 is a high performance, self-launching sail plane with a 50-to-1 glide ratio. That means if you're a mile high, you can sail for 50 miles on still air. Or you can rent a super-decathlon for tail-wheel checkouts or aerobatic flying for $110 and $115 an hour, respectively, including instruction. Each plane fits only two people — a pilot and passenger or student and instructor. The two owners/instructors are commercial airline pilots with a combined 40,000 hours in the air. Santa Fe Soaring is open seven days a week, year round, from 9 AM to 5 PM. Flights are by appointment only — it's best to call a week ahead, though you could take your chances and just show up.

Soccer

America has long played catchup with Europe in its appreciation for the game of soccer. In Santa Fe as elsewhere in the country, however, the sport is rapidly gaining popularity with some 1,500 kids and upward of 500 adults playing the game. Along with this popularity have come increasingly more vocal demands for equal time — and equal playing

The PoPay Foot Race is held every year in July in conjunction with
the Eight Northern Indian Pueblos Arts and Crafts Show.

fields — with other sports. Accused for years of treating soccer players like second-class citizens, the City of Santa Fe is finally rising to the challenge with five soccer fields, the only ones in the city dedicated to the sport, due to open in 1999 at the brand-new Municipal Recreation Complex, 205 Caja del Rio Road, 986-6931, in south Santa Fe.

Adults belong to the Santa Fe Soccer Club, 471-3004, a member of the New Mexico State Soccer Association in Albuquerque. The club has nearly 600 members and 36 teams, about a dozen of them coed and the rest all men, including two new seniors teams — one for players between 30 and 39 and the other for men 40 and older. At this writing, there weren't enough players for an all-women's team. Because the club has been playing in summer, it's out of synch with the rest of the state, including its own association, and will remain so until the fields open at the Municipal Recreation Center. Until then, the club will continue playing in summer on Tuesday, Wednesday and Thursday nights starting at 6:15 PM at the Fort Marcy Ballpark/Mager's Field Sports Complex, 490 Washington Avenue in downtown Santa Fe, and Villa Linda Park, Rodeo Road and Mall Circle, at the southern end of the city. The men's A and B divisions play Saturday at 9 AM, 11 AM and 1 PM at the old Santa Fe polo grounds.

Capital Soccer Club, 984-2891, is the select club for youths from 1st through 8th grades. The Northern New Mexico Soccer Association, 982-0878, is for beginning soccer players. The clubs register kids in May and play from August through October in a variety of locations — Fort Marcy, 490 Washington Avenue; Villa Linda Park, Rodeo Road and Mall Circle; Salvador Perez Park, 601 Alta Vista; and Ashbaugh Park, Cerrillos Road and Fourth Street.

Softball

Greater Santa Fe
Softball Association
3238 Nizhoni Dr. • 473-3933

The Greater Santa Fe Softball Association is a private organization that in 1997 had 2,700 registered players from age 15 (with parental consent) to 67 in women's, men's and coed leagues. Teams start practice in March with games beginning in April and continuing through September five nights a week. Tournaments are played on the weekend at the new Municipal Recreation Complex, 205 Caja del Rio Road, 986-6931, off Airport Road in south Santa Fe. The league plays four games per night starting at 4:45 PM with a new game on the hour. Lights go out after 10 PM, precluding any extra innings.

Swimming

The City of Santa Fe has four swimming pools — three indoor and one outdoor — with schedules, classes and prices unique to each facility. Call the individual pool or pick up a copy of the City of Santa Fe Parks and Recreation Department's annual *Activity Guide*, which has a complete schedule for each pool. Check with the Recreation Division, 438-1485, for special programs and teams. For private pools, see our the Fitness Centers and Gyms section in this chapter.

Alto Park and Bicentennial Pool, 1121 Alto Street, 984-6773

Fort Marcy Swimming Pool, 490 Washington Avenue, 984-6725

Salvador Perez Park and Pool, 601 Alta Vista Street, 984-6755

Tino Griego Pool, 1730 Llano Street, 473-7270

Tennis

Santa Fe has public tennis courts throughout the city, all of them outdoors. Call the individual facility, if possible, or the City of Santa Fe Parks and Recreation, 438-1485, for hours, lighting, rules, etc. as well as for information about instruction for children and adults. There is no charge to use the courts, which are available on a first-come, first-served basis only.

Alto Park & Bicentennial Pool, 1121 Alto Street, 984-6773

Atalaya Park, 717 Camino Cabra

Chamisa Tennis Courts, Dr. Richard Angle Park, Calle Medico

Fort Marcy Ballpark/Mager's Field Sports Complex, 490 Washington Avenue, 984-6725

Galisteo Tennis Courts, 2721 Galisteo Street

Herb Martinez Park, 2240 Camino Carlos Rey

Larragoite Park, Agua Fría Street and Avenida Cristobal Colon

Salvador Perez Park, 601 Alta Vista Street, 984-6755

Private Courts

El Gancho Fitness, Swim and Racquet Club
Old Las Vegas Hwy. • 988-5000

El Gancho is a members-only club with the largest tennis facilities in Santa Fe. It has seven outdoor courts, of which two are clay and three are lighted, and two permanent indoor courts for an extra fee of $6 per half-hour in summer and $12 per half-hour in winter. El Gancho has four on-site tennis pros, leagues and tournaments. For details on membership, see our write-up under the Fitness Centers and Gyms section in this chapter.

Sangre de Cristo Racquet Club
1755 Camino Corrales • 983-7978

Sangre de Cristo Racquet Club is a private tennis club with six outdoor courts, including one clay court and another with lights and heat, and an indoor court in a fabric "bubble." The club also has an outdoor heated swimming pool for seasonal use only. Individual memberships require a $600 initiation fee and monthly dues of $73. Family memberships cost $800 for initiation and $102 a month. Junior memberships run $54.25 per month plus a $300 initiation fee. The per-diem fee for nonmembers is $20. Sangre de Cristo has two tennis pros, a full-service pro shop and two sanctioned tournaments

Shellaberger Tennis Center
College of Santa Fe, 1600 St. Michael's Dr. • 473-6144

Located on the campus of the College of Santa Fe, Shellaberger Tennis Center is the only club in Santa Fe exclusively for tennis. The center has seven outdoor courts, including four with tournament-quality lighting.

Members can join leagues, compete in tournaments and take lessons from pros. The club has anywhere between one and four pros on site, depending on the season. The club will even arrange matches for you with a day's notice. Membership begins with a $275 initiation fee and costs $33 monthly. Nonmembers pay $5 per day for a maximum of five days per year.

Ultimate Frisbee

Santa Fe Ultimate
2886 Clark Ct. • 473-5984

There are two requirements to play for the only ultimate Frisbee team in the city: lots of enthusiasm and an ability to run. Of course, a strong, controlled throwing arm won't hurt either. But mostly, the idea is to have fun at the game, which is like a blend of football and soccer using a Frisbee instead of a ball. There's no tackle in this game, nor can you run with the disc. You need to get the Frisbee from one end of the field to another by tossing it from player to player. Santa Fe Ultimate is sanctioned by the Ultimate Players Association, based out of Colorado. The team has a roster of about 15 steady players, most of them outdoor sports enthusiasts (rock climbers, mountain bikers, etc.) who show up regularly at Ashbaugh Park (Cerrillos Road and Fourth Street), where the team plays Monday, Wednesday and sometimes Friday (if enough people come) from about 6 PM to dark, three seasons out of the year. Another 10 show up when they feel like it. "This is Santa Fe. People have their own agenda," one player noted. Weekends are reserved for tournaments, which generally total four or five a year. The team hosts an annual tournament that in 1997 attracted 21 teams from throughout the Southwest.

Volleyball

Santa Fe Volleyball Club
471-0409

The Santa Fe Volleyball Club is a private outdoor league that plays in summer and fall and often requests facilities from the city.

Santa Fe Parks and Recreation Department
1142 Siler Rd. • 473-1492

The City of Santa Fe sponsors both a coed and an all-women's volleyball team in a season that begins in early October and ends in early March with tournaments. Register early because the Parks and Recreation Division can accommodate only a limited number of teams.

Whitewater Rafting/ Kayaking/Floating

Right here in the high desert of northern New Mexico, you'll experience some of the finest whitewater rafting in the West. Come spring, with the melting of the winter's snowpack, the Rio Grande, Red River and Rio Chama swell their banks with churning, fast-moving water that makes for some mighty hairy rapids. Even the most jaded rafter will get a thrill along with astoundingly beautiful scenery. Try it for yourself and you'll see why Congress officially designated these magnificent rivers as "wild and scenic." Among the more popular rafting spots is the Taos Box of the Rio Grande, so-called because you'll pass through wild rapids boxed in by the sheer cliffs of the Rio Grande Gorge, which, in places, is nearly 1,000 feet deep; and the Rio Chama, which flows through canyons of pink, red and mauve sandstone or Ponderosa pine.

Because of the unpredictability of the rivers, you're advised to do some careful research and advanced scouting before venturing out on your own — and even then, you should do so only if you're highly experienced. The Rio Grande has some dangerous and, in certain sections, impassible stretches of water. Call the Bureau of Land Management in Taos, 758-8148, for up-to-date information on the rivers. Or hire a professional outfitter, whose business is to know the rivers and equip you with good gear and knowledgeable guides. You can choose trips lasting from a half-day to five days, from flat-out easy to downright dangerous. Call the BLM at 758-8851 for a list of New Mexico whitewater touring companies or call the local outfitters listed below:

Known World Guides
825 Early St. • 988-9609, (800) 983-7756

Known World offers a variety of rafting excursions in northern New Mexico, including custom trips and moonlight floats. Your rafting trip can last anywhere from a half-day to a week in the upper Rio Grande from the Colorado border to the Lower Gorge, perhaps, or just the Taos Box or White Rock Canyon, where you can explore Anasazi ruins. Known World serves fresh food throughout the trip and can accommodate all dietary needs. Ask about group rates and multiple-day discounts.

Kokopelli Rafting Adventures
541 Cordova Rd. • 983-3734, (800) 879-9035

Kokopelli Rafting Adventures can provide you with an unforgettable river trip in any of eight prearranged trips that include everything from a relaxing float in the Rio Grande to an exciting Class IV whitewater adventure in the Taos Box of the Rio Grande Gorge. Trips range from a half-day to overnight. Kokopelli provides snacks on shorter trips, full lunches on day-long trips and all meals for overnights.

Santa Fe Rafting Company
P.O. Box 23525, Santa Fe, NM 87502 • 988-4914, (800) 467-7238

Santa Fe Rafting Company provides a variety of trips to make everyone from families to whitewater enthusiasts happy. Certified guides not only lead you through rapids but also identify the flora, fauna and geological attractions along the way. You can paddle yourself or sit back and let your guides do the rowing

Southwest Wilderness Center
P.O. Box 9380, Santa Fe, NM 87504 • 983-7262, (800) 869-7238

Enjoy the thrill of whitewater or the serenity of a float on a half-day, full-day or overnight trip with Southwest Wilderness Center. Southwest offers trips in the Rio Grande Gorge, including the exciting Taos Box; through Indian country in calm water with no rapids; in White Rock Canyon, which is suitable for the whole family; and the "wild and scenic" Rio Chama. Quality meals are included with your trip. Discounts are available for groups of 10 or more.

Wild River Sports
**1303 Cerrillos Rd. • 982-7040,
(888) 869-7238**

Wild River Sports is a retail shop that sells canoes, kayaks, rafts and all the accessories you need or could imagine needing for a rafting adventure. The store also acts as a sort of rafting travel agent, booking half-day, full-day and multiday whitewater and floating trips with a variety of companies, including many listed in this book. You can also book hiking, fly-fishing and archaeological excursions through Wild River. Call or simply show up at the store to see what's available to suit your outdoor fantasies. Hours are typically 9 AM to 7 PM Monday through Friday and 9 AM to 9 PM Saturday and Sunday.

The sun shines brightly here, even in winter. Wear sunscreen and take an extra supply with you for a midday application.

Winter Sports

For some, the idea of "winter" in Santa Fe may stir images of short-sleeved golfing and tennis. After all, this is the Southwest isn't it? Well, yes — but we're not Phoenix. Santa Fe gets a real winter, complete with snow and frigid temperatures. Winter usually begins in late October, settles in for real in January — the coldest month of the year here — and disappears sometime in March or April. In good snow years, you can still see patches of snow on the Sangre de Cristo Mountains above Santa Fe on the Fourth of July. Thanks to our elevation and the surrounding mountains, snow on Memorial Day is not unheard of. And, due to our relatively southerly location, neither is sweatshirt weather in March. Even in winter, some 70 percent of the days here are sunny, and a normal winter brings only a few below-zero spells. To put it simply, "sunny" doesn't mean "warm" here.

Since it has snow and mountains, northern New Mexico boasts the lion's share of the state's ski areas. Within a two-hour drive of Santa Fe, you have access to the Santa Fe Ski Area, Taos Ski Valley, Angel Fire Ski Resort, Red River Ski Area, Ski Rio, Sipapu Ski Area and Sandia Peak Ski Area. You'll also find The Enchanted Forest and Capulin cross-country ski areas and many places to head off on your own for Nordic skiing, snowshoeing or winter hiking.

You can bring your sled or inner tubes up to Hyde State Park, just outside of Santa Fe on N.M. Highway 475, or to city parks such as Patrick Smith Park at 1001 Canyon Road, or Herb Martinez Park, 2240 Camino Carlos Rey, which have hills that make good tubing runs.

Safety Tips and Planning

Before you go off skiing, snowshoeing or winter hiking, please keep these tips in mind.

• You're at a high altitude here, which affects your heart, lungs and overall energy. Give yourself time to adjust before you do anything excessively strenuous. Santa Fe sits at 7,000 feet — the top of the Santa Fe Ski Area is 12,000 feet above sea level.

• The weather can be volatile. Never assume that the clear, sunny early morning conditions will remain. Be prepared for weather changes, especially if you're headed for the back country. Tell people where you're going and when you plan to be back. Take a backpack with extra clothing, matches, a space blanket, food, water and whatever else you'll need if you have to spend the night in sub-freezing temperatures.

• The sun shines brightly here, even in winter. Wear sunscreen and take an extra supply with you for a midday application.

• Northern New Mexico's air is dry, and winter exertion can require a lot from your body. Drink fluids whenever possible. And remember, alcohol has stronger effects at higher altitudes and can contribute to dehydration.

• If you want to ski during the Christmas holidays or spring break, plan ahead. New Mexico's ski areas are popular and, like all ski resorts everywhere, tend to attract more visitors these times of year.

• Need to rent equipment? Renting at the ski areas is the most convenient, but on busy days you may have to wait and occasionally — say during the Christmas holidays or over spring break — all the rentals in your size may be gone before you get there. Our advice: Arrive early during peak ski times (it makes parking easier too) or rent ahead of time in Santa Fe's in-town ski shops. Most will let you rent your equipment the night before at no additional charge. Some will even loan you a ski rack to take it up to the mountain.

• Driving can be treacherous after a winter storm. Although all the ski areas do their best to keep roads clear, some days you'll be happier with chains on your tires or four-wheel drive vehicles.

• If you plan on snowshoeing or Nordic skiing, dress in layers. Begin with long underwear that will wick perspiration away from your body, then continue with light, comfortable insulated clothing that will move with you. Two pairs of socks give both warmth and blister protection. Top it all off with a breathable waterproof shell or sleeveless vest.

Downhill Skiing

Skiing is big business here and an important boost to the state's economy during the off-season. More than a million skiers a year explore the pleasure of the state's generally uncrowded slopes, sunny winters and abundant snow each winter. The sport had an economic impact of $250 million on New Mexico in the 1996-97 season, counting everything from lift tickets and lunches to gasoline and hotel rooms. According to a study by the University of New Mexico, the average skier spends $92 a day in New Mexico. The average length of stay is 4.5 days.

Santa Fe makes an excellent base for a ski vacation. The Rocky Mountains, the Jemez Mountains and the Sandia Mountains are our playground. You can spend a day at any of the state's seven northern ski areas, which offer a variety of terrain, or head to Sandia Peak Ski Area outside of Albuquerque and easily accessible to the south. After a day of fun on the slopes, come back to Santa Fe for lodging and dining.

In most years, the downhill ski areas open around Thanksgiving and close in mid-April. Most operate from 9 AM to 4 PM daily during the ski season and offer food and snacks, lockers, emergency first aid and a shop where you can buy sunscreen, goggles and whatever else you need for a day of skiing or snowboarding. All the areas have rental shops with a variety of equipment for children and adults. To rent, you usually need to leave a deposit on a credit card and perhaps a driver's license. If you wish, you can rent snowboards, regular and high-performance skis, boots and poles at several in-town ski shops. If you're skiing outside of Santa Fe, you might save time by renting equipment in town the day before and taking it with you.

Most areas offer morning and afternoon lessons, and private and semiprivate sessions can be arranged on request. Some ski areas promote bargain weeks, early or late-season discounts, special deals for first-time skiers, multi-day discounts and other enticements to persuade you to come. Children and older skiers usually get a break on ticket prices. Ask about discounts when you call to make your reservations.

If you've never skied before, be sure to inquire about beginner packages. The ski areas encourage people to take up the sport by offering the lessons, rentals and lift tickets at a good price. And if you don't have clothes for skiing and don't want to make a big investment, check around. Some ski shops will also rent you a ski bib, insulated ski pants and a jacket.

In this section, we offer you a glimpse of the ski areas near Santa Fe. All prices are for the 1997-98 season.

FYI

Unless otherwise noted, the area code for all phone numbers listed in this guide is 505.

Santa Fe Ski Area
16 miles northeast of Santa Fe on Hyde Park Rd. (N.M. Hwy. 475) • 982-4429, 983-9155 (snowline), 857-8977 (recorded information), (800) 776-SNOW

The Santa Fe Ski Area, with a 12,000-foot elevation at the mountain top, offers visitors the chance to ski one of the 10 highest ski peaks in the United States. From the wide slopes of Broadway to the challenging, tree-studded Tequila Sunrise, Santa Fe has terrain to please skiers and snowboarders of all abilities. The area keeps strong intermediate and advanced skiers interested and has gentle trails for beginners.

Part of the Santa Fe Ski Area's appeal lies in its convenience. The slopes are an easy (most of the time) 45-minute drive from the Santa Fe Plaza. Skiers from Santa Fe, Albuquerque and elsewhere in New Mexico as well as visitors from Texas, Oklahoma, California, other states and even other countries enjoy themselves here. It's not unusual for conventioneers who come to town between Thanksgiving and Easter to stay an extra day just for the skiing.

Photo: Don Strel/Southwest Assignments

Annual events and races on the slopes are fun for both spectators and skiers.

The ski area covers 550 acres of the Santa Fe National Forest and is leased from the U.S. Forest Service. There are 38 named trails: 20 percent "easiest," 40 percent "more difficult" and 40 percent "most difficult." Lift capacity is 7,300 skiers, but normal business is a comfortable 3,500 skiers a day.

One of Santa Fe Ski Area's strengths is its family focus. The youngest children head for Chipmunk Corner Children's Center, a safe and convenient place to learn the sport or to be cared for while their parents ski. The full-service facility offers convenient separate ticketing and equipment rental for kids, a tow all their own, a cozy lunchroom, a playroom and more. The outdoor learning area is fenced for snow play as well as beginning skiing. Instructors receive special training for helping the little ones. Chipmunk Corner instruction is reserved for ages 4 to 9. For children too young to ski, the area offers a nursery with day care and snow play. Day-care slots are limited, so be sure to make reservations.

When they graduate from Chipmunk Corner, children can try Adventure Land, a ski playground complete with roller-coaster bumps, an obstacle course and the opportunity to "ski the trees." Adults who want to ski here must be accompanied by a child. The area is just off the Lower Broadway run beneath the Super Chief Chairlift.

For older children who live in the Santa Fe vicinity, the ski area features popular weekend lesson programs — Pre-White Tornado, White Tornados, Thunderbirds, Roadrunners and Saturday Shredders — all designed to accommodate a variety of needs and abilities. The seven-session classes run from January through March on Saturdays and Sundays. The Tesuque Peak Flyers provide recreational racing coaching and contests for advanced intermediate skiers ages 7 to 13. The Santa Fe Adventure Team offers skiing challenges for children of the same ages and ability who are not interested in racing. In conjunction with the Santa Fe Public Schools and other private and public schools in the area, the Santa Fe Ski Area also offers discounted-rate classes during the week for elementary school children.

Finally, serious young skiers of intermediate ability or better can join the Santa Fe Ski Team. The team begins its dryland training in October and starts to work on the snow when the ski area opens. The team's business is handled by a board of parents and community volunteers, and their financial support comes from training fees, race revenue and fund-raising events such as the Santa Fe Ski Swap. Held each November, the Swap is a great place to pick up used equipment. (See our Annual Events chapter.)

Now that the kids are taken care of, let's go skiing!

To get skiers to the mountain top, the area offers a quad chairlift, a triple chairlift, two double chairs, a poma and two "mighty mite" surface lifts for beginners. The top of the triple chair unloads passengers at the state's highest elevation for skiing — 12,000 feet. If you ski a short way from the apex, you'll look down toward Santa Fe, west to Mount Taylor and north toward the Colorado border. The vista of mountains and valleys, mesas and river beds weaves together, sometimes with a band of low-lying fog or misty clouds, in blues and tans, reds, pinks and warm beige. From there you can ski down 3 miles to the base.

Average annual snowfall here is 225 inches, and snowmaking covers 30 percent of the mountain. On a winter night, if you look toward the Sangre de Cristo Mountains from Santa Fe, you'll see the lights of the snowcats bobbing back and forth as the big machines groom the slopes for the next day's skiing. The Santa Fe Ski Area frequently receives overnight storms that drop light powder snow. If you want to make first tracks in the powder, leave extra early. The new snow delights skiers — but not drivers.

If you break a ski or need advice while you're on the mountain, members of Santa Fe's professional ski patrol can help. For more serious situations, they can use their extensive knowledge of first aid, CPR, mountain rescue and other emergency skills. Patrol members also enforce safety rules and have been known to pull lift tickets from out-of-control skiers.

If you get hungry while you're on the mountain, you can grab a bowl of soup, a burger, the daily special or a plate of pasta at La Casa Cafeteria and Outdoor Grill at the base area. The restaurant is open from 9 AM to 4 PM and serves a variety of hot and cold snacks as well as full meals. Totemoff's at mid-mountain of-

fers an outdoor grill with burgers and other ski fare from 11 AM to 2 PM. Totemoff's also is the only place to buy beer or wine at the ski area.

Need a trail map or have questions? Skier Service personnel are usually available near the lockers in the main building and in a stone hut near the base of the quad lift. They'll help with lost and found items, distribute maps and even offer sunscreen to those who came unprepared. You can buy sunscreen, extra socks or a whole new ski outfit at the Wintermill in the main La Casa building.

For rental equipment, the Santa Fe Ski Area's rental shop offers an inventory of 1,400 skis and 75 snowboards from beginner to high-performance and demo models. Skis — including the new super sidecuts — poles, boots and bindings are available.

How about a lesson? The Santa Fe Ski Area has more than 70 ski and snowboard instructors, all professionally certified. Group lessons begin at 10 AM and 2 PM. Or you can work with a private instructor; private lessons can be arranged hourly, and reservations are usually required.

Just as it does for kids, the Santa Fe Ski Area offers special ski programs for grownups, including classes for women with women instructors, classes designed to help people who want to race, classes just for older skiers and more.

Depending on the weather and the amount of snow, the Santa Fe Ski Area builds a snowboard park with jumps, bowls, half-pipes and all the other attractions boarders love. More often than not, Santa Fe's black diamond runs develop respectable moguls for those who want to try their skill in the bumps. The Santa Fe Ski Area has recreational racing on a coin-op NASTAR course. The race course is normally open Thursday through Sunday, but recreational racers may be pre-empted for special events.

No matter how much fun you're having, you can't spend the night. The Santa Fe Ski Area is strictly a day resort with no slope-side lodging. If you're staying at a hotel, ask if it

www.insiders.com

See this and many other **Insiders' Guide®** destinations online — in their entirety.

Visit us today!

has a ski shuttle or call the Santa Fe Ski Shuttle, 820-7541, for information.

Special annual events at the Santa Fe Ski Area include the Gladfelter Memorial Bump Run for mogul hounds, the Southwest Snowboard Championships, WinterFiesta and the Jimmie Heuga Ski Express to benefit people with multiple sclerosis. (See our Annual Events chapter.)

Here is a summary of Santa Fe Ski Area rates:

Adult all-day all-lift tickets cost $39; half-day tickets, morning or afternoon are $26. Beginner chairlift tickets are $20.

For children (age 12 and younger) all-day, all-lift tickets cost $24. Children shorter than 46 inches tall in their ski boots can ski for free. Super seniors, ages 72 and older, ski free; for other seniors, ages 62 to 71, all-day, all-lift tickets are $24.

Equipment rental per day for skis, boots and poles is $15 for adults and $12 for children. Snowboard rental is $22 or $30 with boots. Children's ski school for ages 4 through 9 costs $68 a day with instruction, lifts and lunch. Unlike many ski areas, Santa Fe doesn't offer off-site ticket purchase. The only place to buy your ski tickets is at the ski area itself. For more information write or drop by the Santa Fe Ski Area's in-town office at 1210 Luisa Street, Suite 5, Santa Fe, NM 87505-4126.

Angel Fire Resort
95 miles north of Santa Fe, 22 miles east of Taos, N.M. Hwy. 434, Angel Fire
• 377-6401, (800) 633-7463 (snow report)

Angel Fire is in the midst of a $40 million, 10-year master plan. Resort management had invested $7 million in the area up through the end of the 1998 season, installing 10 new runs and expanding snowmaking to cover more than 55 percent of the mountain. The area also doubled the width of its snowboard park and added more obstacles for boarders to enjoy. The improvements will continue for several more seasons, much to the delight of New Mexico residents and visitors who delight in the broad runs and relaxed atmosphere of this popular resort.

Beginners especially love Angel Fire because they have their own easy slope and their own chairlift. For those just finding their snow legs or adjusting to the altitude, the poetically named Dreamcatcher lift gives a slow-moving ride that reduces anxiety and makes learning to ski easier. Beginners can get a feeling for the snow and the equipment at their own pace, without pressure from more advanced skiers.

Children feel comfortable here too. Angel Fire prides itself on its family-friendly atmosphere. The programs are so popular, in fact, that all children's classes require reservations a minimum of two days in advance. The resort has two programs for kids through age 12 — one for those who are too young to ski or are not interested in skiing or snowboarding. The Angel Fire Resort Day Camp Program offers structured, supervised, creative activities for non-skiing kids and accepts infants as young as 6 weeks and children as old as 11. At the day camp, kids have fun indoors and outside with activities including art, music, movies, games and more. For kids who are eager to learn a new sport, the Children's Ski and Snowboard Center offers classes for ages 3 to 12. The package includes lessons, lift tickets, equipment rental, snacks and lunch with full-day programs for $70. The youngsters are grouped by age and ability. For the youngest, Angel Fire participates in *SKI* magazine's SKIwee program, a nationwide program for children between the ages of 3 and 5. Children from families lucky enough to ski at several different resorts during a season can continue their learning with the continuity of these programs. Older children can join the Mountain Adventures Program or, if they want to snowboard, the Angel Fire Riders.

Angel Fire is a fine place for adults to learn to ski too. The ski school has between 70 and 85 instructors, and you can take a group lesson with people of your same ability level or a private class. Angel Fire also offers equipment and instruction to accommodate skiers with physical and mental disabilities. The staff includes instructors who can teach in languages other than English.

For skiers and snowboarders of all ages, Angel Fire's biggest claim to fame is New Mexico's first and only high-speed detachable quad, the four-person Chile Express. The lift, installed for the 1996-97 season, whisks you up the mountain in record time. And less time on the lift, of course, means more time on the snow. You can cruise more than 10 miles of skiable terrain, including smooth broad slopes.

Angel Fire Mountain offers a nice mix of skiing challenges. Of the 62 runs, 33 percent are suitable for beginners, 51 percent for intermediate skiers and 16 percent more advanced skiers. The resort has six lifts — four double chairs and a rope tow in addition to the Chile Express — which can handle 5,770 skiers per hour at full capacity. Angel Fire has a vertical drop of 2,050 feet, with a base elevation of 8,600 feet. Annual snowfall is 220 inches on average.

When the lifts close, you can still have fun on the slope-side tubing run. Between 5 and 7 PM you can rent a tube and slip and slide beneath the lights to your heart's content. (You have to be age 6 or older to join the fun.)

The resort also offers snowmobiling, ice fishing, sleigh rides, helicopter rides, hot-air balloon rides and more. At the base of the ski mountain, facilities include the ticket sales office, a rental and repair shop, the ski school and ski patrol offices, retail shops and the Angel Fire Resort Hotel. The hotel has convenient slope-side lodging, an après-ski lounge, an indoor pool and hot tub and two restaurants. You can ride the town shuttle to other businesses and lodgings.

Angel Fire's trademark event is the annual Shovel Race, which draws competitors and spectators from around the country and television coverage from ESPN. Angel Fire's World Shovel Race Championships was recently voted "The Most Unique Event of the Year" by *Event Business News*. The race has three major categories. Competitors in the Production Class, the simplest event, slide down the hill on plain, waxed snow shovels. In the Modified

Speed Class contenders build aerodynamic contraptions around the shovel, aiming for speed. It's often hard to find the shovel in these sleek machines, but it has to be in contact with the snow during the race for the machine to qualify. Finally, the Modified Unique Class uses the shovel as the base for a sort of snow-country art work — a ski-slope float like those you might see in a parade. Designs have included a chicken sandwich, the Taj Mahal and an entire living room. The race always draws crowds of enthusiastic spectators.

Angel Fire created the Nordic Cross-Country Center beginning with the 1997-98 ski season. Snow transforms the resort's 18-hole golf course into a cross-country oasis nestled among the slender aspen and rolling valleys. The center welcomes families who enjoy the unhurried charm of traditional Nordic skiing and who are interested in experimenting with the new, highly aerobic skate technique. Skiers will find 15 kilometers of groomed track and skate lanes and mountain views that make you want to savor the moment. Skiers can rent equipment and sign up for lessons at the center.

Opened in 1966, Angel Fire is a year-round resort offering golf, fishing, mountain biking and a range of special events in the summer.

Adult all-day all-lift tickets cost $36. Adult half-day tickets, morning or afternoon, are $27. Seniors age 64 and older ski free. For children (age 12 and younger) all-day, all-lift tickets cost $20. Children's ski school costs $70 a day including lessons, rental equipment and lunch. Basic downhill equipment rental per day for skis, boots and poles is $15 for adults and $12 per child. Snowboard rental is $25 including boots.

A Nordic trail pass for children and adults is $5 a day or $3 for a half-day. Ski rental for adults or children ranges from $10 for standard rentals to $15 for the skate skis, with boots and poles included. Snowshoe rentals are $10.

Pajarito Mountain Ski Area
45 miles from Santa Fe, 7 miles from Los Alamos off N.M. Highway 501 on Camp May Rd. • 662-5725, 662-SNOW (skiing conditions), (888) 662-SNOW (snow conditions and general information)

Pajarito stands out from New Mexico's

other ski areas in several respects. For starters, it is run by the nonprofit tax-exempt Los Alamos Ski Club, a venerable and enthusiastic group of men and women. The club started 54 years ago to enliven the winter for the scientists and GI's working on the atomic bomb in Los Alamos, a beautiful, isolated spot in the Jemez Mountains. The club moved from an earlier site in search of better snow and came to Pajarito Mountain in the early 1960s. Volunteers cleared trees for the runs, built a cozy lodge and installed the first lift.

Today, the club has some 3,500 members who elect a board of directors that hires the general manager and other paid staff. To be a member you must live or work in Los Alamos, but to ski here you just need the price of a ticket. (If the slopes get so crowded that the members have to wait in line any significant amount of time, the area will reduce its solicitations to nonmember skiers.)

Other things of less historic and, perhaps, more practical interest differentiate Pajarito from northern New Mexico's other ski havens. The area is not a resort, but a ski hill. You won't find overnight accommodations, valet parking, ski shuttles, hot tubs, massages, day care or après-ski activities here — or even a beer to go with your lunch. You will discover a challenging mountain with enough cruiser runs

to keep intermediates and beginners happy too.

"We're a skiers' mountain with a good variety of slopes and groomed and ungroomed areas, nice runs through the trees and good bumps," said Sara Kauppila, the area's spokeswoman. Pajarito began marketing itself for the 1996-97 season, but it is still largely undiscovered and never plans to become a "ski resort."

Perched on a ridge above Los Alamos National Laboratory, the area receives an average snowfall of 143 inches. There's no snowmaking equipment here. Since the area depends totally on the natural stuff, Pajarito is usually among the last of New Mexico's ski areas to open, normally getting sufficient snow by mid-December. Pajarito usually closes some time in April. The area operates only on Wednesday, Saturday, Sunday and federal holidays except Christmas Day. On Wednesday, the mountain is about 50 percent open.

The mountain has a peak elevation of 10,441 feet, a vertical drop of 1,410 feet and 37 trails, of which 80 percent are either intermediate or most difficult. Pajarito's skiers ride their choice of five lifts — three doubles, a triple and a quad — to the mountain top. The views are wonderful. From the top of the Aspen chairlift, skiers can see part of the Valle

Photo: Ben Blankenburg

Snowboarding is very popular at Angel Fire Resort.

Grande, a huge volcanic crater that now forms an expansive valley. The lifts can accommodate 6,500 skiers per hour.

The area's cafeteria and ski school occupy the 13,000-square-foot lodge, and the ski patrol office is nearby in a separate building. Pajarito is one of the few mountains that still has an all-volunteer ski patrol, stemming from the days when volunteers ran the whole area.

You can get lessons in telemark skiing and snowboarding as well as alpine skiing here. The area offers private and group classes for children and adults. On Wednesday, the ski club offers classes for school groups from Española, Pojoaque and the Jemez Valley. The Los Alamos Ski Racing Club operates a youth racing program. Challenge New Mexico uses Pajarito to introduce disabled children and adults to the world of skiing.

The year's major event at Pajarito is Skiesta, held the end of March. The welcome-to-spring party comes complete with ski-boot dances, fun races and costumes.

Adult all-day all-lift tickets cost $32 on weekends and $25 on Wednesday. Beginner lift tickets are $21 on weekends and $16 on Wednesday. Adult half-day tickets (afternoon only) are $23 on weekends or $19 on Wednesday. Seniors age 65 to 75 ski for $21 on weekends and $17 on Wednesday. Seniors age 75 and older ski free with ID.

For children (age 12 and younger) an all-day, all-lift ticket costs $21 on weekends and $17 on Wednesday. Children's half-day tickets are $16, $14 on Wednesday or $13 for the beginner lift. The area does not offers an inclusive children's ski school package, but lessons for children are available.

Equipment rental per day for boots, skis and poles is $13 for adults, $9 per child. Snowboard rentals cost $19 or $26 with boots.

Red River Ski Area
106 miles from Santa Fe, N.M. Hwy. 38, Red River • 754-2223, 754-2220 (snow phone)

There aren't many ski towns where you'll find old mines on the slopes — and that's only one of the things that makes Red River Ski

FYI

Unless otherwise noted, the area code for all phone numbers listed in this guide is 505.

Area special. Established in 1959, this family-friendly area has been compared to a dude ranch for skiers. The ski mountain towers above a town settled more than 100 years ago by hardy souls in search of gold. The setting gives Red River its Old West flavor. Some visitors have compared a visit to Red River to a trip back in history, to the simpler days when everything you needed was on Main Street.

Red River has been attracting happy skiers, many of them from Texas, Oklahoma and Louisiana, for decades. A key to the resort's success is that the area offers plenty of easily accessible diversions for non-skiers. If Grandpa doesn't ski, he can watch the grandkids take a few runs on the ski slopes, then walk or ride the free trolley back to Main Street. He can explore the shops, arrange a snowmobile ride or a Nordic ski lesson, enjoy a pleasant lunch, curl up with a book, schedule a massage or even take a nap. Red River boasts the most consistent skier attendance in the Rockies, in part because of the range of activities the village and the ski area offer. It's busy here even during years when the snow gods don't send New Mexico their blessings.

Red River has 57 trails, evenly divided among expert, intermediate and beginner, and three mountain restaurants. The trails are served by seven lifts — four doubles, two triples and a surface tow. Lift capacity is 7,920 per hour, second only to Taos, so skiers hardly ever have to wait.

To supplement the average snowfall of 214 inches, snowmaking covers about 75 percent of the Red River mountain. More snowmaking capacity was part of the area's improvements in the 1997-98 season. The area has a vertical drop of 1,600 feet and a peak elevation of 10,350 feet. Before you ski down, you can stop at the Ski Tip Restaurant on top of the mountain for hot chocolate, lunch or a snack. The restaurant is a favorite rendezvous place for families. From there, beginners can ski easy runs all the way to the base area. That's another reason beginners like this place — they get to see the views from the top of the mountain AND come down safely. Advanced hot doggers can take the more challenging runs.

Another place to visit is the Star Mining Camp, an attraction that's especially popular with children. You can ski right up to an old miner's cabin and through a tepee. The reconstruction of the Old Buffalo Mine includes a plaque that discusses its operation and some of the old equipment. The camp also has tree houses for kids to explore and an old Western-style fort complete with wooden cows. The camp stands in an aspen grove, and the terrain is flat enough that even the most novice skiers usually have little trouble. The camp adds to Red River's extensive beginner area — some might call it beginner paradise.

But the expert skiers aren't ignored, either. New for the 1997-98 season were two additional black diamond runs with a mining town theme: Tailings and E Town Ditch, named for the nearby Elizabeth Town mine. Red River also welcomes snowboarders and offers a terrain park.

Once they've settled in, visitors appreciate Red River for its convenience. To start with, you won't have to hunt for a parking place because 90 percent of the lodging sits within walking distance of the slopes. Two of the six chairlifts rise directly from town. If you need rental equipment, the ski area itself operates two rental shops, one on Main Street and one in the Ski Chalet at the area's base. You can book packages of lessons and lift tickets there and rent what you need for skiing, including super side-cut skis.

To make it less expensive for families to enjoy the sport, many hotels and lodges participate in the Kids Ski Free/Stay Free program. For each paying parent who stays a minimum of three nights and purchases at least a three-day lift ticket, one child stays for free and receives free lift tickets for the same number of days. The area reports that 43 percent of lift tickets during the 1996-97 season went to people younger than 19.

You can take lessons at Red River, choosing from a range of classes for children and adults. The snowboard school at the Bobcat Terrain Park provides beginning and advanced lessons. The youth center hosts ski programs for ages 4 and older, and Buckaroo Child Care Center cares for infants and children ages 6 months to 4 years. Red River's adult programs include all the basics as well as specialty workshops for bumps, powder snow and racing. The area offers recreational racing on the NASTAR course.

Special events include torchlight parades every Saturday night and Mardi Gras, held each February coinciding with Mardi Gras in New Orleans. The area's single biggest event, Mardi Gras includes family costume balls featuring a band brought in from Homa, Louisiana. A slope-side parade complete with floats on skis, Cajun cooking and other activities add to the fun. Mardi Gras brings a capacity crowd to Red River, but it's normally easy to find a room here. The area caters to 500,000 people during the summer and about 200,000 in the winter. As a popular summer destination, Red River offers scenic chairlift rides, jeep tours, horseback riding, camping, hiking, biking, fishing and more.

Adult all-day all-lift tickets cost $37, and adult half-day tickets are $27. Seniors age 60 to 69 ski for $23; seniors age 70 and older ski free. For teens, all-day, all-lift tickets are $30 or $21 for a half-day. Children's (age 12 and younger) all-day, all-lift ticket cost $23; children's half-day tickets are $16. A children's ski school package is $60 per day all inclusive (lessons, rentals and lunch) for ages 4 to 10. Equipment rental per day for boots, skis and poles is $14 for adults and $9 per child. Snowboards rent for $24 including boots.

Sandia Peak Ski Area
35 miles from Santa Fe on N.M. Hwy. 536 • 242-9133, 857-8977 (snow report)

Albuquerque skiers appreciate the conve-

INSIDERS' TIP

Need a ride to the Santa Fe Ski Area? Check at your hotel — some offer ski shuttles — or call Santa Fe Ski Shuttle, 820-7541. For shuttle service from the town of Taos to Taos Ski Valley, try The Pride of Taos, 758-8340, or Faust's Transportation, 758-3410.

nience of this area. You can either drive the twisting, scenic road to the ski slopes or ride the Sandia Peak Tramway, a spectacular trip up the face of the Sandia Mountains to Sandia Crest.

Located in the Cibola National Forest about 30 minutes from Albuquerque, Sandia Peak has 30 runs, 35 percent of them for beginners, 55 percent for intermediates and a few expert trails. Skiers chose from six lifts — four doubles and two tows. Capacity is 4,500 skiers per hour. Vertical drop is 1,700 feet. The area encompasses 200 acres and has snowmaking equipment for 30 acres of the runs. The base elevation here is 8,678 feet, and the peak is 10,378 feet. Though Sandia Peak is high, it is slightly farther south than most ski resorts so it tends to have a shorter season, generally opening in mid-December and closing in March, depending on the snow.

Sandia Peak has a base lodge that offers rental service and a cafeteria. Kids have their own warming hut and a separate area in which to learn to ski safely. Sandia also offers a package of lessons for senior skiers. The staff teaches all types of lessons through the ski school, but there's no on-site day care. Your best bet is to make arrangements for babysitting in Santa Fe or Albuquerque.

Among the area's special activities is Ski and Tee Day, an event that combines a morning ski race with nine holes of golf at a course in Albuquerque the same afternoon.

Adult all-day, all-lift tickets cost $32 or $22 for a half-day. Children's tickets are $22 all day or $14 for a half-day, and kids shorter than 46 inches in ski boots ski free. Seniors age 62 to 71 ski for $22 all day or $14 for a half-day. Seniors age 72 and older ski free. For children (age 12 and younger), all-day, all-lift tickets are $22; half-day tickets are $14. The Children's Ski School costs $60 a day for rentals, lessons and lunch for ages 4 through 10. Equipment rental per day for boots, skis and poles is $14 adults and $9 per child. Snowboard rental packages are $24.

In addition to the ski area itself, you can buy your tickets, sign up for classes and rent equipment at the Ski Service Center, 2225A Wyoming Boulevard in Albuquerque's Hoffmantown Center, 292-4401.

Sipapu Ski Area
65 miles from Santa Fe, 22 miles southeast of Taos on N.M. Hwy. 518
• 587-2240, (800) 587-2240

This little skiing village hidden in a canyon in the Sangre de Cristo Mountains exudes a woodsy, family-friendly atmosphere. Telemarkers have discovered Sipapu with a passion and love its trails cut through the trees and uncrowded conditions. They share the slopes with skiers and snowboarders.

Owned and operated by the Bolander family, who founded it in 1952, Sipapu caters to folks looking for value and a noncommercial skiing experience. You can get a room and a lift ticket here for $45!

The area's 20 runs offer something for everyone: 25 percent are classified beginner; 50 percent are intermediate; and 25 percent are advanced. Skiers can ride a triple chair or two tows, with a capacity of 2,900 skiers an hour.

Sipapu's base elevation is 8,200 feet, and its peak is at 9,065 feet. There are 37 skiable acres here. The season usually opens the week before Christmas and runs through March. Average snowfall is 110 inches, supplemented with snowmaking on 45 percent of the trails.

Classes tend to be very small and offer an opportunity for personalized learning, even in a group setting. Sipapu guarantees that you'll be able to accomplish your skiing goals at the end of the lesson or you get another lesson for free. In addition to traditional downhill classes, Sipapu offers telemark and cross-country skiing and snowboard classes. Besides teaching visiting families, Sipapu offers ski lessons to students at more than 35 nearby northern New Mexico schools. More than 17,000 students participate each year. Because of the area's small staff, day care is available only through prior arrangement.

Among the special ski events, Sipapu

INSIDERS' TIP

A recent issue of *Skiing* magazine rated Santa Fe second among the most livable ski towns in the United States.

Photo: Don Strel/Southwest Assignments

The Santa Fe Ski Area, located just 15 miles from Santa Fe in the Sangre de Christo Mountains, offers beginner to expert terrain.

goes all out for Presidents' Day in February with races, games, music, a costume contest and Clowns Day. A huge castle built completely of snow provides a centerpiece for the event.

At the base area you'll find a folksy lodge with a big fireplace, a restaurant that serves New Mexican food as well as standard American offerings, a lounge, a shop for equipment rental, a gift shop and a place to buy groceries and gasoline. The area has accommodations for 175 people at a motel, in family-style cabins and a dormitory. In the summer — beginning about mid-May when the snow has disappeared — you can play disc golf on Sipapu's 18-basket course. The game, something like regular golf only played with Frisbees and baskets, is appropriate for players of all ages. Best of all, it's free to play on the Sipapu course.

Adult all-day tickets are $27 or $20 for a half-day. Children's tickets are $21 all day or $16 a half-day. Children age 5 and younger ski free. Seniors between 65 and 69 pay $20; those 70 and older ski free. Children's ski school, including equipment rental and lessons, is $37 per day. Rental of skis, boots and poles is $11 a day for adults and $9 for children. Snowboards with boots rent for $25; snowshoes or cross-country skis, boots and poles rent for $9 per package for adults or children.

Ski Rio
110 miles from Santa Fe on N.M. Hwy. 196, 8 miles east of the junction with N.M. Hwy. 522 • 758-7707 (snow conditions), (800) 2ASKRIO (reservations)

Nestled in the Sangre de Cristo Mountains practically at the Colorado border, Ski Rio is the northernmost ski area in New Mexico and the state's newest place to ski.

Ski Rio has a base elevation of 9,500 feet and a peak elevation of 11,650 feet. The resort includes 810 skiable acres. Ski Rio gets 260 inches of snow a year and supplements that with snowmaking. The area has 83 named trails, of which 30 percent are beginner, 50 percent intermediate and 20 percent expert. Otherwise, skiers reach the slopes on six lifts — two triples, a double and three tows. The

area can accommodate 5,500 skiers per hour. The longest run is 3.5 miles.

Expert skiers also can arrange to ride a snowcat — a machine that looks like a tractor with tank tread — to Carmello Peak on select days to ski the black diamond runs there.

Ski Rio welcomes snowboarders and built two snowboard parks to keep them happy. Bullet Proof Snowboard Park at Carmello Peak and the central Chutes and Ladders park offer plenty of challenges and a place to snowboard away from the skiing crowd. Ski Rio has hosted the Ride New Mexico Snowboard Series, a free, grassroots competition sanctioned by the United States Amateur Snowboard Association. The association's goal is to promote the safe and responsible image of snowboarding. The competition is held once a month for three months, with prizes for the top competitors.

In addition to alpine skiing and snowboarding, Ski Rio offers Nordic skiing and snowskating. The area's rental Sled Dog Snowskates, which come with prefitted boots, enable the wearer to glide on snow — part in-line skating, part snowboarding, part skiing, part ice-skating. Ski Rio says its Park Sled Dogs is the only snowskating park in the United States. The park offers everything from smooth "exhibition" space to speed bumps, stair steps and glade snowskating.

For Nordic skiers, Ski Rio has 21 kilometers of groomed trails at its cross-country area. Skiers can cruise past meadows and in and out of the woods through spruce, fir and aspen. It's not uncommon to spot deer, elk and other animals. Of the 17 tracks, 11 are suitable for beginners.

At the base area you'll find ski rentals, a sports shop, the Day Lodge restaurant and Piñatas bar. You'll also find three options for lodging, including two on-slope choices.

Ski Rio offers a full-service ski school with classes for children and adults. All kids programs require reservations. Ski Rio participates in the national Ski Wee program.

One final note: For the 1997-98 season, Ski Rio was open for consecutive days during both Christmas and spring break and on Friday, Saturday and Sunday other weeks. The resort also planned to be open Mondays for Martin Luther King Day and President's Day Weekend.

Adult tickets are $33 for all day or $26 for a half-day; junior tickets are $23 for a full day or $21 for a half-day. Children 6 and younger ski free, as do seniors 65 and older. Active military personnel can buy tickets for $23. Morning and afternoon tickets are available. An all-inclusive full-day children's ski school package is $55. Basic ski rental costs $13 for adults and $10 for kids. Snowboards rent for $18 or $25 with boots. A cross-country pass is $8 for adults and $7 for juniors. Equipment rents for $10 for adults and $7 for youth.

Taos Ski Valley
80 miles from Santa Fe on N.M. Hwy. 150, 18 miles northeast of Taos
• 776-2291, 776-2916 (snow conditions), (800) 776-1111 (information)

When visitors think of skiing in New Mexico, they usually think of Taos, the state's most famous ski resort. *Skiing Magazine* ranks Taos Ski Valley in the top 10 resorts in the United States as well as in the top 10 for getting the most for your money.

Taos Ski Valley's longstanding popularity among skiing fanatics confirms the media's praise. Visitors return year after year, in part because of the resort's well-regarded Learn to Ski Better week. Taos also attracts many first-time visitors who learn about it through the area's extensive national marketing program, ads in major ski publications, an active group sales program and through the area's clever Internet site.

Founded in 1956 by Swiss skier and entrepreneur Ernie Blake and now run by his family, Taos Ski Valley established its fame on the challenge of its terrain and the European quality of the resort itself. With a base elevation of 9,207 feet and a peak elevation of 11,819 feet, Taos has a vertical drop of 2,612 feet. The longest run is more than 5 miles.

Taos boasts 321 inches of snow a year and is famous for its light, dry powder. The area can supplement nature's efforts with snowmaking on 95 percent of the beginner and intermediate terrain.

To reach the slopes, the area offers skiers four quad lifts, a triple, five doubles and a surface lift. The 11 lifts can handle 15,300 skiers per hour — the largest skier capacity of any New Mexico ski area. Al's Run, directly under

the No. 5 lift, is a marathon of bumps where you'll find hard-core, hard-muscled mogul hounds. Taos offers chutes, bowls and ski runs you have take off your skis and hike to. Experts who enjoy a challenge love to ski the ridge, an area above the named runs that involves a strenuous, high-altitude climb before you start to ski.

Although the mountain is a skilled skier's paradise, there's more than enough terrain here for beginners and intermediates. Of the 72 named runs, 49 percent are ranked as "blues" or "greens."

While some who ski here go home with stories of the steep High Traverse or the powder challenge on Lower Stauffenberg, others can speak of their skiing breakthroughs during the Learn to Ski and Learn to Ski Better weeks. *Snow Country Magazine* has ranked Taos' Ernie Blake Ski School as one of the best in the United States. The Ski Week programs, offered throughout the season, match students of similar ability with a teacher who can help them move on to the next level of skiing. Taos also offers special programs for women, older skiers and teens and has Super Ski Weeks for intermediate or advanced skiers who want intensive drills and exercises and specific instructions in racing, moguls and adventure skiing. You can also take a class or a workshop in telemark or mogul skiing. For the most novice, Taos's traditional Yellowbird Programs cater to first- and second-day skiers with morning and afternoon lessons, a lift ticket and a discount on rentals. Private and group lessons are available.

Taos KinderKare provides a safe atmosphere for children six weeks to 2 years of age at $55 per day. The Junior Elite ski program teaches youngsters ages 3 to 12 how to ski. The children's programs have an 18,000-square-foot center with its own ticket counter, ski rental and accessory shop, and cafeteria.

Recent improvements at the area include reshaping and recontouring some runs to improve skiing and reduce congestion. Taos also added a new teen lift ticket to make family skiing more affordable.

What hasn't changed here is the prohibition of snowboarders. Taos is one of the few areas in the country where skiers don't have to share the slopes. The area has an independent, noncorporate spirit — in addition to the Blake family, other skiing families own the lodges in the valley, and there's not a franchise outfit among them. Most of the innkeepers, not surprisingly, are skiers themselves who found the valley's conditions irresistible.

As if the skiing itself wasn't enough, special events add to the area's attraction. In mid-December, Taos Ski Valley offers a Brewmaster's Festival at the Resort Center featuring about 25 New Mexico, Colorado, Utah and Wyoming microbrews. Participants can sample food from local restaurants, enjoy live entertainment and take home a souvenir glass, all for the price of admission ($15 in 1997). The area's most popular tradition, the Winter Wine Festival during the third week in January, is one of the oldest ski/wine festivals in the country. Started in 1985, the weeklong festival involves some 20 winemakers and includes on-mountain tastings, seminars, winemaker dinners and Le Grande Tasting, which includes food from local restaurants. A ski and golf weekend in mid-March is open to four-person teams.

At the Resort Center, you'll find places to purchase equipment and sportswear and to rent skis, boots and poles, including high-performance and demo models. You can eat at Tenderfoot Katie's Cafeteria or on the Longhorn Barbecue deck. At the Martini Tree Bar, you can have a cocktail and listen to live music. Affordable family dining is a tradition at Rhoda's Restaurant. You can also eat at two on-mountain restaurants, The Phoenix and Whistlestop Cafe.

You can stay in slope-side accommodations within walking distance of the lifts or elsewhere in the valley. You'll find about 20 lodges, but no high rises. Most lodges have their own restaurants and offer après-ski and evening entertainment. Another popular option is to stay in the town of Taos and ride the shuttle to the ski valley and back.

With more than 80 galleries, seven museums and numerous restaurants serving traditional northern New Mexican cuisine and gourmet fare, the nearby town of Taos certainly adds to the skier's overall experience — and gives nonskiers plenty to do. The shops here offer high-quality weaving, furniture, pottery, jewelry and more. And historic Taos Pueblo, which provides guided tours, is just a short drive away.

Adult all-day all-lift tickets cost $40. Half-day tickets, morning or afternoon, are $27. Super seniors, ages 70 and older, ski free; seniors age 65 to 69 pay $25 for all-day, all-lift tickets. Teens (age 13 to 16) ski for $30 all day or $21 for a half-day. For children (age 12 and younger) all-day, all-lift tickets are $25 and half-day tickets are $19. Taos offers lower rates on lift tickets from late November until mid-December and for the last two weeks of the season. It also adds $5 to lift-ticket prices from December 27 through 31.

Equipment rental per day for skis, boots and poles is $11 for adults and $7 for children. Junior Elite ski school for ages 3 to 12 costs $66 a day with instruction, lifts and lunch. Shuttles from town are $5 a person one way.

Cross-Country Skiing, Snowshoeing and Snowplay

You can snowshoe and cross-country ski on many hiking trails in the Santa Fe area and throughout northern New Mexico. For novice cross-country skiers or families with small children, the Black Canyon Trail in Hyde Park near Santa Fe may provide an enjoyable outing. This 1-mile round-trip route offers nice scenery, gentle to moderate slopes and picnic tables where you can enjoy lunch. Slightly more experienced skiers head for the Aspen Vista Road, just past Hyde Park on N.M. 475 on the way to the Santa Fe Ski Area. You'll get to practice your uphill technique as you climb from 10,000 to 12,000 feet in about 6 miles. Coming back can be a fast trip!

Due to improvements in equipment and a growing desire to get away from it all in the winter, snowshoeing has become increasingly popular. Snowshoe construction has improved, resulting in lighter shoes with curled toes that don't get buried in the powder. Aluminum and synthetic decking has improved flotation over the snow. Sporting goods stores that sell or rent this equipment — and who may carry state-of-the-art demo models — often can give you advice on where to go. Of-

Angel Fire is an excellent ski area for families and beginners.

ten, the technicians and staff members at these stores are fanatic outdoors people. Don't hesitate to ask them for their suggestions and their favorite runs. You'll also find several guidebooks to cross-country skiing available locally. Santa Fe Community College offers classes that will teach you Nordic skiing and show you some good places to try your new skills.

Capulin Springs
Cross Country Ski Area
and Capulin Snowplay Area
60 miles south of Santa Fe, 1.5 miles past Sandia Park Ski Area on N.M. Hwy. 536 • 384-2209, (800) 484-2319 code 8754

At Capulin skiers will find a 10-kilometer groomed trail system with set tracks and a skating lane. You can also rent snowshoes and enjoy snowplay and tubing areas for the whole family. In the Cibola National Forest, Capulin offers skiers panoramic views from trails that wind through the Douglas fir, ponderosa pine and aspen forests.

Tubing is available on two architecturally designed hills — a big hill and the toddler's hill, both of which are shaped and supervised for safety. The snow is groomed by machine to smooth out the bumps. Use of the hills is limited to tubes and soft snowplay equipment to keep visitors safe.

If you get hungry, you can get a bite to eat or a drink at the area snack bar. Capulin is usually open from mid-December through mid-March, depending on the snow conditions. It operates Wednesday through Sunday except for the Christmas holiday break, when the area is open daily. Capulin is open all holidays. Ask about bargain days, free snowshoe demonstrations, passes for seniors and other specials. Capulin offers morning and afternoon lessons for children and adults.

Use of the track costs $5 for adults and $3 for children 12 and younger. Rental of boots, skis and poles is $12.50 for adults and $10.50 for children and seniors. A combination package with rentals, lessons and a trail pass is

$25. A beginner package with equipment rental and a lesson is also $25. An all-day tubing ticket is $2 for ages 12 and younger and $3 for adults. Tube rental is $5 a day, and helmets are $2. All-day secure, patrolled parking is $4 per space.

Enchanted Forest
Cross Country Ski Area
106 miles from Santa Fe, 3.5 miles east of Red River on N.M. Hwy. 38 • 754-2374 (Miller's Crossing ski store)

You'll find 36 kilometers of 12-foot-wide trails at Enchanted Forest, a five-minute drive from the heart of the village of Red River. New Mexico's largest full-service cross-country ski area, it offers groomed and natural trails through 1,400 acres of aspen groves and sweeping meadows in the Carson National Forest. The area usually opens before Thanksgiving and serves skiers into April, depending on the weather.

Skiers can explore 32 courses, mainly trails winding through the trees. The system is groomed with one side tracked for diagonal stride (the more conventional cross-country skiing) and the other side smooth for snowshoeing and freestyle or skate-skiing. You'll cruise on trails such as Face Flop Drop and Jabberwocky and find warming huts stocked with snacks and hot drinks along the way. The alpine vistas and the solitude of the Rocky Mountain forest is spectacular. The Enchanted Forest receives an average of 240 inches of snow a year — about two feet more than the Red River Ski Area.

Owners John and Judy Miller opened the area in 1985 with a special-use permit from the Carson National Forest and have been catering to cross-country skiers and their families ever since.

For beginners or skiers new to the area, the best place to start is at Miller's Crossing, the in-town headquarters at 212 W. Main Street in Red River. You can rent equipment, make arrangements for instruction and even line up a ride to the area if you're a beginner, a spe-

INSIDERS' TIP

Anyone who can prove he or she is president of something skis free on President's Day at Sipapu.

Photo: Don Strel/Southwest Assignments

Swooshing down a snowy mountainside will take your breath away.

cial service offered to encourage people to try the sport. The shop also offers advice on waxing and will tune your skis. In addition to Nordic skiing, Enchanted Forest has snowshoeing, sledding, and backcountry and high-performance skiing. Special events at Enchanted Forest include a *luminaria* tour on Christmas day and moonlight ski tours on the Saturdays closest to the full moon.

Passes are $10 for adults, $7 for teens (age 13 to 18) and seniors and $3 for children age 12 and younger. Skiers older than 60 pay $6, and those older than 70 ski free. Rentals are $10.50 for adults and $7 for children 12 and younger. A child's learn-to-ski package is $23.

Ski/Snowboard Shops

In addition to these shops, all in Santa Fe, you can rent equipment at all New Mexico ski areas. You'll also find private ski shops in Taos, Angelfire, Los Alamos, Albuquerque and elsewhere.

Alpine Sports
121 Sandoval St. • 983-5155

In business for more than 30 years, Alpine Sports is a full-service sporting goods store. Upstairs you'll discover a fine selection of new, top-of-the-line equipment, ski wear, sportswear and accessories. Downstairs in the rental department, you'll find all kinds of winter-sports equipment — Nordic and alpine skis, snowboards and snowshoes. Ask about group rates. Alpine's staff includes seasoned skiers who know how to match customers to equipment. The shop has skilled boot fitters at your service.

Base Camp
322 Montezuma Ave. • 982-9707

This long-established, full-service shop is the winter headquarters for cross-country and telemark skiing equipment, snowshoes of all sorts and stuff to keep you warm. Base Camp does not rent equipment for alpine skiing. It's also known for wilderness gear and fly-fishing paraphernalia. You'll find information about good places to cross-country ski, and the knowledgeable staff can steer you toward clinics, lessons or workshops to improve your technique. In addition to rentals, this shop sells everything from socks to mountaineering equipment.

Beyond Waves Mountain Surf Shop
333 Montezuma Ave. • 988-2240

This store caters to snowboarders. You can rent or buy Avalanche boards as well as outerwear and boots, hats, sunglasses and other accessories. The shop will also wax, base, tune and repair your snowboard.

Bike'n Sport
521 St. Francis Dr. • 820-0809

Snowshoes are a winter specialty here, with many different types available for rent or sale. You'll also find a nice selection of cross-country skis, telemark equipment and snowboards with the latest in bindings and boots. Bike'n Sport, a full-line mountain bike shop in the summer, also carries clothing and accessories. The staff can offer you plenty of suggestions on where to take your snowshoes for a day of fun.

Cottam's Ski Rentals
Hyde Park Rd. • 982-0495

This stone house in Hyde Park, right along the highway, offers a range of high-performance ski equipment, snowboards, children's equipment and even some sleds. In addition to downhill skis and snowboards for children

and adults, you'll also find waxless cross-country skis for rent. The shop offers complete ski tuning. Cottam's also has four stores in Taos and a shop in Albuquerque.

Santa Fe Mountain Sports
518 Old Santa Fe Tr. • 988-3337

Outdoor sports enthusiasts of all varieties will find something to their liking at Santa Fe Mountain Sports. In addition to a fully stocked retail store, Mountain Sports has rentals galore — downhill ski equipment including high-performance super side-cut skis, snowboards by Killer Loop and Rosignol, snowshoes and cross-country skis. The shop will even do rentals for children for an entire ski season. You can get binding adjustments, ski repair and tune ups in its full-service shop. If you ask, the staff will give you tips on where to snowshoe or ski. In the summer, look for bike rentals.

Ski Tech Ski Rentals
905 St. Francis Dr. • 983-5512

This family-owned business specializes in service and has been serving Santa Fe skiers for about 10 years. You can rent all the ski equipment you need as well as adult-size jackets, pants and bibs. In addition to an assortment of downhill skis, you'll find snowboards and cross-country equipment. The full-service shop offers ski repair, tune ups, binding adjustments and overnight service. In addition to the St. Francis Drive store, Ski Tech also offers rentals at the Glorieta Conference Center in Glorieta and at Fort Marcy Compound, 320 Artist Road.

The Skiers Edge
1836 Cerrillos Rd. • 983-1025

You'll discover a selection of K2 and Avalanche snowboards here as well as skis to suit all levels and ages including high-performance models and parabolics. The shop gets new equipment annually. You can rent bibs and powder pants to keep the cold out. The Skiers Edge sells equipment and accessories.

Wild Mountain Outfitters
541 W. Cordova Rd. • 986-1152

This is one of the biggest ski shops in Santa Fe specializing in cross-country and telemark equipment. You'll find new and rental skis as well as snowshoes. The shop offers a basic touring rental package and new demo skis for customers considering purchasing new equipment. Wild Mountain Outfitters also sells clothing, accessories and gear of all sorts. You'll find a nice selection of books on cross-country skiing and telemarking here as well as mountain guide books about skiing in other states. The management suggests reservations for equipment rental on weekends.

Rodeo de Santa Fe brings well-trained cow ponies and the professional cowboys and barrel racers who ride them to compete for honor, glory and even a little cash.

Spectator Sports

The arts, not sports, draw the spectators in Santa Fe. Next in spectator popularity comes the state legislature's annual session and Santa Fe City Council's twice-a-month meetings. And Santa Fe parents and grandparents turn out with enthusiasm to see their offspring play high school baseball, soccer, basketball and football.

Other than that, spectator sports here mean horses. Rodeo de Santa Fe brings well-trained cow ponies and the professional cowboys and barrel racers who ride them to compete for honor, glory and even a little cash. At the Downs at Santa Fe, you'll see sleek quarter horses and thoroughbreds run for the money.

New Mexico's largest spectator event, the International Balloon Fiesta, comes to Albuquerque each October, bringing with it more than a million spectators from throughout the United States and around the world. The Balloon Fiesta helps fill Santa Fe's hotels and restaurants and draws visitors to the city's attractions.

To watch traditional sports such as hockey, college basketball and minor league baseball, Santa Feans travel to Albuquerque, which is about 60 miles away.

Here's the rundown of major spectator sports in Santa Fe and Albuquerque. Please call for specific schedule information.

Santa Fe

Rodeo de Santa Fe
Santa Fe Rodeo Grounds, Rodeo Rd. at Richards Ave. • 471-4300

Santa Fe loves its rodeo and has supported this event since 1949. Sanctioned by the Professional Rodeo Cowboys Association, the rodeo runs for four days and traditionally opens the Thursday after the Fourth of July weekend.

You'll find all the required competitions here — bareback and saddle bronc riding, steer wrestling, barrel racing and the ever-popular bull riding. Cowboys come from throughout the Southwest to test their skill, and the rodeo also attracts a fair share of local talent. Unlike most professional sports, the cowboys aren't paid. Not only do they have to come up with their own entry fees, but they also cover the cost of transporting and feeding their horses, overnight rooms, medical and rehab bills and all other expenses. For some, a good year is breaking even. Those who don't place in the money go home with only their memories — and the appreciation of the Santa Fe audience.

The rodeo features evening shows and a matinee. A rodeo queen and princess are crowned one evening, and the royalty from

Fiesta de Santa Fe are featured guests at another performance (see our Annual Events chapter).

Rodeo de Santa Fe has always welcomed families. Some little buckaroos watch from right behind the fence. Kids can compete in mutton busting, which gives them a chance to ride a bucking sheep. Or they can join a calf scramble, the goal of which is to capture a red ribbon from the tail of a uncooperative calf.

Before the rodeo starts, there's live entertainment on the grounds, and you can buy the food that goes with the fun — burgers, hot dogs, popcorn, cotton candy, cold drinks and hot coffee. Ticket prices range from $4 to $14, with a limited number of box seats available. Parking is free.

The rodeo is the centerpiece of Western Days in Santa Fe, a summer festival that celebrates Santa Fe's Western heritage. (See our Annual Events chapter.)

Albuquerque

International Balloon Fiesta
Balloon Fiesta State Park, Osuna Rd. near I-25, Albuquerque • 821-1000

Some 1.5 million people visit to watch about 1,000 balloons, including some whimsical special shapes. Attractions include four mass ascensions that fill the sky with color, evening balloon glows, special shape "rodeos" and contests that test pilots' skills. See our Annual Events chapter for more information.

Albuquerque Dukes Baseball
Albuquerque Sports Stadium, University and Cesar Chavez Blvds., Albuquerque • 243-1791

The Albuquerque Dukes have been a top farm club of the Los Angeles Dodgers since

FYI

Unless otherwise noted, the area code for all phone numbers listed in this guide is 505.

1972. As a Class AAA franchise, one of only 28 in North America, the Dukes are just a heartbeat away from the major leagues. During the club's existence, the Dukes have won eight Pacific Coast League Championships, more than any other team in the league.

Many Albuquerque Dukes have been called up to play for the Dodgers, including four of the last five National League Rookies of the Year. Even Dukes' managers have gone on to the major leagues, including Tommy Lasorda, who managed the Dukes in 1972. World Series Most Valuable Player John Wetteland played with the Dukes for the 1989-91 seasons.

The Dukes play from April through August with a home schedule of about 70 games. They play afternoon and evening games and double hitters. The team is big on promotions — group outings for businesses, give-aways for kids and fun stuff for the whole family.

Tickets are $5 for box seats and $4 for general admission. You can also watch the game from your car or on a picnic blanket in the outfield drive-in area.

Lobos Football and Basketball
University Stadium (football) or University Arena (basketball), University and Cesar Chavez Blvds., Albuquerque • 925-LOBO, 925-5626

The Lobos may be the University of New Mexico's team, but Albuquerque loves them. So do UNM alumni around the state — and anyone who's looking for good college ball. As members of the Western Athletic Conference, the Lobos face tough competitors, and the crowd appreciates their fighting spirit. In recent seasons under coach Dave Bliss, the Lobos men's basketball team has placed near the top of the WAC rankings and gone on to do well in national tournaments. Men's bas-

INSIDERS' TIP

Don't let clouds scare you away from a Rodeo de Santa Fe matinee. Even if the stadium is blessed with an afternoon rain, it's usually over in less than 20 minutes. Depending on how hard it rains, the rodeo may proceed through the showers — with the cowboys and the stock grateful for the cooler temperatures.

Cowboys from throughout the Southwest test their skills at Rodeo de Santa Fe.

Photo: Don Strel/Southwest Assignments

ketball begins in mid-November and ends in mid-March. In 1996 and 1997, the Lobos played in the prestigious NCAA competition, where they faced some of the best teams in the country.

The Lobos play all home games in University Arena, fondly known as The Pit. A game in the Pit is a worthy experience even if, God forbid, the Lobos lose. There's not a bad seat in the house, although some are a long view to the floor. Lobos fans are famous for their rousing support, which is recorded on a noise meter that's part of the scoreboard. The volume can go to the top of the scale during

games with the Lobos' major rivals, Utah, University of Texas at El Paso and Arizona. Luc Longley, who now plays for the champion Chicago Bulls, played college ball here. Because of the Lobos men's basketball success in recent years, games may sell out. If you think you'll be around to watch, call to check on ticket availability and make a reservation.

Football, with a season that runs from late August to November, is the second-most popular campus sport. On warm fall days fans come early to enjoy tailgate picnics in the parking lot. Stoney Case, now with the Arizona Cardinals, was the most recent Lo-

The University of New Mexico has first-rate college football and basketball, and in recent years placed in the top 20.

bos player to go on to the pros. Terance Mathis and David Sloan also played football here. The Lobos play both afternoon and evening games. It can get chilly at night or late in the season, so bring a blanket. Early season afternoon games can be hot, so bring your hat and sunscreen. Welcome to New Mexico!

Tickets for both football and basketball are $11 for reserved adult seats. Parking is free, but unless you come early, expect to walk a block or so to the stadiums. Game-day traffic can be intense. If you're driving from Santa Fe, leave two hours before game time.

In addition to men's basketball and football, UNM offers many other sporting events at which spectators are welcome, among then women's basketball and men's baseball.

New Mexico Scorpions Hockey Club

Tingley Coliseum, New Mexico State Fair Grounds, 300 San Pedro N.E., Albuquerque • 232-PUCK, (800) 4-SCORPS

The Scorpions, New Mexico's first-ever hockey team, played their inaugural season in 1996-97 as one of the six original teams in the new Western Professional Hockey League. They made their debut with 10 consecutive victories. The Scorps competition includes the Austin Ice Bats, Amarillo Rattlers and the El Paso Buzzards. Former Albuquerque Duke John Wetteland is one of the team's co-owners.

The team plays more than 60 games a season, half at home and half on the road. The season runs from mid October to early May. The Scorpions transform Tingley Coliseum, which hosts the New Mexico State Fair Rodeo and rock concerts, into an hockey stadium for their games. What a surprise to find ice where sawdust used to be!

The Scorpions practice at Blades Multiplex in Rio Rancho just west of Albuquerque. To help the sport grow in New Mexico, they offer clinics for coaches and kids and a free guide to help New Mexicans follow the action. The Scorpions' free brochure, "A Fan's Guide to the Coolest Game in the Desert" explains the rules, the equipment and the officials' calls. Among other things, the publication gives a short history of hockey. It claims that an Indian tribe in Eastern Canada originated the modern sport as a ball and stick game played on icy ponds. Its name came from the cries of "Ho Ghee" (meaning "it hurts") whenever a player was accidently hit with a stick.

Tickets range from $5 to $18. Parking is free.

Like Santa Fe itself, the real estate market here is eclectic, diversified, sophisticated and, compared to many other places in the country, expensive.

Real Estate

Let's assume, for a happy moment, that not only have you decided to move to Santa Fe, but also you can spend as much or as little as you decide on your housing. Among the options:

• You can buy a quaint old adobe in walking distance to the Plaza.

• You can live in a house with property that gives you access to the Santa Fe River or a historic *acequia*, or irrigation ditch.

• You can settle into a neighborhood with sidewalks, paved streets and potential friends for your children right next door.

• You can buy in an area with hiking trails, parks and other amenities.

• You might purchase a 10-acre lot, hire an architect and use a custom builder to create the best of Santa Fe style.

• You could fall in love with a new, energy-efficient house at the end of a bumpy dirt road with gorgeous views and plenty of privacy.

• You could relocate to a condominium development complete with full-time security, a health club and a dining room.

• You might live in a mobile home park or an apartment complex.

• Or, you could choose to move to a ranch with horses and maybe even llamas and buffalo.

Like Santa Fe itself, the real estate market here is eclectic, diversified, sophisticated and, compared to many other places in the country, expensive. Real estate is big business in Santa Fe and — because of Santa Fe's impact as the state capital and a trend-setter — throughout much of northern New Mexico.

Look in the Santa Fe phone book and you'll find 13 pages of advertising listings for real estate agents and companies. The Santa Fe Association of Realtors has 650 members, all of whom are sincerely interested in making a living in the profession.

The Financial Picture

The early 1990s brought a flood of buyers to Santa Fe's real estate market. Demand was high, and prices skyrocketed. Houses sold quickly, and customers had to act fast, often at full listing price, to get the home they wanted. The market has gotten better for buyers since 1993-94 when homes reached peak prices.

Santa Fe isn't quite the hot spot it once was. For the first quarter of 1997, for example, information from the Santa Fe Association of Realtors showed that the median price for homes sold in the city of Santa Fe had dipped from $165,000 for that period the previous year to $156,000. That compares with an average of $200,000 for the entire year of 1995.

Outside the city limits, Santa Fe County median prices remained level for the quarter at $215,000. For the first half of 1997, 276 homes sold within the city, compared to 272 for the first half of 1996. Santa Fe County statistics show 176 units sold for the first half of 1997, compared to 189 units for the same time the prior year.

In late 1997, buyers had their pick of plenty of property on the market, inside and outside the city limits. They could choose from: 305 listings below $150,000; 645 listings between

---

INSIDERS' TIP

The great 20th-century architect Frank Lloyd Wright designed only one adobe house, the Pottery House, which was eventually built on a hillside overlooking Santa Fe. The owner purchased the plans from the Frank Lloyd Wright Foundation and construction began in 1984. The home is shaped like a football.

$150,000 and $300,000; 316 listings between $300,000 and $500,000; 151 listings between $500,000 and $750,000; 72 listings between $750,000 and $1 million; and 81 listings above $1 million — an all time high for that price range. Agents dealing with the most expensive properties note that Santa Fe competes for buyers in this price range with places such as Aspen and Telluride, Colorado, and Jackson Hole, Wyoming. These communities have become so expensive that some buyers now see Santa Fe's million-dollar properties as a bargain.

In July 1997, 143 homes sold in Santa Fe and the surrounding areas, according to data from the Multiple Listing Service reports of the Santa Fe Association of Realtors. Six of those homes sold for more than a million dollars; 10 of them were purchased for less than $100,000.

The 1997 real estate market could be described as slow, sometimes uneven, but benefitting from low interest rates and buyer demands. Prices seem to have stabilized, Realtors report, with buyers in control. Third-quarter sales showed an increase of 7 percent, and median sales price was $185,000 — a 3 percent increase over the same period in 1996.

"There's a huge inventory of property for sale and I think it will be a long time until prices rise," Realtor Susan Varela said. "Land sales have suffered even more than home sales. Because prices for homes are so low, people can buy a home already built for less than they can buy the land and build their own home."

An Overview

Merrily Pierson, president of the Santa Fe Association of Realtors in 1997, noted that in Santa Fe, location probably has the single biggest impact on a property's price. Whereas in many communities proximity to downtown is a negative factor, in Santa Fe it's a strong selling point.

"Values in Santa Fe are relative to the dis-tance a home is from the Plaza," Pierson said. "The closer to the Plaza, the more a home is worth. For resale appreciation, a buyer is smarter to purchase a house that needs work in a good location rather than a better house farther from the Plaza."

But property values are not simply equated with a home's location and size. They are also determined by views, open space, lack of highway noise, established landscaping and "Santa Fe style" — smooth plaster walls, *vigas*, *bancos*, tile floors and other amenities. (See our close-up in this chapter for more on Santa Fe style.) Santa Fe style can be found in homes of every price range.

For many buyers, the biggest surprise is what their money will buy. The real estate dollar doesn't stretch far here. Most Realtors can tell stories of newcomers who see the east side, one of the city's most prestigious areas, and think they've discovered it. Surely, they think, we'll find a bargain here, a little fixer-upper. And they're more than surprised at the $200 to $300 per square foot price these homes sell for.

Other newcomers are surprised to learn that Santa Fe has no industrial section where they can find a building to remodel into lofts. Still others find it odd to discover homes worth a half-million dollars or more down dusty dirt roads.

In recent years, thanks to initiatives involving the City of Santa Fe, Santa Fe County and private agencies, more housing is available for Santa Fe's working families of average income. In Tierra Contenta, one of the city's newest neighborhoods, three-bedroom, two-bath homes sell for between $120,000 and $160,000. Builders in this neighborhood use the latest techniques to come up with a high-quality home at lower per-foot cost.

What are Santa Fe's desirable areas? Well, it depends on what you want and how much you can spend. A buyer for whom money is no object might select a golf course home at Las Campanas or a historic east side adobe

— or make one of several other wonderful choices. A person who's minding a budget might buy a great house with a convenient location in Tierra Contenta, settle into the more suburban Eldorado area or come up with a fine house elsewhere in the city or county. Buyers looking for homes on larger acreage concentrate their search beyond the city limits. Some have begun exploring areas such as Galisteo, Lamy and La Cienega.

Some Things to Consider

In her book, *Understanding and Buying Santa Fe Real Estate*, Realtor Karen Walker offers some advice for potential real estate buyers. Here are a few of her observations:

• Before you make a commitment, ask to see and take time to read any restrictive covenants from neighborhood associations. Educate yourself about zoning and building regulations from the city and county that apply to the area you're considering. Don't assume that you can build a guest house, put up outside lights or paint your window frames green.

Examples of city or county restrictions are the escarpment ordinance, which restricts building on hillsides; terrain management requirements, which govern the building of roads and structures on steep terrain; and historic district requirements that dictate what kinds of changes can be made to the exteriors of vintage buildings. Building code and zoning restraints may require setbacks of construction from lot lines and might limit the percentage of your building site you can cover with "improvements." Both the city and the county have archaeological ordinances that require researchers to be informed if you find Indian pottery, bones or other ancient artifacts on the site where you planned to build your dream house.

Santa Fe's City Hall takes its zoning regulations seriously. A few years ago a homeowner was required to remove a third story he'd added because the construction violated the city's height restrictions for his neighborhood.

• Buyers looking at property should make sure that they'll have access to it. Don't assume that because you drove there, the road will be yours along with the land. Also, ask if the area has plans for any new roads, which could have an impact on your property in terms of noise, dust or access.

• Views, a strong selling point for some Santa Fe properties, can come with a down side — wind and noise. Often, the same lot placement that gives a home a nice look at the mountains or the lights of the city leaves the place exposed to the wind. With Santa Fe's prevailing westerly winds, the traffic sounds will travel to the east.

• If land near the home or lot you're considering is vacant, ask what the owner plans for it and what kind of structure could be built there. Your neighbor could one day be a convenience store!

• Find out if the lot has city water and sewer service. Much of the property in the northern quadrants of the city is not connected to city sewer even though it is inside the city limits. Instead, septic systems serve these homes. Some of the land in the eastern and southeastern parts of the city has neither city sewer nor city water; you'll need a well and a septic system here. Speaking of water, you won't find many homes with pools in the Santa Fe area, partly because the climate only allows a few months of outdoor swimming and partly because of the region's concerns about water availability and focus on water conservation.

• The higher in elevation your home is, the more snow you'll encounter. Notice the number of four-wheel-drive vehicles on Santa Fe's streets? Many of these aren't just for show — the drivers need them to get home after a storm. If you're looking at property in the summer, be sure to ask what the roads are like in the winter.

• The older the home you buy, the more it will cost to heat and keep up unless it has been renovated and insulated. Santa Fe charm comes at a price.

Rentals

A recent survey of the Santa Fe rental market revealed that the city had about 12,000 rental units, including some 2,000 mobile homes. Fortunately for renters, the glut of property on the market for sale has greatly improved the rental situation, creating more options and making landlords compete for customers and provide better service.

In addition to single-family homes available for rent throughout the city, Santa Fe has some apartment complexes. There are roughly 25 apartment complexes with 30 units or more as well as seven complexes with more than 200 rental units. Apartments and rental homes are scattered around the city, but the largest concentration of apartment complexes can be found in the Zia Road, Airport Road, St. Francis Drive, Rodeo Road and in the southern part of town. Among the choices are Shadowridge, 941 Calle Mejia; Dos Santos, 2210 San Miguel Chavez Road; Rancho Vizcaya Apartments, 2500 Sawmill Road; Tierra de Zia Apartments, 2600 W. Zia Road; and Zia Vista Apartments at 2501 W. Zia Road.

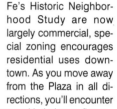

www.insiders.com

See this and many other **Insiders' Guide®** destinations online — in their entirety.

Visit us today!

In the late 1980s and early 1990s, Santa Fe real estate was hot, and rentals were both expensive and harder to find. But in August 1994 — about the same time that the real estate market dropped — a slump in rental activities began.

"Sometimes people may find that it's difficult to get what they're looking for in Santa Fe's rental market, but that may be because they're looking for something that isn't realistic," Patty Ashton of Cyrano's property management company said. "They want a place with three bedrooms and two baths in walking distance to downtown for $800 a month."

She advises people looking for property to rent to get the newspaper early, check the classified ads and begin making calls at 7 AM. A two- or three-bedroom home for rent in the $800 to $1,100 price range will go quickly.

In a complex of 30 units or more, average rent for a one-bedroom apartment is $525. For an efficiency apartment, it's hard to find anything lower than $500. Prices rise from there, depending on size and location. At the other end of the scale, you'll find a custom 5,000-square-foot house renting for $5,000 a month.

In Santa Fe, incidently, the market is its own rent control. When there's plenty of prop-

erty for rent, the owners or their agents may be inclined to lower the cost. And if there's more demand than units available, landlords won't be in the mood to dicker on price.

Santa Fe Neighborhoods

Santa Fe was born around the Plaza and along the Santa Fe River, and the city's oldest neighborhoods are downtown. People have been living in the Barrio Analco area, for example, since the city's founding in 1610. Although this area and many of the 12 other neighborhoods included in the City of Santa Fe's Historic Neighborhood Study are now largely commercial, special zoning encourages residential uses downtown. As you move away from the Plaza in all directions, you'll encounter newer residential areas with their own flavor.

Unlike many communities, Santa Fe generally defines its neighborhoods in terms of geographical locations rather than specific streets, parks, the names of builders or subway stops. The developers of newer subdivisions name their projects, but these "neighborhoods" are the exception. Because of Santa Fe's long history of Catholicism, many people were more likely to identify themselves in terms of the parish where they went to church rather than the neighborhood, and parish boundaries included many different neighborhoods.

In Santa Fe, more so than in many communities in the country, the housing tends to look similar in many sections of town. This is Santa Fe style in its variations. (Please see our close-up in this chapter.) You will, however, find some differences. Generally, more expensive neighborhoods offer more acreage with your home. But this isn't necessarily true on the east side, where a home worth a half-million dollars or more may have little accompanying land. One of the charming quirks of the city's older neighborhoods, and a part of Santa Fe that is disappearing with its growth, is that a million-dollar home may be next to a less expensive house, built by its owners and their children. This economic mix has been replicated in some of the city's newer devel-

Photo: Chris Corrie

The backdrop of the Sangre de Cristo Mountains adds
to the attraction of many Santa Fe properties.

opments, which advertise the diversity of single-family homes at a variety of prices, with townhouses and apartments as one of their drawing cards. Both Tierra Contenta, Santa Fe's affordable housing development, and the upper-end Frijoles Village advertise a return to diversity as part of their attraction.

Some of Santa Fe's residential areas have sidewalks, paved streets, parks and other amenities. Other homes — including million-dollar estates — lie off dirt roads with no curbs or gutters, no parks and no bus service.

Here's a brief guide to Santa Fe's residential areas. Prices were accurate as of late 1997.

Downtown/East Side

Unlike many cities, Santa Fe's downtown, which includes the areas closest to the Plaza, is a prestigious place to live. This historic area, surrounded by winding streets, galleries and towering old trees, is a mixture of historic homes that have been restored and modest houses that haven't been prettied up. The boundaries overlap with the east side, South Capitol area and Guadalupe Street, but to the north E. Palace Avenue, with its big cotton-woods and Spanish Pueblo- and Territorial-style homes set back from the street, is one of the area's trademarks and boundaries.

Guadalupe Street defines the downtown area to the west. The median home price range in this area is $349,122.

Styles tend to be more eclectic downtown than on the adjoining east side. You'll find stone houses as well as vintage hybrids that blend Santa Fe style and Western ranch design. Because the downtown area is largely commercial, residential property here is at a premium.

If you live downtown, you can take your morning jog along the Santa Fe River, stop in a cafe for coffee and a muffin and do gourmet grocery shopping at Kaune Food Town, 511 Old Santa Fe Trail. You can walk to the Plaza. You'll have easy access to the Santa Fe River Park along Alameda Street (from Palace Avenue to Agua Fría/Guadalupe streets), with its picnic tables and walking path, and to quiet Hillside Park, 301 E. Marcy Street, with its statue of late Santa Fe artist Tommy Macaione. If you work at City Hall, the main post office or for the state in any of its downtown offices, you can stroll home for lunch.

The city keeps a close eye on construction, remodeling and renovation in this area to preserve Santa Fe's historic feel. Don't buy a home in any of the city's historic neighborhoods and plan on major new construction, demolition or extensive renovation unless you have the time, money and inclination to follow all the rules.

The east side is marked by real adobe houses on narrow, twisting streets. It's one of Santa Fe's most expensive areas with prices rising to $200 per square foot or higher. But not everyone who lives here is rich. Many of the homes are owned by families who bought or built them before Santa Fe became chic. The boundaries here are nebulous, but Old Santa Fe Trail to the west and Camino Cabra to the east are the general markers. Camino San Acacio, Camino Don Miguel, Canyon Road, Acequia Madre, Garcia Street and Camino del Monte Sol are among the neighborhood's defining streets.

You don't get earth-shaking views or huge estates in the heart of the east side, but, as some people see it, you get something better: an old Santa Fe neighborhood and genuine charm. The classic adobe look of the east side has influenced much of contemporary Santa Fe's construction. The city's oldest and best preserved Pueblo and Territorial architecture is within this and the downtown district. Earthtone walls predominate, although you may find some white walls and decorative murals beneath *portals*. Buildings here tend to be true adobe with mud-plaster finish. The historic district ordinance requires that the walls be at least 8 inches thick and specifies that "geometrically straight facade lines shall be avoided" to emphasize the plasticity of the adobe look. The characteristic effect is that of long and low. The two-story construction you'll see is accompanied by setbacks, *portals*, and a second-floor balcony to visually reduce the height and mass of the structure. Roofs tend to be flat with a slight slope. Wooden lintels and other artistic finishing touches enhance many east side homes.

The lower section of Canyon Road is a mixture of businesses and residential buildings and has become increasingly commer-

cial over the past decade. Canyon Road (see our Attractions chapter) offers galleries, shops and restaurants as well as wonderful ambiance. Garcia Street, Delgado Street and Camino del Monte Sol also mix businesses and residences. Acequia Madre is residential except for Acequia Madre Elementary School, 700 Acequia Madre. Patrick Smith Park, 1001 Canyon Road, offers a pleasant expanse of grass for soccer and baseball, picnic spots, swings and basketball courts along the Santa Fe River east of junction of Canyon Road and Acequia Madre.

As you move away from the heart of the east side, the terrain becomes more hilly. Cerro Gordo and Upper Canyon roads are long-established areas where new mansions abut ancient adobe homes. St. John's College, 1160 Camino Cruz Blanca, and Cristo Rey Church, 1120 Canyon Road, are among this area's landmarks. The Wilderness Gate development in the foothills behind St. John's College offers exclusive homes, many with exquisite views of Santa Fe, on multi-acre lots secluded amid the ponderosa pines.

Another relatively definable section of the east side is known as the Museum Area because the Wheelwright Museum of the American Indian, the Museum of International Folk Arts and the Museum of Indian Arts and Culture are all here just off Camino Lejo. (Please see our Attractions chapter.) As late as 1950, much of this rolling, piñon-covered land remained undeveloped. City planners consider the area "visually important" due to its proximity to the east side neighborhoods — and many buyers like it for the same reason. Some lots here may include ruts created by heavy wagons that traveled the historic Santa Fe Trail.

Heading north along the Old Taos Highway, Bishops Lodge Road or Hyde Park Road, you get a sense of the countryside. This area, which is also known as the northeast or the near north side, is more sparsely populated.

You're likely to see jackrabbits and coyotes along the dirt roads. Many of the homes sit on large lots with fine views of the mountains. Townhouses tend to be hidden among piñon and juniper trees or positioned to capture the views. Some of the property borders on *arroyos*, or sandy washes, areas that can be great places for walking as long as it isn't during a rainstorm! You won't find many sidewalks in this part of town. The city's Fort Marcy/Mager's Field Sports Complex, 490 Washington Avenue, is the closest place for kids to swim or play baseball or soccer.

Southeast

This area includes the South Capitol neighborhood, one of Santa Fe's most architecturally diverse areas with lots of seasoned homes and some quaint old apartment buildings. Some residents live in California bungalows, a rarity in Santa Fe. You'll also discover brick homes and even a lawn or two. Old Santa Fe Trail provides the border to the east, and Galisteo Street frames it to the west. Paseo de Peralta and Cordova Road are, roughly, the north and south boundaries. The median home price range in this area of town is $308,875.

This predominantly residential area includes the Don Gaspar Historic District, which was subdivided as a residential development during the 1890s. For the first time in Santa Fe's history, people here were able to build with materials other than stone, wood and adobe, thanks to the railroad. Santa Fe families got to experiment with materials and styles popular in the East, West and Midwest including Italianate, Mansard, Queen Anne and Craftsman Bungalow. You'll find gabled and hipped roofs here, gracefully intermixed among small Santa Fe-style, flat-roofed adobes. The city leaders' strong negative reaction to this imported look sparked renewed interest in preserving Santa Fe's historic adobe architecture.

Chinese elms shade the streets here, and the ground is good for gardens. Wood Gormley Elementary School, 141 E. Booth Street, serves the area. You'll find paved streets, concrete driveways and sidewalks. Continue out Old Santa Fe Trail to the southeast, and you'll come upon homes in a semi-rural area in the piñon and juniper forests of the Sangre de Cristo foothills. Many people who live here have tremendous views of the Sandia and Ortiz Mountains. Much of this land is regulated by strict requirements that limit building on slopes, protect the views of the foothills from town (including limits on glare from windows) and restrict the construction of new roads.

Among the more established residential areas in the southeast section is the Sol y Lomas neighborhood, just across Old Pecos Trail and accessed by Sol y Lomas Road. The neighborhood has a country feeling and expansive homes. The residential area commonly known as the Hospital/E.J. Martinez neighborhood is bordered by Old Santa Fe Trail, St. Francis Drive, Galisteo Street and Cordova Road. It includes three- and four-bedroom homes, most surrounded by native landscaping with some sidewalks and some paved streets. Homes here are graciously set back from the road, and neighbors have an easier opportunity to get to know each other. E.J. Martinez School, 401 W. San Mateo Road, St. Vincent Hospital, which borders the neighborhood at 455 St. Michael's Drive, and the lovely Harvey Cornell Rose Garden, 1203 Galisteo Parkway, are among this area's landmarks.

Farther out old Pecos Trail is Quail Run, a gated condominium development of 265 units from studios up to four-bedroom homes, complete with a health club, restaurant and nine-hole golf course. The majority of people who live here have moved from elsewhere in Santa Fe. Housing choices at Quail Run on the eight units unsold in late 1997 ranged from $375,000 to about $600,000.

Northwest

The oldest of these neighborhoods began as clusters of Hispanic ranches on the outskirts of Santa Fe's more densely developed Plaza area. The land was plotted in long, narrow parcels so the maximum number of owners could have access to the water in the acequias and from the Santa Fe River for their farms and gardens. The earliest houses were constructed of adobe in the traditional Pueblo style and fronted directly onto the narrow dirt streets. In the third quarter of 1997, the homes that sold in this area ranged in price from $103,000 to $224,000.

With the coming of the railroad and construction of its depot and rail yards in the area, the near west side and Guadalupe districts became a core of economic and social activity. As Santa Fe grew during the 20th century, families continued the long-established practice of subdividing their property among descendants. This created the west side's large number of small, oddly shaped lots. You'll notice many owner-built homes here, adding to the eclectic look.

The Guadalupe Street Neighborhood

The Guadalupe area continues as a commercial center with retail shops and restaurants designed to attract both local and visitor business (see our Shopping chapter). It roughly borders both sides of Guadalupe Street from Don Diego Avenue to Agua Fría Street. In addition to old Pueblo-style homes, the Guadalupe area includes bungalows such as those you see in the South Capitol district. The Santuario de Guadalupe, 100 Guadalupe Street, is one of the area's — and Santa Fe's — landmarks.

The Near West Side

About 25 years ago, the construction of St. Francis Drive separated the Guadalupe/near west side district from the west side. Agua Fría Street from Guadalupe Street to St. Francis Drive is the heart of the near west side. The near west side is probably as close as Santa Fe gets to America's perception of "inner city." Because this area contains the least expensive property in what is still considered the downtown area, it has undergone tremendous change in the last decade.

A gentrified adobe, newly replastered and remodeled to include expensive wooden casement windows, may sit next to a home that looks much the same as it did 50 years ago. The Santa Fe Boys and Girls Club, 730 Alto Street, is one of the landmarks of this area.

The West Side

From St. Francis Drive south, the area between Alameda and Agua Fría streets roughly to Hickox Street is known as the West Side. It's an eclectic, nonglitzy family area, characterized by the remnants of its agricultural days. St. Anne's Church, 511 Alicia Street, and Larragoite Elementary School, 1604 Agua Fría Street, are among its landmarks. There's some commercial development mixed with the residential here.

You'll find mid-priced houses along with a scattering of apartments and rental units. Because of the casual zoning, values don't increase as fast on the west side as they do elsewhere. Many Santa Fe natives who grew up here or on the near west side hold fond memories of these neighborhoods.

Casa Solana/ Michelle Drive

Just north of Alameda Street bordered by Solana Drive to the south and St. Francis Drive to the west is Casa Solana, a family area with sidewalks, paved streets and mature landscaping including some beautiful big trees. Here you'll see kids riding their bikes, parents pushing strollers and gray-haired gardeners hard at work. You'll find a real sense of neighborhood here.

Developer Allen Stamm built these homes in the 1960s, and they're beloved for their *vigas*, hardwood floors, fireplaces and solid construction. Gonzales Elementary School, 851 W. Alameda Street, serves this area. For many decades, until the new landfill opened in 1997, Casa Solana did its civic duty by offering a thoroughfare to garbage trucks and people who hauled their own trash up Camino de las Crucitas to the city dump at the intersection of Buckman Road. From the old dump the views soar to 360-degree vistas which encompass the Jémez, Sangre de Cristo, Sandia and Ortiz mountains. A permanent art display made of old refrigerators, "Stonefridge," is scheduled to be installed on the site.

Barrio de la Canada

This small residential area, just off Camino Alire and West Alameda Street, offers family-size homes and quiet streets because of limited access. The neighborhood's Santa Fe style includes decorative elements such as arches, and many homes are framed with native landscaping or small lawns.

Casa Alegre

Bordered by Agua Fría Street to the west, Cerrillos Road to the east with a commercial buffer, San Jose Avenue, to the north and Maes Road to the south, Casa Alegre, also an Allen Stamm project, was built in the 1950s. Although the houses are smaller than those in Casa Solana, they have the same nice amenities. After World War II, the area provided homes to GIs and their families, some of whom still live in the same homes today. The Gregory Lopez Park, 1230 San Felipe Road, gives kids a place to play. The area's landmarks are Salazar Elementary School, 1300 Osage Avenue, and St. John the Baptist Catholic Church, 1301 Osage Avenue, just across the street from the school.

Kaune Neighborhood

Another Stamm family area with parks, schools and churches, Kaune is accessed primarily from Monterey Drive just off Cerrillos Road. The neighborhood is officially known as the Casa Linda neighborhood, but most folks call it the Kaune area because of Kaune Elementary School, 1409 Monterey Drive, which serves the families here. The school, planned by famed Santa Fe architect John Gaw Meem, was named for Alfred Kaune, a past president of the Santa Fe School Board and part of the family that owned Kaune gourmet grocery stores.

The homes here include hardwood floors, *vigas* and other Santa Fe-style amenities. Buyers can chose between Spanish Pueblo, Territorial or California flat roof styles for their homes. The 128 units originally sold for between $9,000 and $14,000 — today you'll easily pay 10 times that price.

West Alameda

From Solano Drive south, West Alameda Street serves as an access road to mixed housing areas. You'll find older, small handmade adobes, manufactured housing and expensive newer construction. As you continue south, you'll discover some designer masterpieces whose very existence bumps the whole area up a notch or two in price. The farther you get from the Plaza, the more rural the area becomes; you'll see horses out here along with some boarding stables. The upscale Puesta del Sol and Piñon Hills developments offer big lots, big views, an openness to variations of Santa Fe style and a country feel.

Southwest

This is the section of Santa Fe where you're most likely to find family-affordable homes and apartments. Most of the construction here is newer, and this part of Santa Fe provides easiest access to Villa Linda Mall, 4250 Cerrillos Road, the Santa Fe Auto Park, 4450 Cerrillos Road, and to Capital High School, 4851 Paseo del Sol. Median home price range here is $136,794.

La Tierra Contenta

The Tierra Contenta neighborhood, part of the city's fast growing southwest sector, began in 1995, ushering in a hopeful new day for Santa Fe's average working family. Run by a nonprofit group created by the city, Tierra Contenta's prices begin at an unheard of (for Santa Fe) $65,000, with most property in the $100,000 range. Located just off Airport Road west of Cerrillos Road, the neighborhood offers parks and open space and works to cultivate a sense of neighborliness among the homeowners. When complete, Tierra Contenta will feature 5,500 units, of which 3,700 will be single-family residences and the rest multifam-

INSIDERS' TIP

Because of the requirements of the Fair Housing Act, Realtors can't steer clients to a certain neighborhood. They also have to decline to answer questions about crime and schools. They can suggest that clients look at police records, watch the crime reports in the newspapers and talk to the public school systems about programs and achievement in different school zones.

Photo:Don Strel/Southwest Assignments

Santa Fe's climate makes interior courtyards and patios practical as well as beautiful. This courtyard is at the Museum of Fine Arts.

ily town houses, duplexes and apartments. The development will also have convenient commercial areas and hundreds of acres of open space with pedestrian walkways and bike trails. Schools and churches are part of the plan. Tierra Contenta was one of the reasons the Ford Foundation awarded the Santa Fe Affordable Housing Roundtable a $100,000 prize in 1996 for success in helping people find affordable housing.

Bellamah

Named after builder Dale Bellamah, this neighborhood features houses designed to suit young families. The neighborhood is characterized by square one-story suburban-style homes with touches of Santa Fe-style. These homes are noted for their logical floor plans, garages and flat or slightly pitched roofs. Bellamah is largely defined by Siringo Road to the north, Richards Avenue to the south and Yucca Street to the north. The area has several parks, including the city's popular Arroyo Chamiso walking/bike trail that runs from Rodeo Road past the Monica Lucero Park on Avenida de la Campanas, crosses Camino Carlos Rey and ends at Yucca Street.

General Franklin E. Miles Park, 1027 Camino Carlos Rey, one of the city's largest parks, offers baseball fields, lit basketball courts, playgrounds for the little guys and grass to roll on for picnics. Francis X. Nava Elementary School, 2655 Siringo Road, sits at the edge of the park. The Herb Martinez/La Resolana Park, 2240 Camino Carlos Rey, has tennis courts and grass, which is often filled with young soccer players. In 1996, the average selling price for a home here was about $131,000.

Rodeo Road Area

Santa Fe residents jokingly refer to this as "the suburbs." Houses are newer and larger than in Bellamah, but the neighborhood feeling is much the same. Your housing dollar goes farther here than in the historic areas. You'll find clusters of townhouses and apartments, commercial centers along Rodeo Road and easy access to Interstate 25. The Park Plaza development of townhouses and some single homes is a popular spot because of its walking trails and common-land construction, which consolidates housing to allow for greenbelts and open space. The new city/

county biking and hiking trail that will ultimately connect Santa Fe from the Guadalupe Street area to the Eldorado subdivision runs through here, offering a fine place for exercise.

Rancho Viejo

This new development on 2,500 acres plans to have model homes opening in the summer of 1998. Located about a mile south of Interstate 25 off of Richards Avenue, the area's master plan includes a mix of commercial and residential uses. The Village at Rancho Viejo, to be built first, will consist of approximately 334 units on 317 acres, with prices ranging from $120,000 for production homes to more than $200,000 for custom-home sites. The average home is expected to sell for about $175,000. Homesites will focus around a central plaza with shops, delis, small businesses and land set aside for a school.

Northwest of Town

U.S. Highway 84/285 serves as the boundary for this area to the east, and Camino La Tierra and Tano Road provide the main access to these properties. The Tano Road neighborhood, La Tierra, La Tierra Nueva and Salva Tierra are among the residential areas here. All are similar — multi-acre lots with expansive views and homes by some of Santa Fe's finest designers and builders. You're likely to find more established homes in the Tano Road area. Dirt roads are the rule, and you won't find any schools, gas stations, churches or shopping opportunities; they're all in Santa Fe. It's about 10 minutes to the Plaza from the intersection of Camino La Tierra and U.S. 84/285, but it can take you 20 minutes or more to reach that junction from a home in the northwest quadrant. The trade-off for what some consider inconvenience: plenty of space, the chance to hear coyotes howl at the moon and breathtaking views. Median home price range here is $550,000.

Las Campanas

This exclusive development includes an 18-hole Jack Nicklaus signature golf course, a beautifully appointed clubhouse with a first-rate restaurant for members and guests and view lots that range from 1 to 10 acres. All

homesites on this 4,700-acre development include gated entries, paved roads and underground utilities. The development has strict covenants that dictate construction and style of homes. Lots begin at $200,000; custom homes sell in the $1 million range and up.

Frijoles Village

A new development in this section of Santa Fe, Frijoles Village expects to begin construction in 1998. Described as a "neo-traditional community," the project will be south of Las Campanas and 5 miles northwest of the Santa Fe Plaza. The community will have 433 lots of various sizes, averaging one-third of an acre. The project's homes will range in price from $160,000 to $400,000, with some less-expensive subsidized housing. The community will be designed with narrow, curving roads and a conformity of exterior color, heights and styles to provide visual unity. Trees will be planted to line the paved streets. An extensive system of foot and bike paths will link the village to a regional trail network. The development will also include parks and a commercial plaza. A school site has been offered to the Santa Fe Public Schools, and the University of New Mexico is considering building a graduate school here. Sixty percent of the development will be open space, and the village will restrict building on its escarpments.

Southeast of Santa Fe

Eldorado and Vicinity

This family-friendly area is Santa Fe's suburbia. When the Eldorado development was first announced, many Santa Fe residents scoffed. Who, they asked, would drive 20 minutes to get to work? Today, Eldorado is nearly a community unto itself, and newer housing developments have sprouted up nearby. Thousands of people live here, enjoying the panorama of mountains and the quiet neighborly feeling. In addition to humans, many kinds of critters, including hawks, coyotes and rabbits, still call this country home.

Unlike much of Santa Fe County, the land here is relatively flat, which makes for easier construction and lower costs. The older homes are arranged in a traditional neighborhood style with several to a block. The newer houses tend to be larger and sit on sprawling lots in this world of sand, sage and piñon. Amenities include a community clubhouse with meeting rooms and a swimming pool and one of Santa Fe's better elementary schools, El Dorado Elementary, 2 Avenida Torreon. In 1996, residents celebrated the opening of the Agora commercial center, complete with a grocery store, at 7 Avenida Grande. Median home price range in this area is $181,675.

Real Estate Agencies

Bear Creek Real Estate Inc.
215 W. San Francisco St., Ste. 200 • 989-3573

This six-agent firm has a separate division that deals exclusively with property in Las Campanas, Santa Fe's high-end golf course development. Bear Creek offers property management as well as residential and commercial sales. Owner Nancy Abruzzo also specializes in finding winter rentals for visiting skiers.

Branch Realty
228 S. St. Francis Dr. • 984-8100

The nine agents in this office focus on commercial real estate. They can help with investment property, exchanges, leases and consultants as well as sales. The firm, established in 1982, prides itself on its "knowledge and effort." Among the company's recent projects have been a new shopping center, Santa Fe first in 13 years.

City Different Realty
130 Grant Ave. • 983-1557

Located in a lovely old brick building — a novelty for adobe-style Santa Fe — this office features six agents, all of whom are brokers with experience from 12 to 20 years in Santa Fe. City Different is by design a small firm, owned and run by four of the brokers, based on a philosophy of bringing together a select group of experienced, top-producing brokers who wish to work cooperatively. The office deals mainly with upper-end properties, but since most business comes through personal referrals it works in other price ranges.

Coldwell Banker Trails West Realty Ltd.
2000 Old Pecos Tr. • 988-7285, (800) 775-5550

With 46 full-time agents, Coldwell Banker represents both buyers and sellers in residential transactions. In business for 16 years, the firm makes extensive use of the Coldwell Banker national web site and national sales programs such as Blue Ribbon & Previews Properties. The office provides ongoing training for its agents.

Robert Dunn Real Estate Inc./Santa Fe
104 S. Capitol St., Ste. 6 • 988-2200, (800) 444-9887

Dunn has been in the real estate business in Santa Fe for 18 years and specializes in residential property including rural areas and land sales. The office's motto is, "We not only introduce people to properties, we introduce them to the community." The office prides itself on its personal service, a factor of its staff of two.

French & French Fine Properties
231 Washington Ave. • 988-8088, (800) 409-7325

French & French led the Santa Fe area real estate market in residential sales in all price ranges in 1997. In addition to 50 agents, three full-time staff supported offices and an extensive advertising marketing strategy, the agency has a 500-page web site. French & French is the exclusive Santa Fe affiliate of Christie's/Great Estates. The firm has been in business since 1984.

Mares Realty and Accent Property Management
1050 Paseo de Peralta • 988-5585, 986-3838

This five-agent office deals with general real estate and property management. Richard E. Mares, the founding broker, has more than 34 years of experience and is among a select number of brokers who are also licensed appraisers. The office is next to the state PERA building across from the State Capitol, and parking is not a problem.

Nichols Agency
1807 Second St., Ste. 10 • 984-3000

Owner/broker Wayne Nichols, who has also been a builder, has been an active part of the Santa Fe real estate scene since 1962. This office, in operation since 1982, has eight agents who deal with residential sales and commercial leasing. The agency touts its extensive professional experience in design, development and property sales as well as its knowledge of Santa Fe planning, urban development and community processes.

The Realty Group Inc., Better Homes & Gardens
The Design Center, 418 Cerrillos Rd., Ste. 28 • 984-0111

This agency says that its extensive national marketing system, the Better Homes & Gardens Home Buying System and Home Marketing System, sets it apart. Buyers throughout the country can learn about Santa Fe homes before they visit. The 10 agents in this office specialize in ranch property as well as commercial and residential listings.

Town & Ranch Inc.
149 W. Alameda St. • 988-3700

This full-service brokerage has 40 licensed agents and includes specialists in ranches and commercial property in separate departments. Although in business only three years, the company boasts New Mexico's largest real estate web site. Of the 40 agents, half are broker associates.

Varela Real Estate Inc.
1526 Cerrillos Rd. • 982-2525

Varela Real Estate, previously known as the Frank Gomez Agency, has been in business since 1949. President Susan Varela, Gomez's daughter, has worked in the office since 1973. The office offers residential and commercial sales and management and leasing services for residential and commercial property. The office has four agents, a commercial property manager and a residential property manager.

Karen Walker Real Estate
300 E. Palace Ave. • 982-0118, (800) 982-0118

Located just across from Santa Fe's popular La Posada Hotel, Walker Real Estate is a small office with just three brokers — all members of the Walker family. They've been in operation since 1973. The Walkers pride themselves on their knowledge of city and county zoning codes, planning requirements and building regulations and restrictions. Walker also is the author of *Understanding and Buying Santa Fe Real Estate*, which has cartoon illustrations by Pat Oliphant.

Christopher Webster Real Estate
54½ Lincoln Ave. • 988-2533

This firm, which has served Santa Fe buyers and sellers since 1976, is the exclusive Sotheby's International Realty affiliate in New Mexico and the only Estates Club International Real Estate affiliate in the state. The 16 associates specialize in marketing and selling premiere properties. Webster advertises extensively, with ads that have included beautiful drawings of the properties represented.

Resources

ADC Referral
107 Camino Sierra Vista • 989-1139

Ready to build or remodel in Santa Fe? Let this free service help you find the architect, design staff and builders you'll need. The process begins with an in-depth interview to help you understand and define your tastes and vision for your home or office. ADC will then assist you in clarifying design needs, establishing a working budget and identifying the scope of service you'll need to get the job done. The initials, incidently, stand for architect, designers and contractors.

Santa Fe Area Homebuilders Association and Haciendas - A Parade of Homes
P.O. Box 2664, Santa Fe 87504-2664
• 982-1774

The Santa Fe Area Homebuilders Association is a trade organization representing more than 530 firms in the Santa Fe area and northern New Mexico. The nonprofit association is dedicated to promoting safe, quality, attractive, cost-effective and affordable housing. The association presents Haciendas — A Parade of Homes each August, and the self-guided tour is an excellent way to get a sense of Santa Fe's diverse residential areas and the variety of housing available here. The program features homes in many neighborhoods, at various price ranges, from many different Santa Fe builders. The association sponsors a related contest that offers prices for top plans and craftsmanship in four price categories. The association also sponsors a home and garden show, spring expositions of products and services and fund-raising events for charity.

Neighborhood Housing Services
1570 Pacheco St., Ste. A • 983-6214,
(800) 429-5499

This private, nonprofit organization helps low- and moderate-income families maintain their homes and provides opportunities for new affordable housing. The agency offers below-market mortgages, assistance with down payments, a home repair program to help families keep property they already own and home-buyer workshops to teach potential buyers much of what they need to know to be successful homeowners. The agency also assisted in the development of the Los Portales affordable housing project in the Tierra Contenta neighborhood off Rodeo Road.

Santa Fe Association of Realtors
510 N. Guadalupe St. • 982-8385

This organization offers education for Realtors and compiles the Multiple Listing Service data about houses on the market and those that have recently sold. The association has about 650 members, all of whom are working to make a living selling real estate in the Santa Fe area. The group has several active committees, including one that lobbies for legislation "for the betterment of homeowners."

Santa Fe Civic Housing Authority
664 Alta Vista St. • 988-2859

The authority works with the city's low-income families to help them find a decent place to rent. The program includes a low-rent public housing program, rental assistance and other projects to help families become more self-sufficient and eventually own their own homes. Funding comes from public and private sources.

Santa Fe County Housing Authority
52 Camino de Jacobo • 471-3903

The county provides housing services for

INSIDERS' TIP

Santa Fe city water comes from snow and rain collected in our mountainous watershed on the eastern boundary of the city and impounded in McClure and Nichols reservoirs. Wells within the city and at the Buckman well field west of Santa Fe add to the supply. The city of Santa Fe completed the purchase of the public water system in June 1995. Outside the city limits, where the greatest population growth has occurred, residents generally rely on ground water from wells as well as some surface water flowing through *acequias*. In 1994, Santa Fe County created the Santa Fe County Water company to help limit the use of private wells.

Santa Fe Style: Simple Beauty

As you look at Santa Fe's neighborhoods or shop for a home or apartment here, you'll notice numerous variations of the phenomenon known as "Santa Fe Style."

Santa Fe style is deceptively simple. Start with a building that blends into its surroundings because it's the same color as the earth around it and because its contours match those of the landscape in which it is built. Typically, Santa Fe style means modified Pueblo or Territorial style — a thick-walled adobe look, with windows to capture the mountains and the sunsets and patios and portals for outdoor living. The doors are likely to be carved wood with a natural finish or perhaps a whimsical painted trim.

In 1918, when an influx of American influences threatened to make Santa Fe look remarkably like Anytown, USA within a generation, artist Carlos Vierra spearheaded the revival of old styles of building. Vierra, and others who joined him in his work to preserve and contemporize Santa Fe's traditional Pueblo and Territorial look, based Santa Fe style on a combination of the longstanding regional architecture with modifications essential for comfortable contemporary living. Vierra concentrated on the appreciation and development of the great advantages Santa Fe had from it adobe roots. He coined the term "Pueblo Revival" for this updated traditional style. Santa Fe architect John Gaw Meem became one of its finest practitioners.

Santa Fe style homes may look unimposing from the outside — perhaps just a simple adobe wall with an attractive gate — and that's part of their understated charm. Inside you may find a lovely courtyard leading to the house itself. Santa Fe style has evolved in the hands of contemporary builders and designers. It often includes passive solar energy features such as orienting a house to the south with windows to capture the sun's heat in winter and floors and walls to absorb that warmth and hold it into the evening.

The smooth plastered or sand-textured walls tend to be neutral colors — a variation on the adobe plaster used outside — or white or off-white. Exterior doors may be hand-hewn panels of pine, antiques garnered from older homes or even imported from Mexico, or original creations crafted from *latillas* or hand-adzed planks. Floors are normally of tile — again in earth tones — or natural stone, brick or wood. American Indian rugs are common finishing touches. More color usually comes in the accents, in the art work on the walls, the brightly painted folk art carvings in the *nichos*, the fresh flowers on the tables, the textiles on the throw pillows.

When tin came to New Mexico in the form of large storage containers used by the United States Army in the mid-19th century, residents quickly adapted this versatile material to a variety of practical and decorative uses. Tin switchplates with cut and stamped designs, mirrors perhaps with fabric or painted decorative touches and other tincraft are subtle parts of Santa Fe style.

Exterior adobe walls around the house or garden serve many uses. In some cases they shield homes from the noise and closeness of the street; in a different setting they carve a secure enclosure from the vast landscape, frame the views and offer a haven for plants, pets and family use.

For definitive information and beautiful pictures, take a look at *Santa Fe Style*, a wonderful book by Christine Mather and Sharon Woods, published by Rizzoni, New York.

— continued on next page

Photo: Don Strel/Southwest Assignments

Classic pueblo elements are part of Santa Fe's signature architecture.

Glossary

Adobe: A brick made of mud and straw, dried in the sun and used as a building material. Adobe is the heart of Santa Fe style because of its sculptural quality. Building with this labor-intensive material tends to be expensive unless you can do it yourself. Many Santa Fe homes that have an adobe-like appearance are built of less expensive cinderblock or frame and stuccoed in earth tones to resemble adobe. "Adobe" is also used to mean "earth-colored."

Banco: These plastered built-in benches, often found near a fireplace, are either crafted of adobe or framed of wood and stuccoed over.

Canale: An outlet to allow water to run off flat roofs, *canales* are a distinctive feature of Santa Fe style. Trouble with *canales* can lead to leaky roofs.

Casita: This term, meaning a small house, is sometimes used to describe a guest house, townhouse or upscale condo.

Corbel: Usually found atop posts or larger support beams, this decorative feature is usually carved and may also be painted.

Coyote fence: Traditionally crafted from juniper branches wired together vertically, coyote fences are used decoratively, for privacy and as wind breaks. The posts ought to be so close together that a coyote can't squeeze through.

Horno: An outdoor beehive-shape oven seen extensively on Indian pueblos.

Kiva fireplace: A rounded sculptural fireplace usually crafted from adobe. You'll normally find these in the corner of a room. *Kiva* fireplaces are often raised from the floor and surrounded with *bancos*.

Latillas: These small branches (approximately 3 inches in diameter), usually of cedar or aspen, are placed above the *vigas* to form the ceiling. They can be laid in various patterns such as herringbone or straight rows.

Lintel: A exposed beam placed over a window or door, *lintels* are sometimes carved or painted.

— continued on next page

Nicho: An small niche or indentation in a wall, usually rounded at the top, *nichos* are designed to display a work of art or family keepsakes. They could be described as traditional built-in shelving.

Portal: A covered porch that is also used as an outdoor walkway, *portals* can stretch across both the back and the front of a building and may be furnished with benches. In their book *Santa Fe Style*, Mather and Woods say the *portal* is the Southwest's most profound contribution to architecture. Santa Fe's best known *portal* is the porch in front of the Palace of the Governors, 105 E. Palace Avenue.

Pueblo style: This classic design is typified in the homes of the Pueblo Indians and the early Spanish. People interested in the subtleties may differentiate later construction using this theme as Spanish Pueblo style, Pueblo Revival style and Spanish Pueblo Revival style. Construction is of adobe or other materials with stucco to resemble the adobe look. Small windows and doorways accent the thick sculptural walls. The oldest of these homes grew organically rather than by floor plan, with more rooms added as the family expanded. Low ceilings, flat roofs, *vigas*, *latillas*, *bancos* and *nichos* mark this style, but these features also may be found in Territorial style and in contemporary variations.

Territorial style: Stuccoed walls finished with brick coping, decorative trim over windows and door frames and sharper corners characterize this traditional architecture. With the opening of the Santa Fe Trail and the coming of the railroad, new materials, such as plate glass for windows, flooded into Santa Fe. The result was a happy marriage of sensuous adobe walls with brick and wood trim for a more formal look.

Saltillo tile: This fired tile from Mexico, available in a variety of earth tones and usually square, is a popular and practical floor covering.

Vigas: Peeled logs used either decoratively or as a ceiling support, *vigas* are the first part of the ceiling to be installed. These massive timbers may span the house or be found in only a few rooms. In Territorial style, the *vigas* are often squared-off and finished with a decorated edging.

---

low-income and elderly people through this program. Included are vouchers that help with the rent and a popular rent-to-buy program in three sites around the city. The elderly, disabled or families with many dependents may be eligible for help; the waiting list is 6 to 12 months.

Tierra Contenta Corporation
369 Montezuma St., Ste. 220 • 983-9755

Santa Fe has begun to meet its need for housing that working families can afford. This nonprofit group is developing more than 800 acres on the south side of Santa Fe into mixed-income single-family and multifamily homes. The neighborhood uses strict design standards sensitive to the environment and replicates the traditional look of old Santa Fe with narrow, pedestrian-oriented streets. Miles of trails, parks and open spaces are part of the corporation's plan. When the neighborhood is fully developed, it will include about 5,000 housing units.

Publications

Apartment Guide
7801 Academy Blvd. NE, Ste. 203, Albuquerque • 821-5212

Although Albuquerque captures most of this guide's focus, you'll learn about Santa Fe rentals here too. The digest-sized booklet contains a map that shows some of the major complexes. The guide is available by calling or on various free racks throughout the city.

Photo: Don Strel/Southwest Assignments

Finishing touches can add a contemporary flavor to Pueblo Revival architecture, which has become Santa Fe's trademark.

Homes Santa Fe
1229 B St. Francis Dr. • 982-2312, (800) 753-3643

This full-size, full-color magazine comes complete with an index of the agencies and agents that advertise inside it. It's available free of charge at real estate offices throughout the city and on news racks.

The Real Estate Book, Santa Fe and North Central New Mexico
369 Montezuma St., Box 201 • 989-4411, (800) 841-3401

This free pocket-size magazine with color photographs is nothing but ads for single-family homes, townhouses and vacant land. It also includes a classified advertising section. You'll find pictures of houses around the city with prices, descriptions and the agent to call for more information.

Santa Fe Real Estate Guide
Santa Fe New Mexican, 202 E. Marcy • 983-3303

Published by *The Santa Fe New Mexican,* this first-rate monthly magazine is jammed with ads and articles. Regular features include a column by the president of the Santa Fe Association of Realtors, a list of building permits recently issued, an update on zoning and annexations that might affect real estate values, a summary of recent home and land sales, a chart of mortgage rates and a look at the rental market for the previous month. It's distributed free all over town.

Santa Fe Showcase
231 Washington Ave. • 988-8088, (800) 409-REAL

This beautiful magazine features some of the properties listed by French and French, one of Santa Fe's largest real estate firms. The agency has published more than 20 issues of this guide, which rivals many magazines in the quality of its printing and reproduction. Even if you're not in the position to buy anything, it's fun to do this kind of catalog shopping.

Understanding and Buying Santa Fe Real Estate
Karen Walker Real Estate, 330 E. Palace Ave. • 982-0118, (800) 982-0118

This paperback book, written by Karen Walker, delves into some of the quirks of the real estate market in Santa Fe. Walker discusses zoning, private covenants, homeowners associations, site selection, utilities, financing methods and sources and what to do if you buy property that includes an *acequia,* or historic irrigation ditch. Cartoons by Pat Oliphant add to the fun.

A number of national publications have rated Santa Fe among the top places in the United States to retire.

Retirement

It's not in the Sunbelt, and it's certainly not cheap. So why is Santa Fe rated among the top spots to retire in the United States? For the same reasons it's attractive to so many other segments of the American population. It's beautiful. It has a healthy, highly livable, four-season climate. Its history is as fascinating as its mixture of cultures. And it's got culture — the other kind — in spades: world-class opera, chamber music, symphony and chorale; flamenco and other live dance; theater; repertory cinema; galleries and museums; and dozens of classes and seminars on any number of topics in the city's public and private institutions of higher learning. The food here is superb, with internationally acclaimed restaurants offering creative fare for the discerning palate and dozens of lower-priced eateries with good, down-home cooking. Active seniors can burn off the extra calories skiing, hiking, golfing, kayaking, swimming or doing any number of activities in an environment that begs to be enjoyed.

But there's something else in Santa Fe, a *je ne sais quoi*, that makes it just a little more attractive for an older population than other cities with similar qualities. Part of that is a relaxed atmosphere and cordiality toward older people unmatched in other cities. Indeed, a number of national publications have rated Santa Fe among the top places in the United States to retire. It beats out retirement communities in Arizona, California, Florida and other states because of the lack of congestion. As one local senior citizen succinctly put it, "You can grow old here."

The number of residents age 65 and older in Santa Fe County increased 47.1 percent between 1980 and 1990. The county estimates the number will have tripled between 1990 and 2020, when residents 65 and older comprise 27 percent of the population.

In this chapter, we tell you about the services and housing options available for the growing senior population in the Santa Fe area. For more news and information by, about and for seniors, pick up a copy of *Prime Time: For New Mexicans 50 Plus* (see our Media chapter), a free, Albuquerque-based monthly tabloid available at newsstands throughout Santa Fe.

Agencies, Services, Social/Support Groups

American Association of Retired Persons (AARP)
P.O. Box 22831, Santa Fe, NM 87502
• 471-4540

AARP is a nonprofit, nonpartisan organization dedicated to helping older Americans live independent, dignified and useful lives. Its Capital City Chapter, No. 381, fulfills this mission by organizing and joining in many community projects such as the Safe Kids/Safe Seniors Program and Foster Grandparents (see the entries under City of Santa Fe Division of Senior Services in this chapter); and the Vials for Life program, which alerts emergency medical technicians that an individual is on medication.

Adult Protective Services
2001 Vivican Way • 827-7450

New Mexico law requires anyone who suspects an adult is being abused, neglected or exploited to report it. That's where Adult Protective Services steps in. A branch of the New Mexico Children, Youth and Families Department, the agency investigates allegations of ill-treatment of people age 18 and older who are unable to protect themselves. The majority of its clients are seniors. Many cases involve family members or acquaintances who are taking advantage of a vulnerable adult, especially his or her checkbook. The agency has no punitive powers but will refer cases either to a social worker or, if it suspects criminal activity, to the police or district attorney. In some cases, Adult Protective Services will provide housecleaning, shopping, transportation and other services to keep an individual from being institutionalized prematurely.

Alzheimer's Association Support Group

5 Camino Pequeño • 982-5906,
(800) 777-8155 (Albuquerque chapter),
(800) 272-3900 (national headquarters)

This is a local support group for caregivers of people with Alzheimer's disease. It's affiliated with the Albuquerque Chapter of the Alzheimer's Association, whose national headquarters are in Chicago. The local group meets the second Tuesday of every month at 7:30 PM at La Residencia, 983-2273, a private nursing home two blocks from the Santa Fe Plaza at 820 Paseo de Peralta.

City of Santa Fe Division of Senior Services

1121 Alto St. • 984-6731

Part of the city's Community Services Department, the Division of Senior Services is a "one-stop shop" for a wide variety of programs and services at minimal cost for adults 60 and older throughout the city and county. The division provides transportation for a suggested donation of 25¢ per trip with 24 hours notice; $1 meals at designated senior centers or delivered to a person's home; preventive health education and services including blood pressure testing, blood sugar and cholesterol screening, hearing and eye tests, breast cancer screening and flu shots; recreation and activities such as Senior Olympics, dancing, travel, ceramics, sculpture, woodcarving and weaving; case management; outreach, information and referrals.

The Senior Services Division sponsors numerous volunteer programs including Retired and Senior Volunteer Program (RSVP), where seniors act as Medicare-Medigap counselors, peer counselors, nutrition counselors, ombudsmen, craft instructors, etc.; Safe Kids/Safe Seniors to prevent accidental injuries; and the

FYI

Unless otherwise noted, the area code for all phone numbers listed in this guide is 505.

USDA Commodities Distribution, which gets food to low-income seniors and disabled clients. It also offers in conjunction with the State Agency on Aging (see subsequent entry) several paying programs for low-income seniors, including Foster Grandparents, which provides a stipend for serving as classroom "grandparents," and Senior Companions, in which individuals 60 and older can supplement their incomes by providing companionship to frail, homebound elderly clients. The division's Respite Program provides R&R for primary caregivers of people with Alzheimer's disease and dementia.

The division operates nine senior centers within 585 square miles, four of them in Santa Fe: **Mary Esther Gonzales Center**, 1121 Alto Street, 984-6731; **Pasatiempo Center**, 668 Alta Vista Street, 984-9859; **Luisa Center**, 1510 Luisa Street, 984-8091; and **Villa Consuelo Center**, 1200 Camino Consuelo, 474-5431.

Desert State Life Management

1500 Fifth St., Ste. 11 • 988-5550

Desert State Life Management is a private, nonprofit organization that provides guardianship services (making healthcare and placement decisions) and conservatorship services (making financial decisions) for mentally incapacitated people. It also manages trusts too small for a bank to handle and can answer questions about durable power of attorney, in which you assign someone to make healthcare decisions for you, and other advanced directives, including living wills. The agency receives federal, state and private grant money, which allows it to charge fees on a sliding scale. Many of its clients are senior citizens who are unable to make life decisions for themselves. Desert State makes all decisions by team process.

Eldercare Alliance

P.O. Box 9550, Santa Fe, NM 87504
• 982-0655

Eldercare Alliance is a group of private, independent professionals who work with the elderly. Its members include a nurse, a certified retirement-housing specialist, a geriatric social worker and a gerontologist. Fees vary with each professional, as does Medicare eligibility. Some use a sliding scale for fees. The alliance also provides free referrals and resources.

Elderhostel
The College of Santa Fe, 1600 St. Michael's Dr. • 473-6267, (800) 456-2673

The College of Santa Fe is the state headquarters for Elderhostel, a Boston-based national travel and education program for people older than 55. It has programs in all 50 states and 47 countries. Elderhostel in northern New Mexico features adventure programs for camping, hiking, climbing or skiing; service programs in which volunteers restore trails in the national forest or adobe structures; theme weeks that focus on the state museums in Santa Fe, the Santa Fe Opera or the Santa Fe Trail; or classes on the American Indian or Hispanic culture. Recent courses have included such topics as "Spanish Colonial Traditions and Customs," "Cultural Encounters: Examining History through Native Eyes," "African Americans in the Southwest," "Legendary Women of the Southwest," "Artistic Traditions in Northern New Mexico: From the Stone Age to the Present;" and "The River of Lost Souls: Aztec, New Mexico and the San Juan River."

Elderhostel courses cost a maximum of $460 for seven days and six nights, including housing, meals and all field trip and course fees. Courses might include up to 22 and a half hours of college-level, noncredit liberal arts courses. Housing ranges from dormitories to hotels. Elderhostel participants may take a companion or spouse of any age older than 21.

55-Alive Mature Driving
De Vargas Ctr., N. Guadalupe St. and Paseo de Peralta • 986-8909

This is a national program sponsored by the American Association of Retired Persons to give people 55 and older a refresher course on safe driving. Instructors teach how to compensate for slower reflexes, impaired vision and hearing, stiff neck and other physical changes that come with age and affect one's driving ability. The eight-hour course is offered once a month in two four-hour sessions, usually on weekday afternoons. The class is limited to 20 people so be sure to call ahead to make a reservation and to get the specific dates and times. The course costs $8 for books and materials and will more than pay for itself because New Mexico laws require auto-insurance companies to give discounts to people 55 and older who have successfully completed the course.

Neighborhood Housing Services of Santa Fe
1570 Pacheco, Ste. A1 • 983-6214, (800) 429-5499

This nonprofit organization offers home-repair help to a variety of clients, including low- to moderate-income senior citizens. Help might come in the form of financial or technical assistance, education or counseling. Neighborhood Housing Services also has a home-purchase program that includes assistance with down payments, low-interest mortgages and, in some cases, construction.

New Mexico State Agency on Aging
La Villa Rivera Bldg., 228 E. Palace Ave. • 827-7640, (800) 432-2080

The State Agency on Aging oversees the delivery of services for the elderly in New Mexico. The agency's responsibilities include administering federal and state funds, evaluating services, providing training and technical assistance, disseminating information on senior programs and issues, advocating on behalf of seniors and offering a forum for questions, comments and recommendations from providers and receivers of services. The agency's Long Term Care Ombudsman Program makes regular visits to nursing homes and other long-term care facilities to identify and help resolve problems. Its Health Insurance and Benefits Assistance Corps trains seniors to serve as peer counselors for other older individuals on Medicare, Medicaid, long-term care insurance and other long-term care financing.

Newcomers Club of Santa Fe
P.O. Box 28933, Santa Fe, NM 87592 • 820-6038

Open to people of all ages, the Newcomers Club of Santa Fe seems to attract primarily

— though not exclusively — seniors, many of whom have chosen Santa Fe as their retirement or second home. The club is a social group that provides an opportunity to meet people, learn about the Santa Fe area, stimulate the intellect and enjoy good food at fine local restaurants. Club activities include discussion groups on books and movies, study groups, bridge groups, theater-going groups, local travel and monthly Sunday brunches. The club meets once a month for membership luncheons that have featured a planetarium show at Santa Fe Community College, history of the Santa Fe Trail, a backstage tour of the Santa Fe Opera and a slide show of the new Georgia O'Keeffe Museum. Membership runs $10 per year. Call for information and an application form.

Older Adults Program
St. Vincent Hospital, 455 St. Michael's Dr. • 820-5376

This is a specialized program specifically for older people at risk of becoming — or who already are — severely depressed, isolated, grief stricken or have difficulties adjusting to changes in their life. Clients go through an intake session before being accepted into the program, which includes art therapy, group therapy, wellness education and other activities. Sessions last four hours and include a hot lunch. Medicare, Medicaid and most supplementary insurance will usually cover the cost. Call for additional information or to make an appointment.

Open Hands
509 Camino de los Marquez • 982-4258

Established in 1980, Open Hands is a private nonprofit agency whose mission is to keep elderly and disabled people living independently in their homes for as long as possible. It offers a variety of services including an adult day-care center that's open five days a week from 8 AM to 5 PM. The day-care center is the only one in the county and accommodates up to 40 adults, including those with Alzheimer's disease or dementia. Activities include physical exercise, art therapy, museum trips and sing-alongs. The client-to-staff ratio is approximately 5-to-1. The center provides transportation in three vans. Open Hands also provides home care, including a home-safety program to build ramps, put in grab bars and weatherize homes for elderly and disabled clients. It operates a loan bank with walkers, wheelchairs, bath stools and other equipment, and it sponsors a support group for caregivers that meets every other Wednesday from noon to 1 PM. Although Open Hands primarily serves low-income people, it doesn't discriminate against the middle class or the wealthy. Its services are available on a sliding scale.

Seniors Reaching Out
Armory for the Arts Complex, 1050 Old Pecos Tr. • 988-5522

Seniors Reaching Out is a nonprofit group that uses theater arts to put a positive spin on aging. Anyone 55 or older with talent or interest in any aspect of performance — be it tradi-

www.insiders.com

See this and many other **Insiders' Guide®** destinations online — in their entirety.

Visit us today!

tional drama, monologues, mime, dancing, etc.— is encouraged to join. A number of the group's 80 paid members, up to 30 or 40 of whom are active, are professional theater people. SRO tries to stage at least two major performances a year along with one-act plays and other shows it takes on the road to retirement and nursing homes, special events and a variety of nontraditional venues. You can also catch the troupe on Santa Fe's public access station, Channel 6, the second Thursday of every month at 8:30 PM. SRO sponsors a Senior Beginning Playwright Group and a program called "Kid and Kin," in which members work with children on theater-based projects for an eventual collaborative performance.

Tax Aid
Mary Esther Gonzales Senior Ctr., 1121 Alto St. • 984-6731
Pasatiempo Senior Ctr., 668 Alta Vista St. • 984-9859
Sponsored by AARP, these free, walk-in clinics are designed to help low-income seniors file income-tax returns. The clinics are open weekdays from 9 AM to 4 PM beginning the first Monday in February through April 15. Clinic volunteers are lay people certified by the Internal Revenue Service. Call 466- 0755 or 983-1750 for more information.

Widowed Persons Program
1937 Camino Lumbre, Santa Fe, NM 87505 (mailing address only) • 473-9783
The Widowed Persons Program is a nonprofit, AARP-sponsored program that provides one-on-one emotional and practical support to widows and widowers. Trained volunteers attempt to contact people whose spouse recently died. First contact comes through a letter with follow-ups by telephone. The group meets the second Sunday of each month at 1:15 PM for lunch at Ponce de Leon Retirement Community. A monthly newsletter lists the entrees for upcoming lunches.

Women in Transition
Santa Fe Community College, 6401 Richards Ave. • 428-1618
Women in Transition is a series of free workshops designed to give widows and other women going through major life changes a better self-image. Part of Santa Fe Community College's Institute for Intercultural Community Leadership, the workshops provide education, information, support and referrals in the community.

Home Healthcare/ Hospice

Kelly Assisted Living
1751 Old Pecos Tr., Ste. P • 982-9171, (800) 541-9818
A subsidiary of Kelly Services for temporary secretarial help, Kelly Assisted Living is a private, Michigan-based company with offices in Santa Fe, Albuquerque and elsewhere in the Southwest that provides healthcare to people who want to live at home but need help with daily activities. Clients include the elderly, people with Alzheimer's disease or other long-term disabilities and patients recovering from stroke, heart attack, surgery or other serious illness. Caregivers are available 24 hours a day, seven days a week to assist with dressing and bathing, prepare meals, help clients walk and get into and out of bed, monitor medication, provide transportation, run errands, do light housekeeping and offer companionship. Kelly charges an hourly rate and does not accept Medicare or Medicaid.

The Partners Program
St. Vincent Hospital, 455 St. Michael's Dr. • 820-5479
The Partners Program offers pastoral care for people who are terminally ill. This is a well-established program that began at Upaya (see our Worship and Spirituality chapter), a local contemplative retreat and study center, and is now under auspices of the Santa Fe Institute for Medicine and Prayer at St. Vincent Hospital. The program's more than three dozen volunteers teach nonsectarian, meditative practices based in Zen Buddhism to help bring peace and acceptance to individuals at any stage of illness or grieving. Partners help nurture a calm, sacred space that emphasizes prayer, deep

listening and mindful silence or meditation. The Partners Program, in conjunction with Sangre de Cristo Hospice (see subsequent entry), provides a series of training sessions twice a year.

Presbyterian Medical Services
1422 Paseo de Peralta • 982-5565
(800) 880-8001

Presbyterian Medical Services is a non-profit corporation that provides medical, dental and human-service programs primarily to underserved populations and communities in the Southwest. In Santa Fe, that includes PMS Community Home Health Care, 988-4156, and The Hospice Center, 988-2211, both based in the downtown area. The home-care program includes skilled nursing; home health aides for personal hygiene needs; physical, occupational and speech therapy; and medical social services. The Hospice Center provides on-call registered nurses specializing in pain and symptom control; medicine; medical supplies and equipment; home-health aides; physical, occupational and speech therapists; volunteers to support both patients and their caregivers; social workers and pastors for emotional and spiritual counseling and referral; and bereavement services. The Hospice Center also operates a support and counseling service for groups, including schools and businesses, and a thrift store whose revenues support the center. PMS is Medicare/Medicaid-certified.

Professional Home Health Care
10 Calle Medico • 982-8581,
(800) 461-1216

In operation since the 1980s, Professional Home Health Care is a private, nonprofit agency whose mission is to keep individuals — from infants to the elderly, the latter comprising the majority of its clients — out of hospitals, nursing homes and other institutions. Professional Home Health Care describes itself as the "Wal-Mart of home healthcare," providing skilled nursing, home-health aides, hospice and other services in clients' homes. The agency covers a large territory in New Mexico, from Sandoval County south of Albuquerque to the Colorado border. It accepts Medicare, Medicaid and private pay clients.

St. Vincent Home Health Services
1601 St. Michael's Dr. • 989-9331

In 1997 St. Vincent Hospital expanded its home healthcare division, making it the largest home healthcare provider in Santa Fe. St. Vincent Home Health Services, now located a couple of miles from the hospital, provides skilled nursing, physical, speech and occupational therapy, home-health aides and medical social work in addition to the durable medical equipment (beds, wheelchairs, etc.), home infusion (IV) and oxygen it has been supplying homebound clients, most of them seniors, since 1991. St. Vincent accepts almost all insurance and payer sources, including Medicare and Medicaid.

Sangre de Cristo Hospice
2074 Galisteo St., Ste. A3 • 982-7172

In Santa Fe since 1995, Sangre de Cristo Hospice is a private organization that cares for dying patients in their own homes or in nursing homes. A group of registered nurses who are on call 24 hours a day provide pain relief and other symptom management as well as emotional support and education. Home-health aides assist with such care as per-

INSIDERS' TIP

For information on nursing homes in Santa Fe and throughout the state, contact the New Mexico State Agency on Aging for its *Guide to New Mexico Nursing Homes*, published for the first time in 1997 by the agency's Long Term Care Ombudsman Program. The guide is a good starting point in a search for a nursing home in New Mexico. It gives a brief description of the facility, Medicare/Medicaid reimbursement rates, inspection scores and a brief rundown of the medical characteristics of its residents.

sonal hygiene, making meals, doing laundry and running errands. A chaplain and a cadre of volunteers, including those from The Partners Program (see previous entry), offer pastoral and emotional counseling for both the dying and the grieving. Medicare, Medicaid or private insurance will cover most care. Financial aid is available for low-income clients.

Staff Builders Home Care
826 Camino de Monte Rey • 983-5408

Staff Builders is a private home-health and hospice-care agency with a staff of registered nurses, physical, occupational and speech therapists, social workers, home-health aides and homemakers. It provides services in Santa Fe and Rio Arriba counties to Medicare, Medicaid and private pay clients, most of them elderly, at an hourly rate.

VNS Health Corp
2960 Rodeo Park Dr. W., No. 2
• 471-1065, (800) 511-0640

VNS Health Corp is a private, full-service home-healthcare agency that provides intermittent, short-term home care enabling patients to get care after an acute illness. Its patient base is primarily, though not exclusively, elderly people. The 37-year-old agency offers nursing services; home-health aides for personal hygiene; physical, occupational and speech therapists; medical social services; durable medical equipment; and IV pharmaceutical services. It accepts Medicare, Medicaid, private insurance and private pay. VNS participates in local health fairs and volunteers time at senior citizen centers for ongoing blood pressure, glucose and oxygen screening.

Retirement Communities

Ponce de Leon Retirement Community
640 Alta Vista St. • 984-8422,
(800) 288-5678

In 1997, Ponce de Leon celebrated its 11th year as a full-service rental retirement community for independent and assisted living. Its 150 apartments include studios and one- and two bedroom units, each with an electronic emergency-call system. Located just five minutes by car from downtown Santa Fe, Ponce de Leon has a distinct Spanish feel with plenty of wrought iron and a lovely interior courtyard with a reflecting pool, shrubbery, flowers and trees. Independent-living rentals include a continental breakfast and either lunch or dinner, transportation, weekly housekeeping, flat linen service and a full activity calendar featuring art exhibits, concerts and other live entertainment, dances, Friday social hours, seminars, art classes, exercise classes and daytrips to Albuquerque, casinos, museums, Indian and Spanish markets and other events and attractions. Assisted living includes three meals a day, daily housekeeping, help with personal hygiene, dispensing and monitoring medication, regular house checks and a separate activity calendar with field trips closer to home. Ponce de Leon offers on-site banking, a country store and a large city park across the street with an indoor swimming pool, tennis courts and lots of benches and picnic tables.

El Castillo Retirement Residences
250 E. Alameda St. • 988-2877

Just a few blocks east of the Plaza and west of chic Canyon Road, El Castillo Retire-

---

INSIDERS' TIP

Twice each year, volunteers from the Santa Fe-based Living Treasures Program choose three northern New Mexicans age 70 or older to be "Living Treasure Elders" in recognition of their spirit, energy and community service. Of the 110 men and women named as living treasures since 1984, 93 have been captured in a book of photo essays called *Living Treasures: Celebration of the Human Spirit*, published in 1997 by Western Edge Press of Santa Fe. The book is widely available in local bookstores and public libraries.

Photo: Ponce de Leon Retirement Community

Santa Fe's senior population has been growing, as have the services available to retirees.

ment Residences offers what it calls "Life Care" for retirees 62 or older and their spouses of any age. Residents pay a onetime, partially tax-deductible entrance fee — a sort of "mortgage" that varies with the size of the apartment and how many will live there — and a monthly service fee for one meal a day in the dining room, scheduled transportation, maintenance, security, a library, an outdoor pool, a pool room and organized activities such as exercise, arts and crafts and tours. Together, these fees constitute a lifetime contract that assures residents they will have all their needs met — including nursing care and assisted living, should either be necessary — for the rest of their lives. El Castillo currently has a long waiting list for its 150 apartments, though it's adding a new building with 19 deluxe two-bedroom, two-bath apartments in 1998. All apartments have private outside entrances.

Vista de Santa Fe
**2400 Legacy Ct. • 471-2400,
(800) 906-9020**

Vista de Santa Fe, on 5.5 landscaped acres, is a rental retirement community for the 55-and-older set. It offers 70 apartments, each with either a patio or balcony and some overlooking open courtyards, for independent living and another 26 beds for assisted living. Independent-living rates include breakfast and dinner; local transportation in the house Cadillac; all utilities; indoor and outdoor maintenance, including housekeeping every two weeks; social services; and activities such as parties with live entertainment, card games, casino excursions, museum visits, movies, shopping, dancing, exercise classes, meditation and visits with volunteers from youth groups, schools and churches. Assisted-care residents receive all the services listed above plus lunch, snacks, 24-hour care by licensed nurses, medication control, physical therapy and personal-hygiene care. Independent residents may also get lunch, medication control, personal-hygiene care and laundry for an additional cost. Vista de Santa Fe provides on-site banking, a notary public and free office facilities including copying, faxing, use of a computer with Internet access. The complex is a few blocks east of Villa Linda Mall and west of Sam's Club. The property is adjacent to the City of Santa Fe's Recreation Trail, a 4.5-mile path for walkers, joggers, skaters and bicyclists.

The Santa Fe public school system enrolls approximately 13,000 students.

Education and Child Care

If you want to learn massage therapy or acupuncture, Santa Fe is the right place.

If you're interested in a class in photography, a workshop in flamenco dancing, an intensive experience in cross-cultural awareness or an afternoon of bird identification, you're in luck.

If you want your child to do well enough in high school to get a scholarship to Harvard, your choices are more limited — but don't despair.

But if you need a Mary Poppins to take care of your toddler, Santa Fe presents a challenge. It's the same story here as in most cities around the United States. Unless Grandma lives close by and delights in caring for the little ones, securing high-quality child care at a reasonable price is as tough as finding a downtown parking place during Indian Market weekend.

In this chapter, we'll take a look at colleges and special post-secondary programs, the Santa Fe Public Schools, private secondary schools and options for child care and baby-sitters. (You'll find special programs and camps for kids in our Kidstuff chapter.)

Colleges and Universities

The names of Santa Fe's two long-established colleges tend to confuse people. After all, you'd except a college called St. John's to have a religious affiliation. And wouldn't The College of Santa Fe come from secular roots?

In fact, St. John's is a nonreligious institution, although theology is taught here along with the "great books" curriculum. And The College of Santa Fe began as an outreach of the Christian Brothers, firmly rooted in Catholicism. Once known as St. Michael's College, CSF is New Mexico's oldest institution of higher education (see our close-up in this chapter).

Santa Fe's popular community college and programs through branches of the University of New Mexico and New Mexico Highlands University add to the mixture of higher education opportunities.

The College of Santa Fe
1600 St. Michael's Dr. • 473-6011, (800) 456-2673

For the past few years, *U.S. News and World Report* has ranked The College of Santa Fe among the top-10 liberal arts colleges in the West. A nationally recognized performing arts department and cinema studies linked to film and video production draw students here from throughout the country. Professional crews use the college's sound stages, offering students a chance to work on productions ranging from full-length features to commercials and music videos. The newest addition to the campus is a multimillion dollar visual arts center, a cluster of five structures for the growing photography and studio arts programs. Opening for the new center was planned for 1998. The college also teaches a business curriculum, creative writing, social science, humanities, science and teacher education programs.

About 1,600 students attend this private, independent college. Roughly half opt for the traditional residential program; the others take graduate courses or work toward their degrees with weekend and evening classes. The CSF campus also hosts scores of Elderhostel programs each year on topics ranging from Native American literature to New Mexico's history. (See our Retirement chapter.)

In addition to the genius and generosity of the Christian Brothers, the college notes its appreciation to the late actress Greer Garson and her husband, Buddy Fogelson, with campus buildings that bear their names. The Garson Communication Center and Studios, Fogelson Library and Greer Garson Theatre all are campus landmarks. Garson, who lived in nearby Pecos, New Mexico, as well as Dallas, Texas, shared her experience and her fortune with CSF students. She acted in several college productions.

FYI

Unless otherwise noted, the area code for all phone numbers listed in this guide is 505.

St. John's College
1160 Camino de la Cruz Blanca • 984-6000

You won't find any big lecture classes on this campus, and students don't chew their nails over which electives to pick. Most of the course of study for a bachelor's of arts is required and most of the work is done in small seminars. The student faculty ratio here is 8 to 1. Instead of textbooks, students read timeless works of Western civilization, the original writing of more than 100 philosophers, scientists, poets, mathematicians, storytellers and composers. Over their four years of study, students take language and math, three years of laboratory science, a year of music and seminars in philosophy, political science, literature, history, economics and psychology.

Established in 1964 on a lovely location near the eastern foothills, Santa Fe's St. John's is an extension of the school's historic Maryland campus, founded as King William's School in Annapolis in 1696. Only Harvard and the College of William and Mary are older.

St. John's ranks in the nation's top 30 colleges for producing graduates who go on to work on higher degrees, with those who earn Ph.D.s evenly split between the sciences and

humanities. The campus offers graduate programs in liberal arts and Eastern studies. Eastern studies includes classical Chinese and Sanskrit and uses texts from India, China and Japan to prompt student discussions.

St. John's invites the public to sample its approach during Community Seminar Day, held twice a year. Tutors, as the faculty are called, lead programs such as "Scientific and Religious Skepticism," which used Shakespeare's *Hamlet* and *Othello* and Descartes' *Meditation* as its texts.

Santa Fe Community College
6401 Richards Ave. • 471-8200

Until 1983, Santa Fe had no community college. One of the few things you might get a majority of Santa Fe residents to agree on is that this institution has been of enormous benefit to local families. Some would call it Santa Fe's pride and joy.

Located on 366 acres in southern Santa Fe, the campus consists of a main classroom/administrative center, the Witter Fitness Center (see our Parks and Recreation chapter) and the 30,000 square-foot early childhood center. The visual arts center, with studios for print making, photography, jewelry, fiber art, painting, sculpture and more is scheduled to open in the fall of 1998.

The college offers associate's degrees in arts and science, which transfer to four-year colleges. Students can get technical and occupational training here too. SFCC also develops custom contract courses for local businesses and industries. In spring 1997, the school's student headcount was 5,471 registered for credit courses. An additional 2,500 or so students per semester sign up for classes in adult basic education, English as a Second Language, literacy and similar programs. In cooperation with Santa Fe schools, SFCC also offers a concurrent enrollment program that gives students both high school and college credit for classes taken on the college campus.

Another reason Santa Fe loves its community college is its extensive continuing education program, noncredit classes ranging from professional development and leadership skills to tennis, Asian cooking, star lore and palm reading. Between 4,000 and 5,000 students enroll each year.

University of New Mexico - Santa Fe

Santa Fe Community College campus, 6401 Richards Ave. • 438-1234

For more than 20 years, the University of New Mexico, based in Albuquerque, has offered graduate and upper-division programs in Santa Fe. UNM began its program at the request of the governor to fill the educational advancement needs of state employees. Until it found a home on the SFCC campus, UNM rented space from various agencies including the College of Santa Fe. Beginning with 50 students, UNM-Santa Fe enrollment now is near 1,000 annually.

Students at UNM-Santa Fe tend to be working professionals returning to school to complete their bachelor's degree or study toward their master's. For student convenience, most courses are scheduled in the evening. Bachelor's degree programs include nursing, speech and hearing and University Studies, a nontraditional program in which students design their own course of study. Master's degree programs include counseling, communications, and educational administration. In addition, UNM offers upper-level and graduate classes in multicultural education, Southwestern studies and more. About half the courses are taught via television from the main campus in Albuquerque. Santa Fe students use the telephone to call in questions or answers.

The UNM office at Santa Fe Community College can provide information to students about main campus programs. They have applications, financial aid information and UNM's undergraduate catalog and graduate bulletins.

New Mexico Highlands University - Santa Fe

Santa Fe Community College campus, 6401 Richards Ave. • 438-1742

New Mexico Highlands University pro-

grams are intended for students who want to earn a bachelor of arts degree in social work, business or education. Most of the students are working people who have associate's degrees and want to continue their education at a four-year institution. In addition to taking courses offered by visiting or adjunct professors, Highlands-Santa Fe students also participate in "distance learning" with televised classes. Highlands has been in operation in Santa Fe since 1994 and normally enrolls between 20 and 30 students each semester.

Institute of American Indian Arts

1600 St. Michael's Dr. • 988-6495

Some of America's leading Indian artists — among them Fritz Scholder, David Bradley, Doug Hyde, Allan Houser, T.C. Cannon and Darren Vigil Gray — have taught and studied at this unique institution. The IAIA stands alone in its focus on teaching American Indian and Alaskan Native arts to Native American students and offers an associate's degree in several arts-related areas. The federal government, on which the IAIA depends for most of its support, has reduced the school budget in recent years, resulting to a decline in both course offerings and enrollment. The IAIA features student and alumni work in its downtown museum (see our Attractions chapter).

Special Schools and Programs

In this section, you'll find schools that offer a variety of programs, some unique to Santa Fe. Included here is a selected sampling of education ranging from weekend seminars that can teach you how to shoot a great photograph or cook up the chile verde of your dreams to major courses of study leading to certification. Santa Fe's two acupuncture schools are among the best in the country.

The Anthropology Film Center

1626 Canyon Rd. • 983-4127

Founded in 1965, The Anthropology Film Center teaches an intensive nine-month course in documentary and ethnographic filmmaking. The program is structured for those who wish to become visual anthropologists and produce ethnographic films for social documentary film writers/directors/producers. The center also offers tutorials in the practical uses of computers in visual anthropology and film.

Located in a large adobe studio on 2 acres of wooded foothills in a quiet canyon off one of the city's most historic roads, the center's campus adds to its attraction. Students have access to a production studio, editing and projection facilities and a specialized library in the fields of visual anthropology, film production, culture and communication.

International Institute of Chinese Medicine
Off Lopez Ln. • 473-5233

Students interested in learning acupuncture and other aspects of Chinese medicine get a taste of China with their studies here. More than half of the institute's teachers received their primary training in China, and more than a third of the 40-some faculty members are Chinese. Michael Zeng, a Chinese M.D. and a Doctor of Oriental Medicine, is the institute's president, director and academic dean. In addition to an extensive medical practice, Zeng has been a senior medical consultant and guest lecturer at colleges across China, the United States and Canada.

The institute offers a four-year Master of Oriental Medicine degree program, a certificate program in Oriental bodywork and a continuing education certificate program for licensed acupuncturists and other healing arts practitioners. Students can also learn to speak and read Chinese. A herbal pharmacy, low-cost clinic, library and student bookstore are part of the institute. Students receive free healthcare at the student clinic. The campus sits on 1.2 acres of land at the foot of the Sangre de Cristo Mountains off Airport Road (see our Healthcare chapter).

New Mexico Academy of Healing Arts
501 Franklin Ave. • 982-6271

Students can become certified massage therapists and learn polarity therapy at this school, which has operated in Santa Fe since 1981. The academy takes a holistic approach to education and uses meditation as a foundation — it's a required class. About 70 percent of the enrollment comes from outside New Mexico. For their massage therapy certification, students choose programs up to 11 months in length, learning anatomy and physiology, aromatherapy and communication skills and ethics. Polarity therapy, a comprehensive healthcare system created by Randolph Stone, draws upon Ayurvedic and Chinese traditions as well as modern physics. Students study to become Registered Polarity Practitioners or Associated Polarity Practitioners and can enroll in dual certification programs. A public clinic offers those enrolled here an opportunity to practice their skills. (See our Healthcare and Wellness chapter .)

Santa Fe Photography and Digital Workshops
Mount Carmel Rd. Ste. 2, Santa Fe • 983-1400

This prestigious program teams amateur and professional photographers with nationally and internationally known photographers who share their insights both technically and artistically. The weeklong workshops, which run year round, attract more than 1,000 students to Santa Fe and take them on site to shoot their pictures. Classes for beginners include aesthetics, technique and an overview of equipment. Professionals can choose from portraits, lighting techniques, fashion and beauty, hand-colored photos, landscape, color work and more. The school also features a free summer lecture series, open to anyone interested, that gives the instructors an opportunity to discuss and show their work.

Santa Fe School of Court Reporting
110 Delgado St. • 983-5699

Since 1985 this downtown school has offered a full court reporting program leading students to speeds of 225 words per minute at 98.5 percent accuracy. Approved and licensed, the school has a student-teacher ratio of 1 to 6 in theory and speed building classes and 1 to 15 in academic areas. The training normally takes 36 months.

School of American Research
660 Garcia St. • 982-3583

If Santa Fe gave an award for the most beautiful and historic campus, the School of American Research would win, hands down. This nonprofit center has supported innovative scholarship and American Indian artists since its founding in 1905. The shaded, beautifully landscaped grounds and historic adobe headquarters speak of Santa Fe's early days as a magnet for the great minds in archaeology. The SAR presents six fellowships to outstanding scholars, giving them nine-month residencies devoted to writing projects related to anthropology, the humanities and the arts. The school shares their work as part of its publication division. The SAR press also publishes books designed for a popular audience on topics including the peoples and cultures of the American Southwest. Three times a year, the School of American Research invites 10 scholars to campus for a week of discussion and debate on issues on the frontier of anthropological research. (These meetings are closed to the public and the media.)

As another part of its educational mission, the SAR produces periodic newsletters, hosts traveling seminars to notable sites in the Southwest and around the world and offers illustrated lectures. The Indian Arts Research Center with its extensive collection of art and artifacts is open to the public through special tours (see our Attractions chapter).

Santa Fe School of Cooking
116 W. San Francisco St. • 983-4511

That great green chile burrito doesn't have to become just a Santa Fe memory. At Santa Fe School of Cooking, you can learn the secrets of traditional New Mexican cuisine in pro-grams that only take a morning or an afternoon. During the summer, the school offers classes as often as six days a week. Conveniently located downtown in the Plaza Mercado building, the teachers/chefs use indigenous Southwestern ingredients to prepare both traditional and contemporary meals. Afterward, the students eat their creations and take home the recipes. Classes range from two to five hours.

Santa Fe School of Cooking also offers extended programs that include field trips to explore the farms and food of northern New Mexican villages and exciting dinners at Santa Fe's best restaurants. The school happily arranges classes and food tours for groups on request.

Southwest Acupuncture College
325 Paseo de Peralta, Ste. 500 • 988-3538

Operating from both Santa Fe and Albuquerque campuses, Southwest Acupuncture College offers a master's of science in Oriental Medicine with extensive national accreditation. Enrollment is open to students age 20 and older who have successfully completed two years of general education at the college level. According to the school's guidelines, they must also possess the "personal credentials and intellectual skills" to obtain admission. The academic program consists of more than 2,500 hours of training in the five branches of classical Oriental medicine: acupuncture, herbal medicine, physical therapy, nutrition and exercise/breathing therapy.

Since its inception in 1980, the for-profit college reports that its graduates have achieved an unsurpassed passage rate on all state and national exams. The preponderance of the curriculum takes a hands-on and clinical approach. Students locate acupuncture points, practice techniques, develop diagnoses and treatment plans, prepare herbal formulas and observe and treat patients. To help

---

INSIDERS' TIP

Looking for a job? The Santa Fe public schools are the second-biggest employer in Santa Fe County (state government is first), with about 1,900 employees. Santa Fe Community College is also in the top 10.

students become proficient, the school operates an active teaching clinic (see our Healthcare and Wellness chapter).

In addition to the master's program, the college offers continuing education classes in specialty topics, seminars with international experts and externships in China.

Southwest Learning Centers Inc.
P.O. Box 8627, Santa Fe 87504 • 989-8898

Southwest Learning Centers is an umbrella organization for many educational activities, all focusing on serving the multi-ethnic population of the Southwest and helping students of all ages learn to appreciate the diversity and vitality of the cultures. Interdisciplinary classes, research projects, conferences, workshops, apprentice programs and community service fall under SLC's focus. Projects include the World Learning Academy, the Center for Indigenous Arts and Cultures, the Native Visions Media Arts Center, Rio Grande Bioregional Project and the Sustainable Education Resource Center, which operates an organic farm.

Southwestern College
Rt. 2, Box 29D • 471-5756

Class offerings in counseling and art therapy bring students here. The college has an accredited two-year residential program as well as other options for full-time, part-time, evening and weekend study. In its literature the college describes its "transformational approach" to education and a style of teaching that is person-centered, holistic, experiential, reflective and ecological. The school traces the roots of the transformational approach to Ralph Waldo Emerson and John Dewey and Carl Jung. The college was dedicated in 1976 and began its programs in 1979.

Plaza Resolana en Santa Fe
401 Old Taos Hwy. • 982-8539

Subtitled "Santa Fe Study and Conference Center," Plaza Resolana presents a variety of workshops with an emphasis on spirituality, local arts and regional culture. Classes attract both residents and visitors who stay at the center. Among the course offerings are Everything is Sacred — Native American Spirituality; River Songs — An Introduction to

Flyfishing; and a retirement planning seminar through the Board of Pension of Presbyterian Church U.S.A. Last summer Plaza Resolana added a popular new performing arts course, "Santa Fe Voices," which treated students to the sounds of the Desert Chorale, the Santa Fe Symphony and the Santa Fe Opera. In addition to its own classes, the center hosts international Elderhostel programs (see our Retirement chapter), and Recursos de Santa Fe uses the center for its writing programs. Plaza Resolana has begun to focus on partnerships with college and universities, seminaries, churches and other nonprofit groups to arrange specially tailored programs. The center is affiliated with the Ghost Ranch Foundation in Abiquiu.

Public School

Santa Fe Public Schools
610 Alta Vista St. • 982-2631

Santa Fe Public Schools serve the City of Santa Fe and much of Santa Fe County. The district includes an early childhood center, 20 elementary schools, four middle/junior high schools and three high schools. The school system enrolls approximately 13,000 students. Santa Fe High, with about 2,000 students, is the largest school in the system. Next to state government, the schools are the biggest employer in Santa Fe County, with about 1,900 employees on the payroll. The district operates on an annual budget of some $50 million, and 96 percent of that comes from the State of New Mexico.

Let's get the bad news out of the way early. More than 30 percent of the students who enter 9th grade don't stay in school to graduate. And if you measure school success by national test scores, the Santa Fe public system would earn a "C". In 5th and 8th grades, students rank around the 50th percentile in reading, math and language usage. The reasons for the public schools' poor performance depend on who's doing the talking, but inadequate funding, children's lack of preparation for school, family stress and low teacher salaries are usually mentioned.

With the hiring of Lee Vargas as superintendent in 1996, the district renewed its com-

Photo: Native American Preparatory School

Native American Preparatory School offers education to American Indians.

mitment to improving student performance, keeping kids in school and enlisting the help of the entire community to accomplish these goals. In 1996, the district inaugurated the Academy, a new school for dropouts, teen parents and others who would benefit from a different approach to education. All involved expect that it will reduce the dropout rate.

One of the strongest hopes for improving the public schools lies with school-community partnerships. The nonprofit Santa Fe Partners in Education, 474-0240, builds links between the community and the public schools to help teachers do their work better. The group underwrites field trips, funds grants for special programs in the classroom, honors innovative teachers and provides supplies. In cooperation with the public schools, Partners hosts the Superintendent's Ball in the spring to raise money for teacher grants and student scholarships and to increase rapport between the schools and the community. Teenage students work as volunteer servers, bakers, decorators and greeters. A black-tie crowd dances to music provided by topnotch high school bands.

Santa Fe Public Schools do some things well. Each school has exceptional teachers among its faculty and students who work hard

and gain notable success. Individual students win national awards, and high school graduates are accepted to major universities and offered scholarships. Some 47 percent of the teachers have a master's degree or better.

The public school system offers diversity among its schools in terms of both programs and enrollment. By ethnicity, the majority of students are Hispanic in all but seven of Santa Fe's public schools; less than three percent of the 13,000 or so students are Indian. Public high schools teach music, theater, computer design, auto mechanics, television production, construction, culinary arts and more in addition to standard academic programs. Students can try 26 different sports in grades 7 through 12.

On the elementary and middle school levels, some schools offer intensive arts programs or focus on science and the environment. You'll find conflict mediation programs, multi-age classes, collaboration with senior citizens, opera, theater and chamber music enrichment, peer counseling, buddy-to-buddy tutoring and literary magazines. Some classes help with the AIDS walk, sponsor food drives or coat and mitten collections or support the Santa Fe Animal Shelter.

Santa Fe also is home to the state-funded

New Mexico School for the Deaf, 1060 Cerrillos Road, 827-6744, which serves deaf and hard-of-hearing children from throughout New Mexico. NMSD offers preschool through 12th-grade education. The campus is home to the James A. Little Theater, a popular venue for lectures and performances. (See our Arts chapter.) Another publicly funded school, Santa Fe Indian School, 1501 Cerrillos Road, 989-6300, is a boarding school for Native American children that enrolls about 500 students in grades 7 through 12. To attend, students must be at least one-quarter Indian.

Private Schools

Almost 25 percent of the city's middle and high school students attend private schools, according to statistics compiled by the New Mexico Department of Education. (The national average is around 14 percent.) Santa Fe has an abundance of private schools from preschool through secondary. For younger students, choices include church-affiliated elementaries, Waldorf and Montessori schools, informal schools and those with a structured academic focus. High school students have several interesting choices, including a new school, the New Mexico Academy for Sciences and Mathematics, planned to open in September 1998.

Not all Santa Fe's private schools are accredited. The State Department of Education, 300 Don Gaspar, 827-6555, can give you a list of all private schools in the Santa Fe area. We do not have room in this guide to list all the private schools in this area. We have listed some of our secondary schools to give you an idea of the range of options available in Santa Fe.

Desert Academy
RR 14, Box 203, La Cienega • 820-7800

With its inception in 1994, Desert Academy filled a niche in Santa Fe's private school galaxy. Among its enrollment, the school welcomes children with learning disabilities; they make up about a third of its roughly 110-student enrollment. On a beautiful site south of Santa Fe in La Cienega, Desert Academy offers a college preparatory program combined with classes designed to encourage both creativity and critical thinking. Student-teacher ratio is 7 to 1, and the school is fully accredited.

Native American Preparatory School
P.O. Box 260, Rowe • 474-6801

This school was the first private college-prep academy in the country with an Indian-only enrollment. Students from about two dozen tribes around the nation come for a four-year program that stresses character and cultural development. The curriculum encompasses academics, community service, the arts and athletics. Full-time enrollment is about 60 students. NAPS began in 1988 as a summer program for Navajo teens, received recognition on "Good Morning America" and expanded by acquiring as its campus the former home of the Pecos River Learning Center, 30 miles northeast of Santa Fe.

Nizhoni School for Global Consciousness
HC75, Box 72, Galisteo • 466-4336

As you'd guess from the name, this isn't your little red school house. Founded by spiritual teacher and author Chris Griscom, Nizhoni's "soul-centered" education focuses on what is described as "the integration of the student's spiritual essence." The class list includes cosmology, herbology, astrology, exercises in consciousness and global communication as well as traditional courses like English and math. The high school accepts both boarders and day students and recruits internationally. Nizhoni also teaches younger children and adults, who can sign up for intensives and short courses including "Memories of Extra-Terrestiality."

Santa Fe Preparatory School
1101 Camino de la Cruz Blanca • 982-1829

Founded in 1961, Santa Fe Preparatory offers first-rate academics and a comprehensive program of sports, arts and community service. Space for the current campus was donated by John Gaw Meem, one of the architects who shaped the look of contemporary Santa Fe. Prep's extensive college counseling program, designed to help each student select the right school and win accep-

A Legacy of Learning

If a sense of astonishment goes with you to Heaven, the Christian Brothers who established St. Michael's High School and College must be amazed and delighted.

What they started in 1859 has undergone some remarkable changes. But the schools they began, the oldest educational institutions in New Mexico, continue to thrive after more than 100 years.

Close-up

Archbishop Jean Baptiste Lamy, the energetic French cleric who supervised the construction of St. Francis Cathedral, Loretto Chapel and Santa Fe's first hospital and orphanage, sent for Brothers of the Christian Schools to help bring Catholic education to the territory. Four Brothers, chosen because they were skilled teachers, left for their American adventure from Clermont, France, on an old steamer. They traveled across the ocean for 14 days, then went by train from New York to St. Louis. They continued by wagon to Kansas City, where they set out for the plains and mountains beyond. They arrived in Santa Fe on October 27, 1859, after 71 days of travel.

Only two weeks later, the hard-working Brothers opened St. Michael's, named in honor of St. Michael the Archangel. Boarding students began to arrive on November 9, 1859, and the school has served Santa Fe families continually ever since. For many years, it was the only source of education beyond an elementary level in the territory. Lamy and the Brothers shared a dream that their school for boys would develop into a college, helping to train the leaders New Mexico needed to move toward statehood and to prepare those who wished to study for the priesthood.

Photo: Don Strel/Southwest Assignments

The old St. Michael's High School and College is now used as an office building for state government. The school was the tallest adobe building of its time. The Christian Brothers built it next to San Miguel Chapel.

The city's newspaper welcomed the Brothers' work and praised the boys in language one seldom hears today. One writer complimented "the cleanly, joyous little fellows, going and coming from the place." The school quickly had 30 boarders and more than 150 day scholars. By the time the Territory of New Mexico granted a charter to the College of the Christian Brothers of New Mexico in 1874, St. Michael's curriculum had expanded to include college courses.

When New Mexico achieved statehood in 1912, St. Michael's was a well-respected religious and academic institution. As the Brothers and Lamy hoped, many of their graduates had contributed to the territory's achievement.

Under Brother Botulph Schneider's 36 years of leadership, the original school gave way to an impressive two-story building with a third story incorporated in a mansard

— continued on next page

roof. A tall central cupola rose at the center, distinguishing the school as the first building of its type in Santa Fe. The walls were adobe, and the college quickly became famous as the Southwest's tallest adobe structure.

A Good Idea Reborn

The Brothers discontinued the college program after the World War I to focus on the high school but didn't let the dream die. Brother Benildus of Mary began the arduous work of raising the money needed to re-establish the college. In 1947, the Brothers bought land that had been used as an Army hospital and re-opened St. Michael's College with a campus of 51 barracks. Scoffers said the venture was doomed because the college sat too far from the center of town. Today, the college touts its convenient central location.

In 1966, St. Michael's College became The College of Santa Fe to more closely reflect its long ties with the community. That same year, the college admitted women for the first time. While the influence of the Christian Brothers is still felt at the College of Santa Fe, 80 percent of the board members are lay people and only a handful of Brothers remain on the faculty.

The Christian Brothers' presence continues strongly at St. Michael's High School, the oldest high school in New Mexico. The high school moved from its downtown location to a large modern campus just off St. Michael's Drive in December 1967. In the fall of 1968, the first girls were admitted as students. (Loretto Academy, an all-girls school operated by the Sisters of Loretto, had just closed.) A Christian Brother still serves as principal at St. Mike's, and five of the current nine board members are Christian Brothers.

tance there, begins in the 9th grade. The language curriculum includes fifth-year work for proficient students and a home-stay trip to Mexico. In addition to a challenging academic program, Prep students can learn lacrosse and field hockey as well as the standard offerings in physical education. The school follows a "no cut" system, which allows everyone the opportunity to join a team. Students can't hide in the crowd here; student-faculty ratio is 9 to 1. Prep has a selective admissions policy and a waiting list for new students. The high school enrolls about 200 students. Prep also offers 7th and 8th grades.

Santa Fe Secondary
230 St. Francis Dr., Ste. 5 • 982-2240

This tiny school (24 students) works with teens in a multi-graded classroom. In addition to traditional academic subjects, including mandatory Latin, students study aikido twice a week and have the opportunity for internships, community service or employment.

St. Catherine Indian School
801 Griffin St. • 982-6258

Founded in 1887, St. Catherine Indian School is the oldest Native American boarding high school in New Mexico. Mother Katharine Drexel of the Roman Catholic Sisters of the Blessed Sacrament established St. Kate's to educate Indian children. (The school expanded her vision in later years to include blacks and children of the poor.) She recruited its first students herself, visiting the pueblos and reservations on horseback. In the early days, parents brought their children to school by wagon and camped on the school grounds. Enrollment is about 180 in grades 7 through 12. The school boasts 1,400 graduates representing more than 25 different Indian cultures including Navajo, Apache, Hopi and the Pueblo Indians. Alumni have gone on to Notre Dame, Georgetown, Dartmouth, Loyola and other major colleges and universities and served as tribal leaders.

Visitors can tour the campus, including a

gallery that displays the pottery, jewelry and other art work of alumni and students. Sales help pay operational costs of the school. (See our Attractions chapter.)

St. Michael's High School
100 Siringo Rd. • 983-7353

This Catholic school offers a traditional college preparatory program and attracts students with an interest in athletics — more than 40 teams compete in 15 separate sports. St. Mike's regularly wins district sports titles and often takes its teams to the state championships. The school also promotes and encourages service projects, a tradition of the LaSallian Brothers of Christian Schools. (Please see our close-up in this chapter for more information.) The high school enrolls about 500 students. St. Mike's also offers grades 7 and 8. There's usually a waiting list to attend.

The Tutorial School
400 Brunn Rd. • 988-1859

With an enrollment that varies between 20 and 50 students, this school is based on a belief that the pursuit of knowledge thrives in an environment "that is free of fear and authority and whatever else interferes with creativity." That means the school also steers away from coercion, reward and punishments, competition, comparison and unsolicited criticism or evaluation. The school has no hierarchical structures, and students and staff members run the school together. Students are not required to attend formal classes or follow a set curriculum. The school advises parents only to send their children here "if you have absolute trust in the ability of children to take charge of their lives and make their own decisions or if you are at least willing to learn to develop that trust."

Child Care

When it comes to child care, Santa Fe isn't much different from the rest of the country. Especially for infants and the 3-and-younger crowd, finding high-quality, affordable child care can be harder than finding opening-night seats to the opera. Of course, some families hire nannies to stay with children in their own homes. Some have relatives who care for their kids. But most moms and dads have to look for outside help.

Santa Fe has a wonderful resource, the Early Childhood Center at Santa Fe Community College, which make parents' plight easier. The center offers a variety of services and programs including information and referrals, on-campus child care, fact sheets to help parents select good child care and training programs for people who wish to go into the child-care business. You can reach them at 6401 Richards Avenue, 438-1354.

Another resource worth checking, the non-profit Santa Fe Home Child Care Niños Program, 473-1109, has information about home day care throughout the city. Call to learn about registered and licensed home day care providers in your area.

To be licensed, a home-care center with one adult present can have four children with a maximum of two children younger than age 2 and must meet other requirements. Rate per child is roughly $95 a week for an infant and $85 for an older child for eight hours of care. With a second adult, a home center can have up to 12 children. Many home day care providers have waiting lists and do not accept infants. The Early Childhood Center at Santa Fe Community College and the Home Child Care help line will not recommend one center or one provider over another, but they give parents a place to start.

Besides in-home day care, most parents have two other basic options: commercial child-care centers and preschools. There are a few excellent facilities here, several good ones, and many that are adequate. The Santa Fe Public Schools have a preschool for children with special needs that enrolls a limited number of other children. Some tribal governments offer their own programs as well. The Santa Fe telephone book lists 25 child-care centers and 36 preschools. Many programs having waiting lists. Fees range from $70 to $120 a week per child.

The National Association for the Education of Young Children accredits high-quality child-care centers and preschools throughout the country. Here's a list of accredited centers in Santa Fe and a few others Santa Fe parents have recommended. Unless otherwise noted, these facilities are open from 7:30 AM to 5:30 PM five days a week.

Day Care and Preschools

Children's Garden
107 W. Barcelona Rd. • 984-9961

This Waldorf school serves eight to 12 children ages 3½ to 6 in preschool and kindergarten. The program operates from 8:30 AM to 3 PM daily. A teacher and an aide work with the students in a group, and cooperative activities and social involvement are some of the program's strong focuses. The school includes creative play, baking and crafts, music, storytelling and puppet shows and seasonal festivals. Natural fibers, wooden toys and outdoor activities add to the children's experience. The school operates out of the Unitarian Church of Santa Fe.

Garcia Street Club
569 Garcia St. • 983-9512

The Garcia Street Club offers child care, preschool and kindergarten for ages 3 to 6 and has served Santa Fe families for more than 50 years. The former residence that houses the school is on the National Register of Historic Places. The year-round operation appeals to parents who work downtown, but also attracts children from around the city. The program offers appropriate activities designed to help the child develop as a whole person. Unlike many preschools, Garcia Street Club does not follow the public schools schedule and does not cancel when the Santa Fe Public Schools declare a snow day. The school is only closed 10 days a year.

Head Start
1150 Canyon Rd. (next to Cristo Rey Church) and other locations • 982-4484

The federal goverhment specifically designed this long-established program to give kids a boost before they start first grade. Families who meet low-income requirements can enroll their 3, 4 and 5 year-olds. Parents do not need to be working or in school for children to qualify, and there is no fee. Ten percent of the children served are kids with special needs.

In addition to the programs' educational and developmental activities, children receive a meal and a snack and medical and dental screening. Besides the Canyon Road school, Head Start offers several other centers in Santa Fe County and plans to operate directly out of some Santa Fe elementary schools. The program encourages family involvement, and at least half the Head Start staff are parents of former Head Start children. The staff holds Child Development Associate credentials.

Santa Fe Community College Childcare Center and Preschool
6401 Richards Ave. • 438-1344

The college offers infant/toddler care, a program for two-year-olds and a preschool program, all designed to suit a child's level of development. Each group has its own bright spacious room and access to a large outdoor play yard. Preference in enrollment goes to SFCC students, and the college reserves about 75 percent of the slots for these kids. The other places are roughly divided between staff/faculty and the general public. There's usually a waiting list for infant care. Kindergartners and preschoolers thrive at this clean, sunny center on the south side of the campus. Adult to child ratio is high here, and the staff is well-trained and professional.

Temple Beth Shalom
205 E. Barcelona Rd. • 982-6888

This well-regarded Santa Fe school serves up to 42 children from age 3 to kindergarten. The schedule offers a balance of activities —

indoor and outdoor, group and solitary play, quiet and energetic. One of the program's main goals is to stimulate a child's desire to learn. The ratio of adults to children is 1 to 7.

Pre-reading and writing are offered to the 3- and 4-year-olds. Children are introduced to Hebrew and Spanish. Kindergartners have a more structured program designed to give them the skills 1st-grade teachers expect. As part of the Temple Beth Shalom's larger community, the school integrates teachings about Jewish life and values into the curriculum.

La Casa Feliz
1060 Cerrillos Rd. • 982-4896

Santa Fe's weekly newspaper, *Santa Fe Reporter*, voted this as Santa Fe's best child care based on comments from its readers. The school also received the Piñon Award for its work from the nonprofit Santa Fe Community Foundation.

Operated on the grounds of the New Mexico School for the Deaf, La Casa Feliz serves an enrollment of 70, infants through age 6, with a staff to child ratio of 1 to 6. The school caters to children by observing what each child needs to learn at his or her own pace. The school's organization gives children choices while also offering consistency. Students have an opportunity to learn sign language and Spanish. Special needs students are integrated into the classrooms. La Casa Feliz is closed for a week during the Christmas holidays and a week during the summer. Otherwise, the school follows the Santa Fe Public School schedule.

La Comunidad de los Niños
1121 Alto St. • 820-1604

A collaboration between the City of Santa Fe and Presbyterian Medical Services, this new center accepts children ages 2 to 5. With a maximum enrollment of 87, the center offers a 1 to 4 adult to child ratio in its 2-year-old program and a 1 to 6 ratio in the preschool. Besides enjoying a clean new building specifically designed for the child care, La Comunidad offers access to the play yard from each classroom and gives kids a choice of indoor or outdoor activities throughout the day. Some spaces are reserved for the children of city employees and for low-income families;

fees are on a sliding scale. The play-based program incorporates sound early childhood theory.

Wee Wonders Learning Center
Agora Shopping Center, 7 Avenida Vista Grande, Ste. B2, Eldorado • 466-4610

This bright new center accepts children from ages 2 months to 5 years old and is the only commercial child-care operation that serves the popular and populous Eldorado area southeast of the city. Wee Wonders operates from 7 AM to 6 PM and accepts school-age children during the summer. In addition to playing in a large outdoor play area, children can learn art, music and Spanish, spend time in the library and go on field trips. Adult-to-child ratio is 1 to 4 in the baby/toddler room and 1 to 8 or less in the preschool.

La Casita Preschool and Kindergarten
438 Alamo Dr. • 983-2803

A nonprofit parent co-op school, La Casita caters to children between the ages of 3 and 6. Parents commit time as well as tuition here. They make up the school's board of directors, serve on committees and get together twice a year to give the building a thorough cleaning. Once a month, parents work in the school along with teachers and bring a snack for the class.

For kids, play is essential here and a wide range of opportunities is available. Established in 1971, La Casita serves about 40 children with two teachers and two parents assigned to each class of 20. Morning and afternoon programs are available; some children are eligible for all-day school, but La Casita is not a day-care center.

Special Child-Care Services

New Vistas Early Childhood Program
1121 Alto St. • 988-3803

This long-established nonprofit agency provides a full scope of services for children from birth to age 3 who have, or are at risk for, developmental delays. In addition to direct work with sometimes fragile little ones, the program helps their parents, teaching them how to work with children to promote optimal development. Services include parental support; speech, physical, occupational and family therapy; home-based assistance; therapeutic programs for toddlers; a lending library; and consultation and coordination of other professional services.

Santa Fe Community College Early Childhood, Family Studies and Teacher Education Community Outreach Programs
6401 Richards Ave. • Nosotros 438-1697

Nosotros helps strengthen the bonds between moms and dads and children from birth to age 5 by teaching the adults skills they need to parent successfully. Using play as a tool for learning, child development specialists work with families individually or in small groups to help parents learn how to better care for their children physically, psychologically and emotionally. A licensed therapist may consult with the parents and children if necessary. The city of Santa Fe provides some of the program's funding; Santa Fe Community College offers the space and staff. Participation is free.

Corazon Respite Care and Emergency Child Care
6401 Richards Ave. • 438-1610

Families with children ages 12 and younger can receive 10 days of child care, in some cases 24 hours a day, through these two programs. Corazon offers consultations with child-care specialists and referrals to other agencies to help families dealing with terminal illness, hospitalization, unexpected parental death, financial crises and other types of stress.

Early Childhood Resource Center and Toy Lending Center
6401 Richards Ave. • 438-1612

You'll find a wealth of goodies here! The Toy Lending Center, affectionately known as TLC, has more than 2,000 toys and playthings for infants and children up to kindergarten age and a small selection of toys for school-age children. Families, teachers and child-care workers may borrow from the collection for free. The resource center offers books, videotapes, films and slide/tape presentations for teachers and caregivers who work with children. The phone number above will also connect you to the Warm Line, where child development specialists will answer questions about children's behaviors and attitudes and suggest ways to solve problems. All these services are free.

Babysitters and Babysitting Services

For a come-to-the-house teen to watch your little ones, the informal parent-sitter referral network may be your ticket to freedom. Your 6-year-old's best friend's oldest sister might be the babysitter of your dreams. Nieces and nephews might know classmates who baby-sit. Your child's teacher may have some ideas. If your favorite sitter can't come when you need her, ask if she or he has any friends who might be interested. Some parents trade kids with families of friends so Mom and Dad get an occasional break and then return the favor. Ask, ask and ask again. Take names and phone numbers. Keep notes. Be generous with your help to other parents.

If you run out of leads, consider the youth group at your church as a resource. Or call Girls Inc., 982-2042, the YMCA, 985-8821, or Santa Fe Community College, 471-8200, and

---

INSIDERS' TIP

Santa Fe has six colleges, which among them enroll about 8,000 students. The largest of these is Santa Fe Community College. More than 13 percent of the city's population goes to college — and that's not counting workshops, seminar and SFCC's popular continuing education programs.

ask if they've done any babysitter training lately. They might have a list of recommended sitters. Employment services at the local colleges can sometimes give you the names and numbers of college kids who like to baby-sit.

If you're in Santa Fe on a family trip and need a vacation from the kids, there are resources to help. And don't feel guilty. After all, it's your vacation too!

Santa Fe has two commercial services that provide babysitters so Mom and Dad can take a break. (Locals can use this service too.)

Santa Fe Kid Connection Inc.
2422 Cerrillos Rd., Ste. 322 • 471-3100

Founded in 1983, Kid Connection offers care for infants and children of all ages. It screens and requires references from all employees and provides sitters for days, evenings, weekends, holidays and overnight. Advance reservations are strongly recom-

mended. Kid Connection charges for a required minimum number of hours and increases the rate depending on the number of children. They offer an annual $75 membership for residents or frequent visitors, which lowers the hourly rate. Among their clientele are many return visitors who appreciate being able to request a sitter their child knows.

Magical Happenings Babysitting Service and Children's Tours
1124 Don Juan • 982-9327, 982-1570

Outings are a speciality of this service, which has been in business since 1990. All sitters are screened, and you'll find former teachers on their roster. This service happily arranges daytrips and explorations for its young clients and will put together a custom tour for your children. Sometimes you can find a sitter on short notice, but it's best to make reservations.

Santa Fe has always been a beacon for alternative lifestyles and ideologies, hence its nickname, "The City Different."

Healthcare and Wellness

Long before the term "alternative medicine" came into vogue — and we're talking centuries, not merely decades — New Mexicans were using herbs and potions, massage and incantations to cure what ailed them. Remedies came not from acupuncturists, aromatherapists or biofeedback, but from *curanderas*, medicine men and other native healers who have long been an integral part of New Mexican society.

Some of their therapies — echinacea and goldenseal for colds, for example, or St. John's Wort for depression — have been "discovered" in recent years by traditional Western medicine, much as Christopher Columbus "discovered" an America that had been home to Indians for centuries. Those particular remedies are so common these days that you can find them in your local Walgreens — at least in Santa Fe, which is home to nine licensed schools of alternative/natural/holistic healing and massage, many of them with international reputations.

Many northern New Mexicans seem comfortable foregoing the customary white coat, black bag and medical degree of European medicine for less institutionalized healing methods such as acupuncture, Ayurvedics and herbs — no doubt because non-Western doctoring has a formidable history here. Of course, Santa Fe has always been a beacon for alternative lifestyles and ideologies, hence its nickname, "The City Different." But long before some savvy marketing person came up with that sound bite, both the ailing and the healers made northern New Mexico a destination to fulfill their medical destinies.

For some, fulfillment may come in more conventional settings such as hospitals and doctors offices. While Santa Fe has only one hospital — St. Vincent — there are a number of medical centers and clinics in town as well as a healthy list of MDs from which to choose, whether you're looking for a general practitioner or a specialist. And choice is certainly the operative word. Unfortunately, Santa Fe has no medical referral services at present to help you select a doctor. But St. Vincent has a number of publications that rate New Mexico physicians, including one put out by Ralph Nader's Public Citizen called *Questionable Doctors: State Listing for New Mexico* and *The Best Doctors in America: Central Region*, by Steven W. Naifeh. (For more information about St. Vincent's medical library, see the entry for St. Vincent Hospital.) Or, you can pick your doctor the old-fashioned way — by word-of-mouth. Walk-in medical care is offered at St. Vincent Hospital, Lovelace and La Familia Medical Center; see the write-ups in this chapter for more information. In the meantime, here are a few places to start.

Traditional Western Medicine

La Familia Medical Center
1035 Alto St. • 982-4425

La Familia is a community health center that provides primary medical care from obstetrics to geriatrics. It also operates a dental clinic that accepts Medicaid patients, a rarity in Santa Fe. The 25-year-old nonprofit medical center is among the primary deliverers of babies in the community. In 1996, it delivered more than 380 infants; by September of the next year, it had already exceeded 400 births. The clinic has seven board-certified family physicians on site; four residents from the University of New Mexico Medical School; two family nurse practitioners; an RN who is also a certified diabetes educator; three full-time dentists and two dental hygienists. La Familia's health providers recognize the validity of alternative medicine and respect its cultural importance, particularly to Hispanic and Native American patients. They often incorporate alternative therapies in patients' healthcare plans, referring them to outside sources if La Familia doesn't offer a particular method.

La Familia started in 1972 as a little neighborhood clinic in a building shared with a day-care center on Santa Fe's west side. Today, it's a full-time medical center with a building of its own that it rents for $1 a year from the City of Santa Fe. At last count, the center had 7,500 registered patients, 60 percent of them uninsured. Most use La Familia's sliding fee scale in some fashion. Many are Medicare patients. The clinic also has a number of patients who can afford to go elsewhere but choose La Familia for its quality comprehensive healthcare. The clinic provides services to all who walk in its doors, regardless of their ability to pay, though it asks for a minimum payment of $12. La Familia accepts all forms of insurance and contracts with HMOs to provide medical care for their patients. It also operates a number of outstanding community outreach programs, including "Prometoras," which promotes community health education through lay advisors who provide information on such topics as prenatal care, diabetes, child immunizations, asthma and breast feeding. It recently opened a lactating center that teaches mothers how to pump their breast milk to leave with their children's caregiver.

La Familia is open from 8 AM to 5 PM Monday, Tuesday, Thursday and Friday and from 9 AM to 8 PM on Wednesday. It also conducts two Saturday dental clinics per month from 8 AM to 5 PM by appointment only. The center accepts walk-in patients but

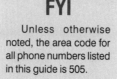

FYI

Unless otherwise noted, the area code for all phone numbers listed in this guide is 505.

asks that you try to call ahead so the staff can fit you into the best available appointment slot or send you to St. Vincent Hospital. La Familia sees an average of 30 walk-ins per day.

Lovelace Health Systems
440 St. Michael's Dr. • 995-2400, (800) 877-7526, ext. 2400

A subsidiary of CIGNA HealthCare, Lovelace is New Mexico's oldest and largest health maintenance organization with headquarters in Albuquerque at 5400 Gibson Boulevard SE, 262-7000, (800) 877-7526. HMOs have earned reputations nationwide as being frustrating mazes of referrals and counter-referrals, but in Santa Fe, at least, many Lovelace staffers — from doctors and nurses to pharmacists and receptionists — seem to sympathize with patients' frustration and try to help them work within the system. Perhaps that's why *U.S. News and World Report* named Lovelace Health Plan the top-ranked HMO in New Mexico last year.

The St. Michael's Drive clinic offers a full range of primary-care services, including family practice, internal medicine, pediatrics, women's health, rehabilitation and fitness, diabetes education, X-rays, laboratory services and a pharmacy. It also provides a number of specialty services on site such as gastroenterology, endocrinology, allergy, urology and nephrology. For other specialties, it contracts with local practitioners — even acupuncturists and other nonorthodox healers, if you meet Lovelace's criteria — or may send a patient to Albuquerque, where its numerous medical centers and contract physicians and hospitals cover up to 43 medical specialties, including cardiology, cosmetic surgery, occupational medicine and orthopedics. Lovelace's Gibson Boulevard hospital in Albuquerque also operates a Level II trauma center, an accredited sleep disorders clinic and the state's largest birthing center.

Lovelace opened its Santa Fe clinic in 1985 in DeVargas Center. Four years later, it moved to brand-new quarters on nearby Alameda Street and, in 1992, opened a second branch on St. Michael's Drive, close to St. Vincent

Hospital. Today, all Santa Fe operations have been consolidated in the St. Michael's Drive clinic, which offers same-day care from 8 AM to 8 PM, seven days a week. The clinic accepts walk-ins but encourages people to call ahead.

St. Vincent Hospital
455 St. Michael's Dr. • 983-3361

St. Vincent is the regional medical center for northern New Mexico and the largest medical facility between Albuquerque and southern Colorado. It's a nonprofit, nonsectarian hospital with 268 beds, more than 200 staff physicians representing 22 medical specialties and more than 475 nurses. With more than 1,350 employees, it is also Santa Fe's largest private employer. Established in 1865 by Sisters of Charity out of Cincinnati, Ohio, St. Vincent was New Mexico's first hospital. It began its days in an old adobe building next to St. Francis Cathedral in downtown Santa Fe. The sisters ran the hospital for more than a century, moving it three times before turning it over to a community-based board of trustees in 1973. In 1977, it moved to its current location on St. Michael's Drive. Today, St. Vincent remains the only hospital in Santa Fe — its "primary service area."

St. Vincent also serves six other New Mexico counties north of Santa Fe to the Colorado border. While four smaller local hospitals also serve this region, many residents from those areas come to St. Vincent for more specialized care. In addition to the usual departments, St. Vincent has a specialized pain clinic, a sleep disorders clinic, a Level II trauma center and comprehensive cancer services. St. Vincent admits more than 10,000 patients a year and treats an additional 11,500 as outpatients. Another 5,000 patients come to the hospital each year for same-day surgery. The emergency room and adjacent FirstCARE unit treat more than 37,000 patients annually, making it the second-busiest acute care facility in New Mexico after University Hospital in Albuquerque. FirstCARE is open for walk-ins from 9 AM to 9 PM. The emergency room is open 24 hours a day.

St. Vincent periodically offers free medical services throughout the year including flu shots and breast cancer screenings. The public may also use the hospital's medical library from 8 AM to 2 PM on weekdays. The hospital is in the process of expanding its consumer health section and has a librarian who specializes in consumer-health issues and information.

Women's Health Services Family Care and Counseling Center
141 Paseo de Peralta, Ste. C • 988-8869

On the southwest corner of the DeVargas Mall parking lot, Women's Health Services is a primary care health center that offers extensive gynecological and family planning services as well as mental healthcare, therapeutic massage and limited laboratory work. Its staff includes physicians, nurse practitioners and master's-level mental health practitioners who provide services on a sliding fee scale. The center also is part of a grant program that covers uninsured patients.

Women's Health Services does not provide either obstetrics or pediatrics, though a good many of its patients are children. Despite the name, many of Women's Health Services patients are men — 10 percent at last count. Women's Health Services opened in 1973 as a self-health education resource center for women. A progeny of the feminist self-help movement, the clinic's initial raison d'être was to give women more information to take better care of themselves. Within a couple of years, it began to provide services and became a full-fledged clinic in the late 1970s. At that time it was staffed by volunteers. It's only been in the last decade that its doctors, nurses and therapists have been on full salary. Although the clinic is geared toward low-income and/or uninsured patients, its waiting room is a true cross-section of Santa Fe. Many women who could afford to go elsewhere choose Women's Health Services because of its reputation for excellent healthcare and for providing patients with information about alternative medicine and suggesting complementary therapies such as acupuncture, herbology and homeopathy.

Presbyterian Medical Services
1422 Paseo de Peralta • 982-5565, (800) 477-7633

Presbyterian Medical Services is the primary provider of mental health and counseling services in Santa Fe County. A nonprofit corporation, its mission is to furnish high-quality, affordable medical, dental, mental health, hospice, retirement and other human services throughout the Southwest, particularly to Hispanic and Native American communities. PMS is the successor to the United Presbyterian Church's medical mission to the Southwest, which began in 1901. When the church could no longer provide financial support, PMS incorporated in 1969 to carry on the work. Although it's an independent organization, it maintains its ties to the church through a covenant with the Presbytery of Santa Fe and the Synod of the Southwest.

www.insiders.com

See this and many other **Insiders' Guide®** destinations online — in their entirety.

Visit us today!

PMS employs about 1,300 people in 38 programs, including primary healthcare centers and agencies; comprehensive mental health care programs; home healthcare and hospice programs; nursing homes; developmental disabilities programs for children and adults; substance abuse treatment; Head Start programs; AIDS and other health education and counseling; and a pharmacy consulting service. PMS also offers the following services:

• **Brain Injury Community Services**, 820 Paseo de Peralta, 986-9633, part of the Santa Fe Community Guidance Center (see subsequent entry), provides case management for individuals with traumatic brain injury by assisting clients and their families in reintegrating into the community.

• **Crisis Response of Santa Fe**, 1422 Paseo de Peralta, Building 2, 820-1440 (office), 820-6333 (hotline), is a suicide prevention program with a hotline and a mobile crisis team, both available 24-hours a day, seven days a week in Santa Fe County. Volunteers trained in short-term telephone crisis intervention operate the hotline to offer immediate suicide counseling as well as information and referrals. The mobile crisis team comprises professionals who respond to suicide, drug/alcohol abuse and psychiatric emergencies.

• **The Hospice Center**, 1422 Paseo de Peralta, Building 2, 988-2211, 988-1477, (800) 880-8001, established in 1991, provides at-home care for people with terminal illnesses and their families. Its registered nurses are specialists in pain and symptom control and are on call 24 hours a day. The center offers regularly scheduled nursing visits; volunteer support services for patients and their families; home health aide services for personal care; social work visits for counseling; pastoral counseling and referral; physical, occupational and speech therapy; bereavement services; medication; medical treatment, equipment and supplies. The center also operates The Hospice Center for Counseling and Support for individuals and groups, including schools or businesses, facing life-threatening illness or experiencing grief or loss.

• **La Nueva Vida** (New Life), 1409 Second Street, 983-9521, provides at-risk youths up to

---

INSIDERS' TIP

Though more of a grocery store than a bona fide member of the healing community, Wild Oats Community Market carries a wide range of dietary supplements, herbs and homeopathic products and tries to hire employees who are knowledgeable about what they sell. You can even get a quickie massage at Wild Oats in an ergonomically correct massage chair complete with a padded, donut-shaped face rest. Wild Oats and its sister store, Alfalfa's Market (located just a few blocks away), offer informative symposia on natural healing and living. Check their bulletin boards or their monthly calendars, available at the customer-service counters. You'll find Wild Oats at 1090 S. St. Francis Drive, 983-5333, and 1708 Llano Street, 473-4943, and Alfalfa's Market at 333 W. Cordova Road, 986-8667.

age 21 with mental health services; residential treatment centers; group homes; alcohol and substance abuse treatment prevention; job placement; and family intervention. It operates two residential treatment centers and a day treatment program for kindergarten through 12th graders.

• **Ortiz Mountain Health Center**, 08A Main Street, Cerrillos, 471-6266. Open since 1995, this is a three-day-a-week primary clinic located in Cerrillos, about 20 miles southwest of Santa Fe. The center provides diagnostic and treatment services, limited pharmacy and laboratory services, prenatal and perinatal care and treatment of minor emergencies. It coordinates with healthcare providers in Santa Fe for referral and speciality care.

• **PMS Home Care**, 1422 Paseo de Peralta, Building 2, 988-2211, 988-1477, (800) 880-8001, provides comprehensive home-care services to residents of Santa Fe County with an emphasis on rehabilitation. Licensed by both Medicaid and Medicare, it provides skilled nursing, home health aides, physical therapy, occupational therapy, speech pathology and medical social services. The staff works with physicians, hospitals, rehabilitation centers, nursing homes and medical equipment suppliers to make a smooth transition to home healthcare.

• **Santa Fe Community Guidance Center**, 820 Paseo de Peralta, 986-9633, is a mental health outpatient facility for day treatment; case management; and supported living and employment. The program provides rehabilitation for the long-term mentally ill through its Spirit Club, 1505 Fifth Street, 986-8827, which focuses on social, recreational and vocational skills.

• **Santa Fe Community Partnership**, 1900 Chamisa Street, 982-8899, founded as a community coalition of organizations and individuals, is primarily an educational organization that aims to increase community awareness about substance abuse and prevention and ensure the existence of treatment and recovery options. Among the programs it has initiated are life-skills training, including parenting; special training for clergy; and a free/low-cost small business employee assistance program to help workers cope with marriage and family issues, alcohol and drug abuse, gambling, depression or financial troubles.

Alternative Healthcare

GRD Clinic
1505 Llano St. • 984-0934

GRD is a holistic healing clinic, which means it takes care of your whole system — body, mind and spirit — rather than just the part that's hurting. Primarily a chiropractic clinic, GRD also offers massage; colonics; facial rejuvenation, an Ayurvedic technique from India that uses facial points for relaxation and healing; and Sat Nam Rasayam, a yoga-based method that uses the body's energy to heal itself. The 14-year-old clinic is owned by Sikhs, for whom holistic health is a religious tenet, though not everyone who works at GRD is Sikh. All practitioners are licensed or certified, if the particular therapy requires it. The clinic refers many patients next door to Acupuncture Associates of America, which is also Sikh-owned. GRD is open Monday through Friday from 9 AM to 6 PM. Some therapists also hold Saturday clinics.

Ojo Caliente Mineral Springs
50 Los Baños Rd. (N.M. Hwy. 285)
• 583-2233, (800) 222-9162

Though located about 50 miles north of Santa Fe, straddling the Rio Arriba County and Taos County lines, Ojo Caliente Mineral Springs is close enough — and special enough — to warrant mention in this chapter. Named by 16th-century explorer Cabeza de Vaca, Ojo Caliente ("Hot Eye") Mineral Springs is the only spa in the world with its particular combination of five naturally hot, bubbling waters that flow from geothermal wells deep beneath the earth. Many people "take the waters" for their purported therapeutic value, others for the sheer pleasure and relaxation. Ojo Caliente's arsenic spring is thought to be the only one outside of Baden-Baden, Germany. In trace amounts, arsenic is supposed to relieve arthritis, rheumatism, stomach ulcers, burns, eczema and a host of other complaints. The spa also has an iron spring, which comes out of the ground at 109 degrees Fahrenheit (the arsenic waters are 113 degrees) into a large pool used for a hot plunge that reportedly rejuvenates the blood. The lithia, soda and sodium springs are primarily for drinking to heal a variety of symptoms, from depression and sluggish kidneys to excess gas.

One of the oldest health spas in North America, Ojo Caliente was once considered a sacred spot by ancient Tewa-speaking Pueblo Indians who lived on a mesa above the present village. Today, the spa is spread out over approximately 1,000 hilly, river-lined acres in the Española Valley . The waters are piped into various pools and tubs, both public and private. The spa offers other services such as therapeutic massage, herbal wraps, facials and salt rubs. The grounds support a quaint old adobe hotel whose rooms have no showers; guests use the public bathhouse. Ojo Caliente is open from 7:30 AM to 9 PM seven days a week year round. The spa closes only on Christmas. On weekends the public tubs cost $11 for 90 minutes, $22 all day. Weekdays are less expensive: $8.50 for 90 minutes, $16.50 all day. Private tubs run $15 for 25 minutes on weekends, including mineral baths, $12 per person during the week.

Parcells Center
121 Lorenzo Rd. • 986-1441, (800) 811-6784

Parcells Center is named for Hazel Parcells, a pioneer in the fields of nutrition and energy healing, who died at age 106 near her home in Las Vegas, New Mexico. Dr. Parcells — a doctor of naturopathy and of chiropractics who held Ph.D.s in nutrition and world religion — founded the center in 1995 to continue her work in natural self-healing. A staff of dedicated professionals operates the Santa Fe center in conjunction with a wide network of expe-

rienced health specialists, many of whom were students and followers of Dr. Parcells. The center promotes the Parcells Method — a regimen outlined in a new book called *Live Better Longer* that includes food cleansing and combining, therapeutic bathing and herbal remedies — and offers classes in its Santa Fe headquarters as well as daylong and weekend workshops in cities around the country. Parcells Center also conducts in-depth courses in natural and nutritional self-healing for health professionals and others seeking certification in the Parcells Method. The center publishes the monthly *Parcells Newsletter*, which provides nutrition and health news, including discoveries from the Parcells Lab. It also sells products Dr. Parcells developed herself, everything from food supplements and homeopathic remedies to bath aids and home appliances.

Ten Thousand Waves Japanese Health Spa
3451 Hyde Park Rd. • 982-9304

Ten Thousand Waves is not just a spa, it's an experience that literally and figuratively bathes your every sense from the moment you enter the premises. To get to the tubs, you pass rock sculptures and plants and climb a few steps that form a bridge over an indoor stream with fish. In the lobby, you're likely to bump into one of the owner's aloof but not unfriendly Akita dogs as you collect your kimono and keys. The dressing rooms, where sandals and towels are stacked for the borrowing, smell pleasantly of the cedar lotion the spa puts out for clients to use after their soak. Once you emerge from the dressing rooms, freshly showered and kimono-clad, you can head for a chlorine free soak in either the clothing-optional public tub ($13 person per day) or one of the spa's luxurious private tubs ($18 to $25 an hour per person), some with a sauna, others with a steam room and one that even has a waterfall. Or, you can go for one of the spa's deservedly famous therapeutic massages. Ten Thousand Waves has more than 100 bodyworkers on its roster, all of them trained in Swedish massage. Many have additional skills such as shiatsu, reflexology, acupressure, Trager, Reiki, Alexander Technique, watsu . . . the list goes on. A standard massage costs $60 an hour, $35 for a half-hour, while a masters massage starts at $78 per hour, $48 for a half hour. It's best to schedule weekday massages a couple of days in advance. Call at least a week ahead of time if you want your massage on the weekend.

The Aquatherapy Institute at Upayah Center
935 Alto St. • 982-5049

The Aquatherapy Institute is exactly what its name implies — a school and clinic for under- and over-water physical therapy. Open since October 1996, the institute offers watsu (shiatsu massage in water) as well as prenatal and neonatal work in water. The institute advocates, but doesn't do, water births. Prenatal water classes are designed to prepare expectant mothers, their newborns and even their partners for birth. The institute claims its method cuts the time and pain of labor by between one- and two-thirds. Classes begin in the last three months of pregnancy and cost up to $1,200 total. Neonatal classes are for babies and are meant to reintroduce newborns to the comfortable water environment they enjoyed for nine months before birth by tapping into their instinct to hold their breath under water. Neonatal classes cost $10 per session for baby, mother and partner. Watsu sessions cost $75 for 75 minutes. The Aquatherapy Institute has two private, chlorine-free pools — one 10 feet in diameter, the other double that size — kept at skin temperature: 96 degrees Fahrenheit. The pools are open from 7 AM to 9 PM Monday through Friday and from 7 AM to 10 PM on Saturday and Sunday. Office hours are Monday through Friday from 10 AM to 3 PM.

Vitality!
513 Camino de los Marquez • 983-5557

Called Vitality Unlimited in a former life, Vitality! is far more than a store — it's an alternative healing center with experts in vitamins, homeopathy, herbs and Chinese patent medicines. On staff are two homeopaths, two doctors of Oriental medicine, a certified nutritionist and two herbalists with a combined expertise of 30 years. Vitality! also offers acupuncture by special appointment and performs urine and saliva testing. Vitality! stocks its shelves with all stripes of alternative over-the-counter health products, including aromatherapy paraphernalia, Chinese patent medicines, flower remedies, herbal supplements and homeopathic pills and potions, not to mention Birkenstock sandals, books, CDs and assorted gift items. It has one of the largest selection of homeopathics and Chinese

INSIDERS' TIP

Contrary to popular myth, the Black Death did not die when the Middle Ages became ancient history. Bubonic plague is endemic to New Mexico, where 41 percent of all cases reported in the United States in 1994 occurred. The state health department gets an average of four to seven reports per year of plague, an acute infectious disease transmitted to humans by fleas from infected rodents. Symptoms include high fever; chills; enlarged, painful lymph nodes (buboes), particularly in the groin; and hemorrhages that turn black. Plague also exists in a virulent and highly contagious pneumonic form, which attacks the lungs. Thanks to antibiotics, few people die in America from any form of the disease.

patent medicines in the Southwest. Vitality! has been around in one form or another for the past 25 years and has earned a solid reputation in Santa Fe and elsewhere around the country, judging from its mailing list. Hours are 10 AM to 6 PM Monday through Saturday.

Student Clinics

International Institute of Chinese Medicine
Lopez Ln. • 438-7328, (800) 377-4561

IICM is a world-renowned graduate school of Chinese medicine that teaches and practices acupuncture, herbology and movement. An important component of the school's curriculum is its advanced student clinic, in which third- and fourth-year students (and occasionally last semester second-year students) see patients from the community under the supervision of a D.O.M. (doctor of Oriental medicine). Visits include a consultation, acupuncture treatment and often an herbal prescription — either a patent medicine or bag of herbs to be brewed into tea. Prescriptions are available at the clinic, generally for less than $10, and may include an ingredient as exotic as silkworm feces or as common as ginger.

IICM opened in 1984 with about 20 students. Today, the school has 220 students divided between its Santa Fe and Albuquerque campuses. Founders Nancy and Michael Zeng are both M.D.s as well as D.O.M.s and are providers for Blue Cross/Blue Shield. They and other faculty members see patients referred by other doctors.

All IICM students memorize the names of each of the 300 herbs used at the school. Patients generally spend an hour at the clinic and return on a weekly basis for six or seven weeks. Sometimes, however, one treatment will do the trick — especially for allergies or pain relief. The first visit costs $7.50. Subsequent visits cost $15 each for the general public, $7.50 for seniors. The clinic also offers a sliding scale for people in financial need. Clinic hours are Monday through Saturday from 9 AM to 6 PM and Thursday evenings from 7 to 9 PM.

New Mexico Academy of Healing Arts
501 Franklin Ave. • 982-6271 office; 982-1001 clinic

The 17-year-old New Mexico Academy of Healing Arts offers certification programs in massage and polarity, a therapy that utilizes bodywork, nutrition and counseling in conjunction with the body's magnetic energy. It also offers student massages to the public for $20 to $30 an hour. The academy's foundation is Swedish massage, though it also teaches other forms of massage including sports massage; cranial-sacral therapy, which aids circulation along the spinal pathway; and orthobionomy, which relies on movement to realign the body

INSIDERS' TIP

Hikers, campers and others who may come into contact with rodents, particularly deer mice, should take special precautions against an extremely rare, but serious and sometimes fatal disease called Hantavirus Pulmonary Syndrome. The primary symptom is difficulty breathing, which quickly progresses to a total inability to breathe. Other symptoms include fever, headache, abdominal, joint, and lower back pain, and sometimes nausea and vomiting. While the risk of infection is small, hikers and campers should take the following precautions: Air out abandoned or unused cabins before occupying them; do not use cabins with signs of rodent infestation; check outdoor campsites for rodent droppings or burrows; avoid sleeping near woodpiles or garbage areas that might attract rodents; avoid sleeping on the bare ground; store food in rodent-proof containers; discard, bury or burn garbage immediately.

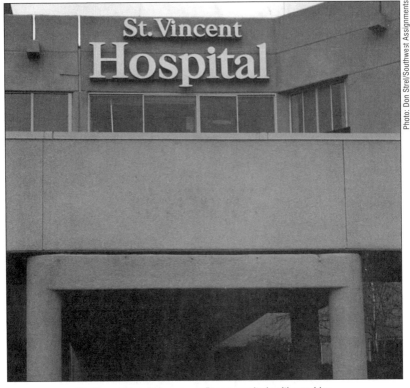

St. Vincent Hospital, a nonprofit community health provider, serves Santa Fe and the surrounding region.

for relief of acute or chronic pain. The student clinic is open from 6 to 9 PM on Thursday and from 8:30 AM to 2:30 PM Friday through Sunday. Call ahead for an appointment.

The Scherer Institute
of Natural Healing
935 Alto St. • 982-8398

The Scherer Institute of Natural Healing opened in 1979 as Dr. Jay Scherer's Academy of Natural Healing. In addition to Swedish massage, the school incorporates aromatherapy, herbology, homeopathy and shiatsu (Japanese pressure-point massage) into its curriculum. Founder Jay Scherer was a naturopathic doctor who died at age 83 in 1990, six years after being named one of Santa Fe's "Living Treasures."

The world-famous Scherer Institute of Natu-

ral Healing holds a couple of two-month student clinics a year where the public can get an hourlong nurturing Swedish massage — the school's specialty — for $15 to $25. The massage clinic is part of the institute's internship program, which requires students halfway through the six-month program to perform 20 massages under supervision. The clinics generally operate January through February and July through August. They're open for business two evenings a week — the days vary, so call in advance — from 6 to 9 PM, and Fridays from 9 AM to 5 PM. In addition to its Swedish massage clinics, the institute offers free shiatsu clinics, medical massage clinics and "specific ailment" clinics. They occur irregularly, so call the institute for details. The school is open from 9 AM to 5 PM Monday through Friday.

Santa Fe Stands Out in AIDS/HIV Care

For a city of only 65,000 people, Santa Fe has an extensive network of AIDS/HIV health services and support groups. That's largely due to efforts by, and in response to,  the city's sizable gay population — a segment of the community, in Santa Fe as elsewhere, that has been hit particularly hard by the AIDS epidemic.

Many gays and lesbians move to Santa Fe because of its reputation for welcoming people who, whatever their orientation, might not be welcome elsewhere. This isn't a new phenomenon; homosexuals have been coming here since the 1920s, during the city's heyday as an arts colony. Indeed, Santa Fe is a gay-friendly town. Its city council has an openly gay member; Mayor Debbie Jaramillo had consistently been a supportive voice for the city's homosexual population, speaking each year at the annual Santa Fe Lesbian, Gay & Bi Pride Parade; and the general population has traditionally been nonjudgmental and accepting.

Over the past two decades, however, gay men were coming to Santa Fe in droves for another reason — to die. They made the pilgrimage in order to succumb to AIDS in a beautiful, mystical place that didn't condemn them for who they were or the disease they had. In a small town like Santa Fe, AIDS touches everybody — with horror at first, then fear and finally compassion, especially for those who've died alone because no support systems existed.

Even before people understood that AIDS is an equal-opportunity killer — when the disease appeared to be uniquely the scourge of gay men, who have been a significant and visible presence in Santa Fe — both the city and state rallied with aggressive treatment and substantial public funding to provide a host of public services. As AIDS widened its net, so did Santa Fe's health community, creating an enviable network of publicly funded support and cutting-edge AIDS treatment, which has turned Santa Fe into a sort of Lourdes for those afflicted with AIDS or HIV-related illnesses. Lots of support comes from Santa Fe's private sector too — particularly from the arts community, which has lost so much talent and friendship to AIDS.

Much of the private funding comes from Santa Fe's numerous fund-raisers throughout the year including AID and Comfort (see subsequent entry), an annual party at the elegant Eldorado hotel whose proceeds help cover HIV-re-

Ken Mullens (left), a client and volunteer of Southwest C.A.R.E. Center, talks with Dr. Trevor Hawkins, director of the center.

— continued on next page

lated bills; the yearly Santa Fe AIDS Walk, which brings out more than 1,000 participants; and Santa Fe Cares' Live at the Lensic, a stage revue that in 1997 featured comedienne Carol Burnett, who lives in Santa Fe, and British actor Michael York.

Anyone even remotely connected to AIDS/HIV work in Santa Fe will necessarily interact with **Southwest C.A.R.E.** (Comprehensive AIDS Treatment, Research and Education), 989-8200, New Mexico's only specialty AIDS/HIV center. Located near downtown Santa Fe at 230 W. Manhattan Street, Suite 300, the center offers under one roof virtually every service someone with AIDS or an HIV-related illness might need. In addition to state-of-the-art medical care, including access to clinical trials, Southwest C.A.R.E. works with the state to provide a full range of practical and emotional support services for its clients. That might include finding a dentist who will treat an HIV-infected person, making referrals for alternative medical treatment,; coordinating home or hospice care;, finding insurance or emergency funding for patients in need, or matching up trained volunteers to visit isolated AIDS patients.

Southwest C.A.R.E. offers medical treatments on a sliding scale. The nonprofit clinic is open Monday through Friday from 8 AM to 5 PM, but there are staffers on call 24 hours a day, seven days a week for emergencies. Locally, call 989-8200. For out-of-town callers, Southwest C.A.R.E. also has a toll-free line at (888) 320-8200. Comprehensive and compassionate services like these have drawn people with AIDS or the HIV infection to Santa Fe for more than a decade. But unlike in the recent past, now they're arriving with some hope. Combination therapy, used aggressively in Santa Fe long before it became de rigueur throughout the nation, has prolonged the lives of many an AIDS sufferer, some of whom are returning to the large urban areas they fled a few years earlier.

For more information about AIDS/HIV resources in Santa Fe, contact any of the following organizations.

AID and Comfort, 1480 S. St. Francis Drive, 989-3399. Founded in 1989, AID and Comfort is a volunteer organization that raises funds to help those with HIV or AIDS pay medical bills. Its main fund-raising event is an annual Thanksgiving Day party and silent auction.

Hope House Inc., 105 E. Marcy Street, 983-8990. Funded primarily by charitable donations, Hope House Inc. runs a private group home for up to eight people with AIDS or HIV.

People of Color AIDS Foundation, 711 Alarid Street, 820-0622. People of Color AIDS Foundation (POCAF) is a nonprofit organization founded to provide HIV/AIDS education, prevention and care to New Mexicans of all races and colors.

Santa Fe Cares, 117 N. Guadalupe Street, Suite B, 986-3820. Santa Fe Cares is a nonprofit community fund-raising and grant-making organization for the treatment, care, education and prevention of HIV/AIDS. Since its founding in 1991, Santa Fe Cares has raised more than $2.5 million from such events as its annual AIDS Walk; "Live at the Lensic," a musical and comedy revue in Santa Fe's beautiful old Lensic movie theater; and Ski for Life, a slalom race at the Santa Fe Ski Area.

Southwest Acupuncture College and Chinese Medical Clinic
411 St. Michael's Dr. • 988-2592

Established in 1980, Southwest Acupuncture College and Chinese Medical Clinic is an accredited four-year master's degree program that teaches the five branches of classical Ori-

ental medicine: acupuncture, herbal medicine, physical therapy, nutrition, and exercise and breathing therapy. Built into the program is clinical experience, which, unlike other colleges, starts in the students' first year and continues throughout the entire program, culminating in more than 1,000 hours of practical

Many Santa Feans pursue a healthy lifestyle.

experience. In addition, the college operates a student clinic, which is open from 9 AM to 9 PM Monday through Thursday and from 9 AM to 5 PM on Friday. The first treatment can take up to an hour and a half and costs a maximum of $9, while subsequent treatments cost up to $18 and usually last an hour. The clinic charges according to a patient's ability to pay. The elderly, handicapped, battered women, substance abusers and patients with AIDS or cancer may be eligible for reduced-cost or free treatments.

Southwestern Counseling Center
Rt. 20 (San Felipe Rd.), Box 29D
• 471-8575

Southwestern Counseling Center is a student clinic under the auspices of Southwestern College, a 22-year-old accredited institution offering masters degrees in counseling and art therapy. The clinic, located on San Felipe Road at Airport Road, has served the Santa Fe community for more than 10 years with low-cost and free counseling services for individuals, couples, families and groups. Clinicians are second-year students working under the supervision of licensed professionals. The clinic charges on a sliding fee scale up to $15 per person. Call ahead for an appointment.

Emergency Numbers

Local:

Police, Fire, Ambulance	911
AIDS Hotline	(800) 545-2437
Environmental Emergency	827-9329
Esperanza Battered Women's Shelter	473-5200
Hantavirus Hotline	(800) 879-3421
Lovelace Health Care Systems Hotline	(800) 366-3401
Rape Crisis Center Hotline	986-9111
St. Vincent Hospital	820-5250
Suicide Hotline	982-2255

National:

Alcohol and Drug Abuse Hotline	(800) 962-8963
Depression and Anxiety Hotline	(800) 234-0038
Missing Children Hotline	(800) 587-4357
National Runaway Switchboard	(800) 621-4000
National Youth Crisis Hotline	(800) 448-4663
Poison control	(800) 432-6866

For such a small metropolis, Santa Fe offers a surprisingly wide variety of homegrown publications to suit almost any taste, lifestyle or political persuasion.

Media

Santa Fe might be small in population, but it's huge in diversity. One need only spend a few hours nursing a latté at the local newsstand-cafe, Downtown Subscription, to witness firsthand the fascinating mix of residents — and visitors — that makes Santa Fe "The City Different."

It's not just what the habitués are drinking or wearing that gives them away; it's also whatever magazine or newspaper they happen to be thumbing through — and there are plenty to choose from at Downtown Subscription, 376 Garcia Street, 983-3085, (see our Restaurants and Shopping chapters) which offers up to 1,000 periodical titles from around the world and around the corner.

It's what comes from around the corner that interests us here. For such a small metropolis — remember, only 65,000 people call this city home — Santa Fe offers a surprisingly wide variety of homegrown publications to suit almost any taste, lifestyle or political persuasion. Also included in this chapter are a number of Albuquerque publications that have enough of a following in Santa Fe to merit mention. At the end of the chapter, you'll find listings of our local and nearby radio and TV stations.

Newspapers

Dailies

Albuquerque Journal
7777 Jefferson St. NE, Albuquerque
• (800) 641-3451

The 117-year-old *Albuquerque Journal* takes great pride in being part of an ever-shrinking pool of independently owned American dailies. The front page announces that the paper is "home-owned and home-operated." Home is Journal Center, an industrial

park owned by publisher Thompson H. Lang. Lang rose to the helm of the family-owned *Journal* in 1971 with the death of his father, C. Thompson Lang. Along with the title of owner/publisher, he inherited a 40-year-old joint operating agreement (JOA) with the *Journal*'s nearest competitor, *The Albuquerque Tribune*.

Despite sharing business operations, the *Journal* and *Tribune* remain separate and competing entities. The *Albuquerque Journal* is unquestionably the dominant news voice in its home town and throughout the state with a daily circulation of 113,253 and 164,021 on Sunday.

For $11.25 a month, *Journal* subscribers get a variety of special sections throughout the week, including "Business Outlook" on Monday; a computer section called "Access" on Tuesday; "Food and Flavor" on Wednesday; Thursday's "Go!" for outdoors and recreation; a Friday entertainment section called "Venue;" "Wheels" on Saturday and a Sunday paper fat with ads as well as its own monthly glossy, *Sage Women's Magazine*.

Journal North
328 Galisteo St. • 988-8881

The upstart *Journal North* — a 17-year-old zoned edition of New Mexico's largest and most widely read newspaper, the *Albuquerque Journal* — is the primary competitor for daily news coverage in Santa Fe and northern New Mexico for the hometown paper, *The Santa Fe New Mexican*. While parochial Santa Feans will always consider it "the other paper," *Journal North* certainly gives *The New Mexican* a run for its money with evenhanded, tightly edited, if somewhat dry coverage of local government and breaking news.

In contrast to *The New Mexican* and especially to the heretofore unapologetically liberal weekly, the *Santa Fe Reporter* (see the entry in our Weeklies section), *Journal North* tends to be conservative in its editorial policy as well as its style, though somewhat less so on both counts than its parent publication, the *Albuquerque Journal*.

Journal North appears seven days a week wrapped around the *Albuquerque Journal*. Its northern New Mexico circulation hovers around 16,000 during the week and 18,000 on Sunday. The Santa Fe circulation rate falls in the 9,000 range.

Journal North often prompts readers to wonder why they seem to get so much news from such a small section. It's because the paper is wall-to-wall news stories with a smattering of display ads in between.

FYI

Unless otherwise noted, the area code for all phone numbers listed in this guide is 505.

Despite being a fixture in Santa Fe for nearly 18 years, *Journal North* can't quite keep up with the 149-year-old *New Mexican*. It's edited and printed in Albuquerque, so its deadlines are far earlier than the *New Mexican's* — sometimes by as much as two and a half hours.

What *Journal North* lacks in local tidbits, it makes up for with columnist Larry Calloway, who gets the inside poop on state government. A veteran political reporter and former Associated Press correspondent, Calloway was *Journal North's* first editor. His thrice-weekly column runs front page in *Journal North* and on the main paper's "State" page elsewhere in New Mexico.

Sunday's *Journal North* recently added a Spanish-language new feature page called "La Gente del Norte" ("People of the North").

The Albuquerque Tribune
7777 Jefferson St. NE, Albuquerque • (800) 665-8742

As a result of a 67-year-old agreement with its primary competitor, the *Albuquerque Journal*, this Scripps-Howard publication will always be the No. 2 newspaper in its home town. So, like Avis, it has to try harder. And it does.

The *Albuquerque Tribune* long ago gave up trying to compete head-to-head on daily news coverage with its business partner and roommate. (*The Tribune* lives in a separate wing of *Albuquerque Journal* headquarters in Journal Center, an industrial park owned by *Journal* publisher Thompson H. Lang.) Instead, it focuses on issue stories and news features,

doing both remarkably well. And it still manages to scoop the *Journal* from time to time on daily news.

With a daily circulation of 27,225, *The Albuquerque Tribune* is about one-fourth the size of the *Journal*. Its Santa Fe circulation is almost nil. But readers can find *The Tribune* at newsstands and in boxes located in key parts of the city, particularly around the state capitol and around the Plaza. *The Tribune* publishes Monday though Saturday and costs 50¢ for a single copy, $5.25 a month to subscribe.

The Santa Fe New Mexican
202 E. Marcy St. • 983-3303

Founded in 1849, Santa Fe's only local daily boasts on its masthead that it's "The West's Oldest Newspaper." But *The New Mexican*, as the locals call it, stands out for another reason: It's one of a steadily declining number of American newspapers that have remained independently owned and operated — though only by the skin of its journalistic teeth.

In 1975, publisher Robert McKinney sold *The Santa Fe New Mexican* to Gannett, the largest newspaper chain in the United States. Less than three years later, however, McKinney sued Gannett for breach of contract. McKinney, a Virginia resident who maintains a hacienda in Santa Fe County, claimed Gannett reneged on its agreement to let him retain editorial and operational control of *The New Mexican*. A jury agreed, and in July 1980, a federal judge ordered Gannett to return the newspaper to McKinney, a onetime assistant secretary of the interior and a former ambassador to Switzerland.

Although it took several years for *The New Mexican* to gain back readership it lost during Gannett's brief reign, the newspaper has once again become a staple — and a favorite target — of locals. Indeed, Santa Feans have a love-hate relationship with *The New Mexican*. Readers, especially local politicians, love to hate the newspaper for its "gotcha" articles, its no-holds-barred editorials and its frequent editing errors. But — and its a big "but" — *The New Mexican* is widely read in Santa Fe, whose slightly left-of-center politics and ideology jibe with the newspaper's editorial leaning.

The proof is in the numbers, and *The New Mexican* has them; its household penetration rate in the city is nearly 61 percent during the week and close to 63 percent on Sunday. That translates to a daily circulation rate, which includes paid subscriptions and street sales, of 23,568 and 25,921 on Sunday.

Many *New Mexican* readers — up to 40 percent, according to some sources — also subscribe to *Journal North*, a zoned edition of the *Albuquerque Journal*. While *The New Mexican* covers the heck out of Santa Fe as both a municipality and the state capital, it tends to ignore the rest of New Mexico and often relegates major national and international news to inside stories or briefs.

Still, some 17,000 subscribers pay from $42.25 for 13 weeks to $162.10 per year for the privilege of getting *The New Mexican* on their doorstep every morning. Many will tell you that "Pasatiempo," the newspaper's Friday arts and entertainment section, alone is worth the subscription price. "Pasatiempo" ("pastime" in Spanish) contains comprehensive, informative and entertaining sections on movies, music, theater, art, dance and all other manner of diversion in and around Santa Fe for the upcoming week. It features primarily local reviewers, who are knowledgeable in their fields and give the skinny on what's good and what's not.

Other weekly sections include Monday's "El Nuevo Mexicano," an all-Spanish news feature page; "Taste," the Wednesday food section; "Outdoors" on Thursday; Saturday's "Teen Page;" and "¿Que Pasa?," a day-by-day calendar of free and nonprofit events and meetings that accompanies the usual array of Sunday sections. *The Sunday New Mexican* is a must-have for jobs and rentals classifieds in the Santa Fe area.

Weeklies

Santa Fe Reporter
132 E. Marcy St. • 988-5541

No doubt, the first issue of the *Santa Fe Reporter* on June 26, 1974, gave the local hometown daily, *The Santa Fe New Mexican*,

the willies. Founding publishers Dick McCord, a former *Newsday* reporter, and Laurel Knowles, a writer for *Women's Wear Daily*, were ready to kick butt. And kick butt they did in the very first issue, with a scoop on commercial flights between Santa Fe and Denver. A mere weekly, and a free one at that, the *Reporter* would beat *The New Mexican* on other occasions over the next two decades on local news and investigative stories.

Under its second publisher, Rockefeller heiress Hope Aldrich, a former *Newsday* reporter and onetime staff writer at the *Reporter* who bought the paper in 1988, the alternative weekly focused on issue reporting, publishing occasional investigative pieces. Last year, she sold it to the owners of *Willamette Week*, out of Willamette, Oregon. For the first time in its 24-year history, the *Reporter* is in the hands of absentee owners. The *Reporter* distributes about 23,000 papers a week and has an estimated readership of 55,000 to 60,000 a week.

Thrifty Nickel
1722 St. Michael's Dr., Ste. D • 473-4111

This free weekly is a favorite among Santa Fe's workday lunch crowd, especially lone diners who thumb through it while downing their green chile cheeseburger or chicken enchiladas with red. The *Thrifty Nickel* is a hefty little tabloid with 24 to 32 pages chock-full of mostly local ads trying to sell everything from cockatiels to used equipment from nearby Los Alamos National Laboratory (the folks who brought you The Bomb). Every once in a while, you'll happen across an ad praising St. Jude or one of the other saints — just another reminder of Santa Fe's Catholic roots.

In addition to merchandise and garage sales, the *Thrifty Nickel* advertises real estate, both sales and rentals; local and national jobs; and, of course, vehicles — lots of them. It also contains a one-page listing of local businesses and services.

Thrifty Nickel distributes 20,000 copies a week to racks throughout Santa Fe County and parts of neighboring Rio Arriba and San Miguel counties. Classifieds run $4 for 10 words and 20¢ for each additional word; display ads start at $8.50 per column inch.

Monthlies

Crosswinds
3701 San Mateo Blvd. NE, Ste. J, Albuquerque • 883-4750

Originally based out of Santa Fe, *Crosswinds* started out nine years ago as a progressive alternative monthly that focused on the environment and what then-publisher Stephen Kress calls the "cutting edge of consciousness." Despite dogged attempts, Kress couldn't shake the community's perception of *Crosswinds* as a New Age newspaper.

Kress sold *Crosswinds* two years ago to publisher Steve Lawrence, a former editor at *Forbes* and the *Financial Times* of Canada, who moved the paper to Albuquerque. While it remains a progressive newspaper — "Smart, Provocative, Useful" is its subtitle — no one's likely to confuse *Crosswinds* with *The Santa Fe Sun* (see our write-up in this chapter).

With recent articles like "Who Owns New Mexico: The 40 Largest Private Landowners;" "Water For the Future: The Most Important Local Agency You've Never Heard Of;" and "Will You Be Put In One of These Places" about New Mexico nursing homes, *Crosswinds* is taking a distinct turn in the direction of investigative journalism.

Crosswinds distributes 60,000 copies a month throughout Albuquerque and northern New Mexico, including 25,000 in Santa Fe, making it the largest alternative weekly in the state. The paper is free.

The Santa Fe Sun
1807 2nd St., No. 29 • 989-8381

Although many will balk at the mere use of the phrase, there's no getting around it: *The Santa Fe Sun* is without a doubt a New Age newspaper — and then some. The free monthly — subtitled New Mexico's Newspaper for Wellness, Sustainability and Creative Community — focuses on spirituality, alternative lifestyles, nontraditional medicine, environmentalism and social consciousness on all levels. The tabloid has undergone changes un-

der publisher Bill Sims. Sims, who bought it in 1997 has movedhis paper into what he calls the "neo-New Age" with the help of electronics. The paper is for sale and may be under new ownership by the time this book is printed.

Quarterlies

New Mexico Kids!
436 Sunset St. • 820-7773

With both children and parents in mind, this free quarterly "magaloid" is geared toward local and visiting families in search of children's activities from Tijeras to Taos — an area that includes Santa Fe, Los Alamos, Albuquerque and points in between. *New Mexico Kids!* got its start in 1992 when publisher Alexis Sabin of Santa Fe discovered that her 4-year-old was one of 25,000 children, including babies and high-schoolers, growing up in a town perceived primarily as an adult playground. It's not that kidstuff doesn't exist here. On the contrary, says Sabin, there's plenty for kids to do in Santa Fe. At that time, however, there wasn't a whole lot of information about what was available and where. So Sabin decided to fill in the void. She compiled what turned out to be a tremendous number of youth activities and published it in a newspaper she called *Santa Fe Kids!* The concept met with so much enthusiasm that she expanded to Albuquerque the following year with a sister publication called, you guessed it, *Albuquerque Kids!* The two papers merged in 1997 to become *New Mexico Kids!* with separate Albuquerque and Santa Fe events calendars.

Each issue usually contains at least two feature stories about seasonal events or activities such as fairs and festivals, hiking, camping or family daytrips; seasonal directories including camps in the summer issue, schools in fall, and winter's "It's Party Time!," which lists places to throw a child's party, party supplies, storytellers, puppeteers, magicians, photographers, etc.; a collection of short articles and announcements called "KIDBITS;" book reviews; community resources and nonprofit organizations; and a seasonal calendar of events with monthly highlights, arts and crafts, classes, dance, music, fairs, festivals, sports and storytelling.

New Mexico Kids! claims 35,000 readers in Santa Fe and Albuquerque, including a small list of out-of-state subscribers who pay $15 a year.

Tumbleweeds
369 Montezuma Ave., Ste. 191
• 984-3171

Tumbleweeds started out in 1991 as a four-page photocopied newsletter called *Tot's Hot News*. In the intervening seven years, it has matured to a full-grown tabloid of 20 or more pages offering support, information and resources on raising children. It's aimed at parents whose children are in their low teens or younger as well as professionals who work with children.

Tumbleweeds includes news and feature articles on all aspects of raising one's own children or working with someone else's. It also contains articles written by and for children as well as a calendar of events. Occasionally it puts out special issues, such as last summer's "Children and the Arts." You can pick up *Tumbleweeds* for free throughout Santa Fe and nearby Española and Los Alamos. Paid subscriptions are available for $10 a year.

Irregular Circulation

Puntos de Vista
702 Felipe Pl. • 982-4083

Puntos de Vista — Spanish for "Points of View" — is a free, grassroots publication that describes itself as a "community-advocacy newsletter that carries important information hard to find elsewhere." It first appeared in 1989 when editor and publisher Joan Chernock churned out 300 copies of a one-page flyer alerting her neighbors about a contaminated public well in their west side neighborhood. Since that time, the newsletter has grown to 24 pages — many written by readers —with a regional distribution of up to 20,000 copies. *Puntos de Vista* appears irregularly three or four times a year — "whenever we have enough money," Chernock says.

Magazines

DESIGNER/builder
2405 Maclovia Ln. • 471-4549

Officially subtitled "A Journal of the Human Environment" — and unofficially, "Architecture's More Than a Pretty Face" — *DESIGNER/builder* started locally in 1994 with an emphasis on Santa Fe. It has since gone international, raising design and building issues around the globe, from the Third World to the First World, and describing all manner of architecture, from mud floors to high-rise buildings. Among the topics *DESIGNER/builder* discusses are cultural issues affecting architecture (and vice versa); urban landscapes; social spaces (i.e., where people congregate such as malls, parks, streets, etc.); alternative building materials and technologies; affordable housing; architectural history and criticism.

Never shy of controversy, *DESIGNER/builder* has run stories deconstructing Nazi architecture, including concentration camps; describing a "vertical village" in Manhattan of Senegalese nationals trying to preserve their culture in a completely foreign landscape by taking over a high-rise and living in it as they would in their villages back home; and discussing a program in San Francisco in which prison convicts create city gardens that supply produce to local restaurants.

Many of the articles featured in *DESIGNER/builder* come from other magazines à la *Utne Reader*. The husband-and-wife team of Kingsley and Jerilou Hammett, publisher and managing editor, respectively, write the rest. *DESIGNER/builder* costs $2.50 at newsstands; $28 for a 12-month subscription.

El Palacio
113 Lincoln Ave. • 827-4361

Founded in 1913, *El Palacio: The Museum of New Mexico Magazine* is the oldest museum publication in the United States. What started out 85 years ago as a weekly pamphlet about the size of one's hand is today a four-color glossy showpiece for the state's museum system: the Palace of the Governors, Museum of Indian Arts & Culture, Laboratory of Anthropology, Museum of International Folk Art, Museum of Fine Arts — all in Santa Fe — and five state monuments. Taking its lead from the museums it represents, *El Palacio* (The Palace) covers New Mexico history, culture, art and anthropology with lively articles accompanied by striking photos and graphics. It's also a darned good substitute, both visually and textually, for those who can't attend museum exhibits or events in person.

An oddly shaped magazine — 10 ¾ " by 8 ¾ " — printed on beautiful stock, *El Palacio* practically jumps out at you on the newsstand. Only 10 years ago, it was a staid, black and white scholarly journal read almost exclusively by museum members and a few hundred academics and professionals. After suspending publication for about eight months, the magazine reappeared in the spring of 1991 with a cleaner, slightly more colorful format. By the very next issue — the first in its 78-year history to incorporate outside advertising — *El Palacio* had metamorphosed into a full-color magazine on the art and culture, history and lore of the Southwest, winning an honorary mention for design from the American Association of Museums. Since that time, the magazine has once again narrowed its focus to New Mexico rather than the entire Southwestern region, garnering a 1995 AAM honorary mention in the process.

El Palacio publishes two or three times each year with an average run of 15,000 issues. Subscriptions are free for the Museum of New Mexico's approximately 6,100 members. Others pay $8 a year or $4.50 an issue

at any of the state museums or at select newsstands and bookstores nationwide.

La Herencia del Norte
P.O. Box 22576, Santa Fe, NM 87504
• 474-2800

Dedicated to the preservation of Hispanic culture, *La Herencia del Norte* ("Heritage of the North") turns 5 this year. In that short time it has carved out a niche for itself, primarily among middle class, highly assimilated Hispanics. "We speak perfect English but have a real affinity to our culture and language," explains founding editor and publisher Ana Pacheco. This elegant, oversized black and white quarterly highlights current issues and trends that directly affect Hispanics in New Mexico. Many newcomers also read to learn more about the history and culture of the region, which is home to the oldest continuous Spanish population in the United States.

The "Norte" (North) in the magazine's title refers not to northern New Mexico, but to the northward route the original settlers took on *El Camino Real* ("The Royal Road") from Chihuahua, Mexico, to southern Colorado. *La Herencia del Norte* distributes 40,000 copies each quarter throughout northern New Mexico and Albuquerque.

localflavor
223 N. Guadalupe St., No. 442
• 988-7560

In a town as obsessed with food as Santa Fe, it's appropriate that there be a magazine here devoted to New Mexico and other types of cuisine. *localflavor* fills that niche,

---

INSIDERS' TIP

Santa Fe might be small, but it's mighty — at least when it comes to readers. A survey by the American Booksellers Association shows Santa Fe had more bookstores per 10,000 people in 1992 than any of the other 75 cities on the list. Santa Fe — population 47,600 at the time the numbers were compiled — surpassed such famously literary cities as San Francisco (No. 14 on the list) and Asheville, North Carolina, (No. 46) home to such literary giants as Carl Sandburg and Thomas Wolfe. The City Different even beat out major college towns like Boston (No. 39); Ann Arbor, Michigan (No. 48); and Madison, Wisconsin (No. 20).

"explor(ing) the world of food and wine from ground to plate."

The oversized black-and-white magazine comes out six times a year, filled with articles and photos profiling chefs throughout New Mexico, though it tends to focus on its home base of Santa Fe. *localflavor* also features first-person prose on food and cooking, recipes, cooking techniques, a wine section and dispatches from around the state. *localflavor* is free, though subscriptions are available for $24 a year.

Mothering
649 Harkle Rd., Ste. F • 984-8116

This 22-year-old bimonthly is a progressive parenting magazine that deals with nearly all aspects of child rearing with articles on topics like home schooling, midwifery, alternative family health and home businesses. It also includes reviews of books, music, films and videos. Subscriptions run $18.95 in the U.S. Single issues cost $5.95 on the newsstand.

New Mexico Magazine
Lew Wallace Bldg., 495 Old Santa Fe Tr. • 827-7447

First published in 1923 as the *Highway Journal*, *New Mexico Magazine* started out as a high-quality internal newsletter of the state Highway Department to promote "interest in good roads through the state" and "advertise to the people of the United States the attractions of New Mexico as a playground and its possibilities as a place of location and business."

Little did editor Ray W. Bennett realize to what extent New Mexico would indeed turn into a playground, nor could he have imagined at the time the beautiful and highly popular magazine his little newsletter would become. The first metamorphosis occurred in 1931, when *Highway Journal* merged with the Game and Fish Department's magazine, *The Conservationist*, to become *New Mexico: The Sunshine State's Recreational and Highway Magazine*.

Six years later, the publication took on its current name and style, becoming the first official state magazine in the nation with a format that would be emulated many times over.

New Mexico Magazine specializes in travel and historical features with regular sections on regional cuisine, literature, arts and culture and high-quality color photographs and illustrations. The magazine's list of contributing authors, photographers and illustrators reads like a "Who's Who" of major New Mexican writers and artists.

New Mexico Magazine has a paid circulation of more than 117,000 with an estimated readership of 500,000. Subscribers pay $23.95 for 12 issues. The newsstand price is $4.95.

Outside
400 Market St. • 989-7100

When *Outside* magazine decided to move its headquarters from Chicago to Santa Fe in 1994, it received less than an open-armed welcome. First the magazine met with loud opposition to locating its offices on the road leading to the Santa Fe Ski Area. So publisher

---

INSIDERS' TIP

Compliments of the Santa Fe Public Library you can have your own personal Internet e-mail account, even if you don't have a computer — in fact, even if you don't have a library card. And it's absolutely free. All you have to do is show up at any of the library's three branches and sign up for a 30- to 45-minute slot (depending on the library) and wait your turn. Ask a librarian to direct you to the correct Web site, then just follow the directions on screen to set up a personal account or to send and receive e-mail. If you already have e-mail but your computer's not handy, you can use the library computers to access your account. If you prefer, you can spend your 30 to 45 minutes browsing the WorldWideWeb or other areas on the Internet.

KUNM-FM

Go into anyone's home or car in Santa Fe, and check the pre-tuned stations on their stereo. Chances are pretty good they'll have their first or second button set to 89.9 FM. That's the home in Santa Fe for KUNM, the state's largest volunteer-operated public radio station and certainly the most diverse.

Broadcasting day and night from the campus of the University of New Mexico in Albuquerque, KUNM provides news, talk and every kind of music imaginable. Its goal is to satisfy a broad spectrum of listeners in a state that's home to New Agers and rednecks, liberals and reactionaries, sophisticates and simple folk and everyone in between.

For that very reason, you'll hear griping from all corners about how KUNM is too progressive or not progressive enough, that it has to much talk or too little, that it plays too much classical music and not enough rock, jazz, folk or vice versa. What no one complains about, however, is the absence — almost — of commercials. But there's a price to pay for that, too: membership.

Twice a year, KUNM holds a weeklong on-the-air fund-raising drive to raise enough money to keep up its eclectic programming. An annual membership costs a minimum of $40 a year for the general public, $20 a year for students, seniors and low-income listeners, though it will happily take whatever listeners can afford, be it $10 or $1,000. Members get KUNM's monthly program guide, "Zounds," which includes a day-by-day listing of on-air events as well as a detailed description of its regularly scheduled programs and times.

Even a cursory glance at the program listings makes it clear that KUNM offers something for everyone.

News hounds can tune in Monday through Friday from 5 to 8:30 AM to hear in-depth news and features on *Morning Edition* and again from 5:30 to 7 PM for *All Things Considered* — both award-winning news magazines from National Public Radio. For local news, tune in at 5 PM Monday through Friday for the 30-minute *KUNM Evening Report*. The station also gives news junkies a weekend fix with NPR's *Weekend Edition*, airing 6 AM Saturday and Sundays at 9 AM.

There's even news about the news Tuesdays at 8:30 AM with *Counterspin*, a critique on the week's stories hosted by Fairness and Accuracy in Reporting (FAIR), a national media watch group.

Musically, KUNM has the widest offering of any station in New Mexico. Its repertoire includes blues, bluegrass, Cajun, classical, country and western, folk, gospel, heavy metal, jazz, Native American music, new rock, oldies, rap, reggae, salsa and Tejano — whew! — to give just a partial list. You can tune in 24 hours a day, seven days a week and rarely, if ever, hear the same thing twice — except, of course, for news.

DJs for the local music programs — which includes all but NPR's weekday classical music show, *Performance Today* — are volunteers who truly know and love the music they play. As nonprofessionals, few affect the classic, *suavecito* radio voice that commercial stations require, though the local newscasters, most of them UNM students, could do with a little more of that polish.

KUNM features a variety of Hispanic programs including *Latino USA*, an English-language radio journal of Hispanic news and culture, on Mondays at 8:30 AM; *Raices*,

— continued on next page

a Latin-American free-form show that plays all genres of Hispanic music on Mondays from 7 to 10 PM and Saturdays from 3 to 6 PM; and Friday night's *Salsa Sabrosa*, three hours of Afro-Caribbean music from Puerto Rico, Cuba, the Dominican Republic, etc. starting at 7 PM.

The station also airs a number of programs for and about Native Americans such as *National Native News* weekdays at 5:25 PM — five minutes of news and issues affecting American Indians; *Native America Calling*, a live call-in show weekdays at 11 AM; and *Singing Wire*, a Sunday afternoon program featuring Native American music from traditional to country-and-western, rock 'n' roll and folk.

The programs mentioned here are only a partial listing of KUNM's offerings. For more information, call the business office at 277-4806. After hours, call the request line at 277-5615 for information about whatever program is airing at that time.

Jim Bailey and Joan LaBabara are among KUNM's staff.

Larry Burke built a showcase office building near downtown's upscale Sanbusco Center. Then he caught flack for not hiring enough locals. And just last year, an ex-employee sued the magazine for civil rights violations. *Outside* prevailed in the lawsuit, but at the cost of more negative publicity, not to mention legal fees.

Still, none of this seems to have hurt *Outside*'s circulation, which at over a half-million is up by 50,000 since the magazine came to Santa Fe four years ago. It has an estimated readership of 1.7 million people. *Outside* is the largest publication based out of "The City Different."

As its name implies, *Outside* covers active outdoor sports such as hiking, climbing, kayaking and cycling (to name just a few) as well as travel, people, politics, art and outdoorsy literature. In addition to its regular monthly magazine, *Outside* publishes two special issues a year — a buying guide for out-

door gear and a travel guide. A 12-month subscription runs $18; special issues are extra. The newsstand price is $3.95 per issue.

Santa Fean
444 Galisteo St. • 983-1444

After a brief hiatus covering politics and local personalities, the 25-year-old *Santa Fean* has returned to its roots as a lifestyle magazine "for the best in Southwest Living." The magazine focuses on art first, followed closely by entertainment, home and garden, and fashion and dining — in that order. Ubiquitous in hotel rooms in northern New Mexico and art galleries throughout the state, the glossy monthly has attracted a sizable out-of-state readership, with 60 percent of its subscriptions outside New Mexico. The remaining 6,000 subscribers are from Santa Fe and elsewhere in the north. The cover price is $2.95, but some hotel guests can pick them up for free in their rooms. A one-year subscription costs $19.97.

THE magazine
520 Franklin Ave. • 982-5785

When Judith Wolf and Guy Cross moved to Santa Fe in 1988, they were amazed to discover that what is reputedly the third-largest art market in the country had no local magazine dedicated to the arts. Sure, there was good old "Pasatiempo," the Friday insert in *The Santa Fe New Mexican* that serves as Santa Fe's what's-happening bible. But they considered "Pasatiempo" primarily a preview vehicle. What Santa Fe needed, they felt, was a critical voice.

That was six years ago. Since then, *THE magazine* has taken off like a rocket with readership all over the country. It even has a handful of international subscribers in places as far flung as Thailand, Japan, South America, Australia and London.

Unlike most art magazines, *THE* is neither glossy nor in color. Yet its matte black-and-white format lends it an air of simple sophistication — not unlike a basic black dress with pearls. At $10\frac{3}{4}$ x $13\frac{1}{4}$, it's also a large magazine — one that stands out on a coffee table. But *THE* is more than just a pretty face. It covers the Santa Fe art scene with articles, reviews and a listing of exhibits and openings. Free for the taking in Santa Fe, *THE* costs $40 for a yearlong subscription and $70 for two years for outsiders.

3D Artist
P.O. Box 4787, Santa Fe 87502
• 424-8945

3D Artist is a locally produced glossy written by readers for freelance artists who make — or aspire to make — a living with computer graphics. The magazine describes itself as "the original 3D how-to publication" and takes credit for inventing such terms as "3D Artist" and "desktop cinematography." *3D Artist* began in 1991 as a newsletter. Two years later, it

upgraded to magazine format, graduating to full color in 1994. Issues run between 32 and 50 pages and appear every six to eight weeks. Subsriptions are $20 for six issues. The newsstand price is $5.

Radio

For a state with only 1.7 million residents and a radio market ranked 233rd out of a possible 266, New Mexico's airwaves carry a surprisingly eclectic collection of sounds. The talk and music come to Santa Fe via 30 or so radio stations, depending on the area, most of them from Albuquerque.

On the music front, listeners can tune in to anything from rap to rock, jazz to Jewish Klezmer music, oldies to opera, classical to Christian — the list goes on and on. If news/talk is your preference, you can choose between left-leaning National Public Radio or conservative poster boy Rush Limbaugh.

Like elsewhere in the country, however, New Mexico's radio options are becoming limited as chains buy out independent stations and homogenize the musical mix. Still, many stations have managed to avoid the Top 40 abyss that seems to be sucking in the larger markets.

You may hear the occasional complaint among country music fans about the notable and surprising absence of classic country stations in the Santa Fe/Albuquerque area. You have to tune in to KUNM's Tuesday night folk show, *The Home of Happy Feet*, to catch such old-timers as Johnny Cash, Patsy Cline, Loretta Lynn or Hank Williams. Still its the rare Santa Fean who doesn't appreciate the wide range of choices for such a small market.

Adult Nostalgic
KTRC 1400 AM, music of the '40s, '50s

and '60s. (Santa Fe)

KIVA 1310 AM, Big Band, crooners. (Albuquerque)

Christian

KFLQ 91.5 FM, music, news/talk. (Albuquerque)

KKIM 1000 AM, news/talk. (Albuquerque)

KLYT 88.3 FM, Christian hit radio, all rock, some news. (Albuquerque)

Classical

KANW 89.1 FM, variable programming includes classical music. (Albuquerque)

KHFM 96.3 FM All music. (Albuquerque)

KSFR 90.7 FM, variable programming includes classical. (Santa Fe)

KUNM 89.9 FM, variable programming includes classical. (See our close-up in this chapter.) (Albuquerque)

Community

KRSN 1490 AM, 23 hours of news/talk/info, one hour daily jazz and/or classical from 5 to 6 PM. (Los Alamos)

KSFR 90.7 FM, local community radio, alternative programming including blues, classical, jazz, opera, Spanish music, news, talk and information. (Santa Fe)

Country

KBFG 95.5 FM, new country, hourly news. (Santa Fe)

KRST 92.3 FM, new country, morning and evening drive-time news, weather, traffic. (Albuquerque)

KTBL 103.3 FM, country favorites. (Albuquerque)

KYBR 92.9 FM, new country, news. (Española.)

Hispanic

KANW 89.1 FM, bilingual, alternative programming includes New Mexican music. (Albuquerque)

KARS 860 AM, music, bilingual news/talk. (Albuquerque)

KDCE 950 AM, Spanish language, music, news, talk. (Española)

KEXT 104.7 FM, Spanish language, music. (Albuquerque)

KLVO 97.7 FM, Spanish language, music. (Albuquerque)

KRZY 105.9 FM, Spanish language, music, news, traffic. (Albuquerque)

KSWV 810 AM, bilingual, music, news, weather, sports. (Santa Fe)

KXKS 1190 AM, all Spanish regional music, news. (Albuquerque)

Jazz

KANW 89.1 FM, variable programming includes jazz in morning drive time. (Albuquerque)

KRZN 105.1 FM, smooth jazz, news. (Albuquerque)

KSFR 90.7 FM, variable community programming includes jazz. (Santa Fe)

KUNM 89.9 FM, variable programming includes jazz. (Albuquerque)

News/Talk

KANW 89.1 FM, variable programming includes Public Radio International and National Public Radio. (Albuquerque)

KKOB 770 AM, news/talk, local and syndicated programs. (Albuquerque)

KRSN 1490 AM, also one hour daily of light jazz. (Los Alamos)

KUNM 89.9 FM, variable programming includes National Public Radio, Pacifica News and Public Radio International. (Albuquerque)

KVSF 1260 AM, morning news/talk. (Santa Fe)

KZSS 610 AM, personal achievement and motivational programming. (Albuquerque)

Public Radio

KANW 89.1 FM, Public Radio International, National Public Radio, variable programming including classical music, jazz, New Mexico music, Native American programming, news and talk shows. (Albuquerque)

KSFR 90.7 FM, local public radio, alternative format including blues, classical, jazz, opera and Spanish music, news/talk/information. (Santa Fe)

KUNM 89.9 FM, National Public Radio, alternative programming. (Albuquerque)

Rock

KBAC 98.1 FM (Radio Free Santa Fe), Pro-

A variety of regional and national papers can be picked up in Santa Fe.

gressive music format includes alternative rock, reggae, world beat, local music and live studio appearances by visiting musicians. (Santa Fe)

KABG 98.5 FM, oldies – '60s and '70s. (Santa Fe)

KBAC 98.1 FM, adult album alternative. (Santa Fe)

KBOM 106.7 FM, oldies — '50s, '60s, '70s. (Santa Fe)

KIOT 102.5 FM, classic rock —'60s, '70s, '80s. (Albuquerque)

KKOB 93.3 FM, pop adult contemporary. (Albuquerque)

KKSS 97.3 FM, contemporary hits/Top 40. (Albuquerque)

KLSK 104.1 FM, classic rock —'60s, '70s, '80s. (Albuquerque)

KMGA 99.5 FM, light rock. (Albuquerque)

KPEK 100.3 FM, adult contemporary. (Albuquerque)

KSFQ 101.1 FM, oldies — '70s. (Los Alamos)

KTEG 107.9 FM, alternative rock. (Albuquerque)

KUNM 89.9 FM, alternative programming includes rock. (Albuquerque)

KYLZ 106.3 FM, urban contemporary/rhythmic crossover, hip-hop, rap, R&B, top 40. (Albuquerque)

KZKL 1580 AM, oldies — '60s. (Albuquerque)

KZRR 94.1 FM, classic rock. (Albuquerque)

Sports

KVSF 1260 AM, sports, morning news/talk. (Santa Fe)

KNML 1050 AM, 24-hour sports; daytime only in Santa Fe (Albuquerque)

Television

As with radio, Santa Fe has few television stations of its own; the majority of network stations come from Albuquerque, the state's largest city. Combining network television with cable, Santa Fe residents have an enviable choice of stations — 50 in all including premium and Pay-Per-View stations.

TCI Cablevision of Santa Fe, 2534 Camino Entrada, 438-2600, is the primary cable provider for Santa Fe County. Surrounding areas

— El Dorado, Tesuque and South Santa Fe, for example — have their own cable systems with different channels. Check *The Santa Fe New Mexican* for details.

Network channels

Channel 2 – KASA (Fox)
Channel 4 – KOB (NBC)
Channel 5 – KNME (PBS)
Channel 7 – KOAT (ABC)
Channel 8 – KLUZ (Univision - Spanish variety)
Channel 11 – KCHF (Christian)
Channel 13 – KRQE (CBS)
Channel 32 – KAZQ (Independent)
Channel 50 – KASY (UPN)

Santa Fe is home to more than 50 active Christian churches; one synagogue and four Jewish congregations; two Buddhist temples and several meditation centers; and dozens of other nondenominational and unaffiliated spiritual centers of every bent.

Worship and Spirituality

"I am always most religious upon a sunshiny day . . ."

Lord Byron wrote those words just a few years before he died in 1824 at age 36. He might have been less glib (and maybe even lived longer) had he experienced Santa Fe, where for 300 days out of the year the sun shines gloriously down across the brooding, protective Sangre de Cristo — "Blood of Christ" — mountain range and the Rio Grande Valley below.

Indeed, it's no accident that this high desert land of magnificent natural beauty, crystal clean air and spectacular sunshine has for centuries drawn spiritual seekers and inspired religious awe among followers of all faiths. From the ancient Anasazi and Athapascan — respective forebears of the region's Pueblo Indians and Navajo and Apache tribes, for whom the land they call "ground of the dancing sun" remains sacred — to today's New Age adherents, who combine ancient mysticism with modern thought, the sky and the very earth beckon. For what is religion if not the spiritual cement that binds humankind to nature and to supernature — what some call "God" and others call "Yahweh," "Allah," "Krishna" or simply "higher power."

The late Fray Angélico Chávez — a Franciscan priest, poet and author from northern New Mexico who wrote some two dozen books about his homeland and the "ánima Hispanica" (Hispanic soul) — understood this clearly when he likened New Mexico to Palestine in both topography and climate. "New Mexican landscape . . . is the holy land," Chávez wrote in his compelling 1974 book, *My Penitente Land*. He called the Rio Grande New Mexico's Jordan River and Santa Fe its Jerusalem. He similarly compared Palestine to Spain, the land from which the first European settlers arrived nearly 450 years ago in what would become New Mexico. "Grazing lands all and most alike in their physical aspects," Chávez wrote, adding that they "share a distinctive underlying human mystique born of that very type of arid landscape." Thus both the *pobladores* (settlers) sanctioned by the Spanish Crown, whose Catholicism was as much as part of their *ánima Hispanica* as their Spanish roots, and the Jews who fled the Spanish Inquisition to the New World in search of religious freedom, sensed a comfortable familiarity in this new land they called "Nuevoméjico," whose appearance and clime approximated not only the home they recently left, but also the ancient biblical soil of their common ancestors.

An ocean and a continent away from the watchful eyes of the inquisitorial Spanish authorities, the colonists and the *conversos* among them — those Spanish Jews who converted to Catholicism rather than face exile, many of whom continued practicing Judaism in secret — lived in relative peace with each other and the natives they found in New Mexico. They had more imminent worries than religious differences, namely survival in the wilderness and a common enemy in Plains Indians.

This atmosphere of religious tolerance extended to Jews but not necessarily to the pueblos. Indians occasionally fell victim to fanatical friars and fearful colonists who suspected witchcraft in such things as fetishes and nature-bound rituals. Despite orders from the homeland to convert the Indians by peaceful means (Spain didn't want to repeat in New Mexico the hostilities Pizarro and Cortés respectively visited upon the Incas in Peru and the Aztecs in Mexico), overzealous missionaries and their followers destroyed Indian *kivas* (sacred underground ceremonial rooms), persecuted medicine men and forced the natives into indentured servitude in exchange for teaching them Christianity.

Tired of their spiritual subordination by the Spaniards' Catholic chauvinism, the Indians made a number of unsuccessful attempts to expel the intruders. It wasn't until the Pueblo Revolt of 1680 that they succeeded. They overthrew the colonists, burned churches, killed priests and forced the Spanish colonial government to flee.

Twelve years later, Spain returned for the "reconquest." This time, however, it resolved to colonize the area without conflict and to live in peaceful coexistence with the natives and their religion. Thus began a new era of religious tolerance that, for the better part of the past 300 years, has remained a constant in Santa Fe and northern New Mexico.

That's not to say tensions didn't exist. The Catholic Church, firmly entrenched in New Mexico, vigorously opposed the Protestant incursion that arrived in the form of missionaries from points east on the Santa Fe Trail after the U.S. invasion and conquest of 1846. (Under Spain, Catholicism was the only legal religion). While hostilities rarely erupted in violence, they came out in other ways. It was not unheard of for Catholic clergymen to drown out Protestant sermons by ringing their church bells as loudly as possible.

Relations between Catholics and Protestants became still more strained with the arrival in 1850 of Jean Baptiste Lamy, a French priest whom the pope named as Santa Fe's first bishop. Lamy attempted to suppress the Protestant movement by subtle means, including wedding local government to the Catholic Church; replacing Hispanic clergy with less tolerant French and Italian priests; sheltering the local Hispanic and Indian population from the Protestant influence of Americans, who were arriving in wagonloads on the Santa Fe Trail; and by making outcasts of Protestant preachers and their converts.

Santa Fe's first Protestant missionary, a Southern Baptist preacher named Hiram Walter Read, arrived in 1849 — three years after the United States conquered New Mexico during the Mexican-American War (see our History chapter) and two years before it became an American territory. Methodist, Presbyterian and Episcopalian missionaries arrived on the heels of the Baptists, while American Jews, many of them German immigrants, predated the Baptists by six years. Documents place Albert Speyers, a Jewish trader from New York, on the Santa Fe Trail as early as 1843. Unlike the Protestants, however, the Jews came not on a religious mission but an economic one. In fact, Santa Fe had no synagogue until 1952 — 76 years after New Mexico's first recorded bar mitzvah.

It wasn't until early in the 20th century that the next wave of spiritual pilgrims came to northern New Mexico. But they differed drastically from their predecessors in that they came not to spread religion but to find it. These were the artists, inspirational writers and thinkers of the East Coast who left the decadence and materialism of their own culture for what they felt was the purity and mysticism of New Mexico. It's largely the legacy of this generation — one that included Georgia O'Keeffe, D.H. Lawrence and Mabel Dodge Luhan — that lends Santa Fe a mystique that has since achieved mythological proportions. However patronizing, they idealized the place, inadvertently advertising it through their artwork and their prose. And people came — as artists and free thinkers in the early part of the century, as hippies and New Age practitioners in more recent generations.

Today, Santa Fe is home to more than 50 active Christian churches; two synagogue and four Jewish congregations; two Buddhist temples and several meditation centers; and dozens of other nondenominational and unaffiliated spiritual centers of every bent.

There's no doubt, however, that Santa Fe is first and foremost a Catholic town. It's a Catholicism so profound that it is an unconscious part of daily life here. Public prayers open government meetings at City Hall, the County Courthouse and the state Legislature. Prayers even preceded sporting events at public schools until a legal challenge in 1997 put an end to the practice, causing an uproar among students and parents. You'll still hear religion taught in some classrooms, though it's not an official part of the curriculum. It might be, however, if it were up to the state Board of Education, which in 1996 attracted national attention after voting to remove evolution as a requirement for biology classes to make way for teaching creationism as described in the Bible. But none of this is to the exclusion of other belief systems. Just open the Yellow Pages to "religion" and you'll find a mindboggling array of choices. Or look in the religion page of Saturday's *Santa Fe New Mexican* for a large listing of spiritual groups along with addresses and phone numbers.

What follows is a small sampling of what Santa Fe has to offer in the spiritual realm. Please note that entries in this chapter are for practicing groups only. For church museums and relics, see our Churches section in the Attractions chapter.

Alaya

Alaya is a Santa Fe-based spiritual organization founded 11 years ago by a Missouri-born man who calls himself Ishvara. Raised as a fundamentalist Christian, Ishvara professes experiencing a profound transcendental metamorphosis in 1987 in Lincoln, Oregon, where he had been operating a metaphysical bookstore for 10 years. That's when he founded "Shambhala," Alaya's original name. The group changed its name in 1997 to avoid confusion with other organizations of the same name. Alaya honors many of the doctrines of conventional religions while remaining free of their structures. The group describes itself as "dedicated to the ongoing awakening of the highest consciousness, as brought forth by Ishvara." Ishvara moved to Santa Fe in 1995, bringing a number of his followers with him. The core group consists of about 15 members.

Baha'i Faith

The local Baha'i community consists of about 80 people throughout Santa Fe County who follow the teachings of the religion's founder, Baha Ullah. They believe in the spiritual unity of humankind; that while the religions of the world are many, their god is one. They advocate simplicity and clarity, world peace, equality of men and women, universal education and an international language and government. They also strive to eliminate wealth, poverty and prejudice. In company with fellow believers around the world, Santa Fe Baha'is hold feasts every 19 days (the length of the Baha'i "month"), celebrations or special observances on holy days, and informal "firesides" — informational meetings open to the public — in private homes several times a month, often followed by a meal.

Buddhism

Santa Fe Buddhists are numerous and varied, some following Japanese lineages, others Vietnamese, Tibetan and Indian Buddhism. The county is home to a number of beautiful Buddhist centers, each as unique as the individuals they attract. Cerro Gordo ("Fat Hill") Temple is located on Santa Fe's rustically fashionable — and fashionably expensive — east side. The temple hosts a number of Buddhist groups who use the austere yet peaceful premises for regularly scheduled meditation practice and special events with visiting teachers. Among the groups that share the temple are Santa Fe Zen Center, which practices *zazen* (sitting meditation); UpayaSangha, a chapter of the Tiep Hien order of Vietnamese Zen master Thich Nhat Hanh; and students of Ngöndro and Vajrakiliya, both forms of Tibetan Buddhism. The temple is on the south side of Cerro Gordo Road — a steep, narrow, winding street named for the turtle-shaped mountain to the north. South of the temple and below it runs the Santa Fe River — a streamlet, really, except in spring when it gushes with mountain runoff.

On Santa Fe's south side, the 69-foot-tall *stupa* (temple) of Kagyu Shenpen Kunchab (KSK) Dharma Center and its 12-foot bronzed spire provides a stunning contrast to Santa Fe's primarily single-story adobe or adobe-colored architecture. Founded in 1975 by meditation master Kalu Rinpoche, who died in 1989, KSK is a Tibetan Buddhist center under the guidance of resident Lama (teacher) Karma Dorje, who oversees a similar center in nearby

Taos. Begun in 1982 and completed four years later, KSK's temple was built in the classic style of stupas throughout Tibet. The blessing post in the Santa Fe spire contains a pearl-like crystal said to have been recovered from the Buddha's cremation. The center regularly sponsors visits by Tibetan Buddhist teachers of all lineages and offers classes in Tibetan art, music and language. Behind the center is Noble Truth Bookstore, 471-5336, which sells literature and other items related to Tibetan Buddhism.

Mountain Cloud Zen Center is a beautiful, remote Buddhist retreat on 23 acres in the foothills of the Sangre de Cristo Mountains. Its members follow a combination of the Rinzai and Soto schools of Zen Buddhism. Their teacher is Robert Aitken, who founded the Diamond Sangha in Hawaii. They hold formal sittings several times a week and four- to seven-day "sesshins" (silent retreats) several times a year in a large, lovely, natural-colored wooden building that does justice to its stunning, rustic setting. It consists of a large, sunny meditation room with windows on three sides and raised wooden platforms upon which sit 24 flat cushions topped by plump round meditation cushions. The indoor corbels supporting the huge wooden ceiling beams (*vigas*) are carved into lotus flowers; the outdoor corbels into cloud designs inspired by Japanese and Tibetan temples. And beneath the building rests a mandala — a ritualistic geometric design symbolic of the universe — that a member created in the shape of a turtle to signify the Native American concept of "Turtle Island" — the Earth. Vipassana students, who practice a form of Thervada Buddhism found primarily in Southeast Asia, rent space at Mountain Cloud for regularly scheduled meditation sessions.

Catholicism

Independent Catholics

The Church of Antioch at Santa Fe is a metaphysical church whose parent organization was founded in 1951 as part of the centu-

ries-old independent Catholic movement. Named for the city in which followers of Jesus were first called Christians, the Church of Antioch looks and sounds much like the Roman Catholic church. It celebrates the Holy Eucharist, practices the sacraments and its priests wear vestments and burn incense. But the churches part ways in apostolic succession (i.e., the true successors of the apostles) and dogma. The Church of Antioch is a metaphysical religion that believes individuals create their own reality and should remain in control of their own lives rather than turn authority over to either pope or priest. It teaches that individuals, not Jesus, save themselves. The church supports freedom of choice in all aspects of an individual's life, from sexual orientation to abortion. Its leader is a woman, the Most Rev. Meri Louise Spruit.

The 10-year-old Church of Antioch at Santa Fe is the seat of the Diocese of the Southwest, which includes six churches and 14 priests throughout New Mexico, Nevada, Colorado and Arizona. The local church has been celebrating mass since 1992 in the Loretto Chapel, famous for its "miraculous" spiral staircase (see the Churches section in our Attractions chapter). About half the church's 100 or so members attend mass on a regular basis at the chapel, now forbidden to Roman Catholics as a place of worship because it's no longer consecrated with the blessed sacraments.

Orthodox Catholics

Holy Trinity Orthodox Church is an Eastern Rite church whose diocese was founded in Antioch, the birth place of Paul and the place where Christians were first called by that name. Orthodox Catholic churches broke from the Roman Catholic church in the 11th century, when the Roman church insisted on the infallibility of the pope and maintained the supremacy in the Trinity of the Father and Son over the Holy Spirit — in other words, that Jesus is purely divine. Orthodox churches believe what's called the Holy Paradox — that Jesus is both human and divine. Holy Trinity parish formed in 1996 when its priest, Father

John Bethancourt, defected from a local Espicopalian church and took a quarter of the congregation with him. At first, only 22 families comprised the new parish, but their numbers quickly grew to 40 households. They eventually bought a ranch-style house in Santa Fe's South Capitol neighborhood, near a number of other houses of worship, and converted it into a church with a couple of bell towers and an interior richly decorated with the ubiquitous icons of orthodox Catholicism. Mass at Holy Trinity is very ornate with singing and chanting from start to finish.

St. Elias the Prophet Greek Orthodox Church is a beautiful white Byzantine structure so unusual for Santa Fe that it seems to stand out for miles. It was built in 1992 in the Dos Griegos (Two Greeks) development in Santa Fe County some 15 miles southeast of downtown Santa Fe. Services are sung in a mixture of Greek and English. The priest wears ornate vestments, and incense burns constantly. About 70 families belong to the 8-year-old St. Elias parish, which worshipped at churches in town before its own church was built. At 7,200 feet altitude, St. Elias is reputedly the highest Greek Orthodox church in the nation — at least according to a Santa Fe mayor, who made a proclamation to that effect.

Roman Catholics

At the junction of Canyon Road and Upper Canyon Roads, where the art galleries and fashionable restaurants make way for homes old and new, beautiful Cristo Rey Church provides a haven for those seeking spiritual solace or simply a peaceful break from shopping and gallery hopping. Designed by internationally acclaimed New Mexico architect John Gaw Meem, the church was built in 1939 in traditional New Mexico mission style. Parishioners provided the land and helped make and lay the more than 150,000 adobe bricks — each weighing between 20 and 40 pounds — it took to complete the church. In 1940, only 14 months after construction commenced, the church was dedicated to commemorate the 400th anniversary of Spain's initial foray into New Mexico by explorer Francisco Vasquez de Coronado. Although only 58 years old, Cristo Rey (Christ the King) is considered

a historic church primarily because of its architecture and decor rather than its age. Today, Cristo Rey serves the growing population of Santa Fe's east side. Its congregation of about 750 families is primarily a mixture of Hispanics and Anglos — the former mostly longtime residents whose families have been here for generations; the latter relatively recent, and affluent, arrivals who share a desire for traditional Catholic worship and social values.

In the heart of downtown Santa Fe, just one block east of the Plaza, stands Santa Fe's most recognized landmark — the majestic, Romanesque-style St. Francis Cathedral. Named for the city's patron saint, St. Francis is without a doubt Santa Fe's most imposing church — and certainly its largest with an active parish of 1,700 families. As a cathedral church, St. Francis is the "mother church" for the Archdiocese of Santa Fe, which covers half of New Mexico, from Socorro County north to the Colorado border and east to the Oklahoma. All major celebrations, including ordinations to the priesthood, take place at St. Francis Cathedral. Indeed, the cathedral is impressive with its vaulted ceilings and a seating capacity of 1,200, including the Conquistadora and Blessed Sacrament chapels. As the seat of the Archdiocese, and the place to which other churches in the diocese look for direction, St. Francis Cathedral is traditional and conservative. Tourists, sometimes busloads at a time, drop in on a daily basis. Unfortunately, tourists sometimes forget that the church is a place of meditation and prayer when it's not being used for services.

San Isidro Church is on the original *Camino Real* — the 2,000-mile "Royal Road" or "King's Highway" from Mexico City to Santa Fe, whose heyday spanned two centuries. "La Iglesia de San Isidro" serves a low-income, largely Hispanic section of Santa Fe County called the Village of Agua Fría. Young families, many of whose kin go back several centuries in Santa Fe, comprise a good portion of the congregation. With up to 250 people regularly attending mass, services wind up being "standing room only," with parishioners spilling into the aisles and out the doors. They come out of devotion to their faith and a love for their pastor, Father Franklin Pretto. Father Pretto is also known as the "Salsa Priest" because his salsa band, Pretto & Parranda, regularly performs at nightclubs around town. To be sure, mass at St. Isidro is a wholly different experience than at St. Francis Cathedral. While Father Pretto follows the rubrics, he's very informal, often inviting members of the congregation to participate in the mass, which they do willingly. San Isidro has no formal choir; instead, church members bring guitars and sing. If no one is so inclined during a particular service, Father Pretto will sit at the piano and lead the congregation in song.

The only post-Vatican II Catholic congregation in Santa Fe, Santa María de la Paz is without doubt the most progressive of the area's Catholic communities. Though very traditional in its devotion to the Eucharist (Holy Communion), Santa María de la Paz celebrates mass in many nontraditional ways that embrace its multicultural congregation. The church has invited Indian dancers to perform on Columbus Day and has held mariachi masses followed by tamales for the feast of Our Lady of Guadalupe. Santa María de la Paz takes pride in its outreach programs, which include support groups for divorced and remarried Catholics and for people with AIDS as well as their loved ones and caregivers. It shares an ecumenical "sister" relationship with two equally progressive houses of worship: St. Bede's Episcopal Church and United Church of Santa Fe. Father Jerome Martinez y Alire describes his parish as "catholic in the best sense of the word" - i.e., liberal and universal in scope.

Charismatic Christian

Calvary Chapel de Santa Fe is only 12 years old, but already it has grown to 1,000 local members, making it the largest nondenominational congregation in Santa Fe. The church describes itself as "conservative charismatic" — a fundamentalist, evangelical congregation that takes the word of the Bible literally, but with a minimum of display such as speaking in tongues or the laying on of hands.

At the other end of the charismatic spectrum is the controversial Potter's House Christian Center, an evangelical Pentecostal church that does indeed practice spontaneous displays of faith. Services at Potter House are exuberant affairs during which people sing, clap, shout, weep, speak in tongues and perform the "laying on of hands." The church also conducts adult baptisms from time to time at either of two municipal swimming pools. One of 995 Potter's Houses throughout the United States, the Santa Fe chapter began in 1979 with 15 people. It has since grown to a regular congregation of more than 400 members who take "spreading the gospel" to heart. The congregation is a mix of all ages and ethnicities, the latter mostly a fairly even mix of Hispanic and Anglo.

Templo Betel is a bilingual Assembly of God congregation that attracts native Spanish speakers, many of them from Mexico and Central America. This is a fundamentalist Pentecostal church that believes in the "manifestation of the Holy Spirit" whether it arrives in the form of speaking in tongues or divine healing. Located on a busy residential street on Santa Fe's west side, Templo Betel has been in existence since the late 1930s. Its present minister, Pastor Facundo Benavidez, has been its preacher for the last 22 years. Membership fluctuates but averages about 65 individuals — a good thing because the church is small and humble. It only holds about 125, and then only if they're packed in tightly. Services are joyful with lots of music and singing that reflect the various Latino cultures the congregation represents.

Eckankar

Santa Fe claims about 35 members of Eckankar, also called the "Religion of the Light and Sound of God." They meet twice a month to read from the sacred writings of Eckankar (pronounced ECK-in-car) and to sing HU — an ancient name for God that serves as a mantra to assist them in finding a conscious connection with ECK, or Holy Spirit. Founded in 1965 by Paul Twitchell, a Kentuckian who died in 1971, Eckankar believes in karma and reincarnation. Its current spiritual leader is Sri Harold Klemp, who is known as the Mahanta, or Living ECK Master.

Judaism

When Chabad Jewish Center set up shop in 1996 in the home of its rabbi, it brought for the first time a fundamentalist Jewish presence to Santa Fe, where for decades, the Reformed, Conservative and Orthodox congregations lived in peaceful coexistence in one synagogue — Temple Beth Shalom. While Chabad wasn't the first to alter that mold — a breakaway reform congregation called Beit Tikva (see entry below) began holding services in a separate location in 1995; the Orthodox group, Pardes Yisroel, moved to its own synagogue — it differs from the other local Jewish groups in that it has an active recruitment policy. Chabad, an acronym that stands for Chachma Bina Das — "wisdom," "understanding" and "knowledge" — is part of the ultratraditional Lubavitcher movement, an Orthodox Jewish sect founded in 1772 in Lubavitch, Russia, that believes in strict adherence to Jewish laws in daily life and religious practice.

Congregation Beit Tikva began in April 1995 with just a dozen families who met at Lutheran Church of the Servant. Five months later — in time for the High Holy Days of Rosh Hashana and Yom Kippur — the congregation had more than quadrupled. Today, 130 families belong to this "traditional reform" congregation whose services include regular Friday night readings from the Torah in Hebrew and English. Beit Tikva's members are largely conservative Jews who have been practicing reform Judaism.

Pardes Yisroel is a small Orthodox Jewish congregation that started in 1984 when a handful of families from the Reformed synagogue, Temple Beth Shalom, decided they wanted a more traditional approach to Judaism. With the help of Beth Shalom's rabbi, the group organized a minion, hired a young rabbi to be its school teacher and officially declared itself Orthodox. At its height, the congregation consisted of 10 Orthodox families who, in highly unorthodox fashion, worshipped in the Reformed synagogue. While such a situation would create shock waves in other cities, it seemed perfectly natural in "The City Different." The departure of its rabbi in 1991 fractured the congregation, leaving it with just a few members. Despite the upheaval, Pardes Yisroel has regrouped and grown to about three dozen core families who in 1997 bought a house on Don Diego Street and converted it

into a synagogue and school. The congregation, which describes itself as "centrist," is lay-led with visiting rabbis for the High Holy Days and other special occasions.

Temple Beth Shalom was the only central place of worship for Jews in Santa Fe and was almost certainly the only synagogue in the country shared by Reform, Conservative and Orthodox Jews. Today, a Reform and a lay-led Conservative congregation share the temple, which is located in a largely residential area shared by a number of houses of worship as well as two museums and a repertory cinema. Although practicing Jews have been in Santa Fe at least since the mid-19th century, they didn't build a synagogue until 1953. During World War II, laymen conducted Sabbath services in the chapel of Bruns General Hospital, a military facility that stood where the College of Santa Fe stands today. (No one's quite sure where Jews met for Sabbath services before that time.) After the war, however, the Santa Fe Jewish Temple and Community Center collected $100 from 18 families toward the purchase of land. It hired nationally renowned local architect John Gaw Meem, whose signature is on a number of Santa Fe churches, to design a synagogue. The temple was dedicated in 1953, but there was no money left to furnish it. The congregation of 40 families sold raffle tickets for $100 each to pay for seats, carpeting, drapes and paving. By 1980, the congregation — now called Temple Beth Shalom — was well-established with a full-time rabbi and a congregation that had quintupled in size to 200 families. It commissioned a new solar sanctuary, completed in 1986, to accommodate the burgeoning congregation. Judging by the temple's growth — its membership currently numbers more than 400 families — another expansion or perhaps even a move is likely.

New Thought

Because of the iconoclastic nature of so many Santa Feans, it's not surprising that New Thought religions have flourished here; at least half a dozen exist in this small city. While they come in a variety of wrappings, most New Thought religions emphasize spiritual healing, the individual and the creative

Penitentes

Driving through the back roads of northern New Mexico, you're likely to pass many a simple, one-room adobe structure, often with no windows and little external evidence of life. What you're looking at is a *morada* — a house of worship used by *penitentes* and that, despite appearances, is teeming with life but of a spiritual nature. Please do not enter.

Penitentes are members of the centuries-old "Hermandad de Nuestro Padre Jesus Nazareno" — Brotherhood of Our Father Jesus of Nazarene — a religious fraternity that traces its roots back to a 16th-century nobleman from Seville named Don Fadríque de Ribera. Ribera was so moved to see pilgrims in Jerusalem carrying heavy crosses along the Via Dolorosa — the route Jesus walked to his crucifixion — that he founded a society to carry on the tradition in Spain. The society grew, spreading to Mexico as Spain expanded its explorations into the New World. There, members carried on the society's rituals of self-flagellation and other bodily punishments to prove their devotion to Christ and their empathy for his suffering.

Penitentes first appeared in New Mexico in the late 18th and early 19th century, a time when priests were at a premium in this growing Catholic outback. With too few priests to go around, *penitentes* openly ministered to the spiritual needs of their communities. But the Church discouraged what it described as their "excesses of most indiscreet corporal penances" and, in time, outrightly forbade their practice of physical penance and eventually forbade them to assemble at all. Thus, *penitentes* became an underground society who practiced their rituals behind the walls of windowless

— continued on next page

Photo: Russ Young

This morada, on the grounds of El Rancho de las Golondrinas, is a copy of a morada in Abiquiú. While real moradas are closed to the public, this one is open for touring.

moradas, out of the eyes of the church, but still very much in the hearts and minds of the community.

Present-day New Mexican *penitentes* keep the tradition alive while maintaining a low profile, as evidenced by their humble *moradas*. While not precisely a secret society, it is certainly a reserved one. The reasons are historical, as we've seen. They're also reverent and pragmatic. The practice of the *penitente* is one of humility, of subserviance to — and a demonstrative empathy for — a suffering Christ expressed in prayer, meditation and physical penance; of community service, whether by feeding the hungry or comforting the dying; and of preserving the culture.

Penitentes wish to avoid the prurient gaze of voyeurs and sensation-seekers who want to witness the rituals of self-flagellation and the rigors of Holy Week, when *penitentes* re-enact Christ's march to Calvary. Please respect their privacy. If you're curious, rent *The Penitent*, a 1988 movie starring Raul Julia and Armand Assante that provides an admittedly melodramatic glimpse of *penitente* society.

power of positive thought. Followers believe that constructive use of the mind will enable them to achieve freedom, power, health and prosperity. The New Thought movement began in the late 19th century on the heels of New England Transcendentalism — a literary and philosophical movement popularized by Ralph Waldo Emerson, Margaret Fuller, Henry David Thoreau and others who believed that God is inherent in humans and in nature and that individual intuition is the highest source of knowledge. New Thought encourages individuals to have a personal relationship with God instead of one whose parameters are defined by a particular organization. Among the New Thought groups in Santa Fe is the Church of Religious Science, a religion founded in the early 20th century by Ernest Holmes. Like its distant cousin, Christian Science, Religious Science believes in healing the body through prayer. Unlike its cousin, however, it does not eschew doctors, medicine or science. The Santa Fe church has about 300 members who tend to be educated professionals involved in an intellectual pursuit of their relationship with God and spirituality. Their minister, the Rev. Bernardo Monserrat, says his church attracts the same kind of people as the Unitarian Church. The difference, he says, is that Unitarians "pray to whom it may concern and we pray to someone that it does concern."

Unity Church of Santa Fe is part of the Unity School of Christianity, founded in 1889 by Charles and Myrtle Fillmore of Kansas City, Missouri. Unity, whose roots lie in the New Thought movement, believes in Christian principles, spiritual values and the healing power of prayer, though not to the exclusion of medical care. Its message is a little nontraditional in that it focuses on the teachings of Jesus, not on the man himself. Members believe that if they follow the teachings of Christ, they will experience peace and joy and love right here on earth. The Santa Fe Church has about 50 members, though sometimes as many as 75 show up for Sunday services at the Santa Fe Woman's Club. Services focus on applying spiritual principles to daily life. About an hour long, they are filled with song and a few minutes of silent meditation.

Symphony of Love is a tiny, evolving New Thought group founded five years ago in Santa Fe. It describes itself as a "nonreligious spiritual fellowship" that rejects institutionalism and dogma. The interfaith group has no formal membership, no board of trustees, no dues or tithes, not even a church. Its main ministry is a public access cable television show called " "Tao of Now" on Channel 6. Symphony of Love began in 1993 as an informal weekly study group loosely affiliated with Brooks Divinity School, part of the First Divine Science Church in Denver. They have continued meeting for in-depth discussions of spiritual literature, spending several months at a time on a portion of the Bible, for example, or the Tao Te Ching of ancient China. The group also offers T'ai Chi and other movement classes for a nominal fee and performs weddings, spiritual coaching and counseling.

Protestant

Episcopalian

Episcopalians made their first official appearance in Santa Fe in 1863 with the arrival from the American northwest of the Right Rev. Josiah C. Talbot. On July 5th of that year, Talbot administered to seven people the holy communion according to the Anglican rite — the first ever in the Spanish speaking Roman Catholic town. Four years later, Good Shepherd Mission was born. It became a parish in 1868, and 10 years later, at the urging of then Gov. Bradford Prince, it changed its name to Church of the Holy Faith — the literal translation for "Santa Fe." Just as New Mexico's Spanish history is inseparable from the Catholic Church, so is its history as a territory — and eventually a state — closely linked to the Episcopal Church. Gov. Bradford Prince, a chief justice of the New Mexico Supreme Court whom U.S. President Rutherford B. Hayes appointed territorial governor in 1889, was chancellor of the diocese for 42 years. Gov. William T. Thornton, who became governor in 1893, belonged to the church's original building committee. Thornton's law partner, T.B. Catron, elected U.S. senator in 1912, belonged to Holy Faith, as did U.S. Senator Bronson Cutting, (he served from 1927 until his death in a plane crash in 1935), who bought *The Santa Fe New Mexican* newspaper in 1912. It was another famous parishioner, architect John Gaw Meem, who in 1927 designed Palen Hall. The hall is attached by a cloister to the east side of the folk-Gothic stone church, now 116 years old. Over the church's main doors is a small window with a Star of David in recognition of the Jewish merchants who donated generously to the church's building fund in 1879. Holy Faith has experienced a number of other alterations since that time, including Conkey House, completed in 1966. Conkey House contains Chapel of the Good Shepherd and Holy Faith Library, which holds more than 5,000 books and tapes by the current bishop, Terence Kelsaw. The collection is estimated to be worth close to $300,000. Holy Faith is a wealthy church. It's also conservative and traditional with worship that follows Rite I, a relatively austere service used by the Anglican Church when it formed in the 16th century. Holy Faith's ceremonies and liturgies are extremely formal with much ritual and spectacular vestments.

Among the newest and most liberal of Santa Fe's churches, St. Bede's was founded in 1962 as a mission of the Church of the Holy Faith. The congregation, which met in a rented building on Cerrillos Road for two years before moving into its own newly built church on San Mateo Road, comprised a few dozen families. At that time, San Mateo was a dusty dirt road on the outskirts of town. Today, it's a bustling residential commuter street that meets with St. Francis Drive to create one of the busiest intersections of the city. The city's growth is clearly reflected at St. Bede's, a thriving church with 210 households and a 10,000-square-foot building on 4.5 acres. In addition to a part-time interim rector, St. Bede's has close to 100 lay liturgical ministers. Worship centers on the Eucharist, Rite II, a less formal ritual than the older, more traditional Rite I. The atmosphere at St. Bede's tends to be informal, or what one parishioner describes as "relaxed spirituality."

Lutheran

Among the last of the mainstream Protestant faiths to send missionaries to Santa Fe were the Lutherans, who arrived in 1914 when Pastor Carl F. Schmid of Albuquerque began visiting the state capital for monthly services. That lasted about two years followed by a 12-year dormant period when Santa Fe had little, if any, Lutheran activity. But in the late 1920s, Santa Fe enjoyed a period of growth that brought more Lutherans to the small city. Services resumed irregularly but with increased frequency until 1938, when the church inaugurated regular Sunday services and officially became Immanuel Lutheran Church. With 230 baptized members, Immanuel Lutheran (Lutheran Church-Missouri Synod) is the largest Lutheran church in Santa Fe as well as being its oldest and most conservative. It worships in a simple Spanish-style adobe structure architect John Gaw Meem designed in 1948. Once past the open *portal* and inside

Photo: The Bishop's Lodge

Bishop Jean Lamy's chapel, now part of the Bishop's Lodge
Resort, is open to the public free of charge.

the church, visitors are greeted with a beautiful collection of banners handmade by members and depicting biblical themes. The altarware — candlesticks, offering plates, missal stand, etc. — are all Nambéware, a special silver-colored metal manufactured near Nambé Pueblo, about 20 minutes north of Santa Fe.

Methodist

With 1,250 members, St. John's United Methodist Church is the largest Protestant congregation in Santa Fe. Its beginnings go back to 1850, when the Rev. E.G. Nicholson set out from his home in Independence, Missouri — not coincidentally the beginning of the Santa Fe Trail — to establish the first Methodist church in the frontier territory of New Mexico. Nicholson managed to achieve his goal in 1853, but not without vigorous opposition by the Catholic Church. The Methodists persisted,

sometimes holding services in an army chapel, other times in the First Presbyterian Church, and their numbers grew. In 1854, they built their own chapel on what is now the site of the First Presbyterian Church. There the church flourished until 1866, when the U.S. Army withdrew from the territory, taking many of the area's Methodists with it. The remaining Methodists persevered, slowly building up their congregation once again until, in 1880 — the year after the first railroad steamed into northern New Mexico — they built their first church on what is now Defouri Street near downtown Santa Fe. They moved their congregation two more times before 1954, when they settled in their present location on Old Pecos Trail.

Presbyterian

The First Presbyterian Church was not the first Protestant Church in New Mexico, but it was the first to survive. The Baptists and Methodists dwindled after the exodus in 1866 by the U.S. Army, which accounted for the majority of the area's Protestants. It was in November 1866 — more than a year after the Civil War ended — that the Rev. David McFarland of Mattoon, Illinois, held the first Presbyterian service in Santa Fe at the Palace of the Governors. Within a few months, he established the First Presbyterian Church. The Presbyterians bought the ruins of an adobe chapel built in 1849 by the Baptists, who had abandoned their mission in Santa Fe. The First Presbyterian Church restored the building — located at what is now the corner of Grant Avenue and Griffin Street — to a useful, if not terribly comfortable, condition and held its first service there in 1867. First Presbyterian would rebuild its church two more times on the same site, consecrating its present structure — a grand Pueblo-style church designed by architect John Gaw Meem — in 1939.

Southern Baptist

The First Baptist Church of Santa Fe was established by missionaries in 1850 and originally operated out of a small church at the corner of Manhattan and Don Gaspar avenues, near what is now downtown Santa Fe. It was the first Protestant Church in the territory, built a year after the arrival of missionary Hiram Walter Reed, who stayed in Santa Fe for two years and moved on. He was succeeded by five more missionaries through 1866, when the Baptists withdrew from the area for lack of worshippers. Today, First Baptist Church is the largest Southern Baptist church in Santa Fe with more than 600 members.

United Church of Christ

The United Church of Santa Fe is part of the United Church of Christ (U.C.C.), a de-

nomination that dates back to the Protestant Reformation and the pilgrims of New England. Like its parent organization, United Church of Santa Fe believes spirituality is inextricably tied to social justice. It's an activist church that has been involved in community projects such as Habitat for Humanity, Esperanza Shelter for Battered Women, the hospitality center at the Penitentiary of New Mexico, St. Elizabeth's Shelter for the needy and the Inter-Faith Council (see entry below). United Church of Santa Fe's liberal bent hearkens back to the United Church of Christ, the first Protestant church to allow women clergy and to ordain an openly gay man.

From the outside, there's nothing particularly remarkable about United Church of Santa Fe. But built into the sanctuary, called a gathering room, is an indoor *acequia* (irrigation channel) there to irrigate the soul. It wraps like the letter "J" around the entire south wall to complete the set of elements — earth, wind, fire and water — contained in and around the church. While its presence is primarily spiritual, the acequia also has a practical function — it's part of the passive solar-heating system that heats the building.

Quakers (Religious Society of Friends)

The Santa Fe Monthly Meeting of Friends gathers every Sunday at 630 Canyon Road in what was once the home and studio of the late Olive Rush (see our Attractions chapter). A Quaker reputed to be the first female artist to move to Santa Fe, Rush left her beautiful, earthy 150-year-old house to the Friends when she died in the mid-'60s. The group had only formed some 10 years earlier when a handful of people met in different homes. Today, about 75 people belong to the Santa Fe Monthly

Meeting of Friends, while other Quakers belong to the Chamisa Friends Meeting, which gathers in another section of town. Between 25 and 40 people show up regularly on Sundays for silent worship and prayerful speaking.

Established in 1647 as a reaction to the extreme Puritan formalism of the Presbyterian Church, the Religious Society of Friends places a high value on conscience, self-examination and social responsibility, embracing pacifism and left-leaning political activism. In Santa Fe, that translates into such affiliations as Concerned Citizens for Nuclear Safety, which opposes the opening of the Waste Isolation Pilot Plant — an underground nuclear waste dump near Carlsbad, New Mexico; Los Alamos Study Group, a grassroots watchdog organization that keeps tabs on Los Alamos National Laboratory and the U.S. Department of Energy; and other progressive organizations and causes.

Sikh

Some 25 miles north of Santa Fe, off the main drag that goes through Española, a large golden dome marks the entrance to Hacienda de Guru Ram Dass, the "gudwara" where the Sikh community attends services Sundays at 11 AM. Inside, worshippers sit with bare feet and covered heads on the floor, singing and chanting and praising God to music. After the service, which usually lasts a couple of hours, they share a vegetarian meal. Española, a small city in both in Santa Fe and Rio Arriba counties, is the headquarters for the Sikh Dharma of the Western Hemisphere.

The Sikh presence in northern New Mexico began in the early 1970s, when Yogi Bhajan, the chief religious authority for Sikhs in the Western Hemisphere, moved to Santa Fe from Los Angeles, bought land in Española and began teaching Kundalini yoga. He soon attracted a following of converts that over the past 25 years has evolved into a community

of 300 people. Members of the Sikh community have a high profile in northern New Mexico not only because of their distinctive white garb and turbans, but also because of their involvement in such arenas as politics, business and especially health. As a "3HO" organization — "healthy, happy, holy" — Sikh Dharma in the West places holistic health high up on its list of religious virtues, and some of its members operate a number of alternative healthcare clinics in northern New Mexico. Other tenets of the Sikh religion, which began in India, include belief in one god who created all humans equally; eating no flesh — meat, fish, fowl or eggs; abstinence from alcohol and drugs; not cutting or removing any body hair, hence the turbans; and wearing white as a sign to each other and the rest of the world that they are of service.

Sufism

Santa Fe followers of the Nimatullahi Sufi Order meet Thursday and Sunday evenings at 405 Greg Avenue in a *khaniqah* with a library and a meditation room decorated with Persian rugs, flowers and calligraphy. Their practice is personal and inward, involving concentrating on unity with God and seeking truth through meditation, selfless service and loving kindness toward others. The *khaniqah* occasionally hosts weeklong open houses with food and meditative music performed by darvishes.

In common with all Sufi orders, Nimatullahi stems from a chain that goes back to the beginning of Islam, with Mohammed considered to be the first Sufi master. Shah Nimatullah Wali, one of the great Sufi masters of Iran, founded the order at the end of the 14th century. He did not delineate a path of asceticism or reclusiveness. Rather, he stressed the integration of the social and the spiritual life based on the invocation of God, reflection, self-examination, meditation and chanting.

INSIDERS' TIP

Pres. Lyndon Baines Johnson married Claudia "Lady Bird" Taylor at St. John's United Methodist Church in Santa Fe, where Lady Bird's brother was a member.

La Conquistadora, who is also known as Our Lady of Reconciliation, is Catholic Santa Fe's best-loved image of the Virgin. The statue has her own chapel in St. Francis Cathedral and is taken on procession as part of the Santa Fe Fiesta.

Unitarian/Universalist

The Unitarian Church of Santa Fe on W. Barcelona Road got started in 1952 as a lay-led fellowship of about two dozen liberal-minded families from Santa Fe and Los Alamos. They were attracted to the church's doctrine of no doctrine. The Unitarian/Universalist Church, once part of the Congregation-

alist movement, functions by a consensus that is constantly in flux because its "eternal truths" are still emerging. For two years after its founding, the Santa Fe Fellowship met at a private club on Garcia Street near downtown Santa Fe. In 1954, they began meeting at Temple Beth Shalom — Santa Fe's first synagogue, completed only a year earlier. There they conducted an active Sunday school which attracted so many children that the youngsters reportedly outnumbered the adults. This forced another move — and another and another — including one to the local Mormon church whose rules against coffee, tea and smoking, even outside, proved difficult to follow.

Finally, in 1968, the 35-member fellowship bought a house it could barely afford, one that allegedly came with a ghost. By 1979, the congregation once again outgrew its quarters and bought the Mormon Church it had rented two decades earlier, its current base of operations. It hired a full-time minister in 1981 and has since renovated and enlarged its church, located in Santa Fe's historic South Capitol area. Today, the Unitarian Church of Santa Fe has 300 members from a variety of religious backgrounds. They're a relatively well-educated and well-heeled group whose members, like their church, tend to be activists with politics that lie somewhere left of center.

Other Religious Groups

New Mexico Faith Communities Against Hate Crimes began two years ago as a coalition of about a dozen Santa Fe spiritual communities that banded together after an incident in which two gay men were harassed and beaten at a shopping trip to a local super-market. The gay-bashing received a lot of attention because of its rarity in Santa Fe, long known for its tolerance of live-and-let-live lifestyles. Originally called Santa Fe Faith Communities Against Hate Crimes, the organization has expanded to include 65 churches and other spiritual communities throughout the state, including 17 in Santa Fe alone. It meets at 7 PM on the third Tuesday of every month at the First Presbyterian Church, which founded the organization. The public is welcome to attend. In addition to operating a hate crimes hotline at 992-7199, the organization currently is working on passage of a hate crimes bill in New Mexico. It's also working with the public schools to develop educational programs about diversity and inclusiveness.

The **Inter-Faith Council of Santa Fe** is a longstanding ecumenical organization that strives to bridge different religious organizations and faith groups in Santa Fe through worship services, concerts and educational programs. Two dozen Santa Fe faith communities belong to the council, which holds such interfaith healing services and spiritual gatherings as its annual autumn Interfaith Thanksgathering; Martin Luther King Jr. memorial celebration; Peace Prayer Day with the Sikh community based out of nearby Española; and an annual potluck supper and sing-along.

Index of Advertisers

Index